BASIC FEDERAL INCOME TAX

Fourth Edition

Gwendolyn Griffith Lieuallen

Partner, Tonkon Torp LLP

Portland, Oregon

The *Emanuel Law Outlines* Series

Wolters Kluwer

Law & Business

Published by Wolters Kluwer Law & Business in New York.

Wolters Kluwer Law & Business serves customers worldwide with CCH, Aspen Publishers, and Kluwer Law International products (www.wolterskluwerlb.com)

To contact Customer Service, e-mail customer.service@wolters kluwer.com, call 1-800-234-1660, fax 1-800-901-9075, or mail correspondence to:

Wolters Kluwer Law & Business
Attn: Order Department
PO Box 990
Frederick, MD 21705

Printed in the United States of America.

4 5 6 7 8 9 0

ISBN 978-0-7355-9775-4

Library of Congress Cataloging-in-Publication Data

Lieuallen, Gwendolyn Griffith, 1957-
    Basic federal income tax / Gwendolyn Griffith Lieuallen. — 4th ed.
        p. cm.—(The Emanuel law outlines series)
Includes index.
ISBN 978-0-7355-9775-4
1. Income tax—Law and legislation—United States—Outlines, syllabi, etc. 2. Tax returns—United States—Outlines, syllabi, etc. I. Title.
KF6369.85.L54 2011
343.7305'2—dc22

                                                                2011018340

About Wolters Kluwer Law & Business

Wolters Kluwer Law & Business is a leading global provider of intelligent information and digital solutions for legal and business professionals in key specialty areas, and respected educational resources for professors and law students. Wolters Kluwer Law & Business connects legal and business professionals as well as those in the education market with timely, specialized authoritative content and information-enabled solutions to support success through productivity, accuracy and mobility.

Serving customers worldwide, Wolters Kluwer Law & Business products include those under the Aspen Publishers, CCH, Kluwer Law International, Loislaw, Best Case, ftwilliam.com and MediRegs family of products.

CCH products have been a trusted resource since 1913, and are highly regarded resources for legal, securities, antitrust and trade regulation, government contracting, banking, pension, payroll, employment and labor, and healthcare reimbursement and compliance professionals.

Aspen Publishers products provide essential information to attorneys, business professionals and law students. Written by preeminent authorities, the product line offers analytical and practical information in a range of specialty practice areas from securities law and intellectual property to mergers and acquisitions and pension/benefits. Aspen's trusted legal education resources provide professors and students with high-quality, up-to-date and effective resources for successful instruction and study in all areas of the law.

Kluwer Law International products provide the global business community with reliable international legal information in English. Legal practitioners, corporate counsel and business executives around the world rely on Kluwer Law journals, looseleafs, books, and electronic products for comprehensive information in many areas of international legal practice.

Loislaw is a comprehensive online legal research product providing legal content to law firm practitioners of various specializations. Loislaw provides attorneys with the ability to quickly and efficiently find the necessary legal information they need, when and where they need it, by facilitating access to primary law as well as state-specific law, records, forms and treatises.

Best Case Solutions is the leading bankruptcy software product to the bankruptcy industry. It provides software and workflow tools to flawlessly streamline petition preparation and the electronic filing process, while timely incorporating ever-changing court requirements.

ftwilliam.com offers employee benefits professionals the highest quality plan documents (retirement, welfare and non-qualified) and government forms (5500/PBGC, 1099 and IRS) software at highly competitive prices.

MediRegs products provide integrated health care compliance content and software solutions for professionals in healthcare, higher education and life sciences, including professionals in accounting, law and consulting.

Wolters Kluwer Law & Business, a division of Wolters Kluwer, is headquartered in New York. Wolters Kluwer is a market-leading global information services company focused on professionals.

**Dedicated
to
Peyton, with love**

Summary of Contents

Table of Contents

CHAPTER 1

GETTING STARTED IN FEDERAL INCOME TAX

CHAPTER 2

IDENTIFYING GROSS INCOME

CHAPTER 3

SPECIFIC INCLUSIONS IN GROSS INCOME

CHAPTER 4

SPECIFIC EXCLUSIONS FROM GROSS INCOME

CHAPTER 5

DEDUCTIONS—IN GENERAL

CHAPTER 6

PERSONAL DEDUCTIONS

CHAPTER 7

BUSINESS AND INVESTMENT DEDUCTIONS

CHAPTER **8**

MIXED BUSINESS AND PERSONAL EXPENSES

CHAPTER 9

TRANSACTIONS IN PROPERTY

CHAPTER **10**

NONRECOGNITION TRANSACTIONS

CHAPTER 11

TIMING OF INCOME AND EXPENSES

CHAPTER 12

CHARACTER OF INCOME AND LOSS

CHAPTER 13

TAX RATES AND CREDITS

CHAPTER 14

IDENTIFYING THE TAXPAYER

CHAPTER 15

TIME VALUE OF MONEY: PRINCIPLES AND APPLICATIONS

CHAPTER 16

PUTTING IT ALL TOGETHER: RECOGNIZING AND ANALYZING COMMON TAX PROBLEMS

Preface

Thank you for buying this book!

In my many years in the classroom, and now as a practicing tax lawyer, I have spent countless hours listening to students and tax professionals alike describe the study of tax law as both fascinating and frustrating.

It's a fascinating subject, not only because it touches almost everyone's life in a very real and direct way, but also because it serves as a pretty good mirror for our society's beliefs and values. But learning tax law can be frustrating as well. It requires learning a whole new language—the language of the Internal Revenue Code and its seemingly endless pages of regulations. It requires faith that what may seem to be a jumble of obscure statutes is really a coherent system whose parts work together in a sensible fashion.

This book offers some of the techniques I've developed over the years to help students and young tax colleagues overcome these frustrations. Chapter 1 begins with the basics, including a systematic method for reading the Internal Revenue Code and grasping these unfamiliar statutes. The succeeding chapters of this book describe in detail the issues of individual taxation that you will be studying throughout the term: what is "income"; what expenses are deductible; the character of income or loss; what tax rates apply; and what tax credits are available. Chapter 16 summarizes the well-established themes and issues of basic income tax, collecting the "families" of tax statutes that govern these issues.

With this edition, we are launching a website that supplements the book. At *www.aspenlawschool .com/books/tax_outline* you will find additional materials and problems, the latest changes made by Congress, and in-depth analysis of some favorite topics professors like to emphasize in class.

This book can't substitute for the hard work of tax study: understanding the Code and regulations, working through example after example, and participating in the discussion in your tax class. What it can do is supplement those sources and help explain the concepts you encounter in class. To make the best use of this book and its accompanying website, I suggest that you:

- Skim the appropriate sections of this outline before the material is covered in class (you will find a casebook correlation chart at the front of the book).

- Review the material in this book in detail after it is discussed in class. Note in the margins of this outline the emphasis that your particular professor places on the various aspects of the material. If your professor delves especially deeply into a topic, check out the book's website for more advanced information and practice.

- Work through the examples and "Quiz Yourself" questions. Make sure you can explain the result in each example, using the Code and case law. Consider creating new examples to work through alone or in your study group. Check out the website for additional problems.

- Use the outline material to supplement the notes or your own outline that you prepare to study for the exam.

- Chapter 16 offers a way of thinking about the material in the rest of this outline as a logical whole. Use it to help you identify the common types of tax transactions and understand how related Code sections work together to govern them.

■ Use the "Capsule Summary" and the Statute Summary Charts as a review just prior to your exam to make sure you can recall fundamental concepts. Use the index to make sure you know all the tax jargon.

My warmest thanks to Wolters Kluwer Law & Business's Carol McGeehan and Barbara Lasoff for their optimism and sensible suggestions—and to my family for their infinite patience—during the writing of this book.

I wish you the best in your first tax course and hope most of all that you will discover that tax can be interesting and even fun. Good luck!

Gwendolyn Griffith Lieuallen
Tonkon Torp LLP

Casebook Correlation Chart

(**Note:** general sections of the outline are omitted for this chart. **NC** = not directly covered by this casebook. For updates to this chart, go to *http://www.aspenlawschool .com/books/tax_outline*.)

Lieuallen: Basic Federal Income Tax Emanuel Law Outline (*by chapter and section heading*)	Burke & Friel: *Taxation of Individual Income* (Ninth Edition, 2010)	Dodge, Fleming, & Geier: *Federal Income Tax: Doctrine, Structure, and Policy: Text, Cases, Problems* (Third Edition, 2004)	Freeland, Lathrope, Lind, & Stephens: *Fundamentals of Federal Income Taxation: Cases and Materials* (Fifteenth Edition, 2009)	Schmalbeck & Zelenak: *Federal Income Taxation* (Third Edition, 2011)	Klein, Bankman, Shaviro & Stark: *Federal Income Taxation* (Fifteenth Edition, 2009)
CHAPTER 1 **GETTING STARTED IN FEDERAL INCOME TAX**					
I. Introduction—The Big Picture	8-19	4-5, 9-16, 767-768	41-44	1-15	1-8
II. The Sources of Federal Income Tax Law	4-8, 1079-1084	29-35, 768-771	5-29, 966-973	30-33	8-11, 42-46
III. Tax Ethics—Tax Return Positions and Sanctions	NC	767	965-966, 973-980, 995-1000	61-69	24-30
IV. Reading the Code	NC	43-44	NC	NC	32-40
V. A Few Words on Tax Policy	NC	117-152	29-41	24-30	11-20
VI. Relationship of the Federal Income Tax to Other Tax Systems	NC	18-23	NC	21-30, 882-884	328-332
CHAPTER 2 **IDENTIFYING GROSS INCOME**					
II. IRC §61	24-25	44-45	46-47	74-78	48-49
III. Definitions of Income	24-50, 217-222, 645-649, 867	37-43, 191-197, 203-208, 223-226, 366-371, 423	46-66	21-23, 71-89, 111-125	50-119, 281-283
IV. Items That Are Not Income	30-32	226-239	64-66	81-110	77-84, 119-138
CHAPTER 3 **SPECIFIC INCLUSIONS IN GROSS INCOME**					
II. Compensation for Services	26-27, 211-212	203-208	46-64	193-196	47-49
III. Gross Income from Business	244-245	46-47	NC	NC	NC
IV. Gains Derived from Dealings in Property	78	45-47	115-116	78-79, 863-865	111-118

Lieuallen: Basic Federal Income Tax Emanuel Law Outline (by chapter and section heading)	Burke & Friel: *Taxation of Individual Income* (Ninth Edition, 2010)	Dodge, Fleming, & Geier: *Federal Income Tax: Doctrine, Structure, and Policy: Text, Cases, Problems* (Third Edition, 2004)	Freeland, Lathrope, Lind, & Stephens: *Fundamentals of Federal Income Taxation: Cases and Materials* (Fifteenth Edition, 2009)	Schmalbeck & Zelenak: *Federal Income Taxation* (Third Edition, 2011)	Klein, Bankman, Shaviro & Stark: *Federal Income Taxation* (Fifteenth Edition, 2009)
CHAPTER 3 continued					
V. Investment Income	30, 148-152, 256-260, 500-501, 598, 646-647	657-665	NC	74	127-131, 596-598
VI. Alimony and Separate Maintenance Payments	847-868	501-505	196-209, 220-226	786-792	320-324
VII. Income from Discharge of Indebtedness	163-178	303-322	163-182	143-148	161-174
VIII. Some Odds and Ends— Prizes, Awards, Helpful Payments, Embezzlements, and Damages	129-130, 182-183, 640, 650-653	197-199	61-63, 105-111, 183-195, 542-547	148-156	73-77, 196-201, 446-449
CHAPTER 4 SPECIFIC EXCLUSIONS FROM GROSS INCOME					
I. Where are We?	NC	462	NC	NC	NC
II. Exclusions–In General	223-228	NC	67-68	15-16	363
III. Death Benefits—§101	143-147	166-168, 177-178	153-162	103-110, 197-200	122-127
IV. Gifts—§102	90-110	155-166, 169-177	68-88	193-196	111-119
V. Interest on State and Local Bonds—§103	223-224	79	245-248	706-711	201-206
VI. Compensation for Personal Injury or Sickness—§104	179-195	268-281	187-195	93-101	154-159
VII. Discharge of Indebtedness Income— §108	159-178	303-322	163-182	233-238	159-174
VIII. Exclusion for Gain on Sale of Personal Residence—§121	111-125	79-80	227-234	284-289, 336-339	206-208
IX. Employment-Related Exclusions	147, 201-222, 225, 451-453	208-222	89-99	125-131, 208-211	51-73
X. Education Provisions	130-139, 227, 446-448	199-202	235-243	131-139	403-404
XI. Payments for Support of Family	227, 851-852	501-510	218-220	NC	320-324
XII. Prizes and Awards	129-130	197-199	105-111	114-116	446-449
XIII. Energy Provisions	NC	NC	NC	NC	NC

Lieuallen: Basic Federal Income Tax Emanuel Law Outline *(by chapter and section heading)*	Burke & Friel: *Taxation of Individual Income* (Ninth Edition, 2010)	Dodge, Fleming, & Geier: *Federal Income Tax: Doctrine, Structure, and Policy: Text, Cases, Problems* (Third Edition, 2004)	Freeland, Lathrope, Lind, & Stephens: *Fundamentals of Federal Income Taxation: Cases and Materials* (Fifteenth Edition, 2009)	Schmalbeck & Zelenak: *Federal Income Taxation* (Third Edition, 2011)	Klein, Bankman, Shaviro & Stark: *Federal Income Taxation* (Fifteenth Edition, 2009)
CHAPTER 5 DEDUCTIONS—IN GENERAL					
II. Role of Deductions	12-15, 253	57-58, 533-537	318-320, 548-551	363	351-355
III. Common Themes of Deduction Controversies	13, 15	58	319	583-584	354-355
CHAPTER 6 PERSONAL DEDUCTIONS					
II. Above-the-Line Deductions	12, 155-157, 345-350, 449-453, 847-851	60, 501-503, 520-521, 605, 611, 856-857	550	363-366	353
III. The Standard Deduction	11-12, 16	462, 767	550	363	353-354
IV. The Itemized Deduction	16	767	550	363-366	353-354
V. Interest—§163	497-514	559-564	481-508	381-394	400-403
VI. Taxes—§164	515-525	550-556	234-235, 243-248, 508-512	79-81, 395-402	404-407
VII. Casualty Losses—§165(c)(3)	527-545	257-260, 522-531	817-827	402-413, 505-513	355-369
VIII. Medical Expenses—§213	547-557	254-257, 512-522	556-567	413-436	369-379
IX. Charitable Contributions—§170	559-594	537-550	794-814	366-381, 441-449	380-400
X. Miscellaneous Expenses—2% Floor	16	558, 589	504	437-439	626
XI. Personal Exemption—§151	16-17	462, 469-475	569-570	38-39, 769-770	353-354, 407
CHAPTER 7 BUSINESS AND INVESTMENT DEDUCTIONS					
II. Trade or Business Expenses—§162	232-264	58-66, 567-585	318-346	527-554, 558-567	545-564
III. Other Deductions	353-364	371-377, 550-556, 559-564	780-794, 817-818	554-558	401, 560, 702
IV. Deductions for Capital Recovery	268-297	60-63, 109-115, 277-279, 577-585, 695-696	406-446	183-193, 621-668	511-545
V. Activities Engaged in For Profit That Are Not Trades or Businesses	16, 353-364, 458-459	588-596	447-478	NC	439-449
VI. Substantiation	380-388, 401-402	557	397	577-578	458-459

Lieuallen: Basic Federal Income Tax Emanuel Law Outline *(by chapter and section heading)*	Burke & Friel: *Taxation of Individual Income* (Ninth Edition, 2010)	Dodge, Fleming, & Geier: *Federal Income Tax: Doctrine, Structure, and Policy: Text, Cases, Problems* (Third Edition, 2004)	Freeland, Lathrope, Lind, & Stephens: *Fundamentals of Federal Income Taxation: Cases and Materials* (Fifteenth Edition, 2009)	Schmalbeck & Zelenak: *Federal Income Taxation* (Third Edition, 2011)	Klein, Bankman, Shaviro & Stark: *Federal Income Taxation* (Fifteenth Edition, 2009)
CHAPTER 8 **MIXED BUSINESS AND PERSONAL EXPENSES**					
II. Origin Test	233-246, 458-459	577-580, 623-628	329-330	529-531	351, 500-506
III. Travel	388-392	633-646	363-382	56-577	452-460, 481-497
IV. Clothing	245-246	632	400-401	603-607	497-500
V. Expenses of Education	417-448	600-607	567-568	592-603	506-510
VI. Meals and Entertainment	393-416	646-653	396-400	577-583	460-477
VII. Home Offices and Vacation Homes—§280A	479-490	614-619	515, 522-527	591-592, 608-620	431-439
VIII. "Luxury" Automobiles and Listed Property—§280F	490-496	614	436-438	NC	451
IX. Hobby Losses—§183	461-477	588-596	515, 520-522	584-591	423-431
X. Gambling Losses	NC	585-588	542-543	239-248	131-133
CHAPTER 9 **TRANSACTIONS IN PROPERTY**					
II. Statutory Analysis—§1001	76-86, 519-521	45-47, 377-382, 413-416	115-152	260-265	37-38, 111, 212-230, 246
III. An Approach to Property Transactions	76-79	NC	115-116	NC	NC
IV. Sales or Other Dispositions of Property	25, 28-30, 224-225, 774-777	400-411, 413-416, 719-721	116-131	157-175, 249-260, 290-292	115-118, 212-230, 235-245
V. Computation of Realized and Recognized Gain or Loss	76-86	420-425, 437-439	132-152	181-182, 265-274, 299, 306-308	234-245
VI. Property Encumbered by Debt	872-900	323-348	135-150	319-320	178-196, 231-234
VII. Basis in Property Received in a Transaction	79-81, 95-104	323-327	116-131	296-305, 317-322, 861-863	111-119, 174-177
VIII. Character of Gain or Loss	NC	45-46	115	301-305	NC

Lieuallen: Basic Federal Income Tax Emanuel Law Outline (by chapter and section heading)	Burke & Friel: *Taxation of Individual Income* (Ninth Edition, 2010)	Dodge, Fleming, & Geier: *Federal Income Tax: Doctrine, Structure, and Policy: Text, Cases, Problems* (Third Edition, 2004)	Freeland, Lathrope, Lind, & Stephens: *Fundamentals of Federal Income Taxation: Cases and Materials* (Fifteenth Edition, 2009)	Schmalbeck & Zelenak: *Federal Income Taxation* (Third Edition, 2011)	Klein, Bankman, Shaviro & Stark: *Federal Income Taxation* (Fifteenth Edition, 2009)
CHAPTER 10 **NONRECOGNITION TRANSACTIONS**					
II. An Approach to the Nonrecognition Provisions	NC	437-440	889-891	275-277	246-247
III. Like-Kind Exchanges—§1031	905-941	440-453	891-911	277-282	247-257
IV. Involuntary Conversions—§1033	946-967	264-268	911-922	283-284	251
V. Spousal and Divorce Transfers—§1041	856-859	505-510	209-218	792-793, 830-835	310-316
CHAPTER 11 **TIMING OF INCOME AND EXPENSES**					
II. The Annual Accounting Concept	703-721	763-766	588-592	140-143	138-153
III. Methods of Accounting	623-691	789-815	592-650	669-694	332-350
IV. Accounting for Inventories	693-701	NC	633-636	670-680, 695-704	538-541
V. Installment Method of Reporting Income	975-979	383-389	830-848	340-348	273-276, 541-545
VI. Restricted Property—§83	637-638	431-436	865-872	221-229	301-310
VII. Special Restrictions on Loss Deductions	1059-1067	874-877	528-542	394	594-596
CHAPTER 12 **CHARACTER OF INCOME AND LOSS**					
II. Who Cares? The Capital/Ordinary Distinction	728-752, 756-777, 1046-1047	53-57	684-702	897-902	545-556
III. An Approach to Characterizing Gain or Loss as Capital or Ordinary	741-749, 753-755	725	684, 710-18, 725-746	903	702-704
IV. Section 1231—Real and Depreciable Property Used in a Trade or Business	781-788	732-736	751-763	909	701-702
V. Calculating Net Capital Gain and Net Capital Loss	733-745	725-732	718-725	902-908	701, 790-791

Lieuallen: Basic Federal Income Tax Emanuel Law Outline *(by chapter and section heading)*	Burke & Friel: *Taxation of Individual Income* (Ninth Edition, 2010)	Dodge, Fleming, & Geier: *Federal Income Tax: Doctrine, Structure, and Policy: Text, Cases, Problems* (Third Edition, 2004)	Freeland, Lathrope, Lind, & Stephens: *Fundamentals of Federal Income Taxation: Cases and Materials* (Fifteenth Edition, 2009)	Schmalbeck & Zelenak: *Federal Income Taxation* (Third Edition, 2011)	Klein, Bankman, Shaviro & Stark: *Federal Income Taxation* (Fifteenth Edition, 2009)
CHAPTER 13 **TAX RATES AND CREDITS**					
II. Tax Rates	17-18	459-462	928-941	847-848	20-22, 621-622
III. The Alternative Minimum Tax	1071-1078	772-774	949-961	751-763	611-620
IV. Tax Credits—In General	18	462-464	941-943	39-41, 439-440	414
V. Dependent Care Credit	454-456	469-474	943-944	768-770	407
VI. Earned Income Tax Credit	NC	475-476	945-946	779-801	414
VII. Education Credits	444-445	604-607	236-238, 945	138	509-510
VIII. Other Credits	225	476-478	943-945, 947-949	767-768	417
CHAPTER 14 **IDENTIFYING THE TAXPAYER**					
II. Persons Subject to Tax	17-18, 825-827	479-480, 493-494	250-251	34-37, 769-771, 847-849	11-12, 22-24
III. Assignment of Income	797-821	480-501	252-283	849-857	623-645
IV. Statutory Responses to Assignment of Income and Related Problems	825-827	496-497	250-252	850-854, 866	645-658
CHAPTER 15 **TIME VALUE OF MONEY: PRINCIPLES AND APPLICATIONS**					
II. Time Value of Money Principles—The Basics	NC	23-29	NC	NC	40-42
III. Original Issue Discount (OID)	1025-1047	665-673	857-865	349-356	264-268
IV. Imputed Interest—§483	1041-1043	NC	863	354	268
V. Below-Market Loans—§7872	829-842	288-291, 497-498	491-498	867-868	NC
VI. The Basic Tax Strategies—Deferral of Income and Acceleration of Deductions	155, 447, 643-645	855-873	675-682	19-20, 879-881	40-42, 576-594

Lieuallen: Basic Federal Income Tax Emanuel Law Outline *(by chapter and section heading)*	Burke & Friel: *Taxation of Individual Income* (Ninth Edition, 2010)	Dodge, Fleming, & Geier: *Federal Income Tax: Doctrine, Structure, and Policy: Text, Cases, Problems* (Third Edition, 2004)	Freeland, Lathrope, Lind, & Stephens: *Fundamentals of Federal Income Taxation: Cases and Materials* (Fifteenth Edition, 2009)	Schmalbeck & Zelenak: *Federal Income Taxation* (Third Edition, 2011)	Klein, Bankman, Shaviro & Stark: *Federal Income Taxation* (Fifteenth Edition, 2009)
CHAPTER 16 **PUTTING IT ALL TOGETHER: RECOGNIZING AND ANALYZING COMMON TAX PROBLEMS**					
II. A Systematic Approach to Tax Problems	5-6, 8	NC	NC	NC	NC
III. Applying the Systematic Approach to Common Types of Transactions	NC	NC	NC	NC	NC
IV. Compensation Transactions	NC	NC	NC	NC	NC
V. Transactions in Property	NC	NC	NC	NC	NC
VI. Personal Expenditure Transactions	NC	NC	NC	NC	NC
VII. Business Transactions	NC	NC	NC	NC	NC
VIII. Intrafamilial Transfers	805	NC	NC	815-817	NC

Capsule Summary

This Capsule Summary is intended for review at the end of the semester. Use it to confirm your understanding of basic concepts and to direct you to areas in which you need further review. Numbers in brackets refer to the pages in the main outline where the topic is discussed.

CHAPTER 1

GETTING STARTED IN FEDERAL INCOME TAX

I. UNDERSTANDING THE BIG PICTURE

The process of computing tax liability is summarized below and can be traced in the Form 1040, included in the Outline. [1-2]

Start with:	Gross Income
Subtract:	Certain Deductions
This produces:	Adjusted Gross Income
Subtract:	Standard Deduction *or* Itemized Deduction and Personal Exemption
This produces:	Taxable Income
Multiply by:	Tax Rate(s)
This produces:	Tentative Tax
Subtract:	Tax Credits
This produces:	Tax Due or Refund

A. Gross income—§61

Gross income includes all income from whatever source derived. IRC §61(a). Income from compensation, dividends, gains from dealings in property, and discharge of debt are common types of income. However, particular Code sections exclude certain types of income from gross income. [2]

B. Deductions

Deductions are subtractions from income in computing taxable income. [2] There are two types of deductions available in computing taxable income:

1. Deductions from gross income in computing adjusted gross income: Certain expenditures are deducted (subtracted) from gross income in computing adjusted gross income (AGI).

2. Deductions from adjusted gross income in computing taxable income: The taxpayer subtracts his or her personal exemptions and subtracts the larger of the standard deduction or the itemized deduction. The standard deduction is a statutorily set amount, and the itemized deduction is the sum of all allowable itemized deductions.

C. Multiply taxable income by the tax rate(s)

The taxpayer's tax rate, which depends on his or her filing status, is multiplied by taxable income to produce the "tentative tax." The tax rates applicable to individuals range from 10% to 35% for ordinary income and 15% (sometimes even 0%) to 28% for capital gain. IRC §1. The alternative minimum tax is a separate tax imposed on some taxpayers, with tax rates of 26% and 28% of alternative minimum taxable income. [2]

D. Subtract available tax credits

A tax credit is a dollar-for-dollar reduction in the amount of tax due. Available tax credits are subtracted from the tentative tax to produce the actual tax due. [2]

E. Seven Fundamental Tax Questions

Tax problems—and the material in this book—can be summarized in seven fundamental tax questions [2-3]

1. **Who is the taxpayer?** Identifying the right taxpayer is critical. Families often try to rearrange income and deductions so as to minimize the tax on the family as a whole, while the IRS seeks to match income and deductions to the right taxpayer. [2] and Chapter 14.

2. **Does the taxpayer have income?** To begin the analysis of a taxpayer's tax liability, it is necessary to identify his or her income in a theoretical sense and in the sense of §61. We construe income broadly. [2-3] and Chapters 2 through 4, 9, and 10.

3. **What deductions may the taxpayer claim?** The income tax is a tax on net income, not gross income. Therefore, taxpayers are entitled to reduce gross income by certain deductions, principally personal and business deductions. We construe deductions narrowly. [3] and Chapters 5 through 8.

4. **In which taxable year should the taxpayer include items in gross income or claim deductions?** Once income and deductions are identified, the next question is when—*in which taxable year*—a taxpayer must include an item of income in gross income and when a taxpayer may claim a deduction. Taxpayers seek to defer income as far into the future as possible, and accelerate deductions to the earliest possible year. [3] and Chapters 11 and 15.

5. **What is the character of the taxpayer's income and loss:** When income or loss arises from the sale or exchange of property, it is necessary to characterize it as ordinary or capital. Taxpayers prefer capital gain to ordinary income, because capital gain is subject to preferential, lower tax rates. Taxpayers prefer ordinary loss to capital loss because the deductibility of capital losses is restricted. [3] and Chapter 12.

6. **To what tax rate is the taxpayer subject?** The particular tax rate(s) to be applied to a taxpayer depends on the taxable income and status of the taxpayer. The tax rate multiplied by the taxpayer's taxable income produces the tentative tax. [3] and Chapter 13.

7. **Is the taxpayer entitled to any tax credits?** The final step in calculating a taxpayer's tax liability is determining and subtracting available tax credits. Tax credits can be refundable (they can result in a refund to the taxpayer) or nonrefundable (the credit can only reduce tax to zero). [3] and Chapter 13.

II. SOURCES OF TAX LAW

Title 26 of the U.S. Code is the statutory base for all federal tax law, including the federal income tax. The Department of the Treasury, through the Internal Revenue Service (IRS), and the courts offer guidance on ambiguous provisions of the Code. [6]

A. Administrative interpretation

The Department of the Treasury issues regulations (temporary, final, or proposed) interpreting various Code provisions as well as revenue rulings, revenue procedures, notices, announcements, private letter rulings, and technical advice memoranda on various issues. [8]

B. Judicial interpretation

The U.S. Tax Court, the U.S. District Courts, the U.S. Court of Federal Claims, and the U.S. Bankruptcy Courts are trial courts for tax matters. Cases are appealed to the appellate court for the circuit in which the taxpayer lives and then to the U.S. Supreme Court. [10-11]

1. **U.S. Tax Court—Litigate without first paying tax:** A taxpayer may adjudicate tax matters in the U.S. Tax Court without first paying the tax, if the taxpayer files a petition within 90 days of the date of the Statutory Notice of Deficiency (90-day letter).

2. **U.S. Bankruptcy Court:** A bankruptcy court has jurisdiction over tax matters of the debtor, and may stay proceedings in the U.S. Tax Court regarding tax matters.

3. **Other courts—Pay first, then litigate:** To litigate in the U.S. District Court or the U.S. Court of Federal Claims, the taxpayer must first pay the tax and file a claim for refund. If that claim is either denied or ignored, the taxpayer can sue for refund.

C. Deference to IRS interpretation

The courts interpret ambiguous statutory material in cases properly brought before them. The courts will properly give deference to an IRS-published, prelitigation interpretation of a Code provision. This means that the court will adopt the IRS's interpretation of a Code provision if it is a "reasonable" interpretation of the statute. The IRS's interpretation need not be the only reasonable interpretation or even the "best" interpretation. It need only be a reasonable interpretation. If, however, there is no published, prelitigation interpretation by the IRS, the courts need not give deference to the IRS's interpretation, and may select the interpretation that seems most reasonable. [13]

III. TAX ETHICS

A taxpayer has a responsibility to file an accurate tax return, and a lawyer can advise a client to take a return position only if he or she abides by the applicable ethical rules imposed by the state bar association. The IRS itself regulates practice before it by imposing certain standards and both preparers and taxpayers are subject to certain penalties if they do not comply with applicable statutes. [14-16]

IV. READING TAX STATUTES

Consider using a five-step process—called parsing—to understand an unfamiliar statute. [17-18]

A. The general rule

Find the statute's general rule and underline it in red.

B. Definitions

Find the statute's terms of art and definitions and highlight these in yellow.

C. Exceptions and special rules

Find the statute's exceptions and special rules and mark them with a green "X."

D. Related statutory material

Find the statute's explicit and implicit references to related material and circle these in blue.

E. Know when this statute is typically implicated

Note the kinds of transactions in which the statute becomes relevant.

V. TAX POLICY

The wisdom of a particular tax statute can be evaluated using three criteria: fairness of the system; its administrative practicality; and its economic impact. [20] These goals are often at odds with each other.

A. Fairness

The U.S. income tax burden is allocated among taxpayers based on their "ability to pay." A "fair" system imposes similar taxes on those with similar abilities to pay (horizontal equity). It is impossible to measure each taxpayer's ability to pay directly, and thus taxable income is the surrogate for a taxpayer's ability to pay. If a tax statute causes the system to be more accurate in distinguishing among various taxpayers' abilities to pay, it is more "fair" than a provision that does not do so. [21]

B. Administrative practicality

A good tax statute will assess and collect tax in a cost-effective manner and will not require undue governmental interference with a taxpayer's life. [22]

C. Economic effects

Taxpayers change their behavior in response to tax statutes, and proponents of a taxing measure must consider the effects (both intended and unintended) that the measure likely will have on taxpayer behavior. [22]

CHAPTER 2

IDENTIFYING GROSS INCOME

I. IRC §61—INCOME

The linchpin of the Code, §61, defines gross income as "all *income* from whatever source derived" (emphasis added). Thus it is important to define "income" in order to determine what is included in gross income (even if later it is excluded by another statute). [28]

II. DEFINITIONS OF INCOME

A. Haig-Simons definition—Theoretical approach

Under this approach, income is the sum of (1) the market value of rights exercised in consumption, plus (2) the change in the value of the store of property rights between the beginning and end of the period in question (usually a taxable year). The Haig-Simons definition defines a comprehensive tax base, but difficulties may arise in measuring all consumption and in valuing assets each year. [28-29]

B. "Economic benefit"—A more practical approach

Under this approach, income is the value of any economic benefit received by the taxpayer regardless of the form of the benefit. [29-31]

1. **Tangible items:** The receipt of cash or other property generates income under this approach, even if it comes from an unusual source, such as a windfall.

2. **Barter:** The exchange of services for services constitutes income to both service providers. See Rev. Rul. 79-24, 1979-2 C.B. 60.

3. **Intangible benefits:** The receipt of an intangible benefit would be included in gross income under this approach. For example, if one taxpayer satisfies another taxpayer's legal obligation, the latter has income in the amount of the satisfaction. *Old Colony Trust Co. v. Commissioner,* 279 U.S. 716 (1929). But noneconomic benefits (such as a sunny day in Oregon) are not income under this principle.

III. CERTAIN ITEMS THAT ARE NOT INCOME

Certain items are not considered income by general understanding of that term in federal tax law, even though they might qualify as "income" under a theoretical definition of income.

A. Imputed income

The value of any services one performs for oneself or one's family and the value of any property used that one owns are imputed income, which is not considered income for purposes of federal income tax. [31-32]

B. Capital recovery

A taxpayer's income from the sale or exchange of property is his or her profit on the transaction, not the total amount received. A taxpayer is entitled to receive his or her capital investment in the property tax-free, although the timing of this recovery is a matter for legislative determination. [33]

C. Loans

Neither the creation nor the repayment of a loan is a taxable event. However, forgiveness or discharge of a loan may generate income to the debtor. [33-34]

D. General welfare exclusion

As a matter of IRS practice, governmental payments made to a person as part of a system of general welfare are not included, unless specifically addressed by the Code. [34]

CHAPTER 3

SPECIFIC INCLUSIONS IN GROSS INCOME

I. SECTION 61

Section 61 provides that gross income includes "all income" from all sources. Courts construe §61 broadly to include most types of income in gross income, unless they are specifically excepted by statute.

II. SPECIFIC ITEMS

Section 61(a) provides a nonexclusive list of types of income specifically included in gross income.

A. Compensation income—§61(a)(1)

Compensation income is the consideration transferred for the performance of services, whether in the form of salary, fees, commissions, or fringe benefits, and whether in the form of cash, property, or other services. [39-41]

1. **Amount included:** The amount of compensation income is the amount of cash received or the fair market value of the property or services received.

2. **Timing issues:** The taxable year in which a taxpayer will include an amount of compensation income will depend on the taxpayer's method of accounting, and if restricted property is involved, the rules of §83.

3. **Character:** Compensation income is ordinary income, potentially taxable at the highest tax rate.

B. Gross income from business—§61(a)(2)

A taxpayer engaged in business as a sole proprietor will include his or her gross income from business and will subtract available deductions from that amount, reporting the net result (income or loss) on the tax return. [41]

C. Gains derived from dealings in property—§61(a)(3)

These are discussed fully in Chapters 9 and 10.

D. Investment income—§61(a)(4)-(7)

Various types of investment income are included in gross income, including dividends, interest (both explicit and imputed), rents, royalties, and income from annuities. [41-46]

1. Imputed interest—OID rules, §§483, 7872: Most loans explicitly provide for interest to be paid. Some, however, provide for no interest or a below-market rate of interest, and the Code often will recharacterize these loans or investments to impute interest to the transactions. [42] and Chapter 15.

2. Annuities—§§61(a)(9), 72: A taxpayer receiving a regular annuity payment is receiving a partial return of his or her invested capital, and the balance of the payment is income. To determine the amount of a payment that is excluded from gross income, multiply the payment by the exclusion ratio. The exclusion ratio is the following fraction:

$$\frac{\text{Investment in the contract}}{\text{Total expected return under the contract}}$$

The amount of the payment in excess of the excluded amount is included in gross income of the taxpayer, subject to certain limitations. [43-46]

E. Alimony—§§61(a)(8), 71

A taxpayer receiving alimony must include it in his or her gross income. The federal definition of alimony governs the tax consequences of alimony payments, regardless of the label used under state law for the payment. [47]

1. Definition of alimony: For a payment to qualify as alimony, it must meet six requirements: (1) it must be paid in cash, not in property or services; (2) the payment must be received by or on behalf of the spouse or former spouse pursuant to a divorce decree or separation instrument; (3) the decree must not designate the payment as nondeductible and nonincludable; (4) the payor and recipient must not be members of the same household at the time of the payment; (5) there must be no obligation to make a payment after the death of the recipient spouse; and (6) the payment must not be, in substance, support for the child of the payor (there is an incentive to characterize child support as alimony because alimony is deductible to the payor, and child support is not deductible).

2. Front-end loaded alimony: If alimony payments vary by more than $15,000 in the first three years, and the payments are greater in the beginning than at the end of the three-year period, they will be "front-end loaded." In that case, the "excess alimony amount" is included in the gross income of the payor spouse and is deducted from the income of the recipient spouse in the third post-separation year.

3. Property settlements: If an amount payable in divorce is not alimony or child support, it may be a property settlement. See Chapter 10.

F. Discharge of indebtedness income—§61(a)(12)

Creation of a loan is not a taxable event to either the creditor or the debtor, for neither has a net economic benefit. If, however, the creditor forgoes collection under the debt, the debtor will have a benefit equal in amount of the debt forgone. This is discharge of indebtedness income and must be included in the debtor's gross income. [50-53]

1. **Enforceable debt:** To have discharge of indebtedness income, there must be an enforceable debt in the first place. See *Zarin v. Commissioner,* 916 F.2d 110 (3d Cir. 1990).

2. **Identifying discharge:** A discharge occurs when the creditor agrees to take something less than he or she originally agreed to take in satisfaction of the loan. Payment of a debt is not discharge, nor is payment of a debt by another, or payment deferral. If the creditor receives what he or she bargained for, even if that amount is different from the amount loaned, there is no discharge.

3. **Contested liability doctrine:** If a taxpayer in good faith disputes the amount of the debt, a subsequent settlement of the debt is treated as the amount of the debt for tax purposes.

4. **Possible exclusion—§108:** Certain types of discharge of indebtedness income are excluded from the gross income of the taxpayer. The newest of these—ripe for testing—is the exclusion of gain on certain foreclosures (discussed in Chapter 4). In general, if a taxpayer excludes discharge of indebtedness income, he or she may also be required to reduce his or her "tax attributes."

III. PRIZES, AWARDS, HELPFUL PAYMENTS, EMBEZZLEMENTS, AND DAMAGES

Code sections other than §61 provide for specific inclusions in gross income, and judicial doctrines also include some amounts in gross income. [54]

A. Prizes and awards—§74

Prizes and awards are included in gross income unless the recipient did nothing to be selected, the recipient is not required to render substantial future services as a condition of receiving the prize, and he ore she immediately transfers the prize to charity. [54]

B. Helpful payments—§§82, 85, 86

Various types of helpful payments are included in gross income, such as unemployment compensation, and a portion of Social Security benefits received, depending on the income of the recipient. [54]

C. Embezzled funds

Embezzlers must include the proceeds of their embezzlements in their gross income unless they can show that the transaction is akin to a loan. See *Gilbert v. Commissioner,* 552 F.2d 478 (2d Cir. 1977). [54-55]

D. Damages

Damages received for injury are includable in a taxpayer's gross income, unless specifically excluded under §104. [55] and Chapter 4(VI)(B).

CHAPTER 4

SPECIFIC EXCLUSIONS FROM GROSS INCOME

I. EXCLUSIONS—IN GENERAL

The Code includes a number of statutes providing that items that are otherwise income will not be included in gross income. Exclusions are construed narrowly; an item must fit within the precise requirements of an exclusion statute in order to be excluded from gross income. [64-65]

II. DEATH BENEFITS—§101

Amounts received under a life insurance policy by reason of the death of the insured are excluded from gross income. Life insurance has its own vocabulary, so make sure you are familiar with the principal terms. [65-67]

A. Transfer for valuable consideration

The exclusion does not apply to payments made under policies that were transferred for valuable consideration; in that case, the exclusion is limited to the purchaser's purchase price under the contract. [67]

B. Chronic or terminal illness

The exclusion extends to amounts paid to or for the care of chronically or terminally ill insureds. [67]

III. GIFTS—§102

The recipient of a gift or an inheritance may exclude the cash or value of the property received from gross income regardless of amount. [67-69]

A. Definition

A gift is a transfer made with detached and disinterested generosity. See *Duberstein v. Commissioner*, 363 U.S. 278 (1960). [68-69]

B. Exceptions

1. **Income from property:** The exclusion does not apply to the income derived from property received by gift.

2. **Employee gifts:** The exclusion does not apply to any transfer made by an employer to an employee; these amounts are considered compensation income, not gifts.

C. Basis—§1015

A recipient of property by gift or inheritance must determine the basis he or she has in the property. [69] and Chapter 9.

1. **Property received by gift:** The recipient of property by gift takes the donor's basis in the gift, plus a portion of any gift tax paid on the transfer. However, if at the time of the gift the fair

market value of the property was less than its basis, for purposes of determining loss on subsequent sale or disposition, the donee takes the fair market value of the gift on the date of the gift. IRC §1015(a).

2. **Property received by inheritance—§1014:** The recipient of property through inheritance takes as his or her basis in the property the fair market value of the property on the date of the decedent's death or the alternate valuation date if that date is elected.

IV. INTEREST ON STATE AND LOCAL BONDS—§103

A taxpayer may exclude the interest paid to the taxpayer on qualifying state and local bonds. [70]

V. COMPENSATION FOR PERSONAL INJURY OR SICKNESS—§104

Section 104 excludes from gross income amounts received as a result of personal physical injury or sickness. This excludes compensatory damages from suit or settlement of personal physical injury actions (in lump sums or in structured settlements), but does not exclude punitive damages (except in very limited situations), previously deducted medical expenses, and pre- or postjudgment interest. [70-71]

VI. DISCHARGE OF INDEBTEDNESS INCOME—§108

Certain types of discharge of indebtedness income may be excluded from gross income. The exclusion is generally conditioned on the taxpayer giving up certain tax benefits. [71-74]

A. **Types of discharge of indebtedness income excluded**

Only certain types of discharge of indebtedness income are excluded under §108. [72-73] Of these, the principal types are the following:

1. **Bankruptcy—§108(a)(1)(A):** If the discharge occurs in a Title 11 (bankruptcy) case, the discharge of indebtedness income is excluded from gross income.

2. **Insolvency—§108(a)(1)(B):** If the discharge occurs at a time the taxpayer is insolvent, the discharge of indebtedness income is excluded from gross income to the extent of the insolvency. Insolvency is the amount of the taxpayer's debts over the fair market value of his or her property.

3. **Certain farm debt—§108(a)(1)(C):** If the discharge is of "qualified farm indebtedness" the discharge of indebtedness income will be excluded from gross income.

4. **Qualified principal residence indebtedness:** If the discharge is of acquisition indebtedness for a taxpayer's principal residence, the discharge will generally be excluded from gross income if the discharge occurs before January 1, 2013. The limit on this exclusion is $2,000,000. IRC §108(a)(1)(E).

5. **Student loans:** Gross income does not include any discharge of a student loan if the discharge is the result of the former student working for a period of time in a nonprofit or governmental setting. IRC §108(f)(1).

B. **"Paying the piper"—§108(b)**

Each dollar of exclusion generally requires a reduction in the taxpayer's tax benefits, i.e., net operating losses, tax credits, capital loss carryovers, and other carryovers. The taxpayer may elect in some circumstances to apply the exclusion amount to reduce the basis of depreciable property. The result of this reduction is that the taxpayer will have a greater amount of income in the future. [73-74]

VII. EXCLUSION FOR GAIN ON SALE OF PRINCIPAL RESIDENCE—§121

Section 121 allows a taxpayer to exclude from gross income $250,000 ($500,000 for joint returns) of gain on the sale of a principal residence, if the taxpayer has owned and used the dwelling as a principal residence for at least two of the past five years. [74-77]

VIII. EMPLOYMENT-RELATED EXCLUSIONS

The Code provides a variety of employment-related exclusions. [77-84]

A. **Meals and lodging—§119**

An employee may exclude from gross income the value of meals and lodging provided by an employer if the meals or lodging are provided for the convenience of the employer, are provided on the business premises of the employer, and in the case of lodging, the employee is required to accept the lodging as a condition of employment. [77-79]

1. **Convenience of the employer:** "Convenience of the employer" means that the employer has a "substantial noncompensatory business reason" for supplying the meals and lodging, considering all the facts and circumstances of the situation.

2. **Business premises:** The business premises of an employer are the grounds of the employer's place of business. The circuits have split on whether the business premises for state police include all public roads and contiguous restaurants.

3. **Condition of employment:** The condition of employment requirement is generally satisfied by showing that the employee is on call for the business of the employer.

B. **Statutory fringe benefits—§132**

The value of any fringe benefit that qualifies as any of eight fringe benefits is excluded from the gross income of the employee. In some cases, the provision of the benefit must meet antidiscrimination rules. [79-81]

1. **No additional cost service—§132(b):** If the employer regularly provides the service to the public and provides it to the employee without incurring any significant additional cost, it will be excluded from the gross income of the employee who receives the service.

2. **Qualified employee discounts—§132(c):** If employees enjoy a discount on property or services provided to the public by the employer, and the discount does not exceed a formulaic percentage, the value of the discount will be excluded from the gross income of the employees taking advantage of the discount.

3. **Working condition fringe—§132(d):** An employee receiving a benefit that would have generated a deduction as a trade or business expense or as depreciation to the employee had he or she purchased the benefit individually may exclude the benefit from gross income.

4. **De minimis fringe—§132(e):** If the benefit provided to the employees is so small that accounting for it would be unreasonable or administratively impractical, it will be excluded from the gross income of the employees receiving it.

5. **Qualified transportation fringe—§132(f):** An employee who receives transit passes, van transportation, or parking may exclude the benefit from gross income, within specified dollar limitations.

6. **Qualified moving expense reimbursement—§132(g):** If an employee receives reimbursement for amounts that would be deductible as moving expenses under §217, he or she may exclude these amounts from gross income.

7. **Athletic facility—§132(j):** The value of an on-premises athletic facility may be excluded from the gross income of an employee if it is operated by the employer and is used mostly by employees.

8. **Qualified retirement planning services—§132(m):** An employer may provide financial planning services, if certain conditions are met.

C. **Insurance premiums and payments—§§79, 105, 106**

The cost of employer-provided health insurance premiums is excluded from the gross income of the employee. When an employee receives benefits, these are excluded from gross income up to the amount of the employee's medical expenses. The employee may also exclude the cost of employer-provided term life insurance attributable to coverage up to $50,000; premiums attributable to excess coverage are includable in the employee's gross income. [81-83]

D. **Dependent care assistance—§129**

The employee may exclude up to $5,000 of employer-provided dependent care assistance in the form of actual care provided or as reimbursement. [83] The exclusion and the dependent care credit (see Chapter 13) may not be claimed for the same expenditure.

E. **Educational assistance—§127**

The employee may exclude up to $5,250 of qualifying educational assistance provided by the employer. [83]

F. **Adoption expenses—§137**

An employer may provide up to $13,170 (in 2011) of adoption assistance to employees, which may be excluded from their gross incomes, subject to certain income limitations. [83]

G. Group legal services—§120

An employer may provide up to $70 per year to provide group legal services plans to employees. [84]

X. EDUCATION PROVISIONS

A. Qualified scholarships—§117

Amounts received as a "qualified scholarship," which generally means amounts received by degree candidates at regularly operated educational institutions for tuition, books, fees, and supplies, are excluded from gross income. A qualified scholarship does not include room and board or amounts paid for services. [84-86]

B. Interest on certain U.S. savings bonds—§135

To the extent the redemption proceeds of certain U.S. savings bonds are used for qualified education expenses, the income element of such redemption is excluded from gross income. Income level restrictions apply. IRC §135. [86]

C. Section 529 plans—§529

Distributions from §529 plans, which are state-sponsored plans for education savings, are excluded from gross income to the extent they are used for qualified education expenses. Unlike many education incentives, these funds can be used for K-12 as well as postsecondary education. [86]

D. Education savings accounts—§530

Distributions from education savings accounts are excluded from gross income to the extent they are used for qualified education expenses. Unlike many education incentives, these funds can be used for K-12 as well as postsecondary education. [86]

XI. PAYMENTS FOR SUPPORT OF FAMILY

A. Child support

A custodial parent may exclude child support received from his or her gross income. [86] Remember, too, that gifts are not included in gross income, so the amounts a family pays to support a family member in college, for example, are not included in the recipient's gross income—they are considered gifts. See Chapter 2.

B. Foster care payments

Qualified foster care payments are excluded from gross income. [86]

CHAPTER 5

DEDUCTIONS—IN GENERAL

I. DEFINITION OF DEDUCTION

A deduction is a subtraction from income in computing adjusted gross income or taxable income. [95]

A. Compare exclusion

By contrast, an exclusion causes an item of income not to be included in gross income. An exclusion and a deduction will have the same tax effect for taxpayers, but will reach this result by very different paths. [95-96] and Chapter 4.

B. Compare tax credit

A tax credit is a dollar-for-dollar reduction in the amount of tax due. [96] and Chapter 13.

II. ROLE OF DEDUCTIONS

Deductions figure prominently in two phases of computation of taxable income. One group of deductions is subtracted from gross income in computing adjusted gross income (AGI). Another group is subtracted from AGI in computing taxable income. See Figure 5A, in text. [97] The benefit of many deductions is limited for higher-income taxpayers, through the mechanism of phaseouts based, directly or indirectly, on adjusted gross income.

III. COMMON THEMES OF DEDUCTION CONTROVERSIES

Three common themes arise in deduction controversies. [99-100]

A. An event

A taxpayer must experience an outlay, an outflow, or a loss in which there is no realistic possibility of recovery of the item. Deductions are narrowly construed, and each and every requirement of a deduction statute must be met. [99]

B. Personal versus business expenses

A common theme in the analysis of deductions is the question whether an expense is "personal" or "business." This distinction is important because, as a general rule, personal expenses are not deductible unless a specific statute provides otherwise. Business expenses are generally deductible. Taxpayers seek to characterize deductions as business-related, rather than personal, in order to deduct them. [99]

C. Expense or capital expenditure?

An expense may be deducted currently, but if an expenditure is for a capital item (a capital expenditure), its cost must be added to basis and be recovered in accordance with the statutory scheme governing capital recovery. Taxpayers prefer to characterize expenditures as expenses rather than capital expenditures in order to accelerate capital recovery. [99-100]

CHAPTER 6

PERSONAL DEDUCTIONS

I. IN GENERAL—§262

While personal expenditures are not generally deductible, specific Code provisions allow a taxpayer to deduct certain personal expenses if statutory requirements are met. [103] Many personal deductions, like some exclusions, are subject to phaseouts based on some measure of income.

II. TWO KINDS OF PERSONAL DEDUCTIONS

A. "Above-the-line" deductions

This group of deductions is subtracted from gross income in computing AGI. Taxpayers seek to increase "above-the-line" deductions because AGI serves as a measure for certain itemized deductions, and lowering AGI will potentially increase the deductible portion of these itemized deductions. [103]

B. "Below-the-line" deductions

This group of deductions is subtracted from AGI in computing taxable income and includes the personal exemption and either the standard or the itemized deduction. The itemized deduction is the sum of a number of deductions including home mortgage interest, taxes, casualty losses, medical expenses, charitable contributions, bad debts, and miscellaneous expenses. [103]

III. "ABOVE-THE-LINE" PERSONAL DEDUCTIONS

A. Alimony—§215

A taxpayer may deduct the amount of alimony or separate maintenance paid during the year. Alimony has a special definition under federal tax law. [104]

B. Moving expenses—§217

A taxpayer may deduct qualifying moving expenses associated with a move to a new place of employment 50 or more miles from the taxpayer's former employment. [104-105]

C. Contributions to regular IRAs—§219

A taxpayer may claim a deduction for certain retirement savings. In general, an individual may deduct the lesser of $5,000 or his or her earned income to an individual retirement account (IRA). Taxpayers 50 years of age and older can make an additional contribution. If the taxpayer participates in a qualified plan and has income in excess of a certain amount, the contribution may be made, but no deduction is allowable. [105]

D. Losses—§165

A taxpayer may deduct losses incurred during a taxable year that are not compensated for by insurance or otherwise. However, an individual taxpayer may deduct only three types of loss. [105-106]

1. **Trade or business losses—§165(c)(1):** A taxpayer may deduct losses incurred in a trade or business. A trade or business is defined below.

2. **Investment losses—§165(c)(2):** A taxpayer may deduct losses incurred in an activity engaged in for profit, which does not constitute a trade or business. For example, losses on the sale of stock would be investment losses, but losses on the sale of a principal residence would not be, as a principal residence is held for personal, rather than investment, purposes.

3. **Casualty losses—§165(c)(3):** A taxpayer may deduct certain casualty losses, such as losses from theft, fire, storm, and flood. Casualty losses up to the amount of casualty gains are deducted from gross income in computing AGI. The remaining deductible losses constitute an itemized deduction to the extent that they exceed 10% of the taxpayer's AGI.

E. Interest on education loans—§221

Up to $2,500 of the interest paid on certain student loans is potentially deductible, as an above-the-line deduction, depending on income limitations. [106-107]

F. Medical savings accounts—§223

A taxpayer subject to a high-deductible health plan can deduct certain contributions to a Health Savings Account (HSA). [107-108]

G. Costs incurred in civil rights or whistleblower actions

A taxpayer who incurs attorneys' fees or other costs in certain civil rights actions may deduct such expenses. There are only a limited number of actions that qualify, and otherwise the taxpayer would probably be required to deduct these amounts as miscellaneous itemized deductions. [108]

IV. THE CHOICE: STANDARD OR ITEMIZED DEDUCTION

A taxpayer may deduct either the standard or the itemized deduction, but not both. The rational taxpayer will choose the larger of the two. The standard deduction is a specified amount based on filing status, and the itemized deduction is the sum of the taxpayer's itemized deductions. [108-109]

V. ITEMIZED DEDUCTIONS

A number of deductions are available to the taxpayer only if he or she claims the itemized deductions. The principal itemized deductions are discussed below.

A. Interest—§163

Personal interest is not deductible. Personal interest is interest other than (1) trade or business interest; (2) qualified residence interest; or (3) investment interest. [111-114]

1. **Qualified residence interest—§163(h):** Qualified residence interest is deductible by individuals. There are two types of qualified residence interest attributable to loans on the taxpayer's principal residence and one other qualifying residence (which the taxpayer uses at least 14 days per year for personal purposes).

      a. Acquisition indebtedness: Interest is deductible on loans up to $1 million, the proceeds of which are used to acquire or construct a qualifying residence, and that are secured by that residence.

      b. Home equity indebtedness: Interest is deductible on loans up to $100,000, which are secured by a principal residence and do not exceed the taxpayer's "equity" in the residence, i.e., the difference between the fair market value and any indebtedness secured by that residence.

    1. Investment interest—§163(d): A taxpayer may deduct interest to finance the purchase of investments, but only to the extent of net income from those investments.

B. Taxes—§164

A taxpayer may deduct state, local, and foreign real property, personal property, and income taxes. [114] Until 2012, taxpayer may elect to deduct state and local sales taxes in lieu of state and local income taxes.

C. Casualty losses—§165(c)(3), (h)

A casualty loss is a loss through complete or partial destruction of property from a sudden, unexpected, and unusual cause such as fire or storm. A taxpayer may deduct casualty losses to the extent that they exceed (1) $100 per event, and (2) 10% of the taxpayer's adjusted gross income. [115-117]

D. Medical expenses—§213

A taxpayer may deduct medical expenses, but only to the extent that they exceed 7.5% of his or her AGI. Medical expenses are expenses for the cure, treatment, or management of a disease or accident and include health insurance premiums paid by the taxpayer but do not include certain other items such as nonprescription drugs and certain elective cosmetic surgery. [117-119]

E. Charitable contributions—§170

A taxpayer may deduct contributions to qualifying charitable organizations. The amount of the deduction is the amount of cash or the fair market value of any property contributed. Limitations based on a taxpayer's AGI are imposed; usually, this is 50% of AGI. The taxpayer must not receive a personal benefit as a result of the contribution. [119-121]

F. Miscellaneous expenses—§67

A number of expenses are deductible only to the extent that they, in the aggregate, exceed 2% of the taxpayer's AGI. These include employee's unreimbursed business expenses and certain investment expenses. [121-122]

VI. PERSONAL EXEMPTION—§151

A taxpayer is entitled to deduct a personal exemption for him- or herself and for any dependent of the taxpayer. [122-123] Only certain individuals, known as qualifying children and qualifying relatives, can be claimed as dependents.

C A P S U L E   S U M M A R Y

CHAPTER 7

BUSINESS AND INVESTMENT DEDUCTIONS

I. IN GENERAL

Net business income is included in a taxpayer's gross income, and net loss from a trade or business constitutes a deduction subject to certain limitations. To compute net income or loss from business, a taxpayer begins with gross income from the business and subtracts available deductions. [131] A taxpayer doing business as a sole proprietor reports this income and the available deductions on Schedule C and the net result (income or loss) is then reported on his or her own tax return, subject to certain limits on losses. A taxpayer who owns rental or royalty property will compute the income and deductions associated with this activity on Schedule E and report the net result (profit or loss) on his or her own tax return, subject to certain limitations. In both situations, it is critical to identify available deductions. [131]

II. ORDINARY AND NECESSARY BUSINESS EXPENSES—§162

A taxpayer may claim a deduction for all the ordinary and necessary expenses paid or incurred in carrying on a trade or business, or while away from home, and rental payments for business property. [132-135]

A. Five requirements

There are five distinct requirements for deduction of an expenditure under §162.

1. **Ordinary:** Ordinary means "usual in the course of general and accepted business practice," arising from a transaction commonly encountered in the type of business in question, even if the expenditure is unique for the particular taxpayers. See *Deputy v. DuPont,* 308 U.S. 488 (1940). In addition, the expenditure must be reasonable in amount, and this particular issue often arises in the area of compensation.

2. **Necessary:** There must be a reasonable connection between the expense and the furtherance of the business. Necessary means "appropriate and helpful" to the business, but the courts are reluctant to second-guess the judgment of business people, except in extreme cases.

3. **Expense:** The expense requirement distinguishes between expenses (which may be deductible) and capital expenditures, which must be capitalized.

4. **Trade or business:** To be deductible, the expense must be incurred in connection with a taxpayer's trade or business. The principal function of the trade or business requirement is to distinguish between personal activities and business activities.

   a. **Definition:** To be engaged in a trade or business, a taxpayer must be involved in an activity with continuity and regularity and must have the primary purpose of creating income or profit rather than merely engaging in a hobby. See *Commissioner v. Groetzinger,* 480 U.S. 23 (1987).

   b. **Hobbies:** A trade or business requires a profit motive, which is not characteristic of hobbies. Hobbies may generate income, and certain deductions may be available under §183.

5. **Carrying on:** The expense must be incurred during the time the taxpayer is actually engaged in carrying on a trade or business.

    a. **Going concern:** A taxpayer is carrying on a trade or business from the date that it is a going concern, i.e., has regular activity in the areas in which the business is organized.

    b. **Pre-opening expenses—§195:** Expenses incurred prior to opening must be capitalized. Up to $5,000 of expenses that would have been deductible if the taxpayer had been engaged in a trade or business when they were incurred can be deducted in the year of opening, but this amount is reduced by the amount by which pre-opening expenses exceed $50,000. Any remaining amount is amortized over 15 years.

B. Limits on deduction

Section 162 is riddled with exceptions and special rules; only the principal exceptions are discussed here. [133-134]

1. **Public policy:** No deduction is allowed for illegal bribes and kickbacks, for fines or similar penalties paid to the government, or for the two-thirds portion of the treble damages of antitrust damages.

2. **Excessive CEO compensation:** There is no deduction for compensation of a chief executive officer of a publicly traded company in excess of $1 million unless it is performance based.

III. OTHER DEDUCTIONS FOR A TRADE OR BUSINESS

A taxpayer engaged in business may deduct other expenses of doing business, including certain charitable contributions, bad debts, interest on debt incurred in connection with the trade or business, taxes, and losses incurred in the business. [135-136]

IV. DEDUCTIONS FOR CAPITAL RECOVERY

A. In general—§263

A taxpayer may not claim a current deduction for capital expenditures, generally defined as "permanent improvements or betterments made to increase the value of any property or estate." [137]

1. **Capital recovery:** When a capital expenditure is made, the cost is said to be "capitalized." The taxpayer will be entitled to recover that capitalized amount at some point during his or her ownership of the asset (capital recovery). "Recovery" means that the taxpayer's economic investment in the asset will constitute a tax benefit, either as a deduction during the ownership of the asset, or at sale when the taxpayer reports as gain the amount received in excess of his or her investment in the property.

2. **Timing:** The timing of capital recovery is completely within the discretion of Congress. Taxpayers prefer to recover capital as soon as possible, preferring accelerated depreciation systems to systems that defer capital recovery until sale or other disposition of the asset.

B. Definition of capital expenditure

Neither the Code nor the regulations offer a precise definition of a capital expenditure. [137-139]

1. **Separate asset test:** If an expenditure creates a separate, identifiable asset with a useful life that will extend substantially beyond the taxable year, the expenditure is probably a capital expenditure. See *Commissioner v. Lincoln Savings & Loan Assn.*, 403 U.S. 345 (1971) and Reg. §1.263-2(a).

2. **Future benefits test:** Even if a separate asset is not created, if an expenditure creates more than an insignificant future benefit, it is a capital expenditure. See *Indopco, Inc. v. Commissioner,* 503 U.S. 79 (1992).

C. Section 179 deduction

Section 179 allows a taxpayer to deduct up to a specified amount attributable to capital expenditures for equipment and tools purchased for the business. This deduction also reduces the basis of the asset(s) by the amount of the deduction claimed. In 2011 the §179 amount is $500,000, reduced by the cost of §179 property the taxpayer places in service that exceeds $2,000,000. The §179 deduction cannot exceed the taxable income of the taxpayer computed without regard to this deduction. [140-141]

D. Modified accelerated cost recovery system (MACRS) deduction for tangible business assets—§§167, 168

MACRS is the method by which taxpayers claim capital recovery for tangible business assets. [141-143]

1. **Dual function of deduction:** The MACRS deduction is a deduction from gross income in computing net business income or loss. Each time the taxpayer claims a MACRS deduction, the basis of the asset is reduced by the same amount (producing the "adjusted basis" of the asset).

2. **Calculation of MACRS deduction:** The MACRS deduction is computed by applying the "applicable recovery method" to the "basis" of the asset over the "applicable recovery period," taking into account "applicable conventions."

   a. **Applicable recovery method:** Three different recovery methods are available under MACRS: straight-line and two accelerated methods.

   b. **Basis:** The basis of an asset is generally its cost, unless it is acquired by some other means.

   c. **Applicable recovery period:** The recovery period for an asset is the period of years over which the taxpayer claims capital recovery for the item. The recovery period for assets is defined by statute or by the IRS.

      i. **Real property:** Residential real property has a recovery period of 27.5 years. Nonresidential real property has a recovery period of 39 years.

      ii. **Personal property:** Personal property can be 3-, 5-, 7-, 10-, 15-, or 20-year property. For example, office furniture is 10-year property.

   d. **Applicable conventions:** The applicable convention expresses the beginning date of capital recovery. Recovery generally begins when property is placed in service, and the conventions provide that regardless of when the property is actually placed in service, it will be deemed placed in service on a particular date. Real property uses a midmonth convention, and personal property a midyear convention.

E. Section 197 intangibles

Section 197 allows a taxpayer to amortize the cost of "section 197 intangibles" ratably over 15 years. A §197 intangible includes purchased goodwill, going-concern value, covenants not to compete, patents, copyrights, secret formulas or processes, and various other intangibles. [144]

V. ACTIVITIES ENGAGED IN FOR PROFIT THAT ARE NOT TRADES OR BUSINESSES

A taxpayer who owns rental property, or property that generates royalties, probably is not engaged in a trade or business. Nevertheless, the taxpayer may deduct the ordinary and necessary expenses incurred to generate this income and may depreciate or amortize assets that are subject to periodic capital recovery. [145]

A. Investment activities

The expenses of carrying on investment activities are deductible, unless the expense must be capitalized (such as commissions on the purchase of stock). The 2% floor of §67 may restrict the availability of these deductions. [145-146]

B. Rental real estate

A taxpayer that holds real or personal property for rental is entitled to deduct the expenses of that property, including interest, taxes, repairs, and the usual deductions for capital recovery. [146-147]

VI. SUBSTANTIATION

A taxpayer must be able to substantiate his or her deductions. [147]

CHAPTER 8

MIXED BUSINESS AND PERSONAL EXPENSES

I. IN GENERAL

Business expenses are usually deductible, while personal expenses are not. Some expenses, however, have a mixed character. They are connected to the taxpayer's business, but also have a connection to his or her personal life. This mixed character raises questions about their deductibility. The Code takes a variety of approaches to these types of expenses. [155]

II. ORIGIN TEST

For an expense to be deductible as a business expense, it must have its origin in the taxpayer's business, not his or her personal life. In making this determination, the courts will inquire into the so-called origin of the expense—the reason the expense was incurred—considering all the facts and circumstances of the situation. See *United States v. Gilmore,* 372 U.S. 39 (1963). [156]

III. TRAVEL

A taxpayer's expenses while traveling away from the taxpayer's tax home primarily for business are deductible. Commuting expenses are not deductible. A taxpayer's tax home is the taxpayer's principal place of business or, if the taxpayer doesn't have one, the taxpayer's primary abode in a real sense. [156-158]

IV. CLOTHING

A taxpayer may deduct the cost of special clothing, such as a uniform, that is required for his or her job or business. But the cost of clothing that can be worn for regular purposes is not deductible. [158]

V. EDUCATION EXPENSES

A taxpayer may deduct the cost of education that improves his or her skills in the taxpayer's current trade or business, or is required as a condition of remaining licensed in that business. Education that prepares a taxpayer for a new trade or business is not deductible. [158-159]

VI. MEALS AND ENTERTAINMENT

Meals and entertainment expenses are subject to the especially stringent rules of §274. First, the meals and entertainment must be sufficiently connected with the trade or business of the taxpayer. Even then, only 50% of the cost of such items is deductible. [159-160]

VII. HOME OFFICES AND VACATION HOMES—§280A

When a taxpayer uses a portion of his or her residence as an office or rents out a vacation home while still using it for part of the year for personal purposes, an allocation must be made between deductible (business) and nondeductible (personal) expenses associated with use of the residence. [160-163]

A. Home offices

In order to deduct any expenses attributable to a home office, the taxpayer must use the office as the principal place of business, or as a place where the taxpayer regularly meets with patients, clients, or customers. [160-162]

1. **Restriction on deductions:** If the taxpayer meets this test, a portion of the expenses allocable to the business activity may be deducted, but not in excess of the gross income from the business minus the sum of the nonbusiness deductions plus business deductions not related to the use of the property.

2. **Remember §121:** Section 121 allows a taxpayer to exclude from gross income some or all of the gain on the sale of a principal residence. This exclusion does not apply to deductions previously claimed for depreciation on a home. Thus, taxpayers must carefully consider whether it is worthwhile to claim such a deduction.

B. Vacation homes

Deductions attributable to rental use of a home cannot exceed the percentage of those expenses equal to the total expenses multiplied by a fraction. The numerator of the fraction is the total number of days the unit is rented at fair rental value, and the denominator is the total number of days during the year in which the unit is used. This limitation does not apply to deductions that are allowable regardless of rental use, such as qualified residence interest. [162-163]

VIII. "LUXURY" AUTOMOBILES AND LISTED PROPERTY—§280F

A. Automobiles

Section 280F limits the amount of MACRS deductions that may be claimed each year for passenger automobiles, thus essentially disallowing depreciation for "luxury" automobiles. [164-166]

B. Listed property

For certain types of property, the taxpayer will be required to use the straight-line method of depreciation unless the predominant use of the property is for business. [165-166]

IX. HOBBY LOSSES—§183

A taxpayer who has no profit motive for an activity may deduct only the expenses associated with the activity to the extent that such expenses are deductible under Code sections that do not require a profit motive (nonbusiness expenses) plus expenses in the amount equal to the gross income from the activity minus the nonbusiness expenses. [166-168]

A. Existence of profit motive—Reg. §1.183-2

Whether a taxpayer has engaged in an activity for profit is to be determined from all of the facts and circumstances of the situation. The regulations offer nine factors indicative of a profit motive. [166-168]

B. Exception—§183(d)

If an activity produces income in three out of the five consecutive years ending in the year in question, it is rebuttably presumed to be engaged in for profit. [168]

X. GAMBLING LOSSES

Gambling losses are deductible only to the extent of gains from gambling. [168-169]

CHAPTER 9

TRANSACTIONS IN PROPERTY

I. SECTION 1001—IN GENERAL

Section 1001 defines realized gain or loss as the difference between the amount realized (what the taxpayer receives in the transaction) and the taxpayer's adjusted basis in the property transferred. [178-180]

II. TRANSACTIONS IN PROPERTY

While most transactions in property are easy to identify—sales or trades of real estate, personal property, or stocks—in some situations it can be difficult to distinguish between sales of property and acceleration of streams of ordinary income. Only the former potentially generates capital gain. [180]

III. REALIZATION EVENT—§1001

A realization event occurs when a taxpayer exchanges property, receiving some materially different item. A "materially different" item of property is one that bestows on a taxpayer a different legal interest than what he or she had before. See *Cottage Savings Association v. Commissioner,* 499 U.S. 554 (1991). Thus, all sales and most exchanges will be realization events. [181-182]

IV. REALIZED GAIN OR LOSS—§1001(a)

Realized gain or loss is equal to the difference between the amount realized on a sale or other disposition of property and the adjusted basis of the property transferred. [182]

A. Amount realized—§1001(b)

A taxpayer's amount realized on the sale or other disposition of property is equal to the sum of the cash and fair market value of property or services received, plus the amount of liabilities assumed by the other party to the transaction. [182-183]

B. Adjusted basis

The adjusted basis of property is equal to its initial basis adjusted upward for improvements and downward for capital recovery (depreciation) deductions. [184-187]

   1. Basis—purchases—§1012: The basis of property is usually equal to its cost. If a taxpayer performs services and receives property in payment, the amount the taxpayer includes in gross income as payment will constitute the basis of the property.

   2. Basis—other transactions: The basis of property received other than by purchase is determined under specific Code sections.

      a. Property received from a decedent—§1014: Property received from a decedent takes a basis equal to its fair market value on the date of death.

b. **Property received by gift—§1015:** If property is received by gift, the donee generally takes the property with the same basis as the donor had in the property, increased by a portion of any gift tax paid. If, at the time of the gift, the adjusted basis of the property in the donor's hands is greater than its fair market value, for purposes of determining loss on sale or other disposition by the donee, the donee's basis is the fair market value of the property on the date of the gift.

c. **Property received in divorce—§1041(d):** Property received incident to a divorce has the same basis that it had immediately prior to the transfer.

V. RECOGNIZED GAIN OR LOSS—§1001(c)

Realized gain or loss is generally recognized unless a specific Code section prohibits or limits recognition. [187-188] and Chapter 10.

VI. TRANSFERS OF ENCUMBERED PROPERTY

A. Amount realized includes liabilities assumed

A taxpayer's amount realized includes the face amount of the liabilities that another party assumes as part of the transaction, regardless of the fair market value of the property. [188-193]

B. Recourse vs. nonrecourse loans

In the sale of property subject to a nonrecourse loan, the greater of the fair market value of the property or the face amount of the loan minus the taxpayer's adjusted basis in the property produces the realized gain or loss on the transaction. If the loan is recourse, however, the transaction is bifurcated: (1) gain or loss equal to the difference between the fair market value of the property and the adjusted basis; and (2) discharge of debt equal to the difference (if any) between the debt discharged and the fair market value of the property. [191-193]

C. Distressed real estate

Distressed real estate can produce several different kinds of transactions: sale; foreclosure; "short sales;" renegotiation with the lender. These can produce very different tax consequences. [193-196]

VII. BASIS OF PROPERTY RECEIVED IN THE SALE OR DISPOSITION

If the taxpayer sells property for cash, there is no need to determine the basis of the property received (since cash neither appreciates nor depreciates in value, there is no need to assign cash a basis for tax purposes). If, however, the taxpayer receives property in an exchange, the basis of that property must be determined, for later the taxpayer may sell or otherwise dispose of the property.

A. Full-recognition transactions

In a transaction in which the selling taxpayer recognizes all realized gain or loss, the property received will have a basis equal to its fair market value. [196]

B. Nonrecognition transactions

In transactions in which the selling taxpayer does not recognize all or part of the realized gain or loss, the property received will have a basis different than its fair market value, determined under specific Code sections. See Chapter 10.

VIII. CHARACTER

The character of the gain or loss recognized will depend on the nature of the asset in the hands of the transferor. See Chapter 12.

CHAPTER 10

NONRECOGNITION TRANSACTIONS

I. IN GENERAL

In some property transactions, realized gain or loss is not recognized in whole or in part at the time of the transaction. These transactions are called nonrecognition transactions and include like-kind exchanges, involuntary conversions, divorce transactions, and other transactions. When realized gain or loss is deferred rather than recognized, the property received in the transaction takes a basis that preserves that realized gain or loss for later recognition. [203-204]

II. LIKE-KIND EXCHANGES—§1031

A. Requirements

There are five requirements for a qualifying like-kind exchange. [204-211]

1. **Exchange of property:** The taxpayer must exchange property for property, rather than selling property or engaging in some other transaction. See *Jordan Marsh Co. v. Commissioner,* 269 F.2d 453 (2d Cir. 1959).

2. **Nature of property—§1031(a)(2):** The property must not be inventory, stocks, bonds, notes, other evidences of indebtedness, interests in a partnership, certificates of trust or beneficial interest, or choses in action.

3. **Property transferred—use:** The taxpayer must have held the relinquished property for use in a trade or business, or for investment. The IRS has recently issued guidance on the application of §1031 to vacation or second homes rented for part of the year.

4. **Property received—use:** The taxpayer must intend to hold the replacement property for use in a trade or business, or for investment. The IRS has recently issued guidance on the application of §1031 to vacation or second homes rented for part of the year.

5. **Like-kind:** The replacement property received must be like-kind to the relinquished property. Like-kind refers to the nature and character of the property rather than to its grade or quality.

a. **Real property:** An exchange of real property for real property is a like-kind exchange regardless of the development status of the two properties. *Koch v. Commissioner*, 71 T.C. 54 (1978).

b. **Depreciable personal property—Reg. §1.1031(a)-1(b):** The regulations offer a safe harbor for determining whether depreciable personal properties are like-kind, in which properties of the same "class" are considered like-kind. Properties outside the same class must be examined under the general like-kind test.

c. **Other personal property:** Intangible and nondepreciable personal property and personal property held for investment must be examined under the general like-kind test.

B. **Effect of qualifying like-kind exchange**

If a taxpayer engages in a qualifying like-kind exchange of property for property, he or she will not recognize any of the realized gain or loss on the transaction. [205]

1. **Effect of boot—§1031(b):** If the taxpayer receives boot (nonlike-kind property), the taxpayer will recognize gain, but not loss, in the amount of the lesser of the fair market value of the boot or the realized gain.

2. **Basis of property received—§1031(d):** The basis of like-kind property received in a like-kind exchange is equal to the basis of the property transferred, plus the gain recognized, minus the fair market value of the boot received, minus any loss recognized, plus any boot paid (additional investment in the property). The basis of any boot (nonlike-kind property) received is its fair market value.

C. **Deferred and three-party exchanges—§1031(a)(3)**

A potential problem arises when the taxpayer wishes to transfer property in a like-kind exchange, but the potential buyer who wants the taxpayer's property does not have suitable property to exchange. This problem can be overcome by creating a deferred exchange, but the property to be received by the taxpayer must be identified within 45 days after the taxpayer relinquishes his or her property and must be received before the earlier of the 180th day after the date the taxpayer relinquishes his or her property or the due date of the taxpayer's return for the year of transfer of the relinquished property. Any intermediary used must meet specific identity requirements to avoid agent status. [211-215]

D. **Effect of mortgages in like-kind exchanges**

1. **One mortgage:** If the property transferred in a like-kind exchange is subject to a mortgage, the transferee's assumption of that mortgage as a part of the transaction is treated as boot to the transferor. The mortgage assumption is also treated as boot for purposes of computing the taxpayer's basis in the property received. [215-221]

2. **Two mortgages:** If both the property transferred and the property received are subject to mortgages assumed in the like-kind exchange, the regulations allow the "netting" of the mortgages. The party with the net relief from liabilities (i.e., whose property was subject to the higher mortgage at the outset) is treated as having received boot in the amount of the net relief from liability. The mortgage netting rule applies only to the computation of gain recognition; the full amounts of the mortgages are considered in the computation of basis of the properties received by each party. [215-221]

3. **Two mortgages plus boot:** The mortgage netting rule allows the party with net assumption of debt to avoid recognition of gain. But this applies only to the mortgage portion of the transaction. If the person with net assumption of debt receives boot, the usual recognition rules will apply so that realized gain will be recognized to the extent of the fair market value of the boot received.

III. INVOLUNTARY CONVERSIONS—§1033

A taxpayer may be able to defer, in whole or in part, recognition of gain on the "involuntary conversion" of property. [221-222]

A. Conversion into similar property

If a taxpayer's property is involuntarily converted into property that is similar or related in service or use, the taxpayer will not recognize any of the realized gain on the conversion. [222-223]

B. Conversion into money

If the taxpayer's property is involuntarily converted into money, the taxpayer may elect to recognize gain in the amount of proceeds that are not reinvested in property similar or related in service or use to the converted property. [222-223]

C. Similar property

Real property used in a trade or business or held for investment must be like-kind to the property converted, invoking the same standard as in §1031. All other property must meet the "similar" standard, which is a stricter standard than "like-kind." The similar standard requires that the properties have the same physical characteristics and that the taxpayer use the properties in the same way. [224]

D. Statutory replacement period

The taxpayer must reinvest within two years after the close of the taxable year in which the taxpayer realizes any portion of the gain on conversion. [224-225]

E. Basis of replacement property

The basis of the replacement property will be the basis of the property converted, plus the gain recognized, minus the unreinvested proceeds of conversion, minus any loss recognized on the conversion. [223]

F. Inapplicable to loss

Section 1033 does not apply to loss realized on the involuntary conversion of property; those losses would be casualty losses, potentially deductible under §165(c)(3) and (h). [225]

IV. SPOUSAL AND DIVORCE TRANSFERS—§1041

A. Nonrecognition

Section 1041 provides that no gain or loss will be recognized on transfers of property between spouses or on transfers incident to a divorce. [226-227]

1. **Incident to a divorce:** A transfer of property is incident to a divorce if it occurs within one year of the date the marriage is terminated, or if it is contemplated by the divorce decree and occurs within six years of the date of termination of the marriage (or later if there is a good reason for the delay).

2. **Indirect transfers:** A transfer usually occurs directly from one spouse to the other. However, a qualifying transfer also can be made to a third person if made by direction or ratification of the other spouse or provided for in the divorce decree.

B. **Effect of qualifying transfer to spouse or former spouse**

The transferor in a §1041 transfer will not recognize gain or loss on the transfer. In addition, the recipient of property will not include any amount in gross income, and will take the property with the same basis as the property had immediately prior to the transfer. [226-227]

C. **Related material**

Consider in connection with §1041 the rules relating to alimony and child support.

CHAPTER 11
TIMING OF INCOME AND EXPENSES

I. THE ANNUAL ACCOUNTING CONCEPT

Federal income tax returns are filed on an annual basis in which taxpayers tote up their income, deductions, and allowable credits for their taxable year, and apply the tax rates for that year to their taxable income. [238-239]

A. **Calendar and fiscal years**

A taxpayer may use a calendar year or a fiscal year (which is a year other than a calendar year). Most individuals use a calendar year. [238]

B. **Problems with annual accounting**

While annual accounting is administratively easy, it can inaccurately measure a taxpayer's ability to pay, particularly for transactions that span more than one taxable year. Several Code sections have evolved to address these difficulties. [239]

1. **The net operating loss deduction—§172:** A taxpayer's excess of deductions over expenses constitutes a net operating loss that the taxpayer may carry back two years and forward twenty years. This allows the taxpayer to more accurately reflect income over a period of years.

2. **Claim of right doctrine and §1341:** A taxpayer must include amounts in gross income over which he or she has a claim of right and unfettered use, even if the taxpayer may be required to return all or a portion of the amount to another person. Section 1341 calculates the tax due if the taxpayer is required to return items previously included in gross income, in a taxpayer-friendly way.

3. **Tax benefit rule—§111:** The recovery of an item that constituted a deduction or credit in a prior year will be income to the taxpayer to the extent of the prior tax benefit. A "recovery" is an event that is fundamentally inconsistent with the previous deduction or credit.

II. METHODS OF ACCOUNTING

A. Cash method of accounting

A taxpayer using the cash method of accounting will report income when it is received, actually or constructively, and will claim deductions when amounts are actually paid (regardless of when they are due). [245-249]

1. Constructive receipt: A taxpayer will be considered to have received items to which he or she had a right and had the ability to claim but did not do so.

2. Restrictions on use of the cash method: Some taxpayers may not use the cash method of accounting, as Congress has determined that it would unreasonably accelerate deductions for these taxpayers.

B. Accrual method of accounting

A taxpayer using the accrual method of accounting will report income when all events that fix the taxpayer's right to the income have occurred, and the amount thereof can be determined with reasonable accuracy. Accrual-method taxpayers will deduct expenses when all events that fix the liability have occurred and its amount can be determined with reasonable accuracy, subject to special rules that defer deductions until "economic performance." [249-253]

III. ACCOUNTING FOR INVENTORIES

Taxpayers engaged in manufacturing and retail activities are required to account for inventories. Under an inventory approach, the taxpayer deducts from gross sales the cost of goods sold to determine the profit from sales for the year. Included in inventory are amounts attributable to the cost of manufacturing or purchasing the product, and certain taxpayers also must include in inventory an amount attributable to indirect costs (administrative costs, for example) under the UNICAP rules. [253-254]

IV. INSTALLMENT METHOD OF REPORTING INCOME—§453

When a taxpayer sells property other than inventory in a sale in which at least one payment will be received after the close of the taxable year, the taxpayer may report the gain realized on the sale over the period of time payments are received by using the installment method. [254-258]

A. Applicable to gain

The installment method is applicable to gain, not loss. It is also not applicable to the interest portion of the transaction; interest is determined and accounted for separately. [254]

B. Amount includable in gross income

The amount of gain to be reported each year is the payment for the year multiplied by the gross profit ratio, which is a fraction the numerator of which is the gross profit (sales price minus adjusted basis) and the denominator of which is the total contract price (amount to be received under the contract). The remaining amount of any payment is excluded from gross income as capital recovery. [255-257]

V. RESTRICTED PROPERTY—§83

In many deferred compensation situations, the taxpayer receives property in exchange for the performance of services that is restricted in some fashion as to transfer or enjoyment. Section 83 defines (1) whether the taxpayer has income; (2) when the taxpayer has income; and (3) how much income the taxpayer has in these situations. [258-261]

A. Income?

A taxpayer potentially has income if there is a "transfer" of property to the taxpayer. An employer's setting aside of funds or property for the taxpayer's benefit is not income if the property can be reached by the employer's general creditors. But if the taxpayer has rights in the property that are not subject to the employer's creditors' claims, the taxpayer may have income. [259]

B. When?

A taxpayer must include the value of the property in gross income in the earlier of the first year in which the taxpayer owns the property without a requirement that he or she perform significant future services (i.e., the property is not subject to a "substantial risk of forfeiture") or the first year in which the property is transferable. [259-260]

C. How much?

The taxpayer includes in gross income the value of the property minus the amount the taxpayer paid for it. A taxpayer who receives restricted property may make what is known as a §83(b) election, in which the taxpayer includes in gross income the value of the property (minus amounts paid for it) within 30 days of receiving it, even though it is restricted. This would be appropriate for restricted property that is expected to greatly increase in value. [260]

VI. SPECIAL LIMITATIONS ON LOSS DEDUCTIONS

In addition to the restrictions on deductible losses of §165(c), discussed above, the Code imposes additional loss restrictions on certain types of losses. These are properly viewed as timing rules because they potentially cause losses incurred in a particular taxable year to be deferred to future taxable years. [261-263]

A. Passive losses—§469

Passive losses are losses from passive activities, i.e., activities that qualify as trades or businesses but in which the taxpayer does not materially participate. Passive losses incurred during a taxable year may be deducted only to the extent of the taxpayer's passive income for that year, and losses that are disallowed under this rule carry forward to future years when the taxpayer has passive income or disposes of the investment generating the passive loss. [261-262]

B. Amounts at risk—§465

A taxpayer's losses from certain activities are limited to a taxpayer's amount "at risk," i.e., the amount by which the taxpayer can be held liable to third parties upon failure of the venture. Losses disallowed by the at-risk rules carry forward to future years in which the taxpayer has amounts at risk. [262]

CHAPTER 12

CHARACTER OF INCOME AND LOSS

I. IN GENERAL

When a taxpayer sells or exchanges property and recognizes gain or loss, the character of that gain or loss—as capital or ordinary—must be determined. [271-272]

II. CAPITAL/ORDINARY DISTINCTION

The capital/ordinary distinction has implications for both income and loss. [272]

A. Income—§1(h)

Tax is imposed on an individual's ordinary income at rates up to 35%. However, the maximum rate on "net capital gain" is potentially much lower, ranging generally from 15% to 28%, with some capital gain escaping tax entirely for taxpayers with relatively small amounts of other kinds of income. Thus, taxpayers prefer to characterize income as capital gain subject to the preferential rate. [272]

B. Loss—§1211

Section 1211 imposes a significant restriction on the deductibility of capital losses. Corporations may deduct capital losses only to the extent of their capital gains. IRC §1211(a). Individuals may deduct capital losses to the extent of their capital gain income, plus $3,000 of ordinary income. IRC §1211(b). Unused capital losses carry forward (and, for corporations, carry back) to other taxable years. [272]

C. Taxpayer preference

Taxpayers prefer capital gain and ordinary loss. [272]

D. Policy

A variety of rationales are suggested for the preference for capital gain, including the general incentive toward savings and investment, preventing lock-in, avoiding bunching of income, and countering the effect of inflation. [273]

III. AN APPROACH TO CHARACTERIZING GAIN OR LOSS

A. An approach to characterization problems

Figure 12A (in text) offers an approach to characterizing gain or loss as capital or ordinary, which requires analysis of the following issues, discussed in the sections that follow. [274-275]

1. Did the taxpayer experience a realization event with respect to which gains or losses are recognized?

2. Did that event constitute a "sale or exchange" of "property"?

3. Was the property a "capital asset"?

4. Was the property a §1231 asset?

5. Do any special recharacterization rules apply?

B. Did the taxpayer experience a realization event with respect to which gains or losses are recognized?

For a taxpayer to have a capital gain or loss, there must be a realization event, and any gains or losses from that event must be recognized. [275]

C. Did that event constitute a "sale or exchange" of "property"?

For the taxpayer to have a capital gain or loss, the recognized gain or loss must arise from the "sale or exchange" of "property." This generally requires a "giving, a receipt, and a causal connection between the two." See *Yarbro v. Commissioner,* 737 F.2d 479 (5th Cir. 1984). Some events that might not otherwise meet this standard are deemed to be sales or exchanges by statute, such as losses from the worthlessness of stock or securities. Moreover, the item in question must constitute a sale or exchange of property, not the prepayment of income. See *Hort v. Commissioner,* 313 U.S. 28 (1941) (lease cancellation payment). [275-277] and Chapter 9.

D. Was the property a "capital asset"?

For the taxpayer to have a capital gain or loss, the recognized gain or loss must be from sale or exchange of a property that qualifies as a "capital asset." [277-282]

1. Excluded categories: Section 1221 defines a capital asset as "property held by the taxpayer (whether or not in connection with his trade or business)" except for eight enumerated categories of property, of which only five are usually important in the basic tax class. Thus, an item is a capital asset *unless* it falls within any of these five categories.

a. Inventory/stock in trade—§1221(a)(1): A taxpayer's stock in trade or inventory held primarily for sale to customers in the ordinary course of business is not a capital asset.

i. Definition: "Primarily" means "of first importance" or "principal." See *Malat v. Riddell,* 383 U.S. 569 (1966).

ii. Dealers: To have inventory, the taxpayer must hold the property primarily for sale to customers in the ordinary course of business. It is the relationship of the taxpayer to the assets, not the taxpayer's status generally, that determines whether assets constitute inventory. See *Van Suetendael v. Commissioner,* 3 T.C.M. 987 (1944), *aff'd,* 152 F.2d 654 (2d Cir. 1945).

iii. Real estate: Whether a taxpayer holds real estate as an investor or as a dealer depends on the analysis of seven factors discussed in *United States v. Winthrop,* 417 F.2d 905 (5th Cir. 1969).

b. Real and depreciable property—§1221(a)(2): Real property used in a trade or business or property used in a trade or business that is subject to depreciation under §167 is not a capital asset. This type of property is §1231 property, discussed below.

c. Creative works—§1221(a)(3): Creative works generated by the taxpayer, such as material subject to copyright, letters, and memoranda are not capital assets. There is an exception for certain musical works, for which the taxpayer may elect capital asset treatment.

d. **Accounts/notes receivable—§1221(a)(4):** A taxpayer's accounts or notes receivable from the sale of inventory are not capital assets.

e. **Supplies—§1221(a)(8):** Supplies and similar items used in a taxpayer's business are not capital assets.

2. **"Related to" the trade or business:** Relying on the case of *Corn Products Refining Co. v. Commissioner,* 350 U.S. 46 (1955), taxpayers asserted that items that were integrally connected with their trade or business should be treated as noncapital assets. In *Arkansas Best Corp. v. Commissioner,* 485 U.S. 212 (1988), the U.S. Supreme Court reexamined *Corn Products*, concluding that the relation of an asset to a taxpayer's business was irrelevant in determining its status as a capital or noncapital asset. In determining whether an item was included in the noncapital category of inventory, certain "inventory substitutes" could be included in that category. The Court limited the holding of *Corn Products* to an application of the inventory substitute idea.

E. Was the property a §1231 asset?

Section 1221(a)(2) excludes from the definition of a capital asset real and depreciable property used in a trade or business or held for investment. But all is not lost. Section 1231 may apply to treat net gains from this kind of property as capital. [285-288]

1. **An approach to §1231:** Figure 12D (in text) offers an approach to characterizing gain or loss arising from §1231 property. The first question is whether the property sold is §1231 property. If the property is not §1231 property, its character is determined under the usual rules set forth in Figure 12A. If the property is §1231 property, the next question is whether the recapture rules of §§1245 or 1250 apply, because recapture income cannot be classified as §1231 gain. Then, the taxpayer determines all of the recognized gains and losses from §1231 assets involving casualties, and if such losses exceed such gains, all are removed from the calculation. If such losses do not exceed gains, all are included, along with all other §1231 gains and losses, and the losses and gains are netted against one another. If the final result is a net loss, all §1231 gains and losses are ordinary. If the final result is a net gain, all gains and losses are capital, except to the extent of unrecaptured §1231 losses during the previous five years.

2. **Section 1231 property:** Section 1231 gains and losses arise from the sale of property used in the trade or business of the taxpayer, or from the involuntary or compulsory conversion of property used in the trade or business, or any capital asset held for more than a year and held in connection with the taxpayer's trade or business.

3. **Recapture rule:** The recapture rule may limit the recharacterization of gains as capital under §1231. If the taxpayer has had, within the previous five years, §1231 losses that were characterized as ordinary, the current year's gain must be characterized as ordinary to the extent of the previous loss.

F. Do any special recharacterization rules apply?

Recognized gain or loss on the sale or exchange of a capital asset will usually be capital. However, the Code may, in certain circumstances, require all or a part of the gain or loss to be characterized as ordinary. [282-285]

1. **Recapture for personal and real property:** The recapture provisions require that upon sale or exchange of property that would otherwise generate capital gain, a portion of the recognized gain be characterized as ordinary. Recapture thus seeks to account for the previous benefit of depreciation deductions taken with respect to the property.

   a. **Personal tangible property—§1245:** On the sale or exchange of depreciable personal property that otherwise qualifies as a capital asset or a §1231 asset generating capital gain, the portion of the gain equal to the lower of the realized gain or depreciation previously claimed with respect to the property will be characterized as ordinary. Any remaining balance will be capital.

   b. **Real property—§1250:** Section 1250 requires recapture of the accelerated portion of depreciation taken with respect to real property to be recaptured upon sale. However, since real property acquired since 1987 has been depreciated using the straight-line method, the practical impact of this provision is minimal today.

2. **Small business stock—§1244:** Individual taxpayers and partnerships may claim a portion of the loss on the sale or worthlessness of small business stock as ordinary rather than capital. The maximum amount considered ordinary is $50,000 for a single taxpayer or $100,000 for a married couple filing a joint return. A small business corporation is a corporation that issues the stock to the taxpayer in exchange for property and must have derived more than 50% of its income from active business sources during the five-year period ending on the date of the loss.

3. **Sales and exchanges between related parties–§ 1239:** If the property is depreciable in the hands of the transferee, the transferor's gain or loss will be ordinary rather than capital. [282-283]

IV. CALCULATING CAPITAL GAIN AND LOSS

The final step in addressing character issues is determining the taxpayer's net capital gain (which is included in the taxpayer's gross income and is taxed at preferential rates) or deductible capital loss, and the net capital loss carryforward. [288-294]

A. **Definitions**

Section 1222 sets forth a number of definitions relating to capital gains and losses that are relevant in calculating capital gain and loss. There are three baskets of capital gain/loss: the 28% group (collectibles); the 25% group (unrecaptured §1250 gain); and the 15%/0% group (everything else). If a taxpayer is in the 10% or 15% bracket for ordinary income, he or she will enjoy the 0% rate on capital gains, but only to the extent theses gains exceed his or her ordinary income. [273, 290-291]

B. **Holding period**

Capital gains and losses must be characterized as long-term or short-term. Long-term gain or loss is gain or loss from the sale of an asset held for more than one year. Short-term gain or loss is gain or loss from the sale of an asset held for one year or less. The period of time during which a taxpayer owns (or is deemed to own) an asset is his or her holding period for the asset. The calculation of a taxpayer's capital gain and loss depends on the taxpayer's holding period of the assets generating capital gain and loss. The holding period usually begins with the taxpayer's acquisition of the asset, but in some cases, the taxpayer's holding period will include another person's holding period for the asset or the taxpayer's holding period for another asset. [289-290]

1. **Exchanged basis property—§1223(1):** For exchange transactions involving the transfer of capital or §1231 assets in which a taxpayer's gain is deferred in whole or in part, the taxpayer's holding period for the property received in the transaction will include the period the taxpayer held the property he or she transferred in the transaction. An example of this is the holding period for property received in a qualifying like-kind exchange.

2. **Transferred basis property—§1223(2):** If a taxpayer receives property in a transaction in which the taxpayer's basis is determined by reference to another person's basis in the same property, the taxpayer's holding period includes the period of time that other person held the property. An example of this is the holding period for a gift.

C. **An approach to calculating net capital gain and net capital loss**

A systematic approach for calculating net capital gain and net capital loss is helpful in solving problems in which the taxpayer disposes of varying kinds of assets. First, the taxpayer's long- and short-term capital gains and losses are categorized into each group (28%; 25%; and 15%/0%). Then, the gains and losses in each group are netted against one another to produce gain or loss in each category. Then, any losses in the short-term, 28% or 15%/0% groups are applied to reduce gains in the other categories. This produces a net gain or a net loss in each category. The maximum rate of tax is the tax rate applicable to the group (such as 28%), but if the taxpayer's regular rate is lower, that rate will apply. [289-293]

CHAPTER 13
TAX RATES AND CREDITS

I. IN GENERAL

The applicable tax rate is applied to taxable income to produce the tentative tax. Available tax credits are subtracted from the tentative tax to produce the actual tax due. [301]

II. TAX RATES

The current tax rate on ordinary income is progressive within a limited range, with tax rates for individuals ranging from 10% to 35% (in 2011). The specific rate applicable to an individual depends on his or her taxable income and filing status. [302]

A. **Sunset 2012**

The current tax rates are scheduled to expire on December 31, 2012, unless Congress acts to extend them or amends the Code. If not, the pre-2001 rates will apply, which are significantly higher and for capital gains, calculated differently. [304]

B. **Children**

Children with sufficient income to owe tax file their own tax returns reporting their gross income and available deductions and credits. In some circumstances a child's parents may claim the child's investment income on the parents' return pursuant to the kiddie tax. [303] and see Chapter 14.

C. Preferential rates on capital gains

Net capital gain is taxed at a maximum rate of 28% (collectibles), 25% (unrecaptured §1250 gain), or 15% or 0% (everything else). If the taxpayer's rate on ordinary income is lower, the taxpayer gets the benefit of that rate. [303]

D. Qualified dividend income

Qualified dividend income is subject to the 15%/0% tax rate regime applicable to capital gains in the 15%/0% category, removing the distinction between capital gain and ordinary income for many corporate distributions. [303-304] This is scheduled to sunset on December 31, 2012 unless Congress acts. If it does not, qualified dividend income will be taxed at the rates applicable to ordinary income.

III. THE ALTERNATIVE MINIMUM TAX

A. In general

The alternative minimum tax (AMT) is a surtax imposed on taxpayers with certain kinds of income or deductions. The purpose of the AMT is to ensure that taxpayers with the kinds of activities that reduce tax through tax-exempt income or significant deductions pays at least some amount of tax. [304]

B. AMTI

The AMT is imposed on "alternative minimum taxable income" (AMTI). AMTI is computed by taking regular taxable income and adding back in certain items that were excluded and certain items that were deducted in the computation of regular taxable income. Important adjustments include the deduction for state taxes, the deduction for personal exemptions, the inclusion of certain tax-exempt interest, and a longer, slower depreciation period for certain assets. [304-305]

C. Exemption/tax rates

The AMT is imposed on AMTI in excess of an exemption amount, which changes frequently. The first $175,000 of AMTI is taxed at 26% and the remaining AMTI is taxed at 28%. [305-306] The AMT often applies to relatively low income taxpayers, and Congress fiddles with the exemption amounts from time to time to reduce the reach of this tax.

IV. TAX CREDITS

A tax credit is a dollar-for-dollar reduction in the amount of tax due. A refundable credit can reduce tax below zero, generating a refund. A nonrefundable credit can only reduce tax to zero and will not generate a refund. [307]

A. Contrast deductions and exclusions

While a tax credit is a dollar-for-dollar reduction in the amount of tax due, a deduction is a subtraction from either gross income or adjusted gross income in computing taxable income. Moreover, if an amount is excluded from gross income, it is never included in the computation of gross income. [307]

B. Credit for tax withheld—§31

Perhaps the most familiar tax credit is the credit for the amount of tax withheld from wages, salaries, bonuses, and similar payments. [307]

C. Dependent care credit—§21

Expenses for care of a dependent are not deductible, because they are personal expenses. Section 21 allows a taxpayer who maintains a household with at least one qualifying individual to claim a nonrefundable tax credit for certain expenses, equal to the taxpayer's "applicable percentage" multiplied by the "employment-related expenses." [308-309]

1. **Qualifying individual:** A qualifying individual is a dependent under the age of 13 for whom the taxpayer is entitled to a deduction as a dependent, or any other dependent or a spouse of a taxpayer who is physically or mentally unable to care for him- or herself.

2. **Applicable percentage:** The taxpayer's applicable percentage ranges from 35% for taxpayers with AGI of $15,000 or less, to 20% for taxpayers with AGI above $43,000.

3. **Employment-related expenses:** Employment-related expenses are those incurred for care of a qualifying individual while the taxpayer works, subject to two limitations.

   a. **Dollar limitation:** Employment-related expenses are limited to $3,000 for one qualifying individual and $6,000 for two or more qualifying individuals.

   b. **Earned income limitation:** Employment-related expenses are limited to the earned income of a single taxpayer, or if a married couple files a joint return, to the earned income of the lesser-earning spouse. Special rules impute an amount of income to students and disabled taxpayers for purposes of this limitation.

4. **Coordination with §129:** Section 129 allows a taxpayer to exclude from gross income up to $5,000 of dependent care assistance provided by an employer. A taxpayer may not claim both the exclusion and the tax credit for the same dollar of dependent care assistance.

D. Earned income tax credit

A low-income eligible individual may claim a refundable tax credit. To compute the amount of the credit, the credit percentage is multiplied by the taxpayer's earned income, up to a certain amount known as the "earned income amount." Then, from that figure is subtracted the taxpayer's phaseout percentage multiplied by the taxpayer's AGI, reduced (but not below zero) by the phaseout amount. These percentages and amounts vary depending on the income and family status of the taxpayer. [309-311]

1. **Eligible individual:** An eligible individual is an individual with a dependent child under the age of 19 or a taxpayer who is a U.S. resident between the ages of 25 and 65 and who cannot be claimed as a dependent on another person's tax return.

2. **Earned income amount:** Earned income includes wages, salary, and self-employment income. See Figure 13C (in text) for earned income amounts.

E. Education credits

Section 25A allows taxpayers to claim tax credits for certain education expenses. The HOPE scholarship credit is a credit of up to $1,500 of qualified education expenses and the lifetime learning credit is a credit equal to 20% of certain expenses. Income level restrictions apply. [312-313]

F. Other tax credits

The Code contains a variety of other tax credits usually given less attention in the basic federal income tax course. [313]

   1. Child tax credit—§24: A taxpayer may claim a credit for $1,000 per child, with income limitations starting at $75,000 for single taxpayers, and $110,000 for married taxpayers. This is a partially refundable credit.

   2. Blind/elderly/disabled tax credit—§22: A taxpayer who qualifies as blind, elderly, or disabled is entitled to an additional tax credit.

   3. Adoption expense credit—§23: A taxpayer who incurs certain qualifying adoption expenses may claim a credit for these expenses, but this credit is phased out as AGI rises.

CHAPTER 14

IDENTIFYING THE TAXPAYER

I. IN GENERAL

The identification of the proper taxpayer to report income and claim deductions is crucial in maintaining a tax system that fairly allocates income among various taxpayers. [321]

II. "PERSONS" SUBJECT TO TAX

Both natural persons and legal entities may be subject to tax.

A. Individuals—§1

Single individuals, including children, file a tax return reporting only their income. Married couples can, and usually do, file a joint return reporting their combined income and deductions. Married couples have the option of filing separately, but usually do not, as this can produce a higher joint tax liability. [321-322]

   1. Child's services income—§73: Income from a child's services is reported on the child's tax return, even if the parent is entitled to the income under state law.

   2. The kiddie tax—§1(g): A child's investment income may be subject to tax at the parental rate, and parents may elect to report a child's investment income on the parents' tax return. A "child" is a person under age 19, or under age 24 if a full-time student.

B. Legal entities

A legal entity—such as a corporation, partnership, estate, or trust—may be required to file a tax return reporting its items of income, deduction, and credit. These are usually beyond the scope of the basic tax class. [322]

III. ASSIGNMENT OF INCOME

In a progressive tax system, an incentive exists for those in high tax brackets to direct income to related persons in lower tax brackets in order to reduce the overall tax imposed on the group. This strategy is known as "assignment of income." Because assignment of income threatens to undermine the integrity of the progressive tax structure, a variety of judicial and legislative responses have arisen over the years to combat it. [322-323]

A. Judicial views on services income

A common scenario involves the taxpayer who performs services for compensation but attempts to direct the compensation to another person (usually a relative in a lower tax bracket) prior to receiving it. [323-325]

1. **Diversion by private agreement:** If a taxpayer who performs services attempts to direct the compensation to another person by private agreement, the taxpayer (not the transferee) will be required to include the amount in gross income. See *Lucas v. Earl,* 281 U.S. 111 (1930).

2. **Diversion by operation of law:** By contrast, if the law governing the legal relationships provides that both the taxpayer and another person have legal rights to the income, the tax consequences will follow from these legal relationships. As a result, the taxpayer and the other party will include their proportionate shares of the income in gross income. See *Poe v. Seaborn,* 282 U.S. 101 (1930).

B. Judicial views on income from property

If an owner of income-producing property gives some interest in the property to another person, the issue arises of which person (the donor or donee) should be taxable on the income from the property. [325-327]

1. **Transfers of property:** If the donor transfers the property itself, the donee will properly report the income from the property.

2. **Transfers of income only:** The general rule is that attempts to transfer only the income from the property to another, without a transfer of the property itself, will be respected only if the income interest is transferred for its entire duration. Otherwise, the donor will be taxed on the income and will be deemed to have made a gift of the income to the donee. See *Blair v. Commissioner,* 300 U.S. 5 (1937); *Helvering v. Horst,* 311 U.S. 112 (1940).

C. Statutory responses to assignment of income and related problems

1. **The kiddie tax—§1(g):** Certain investment income of a child under the age of 14 must be taxed at his or her parents' tax rate. The special tax rate applies only to "unearned income" in excess of $1,900. The parents have the option of including the child's investment income on their own returns. [329-330]

2. **Reallocation of income and deductions—§482:** Under the broad statutory authority granted in §482, the IRS may reallocate among related entities items of gross income, deduction, and credit if necessary to prevent the evasion of tax or clearly to reflect income. This statute goes far beyond assignment of income principles, giving the IRS a powerful tool with which to combat the misallocation of tax items among related entities. [330]

CHAPTER 15

TIME VALUE OF MONEY: PRINCIPLES AND APPLICATIONS

I. IN GENERAL

While the concept of the time value of money is not specifically invoked in any tax statute, its principles permeate much tax-planning activity. Taxpayers invoke basic time value of money concepts when they attempt to defer income and accelerate deductions. The IRS and ultimately Congress may seek to block these strategies by accelerating income and precluding the early deduction of expenses. [335]

II. INTEREST

Interest is the cost of using money. A lender charges the borrower interest for the privilege of using the lender's funds during the period of the loan, and thus the lender is said to "earn interest" on the loan. Interest is what creates the concept of the "time value of money." A specified sum of money will earn interest at the market rate over a period of time; thus, the value of that sum a year in the future will be the sum plus the interest earned during the year. [336]

A. Simple interest

Simple interest is calculated as a percentage of the principal sum only. [336]

B. Compound interest

Compound interest is computed by applying the interest rate to both the principal sum and the accrued but unpaid interest. Compounding generally occurs daily, monthly, half-yearly, or annually. [337]

III. VALUING AMOUNTS

A. Future value

Future value is the value of a sum of money invested for a specified period at a specified interest rate. The future value of a sum will be the amount that an investor will have at the maturity of the investment, given the number of years to maturity and the rate of return (i.e., the interest rate) of the investment. Future value can be calculated using present and future value tables [see Figure 15A, in text] or by using the following formula: [337]

$$FV = PV(1+i)^n$$

B. Present value

Present value is the current value, given an assumed interest rate, of the right to a stated amount in the future. Another way to express this is that present value is the sum that must be invested today at a given interest rate to produce a stated sum in the future. Present value can be calculated using present and future value tables [see Figure 15A, in text] or by using the following formula: [337]

$$PV = \frac{FV}{(1+i)^n}$$

IV. SPECIFIC TIME VALUE OF MONEY APPLICATIONS

The Code recognizes time value of money principles in specific applications, even though it does not import the concept on a global basis.

A. Applicable federal rates

The IRS publishes interest rates monthly for calculations under various Code provisions such as imputed interest and interest on tax over- and underpayments. [339]

B. Tax under- and overpayments—§6621

The U.S. government pays interest on tax overpayments and taxpayers must pay interest on tax underpayments. The interest rate is published from time to time by the IRS. [339]

C. Original issue discount (OID)

While most debt instruments provide for a market rate of interest payable currently or otherwise, some debt instruments may not specifically provide for market interest. Yet these instruments do pay interest in an economic sense, for no creditor would lend money without compensation. Without the OID rules, such instruments might create two misstatements of tax reality. First, repayment of the principal plus an additional sum might be considered a return of capital and capital gain rather than interest, which is ordinary income. Second, the creditor might defer the inclusion of any income until maturity even though presumably the interest is accruing during the entire outstanding period of the loan. The OID rules, while complicated in the extreme, seek to address these character and timing issues. [340]

D. Imputed interest—§483

Section 483 imputes to the creditor interest on certain loans made in connection with sales or exchanges of property to which the OID rules do not apply. [340-342]

1. **General approach:** The creditor must include in gross income the total unstated interest ratably over the term of the contract. IRC §483(a).

   a. **Which loans?** Section 483 applies to contracts for the sale or exchange of property for which at least one payment is due more than one year after the date of the contract. IRC §483(c).

   b. **Total unstated interest:** Total unstated interest is the excess of the total payments due under the contract, over the sum of the present values of those payments and the present value of any payment provided for in the contract, using a discount rate equal to the applicable federal rate. IRC §483(b).

2. **Correlative effects of imputed interest:** The imputation of interest under §483 reduces the amount characterized as the amount realized (principal) by the parties to the transaction. This reduces the gain (usually capital) reported by the seller of the property and, in turn, reduces the basis of the purchaser in the property. Moreover, the purchaser of the property, who is deemed to pay interest, may be able to deduct that interest, if the deduction requirements of §163 are met.

3. **Exceptions to §483:** Section 483 does not apply to sales not exceeding $3,000 and to any debt instrument to which the OID rules apply.

E. Below-market loans—§7872

If a taxpayer makes a loan to another that does not provide for market interest, the transaction may be recharacterized to ensure that the creditor includes market interest in his or her gross income and that any other aspects of the transaction (such as compensation or gifts, for example) are properly taken into account. IRC §7872(a). [342-344]

1. General approach: Below-market "demand," "term," and "gift" loans are recharacterized so that the creditor includes the appropriate amount of interest in gross income. IRC §7872(a)(1).

   a. Demand and gift loans: For demand and gift loans, the forgone interest is treated as transferred from the lender to the borrower and retransferred from the borrower to the lender on the last day of the taxable year. IRC §7872(a)(1). Each leg of the transaction is characterized in accordance with its substance. For a gift loan, for example, the first leg (lender to borrower) is treated as a gift, and the second leg (borrower to lender) is treated as interest.

   b. Other types of loans: For other types of loans, first compute the excess of the amount loaned over the present value of all payments to be received under the loan. The lender is deemed to have transferred this amount to the borrower on the date the loan is made, and the below-market loan is treated as having OID in that same amount. The transfer from the lender to the borrower is characterized in accordance with its substance (e.g., compensation), and the characterization of the loan as having OID means that the lender must include the OID in gross income over the period of the loan.

   i. Demand loan: A demand loan is a loan payable on demand of the creditor.

   ii. Term loan: A term loan is a loan payable on a certain date that is fixed or determinable. IRC §7872(f)(6).

   iii. Gift loan: A gift loan is a loan in the context of which the creditor's forbearance of interest is most appropriately viewed as a gift. IRC §7872(f)(3).

   iv. Below-market loan: A demand loan is below market if its stated interest rate is less than the applicable federal rate at the time the loan is made. IRC §7872(e)(1)(A). A term loan is below market if the amount loaned is greater than the present value of the payments due under the loan, using the applicable federal rate as the discount rate. IRC §7872(e)(1)(B).

2. Exceptions to §7872: Section 7872 doesn't apply to gift loans between individuals, to compensation-related loans, and to shareholder loans if the total outstanding principal amount of such loans does not exceed $10,000. IRC §7872(c)(2),(3). Section 7872 also does not apply to any loan to which either the OID rules or §483 applies. IRC §7872(f)(8).

V. BASIC TAX STRATEGIES: INCOME DEFERRAL, ACCELERATION OF DEDUCTIONS, AND CLAIMING TAX CREDITS

Time value of money principles inspire the most basic tax strategies. The best of all tax strategies from the taxpayer's point of view is the exclusion of amounts from gross income entirely (so that tax will never be due on these amounts) or a deduction for the full amount of an expenditure (that shelters the same amount of income from tax). However, exclusions are relatively rare in the Code, and deductions are limited. Most strategies rely on a delay in tax; the taxpayer invests the amount that would otherwise be paid in tax and earns interest on that amount. The tax ultimately will be due, but the taxpayer who has invested the saved tax will usually come out ahead. [344]

A. Income deferral

A taxpayer may seek to defer the inclusion of an amount of gross income to a future year. This requires that the taxpayer have a sufficient ownership interest in the funds so that they are invested for his or her benefit but have an interest that will not require the taxpayer to include the amounts in gross income currently. Many income deferral strategies also assume that the taxpayer will be in a lower tax bracket when amounts will be included in his or her gross income (e.g., at retirement). Examples of income deferral strategies include the following [345-347]:

1. **Method of accounting:** A taxpayer may attempt to take advantage of the rules of his or her particular method of accounting to defer income to future years. Consider in this context the limitations on the use of the cash method of accounting and the doctrine of constructive receipt as limitations on the cash method taxpayer's ability to defer items of gross income.

2. **Realization principle:** Because income from the sale or exchange of property must be realized before it can be recognized, taxpayers may invest in property to defer the recognition of income until sale. Consider also in this context the effect of §1014, which by giving an heir a fair market value basis in property received from a decedent, encourages taxpayers to hold property until death and thus to exclude from the income tax the appreciation in the property prior to death.

3. **Nonrecognition provisions:** Certain nonrecognition provisions may allow the taxpayer to defer the recognition of gain on the disposition of property. These include like-kind exchanges, spousal and divorce transactions, and involuntary conversions.

4. **Retirement planning:** Most of retirement planning is based on the income deferral strategy. Employers' contributions to retirement plans are not included in the gross income of the employee until retirement, and the fund earns interest for the benefit of the employee during the employee's working years.

5. **Education savings incentives:** Section 529 plans and education savings accounts allow taxpayers to invest money but not be taxed on the earnings until distribution, and then only if the distributions are not used for qualified education expenses.

B. Deduction acceleration strategies

Taxpayers prefer to accelerate and maximize deductions because a deduction "shelters" an amount of income from tax. The tax benefit from a deduction is equal to the amount of the deduction multiplied by the taxpayer's tax rate. Examples of deduction strategies include the following [347-348]:

1. **Method of accounting:** A taxpayer may attempt to take advantage of the particular rules of his or her method of accounting to accelerate deductions. Consider in this context the limitations placed on deductions of prepayments for cash method taxpayers and the economic performance rules for accrual-method taxpayers.

2. **Capital recovery:** A taxpayer prefers accelerated capital recovery for investment in assets. For example, a taxpayer usually will claim double-declining balance depreciation rather than straight-line depreciation for an asset for which the double-declining balance method is available. Consider in this context §179 deductions, the MACRS method of capital recovery, §195

(amortization of pre-opening expenses), and §197 (amortization of intangibles). But consider the effect of recapture on the claiming of capital recovery deductions.

3. **Loss limitations:** Various loss limitations restrict taxpayers' ability to claim a deduction for certain losses. Consider in this context the capital loss restrictions (§1211), the passive loss restrictions (§469), the at-risk limitations (§465), and the rules against the recognition of losses in certain transactions (§165 and various nonrecognition rules).

CHAPTER 16
PUTTING IT ALL TOGETHER: RECOGNIZING AND ANALYZING COMMON TAX PROBLEMS

I. A SYSTEMATIC APPROACH TO TAX PROBLEMS

One approach to ensuring a complete analysis of a tax question is to take the approach described in Figure 16A.

A. Understand the events

The very first step in any tax problem is to study the facts of a transaction carefully. Be sure you understand who did what with whom, when, why, and how. It may be helpful to draw the transaction to ensure that you understand its various components. [356]

B. What is the call of the question?

A specific tax question may accompany a set of facts. More commonly, however, the facts end with a general question such as "What are the tax consequences of these transactions?" or "Advise the taxpayer." These raise two different kinds of tax problems. [357]

1. **Reactive problem:** In a reactive problem, events have occurred already, and the problem is to determine their tax consequences. Consider the alternative characterizations of the transaction, and conclude as to which one is most appropriate.

2. **Proactive (planning) problem:** In a proactive problem, the taxpayer is typically considering a transaction and seeks advice on how best to structure it. Consider alternative means to achieve the taxpayer's goals, and choose the one that produces the best overall tax and nontax consequences.

C. Recognize the transaction: what *is* it for tax purposes?

The transaction must be characterized, and is usually one of several frequently encountered transactions, such as a compensation or property transaction. [357-358]

D. Ask the seven fundamental tax questions [358-360]

There are seven fundamental issues in tax, all or some of which may be relevant to a particular transaction.

1. **Who is the relevant taxpayer?**

2. **Does the taxpayer have income?**

3. **What deductions may the taxpayer claim?**

    4. What is the character of income or loss?

    5. When must a taxpayer include an item in gross income, and when may a taxpayer claim a deduction?

    6. What is the taxpayer's rate of tax?

    7. Is the taxpayer entitled to any credits?

E. Identify and apply the applicable Code sections

The characterization of the transaction as a type is very helpful in identifying potentially applicable statutes and concepts. Once potentially applicable rules are identified, requirements of each statute is examined with the facts in mind to determine if the concept or statute actually applies.

F. Give advice

In the final step, recall that the point of the exercise is tax advice. Whether advising the taxpayer or the government, the tax problem posed must be addressed. Consider in this context what would be an appropriate return position or structure for a transaction, advice with respect to a tax controversy, or an appropriate government position. Basic tax strategies such as income deferral, deduction acceleration, and the claiming of credits should be considered, along with congressional and judicial responses to these techniques.

II. COMMONLY ENCOUNTERED TRANSACTIONS

Commonly encountered transactions can be analyzed using the systematic approach.

A. Compensation transactions [360-364]

    1. Recognizing this transaction: To recognize the basic transaction, look for a person performing services in exchange for value or a promise to transfer value.

    2. Tax analysis: For the payor, the essential question is whether a deduction is available for amounts paid for services. For the service provider, the essential question is whether he or she has income, and if so, how much and when it will be included in gross income. The expenses of performing services may be deductible, and compensation income will be ordinary income, potentially taxable at the highest tax rate. Advice to taxpayers in compensation transactions generally focuses on strategies to accelerate the deduction to the payor and defer the inclusion of income to the service provider.

B. Transactions in property [364-367]

A second major category of commonly encountered transactions is the sale or other disposition of property, including sales and various types of exchanges. (Gifts are treated as intrafamilial transfers, discussed below.)

    1. Recognizing this transaction: Transactions in property involve a taxpayer transferring an item of property that he or she owns, usually in exchange for value. In a gift transaction, the donor will not receive value for the property, but in nongift contexts, we assume that the seller will dispose of the property at fair market value.

2. **Tax analysis:** The tax problem may be posed for the buyer, the seller, or both. For the seller, the essential questions are the amount of gain or loss to be recognized on the transaction and the character of that gain or loss. Sales or exchanges of property may generate capital gain or loss, subject to the preferential rate for net capital gain and the capital loss restrictions of §1211. If the seller has received something other than cash in the transactions, the basis of that property must be computed. For the buyer, the essential question is the basis of the property acquired. Advice to taxpayers in this situation centers on the computation of realized and recognized gain or loss and strategies to exclude or defer income and accelerate loss.

C. Personal expenditure transactions [367-369]

1. **Recognizing this transaction:** In a personal expenditure transaction, the taxpayer is making expenditures for essentially personal items that would not be deductible but for specific Code sections that allow deduction.

2. **Tax analysis:** The crucial questions for the taxpayer are whether he or she is entitled to claim a deduction for these amounts, and when. Income issues may arise if the taxpayer has been compensated for personal losses or physical injuries. Advice to taxpayers in personal expenditure transactions involves identification of allowable deductions and acceleration of these deductions to the earliest possible year.

D. Business transactions [370-372]

1. **Recognizing this transaction:** Business transactions generally involve a taxpayer's sale of inventory or services for profit. Look for a taxpayer potentially engaged in business—the regular undertaking of an activity for profit.

2. **Tax analysis:** For the business taxpayer, the essential question is the net income from the business, which requires a determination of the taxpayer's gross business income and available deductions. Timing issues (including inventory issues) generally figure prominently in the computation of income and deductions. The character of the business income generally will be ordinary, potentially subject to the highest rate of tax. Advice in business transactions involves calculation of gross income from business and identification of available deductions and credits.

E. Intrafamilial transfers [372-373]

1. **Recognizing this transaction:** In this type of transaction, members of a family are transferring money or property among themselves, and the typical transactions include gifts, divorce transfers, and inheritances.

2. **Tax analysis:** The tax consequences to the transferor and transferee of any intrafamilial transfer must be considered.

   a. **Gifts—§§102, 1015:** The making of a gift is not a taxable event to the transferor, and thus the transferor realizes and recognizes no gain or loss on the transfer (unless it is a partial sale, which is properly treated as a sale transaction). The transferee generally receives property tax-free, i.e., without being required to include its value in gross income. The recipient of a gift takes the property with the same basis the property had in the hands of the donor, unless the property's fair market value was less than its basis at the time of the gift. In that situation, for purposes of determining loss only, the donee takes the fair market value of the property on the date of the gift as his or her basis.

b. Inheritances—§§102, 1014: The recipient of property by bequest or inheritance need not include its value in gross income, and takes the property with a basis equal to fair market value on the date of death or at the alternate valuation date six months later, if elected.

c. Divorce transfers—§§71, 215, 1041: The payment of alimony (federally defined) constitutes a deduction to the payor and is includable in the gross income of the recipient. The payment of child support, by contrast, generates no deduction to the payor and no income to the recipient. The transferor of property "incident to a divorce" recognizes no gain or loss on the transfer, and the recipient of the property need not include its value in gross income. The recipient takes the property with the same basis it had immediately before the transfer.

d. Assignment of income and the "kiddie tax"—§1(g): Taxpayers in high tax brackets may attempt to allocate income from services or property to related taxpayers in lower tax brackets. Attempted assignments of services income or income from property that constitutes a "carved-out interest" will not be respected by the IRS or courts, and the transferor will be taxed on the income purportedly assigned. Taxpayers may, however, transfer property to another so that the income from that property is properly taxed to the transferee. The "kiddie tax," however, serves as a check on this strategy by requiring certain unearned income of children to be taxed at their parents' tax rate rather than their lower individual rates.

e. Advice: Advice in intrafamilial transfers centers around ensuring that the transfer is tax-free to both the transferor and transferee, computing the basis of the property transferred, and identifying proper (and improper) assignments of income.

CHAPTER 1

GETTING STARTED IN FEDERAL INCOME TAX

ChapterScope ▬▬▬▬▬▬▬▬▬▬▬▬▬▬▬▬▬▬▬▬▬▬▬▬▬▬▬▬▬▬

To help a student get started in the process of learning federal income tax, this chapter provides some background information on the U.S. tax system, the Code, and the calculation of tax. Key concepts in this chapter include:

- **Calculation of tax:** The process of calculating the tax and the seven fundamental tax questions.

- **Sources of federal tax law:** The sources of tax law, including the U.S. Constitution, the Internal Revenue Code, and various judicial and administrative interpretations of the Code.

- **Tax procedure:** How tax controversies become tax cases, the administrative pathway they follow, and the various courts with jurisdiction over tax matters.

- **Tax ethics:** The standards governing clients and lawyers in taking a position on a tax return.

- **Parsing—a five-step approach to tax statutes:** Parsing offers a five-step approach to understanding an unfamiliar tax statute.

- **Tax policy:** The concepts of fairness, administrative practicality, and rational economic effects often serve as measures of a "good" tax system.

I. INTRODUCTION—THE BIG PICTURE

Learning tax law requires an understanding of general tax concepts, an array of tax statutes, and a grasp of the big picture—the role of specific concepts and statutes in the tax law as a whole. Along the way, the student of federal income tax will learn a new language (the language of the *Internal Revenue Code*—called the "Code"—and regulations) as well as the process of statutory interpretation.

A. Computation of tax

The federal income tax imposes a tax on the ***taxable income*** of an individual (or other taxable entity). The computation of that tax is the point of the Code, regulations, and judicial and administrative interpretations of the law. Computation of the tax due for an individual can be expressed most simply as the following process:

Start with:	Gross Income
Subtract:	Certain Deductions
This produces:	Adjusted Gross Income (AGI)
Then Subtract:	The Standard or The Itemized Deduction
And Subtract:	Personal Exemptions
This produces:	Taxable Income
Multiply by:	The Applicable Tax Rate(s)
This produces:	Tentative Tax
Then Subtract:	Tax Credits
Finally! This produces:	**Tax Due (if positive number) or Refund (if negative number)**

1. **Explanation of process:** The computation of the tax due begins with ***gross income,*** which means all of a taxpayer's income. IRC §61. From gross income, certain ***deductions*** are subtracted to produce ***adjusted gross income*** (AGI). IRC §62. From AGI, a taxpayer subtracts either the ***standard*** or the ***itemized deduction*** (but not both) and his or her ***personal exemptions.*** IRC §63. This produces ***taxable income,*** against which the applicable ***tax rate*** is multiplied to produce the tentative tax. It is "tentative" because one step remains: to subtract, on a dollar-for-dollar basis, any available ***tax credits.*** The ending point is the actual tax due (if a positive number) or a possible refund for the taxpayer (if a negative number).

2. **Multiple processes, multiple rates:** As later chapters will discuss, there isn't just one tax rate. Different kinds of income are subject to different rates of tax. Also, the process described above is used to calculate a taxpayer's ***regular tax liability.*** A second, similar process is also involved: the computation of the ***alternative minimum tax.*** See Chapter 13 (III). But for now, we can focus solely on a taxpayer's regular tax liability.

3. **A note on arithmetic:** Tax requires no advanced math skills, just the ability to add, subtract, multiply, and divide. Later in the text, some formulas will be presented; while these may at first seem intimidating, they are based on these simple arithmetic functions. Outside of some graduate tax schools, professors are usually less interested in computations than in analysis of the legal issues that arise in the computation of taxable income. If you are math-wary, don't despair. You will probably find tax less arithmetically oriented than you think.

B. **Seven fundamental tax questions**

Tax concepts and Code sections cluster around seven fundamental questions. These issues provide an organizational structure for this outline and for many tax casebooks. And, as discussed in detail in Chapter 16, these issues can be used to successfully analyze unfamiliar tax problems on exams and in practice.

1. **Who is the taxpayer?** Tax is a transactional subject, typically involving two or more taxpayers. Identifying the relevant taxpayer is crucial, as is identifying strategies a taxpayer may use to direct income or deductions to others to improve his or her own tax situation. Because analysis of these types of issues requires an understanding of income and deductions, the discussion of "Who is the taxpayer?" is deferred until Chapter 14.

2. **Does the taxpayer have income?** The federal income tax is concerned with a tax on income, and therefore the starting place is whether the taxpayer has items of income that will be included in his or her gross income. This requires an understanding of the concept of income. It also requires a grasp of the myriad tax statutes that include particular items of income in, or exclude particular items of income from, a taxpayer's gross income. Chapters 2, 3, 4, 9, and 10 address these issues.

3. **What deductions may the taxpayer claim?** Because the income tax is a tax not on gross income but on something less, *deductions* constitute an essential step in the computation of the tax base. Deductions may be business related or personal, but whatever their nature, they are a matter of legislative grace: A taxpayer must be able to point to a specific statute as justification in order to claim a deduction. Chapters 5–8 address deduction issues.

4. **In which taxable year should the taxpayer include items in gross income or claim deductions?** Federal income tax law uses a system of measuring income and collecting tax on an annual basis. Therefore, it becomes important to determine when (in which year) a taxpayer must include an amount in gross income, or may claim a deduction. For many items, the proper reporting year is clear. But for transactions that occur over several years, selection of the proper year can have important tax implications for the taxpayer. Moreover, taxpayers invoke timing rules in the *income deferral* and *deduction acceleration* strategies they use to save taxes. Chapters 10 and 11 address timing issues, and Chapter 15 discusses the time value of money principles that underlie many tax planning strategies.

5. **What is the character of the taxpayer's income and loss?** The federal income tax differentiates among some types of income and loss, giving tax preference to some types and imposing limits on others. Principal among these is the distinction between *ordinary income* or *loss* and *capital gain* or *loss*. *Net capital gain* is subject to a preferential rate as compared to the rates for *ordinary income,* and the *deduction* for *capital losses* is limited to an individual's *capital gains* plus $3,000 of ordinary income. Thus, characterizing income and loss as capital or ordinary can have a significant impact on tax liability. Character issues are discussed in Chapter 12.

6. **To what tax rate is the taxpayer subject?** The particular tax rate(s) to be applied to a taxpayer depends on the taxable income and status of that taxpayer. The tax rate multiplied by the taxpayer's taxable income produces the tentative tax. Chapter 13 discusses the tax rate issue, including the alternative minimum tax rates.

7. **Is the taxpayer entitled to any tax credits?** *Tax credits* are subtracted on a dollar-for-dollar basis from the taxpayer's tentative tax. Tax credits are the subject of Chapter 13.

C. **Tax Form 1040—A detailed road map**

The basic federal income tax course is *not* a tax preparation course. But the individual income tax return, the **Form 1040,** provides an excellent road map for the course and a way to organize the massive amounts of information in the course. Figure 1A reproduces the 2010 basic form. Take a moment now to see how Form 1040 presents the seven basic issues of tax. The schedules to the 1040 and updated forms and instructions can be found on the IRS website in .pdf format at *www.irs.gov.*

Figure 1A
Tax Form 1040

Form **1040**	Department of the Treasury—Internal Revenue Service **U.S. Individual Income Tax Return** 2010	(99)	IRS Use Only—Do not write or staple in this space.

For the year Jan. 1–Dec. 31, 2010, or other tax year beginning , 2010, ending , 20   OMB No. 1545-0074

Name, Address, and SSN

See separate instructions.

PRINT CLEARLY

Your first name and initial | Last name | **Your social security number**

If a joint return, spouse's first name and initial | Last name | **Spouse's social security number**

Home address (number and street). If you have a P.O. box, see instructions. | Apt. no.

City, town or post office, state, and ZIP code. If you have a foreign address, see instructions.

▲ Make sure the SSN(s) above and on line 6c are correct.

Checking a box below will not change your tax or refund.

Presidential Election Campaign ► Check here if you, or your spouse if filing jointly, want $3 to go to this fund . . . . . . ►   ☐ You   ☐ Spouse

Filing Status

Check only one box.

1 ☐ Single
2 ☐ Married filing jointly (even if only one had income)
3 ☐ Married filing separately. Enter spouse's SSN above and full name here. ►
4 ☐ Head of household (with qualifying person). (See instructions.) If the qualifying person is a child but not your dependent, enter this child's name here. ►
5 ☐ Qualifying widow(er) with dependent child

Exemptions

If more than four dependents, see instructions and check here ► ☐

6a ☐ **Yourself.** If someone can claim you as a dependent, **do not** check box 6a . . . . .
 b ☐ **Spouse** . . . .
 c **Dependents:**

(1) First name Last name	(2) Dependent's social security number	(3) Dependent's relationship to you	(4) ✓ if child under age 17 qualifying for child tax credit (see page 15)
			☐
			☐
			☐
			☐

Boxes checked on 6a and 6b ___
No. of children on 6c who:
• lived with you ___
• did not live with you due to divorce or separation (see instructions) ___
Dependents on 6c not entered above ___
Add numbers on lines above ► ___

 d Total number of exemptions claimed . . . .

Income

Attach Form(s) W-2 here. Also attach Forms W-2G and 1099-R if tax was withheld.

If you did not get a W-2, see page 20.

Enclose, but do not attach, any payment. Also, please use Form 1040-V.

7	Wages, salaries, tips, etc. Attach Form(s) W-2	7	
8a	**Taxable** interest. Attach Schedule B if required	8a	
b	**Tax-exempt** interest. **Do not** include on line 8a . . .	8b	
9a	Ordinary dividends. Attach Schedule B if required	9a	
b	Qualified dividends	9b	
10	Taxable refunds, credits, or offsets of state and local income taxes	10	
11	Alimony received	11	
12	Business income or (loss). Attach Schedule C or C-EZ	12	
13	Capital gain or (loss). Attach Schedule D if required. If not required, check here ► ☐	13	
14	Other gains or (losses). Attach Form 4797	14	
15a	IRA distributions .	15a	b Taxable amount . . .	15b	
16a	Pensions and annuities	16a	b Taxable amount . . .	16b	
17	Rental real estate, royalties, partnerships, S corporations, trusts, etc. Attach Schedule E	17	
18	Farm income or (loss). Attach Schedule F	18	
19	Unemployment compensation	19	
20a	Social security benefits	20a	b Taxable amount . . .	20b	
21	Other income. List type and amount	21	
22	Combine the amounts in the far right column for lines 7 through 21. This is your **total income** ►	22	

Adjusted Gross Income

23	Educator expenses	23	
24	Certain business expenses of reservists, performing artists, and fee-basis government officials. Attach Form 2106 or 2106-EZ	24	
25	Health savings account deduction. Attach Form 8889 .	25	
26	Moving expenses. Attach Form 3903	26	
27	One-half of self-employment tax. Attach Schedule SE .	27	
28	Self-employed SEP, SIMPLE, and qualified plans . .	28	
29	Self-employed health insurance deduction	29	
30	Penalty on early withdrawal of savings	30	
31a	Alimony paid b Recipient's SSN ►	31a	
32	IRA deduction	32	
33	Student loan interest deduction	33	
34	Tuition and fees. Attach Form 8917	34	
35	Domestic production activities deduction. Attach Form 8903	35	
36	Add lines 23 through 31a and 32 through 35	36	
37	Subtract line 36 from line 22. This is your **adjusted gross income** . . . . . ►	37	

For Disclosure, Privacy Act, and Paperwork Reduction Act Notice, see separate instructions.   Cat. No. 11320B   Form **1040** (2010)

Figure 1A [continued]

Form 1040 (2010)   Page **2**

Tax and Credits	38	Amount from line 37 (adjusted gross income)	38	
	39a	Check if: ☐ **You** were born before January 2, 1946, ☐ Blind. ☐ **Spouse** was born before January 2, 1946, ☐ Blind. } Total boxes checked ▶ 39a	
	b	If your spouse itemizes on a separate return or you were a dual-status alien, check here ▶ 39b ☐	
	40	**Itemized deductions** (from Schedule A) **or** your **standard deduction** (see instructions)	40	
	41	Subtract line 40 from line 38	41	
	42	**Exemptions.** Multiply $3,650 by the number on line 6d.	42	
	43	**Taxable income.** Subtract line 42 from line 41. If line 42 is more than line 41, enter -0- . .	43	
	44	**Tax** (see instructions). Check if any tax is from: **a** ☐ Form(s) 8814 **b** ☐ Form 4972 .	44	
	45	**Alternative minimum tax** (see instructions). Attach Form 6251	45	
	46	Add lines 44 and 45 . . . . ▶	46	
	47	Foreign tax credit. Attach Form 1116 if required . . .	47		
	48	Credit for child and dependent care expenses. Attach Form 2441	48		
	49	Education credits from Form 8863, line 23 . . .	49		
	50	Retirement savings contributions credit. Attach Form 8880	50		
	51	Child tax credit (see instructions)	51		
	52	Residential energy credits. Attach Form 5695 . . .	52		
	53	Other credits from Form: **a** ☐ 3800 **b** ☐ 8801 **c** ☐	53		
	54	Add lines 47 through 53. These are your **total credits**	54	
	55	Subtract line 54 from line 46. If line 54 is more than line 46, enter -0- . . . . ▶	55	
Other Taxes	56	Self-employment tax. Attach Schedule SE	56	
	57	Unreported social security and Medicare tax from Form: **a** ☐ 4137 **b** ☐ 8919 . .	57	
	58	Additional tax on IRAs, other qualified retirement plans, etc. Attach Form 5329 if required . .	58	
	59	**a** ☐ Form(s) W-2, box 9 **b** ☐ Schedule H **c** ☐ Form 5405, line 16 . .	59	
	60	Add lines 55 through 59. This is your **total tax** . . . . ▶	60	
Payments	61	Federal income tax withheld from Forms W-2 and 1099 . .	61		
	62	2010 estimated tax payments and amount applied from 2009 return	62		
	63	Making work pay credit. Attach Schedule M	63		
If you have a qualifying child, attach Schedule EIC.	64a	**Earned income credit (EIC)**	64a		
	b	Nontaxable combat pay election	64b			
	65	Additional child tax credit. Attach Form 8812	65		
	66	American opportunity credit from Form 8863, line 14 . . .	66		
	67	First-time homebuyer credit from Form 5405, line 10 . . .	67		
	68	Amount paid with request for extension to file . . .	68		
	69	Excess social security and tier 1 RRTA tax withheld . . .	69		
	70	Credit for federal tax on fuels. Attach Form 4136 . . .	70		
	71	Credits from Form: **a** ☐ 2439 **b** ☐ 8839 **c** ☐ 8801 **d** ☐ 8885	71		
	72	Add lines 61, 62, 63, 64a, and 65 through 71. These are your **total payments** . . . . ▶	72	
Refund	73	If line 72 is more than line 60, subtract line 60 from line 72. This is the amount you **overpaid**	73	
	74a	Amount of line 73 you want **refunded to you.** If Form 8888 is attached, check here . ▶ ☐	74a	
Direct deposit? ▶ See instructions.	b	Routing number [ ] ▶ **c** Type: ☐ Checking ☐ Savings		
	d	Account number [ ]		
	75	Amount of line 73 you want **applied to your 2011 estimated tax** ▶	75		
Amount You Owe	76	**Amount you owe.** Subtract line 72 from line 60. For details on how to pay, see instructions ▶	76	
	77	Estimated tax penalty (see instructions)	77		

Third Party Designee	Do you want to allow another person to discuss this return with the IRS (see instructions)? ☐ **Yes.** Complete below. ☐ **No**
	Designee's name ▶ Phone no. ▶ Personal identification number (PIN) ▶ [ ]

Sign Here

Joint return? See page 12. Keep a copy for your records.

Under penalties of perjury, I declare that I have examined this return and accompanying schedules and statements, and to the best of my knowledge and belief, they are true, correct, and complete. Declaration of preparer (other than taxpayer) is based on all information of which preparer has any knowledge.

Your signature	Date	Your occupation	Daytime phone number
Spouse's signature. If a joint return, **both** must sign.	Date	Spouse's occupation	

Paid Preparer Use Only

Print/Type preparer's name	Preparer's signature	Date	Check ☐ if self-employed	PTIN
Firm's name ▶			Firm's EIN ▶	
Firm's address ▶			Phone no.	

Form **1040** (2010)

1. **Who is the taxpayer?** Notice that Form 1040 begins with issues relating to the status of the taxpayer. Filing status (Lines 1–5) and *dependents* (Lines 6c) are important in defining the *personal exemption* (Line 42) and tax rate (Line 44).

2. **Income issues:** The Form 1040 continues by addressing items of income. Lines 7–20 list common types of income that must be included in gross income, with a catchall category of "other income" on line 21.

3. **Deduction issues:** In Lines 23–35, Form 1040 addresses *deductions* for various expenses. Lines 23–35 list the items deductible in computing adjusted gross income, and the *itemized deductions* are listed on Schedule A, which in turn are summarized on Line 40 of Form 1040.

4. **Timing issues:** Timing issues are not immediately apparent on the Form 1040. Yet each item of income and deduction raises the issue of whether the current tax year is the proper year for claiming a deduction or reporting income.

5. **Character issues:** Schedule D to Form 1040 requires information on the sale or exchange of *capital assets,* and the result of the computations on Schedule D are reported on Line 13 of Form 1040.

6. **Tax rate issues:** The taxpayer's tax liability appears on Line 44, which the taxpayer can compute from tax tables published by the IRS.

7. **Tax credit issues:** Once the appropriate tax rate is applied to a taxpayer's taxable income, tax credits produce a dollar-for-dollar reduction in the amount of tax due. The basic issues really are simple: is the taxpayer entitled to a tax credit, and if so, how much? Lines 47 - 53 of Form 1040 address credit issues.

II. THE SOURCES OF FEDERAL INCOME TAX LAW

A. The U.S. Constitution—And how the Code is created

The U.S. Constitution is a source of tax law just as it is a source of law for other kinds of law. Article I, §8 of the Constitution empowers Congress "to lay and collect Taxes, Duties, Imposts and Excises . . . ." However, §8 limits the taxing power in three ways: direct taxes must be apportioned among the states; bills for raising revenue must originate in the U.S. House of Representatives; and taxes must be "uniform throughout the United States." Although the U.S. Constitution is a source of tax law, modern courts rarely rely on the Constitution to limit Congress's taxing authority.

1. **Direct taxes:** The "direct tax" issue is no longer controversial because the Sixteenth Amendment (adopted in 1913, the year of the first individual income tax) allows Congress to tax "incomes" without apportionment.

2. **Origination:** Although tax bills must originate in the House of Representatives, a tax bill follows the usual pathway toward enactment, which allows for amendment by the Senate and conferences between the House and Senate to reach compromise.

3. **Uniformity:** Taxes must be geographically uniform throughout the United States. However, the uniformity clause does not prohibit a tax statute from distinguishing among various types or sources of income or from imposing different rate structures on taxpayers of different status (as long as that status is not based on geographic locale).

B. The Internal Revenue Code

1. **The Code:** Title 26 of the U.S. Code, known in this outline as "the Code," or "IRC," contains the rules for income, gift, estate, excise, and employment taxes. The basic federal income tax course is generally devoted to income taxation only, and usually only the income taxation of *individuals,* with a nod to basic income taxation of entities such as trusts or corporations. The starting place for analysis of any tax problem is the Code, with an inquiry into the tax statutes potentially applicable to the problem.

2. **Don't forget—Tax law is how the federal government raises money:** The process of tax legislation is intimately tied to the creation and implementation of the federal budget. The House and Senate receive the budget from the president, and then begin their own process of creating, ultimately, a joint resolution approving the budget. Then, the tax-writing committees get busy writing their tax bills. The budget resolution isn't law, but it acts as a guide for both taxing and spending bills, which must conform to the budget resolution.

3. **Some things, like sausage and legislation, you *don't* want to see made:** The House generates a tax bill, which goes to the Senate. The Senate objects to some provisions, wants to change others, and wants new provisions included. So the Joint Committee on Taxation—made up of representatives from the House and the Senate—is responsible for generating agreement and producing a tax bill. This bill also coordinates the taxing provisions with the budget revenue provisions, and the result is a "reconciliation bill." The chairs of the House and Senate tax committees manage this bill through Congress on a tight time schedule that allows for limited debate.

   a. **More than you want to know—The Byrd rule:** The Byrd rule was enacted originally in 1974, and made permanent in 1990. It is a Senate rule that functions to enforce the budget resolution during the debate on reconciliation bills. This rule permits Senate members to object to any "extraneous" provisions in a reconciliation bill; if the objection is carried, it requires three-fifths of the Senate to waive the rule to keep it in the bill. There aren't very many kinds of objections a senator can make, but one kind that is available is an objection to a provision that would increase net outlays or decrease revenues for a fiscal year beyond those covered by the reconciliation bill.

   b. **So what?** The Economic Growth and Tax Relief Reconciliation Act of 2001 (P.L. 107-16) (EGTRRA) changed tax rates and other tax provisions in the years 2001 through 2010. The Act included a "sunset provision" that provided that all provisions and amendments made by the Act would not apply to any taxable year beginning after December 31, 2010. At practically the last hour, Congress enacted the Tax Relief, Unemployment Insurance Reauthorization, and Job Creation Act of 2010, Pub. L. 111-312, 111th Cong., 2nd Sess. (the 2010 Tax Relief Act). The 2010 Act extended many of the provisions of EGTRRA for two additional years, and made others permanent. Important sections of the Code are still subject to this sunset provision, which will apply on December 31, 2012. Look for the word "sunset" in the text to determine which provisions are scheduled to return to their pre-2001 incarnation as of that date.

   c. **Tax law changes every year:** One of the challenges of understanding tax law is that the statutes change every year—and often more than once a year. Fortunately, income tax principles remain largely the same year after year, and most tax professors focus on these principles and not on the arcane details of obscure Code provisions.

i.   **Inflation adjustments:** Many Code provisions have dollar amounts that are adjusted for inflation each year. The IRS publishes the new numbers annually in the ***Internal Revenue Bulletin.*** See Rev. Proc. 2011-2 I.R.B. 297.

ii.   **Scheduled increases/decreases:** Some Code provisions have dollar amounts, percentages, etc., that are scheduled to increase or decrease over time.

C.   Administrative interpretations of the Code

Section 7805 authorizes the Secretary of the Treasury or the Secretary's delegate to prescribe "all needful rules and regulations" for the administration of the tax system.

1.   **The Internal Revenue Service:** The ***Internal Revenue Service*** (referred to in this outline as the **IRS**), a bureau of the Department of the Treasury, issues various types of administrative interpretations of the Code.

2.   **Regulations:** In issuing regulations, the Department of the Treasury must comply with the Administrative Procedures Act (APA), which requires public notice of new rules and opportunity for public comment. Transcripts of hearings and other opportunities for comments often provide insight into the purpose and proper interpretation of a tax statute.

   a.   **General/specific authority regulations:** A regulation that simply provides guidance on a statutory provision under the general authority granted by §7805 is often called a ***general authority regulation.*** Sometimes, however, Congress will specifically instruct Treasury to issue regulations interpreting a provision; regulations issued under this type of authority are known as ***specific authority regulations.*** While the courts give ***deference*** to both types of regulations, they tend to grant specific authority regulations a greater degree of deference than general authority regulations. See discussion of deference, this chapter, section (II)(D)(2).

   b.   **Types of regulations: Regulations can be final, temporary, or proposed.**

      i.   **Final regulations:** These regulations have the force and effect of law. They are typically cited as Treas. Reg. or simply Reg.

      ii.   **Temporary regulations:** These regulations are in force, but their temporary label suggests that the IRS may revise them in the future. Temporary regulations are identified by their "T" designation. See, for example, Reg. §1.1041-1T.

      iii.   **Proposed regulations:** These regulations are still in the public comment stage of development and are not yet in force, but do serve to indicate the IRS's position on a particular subject. Sometimes they provide that taxpayers may rely on them. They are cited as Prop. Reg.

3.   **Other published administrative guidance:** The IRS issues other types of guidance that are not subject to the APA. These are published weekly in the ***Internal Revenue Bulletin*** (cited as I.R.B.) and compiled annually in the ***Cumulative Bulletin*** (cited as C.B.).

   a.   **Revenue Rulings:** ***Revenue Rulings*** (cited as Rev. Rul.) apply the law to a specific set of facts and draw conclusions on the application of the law. Taxpayers may rely on Revenue Rulings in preparing their tax returns if their own facts and circumstances are substantially the same as in the ruling.

   b. **Revenue Procedures:** *Revenue Procedures* (cited as Rev. Proc.) set forth the rights and duties of taxpayers in dealing with the IRS on an administrative matter, such as seeking a private letter ruling. Revenue Procedures do not deal with substantive tax issues. If the IRS deviates from its stated policy published in a Revenue Procedure, a taxpayer has no right to the benefit of a particular procedure.

   c. **Notices and Announcements:** These authorities set forth the IRS's views or a procedure on a matter of transitory importance, such as the procedure for seeking an extension of filing dates due to natural disasters. Taxpayers may rely on notices and announcements in preparing their tax returns.

4. **Forms, instructions, and publications:** An important source of guidance for taxpayers is the forms and instructions, as well as information publications, issued by the Internal Revenue Service. However, IRS forms, instructions, and publications do not bind the IRS with respect to a particular interpretation of the law.

5. **Internal Revenue Manual:** The *Internal Revenue Manual* (cited as I.R.M.) sets forth the IRS's internal procedures in the administration of the Code. It provides useful information on how the IRS will conduct *audits* and related matters, but taxpayers are not entitled to rely on it to require the IRS to follow any particular procedure or take any specific action.

6. **Actions on decisions:** The IRS often publishes its decision to follow, appeal, or not follow without appeal, a decision of a trial court in what is known as an *Action on Decision* (cited as A.O.D.). In addition, the IRS indicates its agreement to abide by an unfavorable decision or intention to continue to contest the issue in an *acquiescence* or *nonacquiescence* published in the Internal Revenue Bulletin.

7. **Written determinations:** The IRS issues several kinds of unpublished authority. These are subject to public disclosure (in redacted form) and are generally available from commercial services but are not published in the Internal Revenue Bulletin. They can also be found on the IRS website. None of these may be used or cited as precedent. IRC §6110(k)(3). However, tax lawyers use written determinations to get a sense of the IRS's views on a particular transaction.

   a. **Private Letter Rulings:** Taxpayers in some circumstances may seek a ruling by the IRS on the application of the law to a specific set of facts. Only the taxpayer to whom the *private letter ruling* is issued can rely on it.

   b. **Technical Advice Memoranda:** During an *audit,* either the IRS revenue agent or the taxpayer may request technical advice from the National Office of the IRS. The response is a **Technical Advice Memorandum** that interprets the law and applies it to the specific set of facts submitted by the agent and taxpayer. It is binding on the IRS, even if the local IRS authorities conducting the audit do not agree with its conclusions.

   c. **Chief Counsel Advice:** The Chief Counsel's office of the IRS may issue a memorandum to IRS personnel interpreting the law on an issue that applies generally to a class of taxpayers or an industry. This advice is not directed to the situation of a particular taxpayer. These are known as *Chief Counsel Advice.*

D. Judicial interpretation of the Code

A number of courts have jurisdiction over tax controversies between the IRS and taxpayers.

Figure 1B
How a Tax Case Gets to Court

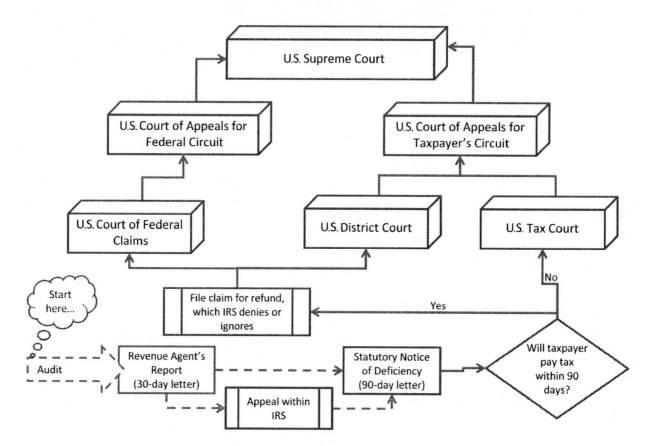

1. **How a tax case gets to court:** Figure 1B—How a Tax Case Gets to Court—summarizes the steps by which a tax case arrives at court. In Figure 1B, the dashed line represents the administrative process that a tax controversy goes through before ripening into an actual case.

   a. **Filing a tax return:** The U.S. tax system is a *self-assessment system,* which means that each taxpayer calculates his or her tax on a tax return he or she files with the IRS.

   b. **Audit:** The IRS may review all or part of a return, raising questions about items reported (or not reported) by the taxpayer. At the conclusion of an audit, the IRS issues a ***Revenue Agent's Report*** (also known as a "*30-day letter*") setting forth proposed changes. This gives the taxpayer 30 days in which to agree (and have additional taxes assessed) or to appeal the findings.

      i. **Three-year statute of limitations:** In general, the IRS has three years from the later of the date of filing or the day a return was due to make additional assessments. §6501(a).

      ii. **Six-year (or longer) statute of limitations:** In certain cases, the three years is extended to six years, such as when there is a substantial omission of items from the return. See §6501(e)(1). In certain circumstances, the statute of limitations can be even longer.

   c. **Administrative controversies:** If the taxpayer does not agree with the changes proposed by the Revenue Agent's Report, he or she may appeal the decision within the IRS and request a conference with the Appeals Division of the IRS.

    i.   **Small cases—less than $50,000 assessment for each year:** The taxpayer sends a brief written statement to the IRS summarizing why he or she disagrees.

    ii.   **Protest, conference, and settlement:** For cases that are not small cases, the taxpayer submits a *Protest* (similar to a brief) setting forth the basis for his or her disagreement with the Revenue Agent's Report. At the conference and thereafter, the appeals agent has the authority to settle the case with the taxpayer.

    iii.   **No settlement—Statutory Notice of Deficiency:** If the case is not resolved at the Appeals Division, the IRS will issue a *Statutory Notice of Deficiency* (also known as a *90-day letter*) seeking to assess additional taxes and setting forth the basis for the IRS's position.

  d. **Judicial determinations:** After receiving a Statutory Notice of Deficiency, the taxpayer must make a decision as to which trial forum he or she prefers. See Figure 1C—Comparison of Trial Forums for Tax Disputes.

Figure 1C
Comparison of Trial Forums for Tax Disputes

Question	U.S. Tax Court	U.S. District Court	U.S. Court of Federal Claims
Pay tax first?	No	Yes	Yes
Jury trial?	No	Available	No

    i.   **U.S. Tax Court:** A taxpayer may file a petition with the *U.S. Tax Court* (formerly the Board of Tax Appeals) within 90 days of receiving a Statutory Notice of Deficiency from the IRS. This is the only forum in which the taxpayer does not have to pay the tax prior to filing. The taxpayer may choose to pay the tax, however, in order to stop the accumulation of interest. All collection efforts are suspended during pendency of the suit. The trial is to a Tax Court judge, not a jury. The Tax Court will apply the law of the circuit to which the taxpayer would appeal. See *Golsen v. Commissioner,* 54 T.C. 742 (1970), *aff'd on another issue,* 445 F.2d 985 (10th Cir.), *cert. denied,* 404 U.S. 940 (1971). The U.S. Tax Court issues three kinds of opinions. A taxpayer may designate the case as a *small tax case* (less than $50,000 at issue), which will result in a nonappealable summary decision. For other than small cases, the Tax Court will issue either a regular opinion (cited as T.C.) or a memorandum decision (cited as T.C. Memo or T.C.M.).

    ii.   **U.S. District Court:** If the taxpayer does not file a petition in the Tax Court within 90 days, his or her only other option for contesting the assessment is to pay the tax and file a *claim for refund,* and have that claim denied (or ignored for six months). Then the taxpayer may file a complaint in *U.S. District Court* for a refund of taxes paid, following a denial of the taxpayer's application for refund prior to filing suit. This is the only forum in which a jury trial is available.

    iii. U.S. Court of Federal Claims: As an alternative to filing in U.S. District Court, a taxpayer may file for refund of taxes paid in the ***U.S. Court of Federal Claims.*** To be eligible to file suit, the taxpayer must have paid the tax and filed a claim for refund, which was denied (or ignored for six months). The trial is to a judge of the U.S. Court of Federal Claims, not a jury.

    iv. Jurisdiction of the U.S. Bankruptcy Courts: The U.S. ***Bankruptcy Courts*** have jurisdiction over any tax issue of a debtor or a bankruptcy estate for which a bankruptcy petition has been filed. 11 U.S.C. §505(a). If a taxpayer commences a proceeding in Bankruptcy Court, actions pending in the Tax Court for that taxpayer are automatically stayed. 11 U.S.C. §362(a)(8). The Bankruptcy Court may decide all tax matters, preempting the jurisdiction of the Tax Court. 11 U.S.C. §362(a), (f). If a Statutory Notice of Deficiency has been issued, the stay stops the running of the 90-day period, although the Bankruptcy Court may (but is not required to) lift the stay and allow the filing of a petition with the Tax Court. 11 U.S.C. §362(c), (d).

  e. Appellate jurisdiction

    i. Circuit Courts of Appeal: From the U.S. District Court and the U.S. Tax Court, appeals go to the U.S. Court of Appeals for the Circuit in which the taxpayer lives or has his or her domicile. Appeal from the Court of Federal Claims is to the U.S. Court of Appeal for the Federal Circuit.

    ii. U.S. Supreme Court: Appeal from the appellate courts for tax decisions is to the U.S. Supreme Court.

  f. Tax procedure: Numerous rules govern the actions of the IRS and taxpayers (and their representatives) in assessing, contesting, and collecting taxes. These rules are generally beyond the scope of the basic income tax course. A passing familiarity with the following rules will usually suffice.

    i. Burden of proof: Under the Tax Court rules, the taxpayer generally bears the ***burden of proof.*** Tax Court Rule 142. There are a few exceptions in which the burden of proof is on the IRS. These generally involve situations in which the IRS is asserting a particular kind of taxpayer behavior, such as fraud, for which it should already have proof before asserting its argument.

    ii. Collection processes: Three major pieces of legislation, in 1988, 1996, and 1998, all known as the ***Taxpayer Bill of Rights*** (I, II, and III, respectively), addressed concerns with IRS collection and other internal processes. Taxpayers have the right to notice and special appeals in the collection process.

    iii. Taxpayer Advocate: The ***Office of the Taxpayer Advocate*** is a special office in the IRS designed to address taxpayer's concerns and help improve the system for taxpayers. This office is intended to be independent of other IRS functions and can require that the IRS respond to inquiries and recommend solutions.

2. The process of statutory interpretation: Because the federal income tax is a creature of statute, most judicial activity in the area focuses on the process of statutory interpretation. An interpretive question arises whenever the taxpayer and the IRS cannot agree on the proper meaning of an ambiguous statutory term.

a. Deference: Courts will give deference to the IRS's prelitigation, published interpretation of a statutory term. This means that a court will adopt the IRS's interpretation of an unclear term (instead of the taxpayer's interpretation or an interpretation the court might devise) if the IRS's interpretation is a reasonable interpretation of congressional intent. The Commissioner's interpretation need not be the only possible interpretation, or even the best interpretation; it need only be a reasonable interpretation. *Chevron U.S.A., Inc. v. Natural Resources Defense Council, Inc.,* 467 U.S. 837 (1984).

    i. Types of authority given deference: Courts give the greatest deference to specific authority regulations. See discussion this chapter, section (II)(C)(2), above. But the courts also give deference to other kinds of regulations, and, to a lesser extent, to Revenue Rulings and other administrative interpretations. Generally, however, less deference is given to authorities the promulgation of which was not subject to the Administrative Procedures Act.

    ii. No deference required: Deference is not accorded an IRS interpretation that was not the subject of a prelitigation, published administrative position. In that situation, the court will determine which interpretation—the taxpayer's, the IRS's, or some other interpretation—is correct, without giving deference to the IRS's interpretation. In addition, courts will adopt a particular interpretation if they believe the term is clear; that is, the interpretation is obvious.

    iii. The effect of deference: It is extremely difficult (but not impossible) for a taxpayer to prevail when making the argument that an IRS regulation should be invalidated.

b. Tools of interpretation: In interpreting the Code, the courts rely on a variety of tools (useful sources of information) to guide them in choosing an interpretation of a statutory term. These include language tools, extrinsic tools, and functional tools.

    i. Language tools: Courts often refer to the literal language of a statute as the best guide to its meaning. But if the language were so clear, there would be no controversy. Therefore, courts often turn to the canons of statutory interpretation (which are not unique to tax law) as a language tool. In addition, courts consistently invoke two specific rules of interpretation for tax statutes: Construe income statutes broadly, and construe deduction and credit statutes narrowly.

    ii. Extrinsic tools: Courts seek guidance in the meaning of a statutory term from a wide variety of extrinsic sources. These include legislative history (hearings, floor debates, statements of the sponsors, and committee reports), the Joint Committee on Taxation's General Explanation of a tax bill, legislative inaction, other statutory schemes, and commentary on a statute.

    iii. Functional tools: Courts also seek to interpret tax statutes consistently with their purpose within a legislative scheme. This requires a court to discern the purpose of a statute and to interpret its particular terms consistently with that purpose. Functional analysis often produces the same result reached by reference to language or extrinsic tools. Yet it can also provide answers where a statute defies interpretation using other tools. Courts develop the purposes of statutes from legislative history, the structure of the larger legislative scheme, and tax policy. See discussion of tax policy this chapter, section (V).

c. **A guide to statutory interpretation cases:** Most statutory interpretation deals with the meaning of one or two ambiguous terms within a tax statute. To understand the interpretative question, identify the following:

  i. **The ambiguous term(s):** Identify the statutory term(s) at issue.

  ii. **The consequences:** Focus on the different tax consequences of the competing interpretations. What results will flow from each interpretation?

  iii. **The process:** What process did the court use in reaching its result? How did it determine the correct interpretation? Did the court give deference to the IRS's interpretation? Why or why not?

  iv. **The result:** Which interpretation did the court choose, and why?

III. TAX ETHICS—TAX RETURN POSITIONS AND SANCTIONS

A. Taxpayer's responsibility for accuracy

Section 6001 requires taxpayers to file tax returns and comply with the Secretary of the Treasury's regulations. Form 1040 requires a taxpayer to sign the return, declaring under penalties of perjury that the return is "true, correct, and complete." The standard for a taxpayer's return position is the same as the standard for positions to be litigated before the U.S. Tax Court: the position must not be *frivolous*—i.e., it must be well grounded in fact and warranted by existing law or a good faith argument for the extension, modification, or reversal of existing law. See Tax Court Rule 33.

B. Taxpayer penalties

1. **The accuracy-related penalty:** A penalty is imposed for any portion of a tax underpayment equal to 20% of any underpayment that is attributable to *negligence,* a *substantial understatement of tax,* or certain other misstatements. IRC §6662(a).

   a. **Negligence or disregard:** Negligence includes any failure to make a reasonable attempt to comply with the tax laws. IRC §6662(c). Disregard includes any careless, reckless, or intentional disregard of rules or regulations. *Id.*

   b. **Substantial understatement of tax:** An understatement of tax is substantial if it exceeds the greater of 10% of the tax required to be shown on the return for the year, or $5,000. IRC §6662(d)(1); Reg. §1.6662-4(b)(1). A tax understatement is the excess of the amount of tax required to be shown on the return over the amount actually shown. IRC §6662(d)(2).

   c. **Exception for supported, disclosed items:** The penalty will not be imposed for any understatement for which the taxpayer had *substantial authority,* or (1) which the taxpayer disclosed on the return, and (2) for which the taxpayer had a *reasonable basis.* IRC §6662(d)(2)(B).

      i. **Substantial authority:** A taxpayer has substantial authority for a position if the weight of authorities supports the position compared with the weight of authorities against it. Reg. §1.6662-4(d)(3). The regulations specify which authorities may be considered in making this comparison. *Id.*

      ii. **Disclosure:** The taxpayer makes the required disclosure on Form 8275.

      iii. Reasonable basis: The prior regulations referred to the reasonable basis standard as being "arguable, but fairly unlikely to prevail in court." Prior Reg. §1.6662-4(d). The legislative history of the accuracy-related penalty suggests that it is somewhat higher than the "not frivolous" standard, but the precise outlines of this standard are not clear.

  2. Lack of economic substance penalty: Section 6662(b)(6) imposes a strict liability 20% penalty for underpayments attributable to any disallowance of a tax benefit because a transaction lacked economic substance, as defined in §7701(o) or otherwise. The parameters of this new penalty and the economic substance rules are not yet known, but certainly the courts will draw upon longstanding law that a transaction must have real economic ramifications (beyond tax benefits) in order to be respected for tax purposes.

  3. The civil fraud penalty: If any part of a tax underpayment is due to *fraud,* a penalty is imposed equal to 75% of that portion of the underpayment. IRC §6663(a). Fraud is defined as an intentional wrongdoing by the taxpayer with the specific intent to evade a tax known to be owed. See *Stoltzfus v. United States*, 398 F.2d 1002 (3d Cir. 1968), cert. denied, 393 U.S. 1020 (1969).

  4. Criminal tax sanctions: Tax fraud is a crime for which criminal sanctions, including prison terms and fines, apply. See IRC §§7201–7207. Criminal tax penalties are generally beyond the scope of most basic tax courses.

C. Lawyer's duty in advising on tax return positions

  1. State ethics rules: A lawyer advising a client of a tax return position is subject to all of the rules and regulations governing law practice of his or her state. Some state bar associations have issued their own ethics opinions regarding the standards of practice for tax lawyers.

  2. Preparer penalties: A tax preparer is subject to penalties if he or she prepares a return or a claim for refund and knows (or reasonably should have known) that the position taken on the return was unreasonable. The penalty on the preparer is the greater of $1,000 per violation or 50% of the compensation received on the transaction.

    a. Tax return preparer: This is the person primarily responsible for taking the position on the return. Reg. §1.6694-1(b). A person who does not sign the return, i.e., an attorney advising a client to take a position on a tax return, can be considered a preparer.

    b. Unreasonable position: A position is unreasonable in the following scenarios.

      i. Tax shelters and reportable transactions: If the return or claim for refund is based on a tax shelter or *reportable transaction,* the position is unreasonable unless it is more likely than not to prevail. IRC §6694(a)(2)(C). The IRS publishes a list of reportable transactions, which are transactions that it views as abusive.

      ii. Other transactions: If the return of claim for refund is based on a position that is not a tax shelter or reportable transaction, the position is unreasonable unless:

        ■ **Undisclosed positions:** If the position is not disclosed on the return or refund claim (by means of a specific IRS form), the position is unreasonable unless there is or was substantial authority for the position. IRC §6694(a)(2)(A).

■ **Disclosed positions:** If the position was disclosed on the return or refund claim (by means of a specific IRS form) the position is unreasonable unless there is or was a reasonable basis for the position. IRC §6694(a)(2)(B).

3. **Circular 230 standard:** The IRS governs practice before it, and has promulgated rules governing that practice in what is known as *Circular 230.* 11 C.F.R. pt. 10. Violation of those rules can lead to sanctions, including being prohibited from practicing before the IRS. A practitioner cannot advise a taxpayer to take a return position or sign a return unless the practitioner believes that the standard of §6694, discussed immediately above, is met.

IV. READING THE CODE

At first, the Code may seem like a foreign language. And indeed, learning to read the Code is like learning a new language—part vocabulary, part syntax. To help you with vocabulary, this outline provides you with definitions within the text. Learning the syntax requires a systematic approach to reading a tax statute, discussed below.

A. Nomenclature of the Code and Regulations

A Code section is divided into a number of subparts, separately identified by letters or numbers. The nomenclature is identical for every Code section. It is helpful to have in mind the name of each separate part, particularly when *parsing* complex Code sections.

1. **From section to subclause:** A Code *section* is the entire statute. Subdivisions are made by parenthetical indicators. The first subdivision is indicated by a parenthetical lowercase letter, such as (a)—this is known as a *subsection.* A subsection may be divided into parts, indicated by a parenthetical Arabic numeral, such as (1)—these are known as *paragraphs.* A paragraph may be divided into parts, indicated by parenthetical uppercase letters, such as (A)—these are known as *subparagraphs.* A subparagraph may be divided into parts, indicated by parenthetical lowercase Roman numerals, such as (iv)—these are known as *clauses.* Clauses may be subdivided into parts, indicated by parenthetical uppercase Roman numerals, such as (I)—these are known as *subclauses* and are not further divided. Finally, language that begins at the left margin without a parenthetical indicator is known as *flush language.*

2. **Summary:** To summarize, the Code's nomenclature is as follows:

   ■ Section—§ symbol or Section

   ■ Subsection—Parenthetical lowercase letter, e.g., (a).

   ■ Paragraph—Parenthetical Arabic numeral, e.g., (1).

   ■ Subparagraph—Parenthetical uppercase letter, e.g., (A).

   ■ Clause—Parenthetical lowercase Roman numeral, e.g., (i).

   ■ Subclause—Parenthetical uppercase Roman numeral, e.g., (II).

   ■ Flush language—Begins at left margin without indicator.

   See Figure 1D—Code Nomenclature. Figure 1D provides an illustration of the Code's nomenclature for a Code section (§163(h)(1)) that students are likely to encounter later in the course.

Figure 1D
Code Nomenclature

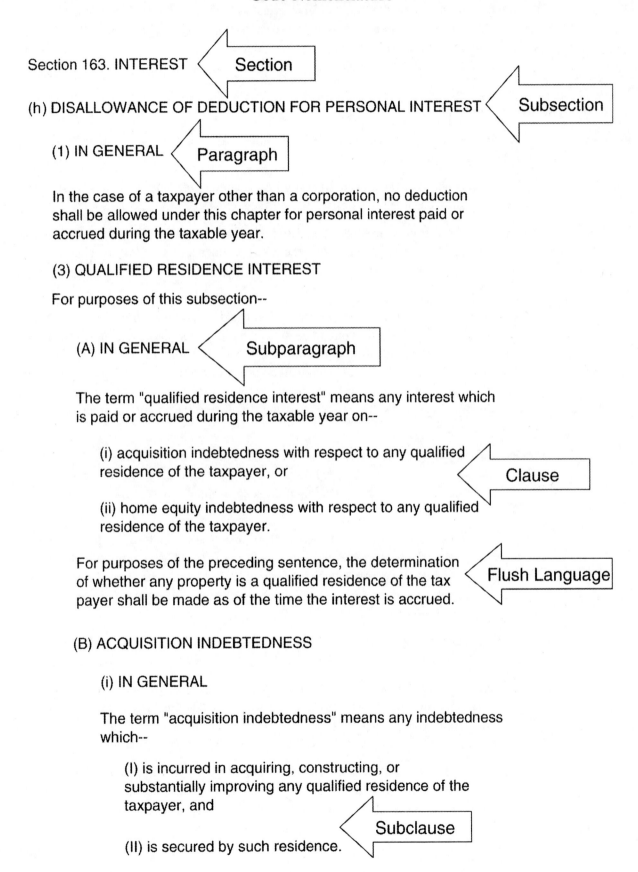

Section 163. INTEREST — Section

(h) DISALLOWANCE OF DEDUCTION FOR PERSONAL INTEREST — Subsection

(1) IN GENERAL — Paragraph

In the case of a taxpayer other than a corporation, no deduction shall be allowed under this chapter for personal interest paid or accrued during the taxable year.

(3) QUALIFIED RESIDENCE INTEREST

For purposes of this subsection--

(A) IN GENERAL — Subparagraph

The term "qualified residence interest" means any interest which is paid or accrued during the taxable year on--

(i) acquisition indebtedness with respect to any qualified residence of the taxpayer, or — Clause

(ii) home equity indebtedness with respect to any qualified residence of the taxpayer.

For purposes of the preceding sentence, the determination of whether any property is a qualified residence of the tax payer shall be made as of the time the interest is accrued. — Flush Language

(B) ACQUISITION INDEBTEDNESS

(i) IN GENERAL

The term "acquisition indebtedness" means any indebtedness which--

(I) is incurred in acquiring, constructing, or substantially improving any qualified residence of the taxpayer, and

(II) is secured by such residence. — Subclause

3. **The Regulations' nomenclature:** The Treasury has its own nomenclature for regulations as well. Income tax regulations generally begin with "1" and include the Code section number, followed by a dash and another number in a series, as in -1, -2, -3, etc. For example, "Treas. Reg. §1.102-1" is a regulation explaining the basics of the gift exclusion of §102. You can locate regulations by Code section number. Procedural regulations usually begin with "301" (e.g., Reg. §301.7701-1) and estate/gift tax regulations usually begin with a "20" or "25" (e.g., Reg. §25.2502-1).

B.   A systematic approach

1. **If . . . then:** Like most statutes, tax statutes are simply expressions of "if . . . then" statements of varying degrees of complexity.

   a. **The requirements for the statute to apply:** A tax statute (like any statutes) does not apply universally. Instead, it applies only if certain facts exist.

   b. **So what? The consequences of the statute:** If the requirements of a statute are met, the next question is, so what? What will be the tax consequences to the taxpayer? (And, if the statute doesn't apply, how do these consequences differ?)

2. **Parsing—A five-step approach to unfamiliar statutes:** Tax statutes are classic examples of what educators euphemistically refer to as "difficult texts." The meaning of a tax statute is difficult for novices to glean with standard reading techniques. The antidote to any difficult text is a systematic approach to identifying the important material within the text. Fortunately, any tax statute can be understood by a five-step method of *parsing* a statute. Parsing a statute is like briefing a case—it identifies the important components of a statute and creates a tool for using the statute to solve problems. These five steps help you find the important information in a statute, in the proper order.

   a. **Step 1. Find the general rule:** Almost every tax statute has a fundamental "if . . . then" statement, which is its general rule. Look for a provision (usually in subsection (a)) that states the basic conditions for application of the section and its consequences. *Underline the general rule in red.*

   b. **Step 2. Find the terms of art and their definitions:** The general rule usually contains a few terms of art or ordinary terms used in a technical sense. The statute often defines the most important of these terms later in the statute. *Highlight the terms of art and their definitions in yellow. If a term is not defined, note this as a candidate for administrative or judicial interpretation.*

   c. **Step 3. Find the exceptions and special rules:** Few tax statutes apply universally; most have special rules, limitations, and exceptions. *Mark these with a big green "X" for later analysis.*

   d. **Step 4. Find related statutory material:** Many statutes work together in groups, and related statutory material must be identified to understand the tax consequences of a particular statute. Related material may appear as a reference to a Code section or as a reference to a concept discussed elsewhere in the Code. *Circle related material in blue.*

   e. **Step 5. Note when the statute is likely to be implicated.** An important part of competence in any arena is recognizing patterns that trigger certain results. In tax, that means knowing when certain statutes are likely to be implicated, i.e., the typical fact pattern in which the statute is relevant. This helps trigger consideration of analogous fact patterns in which the statute may be relevant. *Note the typical situation implicating the statute in the margin in black.*

Example: See Figure 1E. (The black-and-white format of this book prevents this example from being parsed in color. However, you can see an example in color on the website, *www.aspenlawschool.com/books/tax_outline.*)

Figure 1E
Example of a Parsed Statute

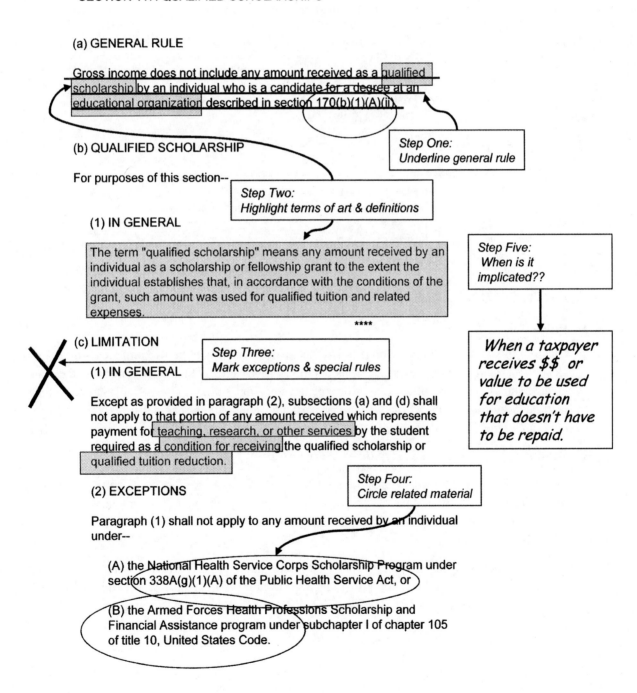

SECTION 117. QUALIFIED SCHOLARSHIPS

(a) GENERAL RULE

Gross income does not include any amount received as a qualified scholarship by an individual who is a candidate for a degree at an educational organization described in section 170(b)(1)(A)(ii).

Step One:
Underline general rule

(b) QUALIFIED SCHOLARSHIP

For purposes of this section--

Step Two:
Highlight terms of art & definitions

(1) IN GENERAL

The term "qualified scholarship" means any amount received by an individual as a scholarship or fellowship grant to the extent the individual establishes that, in accordance with the conditions of the grant, such amount was used for qualified tuition and related expenses.

****

Step Five:
When is it implicated??

When a taxpayer receives $$ or value to be used for education that doesn't have to be repaid.

(c) LIMITATION

Step Three:
Mark exceptions & special rules

(1) IN GENERAL

Except as provided in paragraph (2), subsections (a) and (d) shall not apply to that portion of any amount received which represents payment for teaching, research, or other services by the student required as a condition for receiving the qualified scholarship or qualified tuition reduction.

(2) EXCEPTIONS

Step Four:
Circle related material

Paragraph (1) shall not apply to any amount received by an individual under--

(A) the National Health Service Corps Scholarship Program under section 338A(g)(1)(A) of the Public Health Service Act, or

(B) the Armed Forces Health Professions Scholarship and Financial Assistance program under subchapter I of chapter 105 of title 10, United States Code.

3. **Statute Summary Charts:** This outline presents statutory material using these five steps: the general rule, definitional issues, special rules and exceptions, related material, and "typically implicated when . . . ." A chart summarizing the material is offered for particularly important statutes. See Figure 1F—Sample Statute Summary Chart. The relevant charts are located at the end of each chapter.

Figure 1F
Sample Statute Summary Chart

Parsing Step	IRC §71
General Rule	Gross income includes alimony payments.
Definitions	**Alimony:** has federal tax law definition, independent of state law labels. Requirements: cash; divorce decree; not designated as nondeductible; not members of same household; no liability to pay beyond recipient's death; no child support. **Front-end loaded alimony:** varies by more than $15,000 in first three years—see technical definition.
Special Rules and Exceptions	Front-end loaded alimony results in income to payor and deduction to payee in third post-separation year.
Related Statutes	**§215:** Deduction to payor for alimony **§1041:** Property transfers in divorce or between spouses
Typically implicated when . . .	Divorce situations, or post-divorce situations.

V. A FEW WORDS ON TAX POLICY

A. Importance

One tool of statutory interpretation is functional analysis, in which the IRS and courts interpret the Code consistently with the policy considerations motivating Congress. Moreover, the federal income tax course is often policy-oriented, requiring students to be able to articulate a methodology for evaluating the wisdom of particular tax statutes. The debate is value laden, but there are some accepted standards for evaluation of a tax statute.

B. Before we dive in . . . who pays taxes, anyway?

The Tax Policy Center (or "TPC," a joint venture of the Urban Institute and the Brookings Institution) estimates that 45% of U.S. households will pay no federal income tax in 2010. Most of these households have low incomes—60% of them have household incomes of less than $20,000.

1. **What's going on out there?** The TPC estimates that the nearly $1 trillion in tax expenditures (see below) have had the effect of reducing the number of people who actually pay federal income tax. It simulated what would happen if the dependent exemption, the itemized deduction, and all personal credits were eliminated. This would result, the TPC estimates, in only 27% of households paying no federal income tax. (One can debate whether it is a good

or bad thing that nearly half of U.S. households do not pay federal income tax, of course.) For more information, see Roberton Williams, "Why Nearly Half of Americans Pay No Federal Income Tax", *Tax Notes*, June 7, 2010.

2. **The tax expenditure issue:** Tax scholars have long argued that there are two parts to the tax system: the part that comprises the provisions necessary to define income and collect tax on it, and the part that comprises a system of tax expenditures under which governmental financial assistance is carried out through special tax provisions. Provisions that allow deductions for home mortgage interest, that provide a tax credit for purchasing energy-efficient windows, or allow a deduction for clean-up of environmental damage are arguably part of the second system of tax expenditures. Tax expenditures can take the form of exclusions, deductions, credits, special tax rates, or deferral opportunities. The benefit given to a taxpayer as a result of a special provision is viewed as a federal expenditure of funds (forgoing the tax that would have otherwise been due) and a transfer of value to that person. The Office of Management and Budget estimated the revenue loss from the top six tax expenditures in 2007 as follows:

   a. **$118.4 billion:** Exclusion of employer contributions for insurance premiums and medical care; see Chapter 4(IX)(D).

   b. **$88 billion:** Deferral of pension and 401K contributions from gross income; see Chapter 15(VI)(C).

   c. **$62.2 billion:** Deductibility of home mortgage interest; see Chapter 6(V)(D).

   d. **$41.8 billion:** Child tax credit; see Chapter 13(VIII)(A).

   e. **$36.5 billion:** Deductibility of personal state and local real property taxes; see Chapter 6(VI).

   f. **$36 billion:** Exclusion of gain on sale of principal residences; see Chapter 4(VIII).

C. **Standards for evaluating tax statutes**

Evaluation of a tax statute involves three general goals that often compete with one another.

1. **Fairness:** Is the statute fair? The income tax burden is intended to be allocated among taxpayers based on their relative abilities to pay tax. A fair tax statute would add to the system's ability to distinguish between taxpayers with different abilities to pay. It would ensure that taxpayers with similar ability to pay are treated similarly for tax purposes *(horizontal equity)*, and taxpayers with different abilities to pay would be treated differently *(vertical equity)*.

   a. **Ability to pay and taxable income:** It is difficult, if not impossible, to directly measure a taxpayer's ability to pay tax. This would require direct inquiry into a taxpayer's relative ability to contribute to the tax burden. "Taxable income" is viewed as a viable substitute or surrogate for direct measurement of a taxpayer's ability to pay.

   b. **A "fair" measure of taxable income:** Taxable income will never be a perfect surrogate for ability to pay. But if it is a good substitute, use of taxable income as the income tax base will tend to impose similar taxes on those with similar abilities to pay and will differentiate among taxpayers with different abilities to pay. Thus, the choice to include an item in gross income or to allow a deduction must make taxable income a closer measure of ability to pay if it is to be a "fair" statute.

2. **Administrative practicality:** Is a statute administratively practical? A statute must not be so complex as to be unworkable or require undue governmental intrusion into the lives of taxpayers. It must also collect revenue at a reasonable cost. The goal of administrative practicality often competes directly with the goal of fairness. As statutes make increasingly fine distinctions among taxpayers with different abilities to pay (presumably making the system fairer), these distinctions tend to increase the complexity of the system as a whole.

3. **Economic effects:** Does the statute have the intended economic effect? Taxpayers respond rationally to any statute, and if a statute creates an incentive to take a particular action, they may indeed do so. In addition, a statute may have some unintended effects on taxpayer behavior. Every tax expenditure can be explained in terms of its expected economic effects. In enacting a tax statute, Congress must attempt to predict its consequences and determine if they are desirable. The modern thinking in tax policy is to make statutes as behaviorally neutral as possible. That doesn't stop Congress from enacting tax measures designed to stimulate the economy, for example. See Chapter 7(IV).

VI. RELATIONSHIP OF THE FEDERAL INCOME TAX TO OTHER TAX SYSTEMS

A. The federal income tax

The primary subject of the income tax is the tax levied by §1 of the Code on the "taxable income" of the individual.

B. Other tax regimes

Other tax systems exist independently of the federal income tax.

1. **Estate and gift tax:** The Code imposes a tax on the transfer of property by decedents in amounts in excess of stated amounts ($5,000,000 in 2011) and on lifetime gifts in excess of $1,000,000. This is not an income tax; it is a tax on transfers. The $5,000,000 lifetime exemption amount is scheduled to sunset on December 31, 2012.

2. **Employment tax:** The Code imposes Social Security, unemployment, and Medicare taxes on the wages of employees and on employers. The employer must deduct and withhold the employee's portion of these taxes, and the employer must pay its share. Employers are also responsible for withholding federal income taxes, but this is merely a method of collection of the income tax, and employment taxes are a separate system of taxation.

3. **State and local tax:** The various states and their political subdivisions impose taxes on their residents. Many states adopt the federal income tax definitions and computations for their own income tax, but state income taxes are separately levied and collected. States and local governments also favor property and sales taxes in generating revenue.

4. **Foreign tax systems:** Foreign countries have their own taxing systems, which may extend to tax U.S. persons engaged in foreign transactions.

VII. NEED TO KNOW MORE?

This book's website *www.aspenlawschool.com/books/tax_outline* contains additional information, including:

- An example of a parsed statute—in color.

- From simple to complex—how tax statutes develop over time.

- Why the regulations are your best friend—how to get the most out of reading the regulations.

- Latest inflation-adjusted limits, etc. for various Code provisions.

- And other materials that will help you get started in federal income tax.

VIII. WHERE ARE WE GOING?

With these preliminary matters out of the way, the next chapters turn to the technical matters of calculating a taxpayer's tax—the determination of gross income, deductions, tax rates, and credits. As a first step in this process, Chapter 2 addresses the theoretical concept of income to identify what items are potentially includable in gross income.

Quiz Yourself on GETTING STARTED IN FEDERAL INCOME TAX

1. Why would a taxpayer disclose the details of a particular return position even though not required to do so by the usual tax return reporting rules? _____

2. The IRS is assessing additional taxes, interest, and penalties against Leona. She is outraged, because in her opinion, "Only the little people pay taxes!" She is further outraged because she relied on an article in *Time* magazine and followed that advice in taking one of her return positions and disclosed that on the return. After calming her down, you must explain what authorities do and do not have "precedential value." How do you do that? _____

3. Willie received a Statutory Notice of Deficiency assessing $13,000,000 in back taxes, interest, and penalties. He hasn't a cent to his name, only a guitar, a collection of records, and an old pickup truck. If Willie wants to contest this assessment, how should he do so? _____

4. Why might a taxpayer prefer to litigate in a U.S. District Court rather than the U.S. Tax Court? _____

5. What is the difference between a Revenue Ruling and a private letter ruling? _____

6. Carla was surprised to hear from her tax preparer that a position she and her tax preparer had taken for years in the past needs to be disclosed on the return or the preparer can't sign the return. What is motivating this change in approach? _____

7. Why would taxpayers be subject only to the "not frivolous" position standard on their own tax returns, while tax preparers are subject to a higher standard? _____

8.   Your congressman proposes a new Code provision that allows a person getting a divorce a deduction of $5,000 in the year the divorce is final. His rationale is that taxpayers have additional expenses in that year, and their taxable income should reflect that reality. You're his aide, and official tax guru. What do you tell him as to the advisability of this? (Disregard budget and budget process implications.) _____

Answers

1.   In order to avoid the substantial understatement penalty of §6662, the taxpayer might choose to fully disclose the details of a transaction. A preparer might advise a taxpayer to disclose in order to avoid the penalties of §6694 if the preparer thought that there was only a reasonable basis for the position and not substantial authority.

2.   Precedential value means, in the tax world, that authorities can be cited as precedent in the Tax Court and that, if they are administrative guidance, the IRS will be bound by such rulings. Court opinions, temporary and final regulations, revenue rulings, and revenue procedures all have precedential value and all bind the IRS except for some court opinions (it is bound by the Supreme Court's opinions, and appellate courts' opinions for tax controversies appealable to that circuit). Authorities that do not have precedential value and do not bind the IRS: private letter rulings and Technical Advice Memoranda addressed to other taxpayers; Chief Counsel Advice; proposed regulations; the Internal Revenue Manual; and forms and instructions issued by the IRS. Also (need it be said?) *Time* magazine—while possibly a source of tax information—does not generate opinions with precedential value.

3.   Willie has two alternatives. He can file a petition in the U.S. Tax Court, if he files within 90 days of the date of the Statutory Notice of Deficiency. If he does so, he won't have to pay the tax unless and until the Tax Court decides against him. But he might want to consider coming under the wing of the Bankruptcy Court—this will stay enforcement proceedings. There is no guarantee that the taxes will be dischargeable in bankruptcy, but maybe he could keep his guitar and truck.

4.   In a U.S. District Court, a taxpayer has the right to a jury trial, while cases in the U.S. Tax Court are tried to a judge, not a jury.

5.   In both private letter rulings and Revenue Rulings, the IRS addresses the application of the tax laws to a particular set of facts. But a private letter ruling is a form of written determination by the IRS, which is addressed to a particular taxpayer in response to the taxpayer's request. It is binding only with respect to that taxpayer. It cannot be used or cited as precedent. A Revenue Ruling is a statement of the law issued by the IRS not addressed to any particular taxpayer, and has precedential value if a taxpayer's facts are the same as those in the Revenue Ruling.

6.   The standards applicable to preparers have changed in recent years. A preparer must have a reasonable basis for any position taken, and if the position isn't disclosed, an even higher standard applies: the substantial authority standard (for non-tax shelters or transactions that are not reportable transactions). It appears that the tax preparer is concerned that the tax return position previously taken would not pass muster under the new standards of §6694. It is supported by a reasonable basis (or the tax preparer could not take the position at all), but the preparer appears concerned that the higher standard might not be met.

7. Taxpayers are not expected to have the same access to or experience with the various administrative interpretations of the Code as tax professionals, so taxpayers would not be able to evaluate whether a particular position met the "reasonable basis" or "more likely than not" standards. However, taxpayers are expected to determine if the positions they are taking are frivolous, a relatively low standard to meet.

8. In advising the congressman, you would focus on the fairness, administrative practicality, and economic effects of this provision.

   Fairness: Does it treat persons similarly situated, as to their ability to pay, in a similar fashion? Doubtful. Certainly the good congressman is correct, that many people getting a divorce have extra expenses associated with that divorce, and this reduces their ability to pay. But the proposal has two faults (at least) in the fairness arena. The first problem is the reach of the statute. It is not limited to people who really have extra expenses, nor does it distinguish the year in which those expenses actually occur. Second, divorce expenses are clearly personal expenses. While some personal expenses are deductible (such as certain medical expenses and casualty losses), in all of these cases you can be pretty sure that the taxpayer is really "out" a significant amount of money. Not so with divorces—in fact, some people (those married to compulsive shoppers, for example) may be saving money by getting a divorce.

   Administrative practicality: It seems to be easy to administer, at least in its current form. The year of divorce is easy to identify, and the people getting a divorce are also easy to identify. However, one might wonder how to distinguish between real divorces and those designed to take advantage of this deduction (see below).

   Economic effects: Here is where you tell your congressman that "this dog won't hunt." Not only does it appear he is supporting divorce, he may in fact appear to be creating an economic incentive for people to get a divorce. It's a political dead end because of these effects.

Exam Tips on
GETTING STARTED IN FEDERAL INCOME TAX

Make sure you understand the "big picture" of how the federal tax is imposed:

Gross Income
− Certain Deductions
= Adjusted Gross Income (AGI)
− Either Standard or Itemized Deduction
− Personal Exemptions
= Taxable Income
x Tax Rate
= Tentative Tax
− Tax Credits
= **Tax Due or Refund Owed**

☛ The most valuable thing you can do at the beginning of the course is to become comfortable reading the Code and applying it.

☛ The first step is finding the Code. Become facile in finding Code and regulations sections in your statute book *before* you need to do this in class. Can you find IRC §102(b)(2)? Or §117(b)(2)(A)? Or §108(f)(2)(C)(iii)? How about Reg. §1.61-2? Or Reg. §1.132-5?

☛ Give parsing, as described in this chapter, a try. Doesn't work for you? Find some other systematic way to approach Code sections.

☛ When you read a tax case, read the statute that the case is based on. Analyze how the taxpayer interpreted the statute and how the IRS interpreted it—and ultimately how the court interpreted it.

☛ Tax professors almost universally allow students to take the Code book into the exam. By that time, you will have "parsed" the important statutes, for later reference. When discussing a tax problem on an exam, it never hurts to cite the statutes involved, but if pressed for time, don't cite to particular subsections, paragraphs, etc.

☛ On a test, an ingenious tax professor often will offer up an imaginary tax statute that you've never seen before, and pose problems from it. This tests your ability to read statutes. Use the parsing approach, and you'll be fine. (The good news: it's usually a relatively simple statute.)

☛ Given the recent important changes in the standards of tax practice, be ready to discuss the propriety of various return positions, and the different standards involved in penalty assessment, tax preparer assessment, and—most important—lawyers' ethical duties in giving tax advice.

☛ Tax procedure, including how cases get to court, is usually tested *indirectly* on tax exams. If a question is about a position that is being challenged by the IRS, it may be helpful to consider what the taxpayer's choices will be for appealing an adverse determination by the IRS.

☞ *Look for:* A taxpayer who has filed a return with a problematic return position.

☞ *Analyze:* The likelihood of success if challenged on the merits, and the taxpayer's options for resolving this controversy.

☛ Policy questions place you in the position of a legislator, an aide, or even an advocate faced with a statute that arguably produces unfair, impractical, or absurd results. Be sure to present both sides of the issues. There is no "right" answer to these questions; you're being tested on your understanding of tax fairness, how tax statutes are administered, and your ability to see expected and unexpected consequences of tax statutes. These questions can be paired with the "new" statute described above.

☛ Given recent discussions about the federal budget, expect a policy question about tax expenditures. Such a question might involve asking you to evaluate one of the "big six" of tax expenditures from a policy point of view.

CHAPTER 2

IDENTIFYING GROSS INCOME

ChapterScope ▬▬▬▬▬▬▬▬▬▬▬▬▬▬▬▬▬▬▬▬▬▬▬▬▬▬▬▬▬▬

This chapter begins the analysis of the substantive rules governing the computation of taxable income. The starting place is the concept of gross income, which is defined in §61 as including all "income" from all sources.

- **IRC Section 61:** Section 61 provides that gross income includes all income from whatever source derived. Section 61's use of the term "income" requires that a definition of income be developed so that transactions potentially generating gross income can be identified.

- **Haig-Simons definition of income:** Under this approach, a taxpayer's "income" for any period is the sum of (1) the market value of rights exercised in consumption, plus (2) the change in the value of the store of property rights between the beginning and end of the period in question. This approach generates a comprehensive tax base but raises complex issues of tax administration.

- **Economic benefit:** A second approach to the definition of income views a taxpayer as having income when he or she receives an economic benefit, whether in cash or property (tangible or intangible).

- **Imputed income:** Imputed income is the value one experiences from performing services for oneself or using one's own property. Imputed income, although perhaps income in a theoretical sense under the two approaches above, is not considered income under our tax system. The principal forms of imputed income are the value of household services by a nonworking spouse and the value of owner-occupied housing.

- **Capital recovery on sales of property:** The income tax is a tax on "income," and therefore the tax should be imposed only on the profit from the sale or disposition of property. The capital a taxpayer invested in the property and has not receovered will not be subject to the income tax.

- **Loans:** An inflow of funds from a loan is not considered income to the debtor because of the offsetting obligation to repay the loan.

- **General welfare payments:** The IRS takes the approach that payments to individuals under governmental programs for general welfare are excluded from gross income.

▬▬▬

I. WHERE ARE WE?

On the long road toward determination of a taxpayer's tax, *gross income* is the starting place. Section 61 requires the inclusion of all items of *income* in a taxpayer's gross income. Therefore, we begin our analysis with a discussion of the definition of "income." If a transaction produces no income for a taxpayer, no amount will be included in gross income, and the transaction will not generate tax for the taxpayer. By contrast, if an amount is considered income it will be included in gross income (and potentially subject to tax) unless specifically excluded by another Code section. This chapter examines two theoretical approaches to income and four items that are excluded from the concept of income.

II. IRC §61

Internal Revenue Code §61(a) defines gross income as follows: "Gross income means all income from whatever source derived. . . ." Section 61 also provides a nonexclusive list of specific items that are included in gross income.

A. Interpretation

The courts interpret this language broadly, in order "to exert the full measure of [Congress's] taxing power under the Sixteenth Amendment to the United States Constitution." *Cesarini v. United States,* 296 F. Supp. 3 (N.D. Ohio 1969), *aff'd per curiam,* 428 F.2d 812 (6th Cir. 1970).

B. What is income?

Section 61 seems circular: It includes in gross income all items of income. This requires a definition of "income" so that transactions potentially generating gross income can be identified.

C. The income tax base

The definition of income is important because it defines the ***tax base*** for the income tax, i.e., the total items on which the income tax is potentially assessed.

III. DEFINITIONS OF INCOME

A. Haig-Simons definition—Theoretical approach

Under this approach, income is the sum of (1) the market value of rights exercised in consumption, plus (2) the change in the value of the store of property rights between the beginning and the end of the period in question (usually the taxable year). H. Simons, *Personal Income Taxation* 50 (1938). This is known as the "Haig-Simons definition of income."

1. **Consumption rights:** This part of the equation measures the expenditures of a taxpayer for all items of consumption. Included are expenditures for basic necessities such as food, clothing, and shelter, as well as for luxuries. The definition potentially includes non-marketplace consumption, i.e., the value of services performed for oneself and the value of property owned and used by the taxpayer. This is known as ***imputed income*** and is discussed more generally in this chapter, Section (IV)(A).

2. **Property rights:** This part of the equation measures the net change in savings over the taxable period. Savings includes bank accounts, stocks and bonds, real estate, and other types of property. A net increase in savings would constitute an addition. A net decrease in savings (a fall in value of an asset, for example) would constitute a subtraction.

    Example: During the taxable year Heidi spent $32,000 on food, clothing, and shelter, another $5,000 on travel and other items, and saved $4,000. Under the Haig-Simons definition of income, her income is $41,000; the sum of her market rights exercised in consumption ($37,000) and the net increase in her property rights ($4,000).

    Example—Changes in property rights: Assume the same facts as in the previous example, except that in the next year Heidi invests her $4,000 savings from the prior year in a mutual fund, which declines in value to $3,000. All of her expenditures remain the same. Her income for the year would be $36,000; the market rights exercised in consumption ($37,000) minus the net change in the value of her property interests ($1,000).

3. **Broad definition:** The Haig-Simons approach constitutes a broad definition of income. It offers a "comprehensive tax base," i.e., a tax base that reflects all potential sources of income from which taxpayers may derive an ability to pay tax.

4. **Criticisms:**

   a. **Practical:** It would be difficult (but not impossible) to measure the value of imputed income and to administer the yearly addition or subtraction of paper "profits or losses" for assets.

   b. **Theoretical:** Some have criticized the Haig-Simon definition as tautological, as it merely states the obvious, that income must be either saved or spent. Others have criticized its neutrality between consumption and savings, and that it is an imperfect surrogate for a taxpayer's ability to pay. See Chapter 1(V)(C).

B. Another approach—Economic benefit

Under this approach, income is the value of *economic benefits* received by the taxpayer. A benefit is broadly defined to include inflows of both cash and noncash items that result in the taxpayer being better off as a result of the receipt. Only economic benefits are considered in this analysis, although "economic" is construed broadly to include not only cash and property but certain other benefits that cause the taxpayer's wealth to increase. Intangible, nonmaterial benefits are excluded, such as one's enjoyment of a job, the beauty of a spring day, or the personal satisfaction of family. While important benefits to individuals, these are not quantifiable and are not considered benefits in the economic sense to be included in gross income.

Example: Ed works as an analyst for Bingo Corporation for a salary of $25,000. One morning he arrives at work to find new, original artwork displayed throughout the building. Ed is an art lover, and his enjoyment of his job increases dramatically as a result of his employer's action. The value of the intangible benefit of a pleasant workplace is not included in Ed's income under the economic benefit theory even though it is a benefit to him, because it is not an "economic" benefit.

1. **Receipt of cash or property:** The receipt of cash or property (whether tangible or intangible) is the receipt of an economic benefit by the taxpayer. The source of the cash or property is not important to this determination, so even receipts from unusual sources constitute income.

   a. **The usual economic benefits:** The usual economic benefits include payments for goods or services, gifts, and transfers of property.

   b. *Commissioner v. Glenshaw Glass Co.,* **348 U.S. 426,** *rehearing denied,* **349 U.S. 925 (1955):** The taxpayers received exemplary damages for fraud and treble damages for antitrust violations by other companies.

      i. **Issue:** Were exemplary and treble damages includable in the taxpayers' gross incomes?

      ii. **Result and rationale:** Treble damages under antitrust law and exemplary damages for fraud are included in recipient's gross income. According to the court, "[U]ndeniable accessions to wealth, clearly realized, and over which the taxpayers have complete dominion" are includable in gross income.

c. **Windfalls:** In *Cesarini v. United States,* 296 F. Supp. 3 (N.D. Ohio 1969), *aff'd per curiam,* 428 F.2d 812 (6th Cir. 1970), a lucky husband and wife found $5,000 inside an old piano they had purchased.

     i. **Issues:** Must the taxpayers include the $5,000 in their gross income? If so, when the piano was purchased, or when the cash was discovered?

     ii. **Result and rationale:** The taxpayers must include the $5,000 in their gross income. Reg. §1.61-14(a) requires taxpayers finding treasure to include it in gross income when reduced to undisputed possession. This regulation is consistent with §61's statutory scheme to include all income in gross income. The court rejected the taxpayers' arguments that §74 (prizes) or §102 (gifts) would exclude this amount from gross income.

2. **Receipt of intangible benefit:** What the taxpayer receives may be something other than cash or a property right. If it constitutes an economic benefit to the taxpayer, it is income within this definition.

a. **Noncash compensation:** In *United States v. Drescher,* 179 F.2d 863 (2d Cir.), *cert. denied,* 340 U.S. 821 (1950), an employer paid $5,000 for an annuity contract naming an employee as the annuitant. Under the terms of the contract, the employer retained possession of the contract until the employee reached age 65, and thereafter the insurance company would pay the annuitant $54.70 monthly until his death. If he died before receiving 120 payments, the remaining payments would be paid to a beneficiary named by the annuitant. The employee had no assignable rights in the contract, and it had no cash, surrender, or loan value.

     i. **Issue:** Must the employee include in his gross income the $5,000 paid by the employer for the annuity contract?

     ii. **Result and rationale:** The employee must include an amount in gross income equal to the value of the contract. The employee received an economic benefit for services rendered to his employer, thus receiving compensation. The absence of assignability or surrender value did not render the benefit valueless. The question of value was to be considered on remand.

b. **Satisfaction of obligation:** In *Old Colony Trust Co. v. Commissioner,* 279 U.S. 716 (1929), an employer entered into a contract with an employee in which the employer agreed to pay the income taxes of the employee.

     i. **Issue:** Did the employer's payment of the taxes constitute additional gross income to the employee?

     ii. **Result and rationale:** The Court concluded that the satisfaction of a taxpayer's obligation (taxes) by another person constitutes an economic benefit to him, resulting in income to the taxpayer.

     Example: Tom agrees to work for The Firm, a law firm offering a competitive salary and benefits. On the first day of work, much to Tom's surprise, the senior partner informs him that The Firm has paid all of his law school debt, a total of $150,000. This transaction will be viewed for tax purposes as the payment of $150,000 of compensation income to Tom followed by Tom's payment of the loans. Thus, Tom will be required to include the $150,000 in gross income. (Notice that because the creditors have been paid in full, Tom has no "discharge of indebtedness income," discussed in Chapter 3(VII).)

c. **Services—Barter:** Revenue Ruling 79-24, 1979-1 C.B. 60, poses the situation in which a lawyer performs legal services for a housepainter, who in turn paints the lawyer's house.

  i. **Issue:** Do the lawyer and housepainter have income as a result of the transaction?

  ii. **Result and rationale:** The lawyer and the housepainter both have income as a result of the transaction, in an amount equal to the fair market value of the services each received. (This is presumed to be an equal amount for each, because neither made an additional payment.)

IV. ITEMS THAT ARE NOT INCOME

A. Imputed income

Imputed income is the fair market value of the taxpayer's performance of services for his or her personal benefit and the value of the taxpayer's personal use of property that he or she owns. The amount of imputed income can be established by reference to what the taxpayer would have to pay to hire the service or rent the property in the marketplace. Imputed income is not considered income for purposes of inclusion in gross income. There is no statutory basis for this principle.

1. **Importance:** The value of any service one performs for oneself, and the rental value of any property that one owns, constitutes imputed income. In terms of dollar value, there are two very significant types of imputed income that are omitted from most measures of gross domestic product.

   a. **Household services:** The value of unpaid family caretaking performed by stay-at-home spouses or partners is an important type of imputed income in the U.S. economy.

   b. **Owner-occupied housing:** The rental value of the home owned by the occupier is also an important type of imputed income.

2. **Compare—Barter:** A barter transaction does not generate imputed income. If a housepainter paints a house for a lawyer in exchange for legal services, neither has imputed income because neither has performed services for him- or herself. Instead, each has performed services for the other and has gross income in the amount of the value of the services obtained from the other. See Rev. Rul. 79-24, 1979-1 C.B. 60, discussed in this chapter, Section (III)(B).

3. **Is it income?** Imputed income appears in theory to be income under either the Haig-Simons or economic benefit definitions of income.

   a. **Haig-Simons:** The Haig-Simons definition includes the market value of rights exercised in consumption. Thus, the value of shelter (housing), child care, and housework constitute consumption, which in turn constitutes income, in theory.

   b. **Economic benefit:** The right to live in a home and the value of child care and housework are economic benefits to the taxpayer. Thus, they are income to the taxpayer, in theory.

   c. **Transactions only?** One possible explanation for the exclusion of imputed income from the definition of income is that a "transaction" is necessary to trigger income. A transaction requires more than one taxpaying unit and some sort of transfer of value between them. The family is treated for this purpose as one taxpaying unit.

4. Policy

    a. Fairness: Some commentators argue that it is unfair to exclude from gross income imputed income because the exclusion results in taxpayers with similar abilities to pay tax being treated differently (a violation of horizontal equity).

    Example: Compare Jack and Jill, a married couple with two children, with Kurt and Kathy, also married with two children. Jack works outside the home, earning taxable income of $50,000, and Jill cares for their two children and home. Kurt and Kathy both work outside the home, with Kurt earning $50,000 in taxable income and Kathy earning $25,000 in taxable income. Kurt and Kathy hire Lola to care for their two children and home while they work, and they pay her $20,000. Both couples are in a 30% tax bracket.

    Current taxation. Kurt and Kathy will pay tax on $75,000 of income while Jack and Jill will pay tax on $50,000 of income. At a 30% rate, this would result in Kurt and Kathy paying $7,500 more in tax.

    Compare consumption rights. Both couples have someone to care for their home and children, at an apparent value of $20,000 (Lola's wages). In fact, Kurt and Kathy have only $5,000 more in available consumption rights than do Jack and Jill and thus should have an additional tax of only $1,500.

    Compare economic benefits. Same analysis as consumption rights; both couples have the economic benefit of a cared-for home and cared-for children.

    A possible solution. Include in Jack and Jill's gross income the $20,000 of imputed income Jill earns taking care of the children and home. This would result in the two couples being taxed similarly.

    b. Administrative practicality: It is difficult to measure the value of owner-occupied housing or the value of family caretaking but it is hardly an impossible task. The annual value of owner-occupied housing could be set as a percentage of property tax value. The value of family caretaking could be conservatively estimated based on the annual cost of hiring household help.

    c. Economic effects: The exclusion of imputed income from gross income may cause desirable or undesirable economic effects, depending on one's value choices.

        i. Marketplace or home? Lesser-earning spouses or partners may choose to stay home rather than work outside the home.

        ii. Own or rent? Taxpayers may choose to own rather than rent items such as homes or equipment.

        iii. Work or play? Taxpayers may choose to perform certain services (e.g., home repair) for themselves rather than hiring a professional. The time they devote to such activities may be more productively spent in other pursuits, such as their own job.

    d. The political question: Imputed income is so far from the average taxpayer's view of the proper subject for taxation that it seems unlikely to become part of the federal income tax.

B. Capital recovery

1. **Definition of capital:** *Capital* is the taxpayer's unrecovered economic investment in property. Upon sale or disposition of that property, the taxpayer has a right to be taxed only on the income (profit) from the transaction, not his or her invested capital. Thus, the taxpayer is entitled to "recover" his or her invested capital. See discussion in Chapter 7(IV)(A).

   Example: Ingrid purchases Blackacre, a parcel of raw land, for $10,000. Five years later she sells Blackacre for $30,000. Ingrid will be taxed only on her income from this sale, which is the difference between her sales price ($30,000) and what she paid for Blackacre ($10,000), or $20,000. She will not be taxed on her invested capital.

2. **Capital recovery—Timing:** While the right to obtain a tax-free recovery of invested capital in property is a constitutional issue, the timing of that recovery is within the discretion of Congress. See discussion in Chapter 7(IV)(E).

   Example: In the above example, Ingrid received her tax-free recovery of capital upon sale at the end of her investment. If Blackacre had been a commercial office building, Ingrid would have been entitled to obtain her tax-free capital recovery during her ownership of the property (through depreciation or MACRS deductions).

3. **Basis:** A taxpayer's economic investment in property is reflected in his or her **basis** in that property. Basis is adjusted downward for capital recovery deductions, producing a taxpayer's **adjusted basis**. See discussion in Chapter 9(V)(C).

C. Loans

The creation of a **loan** does not generate income for either the debtor or the creditor. A loan is defined as the "unconditional and legally enforceable obligation for the repayment of money." *Autenreith v. Commissioner,* 115 F.2d 856 (3d Cir. 1940). The inflow of funds (the loan proceeds) to the debtor, which might otherwise be viewed as an economic benefit, is offset by the debtor's obligation to repay the debt. Similarly, the creditor's receipt of the debtor's note or other evidence of indebtedness, which could be viewed as the receipt of an economic benefit, is offset by the outflow of the loan proceeds. Repayment of the loan does not generate income for either party. The creditor's inflow (repayment) is offset by the creditor's return of the note. The debtor's receipt of his or her note, even if it qualifies as an economic benefit (which it may not), is offset by repayment. Thus neither the making of the loan nor repayment generates income to the parties to the loan.

1. **Loan and use of proceeds are separate transactions.** As a general rule, the loan is treated as an independent transaction from the debtor's use of the loan proceeds. Each transaction generates its own tax consequences; the consequences of the use of proceeds do not affect the loan transaction. *Vukasovich, Inc. v. Commissioner,* 790 F.2d 1409 (9th Cir. 1986).

   Example: Rita borrows $100,000 from Friendly Bank and uses it to purchase Blackacre, a parcel of raw land. She intends to hold Blackacre until the loan is due, then sell it, repay the loan, and keep the profit. Unfortunately, toxic waste is found on Blackacre, and its value falls to $20,000. When the loan is due, Rita sells Blackacre and repays the bank in full, using $80,000 of her own savings to fully repay the loan. The tax consequences of the loan are independent of the real estate transaction. The loan and its repayment generate no tax consequences. On the real estate transaction, Rita has an $80,000 loss.

2. **Discharge of indebtedness income:** If the debtor's obligation to repay is canceled in whole or in part, the debtor will have discharge of indebtedness income in the amount of the cancellation. See discussion in Chapter 3(VII).

3. **Possible exclusion—§108:** Section 108 provides an exclusion from gross income for discharge of indebtedness income in certain circumstances. See discussion in Chapter 4(VII).

D. **General welfare exclusion**

Through longstanding policy, the IRS takes the position that payments to individuals by governmental units under legislatively provided social benefit programs for the *promotion of the general welfare* are excludable from gross income. There is no perfect theory for this exclusion. However, if the Code specifically addresses payments, the provisions of the Code will trump this policy.

Example: Christine is a low-income homeowner who receives a $500 grant from her city to assist her in weatherizing the windows in her home. This payment is excluded from Christine's gross income. See Rev. Rul. 76-395, 1976-2 C.B. 16.

V. NEED TO KNOW MORE?

This book's website *www.aspenlawschool.com/books/tax_outline* contains additional information, including:

- Specific examples of items that are (or are not) income.
- The relationship of whether income exists and when it exists.
- Other examples of imputed income.
- And other material that will help you learn to identify "income" for tax purposes.

VI. WHERE ARE WE GOING?

With an idea of what theoretically constitutes income in mind, we now move to an analysis of items specifically included in gross income. Section 61 provides a nonexclusive list of items of income that are included in gross income, and other statutes supplement this list with additional inclusions in gross income. These are addressed in Chapter 3.

Quiz Yourself on
IDENTIFYING GROSS INCOME

9. Why wouldn't a tax system based on the Haig-Simons approach to measuring income be a good idea? Or would it? _____

10. What is the difference between "income" and "gross income"? _____

11. This year, Bev earned $100,000 in salary as a lawyer. She spent $40,000 on housing, $10,000 on clothing, and $5,000 on food. She spent $25,000 on other items. The rest she invested in a Certificate of Deposit earning 5%. Using the Haig-Simons definition of income, what is Bev's income? _____

12. Assume that Bev (from the previous question) liquidated the CD in the next year and invested the proceeds ($10,500) in stock in EndRun Co. During that year the value of the stock plummeted to $1,000. What effect does this have on Bev's income in the later year, using the Haig-Simons definition of income? _____

13. Nick's grandparents pay off his student loans for him as a graduation present. Does this result in income to Nick under the economic benefit theory of income? _____

14. After graduation, Nick had identical job offers in Utah and Texas. He chooses to work in Utah rather than Texas, because he loves to ski. Does Nick have income as a result of this choice?

_____

15. Ken borrowed $15,000 from his credit union to buy a car. Does he have income when he receives the loan proceeds, under the economic benefit theory of income? Why or why not?

_____

16. Martha is the ultimate stay-at-home mother. She raises the children and, in her spare time, she decorates the home she and her husband own, repairs their appliances if they break, creates fabulous meals on a shoestring, and gives advice on cooking, cleaning, and crafts to her many friends, neighbors, and acquaintances. What is her "income" from these activities? _____

17. Don purchased a parcel of unimproved real estate for $500,000. His plans for building an office complex on the property never matured and several years later he sold the parcel for $750,000. What is Don's "income" from the sale of the parcel and why? _____

18. Donna provides legal services to Mandy in exchange for Mandy's boarding Donna's dogs while she travels. Do Donna or Mandy have income from this exchange? _____

19. Lana has saved $10,000. She purchases 100 shares of ABC stock with this money. Does she have income as a result of this transaction? _____

20. Heidi purchased an insurance policy. Her broker gave her a check to reimburse her for the first year's premium. Heidi later discovered that this was an illegal practice called "rebating." What are the tax consequences to Heidi of this event? _____

Answers

9. There are two principal criticisms of the Haig-Simons approach to measuring income. First, there are practical concerns. This approach would require, for example, that a taxpayer's net change in the value of property rights be measured each year. So a taxpayer who owned real estate would have to obtain an appraisal each year or rely on some other measure of value to report gain or loss. Moreover, taxpayers would not necessarily have cash with which to pay taxes on gains that accrue without a sale or exchange. The second criticism is theoretical. These criticisms include it being tautological (it states the obvious) and that it does not measure a taxpayer's ability to pay more accurately than other approaches.

10. "Income" is the theoretical concept of inflows to a person that could make up the tax base, and the parameters of income will differ depending on which approach one adopts. "Gross income" is the statutory term used of §61 to mean "all income, from whatever source derived." It is the beginning place for the calculation of taxable income, defining the tax base on which the income tax is levied.

11. Under the Haig-Simons definition of income, Bev's income is the sum of (1) all rights she exercised in consumption, plus (2) the change in the value of her property rights from the beginning to the end of the taxable period. Bev exercised $80,000 in consumption rights. She also had a net increase in property rights of $10,000 (the CD) plus whatever interest accrued on that amount during that year. Thus, her total income (under this theory) is $100,000, plus interest, for the year, exactly the same as what she earned.

12. Bev started with a property right worth $10,500 and ended with a property right worth $1,000. In the Haig-Simons definition of income, the net decrease in property rights ($9,500) is a reduction in her income for that year.

13. When Nick is relieved of the obligation of paying the loans, this is an economic benefit to him, and so he has income. Later chapters will discuss specific exclusions for gifts. See Chapter 4(IV).

14. The economic benefit theory of income does not include in gross income nontangible, personal benefits. The value of Nick of being near the ski slopes does not result in income to him.

15. Even though loan proceeds flow into his checking account, Ken does not experience an economic benefit from taking out the loan because he has an offsetting obligation to repay it.

16. Imputed income is the value of the use of property one owns, or the services one performs for oneself. The value of all of Martha's activities that she performs for herself and family (child care, decorating, cooking, etc.) constitute imputed income. Also, one-half of the rental value of her home is imputed income to her (the other one-half is imputed to her co-owner, her husband). The advice she gives to others is not imputed income, as it is not services she provides for herself (nor does she appear to be receiving income for this activity). However, under our system of taxation, imputed income is not included in gross income. This avoids the difficult question of how to value these services.

17. Don's income from the sale of the real estate is $250,000, the difference between the sales price ($750,000) and his cost of the property ($500,000). Don is entitled to recover his capital investment in the property tax-free, and be taxed only on the gain he experiences on the sale.

18. Both have income. This is a barter transaction, in which the value of the services exchanged will be income to both parties. It will probably be easier to value the services based on the standard fee for boarding dogs, so each will have income equal to that fee.

19. No. Lana has simply transformed money into property; she has had no increase or decrease in income under any theory. However, if she receives dividends on the stock, that would be income to her.

20. Heidi has income in the amount of the rebate check given to her by the broker. Income from an illegal source is still "income." *Rickard v. Commissioner,* TC Memo 2010-159.

Exam Tips *on* IDENTIFYING GROSS INCOME

☛ If the question is whether the taxpayer has "income," determine what theory is being used to define gross income. Is this a theoretical question of comparing a broad tax base (Haig-Simons) with the more practical statutory scheme? Or is this a question based solely on a single theory, or on the statutory system of the Code?

☛ Questions requiring identification of gross income focus on a taxpayer receiving "stuff" of value, including:

☞ Cash

☞ Property

☞ Services

☞ The use of the taxpayer's own property, or the value of the taxpayer's own services (imputed income)

☞ Discharge of debt

☛ Questions requiring identification of gross income also focus on the few things that are *not* income in our system:

☞ Loan proceeds are not income, because of the offsetting obligation to repay.

☞ Capital recovery is not income; a taxpayer is entitled to recover his or her invested capital without tax.

☞ Imputed income is not income in our system, but is income under other theories.

☞ Noneconomic benefits, such as living in a beautiful place or the enjoyment of one's job, are not income.

☛ Some questions combine a nontaxable receipt and a later development that might change the result.

☞ Example: In Year One, Kelly borrows $45,000 from Alex. That isn't income, because Kelly is required to pay Alex back. But later, Alex forgives the debt. This is income to Kelly in the year of forgiveness, because she has been discharged of the obligation. (It might, however, be excludable under a specific statutory rule, but that's for a later chapter.)

☛ Questions involving barter are common—on exams and in practice. A barter transaction involves the exchange of goods or services, and is distinguishable from imputed income, which involves the use of property or services for oneself.

CHAPTER 3

SPECIFIC INCLUSIONS IN GROSS INCOME

ChapterScope ━━━━━━━━━━━━━━━━━━━━━━━━━━━━━━━━

The previous chapter discussed the concept of income. This chapter addresses the specific items listed in §61 as included in gross income and discusses some items brought into gross income by other Code sections and judicial decisions. Some important kinds of income include:

- **Services income:** Compensation for services is included in gross income of the service provider, whether in the form of cash, property, or other services.

- **Investment income:** Income from investments, including interest, dividends, annuities, rents, and royalties, is included in the gross income of the recipient.

- **Alimony:** Alimony, which has a specific federal definition independent of state law labels, is includable in the gross income of the recipient.

- **Discharge of indebtedness income:** Income from the discharge or cancellation of indebtedness is included in the gross income of the debtor.

- **Other income:** Gross income includes a number of other items of income, including certain prizes and awards, a portion of social security payments, and a variety of payments that are normally beyond the scope of the federal income tax course.

I. WHERE ARE WE?

We are still at the starting gate of computing a taxpayer's ultimate tax liability. Remember: If an item is excluded from gross income, it will never be taxed. So it is very important to determine what is—and is not—included in gross income. Moreover, being able to identify different kinds of gross income is important because certain types of income potentially lead to tax benefits—exclusions, deductions, and credits. For example, §108 potentially allows an exclusion from gross income for discharge of indebtedness income, but not for other types of gross income.

II. COMPENSATION FOR SERVICES

Section 61(a)(1) includes in gross income *compensation for services,* including fees, commissions, fringe benefits, and similar items, whether performed as an employee or otherwise.

A. Identifying the transaction

To identify a transaction involving compensation for services, look for two related events.

1. **Provision of services:** One taxpayer provides services for another, or promises to do so (e.g., signing bonuses for athletes).

2. **Compensation:** The person receiving the benefit of the services (or a person related to the recipient of the benefit) transfers money or other property (or the promise of money or other property) to the service provider.

   Example: Mildred drafts a will for Nelson, who pays her $300. Mildred has $300 income from compensation for her services.

   Example: Ollie agrees to live in Paula's mountain cabin for the winter to tend Paula's livestock. Ollie is performing services for Paula in exchange for the benefit of living in the cabin. His income is the fair market value of the rental. This income may be excluded from his gross income by §119; see discussion in Chapter 4(IX)(B).

   Example: George agrees to fix two meals per week for Fred, who is disabled and cannot prepare his own food. George receives nothing in return for his meal preparation. This transaction is not compensation, for although George has provided services to Fred, George has received nothing tangible in return.

   Example: Rudy repairs Steve's car, and Steve gives Rudy a TV worth $300 in exchange. Rudy has income from compensation equal to the fair market value of the TV—$300.

B. Forms of compensation

The form of the compensation does not matter for federal income tax purposes. The service provider must include in gross income the amount of money, or *fair market value* of the property or services, received as compensation.

1. **Cash/check:** The gross amount of wages or salary (not reduced by withholdings) is included in the gross income of the service provider. Wages include tips.

2. **Property:** The fair market value of property received as compensation is included in gross income of the service provider. The objective fair market value, i.e., the value at which goods will changes hands between unrelated buyers and sellers, must be used in determining the amount to be included. See *Rooney v. Commissioner,* 88 T.C. 523 (1987). The service provider will then have a "basis" in the property equal to the amount he or she included in gross income. Property can include items such as the employer's inventory (a car or washing machine) or can include stock or stock options or other rights with respect to the employer.

3. **Barter of services:** If taxpayers exchange services, each has income equal to the fair market value of the services received. See discussion of Rev. Rul. 79-24 in Chapter 2(III)(B).

4. **Income taxes paid:** If the person paying compensation income to another also pays the income taxes on such compensation, the amount paid as taxes is also compensation income. See *Old Colony Trust Co. v. Commissioner,* 279 U.S. 716 (1929). The payment of the taxes increases the amount of compensation income, which in turn increases the amount of the taxes on the income.

C. Related issues

1. **Exclusions:** Various Code sections provide exclusions from gross income for certain types of compensation income, such as fringe benefits. See discussion in Chapter 4(IX)(C).

2. **Timing:** The question of *whether* a taxpayer has income is related to—but independent of—the question of *when* a taxpayer has income. The taxpayer may provide services in one year but be paid in a later *taxable* year. This transaction will generate compensation income

for the servic*e provider*, but in which taxable year that person must include the income in gross income depends on a number of factors. See generally Chapter 11.

3. **Character:** Compensation income is ordinary income. See generally Chapter 12.

III. GROSS INCOME FROM BUSINESS

Although §61(a)(2) includes in gross income the taxpayer's gross *income from business,* the taxpayer actually reports the net result (net income or loss) from business activities on his or her own tax return, having calculated that result by tallying up gross income from business and subtracting available deductions. Net income is included in the taxpayer's gross income, and net loss may be deductible.

A. Identifying business income

To identify potential business income, look for a taxpayer selling goods or services or engaging in other regular activity with an intention to make a profit. In the basic tax course, most business income issues are presented as a taxpayer conducting business through a sole proprietorship. Such a taxpayer computes the net income or loss from the business on Schedule C of the tax return and the result is ultimately reported on Form 1040, Line 12 (see Figure 1A). Net income is included in gross income.

B. Related issues

1. **Trade or business expenses:** In computing net income or loss, the taxpayer deducts certain business expenses. See generally Chapter 7.

2. **Losses:** There are special restrictions on the deductibility of losses. See discussion in Chapter 11(VII).

3. **Character:** Income from business activity is ordinary, not capital. See discussion in Chapter 12.

IV. GAINS DERIVED FROM DEALINGS IN PROPERTY

Section 61(a)(3) includes *gains derived from dealings in property* in gross income. When a taxpayer sells or exchanges property, the taxpayer must compute the gain or loss from the transaction and determine if any statutes limit the amount of gain to be included in gross income or the amount of loss to be deducted. Losses generally offset gains, and the taxpayer will report the net figure as gain or loss from dealings in property. This very important topic in federal income tax is discussed fully in Chapters 9 and 10.

V. INVESTMENT INCOME

Section 61 includes in a taxpayer's gross income various types of *investment income.*

A. Identifying investment income

Investment income generally means income from profit-motivated activities that do not rise to the level of a *trade or business.*

1. **Trade or business:** In order to be engaged in a trade or business, the taxpayer must be involved in the activity with regularity and continuity and must have as his or her primary motivation for engaging in the activity an expectation of profit. *Commissioner v. Groetzinger,* 480 U.S. 23 (1987).

2. **Investment activity:** The activities of owning stock and buying and selling for one's own account are not a trade or business, regardless of frequency of trades or the amount of time devoted to the activity. *Higgins v. Commissioner,* 312 U.S. 212 (1941).

B. Dividends

Section 61(a)(7) includes **dividends** in a taxpayer's gross income. Dividends are amounts paid by a corporation to a shareholder in his or her capacity as a shareholder from the earnings and profits of the corporation. IRC §301(c)(1). Payments made to a shareholder other than in his or her capacity as a shareholder are *not* dividends and must be classified as some other type of payment, such as salary or rent.

Example: Victor is the sole shareholder of a profitable corporation. He also rents an office building to the corporation. The corporation pays Victor an annual lump sum of $100,000. This payment must be divided between rent payments for the building and dividends paid by the corporation. If a reasonable rental for the office building is $40,000, the remaining $60,000 must be a dividend, which must be included in Victor's gross income.

C. Interest

Section 61(a)(4) includes **interest** in a taxpayer's gross income.

1. **Definition:** Interest is the amount paid by a debtor to a creditor for the use of borrowed money. *Deputy v. DuPont,* 308 U.S. 488 (1940). The label given to a payment is not determinative. If it meets the definition of interest, and is not some other kind of payment, it qualifies as interest. See Rev. Rul. 60-188, 1960-1 C.B. 54. Interest depends on the existence of an underlying debt, which is defined as the "unconditional and legally enforceable obligation for the repayment of money." *Autenreith v. Commissioner,* 115 F.2d 856 (3d Cir. 1940).

   Example: Wendy lends Yolanda $5,000 at 10% interest for five years. Each year that the debt is outstanding, Yolanda pays Wendy $500 as interest. Wendy must include the $500 yearly interest payment in her gross income.

2. **"Hidden" interest payments:** Federal income tax law assumes that creditors will require debtors to pay market interest, even if the loan appears to provide for a below-market rate of interest or no interest at all. Such a transaction will be ***"recharacterized"*** for tax purposes, i.e., it will be recast in another form to reveal the hidden interest payment. In the recharacterization, the creditor will be deemed to receive, and the debtor will be deemed to pay, an appropriate amount of interest. See generally Chapter 15.

3. **Related issues**

   a. **Timing:** The year in which the creditor includes the interest in income depends on the creditor's method of accounting. See discussion in Chapter 11(III).

   b. **Character:** Interest is ordinary income. See generally Chapter 12.

   c. **Exclusion for interest on certain state and local bonds:** See discussion of §103 in Chapter 4(V).

    d. Deduction: The payor of interest may be able to deduct the interest paid or accrued. See discussion in Chapters 6(VI) and 7(III)(A).

D. Rental income

Section 61(a)(5) includes *rents* in a taxpayer's gross income.

  1. Definition: Rental income is the amount paid by the lessee of property to the lessor for the use of tangible property. Reg. §1.61-8(a).

    Example: Felicia owns Whiteacre, an office building. She leases Whiteacre to Sylvia for ten years at an annual rent of $640,000. Felicia must include the rental income of $640,000 per year in her gross income.

  2. Related issues

    a. Timing of inclusion: The year in which the taxpayer includes rental income depends on his or her method of accounting. See discussion in Chapter 11(III).

    b. Deduction of rent by lessee: A lessee using premises for business purposes may be able to deduct the rental payment. See discussion in Chapter 7(II)(A).

E. Royalty income

Section 61(a)(6) includes *royalty* income in the gross income of the recipient.

  1. Identifying royalty income: Royalty income is the amount paid for the use of intangible property, such as a copyright, trademark, or patent. Reg. §1.61-8(a). Royalty income also includes the payment (in money or in kind) made by an operator of oil and gas properties to the owner as a portion of the oil and gas mined from the property. *Shamrock Oil and Gas Corp. v. Commissioner,* 346 F.2d 377 (5th Cir. 1965).

    Example: Brian wrote a book about a famous local poet. Under his contract with the publisher, he is entitled to a royalty of 15% of the gross sales from the book. He receives his first royalty payment of $1,500 from the publisher, which he must include in his gross income.

  2. Related issues

    a. Timing: In which taxable year the taxpayer includes royalty income depends on his or her method of accounting. See discussion in Chapter 11(III).

    b. Deduction: The payor may be able to deduct the royalty payment.

F. Income derived from annuities

Section 61(a)(9) includes income from *annuities* in a taxpayer's gross income.

  1. What is an annuity? In general, an annuity is a stream of payments from one person to another. In business and tax circles, an annuity is a kind of investment in which a company promises to pay an amount of money monthly to a person in exchange for the person paying premiums (in a lump sum or over time) to the issuer of the annuity. An annuity can be an "immediate annuity," in which the person purchasing the annuity begins to receive monthly payments right away, or it can be a "tax-deferred annuity," in which the payments won't begin until sometime in the future. The annuity can last for the lifetime of the taxpayer, or the joint lifetimes of the taxpayer and another person, such as his or her spouse. The issuer of the annuity invests the premiums in order to satisfy its future promise to pay the taxpayer. The annuity contract can have any number of choices for the taxpayer to withdraw his or her money: withdrawing amounts from time to time; electing to receive periodic (usually monthly or annual) amounts; or withdrawing the entire amount in a lump sum. It is common for taxpayers to use annuities in retirement planning.

2. **The tax problem:** Recall that a taxpayer can be taxed only on the income realized from property; he or she is entitled to a tax-free return of his or her investment. See discussion in Chapter 2(IV)(B). If a taxpayer receives a lump-sum payment pursuant to an annuity contract, there will be no problem in identifying the amount of income from the contract: it will be the excess of the sum received over the cost of the annuity to the taxpayer. But what if the taxpayer withdraws amounts from time to time or receives periodic payments? How much of each payment is income and how much is a tax-free return of the taxpayer's invested capital? The annuity taxation rules allocate a portion of each payment between capital and income.

3. **Statutory analysis—§72**

   a. **General rule:** Gross income includes amounts received as an annuity under an annuity, life insurance, or endowment contract. IRC §72(a). Section 72(b), however, excludes from gross income the portion of a periodic annuity payment equal to the payment multiplied by the *exclusion ratio.* IRC §72(b)(1).

   b. **Definitional issues:** To determine the portion of an annuity payment that is excluded from gross income, multiply the payment by a fraction, called the "exclusion ratio." The numerator of this fraction is the taxpayer's *"investment in the contract."* The denominator is the *"expected return under the contract."* IRC §72(b)(1). Both figures are calculated at the annuity starting date. IRC §72(b)(1). See Figure 3A—Exclusion Ratio—§72.

Figure 3A
Exclusion Ratio of Section 72

Amount of annuity payment included in gross income is equal to:

$$\text{Annuity payment} \quad \times \quad \frac{\text{Taxpayer's Investment in the Contract*}}{\text{Total Expected Return**}}$$

* *Investment in the Contract* = total premiums paid, less amounts previously withdrawn tax-free
** *Total Expected Return* = the total amount to be received under the contract, given the taxpayer's age and the type of contract

   i. **Investment in contract:** The taxpayer's *investment in the contract* is equal to the total premiums paid, less any amounts previously withdrawn that were excluded from gross income. IRC §72(c)(1).

   ii. **Total expected return:** The calculation of *total expected return* depends on the nature of the contract. If the contract pays a fixed amount, the total expected return is the total amount to be received under the contract. IRC §72(c)(3)(B). If the contract depends on the life of the annuitant (or the annuitant and spouse), the total expected return is the life expectancy of the taxpayer at the starting date multiplied by the annual amount to be received. IRC §72(c)(3)(A).

   Example—immediate annuity: Peggy, age 65, has saved $250,000 for retirement (not in an IRA or other qualified retirement plan). Wanting to relieve herself of the stress of wondering whether this will last for her lifetime, Peggy invests all of it in an immediate annuity that will pay her $1,666 per month for her lifetime. At age 65, she has a life expectancy of 20 years. In the first year, Peggy receives $20,000 ($1,666 × 12 months). To determine how much of the $20,000 she must include in gross income, the annual payment is multiplied by the exclusion ratio, the numerator of which is her investment in the contract ($250,000) and the denominator of which is her life expectancy multiplied by the annual payments to her of $20,000:

$$\$20,000 \quad \times \quad \frac{\$250,000}{\$400,000} = \$20,000 \quad \times \quad 62.5\%$$

Application of the exclusion ratio results in 62.5% of each payment being excluded from gross income, so that the amount of each payment that is included is 37.5%. Therefore, of each annual amount of $20,000, Peggy must include $7,500 in her gross income and may exclude the rest.

Example—tax-deferred annuity. George, age 45, purchases a premium annuity contract from Friendly Insurance Company for a single premium of $50,000. Under the terms of the policy, he is entitled to a monthly payment of $500 beginning on January 1 of the year he turns 65 and continuing until his death. Assume he has a life expectancy of 20 years when he turns 65.

The purchase of the policy is not a taxable event to George. During the 20 years that Friendly invests George's $50,000, George is not taxed on the investment income.

In the year George turns 65, he receives monthly payments of $500 for a total annual payment of $6,000. To determine how much of this payment is income, George applies the exclusion ratio to the annual payment, as follows

$$\text{Payment} \quad \times \quad \frac{\text{Investment in the Contract}}{\text{Total Expected Return}} = \text{Excluded percentage}$$

$$\$6,000 \quad \times \quad \frac{\$50,000}{\$120,000*}$$

$$*(6,000 \quad \times \quad 20 \text{ years})$$

$$\$6,000 \quad \times \quad 41.67\% = \$2,500 \text{ (amount excluded)}$$

Thus, of the $6,000 payment George receives each year, 58.33% ($3,500) must be included in gross income, and the remaining 41.67% ($2,500) is a tax-free return of capital.

c. **Special rules and exceptions:** For contracts based on the taxpayer's life, if the taxpayer's actual life span matches his or her actuarially determined life expectancy, at death he or she will have fully recovered invested capital and will have reported the proper amount of income. If the taxpayer dies earlier or lives longer than expected, the exclusion ratio will overstate or understate, respectively, the income from the contract. Two special rules address this problem.

i. **Exclusion limitation:** The total exclusion allowed under §72(b) is limited to the taxpayer's investment in the contract (i.e., his or her basis). IRC §72(b)(2).

Example: Consider George from the previous example. Notice that if George lives exactly 20 years from the annuity payment starting date, he will have recovered his full $50,000 investment in the contract (20 years of excluding $2,500 from each annual payment, with some rounding error). Assume, however, that George lives past age 85. If the exclusion ratio were applied to payments in those years, George would be excluding more than his initial investment of $50,000, and thus his income would be understated. Therefore, once George fully recovers his invested capital, all additional payments are income to him.

ii. **Deduction for unrecovered investment:** If the taxpayer dies before recovering his or her investment in the contract, and the payments end by reason of the taxpayer's death, the taxpayer's executor will be able to claim a deduction on the taxpayer's last income tax return for the unrecovered portion of the investment. IRC §72(b)(3).

Example: Consider George from the previous two examples, but assume that George dies on January 1 exactly five years after the annuity starting date, rather than surviving to his life expectancy of 85. Having properly applied the exclusion ratio during the first five years of the annuity payments, George will have recovered, tax-free, only $12,500 of his $50,000 investment in the contract. On his income tax return for the year of his death, George's executor will claim a deduction equal to the unrecovered amount of $37,500 ($50,000 – $12,500).

iii. **Nonperiodic withdrawals.** As a practical matter, annuities are often marketed to and used by taxpayers as a tax-deferred investment. Amounts invested in an annuity compound tax-free until they are withdrawn. The approach described above in connection with the exclusion ratio applies after the annuity has been *"annuitized,"* i.e., a payout time has been selected. In many cases, annuities are not annuitized. Instead, the owner withdraws a lump sum from the annuity from time to time. In that case, the entire amount is considered income, unless it exceeds the amount by which the cash value of the annuity exceeds the taxpayer's investment in the contract. Any amount by which the withdrawal exceeds that figure is excluded. IRC §72(e)(2)(B), (e)(3).

Example: Lisa purchased an annuity for $14,000. In time, its cash value increases to $30,000. Lisa withdraws $8,000 from her annuity as a nonperiodic withdrawal. All of the $8,000 is included in her gross income because it is less than the amount by which the cash value of the annuity ($30,000) exceeds her investment in the contract ($14,000). If, however, Lisa had withdrawn $22,000, $6,000 would be considered a tax-free return of her investment.

d. **Related material**

i. **Life insurance contracts:** For a discussion of the exclusion of life insurance proceeds payable upon death, see Chapter 4(III).

ii. **Installment sales:** For similar timing rules in installment sales, see discussion in Chapter 11(V).

e. **Be alert for annuity issues:** Section 72 is typically implicated when a taxpayer has purchased an annuity and begins to receive income from it. This section is also applied when a taxpayer starts to receive distributions from an IRA or other retirement account.

VI. ALIMONY AND SEPARATE MAINTENANCE PAYMENTS

Section 61(a)(8) includes *alimony* and *separate maintenance payments* in the recipient's gross income. Section 71(a) confirms this inclusion.

A. Identifying alimony income

Look for a divorce situation in which one former spouse pays support (other than *child support*) to the other. Make sure that the payment meets the strict federal definition of alimony; its state law label is irrelevant.

B. Statutory analysis—§71

1. **General rule:** The recipient of alimony or separate maintenance must include it in his or her gross income. IRC §71(a).

2. **Definitional issues:** The Code defines alimony, and state law labels are irrelevant. In order to qualify as alimony for federal tax law purposes, the payment must satisfy the following six requirements.

   a. **Cash:** The payment must be in cash, rather than any other type of property (*not* stocks, bonds, or diamond rings). IRC §71(b)(1).

   b. **Receipt under decree:** The payment must be received by (or on behalf of) the spouse pursuant to a divorce decree or separation instrument. IRC §71(b)(1)(A), (2)(A). The payor spouse may pay the recipient spouse directly, or the payor spouse may pay a third party on behalf of the former spouse. IRC §71(b)(1)(A); Temp. Reg. §1.71-1T(b), A-6. Common examples of payments on behalf of a former spouse include a mortgage payment, the payment of health insurance premiums, or the payment of the recipient spouse's tuition. Rev. Rul. 62-106, 1962-2 C.B. 21.

      Example: Toya and Frank are getting a divorce. Under the divorce decree, Toya is awarded the marital home and Frank is ordered to make the mortgage payment each month to Friendly Bank. Assuming the other requirements for alimony are met, this payment would qualify as a payment received "on behalf of" a spouse pursuant to a divorce decree and would constitute alimony.

   c. **Private ordering:** The divorce decree or separation instrument must not designate the payment as nondeductible/non-includable. IRC §71(b)(1)(B). The parties have the power to determine which spouse will pay tax on the alimony income and generally will choose the approach that lowers the tax on the couple as a unit. Generally, the payor will wish to claim the deduction, because he or she will be in a higher tax bracket than the recipient. If, however, the payor's tax bracket is lower, the parties should specify in the decree that the payment is nondeductible to the payor and non-includable to the recipient.

      Example: Karl and Linda are getting a divorce. Karl anticipates that his tax bracket will be 33% after the divorce, and Linda expects that hers will be 15%. Under the terms of the divorce decree, Karl is to pay Linda $1,000 per month for four years. Compare the effects of treating this $12,000 annual payment as deductible and nondeductible alimony:

      Treatment as deductible to payor and includable to recipient. Treating the payments as deductible to Karl and includable in Linda's gross income means that Linda will be taxed on the $12,000 annual payment. Linda includes the $12,000 in gross income and pays a tax of $1,800 on it ($12,000 × 15%). Thus, the total tax on the $12,000 is $1,800. Because Karl deducts the alimony payment, he is not taxed on the income that generated the payment.

Treatment as nondeductible to payor and non-includable to recipient. Treating the payments as nondeductible to Karl and excluded from Linda's gross income means that Karl will earn the funds to make the payment, and will be taxed on them without an offsetting deduction. Linda will not be taxed on this amount. Karl will pay a tax of $3,960 ($12,000 × 33%) on this amount.

Comparison. Rational taxpayers would clearly opt to treat this payment as deductible to Karl (assuming it otherwise meets the requirements for alimony) because this treatment saves the parties $2,160 in tax, equal to the difference between the tax Karl would pay and the tax Linda would pay on the annual alimony payment. This will become part of the divorce negotiation.

d. No "live-in" divorces! The payor and recipient must not be members of the same household at the time of the payment. IRC §71(b)(1)(C).

e. No payment if recipient dies: There must be no liability to make payments beyond the death of the recipient spouse. IRC §71(b)(1)(D). Think of alimony as "support" for the recipient spouse. If that spouse dies, he or she no longer needs support. Thus, alimony must end at the death of the recipient spouse. If the parties intended an amount to be a deferred payment of property (rather than a support payment) they would make arrangements for payment to be made to the estate of the recipient spouse in the event of his or her death. This would not qualify as alimony. In addition, there must be no "substitute payments" to replace payments to the recipient spouse after the latter's death. Treas. Reg. §1.71-1T(b); see *Okerson v. Commissioner,* 123 T.C. 258 (2000). If the decree or order is silent on this issue, look to state law to determine whether the payment would be required if the recipient spouse dies.

Example: Karl and Linda are getting a divorce. Karl owns a business in which Linda has an interest. The parties agree that Karl will receive the business and will pay Linda $50,000 each year for seven years. In the event of Linda's death prior to the last payment, Karl will pay the amounts into a trust established by Linda's will for the benefit of her children from a prior marriage. The $50,000 annual payment does not qualify as alimony, because it survives the death of the recipient spouse. Instead, it is a property settlement.

f. Not child support: Child support is excluded from gross income of the custodial spouse. IRC §71(c)(1); see discussion in Chapter 4(XI)(A). Thus, in order to qualify as alimony, the payment must not be, in substance, a payment for the support of a child of the payor. IRC §71(c)(2); Reg. §1.71-1T(c), A-16. The decree will generally fix an amount for support of a child; this amount is not alimony. If the payment is tied to a contingency of a child (such as attaining majority), it will be considered child support, even if it is called and otherwise qualifies as alimony. IRC §71(c)(2)(A).

Example: In Toya and Frank's divorce, Frank's obligation to pay the mortgage ends on the earlier of April 13, 2012 (which just happens to be the date on which his youngest daughter turns 18), or the date of the last-to-die of his children. This would be a payment tied to a contingency of a minor child and would be considered child support rather than alimony.

3. **Special rules and exceptions—"Front-end loaded" alimony:** This special rule ferrets out disguised property settlements, reducing the benefit of the deduction to the payor and the detriment of the inclusion to the recipient in those situations.

   a. **General approach:** If alimony payments are front-end loaded, the statute requires an adjustment in the third taxable year. In that year, the payor includes the *excess alimony payments* in gross income, and the recipient is entitled to a deduction in computing adjusted gross income (AGI) in the same amount. IRC §71(f)(1)(A), (B).

   b. **Third year:** The adjustment is made in the taxable year beginning in the third post-separation year. The first post-separation year is the first calendar year in which alimony is paid, and the next two years are the second and third post-separation years. IRC §71(f)(6).

   Example: Rita and Jeff are getting a divorce. Jeff is to pay Rita $100,000 on January 1, Year One; $50,000 on January 1, Year Two; and $25,000 on January 1, Year Three. Assume that the payments qualify as alimony. Because they are front-end loaded, in the third post-separation year Jeff will include in gross income, and Rita will deduct, the excess alimony amount.

   c. **Identifying excess alimony payments:** A front-end loaded payment is exactly what it sounds like—a payment that is relatively large in the early year or years, compared with later payments. The statute focuses only on the first three years following the divorce; payments in the fourth year and thereafter are irrelevant. The statute provides a very complicated definition of excess alimony payments, the calculation of which is outlined in the steps of Figure 3B—Front-End Loaded Alimony Payments. In general, however, there must be a variance among the payments due during the three-year period of more than $15,000 in order for the front-end loading rules to apply.

Figure 3B
Front-End Loaded Alimony Payments

(Y = year)	
Step 1	Calculate the excess alimony payment for the *second* post-separation year. Alimony Y2 − (Alimony Y3 + $15,000) = excess payment for second post-separation year.
Step 2	Calculate the excess alimony payment for the *first* post-separation year. $$\text{Alimony Y1} - \left[\left\{ \frac{(\text{Alimony Y2} - \text{Excess Payment Y2}) + \text{Alimony Y3}}{2} \right\} + \$15,000 \right] = \text{excess payment for the \textit{first} post-separation year}$$
Step 3	Calculate the excess alimony payment: sum of steps 1 and 2.
Step 4	Determine the consequences to payor and recipient in third post-separation year: *Deduction to recipient* in the amount of excess alimony payment. *Inclusion to payor* in the amount of excess alimony payment.

Example: Molly and Neil are getting a divorce, and they agree that Molly will pay Neil $60,000 in the first year after their divorce, $30,000 in the second year, and $10,000 in the third year. Assume that the payments otherwise qualify as alimony, and Molly deducts these payments and Neil includes them in his gross income in the years the payments are made. These payments likely are front-end loaded because they vary by more than $15,000 during the three years. The calculation of the excess alimony payment confirms that indeed the amounts are front-end loaded. Neil will receive a deduction for the third year equal to the excess alimony payment, and Molly will include that amount in gross income in the third year. The excess alimony payment is calculated as follows:

- *Step 1:* Calculate the excess alimony payment for the *second* post-separation year.

- $30,000 – ($10,000 + $15,000) = $5,000

- *Step 2:* Calculate the excess alimony payment for the *first* post-separation year.

$$\$60{,}000 - \left[\left\{ \frac{(\$30{,}000 - 5{,}000) + 10{,}000}{2} \right\} + \$15{,}000 \right]$$

$60,000 – $32,500 = $27,500

- *Step 3:* Calculate the excess alimony payment: The sum of steps 1 and 2.

$27,500 + 5,000 = $32,500

- *Step 4:* Determine the consequences to payor and recipient in the third post-separation year:

$32,500 deduction from AGI to Neil
$32,500 inclusion in gross income for Molly

4. Related material

a. Deduction: For a discussion of the deduction for alimony available to the payor, see Chapter 6(II).

b. Child support: For a discussion of the exclusion of child support from the gross income of the recipient, see Chapter 4(XI)(A).

c. Property transfers: For a discussion of the treatment of property transfers in divorce, see Chapter 10(V).

5. Be alert for alimony issues:
Section 71 is typically implicated only in divorce or post-divorce situations and must be coordinated with the deduction for alimony by the payor and property settlements. The principal issue in alimony is whether it qualifies under the federal definition of alimony.

VII. INCOME FROM DISCHARGE OF INDEBTEDNESS

Section 61(a)(12) includes income from *discharge of indebtedness* in a debtor's gross income.

A. Recognizing the basic transaction

The making of a loan is not a taxable event for either the debtor or the creditor. See discussion in Chapter 2(IV)(C). But when the creditor forgives or discharges all or part of the loan, the debtor has income in the amount of the forgiveness or discharge. To identify a potential discharge of debt situation, look for a creditor accepting (or being required to accept), in satisfaction of a debt, less than the creditor originally contracted to receive.

B. Loan repayment—A tax nonevent

When the debtor repays the principal amount of the loan in full, this is not a tax event for either the debtor or the creditor. Neither party is better or worse off because of the repayment. Interest payments are treated separately. They constitute income to the creditor and may generate a deduction to the debtor.

Example: Megan borrows $25,000 from Friendly Bank. Megan has no income as a result of the loan, and Friendly Bank has no deduction. When, five years later, Megan repays the debt in full, neither she nor Friendly Bank have any tax consequences as a result of the repayment. If Megan has paid interest during the five-year period, that transaction is accounted for separately, with Friendly Bank including the interest in its gross income and Megan potentially taking a deduction for the interest paid.

C. The forgiveness transaction—A tax event

In a forgiveness or discharge situation, the creditor accepts, in satisfaction of all or part of the debt, something less than the creditor originally agreed to receive in payment of the debt.

1. **Debtor's tax consequences—Income:** The debtor has income from a ***discharge of indebtedness*** event, in the amount of the discharge. There are two different rationales for this income.

    a. **"Freeing of assets" theory—*United States v. Kirby Lumber Co.*, 284 U.S. 1 (1931):** *Kirby Lumber* suggests that the discharge event "frees up" assets of the debtor, generating income to the debtor. This rationale is problematic, because not every discharge frees assets of the debtor.

    b. **Economic benefit rationale:** The more comprehensive explanation is that the debtor has income because discharge removes all or part of the offsetting obligation to repay, which prevented the debtor from having income at the creation of the loan. Thus the debtor has enjoyment of the loan proceeds (in whole or in part) without the offsetting obligation to repay, resulting in a net economic benefit to the debtor.

2. **Creditor's tax consequences—Possible deduction:** In a discharge situation, the creditor receives less than it had originally loaned and may be entitled to a deduction. See discussion in Chapter 7(III)(C).

D. Definition of discharge

Discharge is "forgiveness of, or release from, an obligation to repay." *United States v. Centennial Savings Bank FSB,* 499 U.S. 573, 580 (1991). Discharge occurs when the taxpayer is relieved of a liability through the creditor (voluntarily or not) canceling or forgiving the obligation to repay, thus taking less than the creditor originally bargained for in satisfaction of the debt.

1. **Common examples of discharge:** The following three examples of discharge illustrate the creditor accepting less than it originally bargained for in satisfaction of the loan.

    a. **"Taking what you can get":** When the creditor perceives that the debtor is unlikely to pay the full amount, the creditor may opt to take what it can get rather than waiting (perhaps in competition with other creditors) for the full amount. The difference between the face amount and the amount paid is the discharge or forgiveness.

Example: Sam borrows $150,000 from Friendly Bank, promising to repay it in two years. Two years later, Sam is teetering on the brink of financial ruin, and offers Friendly Bank $35,000 in satisfaction of the debt. Friendly Bank accepts this offer. Sam has $115,000 of discharge of indebtedness income because the creditor has accepted $35,000 in satisfaction of a $150,000 debt.

b. **Antideficiency statutes:** Some states have *antideficiency statutes,* which protect mortgagors from personal liability when foreclosure proceeds are insufficient to satisfy the mortgage on a personal residence. If an antideficiency statute operates to cancel the underlying obligation, this cancellation may constitute a discharge. However, some antideficiency statutes simply make the debt nonrecourse, which changes the tax treatment of a foreclosure. See discussion in Chapter 9(VI).

c. **Repayment obligation:** A cancellation of a debt that is conditional upon the obligation to repay sometime in the future upon the occurrence of certain events will be a discharge at the time of cancellation of the original debt. By contrast, a cancellation that takes effect sometime in the future is not a discharge until that future time. See, e.g., *Jelle v. Commissioner,* 116 T.C. 63 (2001).

2. **Common examples of nondischarge:** Be careful—it is tempting to apply the discharge of debt concept to situations that do not involve an actual discharge of debt.

a. **No real debt, no discharge:** In *Zarin v. Commissioner,* 916 F.2d 110 (3d Cir. 1990), the taxpayer, Zarin, was a compulsive gambler. Resorts, a casino, extended credit to him in the form of allowing him to purchase gambling chips in the amount of $3,000,000 in violation of state law. Zarin and Resorts agreed that Zarin would pay $500,000 in satisfaction of the debt, and he did so.

   i. **Issue:** Did Zarin have $2,500,000 of discharge of debt income (the difference between the loan and the payment)?

   ii. **Result and rationale:** Zarin had no discharge of debt income because there was no debt. Section 108 requires either that (1) the taxpayer be liable for the debt, or (2) the taxpayer hold property subject to the debt. The debt was unenforceable under state law, so Zarin was not liable for the debt.

b. **Contested liability doctrine:** If a taxpayer in good faith disputes the amount of the debt, a subsequent settlement of the debt is treated as the amount of the debt for tax purposes. *N. Sobel, Inc. v. Commissioner,* 40 B.T.A. 1263 (1939).

Example: Paula borrowed $10,000 from Quinton, and agreed to repay him in two years. In connection with this loan, both parties agreed to undertake certain tasks. When payment became due, Paula argued in good faith that Quinton did not fulfill his obligations under the loan. They settled their dispute by agreeing that Paula would pay $8,500 to Quinton in full payment of the debt. For tax purposes, the original loan is treated as $8,500, not $10,000.

c. **Payment of debt:** If the taxpayer pays the debt, actually or constructively, there is no discharge of the debt. In Rev. Rul. 84-176, 1984-2 C.B. 34, the taxpayer owed X $1,000 for goods it had purchased. But X breached its contract with the taxpayer for the shipment of other goods, and the taxpayer refused to pay the $1,000 and claimed damages. Eventually, they settled the dispute by having the taxpayer pay $500 to X in exchange for a release of the damages claim. The taxpayer wanted to characterize the transaction as $500 of discharge of indebtedness income because the taxpayer could claim an exclusion for this amount under §108. The IRS characterized this transaction as the payment of $500 in damages by X to the taxpayer, which constituted gross income. But the character of the income was not discharge of indebtedness income and therefore no §108 exclusion was available.

d. Repayment by another: Repayment of a taxpayer's debt by the taxpayer or another person does not create discharge of indebtedness income because the creditor has not taken less than the originally agreed-upon amount. Instead, the repayment by another may be another type of income to the taxpayer, includable in his or her gross income.

Example: Stephanie owes $40,000 in student loans. The Firm offers her a job at a nice salary, and one of the fringe benefits is that if she works for a year, The Firm will pay off her student loans in full. If The Firm pays her loans, Stephanie will not have discharge of indebtedness income because her creditors have received payment in full. Instead, she will have compensation income in the amount The Firm paid the creditors. The distinction can make a big difference in the application of §108. See Chapter 4(VII).

e. No discharge event—No income: If the creditor receives what it bargained for, there is no discharge. In the usual situation, it will be easy to see whether the creditor received the principal amount in repayment. But in some unusual situations, the creditor may receive exactly what it bargained for, even if that is not what it originally loaned the debtor.

Example: Theresa borrowed $50,000 from Uly. Under the terms of the loan, Theresa was to repay Uly in two years in the amount of the lesser of $50,000 or her gross income for the year. Two years later, Theresa's gross income was $45,000 and she repaid Uly that amount. Theresa has no discharge of indebtedness because Uly received in repayment exactly what he bargained for—no more and no less.

E. Income possibly excluded

A taxpayer with discharge of indebtedness income may be able to exclude the income from gross income because of a specific exclusion available under the Code.

1. Gift: If the discharge is intended as a gift, there is no income to the taxpayer. See discussion in Chapter 4(IV).

Example: Gerry borrows $1,500 from his father in order to study for the bar exam. When Gerry passes the exam, his father is so pleased that he forgives the debt. It is likely that the forgiveness is intended as a gift, and Gerry may therefore exclude from his gross income the $1,500 that would otherwise be included as discharge of indebtedness income.

2. Section 108: Section 108 provides an exclusion from gross income for certain types of discharge of indebtedness income. See discussion in Chapter 4(VII).

VIII. SOME ODDS AND ENDS—PRIZES, AWARDS, HELPFUL PAYMENTS, EMBEZZLEMENTS, AND DAMAGES

Code sections other than §61 and certain judicial doctrines also specifically include items in gross income.

A. Prizes and awards—§74

1. **General rule:** Gross income includes amounts received as prizes and awards. IRC §74(a). Similarly, rewards paid for taking certain actions, such as giving information leading to conviction of a crime, are also includable in gross income. See *Roco v. Commissioner*, 121 T.C. 160 (2003) (amounts received under *qui tam* action under False Claims Act includable in gross income).

2. **Definitional issue:** Prizes and awards include amounts received in contests, door prizes, radio and television promotions and games, and employee prizes. Reg. §1.74-1(a)(1).

3. **Special rules and exceptions—limited exclusion:** The amount of the prize or award will be excluded from the gross income of the recipient if three conditions are met. See Chapter 4(XII).

B. Helpful payments

1. **Moving expenses:** Section 82 includes in gross income any payment or reimbursement for moving expenses relating to employment or self-employment. For a discussion of and exclusion for qualified moving expenses, see Chapter 4(VII)(C) and for a discussion of the deduction for moving expenses, see Chapter 6(II)(B).

2. **Unemployment compensation:** Section 85 includes unemployment compensation in gross income. From time to time, Congress will allow recipients of unemployment compensation to exclude some amount from gross income, as it did in 2009 by allowing a $2,400 exclusion, which has since expired.

3. **Social Security benefits:** A portion of Social Security benefits (including disability benefits) is included in gross income if a taxpayer's modified adjusted gross income (MAGI) exceeds a certain base amount. IRC §86. The amount included is either 50% or 85% of the Social Security benefits received. The computation of this inclusion is extremely complex and the entire concept of including Social Security benefits in gross income has been criticized as creating a double income tax—once on the income earned (from which Social Security taxes were withheld) and then again upon benefits being received.

4. **Disability payments:** If a taxpayer receives disability payments attributable to premiums paid by his or her employer that were excluded from gross income, the payments will be included in the taxpayer's gross income. See discussion in Chapter 4(IX)(D).

C. Embezzled funds

Illegal income of all sorts, including income from theft or embezzlement, is included in gross income. An embezzler must include the proceeds of embezzlement in his or her gross income, unless he or she repays the money in the same taxable year as the embezzlement. *James v. United States*, 366 U.S. 213 (1961); *Collins v. Commissioner*, 3 F.3d 625 (2d Cir. 1993).

D. Damages

Damages received for injury are includable in gross income, unless a statute specifically allows exclusion. (See, e.g., §104, which allows an exclusion for personal physical injury recoveries, discussed in Chapter 4(VI).) When damages are received for loss profits, the damages are simply a substitute for those profits, which would be taxable. See *Raytheon Production Corp. v. Commissioner*, 144 F.2d 110 (1st Cir. 1944), cert. denied 323 U.S. 779 (1944).

IX. NEED TO KNOW MORE?

This book's website *www.aspenlawschool.com/books/tax_outline* contains additional information, including:

- Examples of how annuity payments are taxed.

- More on alimony—and especially the front-end loaded rules.

- How discharge of indebtedness income works in the real world.

- A discussion of *Bradford v. Commissioner*, 233 F.2d 935 (6th Cir. 1956).

- And other materials that will help you identify gross income.

X. WHERE ARE WE GOING?

This chapter has discussed the list of items of income specifically included in a taxpayer's gross income under §61 and related statutes. However, not all items that would otherwise qualify as "income" are actually included in gross income. Various Code sections exclude some items from gross income, and Chapter 4 explores these items in detail.

Quiz Yourself on SPECIFIC INCLUSIONS IN GROSS INCOME

21. Diane's employer falls on hard times. Instead of giving her a paycheck, the employer gives her a used car worth $3,500. Will Diane have gross income as a result of this transaction?

———————————

22. Michael, a noted basketball player, realizes that he needs a plan for his retirement. He pays a $500,000 one-time premium for an annuity, which will pay him $40,000 per year for the rest of his life. At the time of the purchase, Michael's life expectancy is 20 years. When Michael receives his first year's payment of $40,000, must he include it in his gross income? ———————————

23. Assume Michael, from the previous question, died on January 30 of the third year in which he received a payment, i.e., he died after receiving $120,000. The terms of the annuity provided that if the annuitant died before the end of his life expectancy, the remaining amounts that would have been

received, based on his life expectancy at the time the annuity began paying, would be paid to his estate or beneficiary. What are the tax consequences if $680,000 is paid to the estate or beneficiary in that year? _____

24. Cindy and Bill are getting a divorce. The divorce decree says that Cindy must pay Bill $100,000 within 30 days of the entering of the decree, $50,000 on the first anniversary of the divorce, and $25,000 on the second anniversary of the divorce, unless Bill dies during this period. They have no children. Will these payments be includable in Bill's income? _____

25. Bruce and Debi are divorced. Under the divorce decree, Bruce is obligated to pay Debi $24,000 per year for ten years. Is this alimony, under the federal definition? _____

26. Aging film star Greta's mansion in Bel Aire is virtually falling apart. She leaves for a trip around the world, and rents it to carpenter-turned-starving-actor Harrison for $200 per month and Harrison's agreement to spend 20 hours a week repairing it. What are the tax consequences to Greta of this arrangement? _____

27. Marc borrowed $1,000,000 from the bank. He absconded to Europe and never paid it back. The bank determined that the amount was uncollectible, and wrote it off. The time period for collection expired. What are the tax consequences of this transaction to Marc? _____

28. Assume the same facts as in the previous question, except that Marc's mother is mortified at her son's behavior, and repays the loan. What are the tax consequences of the loan and its repayment to Marc? _____

29. Frieda owed $40,000 on her credit card. She convinced the credit card company to accept a reduced amount of $25,000 in full satisfaction of the debt. What are the tax consequences of this transaction to Frieda? What if Frieda had been disputing some of the charges with the credit card company at the time of the discharge? _____

30. Rookie pitcher Greg listened to his parents' advice and purchased disability income insurance. It's a good thing he did, because in his very first major league game, he injured his shoulder and was released from the team. He receives payments from the insurance company. What is the tax treatment of these payments to Greg? _____

31. Bea was selected to win a Nobel Prize for her work in chemistry. She immediately donated the monetary prize to the Red Cross. Will she be taxed on this award? _____

32. Carlotta was a bookkeeper for ABC Corp who felt she was underpaid. She took matters into her own hands, and embezzled $50,000 from the company before being discovered. She promises to repay the money as soon as possible. What are the tax consequences to Carlotta? _____

33. Of the following, which is *not* includable in an individual taxpayer's gross income?

(a) Dividends received from corporations

(b) Royalties received from the licensing of patents

(c) Unemployment compensation received from the government

(d) Interest on a loan made to a relative

(e) Loan proceeds received from a credit union

Answers

21. Section 61(a) provides that gross income includes all income from whatever source derived, including income from services. Diane has gross income of $3,500, which is the value of the car she received from her employer as payment for services.

22. Michael must include some of each payment in his gross income. Section 72 determines the amount to be included. Michael must multiply each payment by the exclusion ratio, the numerator of which is his investment in the contract and the denominator of which is the expected total return of the contract. The resulting number will be the nontaxable amount (his capital recovery) and the rest he must include in gross income. The expected total return is calculated by taking Michael's life expectancy and multiplying it by the annual payment on the contract ($40,000 × 20 years = $800,000). In Michael's case, the exclusion ratio produces the following result for each payment:

$$\$40,000 \quad \times \quad \frac{500,000}{800,000} =$$

$$\$40,000 \quad \times \quad 62.5\% \quad = \$25,000$$

The remaining $15,000 of each payment is included in Michael's gross income.

23. Michael's death after receiving three payments of $40,000 results in the estate or beneficiary being entitled to claim an exclusion of $425,000 of the total amount received. This is Michael's unrecovered investment in the contract at the time of his death. (Total contract cost was $500,000, and he had recovered $75,000 tax-free.) Thus, of the $680,000 received, only $255,000 is includable in the estate or beneficiary's gross income. Taking all payments into consideration, the right result is reached: the total contract cost of $500,000 is recovered tax free (Michael claimed $75,000 and the estate/beneficiary claimed $425,000) and the $300,000 of income is reported ($45,000 by Michael and $255,000 by the estate/beneficiary).

24. These payments appear to meet the requirements of alimony: They are made in cash and received under a divorce decree; the parties aren't living together; the payments stop if the recipient dies; and they are not disguised child support. Thus, they should be included in Bill's gross income. However, because the payments vary by more than $15,000 per year, they will be considered "front-end loaded" and be subject to the special rules of §71(f). This section requires that the amount of so-called excess alimony payments be included in the income of the payor in the third post-separation year. To determine the excess alimony payment, a rather complex calculation must be completed, as follows:

Step 1: Compute the excess payment for the second post-separation year. (IRC §71(f)(4))

Alimony paid Y2 − (Alimony Y3 + $15,000)

$50,000 − ($25,000 + $15,000)

$50,000 − $40,000 = $10,000 + excess payment for second post-separation year.

Step 2: Compute the excess payment for the first post-separation year. (IRC §71(f)(3))

$$\$100,000 - \left\{ \left[\frac{(\$50,000 - 10,000) + \$25,000)}{2} \right] + \$15,000 \right\}$$

$100,000 – ($32,500 + $15,000)

$100,000 – $47,500

$52,500 = excess payment for first post-separation year.

Step 3: Add the two excess payments together:

$10,000   second year

+   52,500   first year

$62,500   total

The total amount is the amount that will be included in Cindy's gross income and deducted from Bill's gross income in computing AGI in the third post-separation year.

25. It is tempting to label this as alimony: It is payable in cash, pursuant to the divorce decree, and presumably the couple are living separately. However, there is no indication that the payments will stop upon the death of the recipient. If they do not cease at that time, the payments will not be alimony. The parties will look first to the terms of the decree for guidance, and if the decree is silent, state law will apply to determine whether the payments cease or are paid to Debi's estate.

26. Greta has rental income, which under §61(a)(5) she must include in gross income. But how much? Focus on the exchange: Greta is providing a home for Harrison, and thus what she receives in exchange is properly considered rental income. This would be $200 per month plus the fair market value of the services Harrison agrees to perform. The best way to measure this is to determine the fair rental value of the house, or, if that is not possible because there simply isn't a rental market for dilapidated mansions, by determining the hourly rate for carpenters.

27. Marc did not have income in the year of the loan because of the offsetting obligation to repay it. However, in the year it is forgiven (written off by the bank) he has discharge of indebtedness income in the amount of $1,000,000 (plus any accrued interest left unpaid).

28. Marc does not have discharge of indebtedness income if his mother repays the loan. This is a benefit to him, which would be income, but, as discussed in the next chapter, would probably be considered a gift that would be excluded from his gross income.

29. Frieda has $15,000 of discharge of indebtedness income that must be included in her gross income unless, as discussed in the next chapter she can fall within any of the exceptions of §108(b), such as the insolvency exception. If Frieda had a legitimate basis for disputing any of these charges, however, the discharge attributable to those amounts would not constitute discharge of indebtedness income under the disputed liability doctrine. Allocation of the discharge among disputed and accepted items is a question of fact.

30. It appears that Greg paid for the disability insurance premiums personally, with after-tax dollars. Therefore, the amounts received would be excluded from his gross income. If instead Greg's employer had paid the premiums, and these premiums were not included in Greg's gross income, the amounts received under the policy would be includable in Greg's gross income.

31. Bea may exclude the prize from her gross income: She didn't do anything to enter the competition; she need not perform any services; and she immediately transferred the award to charity.

32. Carlotta must include the $50,000 in her gross income. Her promise to repay the funds does not affect this result. In fact, it is very unlikely that any embezzler will be able to meet the four requirements of *James v. United States, supra.*

33. (e). The receipt of loan proceeds is not income because of the offsetting obligation to repay the debt. All of the other types of income are included in gross income.

Exam Tips on
SPECIFIC INCLUSIONS IN GROSS INCOME

☛ Tax questions typically involve transactions between two or more people. Which person's tax consequences are you asked to address in the question?

☛ Recall the principles of Chapter 2—some receipts aren't income, by definition. If these rules apply, you do not reach the specific statutory inclusions in gross income. These excluded amounts are:

☞ Loan proceeds

☞ Capital recovery

☞ Imputed income

☛ Questions about income inclusion involve the taxpayer's receipt of something of value. Identify the transfer of things of value, such as:

☞ Cash or check

☞ Services

☞ Property

☛ Section 61 is the cornerstone of basic income tax. Expect a question about whether a type of income is included in gross income.

☛ Compensation for services is a common transaction.

☞ *Look for:* Someone providing services to another in exchange for something of value.

☞ *Analyze:* Focus on the service provider—what he or she did, and what is received. The fair market value of services or property received is gross income to the service provider.

☛ Most, if not all, kinds of investment income is includable in gross income. Dividends, rents, royalties, and interest are all includable.

☛ In a divorce setting, one party may pay alimony to the other. Be sure to analyze the transaction from both sides, and include any alimony in the gross income of the recipient.

☞ *Look for:* The payment of cash from one party to the other in a divorce setting

☞ *Analyze:* Are the requirements for alimony met? Are the payments front-end loaded?

☛ Understand loan transactions. A loan isn't a taxable event, nor is the repayment of the loan principal. When a taxpayer takes out a loan, what he or she does with the proceeds (buys a house, for example) is an independent transaction, even if the seller of the property is the one making the loan (seller financing).

☛ Be able to identify discharge of debt situations.

☞ *Look for:* A loan from one party to the other, and then the lender doing something that reduces or eliminates the debt, or a discharge by operation of law.

☞ *Analyze:* How much discharge income does the taxpayer have? In later chapters we will consider possible exclusions.

☛ Some payments are partially includable in gross income, such as:

☞ Some annuity payments

☞ Some Social Security payments

☛ Most receipts are includable in gross income. If in doubt, include an item in gross income, because gross income is a broad category that involves much more than what is specifically enumerated.

 STATUTE SUMMARY CHARTS

Statute Summary—§72

Parsing Step	IRC §72
General Rule	The amount of each payment that is excluded from Gross Income is equal to the amount of the payment multiplied by the Exclusion Ratio.
Definitions	**Annuity:** a stream of payments, usually from payment of premiums in exchange for a promise of payments from an annuity company. **Exclusion Ratio:** Total Investment/Total Expected Return.
Special Rules and Exceptions	If annuitant dies early, deduction for unrecovered investment in annuity. If annuitant lives longer than life expectancy, all amounts will be included in gross income after total investment recovered tax-free.
Related Statutes	**§101:** Tax treatment of insurance **§453:** Similar method for installment contracts
Typically implicated when . . .	A taxpayer receives a distribution from an annuity or from an IRA or retirement plan and must determine how much of the payment is income and how much is a tax-free return of capital.

Statute Summary—§71

Parsing Step	IRC §71
General Rule	Gross income includes alimony payments.
Definitions	**Alimony:** has federal tax law definition, independent of state law labels. Requirements: cash; divorce decree; not designated as nondeductible; not members of same household; no liability to pay beyond recipient's death; not child support. **Front–end loaded alimony**: varies by more than $15,000 in first three years—see technical definition.
Special Rules and Exceptions	Front-end loaded alimony results in income to payor and deduction to payee in third post-separation year.
Related Statutes	**§215:** Deduction to payor for alimony **§1041:** Property transfers in divorce or between spouses
Typically implicated when . . .	Divorce situations, or post-divorce situations.

CHAPTER 4

SPECIFIC EXCLUSIONS FROM GROSS INCOME

ChapterScope _____

This chapter addresses specific statutory exclusions from gross income: items that constitute "income" within the meaning of §61 but are not included in a taxpayer's gross income because of a specific exception in the Code.

- **Interpret narrowly:** Exclusions are matters of legislative grace, and in order for an item to be excluded from gross income, it must meet the specific requirements of a statute allowing an exclusion.

- **Life insurance payments:** Section 101 excludes from the gross income of the beneficiary the proceeds of life insurance policies payable upon the death of the insured.

- **Gifts and bequests:** Section 102 excludes gifts and bequests (regardless of amount) from the gross income of the recipient of the gift.

- **Damages for personal physical injury:** Section 104 excludes from gross income amounts received as compensation for personal physical injuries or sickness.

- **Discharge of indebtedness income:** Section 108 excludes discharge of indebtedness income from gross income, if certain conditions are met. A taxpayer excluding amounts under §108 may be required to reduce certain tax benefits that he or she would otherwise enjoy.

- **Employment-related exclusions:** A variety of Code sections provide exclusions for certain types of compensation income, including certain meals and lodging (§119), life (§79) and health (§106) insurance premiums, and fringe benefits (§132).

- **Gain on sale of principal residence:** All or a portion of the gain on the sale of a taxpayer's principal residence is excludable from gross income if certain conditions are met.

- **Other exclusions:** Various other Code provisions allow a taxpayer to exclude certain items that would otherwise qualify as income from his or her gross income. These include interest on certain savings bonds, qualified scholarships, and child support.

I. WHERE ARE WE?

We are still trying to define gross income, the starting place for the computation of a taxpayer's tax. Although gross income is a very broad concept, Congress has determined that certain kinds of income are not appropriate for inclusion in gross income—if and only if certain conditions are met.

II. EXCLUSIONS—IN GENERAL

A. Exclusions—Definition

An *exclusion* from gross income means that the item is simply not included in gross income, so that it never enters the computation of taxable income.

1. **Compare deduction:** An exclusion means that the item is not included in gross income at all. A *deduction* is a subtraction from income in computing taxable income. Both a deduction and exclusion will reduce tax liability by the amount of the item multiplied by the taxpayer's tax rate. However, the process by which each works is very different. Excluding an item from gross income means that the item will forever escape the income tax. A deduction, by contrast, will offset an equal amount of income so that the amount of income will not be taxed.

   Example: Angela's taxable income is $40,000. Assume that she is in a flat 20% income tax bracket, so that she pays $8,000 of tax. If she discovers that she is entitled to exclude $5,000 of income so that her taxable income is $35,000, she will pay only $7,000 of tax, saving $1,000. The tax savings of $1,000 is equal to the exclusion ($5,000) multiplied by Angela's tax rate (20%). The same result is obtained if Angela is entitled to a deduction of $5,000.

   Example: Dave's taxable income is $50,000. Assume that he is in a flat 30% income tax bracket. He pays $15,000 in tax. If he discovers an additional $5,000 deduction to which he is entitled, he will reduce his taxable income to $45,000 and will pay a tax of $13,500. Dave's tax savings of $1,500 is equal to the deduction ($5,000) multiplied by his tax rate (30%).

2. **Compare credit:** A *tax credit* (discussed generally in Chapter 13) is a dollar-for-dollar reduction in the amount of tax due. An exclusion is very different from a credit in operation. An exclusion prevents an item from being included in the computation of taxable income, allowing it to escape taxation entirely. By contrast, a credit simply reduces the amount of tax imposed on taxable income. The value of an exclusion is the amount of the exclusion multiplied by the taxpayer's tax rate, and its value is higher for taxpayers in high brackets than for taxpayers at lower brackets. A tax credit, by contrast, results in a tax savings equal to the amount of credit and thus has the same value for high- and low-bracket taxpayers.

3. **Compare deferral:** An exclusion exempts an amount from gross income altogether, so that it is never subject to tax. *Deferral* statutes push into the future the potential inclusion of amounts in gross income, so these amounts may be included in a taxpayer's gross income in a later year. Taxpayers like deferral statutes, even if the tax must ultimately be paid, because they have the use of the funds in the interim periods.

B. Construction

While the courts construe §61 broadly, they construe exclusions narrowly. See *United States v. Centennial Savings Bank FSB,* 499 U.S. 573, 583–584 (1991).

C. Phaseouts of benefits based on income

Many Code sections that grant a tax benefit, such as an exclusion from gross income, reduce or remove that benefit for taxpayers with high incomes. While *phaseouts* are rarer for exclusions than they are for deductions, Congress often use them for statutes that place a dollar limit on the amount of the benefit that can be obtained.

1. **Phaseouts generally:** Statutes that phase out a tax benefit typically deny a portion of the benefit beginning at a certain income level, so that the benefit is completely denied to taxpayers at a specified income level. Income is usually measured by reference to adjusted gross income, with certain adjustments. The phaseout income levels are usually different for single and married taxpayers, and for married taxpayers filing separately. The statute specifies the income levels, and often (but not always) provides for an inflation adjustment, which the IRS calculates and publishes each year in the Internal Revenue Bulletin. See, e.g., Rev. Proc. 2011-2 I.R.B. 297.

2. **What you need to know:** Most professors don't test on the specific phaseouts because they change annually. So you don't need to know the exact amounts. However, you do need to know which statutes have phaseouts. You also need to know how phaseouts work. Typically, a phaseout reduces a tax benefit by a dollar amount that is calculated according to a formula.

   Example: An employer may provide up to a certain dollar amount of adoption assistance to a taxpayer under §137. Let's assume that this maximum exclusion is $15,000. The statute may reduce that dollar amount by an amount that bears the same relation to $15,000 as the taxpayer's AGI minus $150,000 bears to $40,000. The arithmetic equation to be solved is:

$$\frac{X}{\$15,000} = \frac{(\text{Taxpayer's AGI} - \$150,000)}{\$40,000}$$

   Therefore, if the taxpayer's AGI is $180,000, the reduction is $11,250, and the taxpayer would only be entitled to $3,750 of excludable assistance, as follows:

$$\frac{\textbf{\$11,250}}{\$15,000} = \frac{(\$180,000 - \$150,000)}{\$40,000}$$

   Once the taxpayer's income rises to $190,000, the taxpayer cannot claim any exclusion for adoption assistance.

III. DEATH BENEFITS—§101

Section 101(a) excludes from gross income amounts received under a *life insurance* policy by reason of the death of the insured.

A. Life insurance—A primer

1. **Why buy insurance?** Taxpayers purchase life insurance for two reasons: income replacement and investment. Many taxpayers purchase life insurance to replace their earnings in the event of their untimely death. This is the "insurance element" of life insurance. But taxpayers also purchase life insurance as a savings device. Like an annuity, the increase in value of the life insurance contract over time is not included in the gross income of the insured.

   a. **Compare other investments:** The savings element in a life insurance policy is treated very differently from other types of savings vehicles such as bank accounts or mutual funds in which income is taxed currently to the owner.

   b. **Policy:** This represents a political preference for life insurance products, as opposed to other types of investment, perhaps in recognition of the importance of life insurance for many taxpayers and the strength of the insurance industry lobby.

2. Vocabulary: Life insurance has its own vocabulary.

    a. Life insurance contract: A life insurance contract is the promise by an insurance company to pay a fixed amount to the beneficiary named by the insured upon the death of the insured.

    b. Insured: The person whose life is insured under the contract, whose death triggers payment under the policy.

    c. Premium: The amount(s) paid for the life insurance contract. The premium may be paid in a single sum or, more commonly, annually. The insured may be the owner, or the owner may be some other person, e.g., a corporation, or a spouse, or a trust.

    d. Term insurance: A *term insurance* policy provides insurance for a stated period, usually a year. The premium pays for insurance for that period, and when that period is over, the insured has no further benefit under the contract. Term insurance becomes more expensive as the insured ages.

    e. Permanent insurance (also known as "whole life" insurance): A *permanent insurance* policy provides insurance for the entire period of the taxpayer's life, as opposed to the stated period of a term policy. Premiums may change over the period or be level throughout. If the premium is level throughout the life of the policy, the insured will be paying more in the early years of the policy than the cost of term insurance, but in later years, the annual premium will be less than required to fund term insurance. Investment of the sum in excess of the amount needed for insurance will earn interest and will pay for the more expensive insurance later in the policy.

    f. Cash value (or "surrender value"): In the early years of a permanent insurance policy, the premium is greater than the amount needed to fund term insurance. The difference (reserve) earns interest that is not taxed to the taxpayer. The reserve is used in the later years of the policy to fund a portion of the premium in the years when the premium for term insurance would be high. During the years in which the reserve exists, the taxpayer may borrow this cash value from the insurance company.

B. Statutory analysis—§101

1. General rule: Section 101(a) excludes from gross income amounts received under a life insurance contract, whether in a lump sum or in a series of payments, by reason of the death of the insured.

Example: Bill purchases a single premium life insurance policy under which the insurance company promises to pay Bill's designated beneficiary $100,000 upon his death. Bill dies, and his son Corey receives the $100,000 proceeds. Corey excludes this amount from his gross income under §101(a).

2. Definitional issues—Life insurance contract: In general, a life insurance contract is the promise of an insurer to pay, upon the death of the insured, an amount to a designated beneficiary in exchange for the payment of premiums. To qualify for the advantageous tax treatment of §101(a), a life insurance contract also must meet specific statutory tests. These are designed to exclude contracts that function primarily as investments rather than insurance.

3. Special rules and exceptions

a. **Accelerated death benefits:** Although §101(a) requires amounts to be paid by reason of the death of the insured, a special rule allows certain accelerated death benefits to fall within the general rule's exclusion. Under certain life insurance contracts, amounts can be withdrawn if the insured is terminally or chronically ill. These amounts will be treated as paid by reason of the death of the insured, i.e., excluded from gross income. IRC §101(g)(1).

b. **Transfer for valuable consideration:** The exclusion does not apply to those who receive proceeds by purchasing a life insurance contract for valuable consideration. In that situation, the exclusion is limited to the buyer's purchase price in the contract; amounts in excess of the purchase price must be included in gross income. IRC §101(a)(2). However, the transfer of a policy to allow payment for long-term care for a terminally or chronically ill insured is not considered assignment of the death benefit. IRC §101(g)(2)(A).

Example: Diane purchased a single premium life insurance policy that will pay her designated beneficiary $100,000 upon her death. While in financial difficulty, Diane assigns all her rights in the insurance contract to a creditor to whom she owes an $80,000 debt, in satisfaction of that debt. The creditor names himself beneficiary. When Diane dies, the creditor receives $100,000 in insurance proceeds. Only $80,000 of this amount is excluded from gross income (as capital recovery). The $20,000 balance is included in the creditor's gross income.

c. **Employee death benefits:** Any amount paid by an employer for death benefits is generally included in the gross income of the recipient, unless the death benefit is part of a life insurance arrangement. However, §101(i) provides an exclusion from gross income for any amount paid by an employer with respect to the death of an employee who is a specified terrorist victim.

4. Related material

a. **Annuities:** For the treatment of amounts payable by reasons other than the death of the insured, see discussion of annuities in Chapter 3(V)(F).

b. **Premiums:** For a discussion of exclusions for an employer's payment of life insurance premiums, see this chapter, Section (IX)(D).

c. **Military death gratuity:** A survivor who receives a qualifying military death gratuity may exclude it from gross income. IRC §134(a), (b)(3)(C).

5. Be alert for life insurance issues: Section 101 is implicated whenever a taxpayer dies covered by insurance.

IV. GIFTS—§102

Section 102(a) excludes from the gross income of the recipient the value of cash or property received by *gift* or *inheritance,* regardless of amount.

A. Policy

Possible justifications for exclusion of gifts include the following:

1. **Support/gifts:** Since most transfers by gift occur within families, it may be difficult to distinguish between gifts and support, and including gifts in gross income would require such a distinction.

2. **Estate and gift tax:** A frequently invoked rationale is that the income tax should not apply to gifts because a separate federal taxing scheme applies to estates and gifts. However, this justification is unfounded because the two tax systems operate independently, and are motivated by different rationales.

B. Statutory analysis

1. **General rule:** Gross income does not include the value of property acquired by gift, bequest, devise, or inheritance. The value of the gift is excluded from the recipient's gross income, regardless of the amount of the gift.

   a. **Compare gift tax:** The donor may be required to pay gift tax on the transfer, and for federal gift tax purposes only, the amount of the gift is relevant.

   b. **Annual gift tax exclusion:** For gift tax purposes, the donor may make a nontaxable gift of up to a specified dollar amount per person per year. This amount is $13,000 in 2011, and is scheduled to increase annually with cost-of-living adjustments. IRC §2503(b). Amounts in excess of the specified dollar amounts are applied to the donor's lifetime exclusion for estate and gift tax. No similar limit applies to amounts excluded from gross income under §102.

      Example: Frieda gives stock in ABC Corporation worth $50,000 to her son Jon as a holiday gift. Jon does not include the $50,000 in his gross income. (Frieda does not take a deduction for the gift, either.) Frieda may have to pay gift tax on the gift because it exceeds the amount she can give free of gift tax each year, but the amount of the gift does not affect the exclusion from Jon's income for federal income tax purposes.

2. **Definitional issue—Gift**

   a. **Intent of transferor:** A gift is a transfer made by a transferor motivated by "detached and disinterested generosity." *Commissioner v. Duberstein,* 363 U.S. 278 (1960).

   b. **Compare compensation:** Transfers made to compensate another for services rendered or in expectation of services to be rendered are not gifts and therefore are not excluded from the recipient's gross income.

      i. *Olk v. United States,* **536 F.2d 876 (9th Cir.),** *cert. denied,* **429 U.S. 920 (1976):** Dealers who received chips from gamblers as tips must include the cash equivalent in gross income, because transfers were not made through pure generosity. Gamblers generally view these so-called gifts as conducive to success at the tables.

      ii. *Goodwin v. United States,* **67 F.3d 149 (8th Cir. 1995):** Congregation members regularly and anonymously gave gifts of cash to a popular pastor. These amounts were gross income to the pastor, not excluded as gifts, because the motivation was to induce him to continue to provide services despite low salary.

   c. **Intrafamilial transfers:** In the gift tax context, intrafamilial transfers are rebuttably presumed to be gifts. In the income tax field, by contrast, courts do not apply a presumption but instead examine the facts and circumstances surrounding each transfer. Intrafamilial transfers usually qualify as gifts because they are motivated by affection and generosity. If, however, the transferor has an expectation of receiving economic value, the transfer will not be considered a gift even if it is made from one family member to another.

Example: Frieda sends her son Jon a check for $1,000. This would probably be a gift, but if there was evidence that the $1,000 was payment for services provided by Jon, the exclusion for gifts would not apply.

d. **Bequests:** Section 102(a) excludes amount received by "bequest, devise or inheritance," covering all the usual ways in which a person receives a gift upon the death of another. Amounts received pursuant to a will dispute are also excludable if the person could have been considered an heir. See *Lyeth v. Hoey,* 305 U.S. 188 (1938). The major definitional problem is determining when a bequest is made on account of some consideration flowing from the beneficiary to the decedent; in that case, the bequest is not excludable. See, e.g., *Wolder v. Commissioner,* 493 F.2d 608 (2d Cir. 1974) (lawyer and client contracted for lawyer to provide lifetime legal services in exchange for a bequest; amounts received under the client's will were not bequests excludable from gross income.)

3. Special rules and exceptions

a. **Income:** The exclusion does not apply to income from property received by gift. IRC §102(b)(1).

Example: Connie's mother gives her Blueacre, a rental property. While Connie may exclude the value of Blueacre from her gross income, she nevertheless must include in her gross income the rental income from Blueacre during her ownership of the property.

b. **Employee gifts:** The exclusion of §102 does not extend to any transfer made by an employer to an employee. IRC §102(c)(1). These amounts are considered compensation, not gifts.

Example: Hilda worked for XYZ Corp. as a bookkeeper for 30 years. At Hilda's retirement party on her last day of work, XYZ gave her a $5,000 gift certificate for a trip to Hawaii. The $5,000 is considered compensation to Hilda and is includable in Hilda's gross income.

4. Related material

a. **Basis:** The recipient of a gift generally takes the same basis as the donor had in the property increased by a portion of any gift tax paid. See discussion in Chapter 9(V)(C).

b. **Fringe benefits:** For transfers of value by employers to employees that may be excluded, see discussion of fringe benefits in this chapter, Section (IX).

c. **Assignment of income:** The transfer of income from property, as compared to the transfer of the property itself, may constitute a prohibited assignment of income. See discussion in Chapter 14(III).

5. Be alert for gift issues:
Section 102 is probably the most widely tested concept in federal income tax. Look for transfers that are motivated by love and affection, or transfers that people would like to be treated as gifts but that arise from other motivations.

V. INTEREST ON STATE AND LOCAL BONDS—§103

Section 61(a)(4) includes interest in gross income, but §103 allows a taxpayer to exclude from gross income interest on certain bonds issued by a state or local government. The details of this exclusion are beyond the scope of most basic tax classes.

VI. COMPENSATION FOR PERSONAL INJURY OR SICKNESS—§104

Section 104(a) excludes from gross income amounts received as compensation for *personal physical injury* or *physical sickness.*

A. Policy

The following rationales have been offered for this exclusion.

1. **No income:** Because the taxpayer is merely placed back in his or her original (undamaged) state, the taxpayer has no benefit and therefore no income from the transaction.

2. **Measurement:** Even if the taxpayer has some amount of income, it is too difficult to measure.

3. **Adding insult to injury:** It would be cruel to an injured taxpayer to include these amounts in income.

B. Statutory analysis—§104

1. **General rule:** A taxpayer may exclude from his or her gross income amounts received for personal physical injury or physical sickness in the form of workers' compensation payments, damages received, and certain amounts received from health insurance not in excess of medical expenses. IRC §104(a).

   a. **Damages—Method of payment:** The exclusion applies whether the damages are received in a lump sum or as periodic payments. IRC §104(a).

   b. **Damages—Suit or settlement:** Damages may be received either as a judgment or in settlement of a claim. IRC §104(a)(2). If in settlement, the proper allocation of damages among claims and types of damages is a question of fact.

      Example: Ian slips and falls on his neighbor's icy steps, and injures his back. His neighbor's insurance company pays Ian $5,000 in settlement of his claim for injury. Ian may exclude the $5,000 from his gross income.

2. **Definitional issues**

   a. **"Personal" physical injury or sickness:** Only amounts received on account of "personal physical injuries" or "physical sickness" are excludable and this requires a direct causal link between the physical injury and the damage recovery. *O'Gilvie v. United States,* 519 U.S. 79 (1996). IRC §104(a)(2). Business injuries and personal nonphysical injuries, such as discrimination, are not excluded.

   b. **"On account of" the injury:** Damages must be received as a result of the injury, i.e., there must be a direct causation between the injury and the damages incurred and received. See *Commissioner v. Schleier,* 515 U.S. 323 (1995).

c. **Emotional distress:** Damages for emotional distress from a nonphysical injury are not excludable. This is true for physical symptoms of emotional distress. But if a sickness is physical, emotional distress events can exacerbate it, which may lead to excludable recoveries. However, amounts received and expended on medical care for emotional distress are excludable, even if the source is a nonphysical injury. IRC §104(a); Prop. Reg. §1.104-1(c)(1).

3. **Special rules and exceptions**

   a. **Punitive damages:** Punitive damages are included in gross income even if received on account of personal physical injury or physical sickness. IRC §104(a)(2). The one exception to this rule is that punitive damages received for wrongful death under a state statute that does not allow for compensatory damages will be excludable. IRC §104(c).

   b. **Previously deducted medical expenses:** The exclusion does not apply to amounts the taxpayer has deducted as medical expenses under §213. IRC §104(a). See Chapter 6(VIII).

      Example: Ian slipped on his neighbor's steps and hurt his back. In the year of his injury he incurred medical expenses, and he properly claimed $2,000 as a deduction on that year's tax return. In the next year he received $5,000 in payments from his neighbor's insurance company. Assuming the entire amount was compensation for personal physical injuries, only $3,000 is excludable from gross income, as the other $2,000 is attributable to previously deducted medical expenses and must be included in gross income. See also Chapter 11(II)(F) (tax benefit rule).

   c. **Interest on judgments:** The exclusion from gross income does not extend to prejudgment interest. *Brabson v. United States,* 73 F.3d 1040 (10th Cir. 1996); *Kovacs v. Commissioner,* 100 T.C. 124 (1993), *aff'd without published opinion,* 25 F.3d 1048 (6th Cir. 1994). Delay damages are treated like prejudgment interest as included in gross income. *Francisco v. United States,* 267 F.3d 303 (3d Cir. 2001).

4. **Related material**

   a. **Health insurance benefits:** For the treatment of health insurance benefits see discussion in this chapter, Section IX(D).

   b. **Deduction:** For the deduction of medical expenses, see discussion in Chapter 6(VIII).

   c. **Attorneys' fees:** For the treatment of attorneys' fees see discussion in Chapter 6(III)(G).

5. **Be alert for damages for injury issues:** Section 104 potentially applies whenever a taxpayer is physically injured and receives compensation for that injury. Be ready to discuss why it doesn't apply in certain cases, e.g., compensation for nonphysical or business injuries, and its coordination with medical expense deductions and reimbursements.

VII. DISCHARGE OF INDEBTEDNESS INCOME—§108

Section 108(a) provides an exclusion for *discharge of indebtedness income* in certain specified circumstances. The exclusion is generally conditioned upon the taxpayer giving up certain tax benefits.

Example: Jolene owes Friendly Bank $100,000. Jolene's assets have a value of $50,000, and her debts total $150,000. In recognition of her dire financial straits, the bank agrees to take $20,000 in satisfaction of the debt. Jolene has discharge of indebtedness income of $80,000, but if she meets one of the conditions of exclusion of §108, she will be able to exclude all or part of the $80,000 of discharge of indebtedness income from her gross income.

A. Policy

Various rationales justify this exclusion.

1. **Blood from a turnip?** It is difficult to collect tax from insolvent taxpayers, so deferral of the tax is the best option.

2. **Subsidy:** For certain types of taxpayers, such as farmers, exclusion or deferral represents a political decision to offer a tax benefit.

B. Statutory analysis—§108

1. **General rule:** A taxpayer may exclude from his or her gross income discharge of indebtedness income if any of the following five conditions apply.

   a. **Bankruptcy:** The discharge occurs in a Title 11 (bankruptcy) case. IRC §108(a)(1)(A).

   b. **Insolvency:** The discharge occurs while the taxpayer is *insolvent* (in this case, the exclusion is limited to the amount of the insolvency). IRC §108(a)(1)(B).

   c. **Qualified principal residence indebtedness:** The discharge is of *acquisition indebtedness* for a taxpayer's *principal residence* when the discharge occurs before January 1, 2013. The limit on this exclusion is $2,000,000. IRC §108(a)(1)(E). For the definition of acquisition indebtedness, see Chapter 6(V)(C). For the definition of a principal residence, see this chapter, Section (VIII).

   Example: Anna purchases a principal residence for $500,000, taking out a loan for $400,000 and paying $100,000 from her savings. Home values plummet, and her home is now worth only $350,000. In 2011, she negotiates with her lender to reduce the debt to $300,000. She is solvent and not in bankruptcy. The discharge of indebtedness income of $100,000 is excluded from her gross income because it is qualified principal residence indebtedness: it was acquisition indebtedness; it is discharged before 2013; and it is less than the statutory limit of $2,000,000. However, as discussed below, Anna will have to reduce her basis in the home by the amount of the income excluded.

   d. **Qualified farm indebtedness:** The indebtedness discharged is *qualified farm indebtedness.* IRC §108(a)(1)(C).

   e. **Student loans:** Gross income does not include any discharge of a student loan if the discharge occurs because the student works for a certain period of time for a nonprofit or governmental organization. IRC §108(f)(1). See Rev. Rul. 2008-34, 2008-1 C.B. 76 (forgiveness under program that refinanced and then forgave student loans if the person worked in a public interest job for a specified period qualified as student loans within the meaning of §108).

   Example: Mary incurs $40,000 in governmental student loans to attend medical school. The lender offers a program under which, if she works for five years in a publicly funded poverty medical program, $25,000 of her loans will be discharged. Mary works for five years in a qualifying program and receives the benefit of the $25,000 discharge. This discharge of indebtedness income is not included in Mary's gross income.

2. Definitional issues

a. **Indebtedness:** In order for §108 to apply, there must be an "indebtedness," which is defined as a debt for which the taxpayer is liable or a debt secured by the taxpayer's property. IRC §108(d)(1). See discussion of *Zarin v. Commissioner* in Chapter 3(VII).

b. **Discharge of indebtedness income:** In order for §108 potentially to apply, there must be discharge of indebtedness income. See discussion in Chapter 3(VII).

c. **Insolvency:** A taxpayer is insolvent if, and to the extent that, his or her liabilities exceed the fair market value of his or her assets. IRC §108(d)(3). Insolvency is determined immediately prior to discharge. IRC §108(d)(3).

d. **Qualified farm indebtedness:** This definition is quite technical, but generally means commercial or governmental debt incurred by a person whose primary business is farming. IRC §108(g)(2).

3. Special rules and exceptions

a. **Paying the piper:** The exclusion from gross income is not "free." For each dollar of exclusion claimed by the taxpayer because of any exclusion other than real property business indebtedness, the taxpayer must also give up a dollar of tax attributes or reduce the basis of his or her depreciable property. IRC §108(b)(1).

   i. **Effect:** Although §108 will protect the taxpayer from the inclusion of discharge of debt income in gross income, the taxpayer will experience a burden in the future—by having fewer tax benefits to enjoy or having property with a lower basis for depreciation and a larger gain on sale.

   ii. **Tax attributes:** Tax attributes are reduced in this order:

   - net operating losses and carryovers,

   - certain tax credits,

   - capital loss carryovers,

   - passive activity loss carryovers, and

   - foreign tax credit carryovers.

   IRC §108(b)(1), (2).

   iii. **Basis reduction:** When the taxpayer's discharge is of qualified principal residence indebtedness, the taxpayer must reduce his or her basis in the property by the amount of the discharge. In that situation, the basis reduction applies only to the principal residence of the taxpayer; if the taxpayer no longer owns that residence, as in foreclosure, no basis reduction is required. In other situations, the taxpayer may elect in certain cases to apply the exclusion amount to reduce the basis of his or her depreciable property, up to the basis of that property. IRC §108(b)(5)(A).

   Example: Kathy has discharge of indebtedness income of $80,000, which is discharged in a Title 11 case. She also has a net operating loss carryforward of $50,000 and depreciable property with a basis of $40,000. Kathy elects to apply the exclusion amount of $80,000 first to the basis of her depreciable property ($40,000), and thereafter she reduces her net operating loss carryover from $50,000 to $10,000.

b. Purchase price adjustment: A discharge of debt of a solvent debtor will be treated as a purchase price adjustment (which has no tax consequences) if the seller of property reduces the debt incurred to acquire the property and the reduction does not occur in a Title 11 case or when the purchaser is insolvent. IRC §108(e)(5).

Example: Larry purchases a backhoe for $35,000, giving the seller $5,000 in cash and a promissory note for $30,000. Later, the purchaser agrees to reduce the amount of the note to $20,000, in light of difficulties Larry is having with the equipment. Assuming Larry is not insolvent and is not participating in a bankruptcy proceeding, the $10,000 reduction (which would otherwise be discharge of indebtedness income) will be treated as a reduction of the original purchase price from $35,000 to $25,000. Therefore, Larry will not have any discharge of indebtedness income. Of course, this reduction will also be reflected in a reduction of basis in the backhoe.

4. Related material

a. Discharge: In order for §108 to apply, there must be discharge of indebtedness income. See discussion in Chapter 3(VII).

b. Sales or other dispositions of encumbered properties: A sale of encumbered property may generate discharge of indebtedness income potentially subject to §108. See discussion in Chapter 9(VI).

c. Net operating losses *(NOLs)*: For a discussion of *NOLs,* a tax attribute, see Chapter 11(II)(D).

5. Be alert for discharge of debt issues: Section 108 potentially applies whenever a taxpayer is excused from repaying a debt. This can happen through action of the creditor or the creditor being precluded from taking action.

VIII. EXCLUSION FOR GAIN ON SALE OF PRINCIPAL RESIDENCE—§121

A taxpayer may exclude from gross income up to $250,000 ($500,000 for joint filers) of the gain on the sale of his or her *principal residence.*

A. Policy

Section 121 is one of several Code provisions favoring investment in real estate, particularly homes. As a practical matter, §121 will result in most sales of taxpayers' principal residences being tax-free.

B. Statutory analysis—§121

1. General rule: A taxpayer may exclude up to $250,000 ($500,000 for joint filers) of qualifying gain on the sale of a principal residence if the following two conditions are met.

a. Principal residence: The taxpayer must have owned and used the property as a principal residence for a period aggregating two or more years during the five-year period ending on the date of the sale or exchange. IRC §121(a).

b. **Once every two years only:** A taxpayer can usually take advantage of this provision only once every two years.

Example: Amanda, a single person, has owned and used Whiteacre as her principal residence for ten years. She has a basis of $40,000 in Whiteacre. Amanda sells Whiteacre for $190,000. Amanda's gain on the sale is $150,000 ($190,000 – $40,000). She may exclude all of this gain from her gross income pursuant to §121.

2. Definitional issues

a. **Principal residence:** The principal residence is the residence where the taxpayer actually lives, based on all the facts and circumstances of the situation. A principal residence can be a nontraditional dwelling, such as a houseboat, a recreational vehicle, or stock in a tenant cooperative. Reg. §1.121-1(b).

b. **Ownership and use:** Ownership and use may be satisfied with nonconcurrent periods of time. For the use requirement, occupancy of the dwelling is required, but short absences, such as for vacation or illness, do not interrupt a period of use. Reg. §1.121-1(c). If a dwelling is used partly for business and partly for residence, only the part attributable to the residence use is eligible for the §121 exclusion. Reg. §1.121-1(e).

Example: Calvin lived in a townhouse that he rented from 2004 through 2008. On January 1, 2009, he purchased this townhouse. On February 1, 2009, Calvin moved into his daughter's home. On March 1, 2011, while still living in his daughter's home, Calvin sold his townhouse. The §121 exclusion will apply to gain from the sale because Calvin owned the townhouse for at least two years out of the five years preceding the sale (from January 1, 2009, until March 1, 2011) and he used the townhouse as his principal residence for at least two years during the five-year period preceding the sale (from 2004 until February 1, 2009).

3. Special rules and exceptions

a. **Nonqualifying use:** Gain will be recognized to the extent it is allocated to periods of "nonqualifying use," i.e., periods of time in years (after 2008) during which the residence was not used as the principal residence of the taxpayer, or his or her spouse or former spouse. The gain included in gross income is the gain on sale, multiplied by a fraction, the numerator of which is period of time of nonqualifying use and the denominator of which is the total period of time the taxpayer owned the property. IRC §121(b)(5). However, a period of nonqualifying use does not include any period after which a taxpayer has used a property as a principal residence.

Example: Marta was a long-time resident of Seattle. In anticipation of retirement, she purchased a second home in Arizona on January 1, 2009 for $125,000. On January 1, 2011, Marta retired and moved into the home. At that time, the home was worth $200,000. Having discovered that there is such a thing as too much sun, she sold the home on January 1, 2013 for $275,000. How much of the gain on this sale may Marta exclude from gross income? Marta multiplies the total gain ($150,000) by a fraction, the numerator of which is the period of her nonqualifying use, i.e., the period of time she owned the property but did not live in it (two years: 2009 and 2010). The denominator of the fraction is her total period of ownership (four years: 2009 through 2012). Therefore Marta must include $75,000 of the gain ($150,000 × 2/4 = $75,000), but may exclude the remaining $75,000 from gross income.

Reduced exclusion: When a taxpayer cannot satisfy the use/ownership test, or needs to use the exclusion more than once in a two-year period, special rules may apply to allow a reduced exclusion. The taxpayer's need to sell must arise from a change in place of employment, health, or other unforeseen circumstances acceptable to the IRS. In those cases, the reduced exclusion is applied by multiplying the maximum gain ($250,000, or $500,000 for joint filers) by a fraction, the numerator of which is the amount of time the taxpayer did own or use the property, or the period of time since the last §121 sale, and the denominator is two years, expressed as days or months. This produces the reduced exclusion to which the taxpayer is entitled.

Example: Lois, who files as a single taxpayer, purchases a house that she uses as her principal residence. Twelve months after the purchase, Lois sells the house due to a change in place of her employment. Lois has not excluded gain under §121 on a prior sale or exchange of property within the last two years. Lois is eligible to exclude up to $125,000 of the gain from the sale of her house (12/24 × $250,000).

b. **Husbands and wives:** A husband and wife will meet the requirements of §121 if *both* or *either* of them meet the ownership and use tests, and *neither* of them has used the §121 exclusion in the past two years. If they don't meet this test, their maximum exclusion will be the sum of their individual exclusions. Reg. §1.121-2(b)(1), (2).

Example: During 2010, newly married taxpayers Harlan and Wynona each sell a residence that each had separately owned and used as a principal residence before their marriage. Each spouse meets the ownership and use tests for his or her respective residence. Neither spouse meets the use requirement for the other spouse's residence. Harlan and Wynona file a joint return for the year of the sales. The gain realized from the sale of Harlan's residence is $200,000. The gain realized from the sale of Wynona's residence is $300,000. Because the ownership and use requirements are met for each residence by each respective spouse, Harlan and Wynona are eligible to exclude up to $250,000 of gain from the sale of each of their residences. However, Wynona may not use Harlan's unused exclusion to exclude gain in excess of her exclusion amount. Therefore, Harlan and Wynona must recognize $50,000 of the gain realized on the sale of Wynona's residence.

c. **Disabled taxpayer:** An elderly or disabled taxpayer who moves to an assisted care facility may have difficulty meeting the use requirement. A special rule allows such taxpayers to claim the exclusion if the taxpayer uses the property as a residence for at least one year out of the five ending on the date of sale. IRC §121(d)(7).

4. **Related material**

   a. **Computation of gain or loss:** For discussion of computing gain or loss on the sale of property, including a principal residence, see Chapter 9(V).

   b. **Office in home:** When a taxpayer claims depreciation for use of part of his or her home as an office, §121 will not protect the gain attributable to that deduction from recognition.

5. **Be alert for sale of principal residence issues:** Section 121 is implicated whenever a taxpayer sells his or her principal residence at a gain. The principal issues are whether the

residence qualifies and the amount of gain that can be excluded. *Remember:* There is no deduction for a loss on the sale of a principal residence.

IX. EMPLOYMENT-RELATED EXCLUSIONS

In the ***employment relationship,*** the employer typically pays the employee wages or salary, but also may provide certain other benefits such as health insurance, child care, or the ubiquitous holiday turkey. Some of these benefits may be excludable from gross income; others are not. In order to exclude an amount from gross income, the employee must be able to point to a specific statutory exclusion that applies to the particular benefit.

A. Policy

While it is clear that amounts paid—whether in cash or property—by an employer to an employee are compensation income to the employee, several rationales exist to exclude some common noncash benefits from the employee's gross income. Some benefits may be difficult to value. Others may be so small that the expense of accounting for them would exceed their value to the employee. Still others are the result of a congressional purpose to encourage the provision of a certain benefit. Section 132 was intended to deal definitively with commonly encountered fringe benefits, although it has not resolved all controversies. Various specific benefits continue to raise questions about whether such amounts constitute compensation and, if so, whether any exclusion applies.

B. Meals and lodging—§119

1. **Judicial limitation on gross income—meals and lodging.** In *Benaglia v. Commissioner,* 36 B.T.A. 838 (1937), *acq.* 1940-1 C.B. 1, Mr. Benaglia was the manager of the Royal Hawaiian Hotel, where he was on call 24 hours a day. He and his wife lived in a suite of rooms at the hotel and ate their meals in the hotel dining room.

   a. **Issue:** Should Mr. Benaglia's gross income be increased by the fair market value of the room and board ($7,845 per year) provided to him by his employer?

   b. **Result and rationale:** Mr. Benaglia may exclude the value of the room and board from his gross income. Because he was required to live in the hotel for the convenience of his employer, the advantage to him was merely incidental, even though it relieved him of an expense he would otherwise bear.

   c. **Comment—Fairness:** It is almost impossible to justify this result on statutory or fairness grounds. Mr. Benaglia did have an economic benefit (food and shelter), and as there was no exclusion in the Code at that time, it seems clear that some amount should be included in his income. To hold otherwise seems patently unfair to similarly situated employees whose employers do not provide food and shelter.

   Example: Consider two employees, Alvin and Betty, both subject to a flat 30% tax rate. Alvin's taxable income is $50,000, and he pays $15,000 in tax. From his remaining $35,000 he pays $10,000 for rent and $5,000 for food. Alvin has $20,000 left over for other expenses. Betty is a firefighter who lives at the fire station. Her taxable income is $50,000, but she lives at the station rent-free and her food is provided by the fire district. Assuming the room and board are not included in her income, Betty pays the same tax, but has $35,000 left over for other expenses. Is this fair? Arguably not if Alvin and Betty's living quarters and food consumption are equivalent. However, there may be a countervailing argument that Betty, left to her own devices, would not choose to live at the fire station at all, and thus the value of the rent/food to her is less than its fair market value.

    d. Comment—Administrative practicality: If any amount were included in Mr. Benaglia's gross income, determining what that amount should be may be difficult. Would "fair market value" be equivalent to what a tourist would have paid, or to the employer's cost?

    e. Comment—Economic effects: The result reached in *Benaglia* might well encourage other employers to require their employees to eat and live on the business premises, which may alter the working relationship in undesirable (or perhaps desirable) ways.

2. Statutory analysis—§119: *Benaglia* was decided before the enactment of §119, which now governs the inclusion of room and board provided to employees.

    a. General rule: An employee may exclude from his or her gross income the value of the meals and lodgings provided by an employer if the following three conditions are met.

        i. Convenience of employer: The meals or lodging must be provided for the ***convenience of the employer.*** IRC §119(a).

        ii. Business premises: The meals or lodging must be provided on the ***business premises*** of the employer. *Id.*

        iii. Lodging—Condition of employment: For lodging, the employee must be required to accept such lodging as a ***condition of employment.*** *Id.*

    b. Definitional issues

        i. Convenience of the employer: This requires that there be a "substantial noncompensatory business reason" for supplying the meals or lodging. Reg. §1.119-1(a)(2). Whether this exists depends on all of the facts and circumstances of the situation. The classic example is the employee who must be "on call" for the employer during meals.

        ii. Business premises: An employer's "business premises" is generally where the employee works. Reg. §119-1(a)(2). Standard business premises are easy to identify. Properties "nearby" the employer's premises probably do not qualify.

        iii. Condition of employment: This requirement is usually satisfied by showing that the employee is on call for the business of the employer. Reg. §1.119-1(b)(3).

        iv. Cash payments don't qualify: The Supreme Court has ruled that cash payments of any kind do not constitute the provision of meals and lodging. This was in the context of meal allowances to police officers who patrolled state highways and ate at restaurants using the meal allowance. *Commissioner v. Kowalski*, 434 U.S. 77 (1977).

3. Special rules and exceptions

    a. Qualified campus lodging: Employees of educational institutions are often provided nearby housing at below-market rent. The value of qualified campus lodging is excluded from the gross income of the employee. IRC §119(d)(1). However, the exclusion does not apply to the excess, if any, of the lesser of (1) 5% of the appraised value of the property; or (2) the average of rentals paid (by other than students and employees) for similar property, over the amount actually paid by the employee. IRC §119(d)(2).

b. **Charges for meals:** Some employers pay their employees a fixed amount for meals. This amount is excluded from the employee's gross income if the other requirements for meals are met, and the employee must make the payment whether or not he or she accepts the meals. IRC §119(b)(3)(A),(B).

4. **Related material**

   a. **Deductions:** For a discussion of deductions for business meals and entertainment, see Chapter 8(VI).

   b. **Business travel:** For a discussion of deductions for lodging while away from home, see Chapters 7(II)(C) and 8(III).

5. **Be alert for meals and lodging issues:** Section 119 is implicated whenever an employer provides lodging or meals (or both) to an employee. This is usually presented as an issue along with a list of other fringe benefits, and the principal question of §119 is whether the benefit is provided as a convenience for the employer (not the employee).

C. Statutory fringe benefits—§132

1. **General rule:** Section 132(a) excludes from the gross income of the recipient the value of any fringe benefit provided by the employer that qualifies as any of the specially defined fringe benefits. The value of a fringe benefit is its fair market value, minus the amount the employee is required to pay for it.

2. **Definitional issues:** The key to §132 is determining whether a particular benefit fits within any of the exclusions.

   a. **Employee:** All of the exclusions require an employer-employee relationship. The employee's use of the benefit will qualify. For qualified employee discounts and no-additional-cost services, use by close family members and surviving spouses generally will also qualify for exclusion. IRC §132(h).

   b. **No-additional-cost service:** A *no-additional-cost service* is one regularly provided to the public by the employer, which the employer can provide to the employee without incurring significant additional cost (disregarding any amount paid by the employee). IRC §132(b).

   Example: Carlo is employed by Dolphin Airways as a counter clerk. All Dolphin employees and immediate family members are entitled to fly on Dolphin flights, on a standby (space available) status, for a flat fee of $25.00 per trip. Carlo and his wife take advantage of this by flying from Atlanta to Miami for $50.00 instead of the usual fare of $640.00. Although he has income (an economic benefit), the value of the benefit net of what Carlo paid is $1,230 (($640 × 2) − 50), and this amount is excludable from gross income as a no-additional-cost service: Dolphin regularly provides this service to the public and incurs no additional cost by providing it to Carlo on a standby basis. In addition, Carlo's spouse's use of the benefit is deemed to be use by the employee.

   c. **Qualified employee discount:** There are three requirements for a *qualified employee discount.*

      i. **An employee discount:** This is the amount of the discount to employees, determined by comparing the price paid by employees to the price paid by the general public. IRC §132(c)(3).

ii. **Qualified property or services:** These are services and property (other than real estate and securities) that the employer sells in the ordinary course of business. IRC §132(c)(4).

iii. **Limitation on discount:** For services, the discount must not be in excess of 20%. IRC §132(c)(1)(B). For property, the discount must not be greater than the "gross profit percentage" at which the property is sold to the public. IRC §132(c)(1)(A). The gross profit percentage is a fraction, the numerator of which is the gross sales price minus the cost of the property, and the denominator of which is the gross sales price, determined for a representative period. IRC §132(c)(2)(A).

Example: Eliza is a professor for Giggleswick University, which offers her a 20% discount at the university bookstore. For a representative period, the aggregate price to the public and cost of bookstore items was $100,000 and $65,000, respectively. Thus, the gross profit percentage is 35% (100,000 – 65,000)/ $100,000). Eliza's discount is a qualified employee discount, as it does not exceed 35%.

d. **Working condition fringe:** This is a benefit to the employee that, if he or she had paid for it personally, would have generated a business deduction as a trade or business expense under §162 or as depreciation under §167. IRC §132(d).

Example: Gerry is a tax lawyer in the employ of the firm of Smith & Jones. Smith & Jones provides Gerry with subscriptions to various tax publications for his offices at both work and home. The cost to the firm is $2,600 per year. While Gerry has income (an economic benefit) as a result of this benefit, the $2,600 value is excluded from Gerry's gross income as a working condition fringe—if he had purchased these items personally, he would have been entitled to a deduction under §162 for the expenditure.

e. **De minimis fringe:** This is the provision of goods or services to the employee with a value so small that the accounting for the benefit would be unreasonable or administratively impractical. IRC §132(e)(1). However, a cash payment cannot be a de minimis fringe benefit regardless of amount.

Example: Ixnel Corporation employees occasionally use the company photocopiers for personal use. In addition, if an employee works late and leaves work after 10 pm, Ixnel will pay for taxi fare home. Finally, Ixnel gives each employee a $25 gift card whenever each department achieves its quarterly goals. The photocopier use and taxi fare are de minimis fringe benefits. However, because gift cards are equivalent to cash, they are not de minimis fringe benefits. Reg. §1.132-6(c).

f. **Qualified transportation fringe:** This means employer-provided transit passes, transportation by van from home to office, or parking near the employer's premises, within specified dollar limits ($120 for a transit pass and $230 for parking, in 2011). IRC §132(f)(1).

g. **Qualified moving expense reimbursement:** This is the amount paid to an employee for expenses that would be deductible as moving expenses under §217. IRC §132(g).

Example: Ivan works for Ixnel Corporation, which transfers him from Pittsburgh to San Antonio. He incurs $5,000 in moving expenses for himself and his family. Ixnel Corporation reimburses him for this amount. He may exclude the $5,000 as a qualified moving expense reimbursement, because this expense would qualify for deduction under §217.

h. **Qualified retirement planning services:** This includes any financial planning advice or consultation provided by an employer related to the retirement plan sponsored by the employer. IRC §132(m)(1).

i. **On-premises athletic facility:** The value of the facility to the employee may be excluded if it is on the business premises of the employer, is operated by the employer, and is used mostly by employees. IRC §132(j)(4).

3. **Special rules and exceptions**

   a. **Nondiscrimination:** The exclusions for no-additional-cost services, qualified employee discounts, and qualified retirement planning services apply only if the benefit is available on substantially the same terms to all employees and the employer does not discriminate in favor of highly compensated employees. IRC §132(j)(1).

   b. **Reciprocal arrangements:** Employers may enter into reciprocal arrangements that allow their respective employees to take advantage of each other's benefits. IRC §132(i).

   c. **Other sections:** Section 132 expressly does not apply to any fringe provided for in another Code section. IRC §132(l).

4. **Related material**

   a. **Moving expenses:** For a discussion of the deduction for moving expenses, see Chapter 6(II)(B).

   b. **Business expense deductions:** For a discussion of items deductible as business expenses or depreciation, see Chapter 7(IV).

5. **Be alert for fringe benefit issues:** Section 132 is typically implicated whenever there is an employer-employee relationship, and the principal question is whether a particular expense qualifies under §132 (or some other fringe benefit exclusion rule).

D. **Insurance premiums and payments**

Many employers pay the premiums on various types of insurance coverage for employees, and often their spouses and dependents. Employees receive insurance payments directly from the insurer after submitting a valid claim or insurance companies pay health care providers on the employees' behalf.

1. **Health and similar insurance—§106**

   a. **Employer-paid premiums:** The employee excludes from gross income the premiums paid by the employer for coverage for the employee, spouse, and dependents under an accident or health plan. IRC §106.

      i. **Accident or health plan:** This is a plan for payments to employees in the event of their personal injury or sickness. Reg. §1.105-5(a). It includes traditional insurance, HMO plans, and long-term care insurance. The exclusion for premiums also extends to the provision of disability insurance.

      ii. **No dollar limitation:** The exclusion applies regardless of the cost of the premiums.

      iii. **Definition of "dependent":** The definition of a "dependent" for health insurance purposes is less stringent than for purposes of claiming the personal exemption. See

Prop. Reg. §1.106-1, which defines dependent as provided in §152, without regard to subsections (b)(1), (b)(2), or (d)(1)(B). Therefore, a married dependent or a dependent with gross income greater than the exemption amount can qualify. The IRS has taken the position that a domestic partner of a taxpayer is not a spouse of the taxpayer for these purposes, even in jurisdictions that require employers to extend benefits to same-sex couples. *See, e.g.,* PLR 200339001.

b. Benefits received by employee: When the employee receives benefits under a health insurance plan, the question is whether the employee must include the amount received in gross income. Section 105(a) includes in the employee's gross income any amounts received for personal injuries or sickness that are attributable to employer-provided premiums or coverage (self-insurance). However, §105(b) excludes amounts otherwise included under §105(a) if they are to reimburse the employee for medical care for the employee or his or her dependents, and if the taxpayer has not deducted the amount under §213. Any amount paid for other benefits—such as wage replacement or disability—are included in gross income, except for payments of loss of bodily function that are paid based on the type of injury.

Example: Karen's employer pays medical insurance premiums for her family coverage, the amount of which is excluded from her gross income under §106. Karen incurs $4,000 of medical expenses resulting from an automobile accident. The insurance company reimburses her 80% ($3,200) of this amount. She may exclude the $3,200 from her gross income, assuming she did not deduct it under §213.

i.   Health savings accounts: An employee covered under a high-deductible health plan may establish a *health savings account.* This allows the employer to contribute to the plan amounts (up to a specified amount per year) that can be used to pay for the employee's health care expenses. The contribution is not included in the employee's gross income, and any interest earned on the plan's funds is excluded from gross income. If distributions are used for qualified medical expenses, these distributions are not included in the employee's gross income. See IRC §223 and discussion in Chapter 6(II).

ii.   Disability insurance premiums: *Disability insurance* pays amounts to an insured person if they are injured and unable to work. Employer-paid premiums for disability insurance are excluded from gross income. Amounts received through disability insurance payments are excluded from gross income if the premiums were either paid by the insured person or were paid by the employer but included in the gross income of the insured employee. IRC §§104(a)(3); 105(a), (b).

Example: Dolores was an employee of Company X. Company X provided disability insurance to each of its employees on a group disability plan and was responsible for paying the premium on the group policy every month. However, each employee was deemed to have received as salary the amount paid for his or her premium each month, and this was included in the employee's taxable salary. If Dolores becomes disabled, the amounts received from the disability policy should be excluded from her gross income.

2. Life insurance premiums: The employee excludes from gross income employer-paid premiums on group term life insurance in an amount not in excess of $50,000 of coverage. IRC §79(a). Group term life insurance is life insurance (1) providing a general death benefit for each member of a group of employees, (2) that is paid for by the employer, and (3) the amount of which is based on a formula generally applicable to all members of the group based on age, years of service, compensation, or position. Reg. §1.79-1(a). Nondiscrimination rules limit this exclusion. IRC §79(d).

3. **Group legal services:** The employee may exclude up to $70 per year of either insurance to provide legal services or the value of legal services provided under a qualified group legal service plan. IRC §120(a).

E. Dependent care assistance—§129

1. **General rule:** An employee may exclude from gross income amounts paid by the employer for *dependent care assistance* pursuant to a qualified dependent care assistance program. IRC §129(a)(1).

2. **Definitional issues**

   a. **Dependent care assistance:** Dependent care assistance is the employer's payment of, or reimbursement of, an employee's payment of employment-related expenses for the care of a dependent unable to care for him- or herself. IRC §129(e)(1).

   b. **Dollar limitation:** A plan may provide any amount of assistance, but the employee may only exclude a maximum of $5,000 ($2,500 for married filing separately). IRC §129(a)(2)(A).

3. **Special rules and exceptions**

   a. **Earned income limitation:** The exclusion is limited to the earned income of the lesser-earning spouse. IRC §129(b)(1)(B).

   b. **Nondiscrimination:** The plan must meet certain requirements, including that the plan not discriminate in favor of highly compensated individuals. IRC §129(d)(2).

   Example: Larry is a single father of one son, age six. Last year he paid $2,000 in day care costs, for which his employer reimbursed him pursuant to a qualified dependent care assistance plan. Larry may exclude from his gross income the $2,000 in dependent care assistance he received from his employer as reimbursement.

4. **Related material—dependent care credit:** For a discussion of the tax credit for dependent care expenditures, see Chapter 13(V).

5. **Be alert for dependent care issues:** Section 129 is one more item in the long list of benefits that may be provided tax-free by employers to employees; consider it whenever an employment relationship exists and a taxpayer pays for care for a family member. Be sure to coordinate with §21, the credit for dependent care.

F. Educational assistance

An employer's expenditures for educational assistance to employees will not be included in the employee's gross income. IRC §127(a)(1). Educational assistance is limited to $5,250 per employee. IRC §127(a)(2).

G. Adoption assistance—§137

An employer can provide tax-free assistance up to $13,170 (in 2011) per child with respect to an employee's "qualified adoption expenses" pursuant to an employer's written adoption expenses program. IRC §137(a). This exclusion has an income phaseout. See this chapter, Section (IX)(G).

H. Frequent flyer miles

Frequent flyer miles accumulated by employees while on business travel—and subsequently used to purchase personal travel—do not constitute gross income to them. See *Charley v. Commissioner,* 91 F.3d 72 (9th Cir. 1996). Announc. 2002-18, 2002-10 IRB 621.

I. Summary—Employment-related exclusions

See Figure 4A—Summary of Employment-Related Exclusions.

Figure 4A
Summary of Employment-Related Exclusions

Code Section of Exclusion	An employee may exclude from gross income certain benefits provided by the employer, including:
§119: Meals and lodging	Certain meals and lodging, subject to convenience of employer and business premises requirements
§132: Statutory fringe benefits	A number of specifically defined fringe benefits, such as de minimis fringes, working condition fringes, etc.
§106: Health insurance	Health insurance premiums paid by the employer
§79: Life insurance	Premiums on $50,000 of term life insurance paid by employer
§120: Group legal services	$70 per year of group legal services benefits
§129: Dependent care assistance	$5,000 of qualified dependent care assistance, subject to earned income limitation (see also IRC §21)
§127: Educational assistance	$5,250 of qualified educational assistance
§137: Adoption assistance	$13,170 (in 2011) of qualified adoption expenses

X. EDUCATION PROVISIONS

A. Qualified scholarships—§117

Section 117 excludes from gross income the amount received as a *qualified scholarship* by students at *qualifying educational institutions.* The legislative history for §117 reveals no rationale for its exclusion of scholarships from gross income. It may reflect a desire to treat similarly those who receive gifts from family to attend school and those who receive "institutional gifts" such as scholarships. While such a rationale is consistent with §117's restrictions as to services, it does not explain the denial of an exclusion for amounts attributable to room and board.

1. **General rule:** A candidate for a degree at a qualifying educational organization may exclude from his or her gross income the amount he or she receives as a qualified scholarship or as a qualified tuition reduction. IRC §117(a).

2. **Definitional issues**

   a. **Qualifying educational organization:** The educational organization must qualify as one under §170(b)(1)(A)(ii), i.e., one that normally maintains a regular faculty and curriculum and normally has a regularly enrolled body of students in attendance where its educational activities are regularly carried on. IRC §117(a).

   b. **Qualified scholarship:** The scholarship or fellowship must be for tuition, books, fees, and supplies (not room and board). IRC §117(b).

   c. **Qualified tuition reduction:** This is a reduction in tuition provided to an employee (or family member of the employee) of the qualifying educational organization, if the benefit does not discriminate in favor of highly compensated employees and is used for undergraduate study. IRC §117(d). Graduate study may be included in certain cases, if the recipient of the benefit is engaged in teaching or research activities at the university. IRC §117(d)(5).

   Example: Wanda is a professor at a small college in the Pacific Northwest. Under the terms of Wanda's employment agreement, her children may attend the college for four years of undergraduate study by paying only 20% of the tuition charged to students whose parents are not employees. Wanda's son Victor opts to do so and thus enjoys a tuition reduction of 80%. Assuming this benefit does not discriminate in favor of highly compensated employees of the college, it is excluded from the gross income of both Victor and Wanda because it is a qualified tuition reduction.

3. **Special rules and exceptions—Not for services:** The exclusion does not apply to any portion of the amount received that represents payment for services—teaching, research, or other services—required as a condition of the grant. IRC §117(c).

   a. **For benefit of grantor:** Programs that represent compensation for past or future services or are primarily for the benefit of the grantor of the scholarship are not excluded from gross income. See *Bingler v. Johnson,* 394 U.S. 741 (1969) (deference to IRS interpretation of Treas. Reg. §1.117-4(c)).

   b. **Athletic scholarships:** If (1) students are expected but not required to participate in athletic events, (2) no particular activity is required in lieu of participation, and (3) no cancellation will occur if the student cannot participate, a student receiving the scholarship may exclude it from gross income Rev. Rul. 77-263, 1977-2 C.B. 47.

   Example: Zach is offered a fellowship at a nationally acclaimed graduate program that will cover his tuition for three years. As a condition of the fellowship he must teach a section of Economics 101. The portion of the fellowship attributable to teaching activities will not be excluded from Zach's gross income.

4. **Related material**

   a. **Prizes and awards:** For a discussion of prizes and awards, see Chapter 3(VIII)(A) and this chapter, Section (XII).

   b. **Educational incentives:** For descriptions of other educational incentives, see discussion in Chapter 13(VII).

5. **Be alert for scholarships:** Section 117 is part of a set of exclusions, deductions, and credits that are potentially implicated whenever a taxpayer or a member of the taxpayer's family attends college or other higher education. The principal issue for scholarships is whether the payment qualifies as an excludable scholarship, and the receipt of a scholarship must be coordinated with the other education tax provisions.

B. **Savings bonds—§135**

Savings bonds are purchased from the U.S. government in multiples of $50. They are "discount" bonds, i.e., their issue price is less than their redemption price at maturity. For example, a $50 savings bond costs $25 today, and is redeemable for $50 at maturity. The $25 difference between the issue price and redemption price is, of course, interest, which is includable in the gross income of the holder of the bond in the year of maturity. Section 135 excludes from the gross income of an individual any amount received upon redemption of any qualified U.S. savings bond if used for higher education expenses. IRC §135(a). There are income limits on this exclusion.

C. **Section 529 plans and education savings accounts**

1. **Section 529 plans:** A *§529 plan* is a plan established under state law designed to create an incentive to save for education. Under this type of plan, the taxpayer is the account owner. He or she designates a beneficiary who will receive the funds, for K-12 or postsecondary education. When a taxpayer makes a contribution to the plan, he or she receives no federal income tax deduction for that contribution, but the investment earnings accrue tax free, i.e., are not includable in the gross income of either the account owner or the beneficiary. IRC §529(c)(1). Distributions from the plan are excluded from income if the distributions are used for qualified educational expenses.

2. **Coverdell education savings accounts:** These are accounts, usually held by banks or brokerage firms, to which taxpayers may contribute up to $2,000 per year. These accounts name a "beneficiary," who is the person whose education is being funded, for K-12 or postsecondary education. No deduction is available for these contributions, but income earned in these accounts is excluded from gross income. IRC §530(a). Distributions from the account are tax-free if the distributions are used for qualified education expenses.

XI. PAYMENTS FOR SUPPORT OF FAMILY

A. **Child support—§71(c).**

Child support is *excluded* from the gross income of the recipient parent. IRC §71(c)(1). Child support is payment for the support of the payor's minor children. *Id.* Amounts not designated child support but that are tied to a contingency involving a minor child of the payor will be considered child support. IRC §71(c)(2).

B. **Foster care payments—§131.**

Qualified foster care payments, i.e., those made from a governmental entity to a person appointed to provide foster care for a child, are excluded from gross income. IRC §131(a).

C. **Qualified disaster relief—§139.**

Payments received as qualified disaster relief to pay reasonable and necessary family living expenses, or funeral expenses, are excluded from gross income. IRC §139(a).

XII. PRIZES AND AWARDS

Prizes and awards are included in the recipient's gross income. See Chapter 3(VIII)(A). However, under certain circumstances, a recipient may exclude a prize or award from gross income. These requirements are: (1) the recipient must have been selected without any action on his or her part to enter the contest, IRC §74(b)(1); (2) the recipient must not be required to render substantial future services as a condition of receiving the prize, IRC §74(b)(2); and (3) the recipient must immediately transfer the prize to charity, IRC §74(b)(3).

Example: Amy's mother secretly entered her name in a drawing for a trip to Hawaii. Much to Amy's surprise, she won the trip, and there were no conditions that she endorse any product or perform any services for any person. Amy enjoyed her trip to Hawaii immensely. However, she must include in her gross income the fair market value of the trip, as §74 includes this amount in gross income, and she fails the third of the three requirements for exclusion—she didn't immediately transfer the trip to charity.

XIII. ENERGY PROVISIONS

Amounts paid by a public utility to or for a taxpayer for the purchase or installation of any energy conservation measure in a dwelling are excluded from gross income. IRC §136(a).

Example: Ted remodeled his home. He received a rebate check for $300 from the public utility because he installed certain windows that would reduce his electricity consumption. The $300 is excluded from Ted's gross income.

XIV. NEED TO KNOW MORE?

This book's website *www.aspenlawschool.com/books/tax_outline* contains additional information, including:

- How phaseouts work for exclusions, with examples.
- More on discharge of indebtedness income, with examples involving discharge of mortgages on primary residences.
- Coordination of education-related exclusions.
- Recognizing qualifying employment-related expenses.
- And other materials that will help you understand statutory exclusions from gross income.

XV. WHERE ARE WE GOING?

With this chapter's discussion of exclusions from gross income, we now have a sense of which items are included in (and excluded from) gross income. These are the items that are potentially subject to the federal income tax. In the next chapter we will turn to *deductions*—the items that are subtracted from gross income in computing taxable income.

Quiz Yourself on
SPECIFIC EXCLUSIONS FROM GROSS INCOME

34. Upon settlement of her grandfather's estate, Rikki received a pair of antique carved mongooses worth $50,000. Her grandfather had won these in a poker game in India many years before. What are the tax consequences of this receipt to Rikki? _____

35. XYZ Corp. falsely filed a criminal complaint against Brenda for passing a bad check. Before the charges were dropped and she was released, she was arrested, handcuffed, searched via pat-down, forced to undress and put on an orange jumpsuit, photographed, and confined to a holding area. Brenda sued XYZ Corp. for false imprisonment, claiming that while she did not suffer any physical injury from her arrest and detention as a result of the incident, she suffered significant emotional injuries: emotional distress; humiliation; mental anguish; and damage to reputation. To treat these, she visited a psychologist for about eight sessions. Brenda won, and was awarded damages of $100,000. May Brenda exclude the $100,000 from gross income? _____

36. DotComInc has debts of $1 million, property with a fair market value of about $50,000 (with a basis of zero), and a net operating loss of $400,000. Negotiating with creditors, DotComInc obtains cancellation of $700,000 worth of debt. What are the tax consequences to the company of this cancellation? _____

37. On each annual Administrative Assistant's Day, ABC Law Firm gives each member of its non-lawyer staff a gift certificate for a spa day. Is the value of the gift certificate includable in the gross incomes of the recipients? _____

38. Sheri is a flight attendant whose employer provides certain fringe benefits, including medical insurance for herself and her husband and the opportunity to fly free on a standby (seats available) basis for her and her family. What are the tax consequences of these fringe benefits to her? _____

39. Not to be outdone by ABC Law Firm in Question 37, FEG Law Firm provides to staff and lawyer associates free breakfasts and lunches, as well as a "personal concierge service," which runs personal errands for them (such as picking up dry cleaning, standing in line for tickets, etc.). The firm explains these benefits as a way to improve morale and help associates and staff balance work and home life expectations. What are the tax consequences of these benefits to the staff and associates? _____

40. Travis bought a home in Year One. He used it as his principal residence in Year One and Year Two. He then decided to change his life: He abandoned his career as a tax lawyer, got his private detective's license, and moved onto a houseboat in Florida. The house sat empty for a couple of years but he sold it in Year Five at a gain of $75,000. What are the tax consequences of this sale to Travis? Assume all transactions occur on the first day of each Year. _____

41. Bob purchased Blackacre for $200,000. A friend loaned him $180,000, secured by the residence, and he paid the rest of the purchase price in cash. Bob used Blackacre as his principal residence for several years. Real estate prices plummeted and Bob fell on hard times. At a time when Bob was insolvent, and the outstanding principal balance of the mortgage was $140,000, Bob negotiated with his friend that he would repay only $100,000 of the loan. What are the tax consequences to Bob? _____

42. Lisa's employer provides her and her family with health insurance, and also provides disability insurance for Lisa. In Years 1 through 5, the employer spent $10,000 on these premiums for Lisa. In Year 4, Lisa became very ill. She incurred $25,000 of medical expenses, of which the insurance company reimbursed her for $20,000. Eventually, she was determined to be disabled, and now receives $2,000 per month under the disability policy. What are the tax consequences of these events to Lisa? _____

43. In Hamm and Brenda's divorce decree, Hamm was to pay Brenda the sum of $1,000 per month until their only child reached age 18, at which time the amount was to be reduced to $250 per month. Hamm has paid $1,000 per month for each of the last five years, and Brenda has not included any amount in her gross income. Is this the correct reporting position? _____

44. Of the following, which are excluded from a taxpayer's gross income?

(a) A $2,000 prize awarded by a taxpayer's employer for "the best idea of the year"

(b) A scholarship for tuition for one year of undergraduate education

(c) A $300 rebate from the local utility company for purchase of an energy efficient appliance

(d) (a) and (b)

(e) (b) and (c)

Answers

34. Section 102(a) excludes from gross income bequests and inheritances. Rikki can exclude from her gross income the value of the carvings. (Her basis in the carvings will be their fair market value as of the date of her grandfather's death. See Chapter 9.)

35. Brenda may exclude the amounts paid for the visits to the psychologist, but the rest of the award must be included in her gross income. The injury was not physical in nature: all of her claims were for emotional distress. In order to exclude an award for damages for personal injury, there must be a direct causal connection between a physical injury and the resulting damages. See *Stadnyk v. Commissioner*, 367 Fed. Appx. 586 (6th Cir. 2010).

36. The adjustment in the amount of its indebtedness results in $700,000 of discharge of indebtedness income to DotComInc. However, because it is insolvent (liabilities exceed assets) it may exclude the discharged amount from gross income under §108(a), up to the amount of insolvency (which, in this case, is greater than the discharged amount). However, it must reduce its net operating loss to zero as a result of this discharge.

37. Under §102(c), any amount paid by an employer to an employee is not considered a gift. Therefore the face value of the gift certificate cannot be excluded from gross income as a gift. It also does not qualify for exclusion as a de minimis fringe benefit because gift certificates are treated as cash equivalents, and cash equivalents can never be de minimis fringes. Therefore, the value of the gift certificates must be included in the staff members' gross incomes.

38. Sheri may exclude from gross income the medical insurance premiums paid by her employer for her and her family (§106) and may exclude as a no-additional-cost fringe benefit (§132) the value of standby flights.

39. If the meals are provided for the convenience of the employer, the value of the meals is excluded from gross income. In this case, the employer's explanation does not support a "convenience of the employer" argument in the usual sense, and no facts suggest that the associates and staff are "on call" during these meal times, as in the *Benaglia* case. The concierge service will be included in the gross incomes of the associates and staff who use the service, and the amount included (unless the use is de minimis) will be the fair market value of such services (presumably valued by reference to the cost of such services in the market).

40. Section 121 requires the taxpayer to own and use the home as a principal residence for at least two of the past five years in order to exclude the gain on sale from gross income. Travis's use of the home qualifies and therefore he may exclude the $75,000 of gain from his gross income. (This assumes that he has not used the exclusion during the past two years.)

41. Bob has discharge of indebtedness income of $40,000. However, because the discharge relates to principal residence indebtedness—Bob's mortgage was to acquire his home—§108(a)(1)(E) applies to exclude this discharge of indebtedness income from Bob's gross income. He must, however, reduce the basis of the home by $40,000. A related question, which would change the result, is whether Bob's friend intended the discharge as a gift; if so, the discharge would be excluded under §102.

42. Lisa may exclude the value of her employer's provision of insurance (both health and disability) from her gross income. IRC §106. She also may exclude the $25,000 of insurance reimbursements as they were for medical expenses. IRC §105(b). (The excess $5,000 not reimbursed by the insurance company may be deductible under §213. See Chapter 6(VIII).) The disability payments she receives will be included in her gross income because her employer paid the premiums, which were not included in Lisa's gross income. IRC §105(b).

43. The payments from Hamm to Brenda should have been bifurcated into alimony ($250/month) and child support ($750/month). The latter is child support because it is tied to the child reaching age 18. Assuming the other requirements for alimony are met, the amount allocable to alimony should have been included in Brenda's gross income. The amount that is child support is excluded from her gross income.

44. The answer is (e). Section 117 provides an exclusion for the scholarship, and §136 excludes the subsidy from the local utility. Although some employee achievement awards are excluded from gross income, this amount of a cash award exceeds the limits of §274(j).

Exam Tips *on*
SPECIFIC EXCLUSIONS FROM GROSS INCOME

☞ Questions about exclusions focus on the taxpayer's receipt of something of value that would otherwise be included in the taxpayer's gross income.

☞ *Look for:* Receipt of property, money, or some other benefit to the taxpayer that would be considered gross income under §61.

☞ *Analyze:* Is there a specific statutory exclusion that exempts it from gross income?

☛ Interpret exclusions narrowly.

☞ Make sure the purported exclusions precisely fit within the requirements of the statute. If in doubt, don't exclude an item; include it in gross income.

☞ Many exclusions (and deductions) have complex limitations based on income. In a test situation, the limitation phaseout figures would usually be given to you and the goal would be to demonstrate your ability to understand how these limitations work and show that you comprehend the structure of the statute.

☛ Understand the difference between the exclusion for gifts for income tax purposes, and the so-called annual exclusion for gift tax purposes.

☞ A person can receive an unlimited amount of gifts, in terms of value, without including them in gross income.

☞ The gift tax exclusion is limited to a dollar amount ($13,000 in 2011); this is the amount any person may give to another person without counting against the donor's lifetime exclusion amount.

☛ **Remember:** Damages for nonphysical injuries are includable in gross income; damages for physical injuries are excludable; punitive and delay damages are included in the gross income.

☛ Section 108 provides a number of potential exclusions from gross income for discharge of indebtedness income.

☞ *Look for:* A discharge of debt situation that generates gross income to the taxpayer, but surrounding circumstances that make it seem somewhat "unfair" to tax the income.

☞ *Analyze:* Does some subsection of §108 apply? If so, are there corresponding reductions in tax benefits? Or is there a gift that would protect otherwise includable discharge of indebtedness income from being taxed? Recent economic conditions make it likely that a professor will test on qualified principal residence indebtedness, through questions involving adjustment of mortgages or foreclosures. Be sure to understand how §108 interacts with §1001, which addresses gain and loss on the sale of property.

☛ Consider the employment situation carefully.

☞ *Look for:* Compensation income in the form of noncash items, such as medical insurance, fringe benefits, dependent care assistance, or other benefits.

☞ *Analyze:* Is there a benefit to the taxpayer that would otherwise be included in his or her gross income? If so, is there a specific statutory exclusion that would prevent it from being included in the taxpayer's gross income?

STATUTE SUMMARY CHARTS

Statute Summary—§101

Parsing Step	IRC §101
General Rule	Life insurance proceeds are excluded from gross income.
Definitions	**Terms of art:** Life insurance contract; premium; insured; term insurance; permanent insurance.
Special Rules and Exceptions	Can accelerate benefits for terminal/chronic illness/still excluded. Exclusion does not apply to policies transferred for valuable consideration.
Related Statutes	**§72:** Annuities
Typically implicated when . . .	A taxpayer dies who is covered by life insurance and someone receives insurance proceeds.

Statute Summary—§102

Parsing Step	IRC §102
General Rule	Gifts and inheritances are excluded from gross income of the recipient, regardless of value of gift or inheritance.
Definitions	**Gift:** A transfer made with detached and disinterested generosity.
Special Rules and Exceptions	Exclusion does not apply to income from property transferred as a gift. Exclusion does not apply to transfers from employers to employees.
Related Statutes	**§1015:** Basis of property received by gift **§1014:** Basis of property received by inheritance
Typically implicated when . . .	A person transfers something of value to another but it isn't an exchange. The question is whether the transaction is a gift or something else.

Statute Summary—§104

Parsing Step	IRC §104
General Rule	Damages received for personal physical injuries are excluded from gross income.
Definitions	**Damages for physical injury:** requires causal connection between the physical injury and the damage recovery.
Special Rules and Exceptions	Punitive damages included in gross income. Amounts expended on medical care for emotional distress from nonphysical injury are excludable.
Related Statutes	**§§105 & 106:** Health insurance premiums and payments **§213:** Deduction for medical expenses
Typically implicated when . . .	A taxpayer is physically injured and receives damages or compensation for that injury.

Statute Summary—§108

Parsing Step	IRC §108
General Rule	Discharge of indebtedness income may be excluded from gross income in certain situations.
Definitions	**Discharge of indebtedness:** requires action by creditor. **Insolvent:** debt is greater than assets. **Qualified principal residence indebtedness:** acquisition debt, not HELOC.
Special Rules and Exceptions	Amount of exclusion usually requires concomitant reduction in tax attributes.
Related Statutes	**§1001:** Foreclosure/sale of encumbered properties **§172:** Net operating losses as tax attribute **§163(h):** Acquisition Indebtedness
Typically implicated when . . .	A taxpayer is excused from repaying a debt: *always* check to see if the taxpayer fits within any of the exclusions that will allow the discharge of indebtedness income to be excluded from gross income.

CHAPTER 5

DEDUCTIONS—IN GENERAL

ChapterScope

Gross income is the starting point for computing a taxpayer's ultimate tax liability. But gross income is certainly not the tax base—the amount on which tax is levied. Certain deductions must be subtracted from gross income to reach taxable income, upon which the income tax is imposed. This chapter explores the concept of a deduction, and the next three chapters discuss various deductions in detail.

- **Definition of a deduction:** A deduction is a subtraction in the calculation of taxable income. Some deductions are subtracted from gross income in computing adjusted gross income (AGI), while others are subtracted from AGI in computing taxable income. In order to claim a deduction, a taxpayer must meet every requirement of the statute, and these statutes are narrowly construed.

- **Standard versus itemized deduction:** In computing taxable income, an individual taxpayer may claim either the standard or the itemized deduction. The standard deduction is an amount set by statute based on filing status, while the itemized deduction is the aggregate of a number of deductions that are available only if the taxpayer files a Schedule A on which he or she lists all of the available deductions.

- **Personal versus business deductions:** Section 262 denies a taxpayer any deduction for personal expenses except for deductions specifically allowed by statute. By contrast, taxpayers generally may claim deductions for the expenses of doing business. A commonly encountered theme is whether a particular expenditure is a personal (nondeductible) or business (deductible) expense.

- **Expense versus capital expenditure:** If an item is not currently deductible, it may constitute a capital expenditure, and the taxpayer may recover his or her investment in the item at some point during ownership of the asset.

I. WHERE ARE WE?

Having established what is—and is not—gross income, we now turn to deductions. These are subtractions from income that must be made to compute taxable income, on which the income tax is levied.

II. ROLE OF DEDUCTIONS

A. Deduction—Definition

A *deduction* is a subtraction from income in the calculation of taxable income.

1. **Compare exclusion:** If an item is excluded from gross income, it never appears in the calculation of taxable income. By contrast, if an item is deducted, it appears as a subtraction from income in the ultimate calculation of taxable income. An exclusion is appropriate for an income (inflow) item, while a deduction is appropriate for an expenditure (outflow) item.

2. **Effect of exclusion:** The tax effects of an exclusion and a deduction are the same, although they reach the same result by different paths. An exclusion prevents an item from being included in gross income, thus protecting it from tax. A deduction "shelters" other income from tax—the subtraction from income potentially results in the same amount of income escaping tax.

3. **Compare credits:** Unlike a deduction, a tax credit is a dollar-for-dollar reduction in the amount of tax due. See generally Chapter 13.

   Example: Compare the effect of a $50 deduction and a $50 tax credit to a taxpayer in the 28% tax bracket. The $50 deduction will reduce the taxpayer's income by $50, reducing tax by $14 ($50 multiplied by the 28% tax rate). The $50 tax credit will reduce the taxpayer's tax by $50 because the tax credit is a dollar-for-dollar reduction in the amount of tax due. In this case, the tax credit is obviously more valuable to the taxpayer than the deduction.

4. **The upside-down subsidy:** Because a deduction reduces tax by the deduction multiplied by the tax rate (see example above), a deduction is more valuable to a high-tax-bracket taxpayer than a low-tax-bracket taxpayer. Thus, a deduction is sometimes referred to as an *upside-down subsidy* because in a graduated tax system, it offers a bigger benefit for the higher-income taxpayer than for the lower-income taxpayer. A tax credit, by contrast, confers the same dollar benefit on all taxpayers regardless of their tax rates.

B. The policies behind deductions

1. **Tax policy in general:** Gross income does not accurately measure a taxpayer's ability to pay (See Chapter 1(V)(C)). Deductions constitute a reduction in gross income to achieve a tax base that more accurately measures a taxpayer's ability to pay. For example, a person who has high medical expenses not covered by insurance will generally have a lower ability to pay than a person without such expenses (all other things being the same). Other deductions are designed to promote certain activities, such as the deduction for charitable deductions. Deductions introduce substantial complexity into the tax system, but the competing claims of tax fairness and the attainment of certain economic objectives often override calls for tax simplification.

2. **Reduction or denial of benefit based on income:** The Code restricts deductions otherwise available in two principal ways: reducing or denying deductions as a taxpayer's income rises to certain levels; and allowing deductions only to the extent these deductions exceed a certain threshold.

   a. **Denial based on income:** As a taxpayer's income rises to a certain level, Congress believes that the deduction is not necessary to either create an incentive to encourage certain activities by that taxpayer or measure the taxpayer's income (and sometimes simply because allowing the deduction to everyone would be too expensive). See, e.g., IRC §221, which allows a deduction for interest on student loans. See Chapter 6(II)(E).

   b. **Denial unless potential deduction exceeds a threshold amount:** In measuring a taxpayer's ability to pay, it is assumed that everyone has a basic level of expenses. The standard deduction is designed to cover these. Only if a taxpayer's losses or expenses exceed a certain threshold amount should they be taken into consideration in measuring his or her ability to pay, i.e., become a deduction. See, e.g., IRC §213, which allows a deduction for medical expenses only to the extent that they exceed 7.5% of AGI.

C. Narrow construction

A deduction is available by statute only—as the courts often say, "by legislative grace." Courts interpret deduction requirements strictly, construing these statutes narrowly. *New Colonial Ice Co v. Helvering,* 292 U.S. 435 (1934).

D. Role of deductions

Deductions occur in two steps of the computation of taxable income. See Figure 5A—Role of Deductions. Deductions that are subtracted in computing *adjusted gross income (AGI)* are known in the tax trade as *"above-the-line"* deductions. Deductions that are subtracted in computing taxable income are known as *"below-the-line"* deductions.

Figure 5A
Role of Deductions

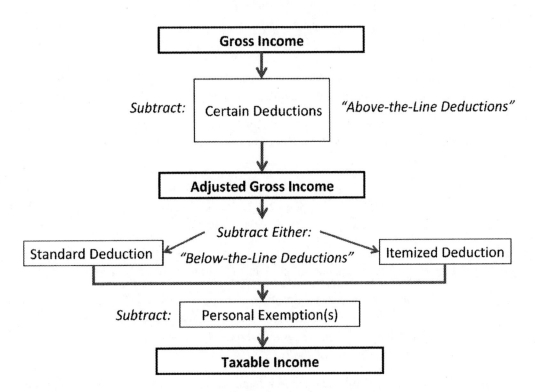

1. **Adjusted gross income:** A number of deductions constitute a subtraction from gross income to produce adjusted gross income. AGI is used as a measure for certain other deductions (such as medical expenses, casualty losses, and entitlement to certain tax benefits), and therefore its determination is important. Taxpayers generally seek to reduce AGI as much as possible because it is often used as a measure for limiting itemized deductions and other tax benefits. Section 62 defines adjusted gross income, allowing the following principal deductions from gross income.

a. **Alimony:** A taxpayer may deduct the amount of alimony he or she pays. IRC §62(a)(10). See IRC §215 and discussion in Chapter 6(II)(A).

b. **Certain retirement savings:** A taxpayer may deduct certain contributions to an Individual Retirement Account (IRA) and other retirement plans. IRC §62(a)(6), (7). See IRC §219 and discussion in Chapter 6(II)(C).

c. **Certain health care expenses:** A taxpayer may deduct certain contributions to health care accounts. IRC §62(a)(16), (19) and discussion in Chapter 6(II)(F).

d. **Moving expenses:** A taxpayer may deduct qualifying moving expenses incurred in moving his or her household to take a new job. IRC §62(a)(15). See IRC §217 and discussion in Chapter 6(II)(B).

e. **Rent and royalty expenses:** A taxpayer earning rents or royalties that do not rise to the level of a trade or business may deduct certain expenses associated with that income. See IRC §62(a)(4) and discussion in Chapter 7(V).

f. **Certain employee expenses:** A taxpayer who is employed may deduct certain reimbursed expenses from AGI. See IRC §62(a)(2) and discussion in Chapter 6(III)(H).

g. **Capital losses:** A taxpayer's capital losses are deductible, subject to the limitations of §1211. IRC §62(a)(3). See generally Chapter 12.

h. **Business losses:** If a taxpayer's expenses of doing business exceed the income from that business, the net loss will be deductible, subject to certain limitations. IRC §62(a)(1). See generally Chapter 7.

i. **Interest on education loans:** The taxpayer's interest expense on education loans is deductible. IRC §62(a)(17). See IRC §221 and discussion in Chapter 6(II). This provision is scheduled to sunset on December 31, 2012.

j. **Qualified tuition:** Through 2011, a taxpayer may deduct up to $4,000 of qualified tuition expenses for higher education, subject to limitations based on income. IRC §222.

2. **Taxable income:** A second group of deductions is subtracted from AGI to produce *taxable income.* Section 63 defines taxable income as adjusted gross income reduced by either the *standard deduction* or the *itemized deduction* (but not both), and the sensible taxpayer will choose to deduct the larger of the two.

a. **Standard deduction:** The standard deduction is the sum of four specific deductions, the most common of which is the *basic standard deduction,* a statutorily fixed amount based on the taxpayer's filing status. The other three are the additional standard deduction, the disaster loss deduction, and the motor vehicle sales tax deduction. IRC §63(c)(1). In theory, the standard deduction, combined with the personal exemption, set a floor of income that should not be taxed because the taxpayer has no ability to contribute to taxes if his or her income is below this combined sum.

b. **Itemized deduction:** The itemized deduction is the sum of a number of deductions, other than the personal exemption and standard deduction. These include home mortgage interest, state and local taxes, casualty losses, medical expenses, charitable contributions, and miscellaneous itemized deductions, all of which are subject to certain limitations.

3. Personal exemption: Each taxpayer is entitled to claim a deduction for *personal exemptions* for him- or herself, a spouse (if a joint return is filed), and any qualifying dependents. This essentially exempts from tax an amount attributable to basic living expenses (although the personal exemption amount is not explicitly tied to a measure of those living expenses). See discussion in Chapter 6(XII).

III. COMMON THEMES OF DEDUCTION CONTROVERSIES

There are several common tax controversy themes involving deductions.

A. An event

To qualify for a deduction, the taxpayer must have experienced an outlay, a loss, or some other event that results in a net outflow—and there must be little if any likelihood of *recovery* of the item that generates the deduction. Deductions are narrowly construed, and therefore the taxpayer's situation must fit within each requirement of a deduction statute to qualify for the deduction. A closely related question is when a taxpayer may claim the deduction—in what taxable year. See generally Chapter 11.

B. Personal versus business deductions

Throughout the deduction provisions of the Code, a common theme emerges—most *personal expenses* are not deductible, and *business expenses* generally are deductible.

1. No deduction for personal expenditures: Section 262 provides that no "personal living or family expenses" are deductible unless a specific statutory provision allows a deduction. Although it can be difficult to identify a personal expense, in general, if an item has more than a minimal connection with a taxpayer's personal (as opposed to business) life, it is likely to be considered a personal expense. See generally Chapter 6.

2. Deduction for business expenses: Section 162 provides a deduction for most commonly encountered business expenses, and other provisions specify other types of business expenditures for which a deduction is allowed. See generally Chapter 7.

3. Policy: There are very different rationales for business and personal deductions.

a. Business deductions: The income tax is generally a tax on net, rather than gross, income. Thus, the Code must provide a deduction for the expenses of creating business income in order to tax only the net increase in wealth of the taxpayer.

b. Personal deductions: If deductions were allowed for all personal expenses, taxable income—the tax base—would be zero. It is sometimes difficult to articulate the rationale for the relatively few personal expenses that are deductible. The income tax often incorporates incentives for specific behavior (such as charitable contributions). It also seeks to tax income actually available to the taxpayer for discretionary expenditure, hence the deductions for alimony, casualty losses, and extraordinary medical expenses.

4. Personal or business? A commonly encountered theme in federal income tax is the question of whether an expenditure is a personal (nondeductible) or business (deductible) expense. Taxpayers generally try to characterize expenses as deductible business expenses, but the IRS may disagree, asserting that the expense has a closer connection with the taxpayer's personal life than his or her business activity and therefore is not deductible. See discussion in Chapters 7(II)(B) and 8(II). Some types of expenditures have a close connection with both aspects of a taxpayer's life. These are particularly troublesome for tax purposes, and Congress has specifically addressed the tax treatment of some such items by statute. See generally Chapter 8.

C. Expense or capital expenditure?

Another commonly encountered theme is the question of whether an expenditure constitutes an *expense* or a *capital expenditure.* If an expenditure is an expense, it will generate a deduction, if the other requirements for deductibility are met. If, however, an expenditure is capital in nature (for the purchase or improvement of real property, for example), the cost or expenditure must be capitalized. This means that the cost is not currently deducted, but instead becomes part of the basis of the property. The taxpayer *may* be able to recover the cost through depreciation or similar deductions during ownership of the property. The line separating expenses from capital expenditures has never been crystal clear, and taxpayers' attempts to characterize an expenditure as a currently deductible expense rather than a capital expenditure (in order to claim the deduction as early as possible) generate a good deal of controversy. See discussion in Chapter 7(IV).

IV. NEED TO KNOW MORE?

This book's website *www.aspenlawschool.com/books/tax_outline* contains additional information, including:

- More on what constitutes an above-the-line and below-the-line deduction—and why it matters.

- More on phaseouts and how they apply to deductions.

- Examples illustrating the common deduction controversies.

- And other materials that will help you begin the analysis of deductions.

V. WHERE ARE WE GOING?

This chapter has introduced the concept and role of deductions and suggested some common themes in controversies between taxpayers and the IRS regarding deductions. The next three chapters examine various deductions in detail, beginning with the principal personal deductions.

Quiz Yourself on
 DEDUCTIONS—IN GENERAL

45. Lee owns a small business, which he runs as a sole proprietorship. His view is: "What's the point of owning a business unless you can run all your expenses through it?" Therefore, he deducts all his living expenses (food, rent, vacations, etc.), in addition to his business expenses, on his Schedule C. What's wrong with that, if anything? _____

46. On his federal income tax return, Double Dip Dan deducted both the standard deduction and his itemized deductions, which exceeded the standard deduction. The IRS assessed additional tax. Why? _____

47. T. C. "Cat" Adorre is a congressman. He is considering proposing a tax code change that would benefit taxpayers who incur expenses in adopting animals from shelters. You are his aide and official tax guru. He asks: "Would it be more beneficial for taxpayers to allow a tax deduction or a tax credit for these expenses? What's the difference, anyway?" _____

48. Jodi runs her hair salon as a sole proprietorship. This year, she invested $50,000 in new styling equipment, an upgrade to her facilities, and a car to be used for business purposes. She intends to deduct all of these costs. Is she correct? (Assume §179 does not apply.) _____

49. What is the rationale for the standard deduction? _____

50. What is the difference between adjusted gross income and taxable income? Why do taxpayers try to minimize AGI? _____

51. Of the following, which are deductible from gross income in computing AGI and which are deductible from AGI in computing taxable income? Medical expenses, personal exemption, standard deduction, moving expenses, retirement savings, capital losses, net personal casualty losses, charitable contributions, alimony. _____

Answers

45. Section 262 disallows a deduction for all "personal, living, and family expenses" unless they are deductible under a specific statute. Most of Lee's living expenses (food, rent, etc.) will not be the subject of any statute allowing deduction. In any event, personal expenses (if deductible) would not be deductible on Lee's Schedule C as part of his business expenses, but elsewhere on his return (Schedule A). They also would be subject to all of the restrictions associated with these deductions. Incidentally, this is the kind of unreasonable return position that could result in penalties, even fraud charges, against Lee. See Chapter 1.

46. Dan is entitled to deduct either the standard deduction or the itemized deduction, but not both. In his case, because his itemized deduction is greater than the standard deduction, he should have deducted only the itemized deduction.

47. A deduction is a subtraction from income in computing taxable income, and its benefit to a taxpayer is equal to the taxpayer's tax rate multiplied by the amount of the deduction. A tax credit is a dollar-for-dollar reduction in a taxpayer's tax. Neither is absolutely "better" than the other, but a deduction does benefit higher-income taxpayers (who are in a higher tax bracket) proportionately more than lower-income taxpayers. By contrast, a tax credit generates the same dollar benefit for all taxpayers who are entitled to it.

48. Jodi's purchase of equipment is a capital expenditure, not a deductible expense. Therefore, she cannot deduct it in the year of acquisition, but instead must recover the cost over time, through MACRS deductions, although §179 may apply to accelerate these deductions. See Chapter 7.

49. In theory, the standard deduction, when combined with the personal exemption, creates a floor of income that will not be taxed because the taxpayer has no ability to pay (to contribute to the national tax obligation) until his or her income rises above that amount. Claiming the standard deduction is substantially simpler than claiming the itemized deduction, so it contributes to the goal of a straightforward, easily administered tax system.

50. Adjusted gross income is the amount computed by subtracting certain items from gross income. Tax is not imposed on AGI, but instead on taxable income, which is the amount computed by subtracting certain items from AGI. Because AGI serves as a measurement for many other tax computations, such as phaseouts for certain tax benefits (e.g., personal casualty losses or medical expenses (see Chapter 6)), reducing AGI tends to increase the likelihood that a taxpayer will benefit from these other reductions.

51. *Deductible in computing AGI:* Moving expenses, retirement savings, capital losses, and alimony. *Deductible in computing taxable income:* personal exemption, standard deduction, personal casualty losses, charitable contributions, medical expenses, and net personal casualty losses.

Exam Tips on
DEDUCTIONS—IN GENERAL

☛ Deduction questions involve an outflow of value from the taxpayer in question to another person.

    ☞ *Look for:* The taxpayer paying someone else for something, in cash or property, or experiencing some other outflow, as in a loss.

    ☞ *Analyze:* Is this item deductible? If so, how much is deductible?

☛ If an expenditure is deductible, is it a deduction from gross income in computing adjusted gross income (an above-the-line deduction)? Or is it deductible from AGI in computing taxable income (a below-the-line deduction)? Make sure you understand why the distinction is important. Deductions are construed narrowly. If in doubt, deny the deduction. The allowance of a deduction is not the whole story. *When* will it be deductible? (See Chapter 11.) Some outlays involve either deductions or credits—or both.

    ☞ Be ready to explain which is more valuable to the taxpayer. A credit is a dollar-for-dollar reduction in tax, so it is usually more valuable, while a deduction is potentially worth the marginal tax rate of the taxpayer multiplied by the amount of the deduction.

    ☞ *Remember:* A taxpayer cannot claim a credit and a deduction for the same dollar of outlay.

CHAPTER 6

PERSONAL DEDUCTIONS

ChapterScope ━━━━━━━━━━━━━━━━━━━━━━━━━━━━━━━━━━━━━━━

Personal expenses are generally nondeductible. However, the Code allows deductions for some kinds of personal expenses. Some of these deductions constitute subtractions from gross income in computing adjusted gross income (AGI); others form part of the itemized deduction, which a taxpayer may claim in lieu of the standard deduction. This chapter discusses the specific requirements for deductibility of personal expenses.

- **Deductions in computing AGI:** A taxpayer may claim certain deductions from gross income in computing AGI. These are often the most valuable deductions to taxpayers because they reduce AGI, which is a measure for entitlement to certain other deductions.

- **Deductions in computing taxable income.** A taxpayer may claim either the standard deduction or the itemized deduction, but not both.

  The standard deduction is the sum of a number of deductions, the most commonly known of which is the basic standard deduction, a statutorily fixed amount that depends on the taxpayer's filing status.

  In lieu of the standard deduction, the taxpayer may claim the itemized deduction, which is also the sum of a number of deductions.

- **Personal exemption:** A taxpayer is entitled to claim a personal exemption for him- or herself, a spouse (if filing jointly), and any qualifying dependents.

I. WHERE ARE WE?

In calculating his or her taxable income, a taxpayer can claim a deduction for certain expenses. In the basic income tax course, *personal deductions* (as opposed to business deductions) are especially important. It is not only important to identify these deductions; it is important to identify them as either deductible from gross income in computing AGI or deductible from AGI in computing taxable income.

II. ABOVE-THE-LINE DEDUCTIONS

The first set of personal deductions discussed here are deductions subtracted from gross income in computing AGI, called in the trade "above-the-line" deductions. All other deductions are "below-the-line" deductions, meaning that they are deductible from AGI in computing taxable income. Taxpayers generally prefer above-the-line deductions because they reduce AGI, which in turn potentially increases certain itemized deductions (such as medical expenses) that use a percentage of AGI as a measure of deductibility. A quick review of Figure 5A, in Chapter 5, is helpful in understanding this concept.

This section discusses the principal deductions that a taxpayer claims as a subtraction from gross income in computing adjusted gross income (AGI). These are defined in §62.

A. Alimony

1. **General rule** Section 215 allows a taxpayer a deduction for the amount of *alimony* or *separate maintenance* paid during the taxable year. This constitutes a deduction from gross income in computing AGI.

2. **Definitional issue—Alimony** Alimony and separate maintenance payments are defined in §71. See discussion of alimony in Chapter 3(VI).

3. **Special rule—Front-end loaded alimony** If alimony is front-end loaded, the payor must include the excess alimony payment in gross income in the third post-separation year. IRC §71(f)(1)(A). See discussion in Chapter 3(VI).

4. **Related material**

   a. **Inclusion:** The recipient of alimony must include it in his or her gross income. IRC §71(a). See discussion in Chapter 3(VI).

   b. **Child support:** *Child support* payments are neither deductible by the payor nor includable to the recipient. IRC §71(c). See discussion in Chapter 4(XI).

   c. **Property settlements:** Transfers of property between spouses or ex-spouses pursuant to a divorce generally produce neither gain nor loss to the parties. IRC §1041(a). See discussion in Chapter 10(V).

5. **Be alert for §215 issues** Section 215 is implicated whenever a divorce situation occurs. The principal issue is whether a payment from a spouse or former spouse to the other spouse or former spouse qualifies as alimony under the federal definition.

B. Moving expenses

1. **General rule:** Section 217 allows a deduction for certain *moving expenses* incurred by a taxpayer in connection with moving to a new place of employment or self-employment. IRC §217(a), (f)(1). This is a deduction from gross income in computing AGI.

2. **Definitional issues:** Moving expenses that may be deducted include the expenses of moving household goods and personal effects and of traveling to the new locale, but do not include meals. IRC §217(b)(1)(A),(B). The mileage rate for moving expenses is lower than for business travel (19 cents/mile for 2011 for moving expenses).

3. **Special rules and exceptions:** Unless the taxpayer is a member of the armed services, the taxpayer's new place of work must be at least 50 miles farther from his or her former residence than his or her former work was from that residence. IRC §217(c)(1), (g)(1).

   Example: Karen is employed in downtown Chicago. She commutes 5 miles to work in the city. She moves outside the city and takes a job with a new employer that is located 60 miles from her former employer. She will qualify for the moving expenses deduction because the location of her new employer is 55 miles longer from her old residence than her old employer's location was from that residence, thereby meeting the 50-mile requirement.

4. **Related material—Coordination with §132: Employer reimbursement** If an employer reimburses an employee for all or a portion of the moving expenses, the employee will be able

to exclude the reimbursement as a fringe benefit under §132. See Chapter 4(VII)(C). Any unreimbursed portion of otherwise qualifying expense would qualify for deduction under §217.

Example: Cliff, currently working in Boston, accepts a new job in Los Angeles. He incurs $7,000 in qualifying expenses of moving to California. His new employer reimburses him for $5,000 of these expenses. Cliff may exclude the $5,000 reimbursement from income (§132) and may deduct the additional $2,000 from gross income in computing AGI (§217).

5. **Be alert for §217 issues** Moving expense issues potentially arise whenever a taxpayer moves in order to take a new job. Section 217 questions are often embedded in larger questions of compensation to a service provider, as part of a litany of fringe benefits that may or may not be includible in gross income.

C. Contributions to regular IRAs

An *"Individual Retirement Account"* (or *IRA*) is an account held in a bank, credit union, or brokerage firm for the benefit of a taxpayer to allow that taxpayer to save for retirement. Each year, the taxpayer may make a contribution to the IRA, which then earns interest or other earnings without tax as long as the funds are in the IRA. There are two kinds of IRAs: *regular IRAs* and *Roth IRAs.* Section 219 allows a taxpayer to claim a deduction in computing AGI only for certain contributions to regular IRAs, not Roth IRAs. When the taxpayer withdraws amounts from a regular IRA, the amount that represents untaxed earnings is included in the taxpayer's gross income. When a taxpayer withdraws amounts from a Roth IRA, no amount is included in gross income.

1. **Contributions limited to earned income:** A taxpayer's maximum annual contribution to an IRA is the lesser of a specified dollar amount or the taxpayer's earned income (salary, wages, and consulting fees, for example). IRC §219(b)(1). A taxpayer may contribute the maximum amount, divided between a regular IRA and a Roth IRA as the taxpayer chooses, subject to certain income limitations applicable to Roth IRAs, but the taxpayer cannot exceed the annual maximum amount. The maximum dollar amount for 2011 is $5,000, and is adjusted for inflation. In addition, taxpayers who have attained age 50 in a particular year may contribute an additional $1,000 per year.

2. **Spousal IRA:** A contribution may be made for a nonworking spouse if the spouses file a joint return, and the total earned income is at least equal to the contribution for both. IRC §219(c)(1), (2).

3. **Participation in qualified plan:** Many employers sponsor a *qualified retirement plan,* to which the employer and employee generally make contributions, subject to special (and complex) rules. If the individual participates in an employer-sponsored qualified plan, the deductible amount will be reduced as AGI rises. The taxpayer participating in a qualified plan may make a nondeductible contribution to a regular IRA regardless of AGI level.

D. Losses

1. **General rule:** Section 165(a) allows a taxpayer to claim a deduction for all "losses not compensated for by insurance or otherwise." §165(c) imposes significant limitations on the deductibility of *losses* for individuals.

2. **Definitional issue—Loss:** A loss is an event that makes the taxpayer economically worse off than he or she was before the event. A loss must be realized, i.e., there must be a realization event that fixes the loss (see Chapter 9(IV)(B)) and there must be no reasonable likelihood that the taxpayer will recoup or recover the loss.

3. **Three types of deductible losses:** Section 165(c) allows individuals to deduct only three types of losses.

   a. **Trade or business losses:** Individuals may deduct losses incurred in a *trade or business.* IRC §165(c)(1). These losses result from a trade or business activity in which expenses exceed income but may be subject to certain restrictions under §§465 and 469. See generally Chapter 7 and Chapter 11(VII).

   b. **Investment losses:** Individuals may deduct losses incurred in *activities entered into for profit,* even if the activity does not rise to the level of a trade or business. IRC §165(c)(2). This category includes losses from rental and royalty-generating activities, as well as losses on the sale or exchange of capital assets, such as real property, stocks, and other types of property. See generally Chapters 7, 9, 10, and 12.

   c. **Personal casualty losses:** Individuals may deduct losses incurred in fire, storm, shipwreck, theft, or other *casualty.* See IRC §165(c)(3) and discussion in this chapter, Section (VII). Personal casualty losses are deductible from gross income to the extent of personal casualty gains. Any remaining losses (net casualty losses) are potentially deductible as part of the itemized deduction.

E. **Interest on education loans**

1. **General rule:** Section 221 allows a taxpayer to deduct a certain amount of *interest* paid on any *qualified education loan.* This is a deduction from gross income in computing AGI. See IRC §221(a). The maximum amount of interest that can be deducted is $2,500 and is subject to a limitation based on modified adjusted gross income (MAGI). Section 221 is scheduled to sunset December 31, 2012.

2. **Definitional issues**

   a. **Qualified education loan:** A qualified education loan is a debt incurred by a taxpayer that is incurred solely to pay *qualified education expenses* of the taxpayer or his or her spouse or dependents. The expenses must be paid within a reasonable time after the loan is incurred. The recipient must be receiving education as an eligible student.

   b. **Eligible student:** The student must be an enrolled student at an acceptable college, university, or trade school.

   c. **Qualified higher education expenses:** These include most of the costs of attending college, university, or trade school, including books, fees, tuition, room, board, equipment, and necessary expenses, including transportation.

3. **Special rule:** The deduction is subject to phaseouts based on modified adjusted gross income of a taxpayer.

4. **Related material—Coordination with other education provisions:** The amount expended for educational expenses must be reduced by any amount received as a scholarship, or which are excluded from gross income under §127 (employer assistance), §135 (interest on U.S.

savings bonds used for education), §529 (qualified tuition programs), or §530 (education savings account distributions). In addition, until December 31, 2011, there is an additional deduction for qualified tuition expenses under §222.

5. **Be alert for education expense issues:** Section 222 (and its cousins, §§25A, 221, 117, and 135) are implicated whenever a taxpayer pays for higher education. The best approach is to identify the qualifying expenditures and how the taxpayer paid for them to determine if any amount, including interest on student loans, is deductible.

F. Certain contributions to medical accounts

Alarming increases in the costs of medical care and health insurance motivated Congress to establish a savings account for medical needs to encourage taxpayers to save for medical expenses: the *"Health Savings Account" (HSA).* A taxpayer may make deductible contributions to an HSA, earnings within the fund grow tax-free (§223(e)(1)), and qualifying distributions are excluded from the gross income of the taxpayer.

1. **General rule:** An eligible taxpayer may claim a deduction from gross income in computing AGI for the amount he or she contributes to an HSA, but the total contribution cannot exceed a specified dollar amount or an amount based on the deductible amount of the taxpayer's health insurance. The deduction is equal to the monthly prorated deductible multiplied by the number of months the taxpayer is participating in the high-deductible health plan, or a specified dollar amount (whichever is less). IRC §223(a), (b)(1),(2).

2. **Definitional issues**

   a. **Eligible individual:** To be eligible, the taxpayer must be covered under a *high-deductible health plan,* which is a health plan (1) with a deductible of at least $1,200 for self-only coverage and at least $2,400 for family coverage, and (2) for which the total out-of-pocket expense annually is not greater than $5,950 (self-only coverage) and $11,900 (family coverage) (2011 amounts). IRC §223(c)(1). The taxpayer may not be eligible for Medicare. IRC §223(b)(7). While the taxpayer cannot have other health insurance, certain kinds of supplemental insurance—such as long-term care insurance—are disregarded. IRC §223(c)(3).

   b. **Qualifying account:** The account must be established with a bank or other approved institution, and may accept contributions only in cash. The funds in the account can be used only for payment of *qualified medical expenses* of the taxpayer or his or her spouse and dependents. The account must be nonforfeitable, i.e., there must be no circumstances in which the taxpayer would have to give amounts in the account to someone else (other than a family member for medical expenses).

   c. **Qualified medical expenses:** Distributions may be used only for those expenses described in §213(d). See this chapter, Section (VIII).

3. **Special rules and exceptions**

   a. **Monthly determination:** Because health insurance is usually provided on a monthly basis, the amount a taxpayer may contribute also is determined on a monthly basis. A taxpayer may contribute and deduct one-twelfth of the annual deductible for any month he or she is eligible to make contributions. IRC §223(b)(2). The statutory limits are $3,050 for individual coverage and $6,150 for family coverage.

Example: Matt has self-only coverage under a high-deductible health plan with a deductible of $3,000 for the months of January through March of Year One. His coverage terminates in April. His maximum contribution to the plan is one-twelfth of the annual deductible ($250) for three months, or $750.

    b. Excise tax: Amounts not used for medical expenses are included in gross income and a 10% excise tax is imposed on these distributions. IRC §223(f)(4).

4. Related material

    a. Distributions excluded from gross income: Distributions from HSAs to pay for qualified medical expenses are excluded from gross income. IRC §223(f)(1).

    b. Exclusion or deduction, not both: If an employer establishes an HSA for employees and makes contributions to it, these contributions are excluded from gross income of the employee and cannot generate a deduction for the employee. The employee can claim the deduction only if he or she contributes to the account.

5. Be alert for medical savings accounts.
This technique is implicated whenever a taxpayer seeks tax-deferred savings opportunities, and must be coordinated with health insurance premium payments and expenditures.

G. Costs incurred in civil rights and whistleblower cases

Amounts received as damages for nonphysical injuries are includable in gross income. See Chapter 4(VI). The costs of pursuing these claims—principally attorneys' fees—are deductible. A taxpayer may claim an above-the-line deduction for attorneys' fees and court costs incurred in connection with any claim for unlawful discrimination and whistleblower actions. IRC §62(a)(20), (21).

H. Certain expenses incurred by individuals

1. Employee reimbursements:
Employees are often reimbursed for their expenses relating to work by their employers. If this reimbursement is included in gross income, the related expense is deductible above-the-line to the extent of the gross income included (but not more than that amount). As a practical matter, employees usually exclude the reimbursement from gross income. The excess potentially qualifies as a miscellaneous itemized deduction. See this chapter, Section (X).

2. Special types of workers:
Certain expenses relating to the work of performing artists, public officials, and Armed Forces reservists are deductible from gross income. Prior to 2012, eligible educators are allowed an above-the-line deduction of up to $250 for the purchase of books and supplies for their classroom. §62(a)(2)(D).

III. THE STANDARD DEDUCTION

A taxpayer must choose either the ***standard deduction*** or the ***itemized deduction.*** A sensible taxpayer will, of course, choose the larger of the two.

A. Definition—Standard deduction

The standard deduction is the sum of the amounts listed in §63(c). Section 63(c) is deceptive, however, because it lists some deductions that have expired (see below).

B. The standard deduction—Amount

1. **Basic standard deduction:** The basic standard deduction is set forth in Figure 6A—Basic Standard Deduction. The basic standard deduction amounts are adjusted annually for inflation.

Figure 6A
Basic Standard Deduction—2011

Filing Status	Standard Deduction (2011)
Married filing jointly	$11,600
Single	$5,800
Head of household	$8,500

2. **Additional amounts:** In addition to the basic standard deduction, a taxpayer may be eligible for additional deductions as part of the standard deduction. These amounts are also adjusted annually for inflation.

   a. **Elderly or blind:** An elderly or blind taxpayer receives an additional amount of $1,150 (for 2011), depending on his or her circumstances. IRC §63(c)(3).

   b. **Certain other expenses:** From time to time, Congress enacts, usually for temporary periods, deductions for certain other expenses. These are designed to create an incentive for taxpayers who do not itemize to take certain actions. An example is the temporary deduction of sales tax on the purchases of automobiles that expired at the end of 2010.

IV. THE ITEMIZED DEDUCTION

When someone says that a taxpayer "itemizes," it means that he or she has decided to forgo the standard deduction and claim the itemized deduction, which is the total of a group of deductions listed on Schedule A to the Form 1040. See Figure 6B—Schedule A. All of the deductions discussed in the following sections are itemized deductions.

Figure 6B
Schedule A (Form 1040) Itemized Deductions

SCHEDULE A (Form 1040)	**Itemized Deductions**	OMB No. 1545-0074
Department of the Treasury Internal Revenue Service (99)	▶ **Attach to Form 1040.** ▶ **See Instructions for Schedule A (Form 1040).**	20**10** Attachment Sequence No. **07**

Name(s) shown on Form 1040 | Your social security number

Medical and Dental Expenses

Caution. Do not include expenses reimbursed or paid by others.

1 Medical and dental expenses (see instructions) . . . . . | 1
2 Enter amount from Form 1040, line 38 | 2 |
3 Multiply line 2 by 7.5% (.075) . . . . | 3
4 Subtract line 3 from line 1. If line 3 is more than line 1, enter -0- . . . . . . | 4

Taxes You Paid

5 State and local **(check only one box):**
    a ☐ Income taxes, **or** } . . . . | 5
    b ☐ General sales taxes }
6 Real estate taxes (see instructions) . . . . | 6
7 New motor vehicle taxes from line 11 of the worksheet on back (for certain vehicles purchased in 2009). Skip this line if you checked box 5b . . . . | 7
8 Other taxes. List type and amount ▶ _____ | 8
9 Add lines 5 through 8 . . . . | 9

Interest You Paid

Note. Your mortgage interest deduction may be limited (see instructions).

10 Home mortgage interest and points reported to you on Form 1098 | 10
11 Home mortgage interest not reported to you on Form 1098. If paid to the person from whom you bought the home, see instructions and show that person's name, identifying no., and address ▶ _____ | 11
12 Points not reported to you on Form 1098. See instructions for special rules . . . . | 12
13 Mortgage insurance premiums (see instructions) . . . . | 13
14 Investment interest. Attach Form 4952 if required. (See instructions.) | 14
15 Add lines 10 through 14 . . . . | 15

Gifts to Charity

If you made a gift and got a benefit for it, see instructions.

16 Gifts by cash or check. If you made any gift of $250 or more, see instructions . . . . | 16
17 Other than by cash or check. If any gift of $250 or more, see instructions. You **must** attach Form 8283 if over $500 . . . | 17
18 Carryover from prior year . . . . | 18
19 Add lines 16 through 18 . . . . | 19

Casualty and Theft Losses

20 Casualty or theft loss(es). Attach Form 4684. (See instructions.) . . . . | 20

Job Expenses and Certain Miscellaneous Deductions

21 Unreimbursed employee expenses—job travel, union dues, job education, etc. Attach Form 2106 or 2106-EZ if required. (See instructions.) ▶ _____ | 21
22 Tax preparation fees . . . . | 22
23 Other expenses—investment, safe deposit box, etc. List type and amount ▶ _____ | 23
24 Add lines 21 through 23 . . . . | 24
25 Enter amount from Form 1040, line 38 | 25 |
26 Multiply line 25 by 2% (.02) . . . . | 26
27 Subtract line 26 from line 24. If line 26 is more than line 24, enter -0- . . . . . . | 27

Other Miscellaneous Deductions

28 Other—from list in instructions. List type and amount ▶ _____ | 28

Total Itemized Deductions

29 Add the amounts in the far right column for lines 4 through 28. Also, enter this amount on Form 1040, line 40 . . . . | 29
30 If you elect to itemize deductions even though they are less than your standard deduction, check here . . . . ▶ ☐

For Paperwork Reduction Act Notice, see Form 1040 instructions.   Cat. No. 17145C   Schedule A (Form 1040) 2010

Figure 6B *[continued]*

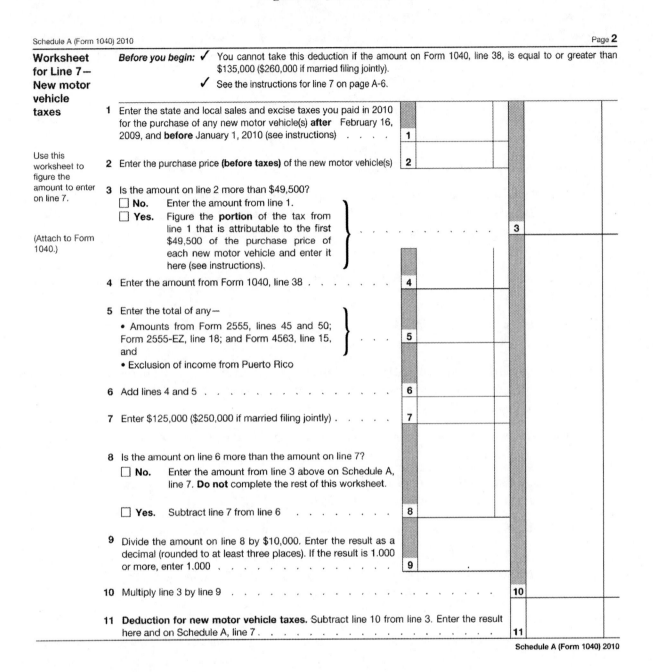

V. INTEREST—§163

A. In general

Section 163(a) allows a deduction for *interest* paid or accrued during the taxable year. (For a discussion of the definition of interest, see Chapter 3(V)(C).) For interest other than trade or business interest, this is an itemized deduction. Section 163 also imposes significant restrictions on the deductibility of interest, for taxpayers other than corporations.

B. No deduction for personal interest

No deduction is allowed for *"personal interest"* paid by an individual. IRC §163(h)(1). Personal interest is interest other than trade or business interest, investment interest, qualified residence interest, and passive activity interests. Common examples of personal interest include:

- interest on credit card debt incurred for personal purposes,

- interest on car loans for cars not used for business purposes, and

- interest on student loans

C. Home mortgage interest—§163(h)(3)

1. **Policy:** Recall that one of the major tax expenditures, which has long been embodied in the Code, is the itemized deduction for home mortgage interest. See Chapter 1(V)(B). This deduction arguably creates the economic effect of stimulating taxpayers to purchase, rather than rent, their principal residences.

2. **General rule:** *Qualified residence interest* is deductible by taxpayers other than corporations. IRC §163(h)(2)(D).

3. **Definitional issues:** The key to understanding the general rule is understanding the definitions.

    a. **Qualified residence interest:** Qualified residence interest is any interest paid or incurred during the year on *acquisition indebtedness* or *home equity indebtedness* for any *qualified residence* of the taxpayer. IRC §163(h)(3)(A).

    b. **Acquisition indebtedness:** In order for a debt to qualify as acquisition indebtedness, it must meet three requirements.

        i.   **Use of funds:** The indebtedness must be incurred to acquire, construct, or substantially improve any qualified residence. IRC §163(h)(3)(B)(i)(I).

        ii. **Security:** The qualified residence must secure the indebtedness. IRC §163(h)(3)(B)(i)(I).

        iii. **Amount:** A taxpayer's aggregate amount of acquisition indebtedness cannot exceed $1,000,000. IRC §163(h)(3)(B)(ii).

             Example: Carla purchases her principal residence for $250,000, paying cash of $50,000 and incurring a mortgage of $200,000. She may deduct the interest on the mortgage because it qualifies as acquisition indebtedness—debt incurred to acquire a principal residence.

    c. **Home equity indebtedness:** In order for a debt to qualify as home equity indebtedness, it must not be acquisition indebtedness, and it must meet three requirements.

        i.   **Equity:** The indebtedness must not exceed the fair market value of the residence minus the acquisition indebtedness on the residence. IRC §163(h)(3)(C)(i)(I), (II).

        ii. **Security:** A qualified residence must secure the indebtedness. *Id.*

        iii. **Amount:** A taxpayer's aggregate amount of home equity indebtedness cannot exceed $100,000. IRC §163(h)(3)(C)(ii).

Example: Debra owns a home with a fair market value of $100,000, which is subject to a mortgage of $60,000. The local bank offers her an arrangement whereby she obtains a credit line of up to 90% of the equity in her home if she places her home as security for the credit. She takes advantage of this arrangement and draws on credit of $25,000. The interest on the credit of $25,000 is deductible as home equity indebtedness because it meets the three requirements: It does not exceed the equity in Debra's home; it is secured by the home; and it does not exceed $100,000.

d. Qualified residence: The qualified residence of a taxpayer is the principal residence of the taxpayer and one other residence designated by the taxpayer that the taxpayer uses for at least two weeks for personal purposes during the year. IRC §163(h)(4)(A)(i)(I), (II).

Example: Aubrey uses his home in Dallas as his principal residence. He also owns two vacation homes, one in Vail and one in Florida, and typically spends about three weeks at each vacation home during the year. All three homes have mortgages on them. Aubrey's principal residence is a qualified residence, and Aubrey will be allowed to designate one of his vacation homes as a qualified residence if he spends at least two weeks there during the year.

4. Special rules and exceptions

a. Construction loans: In a construction loan, the taxpayer typically receives temporary financing for the construction period and replaces that loan with a permanent mortgage (known as permanent financing) once the residence is completed. Because the taxpayer cannot occupy a residence under construction, the question arises whether construction financing will produce qualified residence interest. The regulations solve this problem by allowing a residence under construction to be treated as a qualified residence for the 24 months ending on the date on which the residence is ready for occupancy. Reg. §1.163-10T(p)(5)(i).

b. Refinancing: In a refinancing transaction, a taxpayer seeks a new loan to replace his or her old one. Although the new loan may be in the same amount as the old one, it is often the case that the new loan's face amount exceeds the balance of the old loan. The refinanced portion can qualify as acquisition indebtedness but only in the amount of the original loan balance at the time of refinancing. IRC §163(h)(3)(B)(i)(I), (II). Any amount in excess of the acquisition indebtedness may qualify as home equity indebtedness up to the $100,000 limit on the aggregate amount of home equity indebtedness. IRC §163(h)(3)(C)(i), (ii).

Example: Andy's principal residence has a fair market value of $250,000. He originally purchased it for $175,000, by paying cash of $50,000 and obtaining a mortgage of $125,000. Over the five years since purchase, he has reduced the mortgage to $100,000. With interest rates dropping, Andy wishes to refinance his mortgage and also hopes to access some of the increased equity in his home. To that end, he arranges for a new loan in the amount of $225,000. With this new loan, he repays the original mortgage of $100,000 and uses the additional $125,000 for personal purposes.

Of the new $225,000 loan, only $200,000 generates qualified residence interest. The refinancing of the original mortgage is acquisition indebtedness but only in the amount of $100,000, the debt existing at the time of refinancing. The additional $125,000 might qualify as home equity indebtedness because it is equal to the difference between the fair market value of the home ($250,000) and the amount of acquisition indebtedness on the home ($100,000). But the dollar limitation applies to limit home equity indebtedness to $100,000. The interest on the remaining $25,000 of the mortgage is not deductible.

   c. **Points:** Points are essentially prepaid interest, paid to a lender in the year a loan is closed to obtain a lower interest rate. Taxpayers want to deduct points in the year of payment, and may do so, provided a number of requirements are met. The IRS has established a safe harbor, so that taxpayers may deduct points paid during a year if the following five requirements are met: (1) the points must be paid in cash in connection with the acquisition of the taxpayer's principal residence; (2) the closing statement must clearly designate the amount to be paid as "points," "loan origination fees," "loan discount," or "discount points"; (3) the points must be computed as a percentage of the stated principal amount of the loan; (4) the points charged must conform with general practice in the area; and (5) the points must be paid from cash provided at closing or in escrow, i.e., they must not be incorporated into the loaned sum. Rev. Proc. 94-27, 1994-1 C.B. 613. Points that do not fall within this safe harbor may still qualify, but the burden will be on the taxpayer to show that the amounts paid are truly prepaid interest rather than some other fee associated with the lending transaction.

   d. **Mortgage insurance premiums:** For loans with high loan-to-value percentages, the lender will often require that the borrower pay the premium on the lender's purchase of insurance that will ensure the repayment of the loan in the event of the borrowers' death or disability. Until December 31, 2011, mortgage insurance premiums are treated as mortgage interest, subject to certain limitations. §163(h)(3)(E). For a discussion of gain or loss on the sale of a principal residence, see Chapter 4(VIII), and for a discussion of trade or business interest, see Chapter 7(III)(A).

5. **Be alert for home mortgage interest deduction issues:** Section 163(h) is implicated whenever a taxpayer purchases a residence using debt to finance the purchase. The principal issues are whether the debt qualifies as acquisition or home equity indebtedness.

D. **Investment interest—§163(d)**

For taxpayers other than corporations, the deduction for ***investment interest*** is limited to the ***net investment income*** of the taxpayer for the year. IRC §163(d)(1). Investment interest is interest on debt that is incurred to purchase investments such as stocks or bonds. Net investment income is the net income from these kinds of investments. If this limitation prevents the deduction of an amount of interest, the disallowed portion is carried forward and treated as incurred by the taxpayer in the next year. In that year, the same limitation and carryforward rules apply. IRC §163(d)(2).

VI. TAXES—§164

Section 164 allows a deduction for certain *taxes* incurred by an individual. The potentially deductible taxes include state, local, and foreign real property taxes; state and local personal property taxes; and state, local, and foreign income taxes. Federal income taxes, federal estate, and certain other taxes are not deductible. IRC §275. Taxpayers in states with high state sales taxes may prefer to take a deduction for state sales taxes, and until the year 2012 they may elect to claim a deduction for sales taxes in lieu of the deduction for state income taxes. §164(b)(5).

VII. CASUALTY LOSSES—§165(c)(3)

A. General rule

A *casualty* occurs when a taxpayer's property is destroyed in a fire, storm, or similar event, or is stolen. A casualty can produce a gain or a loss. For example, consider property that the taxpayer bought for $1,000, but that appreciated in value to $10,000. It is stolen and the taxpayer receives insurance proceeds of $10,000. That taxpayer would have a *casualty gain* of $9,000—the difference between the insurance proceeds and the taxpayer's cost of the property. (See discussion of IRC §1033 in Chapter 10(IV).) That casualty gain must be included in gross income. If that same property were not insured, however, the taxpayer would have a *casualty loss* of $1,000, because the measure of loss is the lesser of the decrease in fair market value or the taxpayer's adjusted basis in the property. Reg. §1.165-7(b)(1).

Section 165(c)(3) allows individuals to claim as a deduction losses of property arising from casualty events such as fires or storms or from theft, but, of course, there are limitations and special rules. In particular, the loss must exceed $100 per event, so that the amount of any loss must first be reduced by $100 before any other rules are applied. IRC §165(h)(1). Think of this as a "deductible," removing from the calculation the many small losses of everyday life. Then, the treatment of casualty losses depends on the total casualty gains and losses of the taxpayer during the year.

1. **More gains than losses:** If a taxpayer's personal casualty gains exceed personal casualty losses for the year, both the gains and losses are treated as capital gains and capital losses. This allows the taxpayer to offset the gains (included in gross income) with the losses (deductible from gross income in computing AGI).

   Example: Dave experienced two casualties during the year. First, his antique car was stolen. His basis in the car was $20,000, and it had a fair market value of (and was insured for) $30,000. Second, his cherished Native American marriage basket with a fair market value and basis of $5,000 (which was uninsured) was stolen. In this situation, Dave has more personal casualty gains ($30,000 – 20,000 = $10,000) than losses ($4,900). He includes the gain in gross income as capital gain and is allowed a deduction for the casualty loss of $4,900 as a capital loss, so that his net figure is a capital gain of $5,100.

2. **More losses than gains:** If personal casualty losses exceed gains, the amount of loss equal to the amount of gain is allowed as a deduction from gross income in computing AGI. The balance is potentially an itemized deduction, but only to the extent this loss exceeds 10% of the taxpayer's AGI. IRC §165(h)(2)(A)(i), (ii).

   Example—No casualty gains: Lindsay's personal collection of antiques, worth $150,000, is destroyed when her storage facility burns to the ground. She had a basis in them of $50,000. She did not have insurance. Lindsay's AGI is $75,000. Lindsay may claim a casualty loss as an itemized deduction in the amount of $42,400, calculated as follows:

   - *Step 1:* Determine the loss: $50,000 (the lower of basis or decrease in value).

   - *Step 2:* Subtract the $100 limitation: $50,000 – $100 = $49,900.

   - *Step 3:* Subtract the 10% AGI limitation. Ten percent of AGI is $7,500. Subtract this from $49,900 to obtain $42,400.

   Lindsay may claim an itemized casualty loss deduction of $42,400.

Example—Casualty gains and losses: Kathy experiences two casualty events during the year. In the first event, her horse, Two Egg, is killed by lightning. Two Egg's basis was $10,000, and he was insured for his fair market value of $40,000. In the second event, a Ming vase with a basis and value of $50,100 was stolen. The vase was not insured. Kathy's AGI (disregarding these events) is $50,000.

- *Step 1:* Include in Kathy's gross income the personal casualty gain of $30,000 ($40,000 insurance proceeds minus Two Egg's basis of $10,000).

- *Step 2:* Subtract as a deduction from gross income in computing AGI the personal casualty loss equal to the amount included in gross income as a personal casualty gain. Kathy's personal casualty loss is the loss from the Ming vase ($50,100) minus the $100 deductible. Thus her casualty loss is $50,000. Of this amount, $30,000 is subtracted as a deduction from gross income in computing AGI.

- *Step 3:* Compute the itemized casualty loss deduction by applying the 10% limitation to the balance of the personal casualty loss. This amount will be deductible to the extent it exceeds 10% of AGI. Ten percent of Kathy's AGI of $50,000 is $5,000. The remaining balance of the casualty loss ($20,000) is deductible to the extent it exceeds $5,000; thus the itemized casualty loss deduction is $15,000.

Summary: Kathy will be allowed a deduction of $45,000 of the total $50,100 loss; $30,000 as offsetting casualty gains and $15,000 as an itemized deduction.

B. Definitional issues—Casualty loss

A casualty loss requires a complete or partial destruction of property from a sudden, unexpected, and unusual event. IRC §165(c)(3), (h)(3)(B). There must be no reasonable possibility of recoupment. In order to claim a loss, the taxpayer must file an insurance claim if the property is insured. IRC §165(h)(4)(E).

1. **Cat owners, beware!** In *Dyer v. Commissioner,* 20 T.C.M. 705 (1961), the taxpayer's Siamese cat destroyed a vase during a neurotic fit. The Tax Court denied a deduction for a casualty loss for the vase, as the fit was not "of the same character" as a fire, storm, or shipwreck.

2. **Suddenness requirement:** Termite damage and similar gradual deteriorations do not occur with sufficient "suddenness" to constitute a casualty. See, e.g., Rev. Rul. 63-232, 1963-2 C.B. 97; *Meersman v. United States,* 370 F.2d 109 (6th Cir. 1966).

3. **Theft:** In *Mary Frances Allen,* 16 T.C. 163 (1951), the Tax Court emphasized that the theft must be proven, and the taxpayer bears the burden of proof. Merely losing an item of property does not generate a casualty loss. A theft occurs in the year of discovery.

4. **Corporate wrongdoing:** Some taxpayers have tried to claim a casualty loss when publicly traded stock they purchased for investment declined in value due to the wrongdoing of corporate officers. The courts and the IRS agree that no casualty loss exists in these circumstances. See, e.g., *Paine v. Commissioner,* 63 T.C. 736, *aff'd without published opinion* 523 F.2d 1053 (5th Cir. 1975).

5. **When to claim the deduction:** Timing is usually only a problem in theft situations. The casualty loss is claimed in the year of discovery, or later if there is a reasonable prospect of recovery. When a taxpayer instigates litigation to recover stolen items, the deduction will likely

be deferred until the litigation is concluded, even if it becomes apparent in the litigation that the taxpayer will be unlikely to recover all of his or her losses. See *Johnson v. United States,* 74 Fed. Cl. 360 (2006).

C. Related material

1. **Casualty gain deferral:** For a discussion of the nonrecognition of gain on involuntary conversions, see Chapter 10(IV).

2. **Capital gains and losses:** For a discussion of the treatment of casualty gains and losses treated as capital gains and losses, including as §1231 gains and losses, see Chapter 12(III), (IV).

D. Be alert for casualty loss issues

Section 164(c)(3) and (h) are implicated whenever a taxpayer experiences some sort of disaster, and the taxpayer's property is damaged or destroyed. The principal issues are whether a potentially deductible loss has occurred, and the measurement of that loss. The AGI limitation prevents many taxpayers from claiming a deduction.

VIII. MEDICAL EXPENSES—§213

A. General rule

Section 213 allows a deduction for *medical expenses* paid or incurred by the taxpayer for care of the taxpayer or his or her spouse or dependents, to the extent these expenses exceed 7.5% of AGI. IRC §213(a). This is an itemized deduction.

Example: Lori's AGI is $45,000. This year she had medical bills of $25,000 associated with a complicated pregnancy. She is uninsured and paid this amount with her savings. To calculate Lori's deduction for medical expenses, subtract 7.5% of her AGI (7.5% x 45,000 = $3,375) from her total medical expenses ($25,000). The result is her itemized medical expense deduction of $21,675:

$$7.5\% \text{ of AGI} = 45,000 \times .075 = \$3,375$$

$$\$25,000 - \$3,375 = \$21,675$$

B. Definitional issues—Medical expenses

Medical expenses are expenditures for the diagnosis, cure, relief, or treatment of disease or bodily malfunction, for medical insurance, and for transportation and lodging while seeking care. IRC §213(d)(1)(A)-(C).

1. **Personal versus medical:** In *Ochs v. Commissioner,* 195 F.2d 692 (2d Cir. 1952), Mrs. Ochs was very ill, and she and her husband enrolled their children in boarding school during her treatment and recovery. The Ochs family sought to deduct the boarding school tuition and fees as medical expenses.

   a. **Issue:** Were the tuition and fees for the children's boarding school medical expenses?

   b. **Result and rationale:** These expenses were personal expenses, not medical expenses. The expenses were made necessary not by the medical condition, but by the taxpayers' decision to have children.

2. Cosmetic surgery: Expenses of cosmetic surgery do not qualify as medical expenses unless the procedure is necessary to ameliorate a deformity arising from a congenital abnormality, a personal injury, or disfiguring disease. IRC §213(d)(9).

3. Rx not required? A taxpayer may deduct certain costs of medical tests, such as a full body scan or pregnancy test, even if they are not prescribed by a doctor. See Rev. Rul. 2007-72, 2007-50 I.R.B 1154.

    a. In general: Expenditures for permanent improvements of a residence or for equipment may be medical expenses if specifically necessary for treatment of a medical condition. Reg. §1.213-1(e)(1)(iii).

    Example: Patricia has a slipped disc in her back. After surgery her physician prescribed physical therapy and a special type of chair. Even though the expenditure for the chair constitutes a capital expenditure, it will probably still constitute a medical expense because it is medically necessary for the treatment of her condition.

    b. Increases in value: If the improvement increases the value of the property, only the excess of the cost of the improvement over its effect on the increased value of the property will be considered a medical expense. *Hollander v. Commissioner,* 219 F.2d 934 (3d Cir. 1955).

    Example—*Gerard v. Commissioner,* 37 T.C. 826 (1962): Mr. Gerard's daughter had cystic fibrosis, and her doctor required her to restrict her daily activities to air-conditioned areas. The Gerards installed central air conditioning in their home and deducted the cost ($1,300) as a medical expense. The installation increased the value of the home by $800. Only the difference ($500) between the cost ($1,300) and the increased value ($800) is a medical expense qualifying for deduction.

C. Special rules and exceptions

    1. Coordinating medical insurance payments: Amounts received as payments under insurance plans reduce a taxpayer's medical expenses. Reg. §1.213-1(a)(3)(ii). For example, a taxpayer who incurs $10,000 in medical expenses but receives an insurance reimbursement of $8,000 will consider only the unreimbursed $2,000 in applying the 7.5% limitation to compute his or her itemized medical expense deduction. Recall, however, that reimbursement from accident and health plans generally are not included in a taxpayer's gross income. See discussion in Chapter 4(IX)(D).

    2. Child of divorced parents: Both divorced parents may treat their child as a dependent for purposes of claiming a deduction for the child's medical expenses. IRC §213(d)(5).

D. Related material

    1. Health insurance premiums and proceeds: A taxpayer may be able to exclude from gross income health insurance premiums paid by an employer and insurance reimbursements for expenses. See discussion in Chapter 4(IX)(D).

    2. Personal injury damages: Compensation for certain personal injuries is excludable from gross income of the injured taxpayer. See discussion in Chapter 4(VI).

    3. Health Savings Accounts: Amounts distributed from HSAs to pay for medical expenses cannot generate a deduction under §213. See IRC §223 and discussion, this chapter, Section (VIII)(D).

E. Be alert for medical expense issues

Section 213 is implicated whenever a taxpayer becomes ill and incurs expenses. Consider whether the expenditure is really a medical expense, and whether the taxpayer can claim a deduction given the AGI limitation.

IX. CHARITABLE CONTRIBUTIONS—§170

A. General rule

Section 170 allows a taxpayer to claim as an itemized deduction his or her *charitable contributions* made during the taxable year to qualifying charitable, educational, or religious organizations. IRC §170(a).

B. Definitional issues—Charitable contribution

1. **Charitable organization:** In order for a gift to be deductible, it must be made to a *qualifying charitable organization* that has §501(c)(3) status under federal law.

   a. **Tax status:** Section 170(a) allows a deduction for contributions to certain entities, including the United States or a state or local instrumentality (if made for public purposes), and to religious, charitable, educational, and similar organizations if no part of the net earnings of the organization inures to the benefit of any private shareholder or other individual. IRC §170(c).

   b. **Public policy—*Bob Jones University v. United States,* 461 U.S. 574 (1983):** Faced with the question whether a racially discriminatory private school could be a charitable organization, the Supreme Court concluded that a "charitable organization" is one that serves the public benefit and does not violate public policy. Racial discrimination was found to violate public policy, and therefore the organization was not charitable.

2. **Private benefit:** In *Ottawa Silica Co. v. United States,* 699 F.2d 1124 (Fed. Cir. 1983), the taxpayer owned large parcels of real estate in a developing area. It donated a 70-acre site to the school district, knowing that the district would construct needed access roads that would make the taxpayer's remaining land more valuable. The taxpayer claimed a deduction for the fair market value of the land donated.

   a. **Issue:** Was the taxpayer entitled to a charitable deduction for the donated land?

   b. **Result and rationale:** No deduction was allowed because the taxpayer received a private benefit from donation of the land. A charitable donation assumes that the donor receives no benefit from the transfer. If the benefits received or expected to be received are substantial—i.e., greater than those inuring to the public from a charitable donation—the quid pro quo of the transfer removes it from the realm of deductibility.

3. **Development—*Hernandez v. Commissioner,* 490 U.S. 680 (1989) and Rev. Rul. 93-73, 1993-2 C.B. 75:** The Church of Scientology qualified as a charitable organization, so that donations to it were deductible by donors. Church of Scientology members pay fixed fees for "auditing," a religious process of becoming aware of one's spirituality through individual training with church representatives. The IRS challenged the deductibility of such payments on the ground that they involved the receipt of a benefit.

    a. Issue: Are auditing fees paid to the Church of Scientology deductible?

    b. Result and rationale: The payments were not deductible because they constituted payment for services rendered rather than a donation.

        i. Majority opinion: The donors acknowledged that the payments were made for auditing but argued that the quid pro quo restriction should not apply to the receipt of a religious benefit. The Court found no such distinction in language of the statute or the development of the law in this area, and declined to advance it because of its implications for other types of purported donations.

        ii. Dissent: The dissent focused on the religious contribution exception, under which the IRS considers other types of payments for attendance at religious services (e.g., pew rents) as deductible contributions, rather than payments for services. According to the dissent, the majority's approach constituted discrimination against the Church of Scientology.

    c. Rev. Rul. 93-73: The IRS withdrew its prior ruling that payments for auditing by Church of Scientology members were nondeductible. It currently takes the position, contrary to *Hernandez,* that such payments are deductible.

C. Special rules and exceptions

    1. Amount: The amount of the contribution is the amount of money or the fair market value of the property contributed. Reg. §1.170A-1(c)(1). The taxpayer must substantiate the value of contributed property and special rules apply to noncash donations such as vehicles or artwork.

        a. Services: There is no deduction for services performed for a charitable organization. Reg. §1.170A-1(g).

        b. Expenses: Unreimbursed expenses incurred on behalf of the charitable organization (including mileage, etc.) are deductible. Reg. §1.170A-1(g). The mileage rate, however, is 14¢ per mile rather than the higher business mileage rate. This is a statutory number, not indexed for inflation.

        c. Blood: One cannot claim a deduction for the donation or sale of one's blood. *Lary v. United States,* 787 F.2d 1538 (11th Cir. 1986).

        d. Personal property: Taxpayers may claim a deduction for donations of personal property only if the items are in "good used condition or better." IRC §170(f)(16). A deduction for any item with a claimed value in excess of $5,000 must be supported by a qualified appraisal. IRC §170(f)(11)(C). Special rules apply to boats, airplanes, and vehicles.

    2. Limitation for individuals: The deduction for contributions by individuals is limited to a percentage of their contribution base.

        a. Public charities—50%: For organizations that qualify as public charities (generally schools, churches, governmental entities, and other publicly supported organizations), the limitation is 50% of the taxpayer's contribution base. IRC §170(b)(1)(A).

        b. Private charities—30%: For other organizations, the limitation is 30% of the taxpayer's contribution base. IRC §170(b)(1)(B).

    c. Definition—Contribution base: A taxpayer's contribution base is his or her AGI, computed disregarding the net operating loss deduction. IRC §170(b)(1)(F).

D. Related material

    1. Business expenses: For a discussion of the business expenses limitation for charitable contributions in excess of the AGI limitation, see Chapter 7(III)(E).

    2. Tax-exempt organizations: While §170 allows a deduction for contributions to certain charitable organizations, §501 addresses the tax status of these entities themselves. Section 501 describes a number of organizations that are exempt from federal income tax, of which the most familiar are §501(c)(3) organizations, which are religious, educational, or scientific entities.

E. Be alert for charitable contribution issues

Section 170 is implicated whenever a taxpayer donates property to some sort of charity. The principal issues are whether a donation has occurred, whether the recipient is a qualifying organization, and whether the limits on donations are exceeded.

X. MISCELLANEOUS EXPENSES—2% FLOOR

A number of expenses that comprise part of the itemized deduction are deductible only to the extent that, in the aggregate, they exceed 2% of the taxpayer's AGI. IRC §67(a). These expenses are commonly referred to as **miscellaneous expenses** and the limitation is commonly referred to as *"the 2% floor."* Of these, the most important are employees' unreimbursed business expenses and expenses incurred in the production of income for activities that are not trades or businesses.

A. Employee business expenses

    1. Employees have a "trade or business": Employees are engaged in the trade or business of performing services for their employers. Thus, the ordinary and necessary expenses they incur (and are not reimbursed for) are deductible, but not on a Schedule C. Instead, these expenses are part of a taxpayer's itemized deduction, and are subject to the 2% floor.

    Example: Jill is a salesperson for Howdoyoudo, Inc., a dating service. Her job involves a significant amount of travel and other expenses for which she is not reimbursed by her employer. In the year in question, Jill's AGI was $150,000, and her expenses incurred as a salesperson were $75,000. Because Jill is engaged in the business of providing services to her employer, she may deduct her employment-related expenses, but only to the extent that these expenses exceed 2% of her AGI. Two percent of her AGI is $3,000, and thus she may deduct $72,000 of her expenses as an itemized deduction (assuming she has no other miscellaneous expenses).

    2. Common nonreimbursed employee business expenses: Travel and entertainment; mileage; dues to professional associations; job search expenses in current occupation; home office deduction of an employee (see Chapter 8(VII)), malpractice insurance premiums; equipment used in the business (see §179 and discussion in Chapter 7(IV)(F)); clerical help; publications; and legal fees.

B. Investment expenses—§212

Section 212 allows a deduction for expenses associated with the production or collection of income, with the management or holding of property that produces income (but not in a trade or business), and with the collection or computation of tax. Commonly encountered expenses include:

- tax preparation or litigation fees; computer programs for tax preparation;

- safety deposit box fees;

- fees for investment advice;

- fees on brokerage accounts (but not commissions, which must be capitalized); tax advice; and

- attorneys' fees for nonbusiness lawsuits, unless covered under §62(a)(19), discussed in this chapter, Section (II)(G).

XI. PERSONAL EXEMPTION—§151

A. Policy

The federal income tax is not intended to be levied on taxpayers who are at the subsistence level. Thus, the deduction for the ***personal exemption*** ensures that this amount goes untaxed.

B. Basic amount

The personal exemption is intended to approximate subsistence living expenses. For certain categories of taxpayers, it is increased to reflect their increased expenses. For 2011, the personal exemption amount is $3,700.

C. Dependents—Definition

The taxpayer receives an additional exemption for each ***dependent.*** IRC §151(c)(1), (2). A dependent is either a ***qualifying child*** or a ***qualifying relative.*** IRC §152(a).

1. **Qualifying children:** These include the taxpayer's children and their descendants, stepchildren, or adopted children, but the child must be under age 19 (or if full-time students, age 24), who shares the taxpayer's principal abode for at least half the taxable year, and who does not provide more than half of their own support. IRC §152(c).

2. **Qualifying relatives:** These include most family members, including the taxpayer's spouse, children, and their descendants (other than qualifying children), parents, siblings, aunts/uncles, and nieces/nephews, as well as others. A qualifying relative's gross income must be below the exemption amount, and the taxpayer must provide more than half the support of that individual. IRC §152(d).

3. **Ineligible individuals:** To be claimed as a dependent, the person cannot be married, filing a joint return, and must not be a nonresident alien (unless domiciled in Mexico or Canada). If a person is claimed as a dependent on a taxpayer's return, that person is treated as having no dependents of his or her own. IRC §152(b).

4. Divorced parents: Generally, the custodial parent will claim the exemption, unless the parents otherwise agree that the noncustodial parent will claim the exemption, and certain conditions are met. IRC §152(e)(1).

XII. NEED TO KNOW MORE?

This book's website *www.aspenlawschool.com/books/tax_outline* contains additional information, including:

- Current amounts for the standard deduction and personal exemption.

- Current status for statutes scheduled for sunset in 2011 or 2012.

- The deduction for qualified tuition expenses, which is in effect until December 31, 2011.

- The overall limitation on itemized deductions and reduction in the personal exemption that are scheduled to reappear in the Code in 2013.

- Donations of IRAs to charity.

- And other materials that will help you master personal deductions.

XIII. WHERE ARE WE GOING?

This chapter has addressed personal deductions available to individuals. We next turn to the deductibility of business-related expenses, for both individuals and entities engaged in business activity.

Quiz Yourself on
PERSONAL DEDUCTIONS

52. Under the terms of their divorce decree, Tom will pay Nicole $10,000 per month as alimony that qualifies under the federal definition, and $1,200 per month as child support. Assume that the alimony meets the federal definition of alimony. May Tom deduct these payments?

_____

53. Dorothy has AGI (without considering the following described events) of $200,000 for last year. During the year, her home in Kansas was destroyed by a tornado. The basis of the home was $250,000 and its fair market value was $500,000. Dorothy had no insurance on the home. What are the tax consequences of this event to Dorothy? _____

54. Assume the same facts as in the previous question, except that Dorothy also received $100,000 from an insurance company attributable to the theft of a very valuable pair of shoes. She had a basis of $20,000 in the shoes. What are the tax consequences to Dorothy, considering *both* events?

_____

55. Avid whale watcher Molly decides to move to Seattle. She purchases a new principal residence on the ocean there for $1.5 million. She takes out a mortgage of $1.2 million from Friendly Bank, and pays for the balance in cash. She owns no other properties. May she deduct the interest on the debt? _____

56. Sam owns a parcel of property on which he has built a new home. During construction, he lived in a dilapidated home on the property. Under applicable land use regulations, only one home suitable for occupancy may exist on this parcel. Now that the new home is ready for its occupancy permit, Sam wants to donate the older home to the local fire department (a governmental unit) for a training exercise in which the old home will be burned to the ground. By removing the old residence, the burning exercise will allow him to move into the new home. He intends to claim a deduction equal to the fair market value of the older home. May he do so? _____

57. Of the following, which is not deductible for federal income tax purposes?

(a) Federal income taxes

(b) State income taxes

(c) State property taxes

(d) State sales and use taxes

(e) None of the above is deductible.

58. Pete's hobby is auto racing. This year, he was in a car wreck and incurred $100,000 in medical expenses. His medical insurance company reimbursed $75,000 of these expenses this year, and he paid for the balance with a $10,000 distribution from a qualifying HSA and the rest with savings. His AGI is $250,000. May Pete deduct any of these medical expenses? _____

59. Tom is an outside sales representative for Oldies but Goodies, Inc. ("OBG"). Under the terms of his their agreement, OBG will reimburse Ton for up to $2,500 of travel expenses associated with his sales activities. This year, Tom incurred $30,000 of such expenses, of which $2,500 were reimbursed by OBG. He also had $500 in other qualifying miscellaneous expenses. His AGI is $140,000. How should Tom treat these expenses? _____

60. Janet, a single taxpayer, has a complicated household. The following people live with her. Assume that none of these individuals plan to claim an exemption for themselves on their own tax return. For whom may she claim a personal exemption on her income tax return? _____

Her daughter, age 16;

Her son, age 23, a full-time college student who lives at college 9 months of the year;

Her stepdaughter from a prior marriage, age 18;

Her mother, age 86, who has Social Security benefits of $1,000 per month;

Her brother, who is currently unemployed;

A foster child, age 12;

Her single niece, age 30, who is visiting the United States for an extended period from her home in Mexico; and

An unrelated boarder, who pays Janet $500 per month for room and board.

61. The parents of a dyslexic child send him to a boarding school where part of the program of the school is devoted to overcoming reading disabilities. May the parents deduct the tuition, room, and board they pay to the school as a medical expense? _____

62. Catherine is employed as a nurse by DocInaBox, Inc., an outpatient clinic. DocInaBox maintains a qualified retirement plan in which Catherine participates. Catherine would like to establish an IRA. May she do so, and if so, how much can she contribute? _____

63. Assume that in the next year, Catherine could not make a deductible contribution to a regular IRA, and that she is not able to qualify for a Roth IRA. Why might she still want to make a contribution to a regular IRA, even though the contribution is not deductible? _____

64. Donald tells Maurice, *"You're fired!"* Maurice then incurs the following expenses: $10,000 in attorneys' fees in an unsuccessful attempt to sue his employer for breach of contract; $1,500 in job search expenses to obtain a similar position; $500 to a moving company to move his things out of his office at Donald's building; and $5,000 in psychological counseling to help him recover from this harrowing experience. Of these, which are deductible—and in what manner? What if Maurice says "I've had it with this business! I'm only going to take a job in a completely different profession . . ."? _____

Answers

52. Section 215 allows Tom a deduction for alimony paid during the taxable year; this is a deduction from gross income in computing AGI. The child support is not deductible.

53. Dorothy's loss on her home is a personal casualty loss, in the amount of $250,000 (the lower of basis or value). Personal casualty losses are deductible, subject to two limitations. First, in computing the deduction, each loss is reduced by $100. Second, personal casualty losses are deductible only to the extent they exceed 10% of AGI. Dorothy's AGI is $200,000, so the personal casualty loss of $249,900 is deductible to the extent it exceeds $20,000. Thus, her personal casualty loss is $229,900. This is a deduction on Dorothy's itemized return, i.e., available to her only if she itemizes, and therefore as a deduction from AGI in computing taxable income.

54. The theft of the shoes and receipt of the insurance proceeds is a constructive sale of that item, so Dorothy realizes $80,000 of gain on that transaction. This is a personal casualty gain. Personal casualty gains offset personal casualty losses, so that the net result is the net personal casualty gain (income) or net personal casualty loss (deduction). The net loss is $249,900 minus $80,000, or $169,900. To the extent this exceeds $20,000 (10% of Dorothy's AGI) it is deductible. Thus, $149,900 is deductible on Dorothy's itemized return, i.e., available to her only if she itemizes, and therefore as a deduction from AGI in computing taxable income.

55. Assuming that the property secures the debt, the interest on the acquisition indebtedness, up to $1,000,000 of debt, is deductible. Molly also may deduct the interest on an additional amount of debt ($100,000) as home equity indebtedness. The remaining interest will be nondeductible.

56. Sam is attempting to take a charitable deduction under §170 of the Code. Normally, a deduction for the fair market value of the property would be available to him (and it would be his burden to prove the value by appraisal). However, in this case, Sam appears to be receiving something of value. Without the burn, he would be in violation of the land use laws, and would have to remove the older

home in some way to make way for the new home. By donating the home, he avoids this cost and places his property in compliance with local law. Although this is a close case, Sam probably is not entitled to a deduction for this donation. However, if Sam could show that the costs of removal were nominal, he may be able to claim a deduction for the property donation.

57. The answer is (a)—federal income taxes. State income and property taxes are deductible, and a taxpayer may, until 2012, choose to deduct sales taxes in lieu of income taxes.

58. The amount Pete received as reimbursement for medical expenses is not included in his gross income (see Chapter 3). The $10,000 distribution from the HSA is not includable in his gross income. The remaining $15,000 is deductible as an itemized deduction as medical expenses to the extent it exceeds 7.5% of his AGI. This limit—7.5% of AGI—is $18,750, and because his remaining expenses are less than that amount, Pete may not deduct any amount as medical expenses as an itemized deduction.

59. The amounts Tom received as reimbursements of travel expenses are not included in his gross income. The excess amount ($27,500) is potentially deductible on his return. However, unreimbursed employee business expenses are deductible by the taxpayer only to the extent that they—along with all other expenses in this category of miscellaneous expenses—exceed 2% of the taxpayer's AGI. This amount is $2,800 ($140,000 × 2%). Thus, combining the $500 of miscellaneous expenses and $27,500 of unreimbursed expenses produces $28,000 of expenses. These are deductible only to the extent that they exceed $2,800. Therefore, $25,200 of these expenses is deductible. This is a deduction on Tom's itemized return, i.e., available to him only if he itemizes, and therefore as a deduction from AGI in computing taxable income. (These deductions might be limited in computing Tom's AMT; see Chapter 13.)

60. In order to claim a personal exemption for any of these people, they must qualify as Janet's "dependent," which requires that they either be a "qualifying child" or a "qualifying relative."

Janet may claim an exemption for her daughter as a "qualifying child," assuming that the daughter lives with Janet for at least half the year and doesn't provide over half of her own support. The stepdaughter will likely not qualify, because Janet no longer is married to the stepdaughter's father. None of the others qualify as a "qualifying child" because of the residence test (the son) and the relationships test (everyone else).

The foster child and the boarder are not "qualifying relatives" because of the lack of formal family relationship to Janet. However, her son, brother, mother, and even her niece may qualify, assuming that their gross incomes are less than the exemption amount ($3,700 each in 2011) and that Janet provides over half of their support. Although it would appear that Janet's mother's income is greater than the exemption amount, only a certain amount of her Social Security benefits will be included in gross income, and it is not clear how much that would be; further investigation is necessary. Even though Janet's niece may be a nonresident alien, she is domiciled in Mexico, and therefore she could be a qualifying relative.

61. Usually, the cost of tuition, room, and board would be a nondeductible personal expense, even if part of the program is involved in treating a medical disorder. This is because the taxpayer is purchasing education, not medical care. See *Barnes v. Commissioner,* TC Memo 1978-339. If, however, the taxpayer can show that a portion of the fees paid are directly connected to remediation of the child's condition, and would not be paid but for that condition, this portion would qualify as a medical expense.

62. Catherine may establish either a Roth IRA or a regular IRA. She may contribute an amount to it that is established by Congress and the IRS each year (for example, in 2011 she may contribute up to

$5,000 to it, unless she is age 50 or older, in which case her contribution could increase to $6,000). If Catherine establishes a regular IRA, she may be able to deduct contributions to it. However, because she participates in her employer's qualified retirement plan, if her AGI exceeds a certain threshold, her deduction will be reduced or eliminated. Most taxpayers seem to prefer to establish and contribute to a Roth IRA, because even though there is no current deduction, distributions from the Roth IRA are not includible in the taxpayer's gross income.

63. If Catherine contributes to a regular IRA, the contribution will grow tax-free until it is distributed to her after retirement. Distributions from the regular IRA will be included in her gross income, but she may believe that the combination of tax-free growth in the IRA and her anticipated lower tax rate in retirement still makes the regular IRA a good deal.

64. Maurice may deduct (but only if he "itemizes"—i.e., claims the itemized deduction) the following: $10,000 of legal fees, $1,500 in job search expenses, and probably the $500 in moving costs to remove his items from Donald's office. All of these will be miscellaneous itemized deductions subject to the 2% floor. The $5,000 in counseling will be a medical expense, which will be deductible as an itemized deduction to the extent it exceeds 7.5% of Maurice's AGI. Maurice's job search expenses will be deductible only if he is looking for a position in his current occupation. Expenses for looking for a position "in a completely different profession" will be capital in nature and nondeductible.

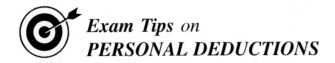

Exam Tips on PERSONAL DEDUCTIONS

☛ Questions involving personal deductions deal with expenditures associated with a taxpayer's personal life. Address these separately from business deductions.

  ☞ *Look for:* Outlays by taxpayers for charity, health, etc.

  ☞ *Analyze:* Deduction by deduction—is this a deductible expense, and if so, how much is deductible?

☛ Know which deductions belong where: "above-the-line" or "below-the-line," i.e., deductible from gross income in computing AGI (above-the-line) or deductible from AGI in computing taxable income (below-the-line). Section 62 is somewhat deceptive, as it includes a number of items deductible above-the-line that are no longer available at all, such as the Section 179A deduction for clean fuel vehicles.

☛ Most taxpayers described on law exams are "itemizers," i.e., they do not take the standard deduction, but instead take the deductions listed on Schedule A as itemized deductions.

☛ Many deductions have specific limitations tied to AGI.

  ☞ *Look for:* Charitable donations, medical expenses, casualty losses, educational loans, miscellaneous expenses, retirement savings.

☞ *Analyze:* Determine if the outlay is deductible at all; if it is, apply the limitations to determine the deductible percentage.

☞ *Don't* allow a taxpayer to claim *both* the standard and itemized deduction.

☞ Personal deductions are usually deductible in the year the outlay is made, if at all, not later. Timing issues are usually not a large feature of these questions. Nevertheless, as a precaution, think about *when* an amount is deductible.

☞ Given recent events, a professor may be interested in testing your knowledge of the tax policy implications of major tax expenditures, particularly the deduction for home mortgage interest. Be ready to discuss the rationales for the deduction for home acquisition indebtedness, home equity indebtedness, and for mortgage insurance premiums and how they may have contributed to recent economic woes, particularly the foreclosure crisis.

☞ *Remember:* Construe deduction statutes narrowly. If in doubt, deny the deduction.

 STATUTE SUMMARY CHARTS

Statute Summary—§163(h)
Qualified Residence Interest

Parsing Step	IRC §163(h)
General Rule	Taxpayers may deduct qualified residence interest as itemized deduction.
Definitions	**Qualified residence:** can include nontraditional residences **Acquisition indebtedness:** limit is $1,000,000 **Home equity indebtedness:** limit is $100,000
Special Rules and Exceptions	Refinancing of acquisition indebtedness Construction loans
Related Statutes	**§121:** Exclusion of gain on sale of principal residence **§165(c):** Denial of loss on sale of principal residence **§1001:** Computation of gain or loss on sale
Typically implicated when . . .	A taxpayer purchases a principal residence using debt to finance the purchase, or refinances an existing debt.

Statute Summary—§165(h)
Personal Casualty Losses

Parsing Step	IRC §165(h)
General Rule	Taxpayers may deduct net casualty losses incurred during the taxable year as an itemized deduction.
Definitions	**Casualty loss:** earthquake, storm, fire, etc. **Net casualty loss:** equal to casualty gains—casualty losses
Special Rules and Exceptions	Net casualty losses are deductible only to extent they exceed: (1) $100 per loss (2) 10% of AGI in the aggregate
Related Statutes	**§61:** Casualty gains are included in gross income **§1033:** Involuntary conversions
Typically implicated when . . .	A taxpayer is involved in natural disasters such as hurricanes or earthquakes and experiences losses of nonbusiness property.

CHAPTER 7

BUSINESS AND INVESTMENT DEDUCTIONS

ChapterScope ───────────────────────────

Gross income includes net income from business and other profit-seeking activities that do not rise to the level of a trade or business. But the federal income tax is not a tax on gross income, and so to compute net income or loss, it is necessary to subtract from this income the various deductions associated with these activities. This chapter explores these deductions in detail.

- **Trade or business expenses:** Section 162 generally allows a taxpayer to deduct all of the ordinary and necessary expenses of carrying on a trade or business, but imposes restrictions on certain types of expenses.

- **Certain other business deductions:** Specific Code sections allow deduction of certain other business expenses, such as interest, taxes, and bad debts.

- **Deductions attributable to investment activities:** Some activities may not rise to the level of a trade or business, but nevertheless be entered into for profit. Certain deductions are allowable for these activities.

- **Capital expenditures:** Section 263 prohibits any deduction for capital expenditures. Instead, a capital expenditure is "capitalized," i.e., the amount expended becomes part of the basis of the property.

- **Capital recovery:** A taxpayer is entitled to recover his or her investment in property, i.e., to be taxed only (for federal income tax purposes) on the income from that property, not the invested capital in the property. The timing of capital recovery, however, is a matter for Congressional discretion and our tax system uses a number of different timing methods for capital recovery, including MACRS, section 179 expense deduction, amortization of intangibles, and deductions for pre-opening expenses.

- **Deductions attributable to nonbusiness, for-profit activities:** Some activities may not rise to the level of a trade or business, but nevertheless are entered into for profit. Certain deductions are allowable for these activities.

I. WHERE ARE WE?

The income and deductions associated with each of a taxpayer's profit-seeking activities will be separately computed (on Schedule C for business and on Schedule E for rents and royalties) and the net result—whether net income or net loss—is reported on the Form 1040. See Figure 1A, Lines 12 and 17. To compute net income or loss, understanding business and investment deductions is critical, and this chapter analyzes these kinds of deductions.

II. TRADE OR BUSINESS EXPENSES—§162

A. General rule

Section 162 allows a deduction for all the ordinary and necessary expenses paid or incurred in carrying on a *trade or business.*

B. Definitional issues

1. **Trade or business:** The principal function of the trade or business requirement is to distinguish the expenses of a taxpayer's business activities from other activities—principally personal activities.

    a. **Judicial interpretation:** Neither the Code nor the regulations define a trade or business. To be engaged in a trade or business, a taxpayer must be involved in an activity with continuity and regularity and must have the primary purpose of creating income or profit rather than merely engaging in a hobby. See *Commissioner v. Groetzinger*, 480 U.S. 23 (1987). An investor in stocks and securities is not carrying on a trade or business, regardless of the frequency or size of transactions. See *Higgins v. Commissioner*, 312 U.S. 212 (1941).

    b. **Profit motive:** A trade or business requires a *profit motive*. The absence of profit motive indicates a personal activity. See IRC §183, and discussion in Chapter 8(IX).

    c. **Trade or business of being an employee:** An employee is in the trade or business of providing services to his or her employer. The unreimbursed expenses of providing these services are deductible (on Schedule A), but are subject to the so-called 2% floor of §67(a), which allows a deduction for such expenses only to the extent they exceed, in the aggregate, 2% of the taxpayer's adjusted gross income. This results in most expenses of the ordinary taxpayer not being deductible.

        Example: Evan is employed by the United Way, and his adjusted gross income is $50,000. This year, he incurred the following unreimbursed expenses associated with his employment: (1) travel and conference costs: $950; (2) professional publications: $250; and (3) supplies: $150. These are his only miscellaneous deductible expenses. Evan may deduct these expenses, if he itemizes, only to the extent that these expenses exceed, in the aggregate, 2% of his adjusted gross income ($1,000). Therefore, of the total $1,350 of expenses, he may claim a deduction for only $350. (If Evan is subject to the alternative minimum tax, all of these expenses may be nondeductible; see Chapter 13 (III)(B).)

2. **"Carrying on" a trade or business:** This requirement exists to prevent the deduction of expenses prior to the time the taxpayer commences a trade or business.

    a. **Going concern:** A taxpayer is carrying on a trade or business from the date that it is a *going concern*. This requires regular activity in the pursuits for which the business was organized. *Richmond Television Corp. v. United States*, 345 F.2d 901 (4th Cir. 1965). Expenses incurred prior to that date are nondeductible capital expenditures. See *Morton Frank v. Commissioner*, 20 T.C. 511 (1953).

        Example: Carla is opening a coffee bar. She rents space, hires a contractor to remodel it, hires staff, and purchases inventory. Until she is ready to sell coffee to customers, however, Carla's coffee bar is not a going concern, and Carla may not deduct expenses incurred under §162.

b. Pre-opening expenses: Section 195 provides for the amortization of certain pre-opening expenses. See this chapter, Section (IV)(I).

3. **Ordinary:** Ordinary means usual in the course of general and accepted business practice, arising from a transaction commonly or frequently encountered in the type of business involved. *Deputy v. DuPont*, 308 U.S. 488, 494–497 (1940).

    a. Common situation—Reasonable compensation: A closely held corporation may attempt to pay shareholder/employees unreasonably high salaries instead of reasonable salaries plus dividends because the corporation can potentially deduct salary, but not dividends. The IRS and courts review the allocation, and may recast a portion of the unreasonable salary as a dividend. They often base a reallocation on the "ordinary" requirement of section 162. See *Harold's Club v. Commissioner*, 340 F.2d 861 (9th Cir. 1965); *Exacto Spring Corp. v. Commissioner*, 196 F.2d 833 (7th Cir. 1999).

    b. Connection with business activity: In *Gilliam v. Commissioner*, 51 T.C.M. 567 (1986-90), Mr. Gilliam was a noted artist with a history of mental disturbance. Anticipating an anxiety attack prior to an airplane trip undertaken for professional purposes, Mr. Gilliam obtained a prescription for a new medication. During the airplane trip he became agitated and attacked another passenger—likely a side effect of the medication. He was arrested and paid legal fees to defend both criminal and civil actions and also paid an amount in settlement of the civil suit.

        i. Issue: May Mr. Gilliam deduct the amounts he paid in connection with the criminal and civil suits?

        ii. Result and rationale: The amounts paid are not ordinary expenses of business and therefore are not deductible. Although Mr. Gilliam was traveling on business during which ordinary expenses might be incurred, these particular expenses did not arise from the business but from his personal medical condition.

4. **Necessary:** The function of the *necessary* requirement is to ensure the requisite connection between the expense and furtherance of the business. "Necessary" means "appropriate and helpful" to the business activity. *Commissioner v. Heininger*, 320 U.S. 467, 471 (1943). Courts are reluctant to substitute their business judgment for that of business people and will disallow an expense as unnecessary only in extreme cases. Moreover, the inherently factual nature of the inquiry makes reversal on appeal highly unusual. This requirement is often used to distinguish between personal and business activity.

5. **Expense:** The *expense* requirement seeks to distinguish between expenses and *capital expenditures*. Only expenditures for expenses are deductible; amounts paid as capital expenditures are not. Instead, amounts that constitute capital expenditures are "capitalized," i.e., they become part of the basis of an item and are potentially subject to capital recovery. See discussion in this chapter, Section (IV).

C. Special rules and exceptions

1. **Traveling expenses:** A taxpayer may deduct the cost of travel for business purposes, including the taxpayer's reasonable expenses of traveling while away from home on business.

a. Standard mileage rate or actual expenses: A taxpayer may deduct the actual expenses of travel. For automobile expenses, however, most taxpayers prefer to simply deduct an amount equal to the number of miles traveled for business purposes, multiplied by the standard mileage rate (51¢ in 2011).

b. Business travel away from home: Commuting expenses are not deductible, and whether a taxpayer is "away from home" on business is a perpetual argument between taxpayers and the IRS. See Chapter 8(III).

2. Health insurance premiums: Section 162(l) allows a self-employed taxpayer to claim a deduction for health insurance for the taxpayer and his or her spouse and children as a trade or business expense.

3. Public policy: Expenses that otherwise meet the requirements of §162, but the payment of which violate ***public policy***, may be nondeductible. The prohibition may arise from the judicial doctrine disallowing expenses that violate public policy, or may arise from a specific statutory prohibition within §162 or other Code sections.

a. *Commissioner v. Heininger*, 360 U.S. 467 (1943):

i. Facts: The federal government successfully prosecuted the taxpayer for using misleading mail order advertising. The taxpayer deducted the legal fees he incurred to defend his business practices. The IRS determined that the expenses were not "ordinary and necessary" because conducting business using illegal methods cannot be considered "ordinary." The BTA ruled that, as a matter of law, the legal fees were not deductible because they were incurred in connection with illegal acts of the taxpayer.

ii. Issue: Does any connection to a taxpayer's illegal activity render expenses non-deductible?

iii. Result and rationale: Reversed. Defending a business against charges of violations of regulatory schemes is the usual and expected course of action and therefore these expenses were ordinary and necessary. While some expenditures may have too close a connection with illegal activity to be deductible, each expenditure must be examined within its context to determine deductibility.

b. Bribes and kickbacks: No deduction is allowed for illegal payments to any governmental employee (domestic or foreign) or illegal bribes or kickbacks to other persons. IRC §162(c).

c. Fines: No deduction is allowed for any fine or similar penalty paid to a government. IRC §162(f).

Example: CCC Trading Co. is indicted on charges relating to insider trading. As part of the settlement of the matter, CCC is required to pay a $200,000 fine. CCC will not be allowed to deduct the payment of the fine as an ordinary and necessary business expense.

d. Treble damages: There is no deduction for the two-thirds portion of antitrust damages attributable to punitive damages. IRC §162(g)(1),(2).

e. Drug trafficking: No deduction is allowed for the expenses incurred in illegal drug trafficking. IRC §280E.

D. Related material

1. **Mixed personal and business expenses:** Some activities may have a connection to both aspects of a taxpayer's life—business and personal. See generally Chapter 8.

2. **When is an expense deductible?** The year in which a taxpayer may claim a deduction depends on the taxpayer's method of accounting. See generally Chapter 11.

3. **Tax credits:** Some expenditures generate tax credits instead of deductions, or a taxpayer may have a choice to claim a deduction or a credit—but not both. See generally Chapter 13.

E. Be alert for business deduction issues

Section 162 is a frequently tested Code section on basic income tax exams. The principal issues focus on the specific requirements of §162. Be especially careful to distinguish between capital expenditures and business expenses.

III. OTHER DEDUCTIONS

A number of specific Code sections allow a taxpayer to deduct particular expenses of carrying on a trade or business. When these expenses are "attributable to a trade or business carried on by the taxpayer," they are subtracted from gross income on Schedule C because they are part of the computation of net business income or loss. See IRC §62(a)(1).

A. Interest

Section 163(a) allows a taxpayer to deduct "all interest paid or incurred within the taxable year on indebtedness." While §163(h)(1) disallows any deduction for personal interest, the definition of personal interest specifically excludes interest attributable to carrying on a trade or business. IRC §163(h)(2)(A). Thus, business interest remains fully deductible.

B. Taxes

Section 164(a) allows a taxpayer a deduction for certain taxes paid or accrued during the taxable year regardless of whether the taxpayer is carrying on a trade or business. For a discussion of nonbusiness taxes as part of the itemized deduction, see Chapter 6(IV).

1. **Deductible taxes:** Deductible taxes include state, local, and foreign real property and income taxes, and state and local personal property taxes. IRC §164(a).

2. **Foreign tax credit:** Instead of deducting foreign taxes paid, a taxpayer may choose to claim a tax credit for certain eligible foreign taxes paid or accrued. IRC §901(a).

C. Losses

Section165(c)(1) allows a deduction for losses incurred in a trade or business. Thus, trade or business losses are fully deductible for individuals conducting a trade or business. Losses can include a net loss from business operations, casualty losses, or theft losses. However, if the taxpayer is not economically at risk for the activity or does not materially participate in it, the loss may be limited by the at-risk rules or the passive activity rules. See Chapter 11(VII).

D. Business bad debts

1. **General rule:** Section 166(a) allows a deduction for the portion of any debt that becomes *worthless* during the taxable year in the amount of the adjusted basis of the debt to the taxpayer. IRC §166(a), (b).

2. **Definitional issues**

   a. **Debt:** Section 166 governs debts that are not securities. These include promissory notes, open account loans, and other informal loans. IRC §166(e).

   b. **Bad debt:** A bad debt is one that is wholly or partially worthless, meaning that the reasonable investor would not view the debt as having any value at all.

   c. **Business versus nonbusiness bad debts:** A *business bad debt* generates a deduction for the taxpayer in computing net income or loss from business. A nonbusiness bad debt is treated as a loss from the sale or exchange of a capital asset, generating a capital loss. See generally Chapter 12.

      i. **Business bad debt:** To qualify as a business bad debt, a debt must be incurred in a trade or business and must become worthless in the course of that trade or business. Reg. §1.166-5(d).

      ii. **Nonbusiness bad debt:** A *nonbusiness bad debt* lacks the requisite connection to the taxpayer's trade or business. IRC §§166(d)(2)(A), (B). This arises in two principal contexts, shareholder loans and employee loans to companies. With respect to shareholder loans, it is clear that the ownership of stock is not a trade or business, so loans made to corporations from stockholders are usually nonbusiness debts because they are not connected with a trade or business. *United States v. Generes*, 405 U.S. 93 (1972). With respect to employee loans, an employee is engaged in the trade or business of performing services for his employer. Therefore, if an employee makes a loan to the employer, and the dominant motivation for making the loan is to protect the employment relationship, the debt should be a business debt. The determination of the dominant motive will be based on all the facts of the situation. See, e.g., *Trent v. Commissioner*, 291 F.2d 669 (2d Cir. 1961).

      Example—Business bad debt: Dale is in the business of making short-term loans to students. In connection with this business, he lends Alicia $2,500. She fails to repay it on time and moves to India. Concluding that the loan is uncollectible, Dale claims a business bad debt deduction of $2,500, his basis in the loan.

E. Charitable contributions

A taxpayer engaged in a trade or business may claim a deduction for charitable contributions to qualifying organizations, subject to the limitations applicable to individuals and corporations. For a discussion of the charitable contribution deduction as part of the itemized deduction, see discussion in Chapter 6(IX).

IV. DEDUCTIONS FOR CAPITAL RECOVERY

A. Capital recovery—in general

Section 263 disallows any deduction for *capital expenditures*, generally defined as "permanent improvements or betterments made to increase the value of any property or estate." Thus, if an expenditure constitutes a capital expenditure, the amount expended is capitalized and is added to (or constitutes) the *basis* of the asset. The taxpayer may *recover* this capital investment at some time during ownership of the asset. This recovery takes the form of a deduction available during ownership, commonly known as *depreciation* or *amortization*. If no such deduction is available, upon disposition of the asset, the taxpayer can take the basis into account in determining gain or loss on sale. See generally Chapter 9.

B. Matching principle

Appropriate capital recovery is said to *match* income and the expenses incurred to produce that income. See generally Chapter 11. For example, if a taxpayer purchases an apartment building to be rented to students, the taxpayer will earn rental income each year for a number of years. In theory, the property will be "used up" over those years, and so deducting a portion of the purchase price as a deduction each year will best reflect the taxpayer's true net income. However, the idea of a property being used up or exhausted on some specific schedule is a fantasy. In fact, a property may rise in value over the period (some real estate, for example) or may fall in value much more quickly than its so-called recovery period (some computer equipment, for example).

C. Depreciable assets

Not all assets are subject to depreciation or amortization. Only tangible assets, used in a trade or business, that are subject to exhaustion, wear and tear, or obsolescence are eligible for depreciation. IRC §§167(a); 168(a). Examples include buildings, equipment, and certain intangible assets such as goodwill. Fine art and collectibles, for example, may not be depreciable. But see *Simon v. Commissioner*, 68 F.3d 41 (2nd Cir. 1995) (antique violin bows depreciable because subject to wear and tear). Raw land certainly isn't depreciable.

D. Definition—Capital expenditure

There is no precise definition of a capital expenditure.

1. **Acquiring assets:** The regulations offer examples of capital expenditures as including the costs of assets such as buildings, machinery and equipment, furniture and fixtures, and "similar property having a useful life substantially beyond the taxable year." Reg. §1.263-2(a). Costs incurred in acquiring or disposing of assets are capital expenditures. The purchase price of an asset is obviously included in this category, along with other expenses of acquiring the property. While it is easy to identify these assets, other assets are trickier. For example, when an existing business expands into new ventures, it is not entirely obvious what parts, if any, of the new business constitute capital expenditures.

   a. **Separate asset test—*Commissioner v. Lincoln Savings & Loan Assn.*, 403 U.S. 345 (1971):** The Supreme Court held that when a *separate and distinct asset* is created, the amounts expended in doing so are capital expenditures.

   b. **Exploring a new venture:** Expenses of researching, investigating, and considering acquiring a new venture are capital expenditures.

c. **Which expenses must be capitalized?** A company producing long-lived assets for sale (inventory) can choose to either buy them or make them. If it purchases them, the costs of the purchases are capital expenditures. See *Encyclopaedia Britannica, Inc. v. Commissioner*, 685 F.2d 212 (7th Cir. 1982). Companies that produce assets themselves should be treated similarly under principles of horizontal equity. They are, under §263A (known as the uniform capitalization, or "UNICAP," rules), which require that the cost of salaries, wages, and administrative expenses be capitalized into the cost of inventory.

Example: M Co. manufactures e-readers. M Co. must include in the capitalized cost of each e-reader not only the cost of raw materials ($30) but also an allocable portion of the total cost of workers and administration ($50). When a reader is sold for $150, M Co. will report $70 of profit.

2. **Future benefits test—*Indopco, Inc. v. Commissioner*, 503 U.S. 79 (1992):** Unilever sought to acquire National Starch (later renamed Indopco) in a friendly takeover. National Starch incurred a variety of expenses in connection with the transaction, including $2.2 million in investment banker's fees and about $500,000 in legal fees.

   a. **Issue:** Were the costs associated with the acquisition capital expenditures or deductible expenses?

   b. **Result and rationale:** These amounts were capital expenditures. The creation of a separate asset (see *Lincoln Savings*) is a sufficient, but not necessary, element to test whether expenditures are capital. If an expenditure creates a more-than-insignificant future benefit to the taxpayer, the expenditure is a capital asset, even if no separate asset is created. In this case, the benefits motivating the acquisition were to last for many years. Hence, the expenditures produced a significant future benefit and were capital expenditures.

   c. **IRS takes a sparing approach to *Indopco:*** *Indopco* theoretically requires the capitalization of many common expenditures, but in rulings and regulations the IRS has limited its application, allowing the deduction of advertising, severance pay, and employee training costs. See, e.g., Rev. Rul. 92-80, 1992-2 C.B. 57; Treas. Reg. §1.263(a)-4, -5.

3. **Deductible repairs:** Whether a particular expenditure is a *repair* of an item (deductible), or constitutes the creation of a new capital asset (which must be capitalized), produces ongoing controversy between taxpayers and the IRS.

   a. **Regulations' standard:** The regulations provide that the "cost of incidental repairs which neither materially add to the value of the property nor appreciably prolong its life" is deductible as a repair. Treas. Reg. §1.162-4. See, e.g., Rev. Rul. 2001-4, 2001-1 C.B. 295, in which expenditures of conducting federally required periodic heavy maintenance inspections of aircraft (along with the repairs required as a result of the inspection) were considered repairs, as they did not significantly extend the useful life of the aircraft.

   b. **Before-and-after test:** In *Plainfield-Union Water Co. v. Commissioner*, 39 T.C. 333 (1962) nonacq. on other grounds, 1964-2 C.B. 8, the Tax Court articulated the approach of comparing the value, use, life expectancy, strength, or capacity of the property before and after the condition that required the making of the expenditure. If the expenditure did not improve these aspects of the property, it would constitute a repair, not a capital expenditure.

c. Application:

i. Repair necessary for ongoing operations: In *Midland Empire Packing Co. v. Commissioner*, 14 T.C. 635 (1950), acq. 1950-2 C.B. 3, a company added a concrete lining to its basement to prevent oil seepage, which was required to continue business and did not prolong the useful life of the building. Held: repair, not capital expenditure.

ii. Environmental remediation: Environmental remediation expenses are generally deductible. However, these expenditures must be capitalized if they create a separate facility (Rev. Rul. 94-38, 1994-1 C.B. 35), are incurred as part of an overall project that improves a facility (*Norwest Corp. and Subsidiaries v. Commissioner*, 108 T.C. 265 (1997)), or are incurred by a company that is subject to the UNICAP rules

Example: Assume M Co. (see example above) makes 50,000 e-readers in a year in which it spends $1,000,000 to clean up hazardous waste at its manufacturing facility. It must add $20 to the inventory cost of each e-reader manufactured in that year. This reduces the profit on the sale of each reader.

iii. Repairing damage to reputation—*Welch v. Helvering*, 290 U.S. 111 (1933): A taxpayer had been an executive in a bankrupt company. When he became a commission agent in the same line of business, he voluntarily paid some of the company's unpaid debts and deducted them as §162 expenses in order to restore his reputation. The Court held that these were nondeductible as ordinary expenses, and properly capitalized as expenditures to restore reputation. Cf. *Jenkins v. Commissioner*, TC Memo 1983-667, in which the Tax Court allowed country singer Conway Twitty to deduct payments he made to disgruntled investors in the failed "Twitty Burger" restaurant venture to protect his reputation as a country singer. Results in this area are fact-specific, and may turn on whether a reputation is destroyed (*Welch*) or only damaged and in need of repair (*Jenkins*).

4. Education for new trade or business: Education undertaken to improve skills in a current job are potentially deductible. *Coughlin v. Commissioner*, 203 F.2d 307 (2d Cir. 1953). However, education that qualifies a taxpayer for a new job or profession is a nondeductible capital expenditure. See Treas. Reg. §1.162-5. See Chapter 8(V).

E. Capital recovery

Unlike an ordinary business expense, a capital expenditure does not generate a deduction for the taxpayer in the year the expenditure is made. But a taxpayer will almost always be allowed at some point in time to "recover" the capital invested in the asset. This means that the taxpayer will be able to offset income by deducting a portion of the capital invested in the asset, either during ownership of the asset or upon disposition. Depreciation deductions, for example, allow a taxpayer to deduct a portion of the cost of an asset each year for a specified period; this deduction constitutes capital recovery.

1. Constitutional issue? The taxpayer has a constitutional right to capital recovery because the federal income tax is a tax on income—not capital. *Eisner v. Macomber*, 252 U.S. 189 (1920). The courts usually accept this principle without much discussion, proceeding on to the question of timing of capital recovery.

2. Timing—Congress's discretion: When a taxpayer will be allowed to recover his or her invested capital is a matter for Congress's discretion. See, e.g., *Burnet v. Sanford & Brooks Co.*,

282 U.S. 359 (1931). Taxpayers want to recover their invested capital as early as possible. See generally Chapter 15. There are three options for capital recovery, all of which are used in the Code for different types of assets.

   a. Capital recovery first: A taxpayer may be allowed to recover his or her capital investment before reporting any income from the asset. An example of this approach is contained in §179, discussed this chapter, Section (IV)(F).

   b. Capital recovery during ownership: A taxpayer may be allowed to recover his or her capital investment on some schedule, apportioning the recovery over his or her ownership of the asset. This is the approach used to recover investment in tangible property (known generally as *depreciation*) or intangible property (known generally as *amortization*).

   c. Capital recovery last: A taxpayer may be required to defer capital recovery until the end of his or her ownership of the asset. This is the system used for nondepreciable property such as raw land.

3. **Relationship of capital recovery to basis:** The basis of a purchased asset is its cost. When a taxpayer claims capital recovery deductions, the basis of the asset is reduced by the amount of the capital recovery claimed. See Chapter 9(V)(C).

   Example: Spencer purchases a residential rental property for $275,000 on January 1, 2011. The property will be depreciated over 27.5 years. Thus, each year (disregarding, for now, any midmonth conventions) Spencer will be entitled to a depreciation deduction of $10,000 ($275,000 divided by 27.5). Each year, the basis of the property will be reduced by that depreciation deduction. At the end of 2013, for example, the basis will be $245,000 ($275,000 minus $30,000).

F. Section 179 deduction

1. **General rule:** Section 179 allows a taxpayer to elect to claim a deduction for the purchase price of a qualifying asset placed in service in a taxable year.

2. **Definitional issues:**

   a. Qualifying assets: A qualifying §179 asset is any tangible property that is §1245 property and that is acquired by purchase for use in the active conduct of a trade or business. IRC §179(d)(1). For example, autos, trucks, computers, telephones, fax machines, tools, and similar items qualify for the §179 election.

   b. Placed in service: The taxpayer must actually deploy the asset in the trade or business during the taxable year in which the asset is purchased.

   c. Election required: The taxpayer must affirmatively elect to apply §179 and the election is irrevocable.

3. **Special rules and exceptions:**

   a. Dollar limits: In 2011, the maximum amount that can be claimed as a §179 deduction is $500,000. However, this amount is reduced by the amount of qualifying property purchased in excess of $2,000,000. IRC §179(b)(1). Congress frequently adjusts the dollar limitations for the §179 deduction to achieve economic (nontax) objectives.

Example: In 2011, D+Co purchased trucks at a cost of $2,300,000 for use in its concrete business. The maximum §179 deduction is $500,000, but this is reduced by the amount of qualifying property placed in service during the year that exceeds $2,000,000. This amount is $300,000. Thus, D+Co can claim a §179 deduction for only $200,000.

b. Taxable income limit: The §179 deduction is limited to the amount of the taxpayer's taxable income from the active conduct of a trade or business. IRC §179(b)(3)(A). Taxable income includes the net income from all of the taxpayer's active trades or businesses. Any amount limited in this way can carry forward to future years, subject to the applicable dollar amount and taxable income restrictions in those years.

Example: In 2011, Mandie purchased $50,000 of kennels and other equipment for her doggie day care business. In that year, she had $25,000 of taxable income from that business and $7,500 of dividends received from investments. Although Mandie had $50,000 of qualifying §179 purchases, she can only deduct $25,000, because that is the amount of her taxable income from the trade or business. She cannot add the $7,500 of dividend income to the limit because that income is not derived from a trade or business.

4. **Related material:** The taxpayer may claim regular depreciation in lieu of the §179 deduction.

5. **Be alert for §179 issues:** Section 179 is implicated whenever a taxpayer purchases an item of tangible personal property for use in a trade or business. The principal issue is whether the taxpayer may claim the election for this property, and the effects of claiming that election (deduction; basis).

G. Modified accelerated cost recovery system (MACRS) deduction for tangible business assets

MACRS is the method by which taxpayers claim capital recovery for tangible assets used in a trade or business or held for the production of income.

1. **Dual function of MACRS deduction:** The MACRS deduction has two functions:

   a. Deduction: The MACRS deduction is a deduction from gross income in computing AGI. IRC §167(a).

   b. Basis reduction: The amount of the MACRS deduction reduces the basis of the asset. IRC §1016(a)(2).

2. **Calculation of MACRS:** The MACRS deduction is computed by applying the applicable recovery method to the basis of the asset over the applicable recovery period, taking into account applicable conventions. While this sounds complicated, it is a relatively straightforward process if the definitions of these terms are kept in mind.

   a. Basis: The *basis* of an asset is generally its *cost*, subject to some particular rules for property acquired other than by purchase. (See Chapter 9(V)(C).) Basis is adjusted downward for capital recovery deductions, producing "adjusted basis." IRC §1016 (a)(2). Improvements are treated as separate assets generating their own MACRS deductions.

   Example: Debra purchases a rental home for $100,000. Over the next five years she properly claims $5,000 of depreciation (MACRS) deductions, reducing her basis to $95,000. She then adds a small apartment on the back of the rental house to increase the rental income from the property. She spends $25,000 on this addition. The original rental home will continue to be depreciated on its existing schedule. Debra will depreciate the addition on the 27.5-year schedule applicable to residential real property beginning on the date it is first rented. Thus, assuming Debra keeps the property, the original rental home will be fully depreciated (i.e., its basis will be zero) five years before the addition is fully depreciated. If Debra sells the rental home, she will use the collective basis of the home and addition at that time as her basis for determining gain or loss.

b. Recovery period: The *recovery period* of an asset is the period of years over which the taxpayer claims capital recovery for the item. Some recovery periods are set forth in the Code (e.g., for real property); for other types of property, the IRS publishes the recovery period. The recovery period might not have any relation whatsoever to the actual life of the asset, but is nevertheless mandatory in computing MACRS deductions. Recovery periods include:

i.   Residential real property—27.5 years recovery period: IRC §168(c).

ii.   Nonresidential real property—39 years recovery period: IRC §168(c).

iii. Other property: Other property can be 3-year, 5-year, 7-year, 10-year, 15-year, or 20-year property. See Rev. Proc. 87-56, 1987-2 C.B. 674, modified by Rev. Proc. 88-22, 1988-1 C.B. 785.

c. Conventions: The applicable convention expresses the beginning date for capital recovery. Recovery begins when the property is *placed in service*, i.e., when it is dedicated to use in a trade or business. Reg. §1.168(d)-1(a). In addition, instead of creating the technical nightmare of computing daily portions of capital recovery for properties placed in service during the year on various days, the MACRS system adopts various conventions. These conventions deem a property to be placed in service at a specific time during the month, quarter, or year, regardless of when the property is actually placed in service.

i.   Midmonth convention: Taxpayers purchasing or selling real property are deemed to make the purchase or sale on the 15th day of the month in which the transaction occurs. IRC §168(d)(4)(B). Thus, if a taxpayer purchases real property on April 28, she is deemed to have purchased it on April 15 for MACRS purposes.

ii.   Half-year convention: For tangible property other than real property, the Code deems a purchase or sale to be made at the middle of the taxpayer's taxable year regardless of when during the year the transaction actually occurs. IRC §168(d)(4)(A). For example, if a taxpayer on a calendar year sells equipment on January 1, he is deemed to have sold it on July 1 for MACRS purposes.

d. Recovery methods: Three different recovery methods are available under MACRS for different types of property; the straight-line method and two accelerated methods. Most professors focus only on the straight-line method in a basic income tax class.

i.   Straight line: Under a straight-line system, the MACRS deduction is taken on a pro rata basis over the recovery period for the property. The cost of the property is divided by the recovery period to determine the annual MACRS deduction. For example, if the cost of the property is $275,000, and the recovery period is 27.5 years, the MACRS deduction is $10,000 per year. The straight-line method *must* be used for buildings and their structural components. A taxpayer may elect to use the straight-line method for other assets as well.

ii. **Accelerated methods:** Under an accelerated method, a larger MACRS deduction is taken in the early years of the useful life of the property than in later years. Taxpayers prefer the accelerated methods because it results in larger deductions earlier in their ownership of property.

e. **Calculating the MACRS deduction—Straight-line system:** Under a straight-line system, the cost of the property is divided by the recovery period to obtain the annual MACRS deduction. If the property is held (or deemed held under the conventions) for less than a full year, the annual figure must be multiplied by the percentage of the year during which the taxpayer held (or is deemed to have held) the property.

Example: Dina purchases Whiteacre, an apartment building, on January 1, 2010, for $330,000. She holds it for two years, selling it on January 1, 2012. During her period of ownership, Dina may claim the following MACRS deductions:

2010: $11,500

This is calculated by taking the Whiteacre's cost ($330,000) and dividing it by the recovery period for residential real property (27.5 years) to produce an annual MACRS deduction of $12,000. However, because of the midmonth convention, Dina is deemed to have purchased Whiteacre on January 15, 2010, and thus she is entitled to only 11.5 months of depreciation during 2010. Multiplying the annual allowance ($12,000) by the percentage of the year she held Whiteacre (11.5/12 or 96%) produces her 2010 MACRS deduction of $11,500.

2011: $12,000

Since Dina held Whiteacre for the full year, she is entitled to the annual MACRS deduction for that year.

2012: $500

Dina sold Whiteacre on January 1, but the midmonth convention deems the sale to have occurred on January 15, 2012. She is therefore entitled to a half-month's MACRS deduction during 2012 equal to the annual MACRS deduction ($12,000) multiplied by the percentage of the year she held the property (0.5/12 or 4%) to produce her 2012 MACRS deduction of $500.

Dina's basis in Whiteacre at the time of sale is $306,000, which is equal to her purchase price ($330,000) reduced by the total MACRS deductions she claimed ($24,000).

f. **Bonus depreciation:** Sometimes, in order to stimulate the economy, Congress enacts special rules that increase the benefit of depreciation. This is intended to create an incentive for taxpayers to invest in property and equipment. Congress did this in 2008 and in 2010. Such a rule might allow a current deduction of a percentage of the total cost of property, or accelerate depreciation deductions for certain kinds of property.

g. **Recapture:** Upon sale of property that has been depreciated, a portion of the gain on sale may be treated as ordinary income. See Chapter 12(III)(E).

H. Amortization of §197 intangibles

1. **In general:** Section 197 was enacted to end years of controversy between taxpayers and the IRS about the appropriate amortization of intangible assets acquired in the purchase and sale of businesses. A taxpayer may claim a deduction in computing AGI for any amortizable §197 intangible equal to the adjusted basis of the intangible divided by 15 years, and may begin claiming the deduction in the month of acquisition of the intangible. IRC §197(a). Like a MACRS deduction, a §197 amortization deduction reduces the basis of the asset in question. IRC §1016(a)(2).

2. **Definition—§197 intangible:** A *§197 intangible* includes purchased (not self-created) goodwill, going-concern value, covenants not to compete, patents, copyrights, formulas or processes, and various other intangibles. IRC §197(d)(1). *Goodwill* is generally defined as the likelihood that customers will return to the old place of business, the tendency of an established business to continue. *Wilmot Fleming Eng. Co. v. Commissioner*, 65 T.C. 847, 860 (1976). In the sale of a business, the seller may promise the buyer not to engage in the same or similar business for a reasonable time after sale, in the same general geographic area as the sold business. This is called a *"covenant not to compete." Going concern value* is the value of an operational business, as compared with the cost of acquiring all of the components of the business and getting them going. *Los Angeles Gas & Elec. Corp. v. R.R. Comm. of Cal.*, 289 U.S. 287 (1933).

   Example: Robyn purchases Kitty Kaverns, an established cat-boarding business. In the purchase, Robyn acquires various tangible assets and also pays $15,000 for the goodwill of Kitty Kaverns. Assuming that the goodwill meets the requirements for an "amortizable §197 intangible," Robyn will be able to amortize this payment over 15 years, i.e., taking a $1,000 deduction each year. She will begin amortizing this intangible in the month of acquisition, so that her first year's amortization deduction will be limited to the number of months that she is open for business in that year.

   Example: Trevor purchases a car-detailing business from Drake. In connection with the sale of the business, Drake promises not to open any type of similar business within 60 miles of the purchased business for 5 years, and Trevor pays Drake $20,000 for this promise. This covenant not to compete is a §197 intangible, which Trevor amortizes over 15 years for an annual amortization deduction of $1,333. Notice that even though the covenant only runs for 5 years, Trevor must amortize it over the statutory 15-year period.

I. Pre-opening expenses—§195:

Expenses that would be deductible but for the "carrying on" requirement of §162(a) may be deductible if the taxpayer properly elects to take advantage of §195(a). A taxpayer may elect to deduct $5,000 in the year the business opens, but this amount must be reduced by the amount the total pre-opening expenses exceed $50,000. IRC §195(b). Any remaining amount must be amortized over 180 months (15 years), much like §197 intangibles (see this chapter, Section IV(H)). General investigatory expenses qualify as start-up expenses, while expenses incurred in acquiring a specific business are capital expenditures. See Rev. Rul. 99-23, 1999-1 C.B. 998.

Example: Sam is planning to open a restaurant. In the month prior to opening, he incurs $8,000 for salaries, utilities, and other expenses that would otherwise qualify as ordinary and necessary business expenses but cannot be deducted because the restaurant is not yet open for business. He may deduct $5,000 in the year of opening, and the remaining $3,000 can be deducted over 15 years ($200/year).

J. Capital recovery—Summary

The Code sections allowing capital recovery for business and investment assets are summarized in Figure 7A.

Figure 7A
Code Sections Allowing Capital Recovery for Business and Investment Assets

Code Section & Topic	Capital Recovery Allowed
§179—Election to expense certain business assets	Taxpayers may elect to claim a deduction for up to a specified amount—$500,000 in 2011—of tangible business assets, subject to overall net income limitation.
§§167, 168 MACRS	Depreciation of tangible business and investment assets for which no §179 election is in effect.
§197—Amortization of intangibles	Allows 15-year, straight-line amortization of intangibles such as goodwill and covenants not to compete.
§195—Pre-opening expenses	May claim up to $5,000 of pre-opening expenses, but this amount is reduced by the amount over $50,000; remaining amounts amortized on straight-line basis over 15 years.

V. ACTIVITIES ENGAGED IN FOR PROFIT THAT ARE NOT TRADES OR BUSINESSES

A. In general

Taxpayers engage in a variety of activities for the purpose of making money, but which do not rise to the level of a trade or business. In the basic income tax class, these principally include investment activities and rental of real estate. Income from all of these activities is includible in gross income (see Chapter 3(V)). The expenses associated with that income are deductible. But because these activities do not qualify as a trade or business, IRC §162 does not apply to allow these deductions. Instead, IRC §212(a) applies to allow deductions for the ordinary and necessary expenses paid or incurred during a taxable year for producing that income or for the management or maintenance of property. The terms "ordinary," "necessary," and "expenses" have the same meaning as they do in IRC §162 and the capital recovery provisions also apply to any depreciable or amortizable asset used in the rental or royalty activity.

B. Investment activities

1. **In general:** No matter how extensive a taxpayer's investments may be, this activity does not rise to the level of a trade or business. A taxpayer may deduct the non-capitalized costs of such activity (fees, subscriptions to investment journals, office expenses, etc) from gross income. But because these expenses are subject to the 2% floor of §67, they usually do not create a deduction for most taxpayers.

   Example: Cedric has an extensive investment portfolio. He spends several hours a day researching stocks and bonds, and making trades for his account. He incurs the following expenses in connection with that activity:

   Subscriptions to investment publications: $5,000

   Attendance at investment conferences: $3,000

   Safety deposit box fees: $500

   Commissions paid on purchases of stock: $10,000

Assume these are Cedric's only miscellaneous deductions, and his adjusted gross income is $100,000. Cedric may not deduct the commissions, because they are a capital expenditure, i.e., commissions are added to the basis of stock purchased or sold. Of the other $8,500, Cedric may deduct only the amount that exceeds 2% of his AGI, or $2,000. Thus, $6,500 is deductible as a miscellaneous itemized deduction on Schedule A. (But consider the effect of the alternative minimum tax, discussed in Chapter 13(III).)

2. **Investment interest:** Interest incurred to purchase investments is deductible to the extent of investment income. IRC §163(d). Investment income is income from dividends, interest, and certain other investments. IRC §164(d)(4).

    Example: Andrea borrows $10,000 to purchase stock in ABC Corporation. She pays $800 in interest per year. Her total investment income is $200. Andrea may deduct $200 of the interest, and the remaining nondeductible amount will carry forward to be deducted in future years, subject to the same limitation.

3. **Investment losses:** Section165(c)(2) allows a taxpayer to take a deduction for losses incurred in an activity engaged in for profit, but that does not rise to the level of a trade or business. For example, theft losses that occur in connection with an investment are deductible. See Rev. Rul. 2009-9, 2009-1 C.B. 735.

    Example—why it matters: Ian entrusted $100,000 to his financial advisor for investment. The financial adviser absconded with all the money. If this is a personal theft loss, it is subject to the restrictions of §165(c)(3), which allows a deduction for theft losses only to the extent they exceed 10% of Ian's adjusted gross income. However, if this is a theft loss associated with an activity engaged in for profit, there is no such limitation, and Ian may deduct the entire loss. Fortunately for taxpayers, the IRS views this as a theft loss under §212, rather than a personal casualty/theft loss under §165(c)(3).

C. Lawsuits

Legal fees in a proceeding that will result in amounts that would be included in gross income are deductible, but are subject to the 2% floor of §67.

Example: Brittany sued a cable network for libel and slander associated with a report about her that appeared on television and on the network's website. She incurred $200,000 in legal fees associated with this lawsuit, which she ultimately lost. Brittany may deduct these legal fees because they were incurred in an attempt to generate income, even though that attempt was unsuccessful.

D. Rental real estate

A taxpayer that holds real or personal property for rental is entitled to deduct the costs of that property, including fees, taxes, interest, repairs, and capital recovery deductions (MACRS and §179 expenses). An individual taxpayer reports the income and expenses on a Schedule E, with the net result (income or loss) reported on the Form 1040. See Chapter 1, Figure 1A. These expenses are not subject to the 2% floor of §67.

Example:

1. **Holding for rental:** In order to deduct expenses, the taxpayer must hold the property for rental, which requires that the taxpayer has made a bona fide offer to rent the property. See

Horrmann v. Commissioner, 17 T.C. 903 (1951). This issue arises when the taxpayer has lived in the property and is converting it to a rental.

2. **Passive loss rules:** The passive loss rules prevent most taxpayers from deducting a loss (expenses in excess of income) attributable to any rental activity. See Chapter 11(VII).

VI. SUBSTANTIATION

Taxpayers bear the burden of proving their entitlement to a deduction by keeping a record of the date, purpose, and amount of expenditure. Sloppy record keepers often rely on the so-called *Cohan rule*: even when no records exist, but it is clear that some expense was incurred, the taxpayer will be entitled to some (rarely all) of the claimed deduction. See *Cohan v. Commissioner*, 39 F.2d 540 (2d Cir. 1930).

VII. NEED TO KNOW MORE?

This book's website *www.aspenlawschool.com/books/tax_outline* contains additional information, including:

- Distinguishing trades or businesses from other activities.

- The Schedule C.

- Computing the §179 deduction.

- Computing the MACRS deduction, and coordinating the various capital recovery deductions.

- Methods of accelerated depreciation.

- And other materials that will help you understand business and investment deductions.

VIII. WHERE ARE WE GOING?

Chapter 6 addressed purely personal deductions, and this chapter has explored purely business deductions. In the next chapter we will turn to expenses that have both personal *and* business connections. The Code has a number of methods of dealing with such expenses, from bifurcating the expense into its component parts, to inquiring into the dominant connection, to disallowing all or a portion of the expense altogether.

Quiz Yourself on BUSINESS AND INVESTMENT DEDUCTIONS

65. Chris's job with Ad-Men, Inc. requires him to develop advertising campaigns for outdoor sports clothing manufacturers. Each year, Chris goes on a lengthy adventure trip, and always takes along a few of the newest items to test and discuss with fellow travelers. He says it gives him all his ideas

for ad campaigns. Chris' employer doesn't reimburse him for these trips. This year, Chris spent $20,000 on a trip to Antarctica, and he wants to deduct this expense. May he do so? _____

66. Clean Machine is a sole proprietorship operating a mobile car-detailing service. This year, the owner, Win, made a number of expenditures, as follows:

Wages to employees	$25,000
Waxes, soaps, etc.	$ 6,000
Licenses	$ 500
Parking fines	$ 600
Advertising	$10,000
Séance to get business advice from deceased father	$ 3,000
Legal fees to settle dispute with car owner	$ 5,000
Legal fees to quiet title to parking lot	$15,000
New van	$35,000

Which of these expenditures are deductible to Win? If not deductible, how should they be treated? _____

67. Jody purchased a rental house on July 1 of Year 1 for $55,000. She rented it for $3,000 in Year 1, and $6,000 in each of Years 2 and 3. She sold it on January 15, Year 4 for $80,000. Assuming no improvements to the home, what is her gain or loss on the sale? _____

68. Grant purchased a bagpipe store from Adam. He purchased the entire bagpipe inventory, a list of all the customers who love bagpipe music, and obtained a promise from Adam not to engage in the retail bagpipe business for five years from the date of sale. He paid Adam $30,000 for the promise. How should Grant treat the $30,000 for tax purposes? _____

69. Kaitlin is the latest teen idol. She embarked upon a concert tour arranged by Carefree Promoters. At just the fourth event, Kaitlin fell off the stage when it suddenly broke into pieces. Kaitlin sued Carefree for negligence resulting in both physical injuries and the humiliation she suffered as a result of the fall. She ultimately settled for a $200,000 payment, which was allocated in the settlement agreement 75% to physical injuries and 25% to emotional injuries. Kaitlin has to pay her lawyer $60,000 in legal fees, and she incurred $40,000 in costs. Assume she had $50,000 of income from her teen idol career in that year. May Kaitlin deduct these costs? _____

70. Baxter is a large animal veterinarian. This year, he returned to his hometown to open a practice. He spent $50,000 on equipment, and on June 1 hired an assistant, Penny, to whom he paid $2,500 per month. He spent $10,000 on fixing up his leased premises and another $5,000 on various miscellaneous expenses associated with opening his business. He was finally ready to open on August 1. His expenses after that date were $35,000. Which expenses are deductible, if any? How should nondeductible expenses be treated? _____

71. Under what circumstances would a taxpayer purchasing eligible property not elect the §179 deduction? _____

72. Lenore purchases the Wallflower Hotel on January 1, Year 1. She expects to be able to claim 12 months of depreciation for the hotel during Year 1. Is she able to do so? Why or why not? _____

73. Xavier makes a loan of $25,000 to Zena. Eventually, it becomes clear that Zena will never repay the loan. What is the proper tax treatment of the loan to Xavier if:

   ■ Xavier is Zena's father? _____

   ■ Xavier is Zena's employer? _____

   ■ Xavier is in the business of making loans to individuals? _____

74. Of the following, which is *not* a capital expenditure?

   (a) Commissions paid on the purchase of stock

   (b) Purchase price of raw land

   (c) The cost of designing and implementing a website

   (d) Expenses for advertising designed to restore customer confidence after a major corporate mistake

   (e) None of the above; they are all capital expenditures

75. Wendy is a practicing lawyer in solo practice. Well aware of how the Internet can be used to destroy reputations, Wendy hires "Reputation Defender"™ a company that constantly monitors what people are saying about her on the Internet and seeks to remove damaging content. May Wendy deduct the cost of this service? _____

76. Richard is a law librarian. He decides to go to law school. He wants to deduct the costs of his education. May he do so? _____

77. After graduating from law school, Sara pays $2,000 for a bar review course, and a $500 application fee to the state bar of Missouri. May she deduct these expenses in the year she incurs them?

   (a) No, they are personal expenses.

   (b) Yes, because they are related to her trade or business of being a lawyer.

   (c) Yes, but they are subject to the 2% floor of §67.

   (d) No, but some or all of these expenses may be capitalized and amortized over Sara's lifetime.

   (e) The application fee will be deductible, but not the expenses of the bar review course.

78. Bonbon owns a rental house. She was paid rental income of $10,000. Her expenses were repairs ($1,500), property management ($3,000), and taxes ($2,500). She also spent $15,000 adding another bedroom to the home. How should Bonbon report these items? _____

79. What is the rationale for allowing depreciation or amortization deductions? _____

80. Felicia is an employee and minority shareholder in Z Corporation. When the corporation falls on bad times, she makes a $15,000 loan to the company to try to keep it afloat. When the company is unable to repay this debt, Felicia claims this as a deduction as a business bad debt. Is she correct in doing so? _____

Answers

65. Section 162 allows a deduction for all of the ordinary and necessary expenses of carrying on a trade or business. Are Chris' travel expenses "ordinary and necessary"? While it may be ordinary and necessary to test products and discuss them with consumers in order to develop advertising, this kind of expenditure probably would be viewed as personal (a vacation) rather than sufficiently related to business. A court would likely invoke the ordinary and necessary standard to deny the deduction. See *Brown v. Commissioner*, 446 F.2d 926 (8th Cir. 1971). (Even if these were deductible, they would be miscellaneous itemized deductions, subject to the 2% floor of §67, and nondeductible for AMT purposes.)

66. Section 162 allows a deduction for all of the ordinary and necessary expenses of carrying on a trade or business. Win's expenses for wages to employees, waxes, soaps, etc., and advertising would certainly fit within this category. The legal fees incurred in the dispute with a car owner would also qualify; even though they might be unique in Win's experience, legal fees are of the usual type of expenses incurred by businesspeople, and therefore considered "ordinary." Similarly, license fees are usually deductible, although there may be some question of when these are deductible (we don't know Win's method of accounting). Parking fines are not deductible, because §162(f) prohibits a deduction for fines or illegal payments. The fees for the séance are almost certainly not deductible; although courts generally don't substitute their judgment for those of businesspeople, in this case, the expenditure would probably not be considered "ordinary" or "necessary." The legal fees to settle the dispute about title to the parking lot are properly capitalized; they are not deductible, but instead become part of the basis in the asset (fee title or lease). Similarly, the van is a capital asset that must be capitalized. However, a portion of the expense may be deducted under §179, which allows up to $250,000 (in 2008) to be deducted instead of capitalized.

67. Jody's basis in the rental home must be adjusted downward to account for MACRS deductions allocable to it. Residential real property is depreciable under MACRS on a straight-line basis, over 27.5 years. Therefore Jody's annual depreciation deduction is $2,000 ($167 monthly). She is entitled to the following depreciation (MACRS) deductions:

Year 1	5½ months	$ 918*
Year 2	12 months	$2,000
Year 3	12 months	$2,000
Year 4	½ month	$ 83
Total		**$5,001**

As a result, her basis is $49,999, and the gain on sale is $30,001.

*Jody is subject to the mid-month convention, in which a purchase of real property is deemed to have occurred on the 15th day of the month of purchase, regardless of the actual day of purchase.

68. The promise from Adam is a "covenant not to compete," one of the so-called §197 intangibles that must be amortized over 15 years—regardless of the actual term of the promise. Therefore, Grant will take a deduction of $2,000 per year for 15 years attributable to the covenant.

69. Kaitlin is in the trade or business of being a teen idol. The lawsuit arises from that business and the expenses of it are deductible as ordinary and necessary business expenses, but only to the extent that they are attributable to income that would be included in gross income. Because the settlement agreement allocates the damages between physical injuries (payment for which would be excluded from Kaitlin's gross income) and emotional damages (payment for which would be included in her gross income), Kaitlin will have to divide her legal fees and expenses accordingly. On her Schedule C for this trade or business, 75% will be nondeductible and 25% will be deductible.

70. The amount that Baxter paid for equipment is a capital expenditure that, except for amounts properly deductible under §179, must be capitalized and depreciated under MACRS. Of his $10,000 of pre-opening expenses ($5,000 to his assistant and $5,000 of miscellaneous expenses) only $5,000 is deductible in the year of opening. The rest is amortizable over 15 years. The expenses incurred after opening are deductible, assuming that they otherwise meet the requirements of being ordinary and necessary.

71. Section 179 allows a taxpayer to elect to claim a deduction for the cost of certain tangible personal property placed in service in the taxpayer's business during a taxable year. However, there are limitations on the election that may cause some taxpayers not to make the election for otherwise qualifying property. First, there is an overall annual limit on the amount of property for which the election has been made, and a taxpayer exceeding that limit would obviously not qualify for the election. Second, the deduction can be claimed only to the extent of the taxpayer's taxable income (not counting this deduction), so a taxpayer that did not have taxable income would not make the election. Finally, a taxpayer can carry forward the election for property that is subject to the election in a year in which the income limitation applies, so a taxpayer with sufficient carryforward would not make the election for property purchased in that year.

72. When a taxpayer acquires real property, he or she is deemed to have acquired it on the midpoint of the month it is acquired, regardless of the day on which it is actually acquired. The function of these conventions is to simplify MACRS calculations. Therefore, Lenore will be able to claim 11 1/2 months of depreciation for Year 1, not a full 12 months.

73. Xavier would like to take a deduction for the bad debt. Ideally, he would like the debt to be a business bad debt, because that leads to an ordinary deduction rather than a capital loss.

- If Xavier is Zena's father, the first question is whether there is a debt at all, or if there were a debt, whether the "badness" of it is really the father making a gift to the daughter. If the debt is bona fide, and it is really a bad debt, it would be a nonbusiness bad debt, as it is family oriented, not related to the business (absent other facts).

- If Xavier is Zena's employer, there is a possibility that this could be considered a business bad debt if Xavier's primary motivation in making the loan was to further the business. If his primary motivation was to be a "nice guy," the debt is a nonbusiness bad debt.

- If Xavier is in the business of making loans, the debt is a business bad debt.

 The distinction between a business and nonbusiness bad debt is important because business bad debts are deductible from gross income in computing adjusted gross income, while a nonbusiness bad debt is deductible only as a short-term capital loss. (See Chapter 12).

74. A capital expenditure is an expenditure that creates a separate asset, or that creates a benefit expected to last beyond the taxable year. The best answer is (e)—all of the above. Each of the expenditures creates an asset or has a benefit beyond the close of the taxable year. However, one might choose. (d) (advertising expenses) as the correct answer because of the IRS's position that these are deductible, despite the fact that under *Indopco*, advertising in general and this kind of advertising in particular could easily be expected to generate benefits beyond the taxable year.

75.   Wendy may probably deduct this expenditure as an ordinary and necessary business expense under §162. Although *Welch v. Helvering*, 290 U.S. 111 (1933), is often cited for the proposition that payments to restore reputation are capital expenditures, Wendy's situation is distinguishable. Her payments are not to restore a ruined reputation, but instead to maintain her good reputation. She would argue that her payments are similar to having a roofing company periodically check and repair damage to a roof, or a painting company repair dings and scratches in the paint on her building. She would rely on *Jenkins v. Commissioner* [TC Memo 1983-667], where Conway Twitty's payments to investors to restore a somewhat tarnished reputation were deductible, as support for her position.

76.   If Richard's job required him to earn a law degree, he would be able to deduct the costs of his law school education. However, if his employer did not require it, the cost would not be deductible because it would qualify him for a new profession. In the latter case, Richard's argument that his information would help him better carry out his current duties would probably fall on deaf Tax Court ears. See *Galligan v. Commissioner*, T.C. Memo. 2002-150.

77.   Of five less-than-perfect answers, the best answer is (d). Sara cannot deduct these expenses, because they are properly capitalized. However, because the application fee qualifies her to join a bar, in theory it is amortizable over some period, perhaps her expected years of practice as a lawyer. See *Sharon v. Commissioner*, 66 T.C. 515 (1976), aff'd 591 F.2d 1273 (9th Cir. 1978), cert. den. 442 U.S. 941 (1979) (costs of admission to bar amortizable over lifetime of attorney).

78.   Bonbon must report the rental income as part of her gross income but may deduct the expenditures for repairs, property management, and taxes as ordinary and necessary expenses of the production of income under §212. Thus, her net income, not considering MACRS deductions, will be $3,000. She will not be able to deduct the costs of the addition, as this is a capital expenditure. She will be able to claim MACRS deductions of some amount for the home and the addition, but these cannot be determined from the facts given.

79.   Depreciation is allowed for capital assets, i.e., those that will last more than one year. To allow a deduction in the year of acquisition would result in a mismatch of income and the costs of producing the income over time—accelerating the deductions while the income would be reported over a number of years. Depreciation deductions match the "using up" of the asset to the income it produces over time. However, the schedule for depreciation (or amortization, for that matter) does not necessarily match up with the actual fall in value of the asset (if any); it is an approximation at best.

80.   This will be the proper reporting position for the transaction if her dominant motive in making the loan was to protect her employment relationship. If the motive was to protect her stock value, the debt will be a nonbusiness bad debt. However, even if it is a business debt—and the business is the employment relationship—it would be deductible as an employee business expense and therefore subject to the 2% floor of §67. See *Graves v. Commissioner*, T.C. Memo 2004-140, 220 Fed. Appx. 601 (9th Cir. 2007).

Exam Tips on BUSINESS AND INVESTMENT DEDUCTIONS

☛ Questions dealing with pure business deductions obviously involve a taxpayer's activities with respect to trade or business.

☞ *Look for:* Usually a sole proprietorship is illustrated in the basic income tax course, but a trade or business can also be carried on by a corporation or partnership.

☞ *Analyze:* Identify the particular outlays. Analyze them expenditure by expenditure. Is an expenditure deductible, and if so, how much is deductible?

☛ Work through the five requirements to test deductibility: ordinary, necessary, incurred in carrying on (not pre-opening), a trade or business, and an expense, not a capital expenditure. If an expense flunks any of these requirements, it is not currently deductible under §162.

☛ Timing questions often arise in these questions.

☞ *Look for:* The taxpayer's method of accounting—cash or accrual (see Chapter 11).

☞ *Analyze:* If an expenditure is deductible, *when* is it deductible?

☛ Watch for expenses that have benefits for a longer period than the taxable year. Usually, these must be capitalized. If so, when will the taxpayer be allowed to recover the invested capital? Over time (as in MACRS) or upon disposition of the investment?

☛ Each professor seems to require a different level of involvement with depreciation and amortization. Check with your professor as to the level of understanding required about the different MACRS methods.

☛ MACRS questions involve some arithmetic skills. Intimidated or pressed for time? Explain how MACRS would be applied to the particular situation, and come back later to do the math if you have time.

☛ Some expenditures have both personal and business connections (see Chapter 8). In that case, usually some or all of the expenditure will be nondeductible.

STATUTE SUMMARY CHARTS

Statute Summary—§162
Ordinary and Necessary Trade or Business Expenses

Parsing Step	IRC §162
General Rule	A deduction is allowed for all of the ordinary and necessary expenses of carrying on a trade or business.
Definitions	**Ordinary and necessary:** no deduction for personal expenses **Trade or business:** requires ongoing, for-profit activity **Carrying on:** no deduction for pre-opening expenses **Expense:** no deduction for capital expenditures
Special Rules and Exceptions	No deduction for fines, kickbacks, or treble damage portions of damage awards. Self-employed can deduct health insurance premiums. Public policy exception—judicial and statutory.
Related Statutes	**§183:** Hobby losses **§179:** Deduction for equipment, etc. **§§167–168:** MACRS deductions **§195:** Amortization of pre-opening expenses
Typically implicated when . . .	A taxpayer makes expenditures for various items that are associated with the taxpayer's business activities.

Chapter 8

MIXED BUSINESS AND PERSONAL EXPENSES

ChapterScope ━━━

As discussed in the previous two chapters, the expenses of conducting business are usually deductible, while personal expenses generally are not (although specific Code sections allow a deduction for certain personal expenses). The previous two chapters have identified and discussed expenses that are clearly business or personal expenditures. Some expenses, however, do not fall neatly into these categories; they are connected with both the business and personal aspects of a taxpayer's life. The dual nature of these expenses raises the difficult tax question of whether they should be deductible in whole or in part. This chapter examines how Congress and the courts have approached a number of mixed business and personal expenses.

- **The origin test:** The origin of an expense determines whether it is most closely related to the business or personal aspect of a taxpayer's life.

- **Specific types of expenses—travel, clothing, education, meals, and entertainment:** Specific approaches have evolved for common dual-nature expenditures. These range from a simple disallowance of part of the expenditure to an inquiry into the taxpayer's subjective intent.

- **Home offices and vacation homes:** A taxpayer using a personal residence as a rental or for business will incur expenses for personal as well as business use of the residence. Section 280A requires bifurcation of these expenses, and imposes significant restrictions on the deductibility of expenses to prevent a taxpayer from claiming a loss attributable to business use of a residence.

- **"Luxury" automobiles and listed property:** Automobiles and certain other types of property (computers, for example) are particularly likely to be used for both business and personal purposes. Section 280F imposes restrictions on capital recovery deductions attributable to these properties.

- **Hobby losses:** Section 183 denies deductions in excess of income for activities not engaged in for profit. The regulations offer nine factors to be used in determining whether a taxpayer is engaged in an activity for profit or as a hobby.

I. WHERE ARE WE?

We are still working our way through deductions on the road to determining taxable income. These deductions, unlike the ones in the previous chapters, have a connection to both the taxpayer's personal life and the taxpayer's business or investment life. The question, then, is whether they are properly deductible, and if so, how—on Schedule C (business income) or E (business or rents/royalties) or elsewhere, perhaps as an itemized deduction on Schedule A?

II. ORIGIN TEST

The *origin* of an expense determines its nature as a business or personal expense.

A. United States v. Gilmore, 372 U.S. 39 (1963)

The taxpayer incurred legal expenses in a divorce action in which the primary issue of controversy was the protection of his ownership of a closely held corporation that also employed him. He argued that the legal expenses were deductible because they related to his business and employment relationships. The Supreme Court disagreed on the grounds that the "origin" of the expense was the divorce, a clearly personal or family matter. Because the origin of the expenses was personal, the expenses were not deductible, regardless of their connection with the taxpayer's business life.

B. Relation to "ordinary and necessary"

Section 162 requires that an expenditure be an ordinary and necessary business expense in order to be deductible. The "ordinary" and "necessary" requirements function in part to distinguish personal expenses from business expenses, denying a deduction for personal expenses even if they have some relation to the business activity. The origin test is most often used for extraordinary, nonrecurring expenses, while the ordinary and necessary definitions are used for ongoing expenditures. Their functions are similar, however, and both can be invoked to deny deduction for a personal expense incurred in business. For a discussion of §162, see Chapter 7(II)(B).

Example: Carol, the sole proprietor of Candy-2-U, hires her son Adam to assist her in delivering candy baskets so that he may earn money for graduate school. She pays him five times the going rate for delivery persons, and seeks to deduct the expense on her Schedule C. In challenging this deduction, the IRS would likely rely on the argument that unreasonably high wages do not qualify as an ordinary expense. Instead, it is partly a payment for services (a deductible business expense) and partly a gift to Adam from Carol (a nondeductible personal expenditure). It would be equally correct to argue that the origin of the expense was partly business (the reasonable part of the wages) and partly personal (the relationship between mother and son). As a result, only the business portion of the payment would be deductible.

III. TRAVEL

A. Basic rule and policy

A taxpayer's expenses while *traveling away from home* primarily for business are deductible. Reg. §1.162-2(b)(1). The rationale for allowing a deduction for expenses of travel and lodging while away from home is that the taxpayer has the burden of substantial continuing expenses that are duplicated when the taxpayer is required to travel for business. See *James v. United States,* 308 F.2d 204, 207 (9th Cir. 1962). The question is whether particular travel is for business, or serves a personal purpose of the taxpayer.

B. Commuting expenses aren't deductible—*Commissioner v. Flowers,* 326 U.S. 465 (1946)

The taxpayer's residence was in Jackson, Mississippi and the offices of his employer were in Mobile, Alabama. Taxpayer sought to deduct the cost of travel between the two cities. The Court established the three requirements for deductibility: (1) the expense must be reasonable and necessary; (2) it must be incurred while "away from home"; and (3) there must be a direct connection between the expenditure and the taxpayer's trade or business or that of the taxpayer's employer. The Court found that this was a personal expense that arose from the personal decision to live in one city and work in another, i.e., it failed the last of the three requirements. Thus, **commuting expenses**—travel from home to work—are not deductible, no matter how long the commute is.

C. Defining "away from home" on business

1. **Business connection at both places:** In *Hantzis v. Commissioner*, 638 F.2d 248 (1st Cir.), cert. denied 452 U.S. 962 (1981), the taxpayer was a second-year law student in Boston, who accepted a summer clerkship with a law firm in New York. She sought to deduct her living expenses in New York, while her husband continued to live in Boston, where he remained employed. The Court denied the deduction because she was not "away from home"—she had no business connection to Boston because she was not employed there (her husband's connection did not extend to her).

2. **Tax home—IRS position:** The IRS interprets a taxpayer's *tax home* as (1) the taxpayer's regular or principal (if more than one regular) place of business; or (2) if the taxpayer has no regular or principal place of business, the taxpayer's regular place of abode in a real and substantial sense, as established through objective tests. These tests examine whether the taxpayer works at the putative home, and maintains a real home there with the usual and expected expenses. If neither (1) nor (2) apply, the taxpayer's home is wherever he or she works. Rev. Rul. 73-529, 1973-2 C.B. 37.

   Example: Char is a law professor at the University of California. She takes a three month leave of absence to accept a position as Special Counsel to the U.S. Senate Ethics Committee. Char's tax home is State X, as that is her regular place of business. Her travel associated with the consulting position (costs of travel and lodging in D.C.) would be deductible as travel incurred principally for business while "away from home."

   a. **No regular or principal place of business:** In *Henderson v. Commissioner*, 143 F.3d 497 (9th Cir. 1998), the taxpayer maintained a home (in a personal sense) at his parents' home in Boise. He traveled as a stagehand for "Disney on Ice" productions throughout the year, and worked in Boise only for one rock concert. The taxpayer sought to deduct the costs of travel. The Court found the taxpayer to be an "itinerant" worker, with no tax home, and therefore the taxpayer could not deduct any cost of being away from home. The Court discussed the policy above; if the taxpayer had no home at which to incur duplicative expenses, there was no policy reason to allow the deduction.

   b. **One-year rule:** A taxpayer is not treated as being away from home on business if the period away exceeds one year. The taxpayer's "realistic expectation" governs, so a taxpayer may deduct expenses for the period of less than a year that a job is realistically expected to last, even if it continues longer, but not for a job that is expected to last more than a year but in fact is completed in less than a year. Rev. Rul. 83-82, 1983-1 C.B. 45; Rev. Rul. 75-432, 1975-2 C.B. 60; Rev. Rul. 60-189, 1960-1 C.B. 60.

   Example: Char's (see previous example) position with the Senate continues for 15 months, and her dean grants her a leave to finish the job. Because Char expected the job to last 3 months, her expenses for the first 3 months would be deductible, but the remaining 12 months' expenses would not be deductible.

3. **Some special rules:** A taxpayer with an office in the home (see this chapter, Section (VII)) may deduct the cost of travel from the home office to other work locations. *Curphey v. Commissioner,* 73 T.C. 766 (1980). A taxpayer may also deduct the cost of travel from home to temporary (less than one year) work locations outside the metropolitan area in which the taxpayer lives. See Rev. Rul. 99-7, 1999-1 C.B. 361.

IV. CLOTHING

Many taxpayers must (or choose to?) wear special clothing to work. Under the origin of the expense rule, taxpayers argue that "but for" the requirements of their job or occupation, they would not purchase or wear such clothing. But the IRS argues in return that clothing is a personal expenditure. Over the years the following principles have evolved. As a general rule, the cost of clothing that is "adaptable for general use" is nondeductible as a personal expense. Generally, this is an objective test, rather than a subjective test of whether the taxpayer would purchase and wear the clothing but for the job requirements. See *Pevsner v. Commissioner,* 628 F.2d 467 (5th Cir. 1980). The cost of a uniform required by an employer or as a result of occupational requirements is generally a deductible expense, but only if the uniform is of a type not suitable for general use. See Rev. Rul. 70-474, 1970-2 C.B. 34. The usefulness of a deduction for an employee is limited, because this expense is subject to the 2% floor of §67(a). See Chapter 6(X).

V. EXPENSES OF EDUCATION

A. The problem—why is the taxpayer pursuing education?

Taxpayers incur expenses for education in the form of tuition, books, fees, and travel in all sorts of contexts. When the taxpayer is engaged in a trade or business and the course has a direct and proximate relationship to a taxpayer's current job, the expenses of such education should be deductible. But when the relationship is less direct, the taxpayer may be pursuing personal, rather than professional, goals and as a result the expenses should be classified as a personal (nondeductible) expense under §262. The problem, as always, is distinguishing between the two.

B. IRS's position—Treas. Reg. §1.162-5

1. **What *is* deductible:** Educational expenses are deductible if they either (1) maintain or improve skills required by the individual in his employment or other trade or business, or (2) allow the taxpayer to meet the express requirements of the taxpayer's employer or applicable law or regulations as a condition of retention in a job or occupation.

   Example: Ava is a corporate bankruptcy lawyer. The state bar association requires that she attend three hours of professional education on child abuse reporting each year. She spends $150 on this course. Even though the content of the program may have little to do with Ava's bankruptcy practice, the course is required as a condition of being a member of the bar, and therefore it is deductible.

2. **What's *not* deductible:** The following expenses of education are not deductible: (1) educational expenses that allow a taxpayer to meet the minimum qualifications for a job or profession; and (2) educational expenses that qualify the taxpayer for a new trade or business.

Example: Bernard clerked for several firms during law school, but graduated at a time when jobs were scarce. He decided to get an LLM in taxation, which cost him $30,000 in tuition. Upon graduation from the LLM program, he passed the bar and was hired by a boutique tax firm. Bernard's expenses for the LLM program are not deductible, for two reasons: they are part of his overall education that qualifies him for the trade or business of being an attorney, and he was not engaged in a trade or business at the time that he incurred them. See *Wassenaar v. Commissioner,* 72 T.C. 1195 (1979).

VI. MEALS AND ENTERTAINMENT

A. The problem—everyone has to eat

In *Moss v. Commissioner,* 758 F.2d 211 (7th Cir. 1985), the partners of a litigation law firm lunched together daily at a diner near the courthouse, where they discussed their cases, received settlement approval, and assigned court calendar duty for the afternoon and following morning. The partners sought to deduct the cost of these meals and the IRS disallowed the deduction. The Court observed that while an argument could be made to disallow any deduction for business meals, on the theory that meals are always a personal expense, some meal expenditures are clearly incurred for the purpose of facilitating business and should be allowed as a deduction. Meals with clients, for example, or monthly business lunches for lawyers in a firm would qualify. But daily lunches went too far: members of the firm had to eat somewhere, and although it saved time to discuss matters over lunch, the meal itself was not an essential element of the business meeting.

B. Meals and entertainment expenses

Meal and entertainment expenses are subject to especially stringent rules in §274. "Meal" expenses are for food and beverages, including tips. "Entertainment" expenses are expenses for amusement, recreation, or entertainment, such as expenses of entertaining at nightclubs, theaters, sporting events, golf, and similar activities. Reg. §1.274-2(b)(1). A taxpayer desiring to deduct any expense for meals or entertainment must run a gauntlet of tests for deductibility, and is likely to find that, in the end, only a portion of the expense is deductible.

1. General requirements

    a. Ordinary and necessary expenses: In order to even begin the analysis of an expense under §274, the expense must first meet the requirements of an "ordinary and necessary business expense" under §162(a). See Chapter 7(II)(B). Section 274, then, focuses on the "business" aspect of the expenditure, subjecting it to more intensive scrutiny to determine if its connection with business is sufficient to justify a deduction.

    b. *Sorry*—Certain really fun expenses are nondeductible: Expenses associated with facilities for entertainment, amusement, or recreation, including dues for such facilities, are nondeductible. IRC §274(a)(1)(B). These include property owned or rented by a taxpayer, such as a yacht, hunting lodge, or hotel suite. In addition, dues for clubs organized for "business, pleasure, recreation or other social purposes" are nondeductible. IRC §274(a)(3).

    c. Special limitations: For meals, any amount that is "lavish" or "extravagant" or is incurred while the taxpayer (or a representative of the taxpayer) is not present is nondeductible. IRC §274(k)(1). For tickets, only the face value is deductible: Extra fees, whether imposed by legitimate ticket agents or scalpers, are not deductible. This is true for skyboxes, where only the face amount of the tickets, multiplied by the number of seats in the box, is deductible. IRC §274(l)(1).

2. Business connection tests: In order to be deductible, Section 274 requires that the taxpayer be able to show that there is a close connection between the taxpayer's business and the expenditure in question. The taxpayer must show that the expenditure is either "directly related to" or "associated with" the business. IRC §274(a)(1)(A); Treas. Reg. §1.274-2(c). While certain expenses (such as the cost of a company picnic) are excepted, for the usual expenses of meals and entertainment, this rule requires taxpayers to prove the connection by showing that business was carried on at, before, or after the event.

3. 50% disallowance rule: If an expense satisfies the requirements discussed above, it is potentially deductible. However, §274(n) allows a deduction for only *50%* of the amount potentially deductible as meal or entertainment expenses. This is designed to allocate the expenditure between its necessarily business and personal elements (and, perhaps, to act as a curb on lavish business lunches?).

C. Business gifts

No deduction is allowed for the cost of ***business gifts*** in excess of $25 per recipient per year. IRC §274(b)(1). For these purposes, a gift is a transfer that is excludible from gross income of the recipient under §102, and husbands and wives are treated as one person for purposes of the gift provisions. For a discussion of gifts, see Chapter 4(IV).

D. Substantiation requirements

Section 274(d) imposes significant ***substantiation*** requirements on taxpayers seeking to deduct expenses. The taxpayer must keep adequate books and records to support (1) the amount of any expense, (2) the circumstances under which it was incurred, (3) the business purpose of the expense, and (4) the business relationship to the taxpayer of the person(s) receiving the benefit of the expense. These requirements have supplanted the so-called *Cohan rule* (see Chapter 7(VI)), which allows taxpayers to estimate business expenses when it is clear that some level of expense has been incurred.

VII. HOME OFFICES AND VACATION HOMES—§280A

A. Policy

Taxpayers may establish offices in their homes in order to deduct the expenses of a portion of the residence such as utilities, repairs, and especially depreciation. Or a taxpayer who owns a vacation home may rent it out for some period of the year and deduct the costs associated with that home. In both cases, Congress is concerned that taxpayers are deducting personal expenses because the business use (in the home office case) is fictional or the percentage of expenses attributable to the rental of the vacation home is overstated. Section 280A severely limits these kinds of deductions, preventing taxpayers from claiming a loss associated with these activities.

B. Statutory analysis—§280A

1. General rule: The complex general rule of §280A contains three parts: a disallowance of deductions, a restoration of certain deductions, and two limitations on allowable deductions.

a. **Disallowance of deductions:** Section 280A(a) disallows any deduction for expenses of a *dwelling unit* that the taxpayer uses as a residence.

b. **Restoration of certain deductions:** Section 280A(b) restores the deduction for expenses that are deductible regardless of whether the taxpayer is engaged in a trade or business, i.e., that are deductible under some other section of the Code (such as qualified residence interest). IRC §280A(c) then restores the deduction for a specified portion of the expenses specifically allocable to business or rental use of the dwelling unit.

c. **Limited allowance of other deductions:** The deductions attributable to the business use of a residence cannot exceed the gross income from the use minus the sum of (1) the deductions allowable without regard to the allowed use (such as deductible mortgage interest) and (2) the trade or business or investment expenses for the activity that are not allocable to the actual use of the property. IRC §280A(c)(5). These would include supplies, advertising, travel, and other §162 expenses that do not arise directly from the use of the home for business. The effect of these limitations is to prevent a deduction for business use of a home to create a loss for tax purposes.

Example: Kristan is an author with a home office that she uses exclusively for researching, writing, and editing magazine articles and talking with editors on the telephone. Her income from writing for the year was $6,000. She had $2,000 of ordinary and necessary business expenses unrelated to her business use of her home. Her expenses that are attributable to her home office are as follows:

Home mortgage interest	$1,400
Property taxes	$1,250
Insurance	$ 375
Utilities	$ 150
MACRS (depreciation)	$1,600

Although §280A(a) disallows a deduction for any expenses associated with business use of a dwelling unit as a residence, certain of Kristan's expenses (her interest and property taxes) will be deductible under §280A(b), which allows a deduction for expenses that are allowable without regard to the taxpayer's trade or business. Moreover, at least a portion of the expenses associated with Kristan's use of her home office will most likely be deductible, as Kristan's use of the office exclusively as her principal place of business for writing qualifies as a use justifying deductions under §280A(c)(1)(A). These expenses, however, may be limited by §280A(c)(5).

Applying the limitation to Kristan's situation, the deductions attributable to the business use of her home will be limited to the gross income from the activity ($6,000), reduced by the sum of (1) the deductions attributable to use that are otherwise allowable regardless of her business use (the interest and taxes, $2,650) and (2) the trade or business expenses not attributable to the business use of the home ($2,000). This produces $1,350, which is the limit on deductions attributable to insurance, utilities, and MACRS. The remaining $775 of these expenses will carry forward and be deductible in future years, subject to the same restriction.

d. **Ordering rule:** If a limitation applies, expenses will be allowed in the following order: interest, taxes, trade or business expenses, and, finally, depreciation.

2. Definitional issues

a. **Dwelling unit:** A dwelling unit includes any typical place of dwelling, including houses, apartments, and condominiums and also includes mobile homes, boats, and recreational vehicles. The term, however, does not include motels, hotels, and inns. IRC §280A(f)(1).

b. **Use as a "residence":** A taxpayer uses a dwelling unit as a *residence* if he or she uses it for personal purposes for a number of days during the taxable year that exceeds the greater of 14 days or 10% of the number of days the unit is rented at a fair rental. IRC §280A(d)(1). Personal use is use by the taxpayer or his or her family, or rental to others at less than a fair rental value. IRC §280A(d)(2).

c. **Place of business:** There are three ways a taxpayer may claim that a home office is a place of business, thus qualifying for the home office deduction. All three require that the portion of the residence used for business be used exclusively for business.

   i. **Principal place of business—*Commissioner v. Soliman*, 506 U.S. 168 (1993):** The portion of the residence may be regularly used as the *principal place of business* for a taxpayer's business. IRC §280A(c). The Supreme Court has defined the principal place of business as the most important, consequential, or influential location, which requires an examination of the relative importance of various places of business and the time spent at various locations. In Rev. Rul. 94-24, 1994-1 C.B. 87, the IRS stated that it will follow *Soliman*, but will examine the time spent at various locations only if the relative importance test doesn't yield a conclusive result. See *Popov v. Commissioner*, 246 F.3d 1190 (9th Cir. 2001) (approach of IRS followed). A home office used for administrative purposes qualifies as a taxpayer's principal place of business if (1) the taxpayer uses the office to conduct administrative or management activities of the taxpayer's trade or business, and (2) there is no other fixed location of the trade or business where the taxpayer conducts substantial administrative or managerial functions of the business. These functions include keeping records, billing patients or other customers, setting up appointments, and forwarding written reports or orders. IRC §280A(c).

   Example: Steve is a self-employed golf teacher. He teaches students at several area golf courses and conducts golf seminars at various hotels around the area. From his home office, he sets up appointments, sends bills, and keeps records of each student's progress. Assuming Steve's home office is used exclusively for this purpose, he should be able to claim a deduction for his home office as the "principal place of business" of his golf teaching business. This will allow him to deduct, among other things, travel expenses between home and the various golf courses, which would otherwise be nondeductible commuting expenses. See this chapter, Section (III).

   ii. **Meeting clients or customers:** The residence may be regularly used as the place where the taxpayer meets with clients or customers of the business. For example, a therapist might use a portion of her home as her office at which she meets patients. IRC §280A(c)(1)(B).

   iii. **Separate structures:** If the home office is located in a separate structure from the residence, it need only be "connected with" the trade or business in order to qualify, which imposes a lesser standard. IRC §280A(c)(1)(C).

3. Special rules and exceptions

    a. Rental of property when taxpayer doesn't use it as a residence: The second limitation applies to rental property that is also used for personal purposes for even one day during the taxable year, but isn't used as a residence (see definition above). The deductions attributable to the rental (other than expenses deductible without regard to rental) cannot exceed the expenses multiplied by a fraction, the numerator of which is the total number of days rented, and the denominator is the total number of days the property is used for either personal or rental purposes. IRC §280A(e).

    Example: Vicki owns a vacation home, which she rented for 358 days during the year, and used for her own vacation for 7 days. Assume that her deductions associated with the rental (other than expenses deductible without regard to rental, such as property taxes) are $10,000. Vicki must multiply the expenses by a fraction, the numerator of which is the number of days rented (358) and the denominator of which is the number of days used for either personal or rental use (365). This produces 98%, and so her expenses will be limited to $10,000 × 98%, or $9,800.

    b. 15-day rental rule: If the taxpayer rents a dwelling unit for fewer than 15 days during the taxable year, the income is excluded from the taxpayer's gross income, but no deductions associated with the rental are allowed. IRC §280A(g).

4. Related material

    a. Otherwise allowable deductions: In order to apply the restrictions of §280A, it is necessary to compute the deductions associated with personal use of a residence, which are allowable without regard to business use. See Chapter 6(V, VI, and VII).

    b. Profit-related expenses: In order to apply the limitations of §280A, it is necessary to compute the potentially deductible expenses that require a business connection in order to be deductible. See generally Chapter 7.

    c. Exclusion for gain on sale of principal residence: Section 121 allows a taxpayer to exclude from gross income all or a portion of the gain on the sale of a principal residence. However, the exclusion doesn't apply to gain attributable to previously deducted depreciation. See Chapter 4(VIII). So taxpayers should think carefully about whether to claim a portion of their home as a home office or other business use, given that they will be giving up a portion of the exclusion on sale.

5. Be alert for §280A issues:
Section 280A is implicated whenever a taxpayer uses real property for both profit-making and personal purposes. Typical scenarios include vacation homes and home offices, or use of a part of a home for business, such as a day care business. The rules of §280A are complex, so if pressed for time, simply explain the general approach of the statute—it allocates all the expenditures between business (deductible) and personal (nondeductible, unless a specific statute applies) based on use or square footage. The expenses attributable to the use of the property cannot generate a loss.

VIII. "LUXURY" AUTOMOBILES AND LISTED PROPERTY—§280F

A. Policy

While depreciation is only available for property used in a trade or business or held for investment, Congress felt the need to further restrict depreciation deductions for certain types of business or investment assets that are likely also to serve personal purposes. Thus, §280F imposes limitations on depreciation deductions for certain types of property, such as boats, airplanes, luxury automobiles, and for certain property (like computers) used for both business and personal use, called *listed property* in §280F.

B. Statutory analysis—§280F

1. **General rules:** Before tackling §280F's general rule, recall that only property used predominately in a trade or business or held for investment is depreciable under the MACRS system or potentially eligible for the §179 expense deduction. Thus, to the extent that property is used for both business/investment and personal purposes, only the portion of the property attributable to business use (expressed as a percentage of use, for example) is depreciable. Going beyond this general principle, §280F imposes two additional limitations on depreciation of certain property.

   a. **Limitation #1—Longer, slower capital recovery for "luxury" automobiles:** The amount of MACRS deductions a taxpayer may claim for so-called "luxury" passenger automobiles is limited to a specified amount, adjusted for inflation (regardless of percentage of business use). IRC §280F(a). The result of this limitation is that §280F imposes a much longer, slower recovery period for most automobiles, although the restrictions are less onerous for clean-fuel vehicles. This reflects Congress's view that the "luxury" component of the cost of the automobile is a personal, nondeductible expenditure but that investment in clean-fuel vehicles should be encouraged. The term "luxury" automobile is misleading; the limitations of §280F can apply to even moderately priced vehicles.

   b. **Limitation #2—Listed property—Straight-line depreciation and recapture:** Listed property that is not used "predominately for qualified business use" must be depreciated using a straight-line method. IRC §280F(b)(1). If business use falls below 51% for listed property that was formerly used predominately in business, the taxpayer must recapture the excess depreciation and must use straight-line depreciation in the future. IRC §280F(b)(2). Recapture requires the taxpayer to include in his or her gross income the excess depreciation, i.e., the amount of depreciation claimed in excess of the amount that would have been allowable under the straight-line method. *Id.*

2. **Definitional issues**

   a. **For limitation #1—Longer recovery periods:** A passenger automobile is any four-wheeled vehicle that is manufactured primarily for use on public streets, roads, and highways, and is rated at 6,000 pounds or less unloaded vehicle weight (or for light trucks and vans, including SUVs built on truck chassis, at 6,000 pounds gross vehicle weight), but excludes certain working vehicles. IRC §280F(d)(5).

b. For limitation #2—Listed property

i. **Listed property:** Listed property includes any passenger automobile, any other property used as a means of transportation (such as a boat, airplane, or motorcycle), any property of a type generally used for entertainment, recreation, or amusement (such as a DVD player), any computer or peripheral equipment, and any other property as specified by the Secretary of the Treasury. IRC §280F(d)(4).

ii. **Excluded—Cell phones and certain computers:** Cell phones are not listed property.

Excluded from the definition of listed property is any computer or peripheral equipment used exclusively at a regular business establishment and owned or leased by the person operating the business. This includes home offices that qualify under §280A. IRC §280F(d)(4)(B). See discussion of home offices this chapter, Section (VII).

iii. **Predominately used in business:** A taxpayer must use property in a qualified business use for more than 50% of the time during the taxable year in order to qualify as predominately in a qualified business use. IRC §280F(b)(3). A qualified business use means any use in a trade or business, but does not include use for the production of income outside of a trade or business. IRC §280F(d)(6)(B).

Example: Erin purchases a personal computer. She uses it 45% of the time for her writing business, 10% to manage her investments and rental property, and 45% for personal purposes. Her use of the property does not constitute "predominately for qualified business use" because her use in a trade or business of writing does not exceed 50%, and she may not add the 10% investment use in computing qualified business use. She will therefore be restricted to using the straight-line method for depreciation (but will be able to depreciate 55% of the property's cost because that percentage is attributable to use in a trade or business or for investment).

3. Special rules and exceptions—employee use: Use of listed property by employees is not considered business use unless the use is for the convenience of the employer and is required as a condition of employment. IRC §280F(d)(3). There must be a clear showing that the employee cannot properly perform the duties of employment without the property. Rev. Rul. 86-129, 1986-2 C.B. 48. This is a very difficult standard to meet.

Example: José is a law professor with an office at the law school with a computer supplied by his employer. José finds that he is much more productive in writing at home, and therefore he purchases a computer for use at home, under a special financing plan offered by his employer. José seeks to deduct the cost as a §179 expense. As an employee, however, he must show that the computer was for the convenience of his employer and was required as a condition of employment in order to deduct its cost. Even though his employer provides a special financing plan, this does not establish that the use was for the employer's convenience, and nothing in these facts suggests that José was required, as a condition of employment, to purchase a computer. Thus, it is unlikely that José will be able to deduct the cost of the computer as a §179 expense.

4. Related material

a. Depreciation: For discussion of depreciation in general, and MACRS in particular, see Chapter 7(III).

b. Section 179: Section 179 deductions are treated like depreciation deductions for purposes of §280F. IRC §280F(d)(1). If both §179 and §280F apply to the purchase of an asset, §280F trumps §179. For a discussion of §179, see Chapter 7(IV)(F).

5. **Be alert for listed property issues:** Most taxpayers engaged in a trade or business have some listed property such as computers or similar equipment. If a taxpayer wants to claim depreciation for expensive cars or other items that can have a substantial personal use component, §280F is implicated.

IX. HOBBY LOSSES—§183

A. Policy

As discussed in Chapter 7(II)(B), a *trade or business* requires regular and continuous activity with the expectation of producing a profit. Most businesses are easy to identify; the taxpayer would not engage in them without some expectation of profit. However, some income-producing activities offer such significant recreational or personal benefits that they raise questions about the taxpayer's *profit motive*. If the activity is engaged in for profit, all of the otherwise deductible expenses associated with the activity should be allowed as a deduction. If the taxpayer does not have a profit motive, however, the activity is properly characterized as personal in nature—a hobby—and expenses should not be deductible. But because the activity may produce income, the taxpayer may claim associated deductions up to the amount of income from the activity. The principal functions of §183 are to identify activities "not engaged in for profit" and restrict deductions associated with them.

B. Statutory analysis—§183

1. **General rule:** A taxpayer engaged in an activity without a profit motive may only deduct certain expenses associated with that activity. These expenses are (1) those that are deductible (under other Code sections) without regard to a profit motive, and (2) expenses in an amount (if any) equal to the gross income from the activity, minus the expenses described in (1). IRC §183(a). A taxpayer may not to generate a loss from a hobby, but is allowed to offset the income from the activity with expenses of producing the income.

   Example: John races cars as a hobby (not for profit). This year he earned $5,000 in race prizes, and had the following two categories of expenses. He had a casualty loss of $6,000 attributable to a crash, and expenses that would otherwise qualify as ordinary and necessary business expenses of $2,500. Assume that of the $6,000 casualty loss, $4,000 is deductible under §165(c) and (h). Since John is engaged in an activity without a profit motive, he may deduct only the deductible portion ($4,000) of the casualty loss (because it is allowable without regard to his profit motive) and $1,000 of the expenses that would be deductible if he had a profit motive. In computing the $1,000 deduction, John subtracts from his gross income from the activity ($5,000) the deductions allowable without regard to his profit motive ($4,000) to determine the allowable deduction ($1,000). The remaining $1,500 of expenses are nondeductible.

2. **Definitional issue—Activity engaged in for profit:** Whether a taxpayer is engaged in an activity for profit depends on all of the facts and circumstances of the situation. The courts emphasize that a taxpayer need have only a sincere and bona fide objective of realizing a profit,

regardless of the reasonableness of that expectation. *Dreicer v. Commissioner*, 78 T.C. 642 (1982). The regulations specify nine factors to be examined in analyzing the taxpayer's profit motive. See Reg. §1.183-2(b).

a. **Nine factors:** The regulations set forth nine factors, none of which are determinative, that are relevant in determining whether the taxpayer has (or does not have) a profit motive.

   i. **Manner of operation:** A taxpayer carrying on the activity in a businesslike manner, keeping books and records, running the business like other similar businesses, and changing methods of operation as necessary to increase profitability, indicates a profit motive. Reg. §1.183-2(b)(1).

   ii. **Expertise:** A taxpayer with expertise in the activity (or who develops or engages others with expertise) is more likely to be viewed as having a profit motive than one without such expertise. The taxpayer also should conduct business in accordance with the best practices of experts, unless he or she can show development of innovative methods for profitability. Reg. §1.183-2(b)(2).

   iii. **Time and effort:** A taxpayer devoting substantial time and effort to an activity is more likely to be considered as having a profit motive than one who dabbles in the activity, particularly if the activity is not particularly enjoyable. A taxpayer who engages others to conduct substantial activity may also be viewed as having a profit motive. Reg. §1.183-2(b)(3).

   iv. **Assets that increase in value:** If assets used in an activity are reasonably likely to increase in value, this may indicate a profit motive. Reg. §1.183-2(b)(4).

   v. **Similar success:** A taxpayer who has had success in similar ventures may be viewed as having a profit motive. Reg. §1.183-2(b)(5).

   vi. **History of income or loss:** While losses during the start-up phase of a business may not indicate a lack of profit motive, losses that continue beyond this period suggest the absence of a profit motive. However, losses arising from unforeseen or unusual events (such as storm or fire) are not indicative of a lack of profit motive. Reg. §1.183-2(b)(6).

   vii. **Amount of occasional profits, if any:** A taxpayer engaging in a venture in which profits, though occasional, would be large in comparison to losses and investment, would generally be viewed as having a profit motive. By contrast, a taxpayer engaging in a venture in which occasional profits would be small compared with losses and investment would generally be viewed as lacking a profit motive. Reg. §1.183-2(b)(7).

   viii. **Taxpayer's financial status:** A taxpayer who does not have substantial income or capital from other sources generally will be viewed as engaged in an activity for profit. By contrast, a taxpayer with substantial income from other sources may not be engaging in an activity for profit, particularly if the activity has personal or recreational elements. Reg. §1.183-2(b)(8).

   ix. **Personal pleasure or recreation:** A taxpayer who engages in an activity for personal purposes may be viewed as lacking a profit motive, especially when the activity involves recreation or other personal elements. However, enjoyment of one's work does not, alone, establish the absence of a profit motive. Reg. §1.183-2(b)(9).

    b. Application—farms: In *Nickerson v. Commissioner,* 700 F.2d 402 (7th Cir. 1983), the taxpayer purchased a farm in anticipation of retiring from the advertising business. The court examined the nine factors, ultimately concluding that Nickerson was engaged in the activity for profit as evidenced by his expectation that the farm would be profitable in future years, his engagement of a tenant farmer to clear and farm the land in his absence, his attempts to improve his expertise, and the absence of pleasurable activities on the fairly dilapidated farm.

3. Special rules and exceptions

    a. Presumption: If the activity produces income for three out of the five consecutive years ending in the year in question, it is rebuttably presumed to be an activity engaged in for profit. IRC §183(d). Moreover, if the activity involves horse breeding, racing, showing, or training, the test is whether the activity showed a profit in two out of the seven consecutive years ending in the year in question. *Id.*

    b. Reporting: If an activity is a hobby, the gross income is reported under "other income" and the deductions, to the extent allowed, are claimed on Schedule A, in the following order: (1) otherwise allowable deductions, such as home mortgage interest; (2) trade or business expenses; and (3) deductions that result in a reduction of basis in property, such as depreciation.

4. Related material

    a. Available deductions—No profit motive: In order to apply §183, it is necessary to understand what deductions are available even if the activity is not engaged in for profit. These can include certain kinds of interest, casualty losses, and other expenditures. See generally Chapter 6.

    b. Tax shelters: Many tax shelters are based on the concept of a trade or business that generates losses. The passive loss rules, which require that a taxpayer participate in the business to claim a loss, prevent this strategy from working to shelter income. See Chapter 11(VII).

5. Be alert for hobby loss issues: Section 183 is implicated when a taxpayer claims to be engaged in a trade or business (and claims deductions for that activity) but the primary motivation for the activity is not profit, but pleasure. Typical scenarios include: farms; horses; dogs; racing of any kind.

X. GAMBLING LOSSES

A. General Rule:

A taxpayer may deduct **gambling losses** to the extent of gambling income. IRC §165(d). This is true whether the gambling is legal or illegal. Gambling losses in excess of gains are most properly viewed as expenditures for the personal enjoyment of gambling.

1. Same-year limitation: Gambling losses can be deducted against gains only in the same year. They cannot be carried forward or back to other years. *Skeeles v. United States,* 95 F. Supp. 242 (Ct.Cl.) cert. denied 341 U.S. 948 (1951).

2. **Deduction limited to gambling income:** Gambling losses in excess of gambling gains cannot be deducted against other kinds of income, such as salary. *Carnahan v. Commissioner*, 9 T.C. 1206 (1947), *aff'd* 176 F.2d 394 (10th Cir. 1949).

B. **How is the loss deductible?**

1. **Professional gamblers:** Professional gamblers may deduct their losses on Schedule C, where they report their gambling winnings. A professional gambler is a person who regularly and continually engages in the activities of gambling with an expectation of profit, even if the person does not hold him-or herself out to others as providing a service. *Commissioner v. Groetzinger*, 480 U.S. 23 (1987).

2. **Others:** A person who does not qualify as a professional gambler must deduct the gambling losses as an itemized deduction on Schedule A. See Rev. Rul. 54-339, 1954-2 C.B. 89.

XI. NEED TO KNOW MORE?

This book's website *www.aspenlawschool.com/books/tax_outline* contains additional information, including:

- Calculating the deductible expenses of a home office or vacation home.

- Coordinating the capital recovery and listed property rules.

- Travel and entertainment expense rules—applying the specific tests.

- And other materials that will help you master mixed business and personal expenditures.

XII. WHERE ARE WE GOING?

This chapter concludes our discussion of deductions, having examined personal, business, and mixed-nature expenditures. We next turn to an in-depth discussion of a type of transaction that can generate gross income or potentially deductible loss—transactions in property, including sales, exchanges, and transfers subject to debt.

Quiz Yourself on
MIXED BUSINESS AND PERSONAL EXPENSES

81. Marco is a state Assistant Attorney General who practices litigation. Recognizing the increasing importance of negotiation and mediation in his practice, he takes two psychology courses at the local college—PSYCH 4840 (Goals, Needs, and Desires) and PSYCH 4300 (Moral Reasoning) and pays for the books and tuition personally (his employer does not reimburse him). May Marco deduct these expenses? What if Marco decides, after taking these courses, to earn a degree in clinical psychology? May he deduct the books and tuition for all of the required courses? _____

82. What is the rationale for the disallowance of 50% of the cost of meals as a deduction under §274(n)? _____

83. Tom is a lawyer in a highly successful private practice. He receives a letter from the IRS questioning his deductions for the following expenses on his tax return:

- Lunches and dinners with other attorneys who refer cases to him: $2,500

- Skybox at local basketball arena where he gives tickets to referral sources

- potential expert witnesses: $50,000

- Attendance at a conference on Trial Techniques at a fishing lodge in Alaska: $6,000

What are the IRS's likely arguments with respect to these expenses, and what should Tom's response be? _____

84. Billie, a cardiovascular surgeon, is considering buying a horse farm and several horses. She's allergic to hay, but her teenage daughters are avid riders, and she currently has to pay an expensive riding academy for her daughters to ride. Billie is a city gal, but longs for the country life. She understands that, at least in the first few years, farms are "losing propositions," but she thinks she can eventually turn a profit by having her daughters board and train other people's horses. In the meantime, she's looking forward to deducting the losses from the farm. You're her tax advisor. What do you tell her? _____

85. Rudy's principal residence is in New York City, but he has a second home in the Adirondacks. Each year, he spends four weeks there, and then rents out the home to vacationers for the rest of the year. In the past, Rudy has reported all of the rent received from the property in his gross income each year, and has deducted 100% of the expenses, including taxes, insurance, and repairs. He also has been depreciating the property on a straight-line basis over 27.5 years. Has Rudy's reporting position been correct? Why or why not? _____

86. Susan is a clinical psychologist in Boston. She sees patients as does any psychologist, and also acts as an expert witness in various trials. Susan owns a townhouse: The bottom floor is her office, and the top floor is her home. In her office, she sees patients, talks with lawyers in person and on the telephone, keeps records, bills insurance companies and lawyers, and does her research. She uses the office exclusively for work. May she deduct expenses associated with the home office? Why or why not? If she can deduct expenses, which ones are deductible? _____

87. Jeff spends most of his time playing poker, entering poker tournaments, and studying poker. This year, he earned $120,000 in winnings, and had $300,000 in losses. Last year, the reverse was true: He had much more winnings than losses. Will Jeff be able to deduct his losses from gambling from this year? If so, how? If not, why not? _____

88. Gerry's business has two locations: manufacturing in City A and retail sales in City B. The two cities are 100 miles apart. Gerry lives in City A, and he goes to the plant there every workday. About three days a week, he travels to City B and back. He travels by car, and has traditionally deducted the travel expense using the standard mileage allowance. Gerry has decided to purchase a small airplane, as he recently earned his pilot's license. Use of the airplane would significantly reduce his travel time between City A and City B—and it would be, as Gerry says, "a lot more fun!" Plus, he says, "I can use it to fly to City C to see my grandchildren—and I can finally travel to see the Ducks play football, wherever they are!" Gerry is looking forward to a "big tax deduction" resulting from his purchase. As Gerry's new tax adviser, what is your advice to him? Will he get "the big deduction"?

_____

89. Steve owns a home in Oregon, and Mike owns a home in Florida. They agree to "swap" houses for three months: Steve lives in Mike's house, and Mike lives in Steve's house from July through September. No cash changes hands. Steve wants to deduct one-fourth (3 months' worth) of repairs, utilities, depreciation, and other expenses associated with his home. Will he be successful?

_____

90. Roma is a celebrity whose occupation is simply "being famous." Frankly, it's hard work. Roma is always on the go, being seen everywhere that matters, and playing cat-and-mouse with the paparazzi. Perfect strangers bombard her with so-called gifts and beg her to tout their products and services. Other jet-setters pay for her travel and meals, send her tickets to major events, and host her for month-long skiing vacations in the Alps. Roma keeps meticulous records of all of her activities and includes all of these items in her gross income (this year: $1,000,000). In addition to being hard work, fame is expensive. Left to her own devices, Roma says, she would wear ratty sweatpants and T-shirts all the time, but she is forced to wear the latest (and weirdest) fashions to maintain her image—after all, image is what makes her profession of being famous possible. This year, her clothing cost $350,000. May Roma deduct her clothing expenses? _____

Answers

81. Educational expenses are deductible if they either (1) maintain or improve skills required by the individual in his employment or other trade or business, or (2) allow the taxpayer to meet the express requirements of the taxpayer's employer or applicable law or regulations as a condition of retention in a job or occupation. Treas. Reg. §1.162-5. In Marco's case, the two initial courses would likely be deductible, as they would help him improve skills required in his trade or business of being employed as a litigation attorney. However, Treas. Reg. §1.162-5 also disallows educational expenses that prepare a person for a new trade or business, so Marco's courses toward a degree in clinical psychology would not likely be deductible in full, although some courses would likely qualify as related to his current trade or business.

82. Some portion of every meal is a personal expenditure: after all, everyone has to eat. If sufficiently connected to a taxpayer's trade or business, a portion of a meal expense might not have been incurred but for business purpose (consider a person who would normally eat a peanut-butter-and-jelly-sandwich at her desk, but who takes a client out to lunch instead). It would be impossible to determine what portion of a meal is personal and what portion of a meal is related to business in every case, so the 50% disallowance is an administratively feasible estimate.

83. The IRS will likely object to all of these deductions as personal expenditures that are not deductible under §262. First, with respect to the skybox, the IRS may have an early win. It is clear that only the cost of tickets (at face value) is deductible. IRC §274(l)(2). If the skybox has twelve seats, Tom may be able to preserve the deduction for the cost of twelve tickets (at face value), if certain tests are met, but he will certainly not receive the additional amount attributable to the cost of the skybox itself.

Meal and entertainment expenses must run a gauntlet of requirements in order to be deductible. First, they must be "ordinary and necessary business expenses" as determined under §162. In this case, these are obviously ordinary expenses, as they are frequently incurred by business owners. They are of the type most business owners view as appropriate to their ability to obtain and retain business, and thus are "necessary." Tom is clearly carrying on a trade or business so there is no problem with pre-opening capitalization, and they do not create a specific benefit beyond the close of the taxable year, so they should not be capitalized under principles of *Indopco*.

Section 274, however, will impose additional requirements. First, with respect to meals, these must not be lavish or extravagant. The lavishness is, of course, a question of fact. Second, for the meals and tickets, the requirement of §274 that may create the most problems is the "business connection" test. Tom may be able to meet the "directly related" test with respect to meals more easily than with respect to the sporting events, because sporting events provide the kind of significant distraction that would preclude the event being directly related to his trade or business. However, Tom may be able to meet the less stringent "associated with" standard, and if so, he will be able to preserve the deduction for meals and/or entertainment. However, even if Tom can meet either business connection test, the amounts expended will still be subject to the 50% limit: only 50% of the amount expended will be deductible. IRC §274(n). It is not clear from the facts whether the amounts deducted are the full costs, or represent 50% of the amounts expended.

As to the conference expenses, the costs of professional conferences are typically an ordinary and necessary business expense, but Tom will have to show that the travel and other costs incurred while away from home were incurred "primarily for business" in order to support this deduction.

84. Billie should be aware that the IRS may well challenge the deduction of losses from the horse farm as "hobby losses" under §183 of the Code. This provision denies a deduction for expenses in excess of income for activities not undertaken "for profit." Whether an activity is engaged in for profit depends on the taxpayer's intention, as evidenced by the nine factors outlined in the regulations. No one factor is determinative. However, a number of factors may work against Billie, including:

- *Time and energy spent on the activity:* As a surgeon, Billie probably has limited time to devote to the business. Relying on teenagers to handle the business is probably not a businesslike plan in the long run. She would need to engage a manager to handle the farm business.

- *Similar success:* Billie apparently has no experience in these matters.

- *Financial situation:* Billie has substantial income from other sources and doesn't need income from the farm to support her family. In fact, she could be expected to seek tax benefits from this activity.

- *Personal enjoyment:* Billie "longs for the country life." She seems to want to support her daughters' wish to ride horses, which would suggest a personal, not profit, motive. On the other hand, she is allergic to hay, which would suggest little pleasure in a horse farm.

If Billie is to make the best possible case for deducting any loss, she should ensure that she takes a businesslike approach to this endeavor, researching best practices and getting the professional help she needs to run the operation. She should be able to show that the farm will increase in value, and that these operations can and do produce profits, even if her particular farm does not. It would be helpful to not have many years of losses in a row.

85. Rudy has been reporting the results of the summer home incorrectly. He is correct in including all of the income from the rental of the property. However, because the property is used partially for personal purposes, the expenses must be allocated between personal and business use. The deductible expenses attributable to the rental (other than expenses deductible without regard to the rental) cannot exceed the total expenses (other than expenses deductible without regard to the rental) multiplied by the percentage of the year the home is rented. While Rudy will be able to deduct all of the property taxes, because these taxes are deductible regardless of rental activity, the rest of the expense will be limited.

86. Susan would like to deduct the expenses of her home office, and it appears that she can do so. She uses the home office exclusively on a regular basis as the principal place of business for her practice. A home office qualifies as a taxpayer's principal place of business if (1) the taxpayer uses the office to conduct administrative or management activities of the taxpayer's trade or business, and (2) there is no other fixed location of the trade or business where the taxpayer conducts substantial administrative or managerial functions of the business. This would appear to be the case for Susan; although she travels to trials, her administrative work is done at the home office and there is no other *fixed* place of business for her practice. As to which expenses are deductible, Susan can already deduct (regardless of the home office) the interest on her mortgage and her property taxes on the property. But because it is a home office, she may also deduct repairs made to that portion of the property and, perhaps most important, she can depreciate that portion of the dwelling. Of course, when she sells the home, she will not be entitled to the exclusion of §121 on the gain from the sale of a principal residence for the portion used as a home office and depreciated.

87. The fact that Jeff spends most of his time playing poker, studying poker, and entering tournaments suggests that he is a professional gambler. If so, he may deduct the poker losses for the year against the poker winnings for the year. He would report the winnings and losses on a Schedule C. However, the net loss for the year would not offset other income, nor may it be carried back to the profitable prior year. If Jeff is not a professional gambler, he may still deduct the poker losses, but again the loss would be limited to the poker winnings. In that case, Jeff would include his winnings as gross income and would deduct the gambling loss as an itemized deduction.

88. As Gerry's new tax adviser, the first question for you to analyze is whether Gerry's travel from City A to City B is commuting (nondeductible) or business travel away from home (deductible)? Even though he seems to have deducted the cost of this travel for years, it is always worthwhile to confirm the accuracy of this reporting position, especially when the client is considering a major change such as purchase of the plane. Gerry's travel is first to his business location in City A, and then to City B. His travel to City B qualifies as business travel, not commuting. If Gerry's only location were in City B, then his travel would be considered as commuting.

   When Gerry purchases the airplane, he is expecting that he will be able to either claim the §179 expense for the entire cost of the plane, or to depreciate it using an accelerated method of depreciation under MACRS. However, the airplane is "listed property," which means that it is of the class of assets that Congress was especially concerned about in terms of use for personal purposes rather than business purposes. In order to depreciate listed property using an accelerated method, or to claim a §179 deduction, the property must be used at least 51% in business. If the property doesn't meet this standard, it can only be depreciated using the straight-line method and no §179 deduction is allowable. In Gerry's case, it is not clear from the facts whether he intends to use the airplane primarily for business (travel between Cities A and B), or whether his primary use will be personal (travel to see his grandchildren and to see his favorite college football team play). As his tax adviser, you will need to explain that the use of the airplane in terms of hours will determine its initial treatment, and then even if it qualifies, if later its business use falls below 51%, Gerry will be forced to recapture the prior deductions.

89. To answer this question fully, you may want to review the materials on barter, Chapter 2(III). Steve and Mike have "bartered" their homes, i.e., traded in-kind use of the homes. Steve and Mike would be required to include in gross income an amount equal to the fair market value of the rental. If they

did so, then each would be able to deduct expenses associated with that rental, subject to the limitations of §280A. Without including this amount in gross income, it is not possible to take the corresponding deduction.

90. Probably not. According to the IRS, the cost of clothing is only deductible if it is not suitable for general use. Although the fashions that Roma purchases would likely not be suitable for general use for the average working person, she certainly wears them in her everyday life and they probably appear in fashion magazines as suitable for a certain group of society. Roma's argument that left to her own devices, she would wear ratty sweatpants and T-shirts is not likely to be successful, as the courts employ an objective test for suitability for general use, not a subjective test of what a taxpayer would do "but for" the requirements of her job.

Exam Tips on
MIXED BUSINESS AND PERSONAL EXPENSES

☛ Mixed business and personal expenses are often a major focus of deduction questions: they offer ample opportunities to test statutory skills.

  ☞ *Look for:* A taxpayer making an expenditure that benefits his or her business, yet is integrally tied to personal enjoyment or lifestyle (food, entertainment, vacations, home life, cars, or trucks).

  ☞ *Analyze:* Find the applicable statute (e.g., §§183, 280A). Which approach does the statute take: nondeductible, partially deductible, deductible in full if requirements are met? Make sure the taxpayer's situation meets the applicable requirements in order to qualify for a deduction.

☛ **Remember:** It is not enough to have expended funds and met the statutory requirements for a deduction. The taxpayer has the duty of substantiating the deduction with adequate records.

☛ Many professors are not interested in the mechanics of the home office/vacation home rules. They just want you to know that these activities cannot generate a deductible loss for a taxpayer. Find out the level of interest your professor has in §280A.

☛ Similarly, professors that don't require a deep understanding of the mechanics of MACRS are also not interested in the mechanics of depreciating listed property. However, the policy behind §280F offers ample opportunity for questions:

  ☞ Do the limitations make sense in an era of Humvees and big SUVs?

  ☞ Do you think this section is effective in achieving its goals? How do taxpayers likely change their behavior in response to the limitations on listed property, for example? Or are gas prices more effective in changing behavior?

☛ Most of the statutes contain objective tests. But §183 is an "intent" test.

☞ *Look for:* Facts relevant to the nine factors evidencing profit motive.

☞ *Analyze:* Analyze each factor as to its particular impact on the taxpayer. Does the question ask you to be an advocate? Or an advisor?

☛ Use the origin of the expense test when there is no statute on point.

☛ **Remember:** Construe deductions narrowly. If in doubt, deny the deduction.

 STATUTE SUMMARY CHARTS

Statute Summary—§280A
Home Offices and Vacation Homes

Parsing Step	IRC §280A
General Rule	Deductions associated with business use of a residence are limited to the gross income from the business reduced by otherwise allowable deductions and trade or business deductions that are not attributable to use of the home.
Definitions	**Dwelling unit:** can include nontraditional residences **Use as residence:** used for personal purposes at least two weeks/year **Principal place of business:** See *Soliman* and specific statutory requirements
Special Rules and Exceptions	Even if the property isn't used as a residence, if used for personal purposes even one day during the year, deductions attributable to personal use are denied (allocate based on days used). 15-day rental rule—if rented for fewer than 15 days during a year, income isn't included and no deductions are allowed.
Related Statutes	**§§162, 163, 164, 165, 166:** Otherwise allowable deductions **§§167, 168, 179, 195:** Deductions attributable to use of the home
Typically implicated when . . .	A taxpayer has a home office, or rents out part of his or her home, or a taxpayer rents a vacation home and uses it for personal purposes.

Statute Summary—§183
Hobby Losses

Parsing Step	IRC §183
General Rule	Deductions are allowed for expenses incurred for an activity not for profit only to the extent they exceed the income from the property reduced by otherwise allowable deductions; cannot generate a loss.
Definitions	**Activity not engaged in for profit:** depends on all the facts and circumstances—see the nine factors in regulations.
Special Rules and Exceptions	Presumption of profit objective if profits in three out of five years (or, for horses, two out of seven years)
Related Statutes	**§162:** Trade or business expenses **§§163, 164, 165:** Typical otherwise allowable expenses **§§167, 168, 179, 195:** Capital recovery
Typically implicated when . . .	A taxpayer with other sources of income engages in some enjoyable activity such as farming, breeding of dogs or other animals, car racing, or similar activities.

CHAPTER 9

TRANSACTIONS IN PROPERTY

ChapterScope

This chapter examines the rules governing the computation of gain or loss from transactions in property, such as sales, exchanges, and foreclosures. This is important, of course, because gross income includes gains from dealings in property, and a loss on the sale or exchange of property can result in a deduction for the taxpayer if certain conditions are met.

- **Section 1001:** Deceptively simple §1001 requires the recognition of gains and losses on the sale or exchange of property, unless some other Code section provides otherwise.

- **An approach to property transactions:** Four straightforward questions provide an approach to any property transaction: (1) has there been a sale or other disposition of property? (2) what is the amount of the gain or loss (realized and recognized) on that sale or disposition? (3) what is the basis of any property received? and (4) what is the character of the gain or loss recognized?

- **The realization concept:** In order to have realized gain or loss on a property transaction, the taxpayer must exchange property for something else, and end up with a different legal entitlement than he or she had before the exchange.

- **Computation of realized gain or loss:** A taxpayer's realized gain is always equal to the difference between the amount realized on the transaction (what the taxpayer received) and his or her adjusted basis in the property transferred. Similarly, realized loss is equal to the difference between the taxpayer's adjusted basis in the property transferred and the amount realized on the transaction. Understanding the computation of adjusted basis and what is included in the amount realized is crucial to computation of realized gain or loss.

- **The effect of loans in sales or other dispositions:** Transfers of encumbered properties raise special questions in the computation of realized gain and loss. Recognizing the common forms of transfers of such property is important in understanding the tax consequences to the seller, buyer, and creditor.

I. WHERE ARE WE?

We are now exploring in detail a specific kind of gross income or loss: *income or loss from dispositions of property.* Section 61(a)(3) includes these gains in gross income, so in a sense we are returning to the computation of gross income. Section 165(c) may allow an individual taxpayer to claim a loss on these transactions, so this is a deduction question as well. Special rules apply to the computation of gains and losses from property transactions, and these are explored in this chapter.

II. STATUTORY ANALYSIS—§1001

A. General rule

Section 1001(c) states that the entire amount of gain or loss on the sale or exchange of property must be recognized, unless some other Code section provides otherwise.

B. Definitional issues

1. **Property:** There is no precise definition of ***property*** for federal income tax purposes. As a starting place, state law defines real and personal property, but federal tax law is ultimately determinative of whether an item qualifies as property. Certainly real property and tangible personal property qualify, as do many items of intangible property, such as copyrights or trademarks. See §1222, discussed in Chapter 12.

2. **Sale or exchange:** Section 1001(c) requires a ***sale or exchange*** of property in order for gain or loss to be recognized. Section 1001(a) uses slightly different language, referring to a "sale or other disposition." Both require that the taxpayer have given up beneficial ownership of property in exchange for something else. Sales, exchanges (trades) of property, involuntary conversions, certain abandonments, and foreclosures qualify, but a gift of property does not because there is no sale or exchange. Mere increases or decreases in the value of property without disposition do not trigger §1001.

3. **Realized gain or loss:** ***Realized gain*** is equal to the excess of the ***amount realized*** on the transaction over the taxpayer's ***adjusted basis*** in the property transferred. ***Realized loss*** is equal to the taxpayer's adjusted basis in the property transferred minus the amount realized on the transaction. In calculating the realized gain or loss on a sale or other disposition, §1001 seeks to measure the taxpayer's economic profit or loss on the investment.

4. **Recognized gain or loss:** ***Recognition*** of gain or loss means that the amount ends up on a taxpayer's tax return as income or a deduction. Recall that a taxpayer must include in gross income gain from dispositions of property (see discussion in Chapter 3(IV)). Taxpayers who receive less in a sale or other disposition than their investment in the property sold *may* be entitled to claim a deduction for the loss on the transaction. A variety of tax statutes exclude gain, prohibit the deduction of loss, or defer the recognition of income or loss to the future. See generally Chapter 10 and discussion of §121 in Chapter 4(VIII).

C. Special rules and exceptions

In real estate transactions, ***property taxes*** typically are allocated between sellers and buyers based on the number of days in the property tax year that each owns the property. Section 1001(b) provides that the amount treated as paid by the purchaser is not included in the seller's amount realized.

Example: On November 1 of Year 1, Joanne paid $3,000 of real property taxes on Whiteacre for the property tax year that began on July 1 of Year 1. Joanne sold Whiteacre to Kyle on January 1 of Year 2. At closing, Kyle reimbursed Joanne for his share of property taxes for the property tax year ($1,500, for half the year). This amount is not included in Joanne's amount realized for federal income tax purposes.

D. Related material

   1. Tax-deferred transactions: Chapter 10 discusses a variety of transactions in which gain or loss is realized, but recognition of that gain or loss is deferred.

   2. Installment method: If a taxpayer sells property and receives payment over time, the taxpayer can recognize the gain over that same time period. IRC §453; see Chapter 11(V).

   3. Exclusions: Even if gain is realized, the Code may provide exclusion for the gain. See, e.g., §121, excluding from gross income the gain from sale of a principal residence. See Chapter 4(VIII).

   4. Denial of deduction of loss: Individual taxpayers may recognize a loss only if §165 allows it. Realized loss, for example, on the sale of a principal residence is not recognized, i.e., is not deductible, because the property was used for personal purposes. See Chapter 4(II)(D).

E. Be alert for §1001 issues: Section 1001 is commonly tested in the basic tax course. Whenever you see a taxpayer selling or exchanging property, using property to satisfy a debt, or otherwise disposing of property, including in foreclosure, §1001 will be implicated. The essential issues are whether a realization event has occurred and the measurement of gain and loss.

III. AN APPROACH TO PROPERTY TRANSACTIONS

Four questions are sufficient to analyze any property transaction. See Figure 9A. As a preliminary matter, it is important to identify the parties to a transaction, and what they exchanged. It is often helpful to draw or chart this. In tax class, we assume that, unless parties are related, they will act rationally. Specifically, they will trade value for value, i.e., the fair market values of the properties transferred by the parties will be equal.

Figure 9A
An Approach to Property Transactions

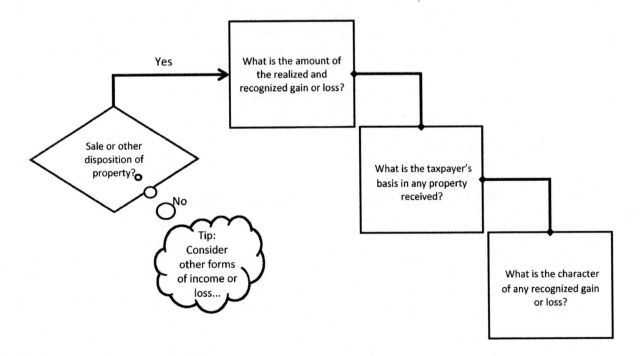

Example: Michael owns Blackacre and Drea owns Whiteacre. Michael sells Blackacre to Drea in exchange for Whiteacre plus $10,000. Michael and Drea are not related. We can assume that Blackacre is worth $10,000 more than Whiteacre. So, if we know Whiteacre's value is $100,000, we know that Blackacre is worth $110,000. However, if Drea and Michael were family members, we would have to consider whether this is a part sale/part gift transaction. In that case, we would need to know the value of both Whiteacre and Blackacre to determine if a gift has been made.

A. Has there been a sale or other disposition of property?

The essential nature of a property transaction is that a taxpayer has some sort of property right, and has sold, exchanged, or bartered it for something else. All of the usual sales and exchanges are covered by this rule, including foreclosure sales and the use of property to satisfy debts. But pure gifts and charitable contributions are not sales or dispositions that trigger realized gain or loss. Sometimes, a gift or charitable contribution can be a part gift and part sale (known as a **bargain sale**).

B. What is the amount of the realized and recognized gain or loss on the transaction?

The meat of §1001 is the calculation of realized gain or loss.

1. **Realized gain or loss:** The formula is deceptively simple: Amount realized minus adjusted basis. Applying the formula requires an understanding of how transactions are structured, what is included as consideration for property, and how basis is calculated. The existence of debt on a property can complicate all of these matters.

2. **Recognized gain or loss:** In general, realized gain or loss is recognized, but many other provisions of the Code provide exceptions and limitations on this rule. See generally Chapter 10.

3. **The relationship between realized and recognized gain or loss.** In order for gain or loss to be recognized, it must first be realized, i.e., the upper limit on recognized gain or loss is realized gain or loss. But sometimes realized gain or loss is not recognized.

C. What is the basis of the property received in the transaction?

If a taxpayer has sold property for cash, this is not a relevant question. But if the taxpayer has received property in exchange, it is necessary to assign a basis to that property. Property received in a fully taxable transaction has a basis equal to its fair market value. If some or all of the gain or loss is not recognized, calculating basis is more difficult. See this chapter, Section (V)(C) and Chapter 10.

D. What is the character of the recognized gain or loss?

If gain or loss on the sale of property is recognized, it must be characterized as ordinary or capital. See generally Chapter 12.

IV. SALES OR OTHER DISPOSITIONS OF PROPERTY

A. Property

The requirement that property be sold or disposed of is not usually an issue because it is usually clear that an item that represents a property right has been sold or otherwise disposed of in a transaction. But for the beginning tax student, it is helpful to think about whether a problem involves a disposition of property or some other type of income. See also Chapter 12(III)(C).

B. The realization requirement

Section 1001 potentially requires recognitions of gain or loss only if a taxpayer has experienced a *realization event,* i.e., some sort of transaction in which it is appropriate to measure the taxpayer's gain or loss. A realization event is a transaction—a sale, exchange, or other disposition for value—in which the taxpayer receives something materially different from that which he or she had before the exchange. To be materially different, the property received must confer different legal interests or entitlements on the taxpayer. This is an easy standard to meet, and most transactions will qualify as realization events.

C. Development of the realization requirement

1. **Realization events—*Eisner v. Macomber,* 252 U.S. 189 (1920):** The taxpayer owned stock in a corporation. The corporation paid a dividend, but not in cash: the taxpayer received a stock dividend in which she received one additional share for every two that she owned. The Commissioner asserted that the stock dividend was income to her, even though the receipt of the stock dividend neither increased her proportionate interest in the corporation nor resulted in her receiving any cash. The Court held that the taxpayer had not "realized or received any income" as a result of the stock dividend, because all of the profits remained in the corporation. The Court relied on the Sixteenth Amendment, an approach that is not favored today. However, the case is typically cited as the origin of the **realization principle,** i.e., that gains and losses must be realized before they will be recognized.

2. ***Helvering v. Bruun,* 309 U.S. 461 (1940):** A tenant erected a building on leased premises, and then surrendered the lease to the landlord, giving up its interest in the building. The landlord (the taxpayer) received the premises with a new building on it, and the IRS asserted that the taxpayer had received gross income equal to the value of the building. The taxpayer argued that the building could not be severed from the land, and therefore it had not realized any income under *Eisner v. Macomber, supra.* The Court held that taxable gain can result even if the value received could not be severed from the original capital investment, and sustained the IRS's determination. The Court distinguished *Eisner v. Macomber, supra,* a situation in which the taxpayer's relationship to the underlying corporate property did not change.

3. **Satisfaction of obligation with property:** When a taxpayer transfers property to another person in satisfaction of an obligation, that transfer is a realization event.

   a. **Payment of compensation:** A taxpayer transferred appreciated stock to its employees as payment under a bonus plan. This transfer was a realization event, resulting in the recognition of gain or loss to the taxpayer. *International Freighting Corp., Inc. v. Commissioner,* 135 F.2d 310 (2d Cir. 1943).

   b. **Distribution from trust or estate:** A trustee distributed appreciated stock to a beneficiary in satisfaction of the beneficiary's claim to a specific dollar amount (a "pecuniary" bequest). This was a realization event resulting in recognition of gain or loss. *Kenan v. Commissioner,* 114 F.2d 217 (2d Cir. 1940). This principle applies whenever property is transferred in satisfaction of a debt, not just in the trusts and estates arena.

4. **Hair-trigger realization—*Cottage Savings Ass'n v. Commissioner,* 499 U.S. 554 (1991):** In the early 1980s, savings and loan institutions (S&Ls) held large numbers of low-interest loans whose value had plummeted during the interest rate rise of the late 1970s. While it would have made economic sense to sell these loans, doing so would have placed the S&Ls at risk of

closure because they would have been required to report losses in excess of those allowed by their regulatory agency, the Federal Home Loan Bank Board (FHLBB). Eventually recognizing this problem, the FHLBB issued a regulation allowing S&Ls to exchange substantially identical mortgages without having to report losses on such exchanges for financial purposes. One such S&L, Cottage Savings, exchanged one package of mortgages for another package of mortgages in a transaction that qualified as "substantially identical" for regulatory purposes. Its basis in the loans transferred was $6.9 million, and it received loans with a value of $4.5 million in exchange. It therefore reported a $2.4 million loss for tax purposes. The IRS argued that Cottage Savings did not realize a loss, citing its long-standing administrative interpretation that the realization principle requires that the properties exchanged be materially different. In the IRS's view, the two mortgage groups did not meet this requirement. The Tax Court held for the taxpayer, and the Sixth Circuit reversed, on the grounds that the loss was not sustained during the taxable year.

a. **Issue:** Does the realization principle incorporate a "material difference" requirement?

b. **Result and rationale:** The realization principle incorporates a material difference require-ment, but to satisfy this requirement, the exchange must simply result in the taxpayer having different legal interests than the taxpayer had before the transaction. Because the exchange of mortgages resulted in Cottage Savings having different legal interests than it had before the exchange, the loss was realized. The Court gave deference to the Commissioner's interpretation of §1001(a) in Reg. §1.1001-1, which requires that proper-ties exchanged be materially different in order for a realization event to occur. However, no deference was given to the IRS's interpretation of "materiality" because there was no prelitigation published interpretation of the term. The IRS's approach of examining the facts and circumstances of the situation was inconsistent with prior case law, the goal of administrative convenience, and the structure of the Code. The minor argument that the loss was not sustained was rejected because the loss was bona fide.

c. **Subsequent developments—Reg. §1.1001-3:** The U.S. Treasury subsequently issued a regulation that provides that any "significant modification" of a debt instrument results in a realization event in which the debt instrument is deemed to be exchanged for a new instrument with the new terms. Reg. §1.1001-3(b). This can result in gain, loss, and discharge of indebtedness income. A "modification" is any alteration of a legal right or obligation of the issuer or holder of a debt instrument. Reg. §1.1001-3(c)(1)(i). In order to be a significant modification, the changes must be economically significant in light of all of the facts and circumstances of the situation. Reg. §1.1001-3(e)(1). The removal of a co-obligor on a debt instrument, for example, is not significant.

V. COMPUTATION OF REALIZED AND RECOGNIZED GAIN OR LOSS

A. **Section 1001 definitions**

1. **Realized gain:** Realized gain is equal to the excess of the amount realized on a transaction over the taxpayer's adjusted basis in the property transferred. IRC §1001(a).

2. **Realized loss:** Realized loss is the excess of the taxpayer's adjusted basis in the property transferred over the amount realized on the transaction. IRC §1001(a).

B. Amount realized

In order to calculate the realized gain or loss, the ***amount realized*** must be determined. The amount realized is the total value that the taxpayer receives in the transaction in exchange for the property transferred. The taxpayer can receive cash, property, services, and the assumption of liabilities as part of the exchange. IRC §1001(b); Reg. §§1.1001-1, -2.

1. **Cash received:** The most common transaction is a sale for cash. The taxpayer sells property to the other party in exchange for an amount of cash equal to the fair market value of the property. The amount of the cash is included in the amount realized.

   Example: Erin owns Pinkacre, a parcel of raw land. She sells Pinkacre to Andrea for $100,000 in cash. Erin's amount realized on this transaction is $100,000.

2. **Property received:** If a taxpayer exchanges property for other property, the amount realized includes the fair market value of the property received in the transaction.

   Example: Tristan owns Blueacre, an apartment building. He exchanges Blueacre for Erin's Pinkacre, which is worth $100,000. Tristan's amount realized is the fair market value of Pinkacre, $100,000.

3. **Services received:** A taxpayer's amount realized includes the fair market value of any services the taxpayer receives as part of the transaction.

   Example: Karin owns Blackacre. She sells Blackacre to Pete in exchange for Pete paving her very long driveway, which would otherwise cost $15,000. Karin's amount realized is the fair market value of Pete's services, or $15,000.

4. **Assumption of liabilities:** In some transactions, the buyer will ***assume*** (take over) all or part of the seller's liabilities in connection with the exchange. In this situation, the amount realized includes the amount of the liability assumed. See Section (VI) of this chapter for a detailed discussion of transfers of encumbered properties.

   Example: Justin owns Yellowacre, an office building. It is worth $200,000, but is subject to a debt of $200,000. Justin transfers Yellowacre to Blake, and Blake agrees to assume the debt to which Yellowacre is subject. Justin's amount realized on this transaction is $200,000, the amount of the debt Blake assumed in connection with this transaction.

5. **Amount realized equals total value received:** Amount realized is the total of the cash received, the fair market value of the property or services received, and the liabilities assumed by the other party to the transaction. For arms-length transactions that include no gift component, the amount realized is always equal to the fair market value of the property transferred. Unless the facts suggest otherwise, you may assume that transactions occur between unrelated parties.

   Example: Leah owns Blackacre, an apartment building. She sells it to William for $60,000 cash and a sports car worth $30,000. Leah's amount realized is $90,000, the total of the cash and the fair market value of the sports car received.

   Example: Patrick owns Whiteacre, a parcel of raw land that is subject to a mortgage of $50,000. He sells it to Hillary for cash of $100,000 and Hillary's assumption of the $50,000 mortgage. Patrick's amount realized on this transaction is $150,000, the total of the cash and assumption of the mortgage.

Example: Betsy owns an antique car worth $100,000. She sells it to Bill for $20,000 cash, a truck worth $30,000, and Bill's assumption of a liability for which Betsy is obligated of $50,000. Betsy's amount realized on this transaction is $100,000, the total of the cash ($20,000), the fair market value of the truck ($30,000), and the assumption of liabilities ($50,000).

C. Adjusted basis

1. Taxpayer's initial basis: In order to calculate realized gain or loss, the adjusted basis of the property transferred must be determined. The adjusted basis of property is its basis when acquired by the taxpayer and adjusted thereafter as required by §1016. Adjusted basis is the way the Code keeps track of a taxpayer's unrecovered economic investment in property for purposes of calculating the taxpayer's gain or loss upon sale or exchange of the property. This discussion applies to most property, but not a taxpayer's inventory. See Chapter 11(IV).

a. Cost: For property acquired by purchase, the purchaser's initial basis is the cost of the property. IRC §1012. The cost of the property is equal to the amount of money paid for the property, the fair market value of the property or services given in exchange for the property, and the face amount of liabilities assumed in acquiring the property. If a taxpayer borrows money to acquire property, the cost includes the amount of borrowed funds.

Example—Cash: Bill purchases Blackacre for $100,000. His initial basis in the property is his purchase price, $100,000.

Example—Cash and property: Allison purchases Whiteacre from Penny, giving Penny $50,000 cash and a parcel of raw land worth $60,000. Allison's initial basis in Whiteacre is its cost, or $110,000, equal to the cash plus the fair market value of the property given Penny to acquire Whiteacre.

Example—borrowed money: Shouka purchases Pinkacre by giving the seller $10,000 of her own funds and $90,000 that she borrowed from Friendly Bank. Her basis in Pinkacre is $100,000.

Example—Cash, property, liabilities: Frank purchases Blueacre by transferring to the seller $30,000 cash and a parcel of real property worth $50,000. Frank also assumes a $40,000 mortgage to which Blueacre is subject. Frank's initial basis in the property is equal to his cost, or $120,000 (the total of the cash, fair market value of the property, and the liability Frank assumes).

i.   Tax cost basis: For property received in exchange for services rendered, the cost is the amount of the income included in gross income as a result of the services transaction (known as tax cost basis).

Example: Mary Ann creates an estate plan for her client, who pays her with a sports car worth $20,000. Mary Ann includes the fair market value of the sports car received ($20,000) in her gross income, and her basis in the sports car is $20,000.

ii. Multiple properties purchased: When a single purchase price results in the acquisition of multiple assets, the taxpayer must allocate the price among the assets based on their relative fair market values. Treas. Reg. §1.61-6(a); *Gamble v. Commissioner*, 68 T.C. 800 (1977).

iii. **Barter:** The adjusted basis of property received in a barter or trade is the fair market value of the property or services received in the exchange. See *Philadelphia Park Amusement Co. v. United States*, 126 F.Supp. 184 (Ct. Cl. 1954).

b. **Property received from a decedent:** The basis of property received from a decedent is the fair market value of the property on the decedent's date of death or, if the alternate valuation date is elected, the value on that date (six months after the date of death). IRC §1014. Property can be received from a decedent by bequest or devise, by disclaimer, or through intestate succession. Property received in this fashion is often referred to as having a *stepped-up basis,* because generally property has a fair market value greater than its basis in the hands of a decedent just before death. However, the property could just as easily have a "stepped-down basis" if its fair market value were less than its basis just before death (although that is not a term in general usage). In that case, however, the decedent would have been well advised to sell the property before death, as the loss inherent in the property will be forever lost for income tax purposes if transferred by devise or inheritance. The date-of-death basis for property received from a decedent has been criticized because it completely exempts from income tax the economic benefit of the increase in value of the property during the decedent's lifetime. While a rationale often heard for this basis rule is that it prevents property from being subjected to both the income tax and the estate tax, this is hardly an adequate explanation. The estate tax, like the gift tax, is a tax on transfers that operates independently of the income tax. Note that in the gift area, the donee generally takes the donor's basis in the property, so that the donee will be taxed on the gain that occurred during both the donor's and the donee's ownership. Not so for property received by inheritance; neither the decedent nor the beneficiary will pay income tax on this gain.

Example: Whitney receives 1,000 shares of XYZ stock pursuant to her grandfather's will. Her grandfather had purchased the stock in 1981 for $10,000, and at his death the stock was worth $150,000. Whitney's basis in the stock will be the value of the stock on the date of her grandfather's death, or $150,000.

c. **Property received by gift:** As a general rule, if property is received by gift, the donee takes the property with the same basis that it had in the hands of the donor, increased by the portion of any gift tax paid by the donor. IRC §1015(a). If, at the time of the gift, the adjusted basis of the property in the hands of the donor is greater than the fair market value of the property, for purposes of determining loss on sale by the donee, the donee's basis in the property is the fair market value of the property at the time of the gift. Under this rule, if the donee sells at a gain, the general rule for determining the donee's basis applies. In order for the special rule to apply, the adjusted basis of the property in the donor's hands must exceed its fair market value on the date of the gift *and* the donee must sell at a loss. Property received by gift is generally referred to as having a *carryover basis,* at least if the special rule does not apply. Technically it has a *transferred basis*. See IRC §7701(a)(42), (43). These basis rules for gifts work in tandem with §102's exclusion from gross income for gifts. (See discussion in Chapter 4(IV).) The donee does not really get a full exclusion of the value of the gift, because he or she takes the property with the donor's basis and may ultimately recognize gain or loss on the sale of the gift property. However, because the donee may be in a lower tax bracket than the donor, it may make sense in a family financial planning situation to cause the donee rather than the donor to realize the gain on sale. Moreover, a donor may not always be able to give away a loss by gifting loss property to the donee. If the donee sells at a loss, the donee will take as his or her basis the fair market value of the property as of the date of the gift rather than the donor's basis. Thus, in this situation, it may make more sense for the donor to sell the property, recognize the loss, and give the proceeds to the donee.

Example—General rule: Alan owns 1,000 shares of ABC stock in which he has a basis of $15,000. The stock is worth $100,000. Alan gives the stock to his daughter Caroline. Caroline will take her father's basis in the shares ($15,000) as her own basis.

Example—Loss property: Alex owns Blackacre, a parcel of raw land in which she has a basis of $50,000. The fair market value of Blackacre is $20,000 on the date Alex gives Blackacre to her sister Jessica. Jessica's basis in Blackacre under the general rule would be $50,000 (Alex's basis). This is the basis used for determining gain: If Jessica later sold Blackacre for $200,000, she would have a $150,000 gain. But, for purposes of determining Jessica's loss on any subsequent sale, the special rule applicable to loss applies because the property's fair market value was less than its adjusted basis in Alex's hands at the time of the gift. If Jessica sells Blackacre for $10,000, her basis would be $20,000, and she would have a $10,000 loss.

Example—No gain or loss: Assume the same facts as in the immediately preceding example. If Jessica sells Blackacre for any amount between $20,000 (its fair market value on the date of the gift) and $50,000 (Alex's basis), she will realize neither gain nor loss on the sale. This is because the basis for determining gain would produce a loss, while the basis for determining loss would produce a gain. For example, assume Jessica sells the property for $30,000. If she takes the basis for determining loss of $20,000, she has a $10,000 gain. If she takes the basis for determining gain of $50,000, she has a $20,000 loss. The regulations conclude that a taxpayer has neither gain nor loss in this situation. See Reg. §1.1015-1(a)(2).

d. Property received in divorce: The recipient of property pursuant to a divorce takes the property with the same basis the property had in the hands of the marital unit. IRC §1041(b)(2). These rules are discussed in detail in Chapter 10(V).

e. Exchanged basis property: In some transactions, a taxpayer gives up property in exchange for other property, and the basis of the property received is calculated in whole or in part by reference to the basis of the property transferred. This is known as *exchanged basis property.* See IRC §7701(a)(44). For example, in a like-kind exchange under §1031, the property received takes a basis that is calculated by reference to the basis of the property transferred. Exchanged basis property is a type of, and is sometimes referred to as, substituted basis property. See IRC §7701(a)(42).

2. Adjustments to basis: A taxpayer must adjust his or her initial basis in property during ownership to reflect additional investment in the property and capital recovery with respect to the property. See IRC §1016.

a. Improvements: Improvements to property result in an increase in the basis of the property. IRC §1016(a); Reg. §1.1016-2.

Example: Tammy purchases Whiteacre, an office building, for $100,000. She then remodels the third floor of Whiteacre for leasing to a particular tenant, at a cost of $65,000. Her initial (cost) basis in Whiteacre was $100,000, and she adds to that basis her improvements of $65,000 for a total adjusted basis for the property and improvements of $165,000.

b. **Capitalized interest and taxes:** A taxpayer may elect to *capitalize,* rather than deduct, otherwise deductible interest and taxes on property used in business or held for investment. IRC §266. If the taxpayer makes this election, the interest and taxes attributable to the property are added to the basis of the property. *Id.*

Example: Emilio purchases Blackacre, a parcel of raw land, for $50,000. He pays the seller $10,000 and promises to pay the balance in equal annual installments for five years with interest at 10%. Taxes on the land are $200 per year. Emilio may elect to capitalize the interest and taxes, so that his interest payments to the seller and the taxes paid are added to the basis of the property. Thus, in the first year after purchase, Emilio would add the $4,000 in interest and $200 in taxes to his basis, increasing his adjusted basis to $54,200.

c. **Capital recovery deductions:** When a taxpayer claims a deduction for capital recovery (MACRS or amortization), the taxpayer must adjust the basis of the property downward by the amount of the capital recovery deduction claimed. See discussion of capital recovery in Chapter 7(IV).

Example: Courtney owns Blueacre, a rental home that she purchased for $100,000. Over the first five years she owns the property, she claims $20,000 in MACRS deductions. This reduces her basis in the property so that her adjusted basis at the end of five years is $80,000.

Example: Jan purchased a computer system for her business in Year 1, which cost $10,000. She made the §179 election for that property and deducted the cost in that year. Her adjusted basis in the computer system is zero, as she has fully recovered her capital in the asset.

D. Recognition

Recognition of gain or loss means that the taxpayer includes the gain in gross income, or that the taxpayer may claim the loss as a deduction. Section 1001(c) requires that all realized gains and losses are to be recognized, unless another Code section provides otherwise.

1. **Tax-deferred transactions:** The Code contains numerous nonrecognition provisions that defer the recognition of realized gain or loss. These are discussed in Chapter 10.

2. **Compare—gain exclusion:** There are a few Code sections that exempt gain from recognition in whole or in part. For example, under certain conditions a taxpayer may exclude from gross income gain on the sale of his or her principal residence. IRC §121. See discussion in Chapter 4(VIII).

3. **Loss restrictions:** The Code contains numerous provisions that restrict the deductibility of losses.

   a. **Capital loss restrictions:** Individuals may deduct capital losses only to the extent of their capital gain, plus $3,000 of ordinary income. IRC §1223. See discussion in Chapter 12(II)(B).

   b. **Section 165(c):** Individuals may deduct only certain types of losses. For example, losses on the sale of assets held for investment may be deductible, but a loss on the sale of one's home is not deductible. IRC §165(c). See discussion in Chapter 6(II)(D).

4. **Part gift/part sale transaction:** If a transaction is partially a gift and partially a sale, often referred to as a *bargain sale,* the transferor will be treated as having realized a gain in the amount by which his or her amount realized exceeds the adjusted basis of the property transferred. However, the transferor may not recognize a loss on the transaction, even if the amount realized is less than the adjusted basis of the property transferred. Reg. §1.1001-1(e).

Example: Dick has a $40,000 basis in Blackacre, which is worth $100,000. He transfers Blackacre to Jane, his daughter. Jane pays him $70,000 for Blackacre. This transaction is partially a gift because Jane paid Dick less than the fair market value of the property, and the other circumstances of the situation (intrafamilial transfer) suggest a gift. Thus, Dick has a realized gain of $30,000, equal to his amount realized ($70,000) minus his adjusted basis in Blackacre ($40,000). He has made a gift to Jane of $30,000.

VI. PROPERTY ENCUMBERED BY DEBT

A. A few terms of art

1. **Liabilities incurred to purchase property:** When a person wants to purchase property such as real estate and doesn't have enough money to do so, another person, usually a bank or the seller, may lend the money to the purchaser to buy the property. The buyer usually puts some of his or her own money (the down payment) together with the loan proceeds to purchase the property from the seller. The purchaser/debtor must usually give a security interest in the property to the lender in order to ensure repayment. If the debtor defaults, the lender will have the ability to sell the property and be repaid from the proceeds (commonly referred to as "foreclosure"). In many states, this is structured as a ***mortgage*** in which the debtor is the mortgagor and the creditor is the mortgagee. Deeds of trust, installment sales contracts, conditional sales contracts, and similar arrangements serve the same function as a mortgage in some jurisdictions but allow the creditor simpler mechanisms for selling the property if the debtor defaults. Here the term "mortgage" will be used to include mortgages and all similar arrangements. See Figure 9B—Typical Mortgage Transaction. As Figure 9B illustrates, there are really two different transactions occurring in this sale: the loan transaction (between the bank and the buyer) and the sale transaction (between the seller and the buyer). This would be true even if the seller were providing the financing; in that case, the seller would simply wear two hats: as seller and as the "bank."

Figure 9B
Typical Mortgage Transaction

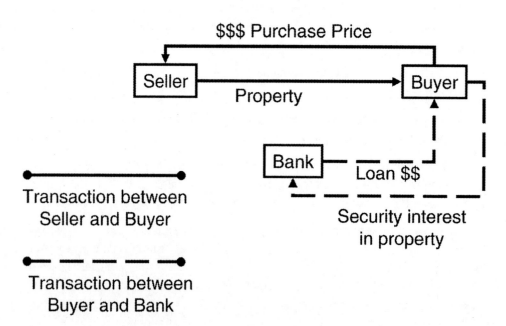

a. **Recourse mortgage:** The most common type of mortgage debt is the ***recourse debt,*** which provides that if the debtor does not repay the loan, the lender may proceed against the debtor's assets for repayment without restriction. Thus, if the borrower does not repay the loan, the lender will seek satisfaction through foreclosure on the property and if that is not sufficient to satisfy the debt, the lender will seek additional payment from the borrower. The debtor's other assets are at risk for this type of debt. Most loans today are recourse loans.

Example: Jared purchases a home for $100,000, making a $20,000 down payment and obtaining a recourse mortgage from Unfriendly Bank for $80,000. He repays $5,000 of the mortgage, but unfortunately an economic downturn causes the fair market value of the property to fall to $50,000. Jared defaults on the loan. Unfriendly Bank causes the property to be sold at foreclosure for its value of $50,000. Jared still owes $75,000 on the loan plus the expenses of the foreclosure sale of $3,000, for a total outstanding obligation of $78,000. The proceeds of sale are applied to Jared's outstanding obligation, reducing it to $28,000. Unfriendly Bank can proceed against Jared for the rest of the debt.

b. **Nonrecourse mortgage:** A less common type of debt is the ***nonrecourse debt,*** which means that the lender has agreed to seek satisfaction only from the property that secures the debt. Thus, if the value of the property is insufficient to repay the debt in full, the lender cannot proceed against the debtor's other assets for repayment of the balance. In a nonrecourse debt situation, the lender, rather than the borrower, bears the risk that the property will decline in value.

c. **State antideficiency statutes:** Some states have statutes that essentially transform recourse obligations into nonrecourse obligations by making it impossible for a lender to pursue certain kinds of debtors for repayment of loans upon default. These typically apply to loans for principal residences, and often have strict requirements. Each state statute is different, and must be analyzed separately. The tax effects of these statues have not been tested.

2. **Transactions occurring after the initial debt is incurred:**

a. **Refinancing:** A taxpayer may wish to refinance an existing debt to obtain a lower interest rate or better terms. The taxpayer takes out a new loan, and uses the proceeds of that loan to repay the existing debt. If the property has increased in value, the taxpayer may be able to borrow more than the balance of the previous debt, and will pocket the additional cash.

Example: Rose borrowed $100,000 to purchase her home, and the interest rate was 7% on that debt. She has reduced the amount of the debt to $90,000. Interest rates have fallen, and her home is worth more than when she purchased it. New Bank agrees to lend her $125,000 at 5% to refinance the existing debt. She uses $90,000 to pay off that debt, and uses the remaining amount ($35,000) to purchase a new car.

b. **Second mortgage or home equity line of credit (HELOC):** If a taxpayer reduces the amount of an existing mortgage, or the property increases in value, the taxpayer may be able to place additional debt on the property to obtain cash. If the property is a residence, see Chapter 6 (V)(C) for a discussion of deductibility of interest on the second mortgage or HELOC.

Example: Matt purchased a home, taking out a mortgage of $100,000 at 7%. The balance on the loan is $90,000. The home has increased in value to $250,000, and Friendly Bank offers to lend him up to 90% of his equity in the home using a home equity line of credit, where he simply writes checks for purchases, which are added to his line of credit, secured by the home. He writes a check for $25,000 to add landscaping to his property. In this transaction, Matt's original loan stays in place, and he adds a second loan to the property, so the total outstanding debt on the property is $115,000.

   c. **Assumption of debt:** An *assumption of debt* occurs when another person explicitly agrees to be responsible for payment of a taxpayer's debt. For state law purposes, this may not relieve the taxpayer of his or her obligation under the debt, but for federal income tax purposes, it is considered a valuable benefit to the taxpayer and included in amount realized. Generally the lender must consent to another person's assumption of an outstanding debt.

   d. **Transfer "subject to debt":** When an encumbered property is sold, most often the debt is repaid to the lender as part of the sale transaction. However, properties can be transferred *subject to* the debt, which means that the seller will transfer the property to the buyer with the debt intact, and the buyer will become the obligor on the debt. This is an implicit assumption of debt, and has the same effect as an assumption of debt. Almost always, the lender must consent to a transfer of property subject to a debt.

B.   The typical transaction—Sale of property and satisfaction of debt

In the typical transaction, the seller who owns mortgaged property agrees to sell a property to the buyer for cash equal to the property's fair market value. The seller repays the lender with some of the sales proceeds and keeps the rest. The seller transfers the property "free and clear" (i.e., without any debt associated with it) to the purchaser. The tax consequences to each party of this transaction are determined independently.

1. **Seller's tax consequences:** The seller will calculate realized gain or loss in accordance with the usual rules: amount realized (the purchase price) minus the seller's adjusted basis in the property. Recognized gain or loss will be equal to realized gain or loss, unless some Code provision limits recognition. Notice that the mortgage amount is irrelevant to the tax consequences of this transaction because the buyer is not assuming the mortgage. The repayment of the loan principal is not a taxable event to the seller.

2. **Buyer's tax consequences:** The buyer's basis in the property will be the buyer's cost of purchasing the property, including both cash and debt.

3. **Lender's tax consequences:** The repayment of the principal amount of the loan is not a taxable event to the lender.

   Example: Sheila owns Blackacre, in which she has an adjusted basis of $70,000. Blackacre is subject to a mortgage of $40,000 from Friendly Bank and has a fair market value of $100,000. Brian purchases Blackacre from Sheila for $100,000 (cash). Sheila repays Friendly Bank with $40,000 of the sales proceeds, which releases its security interest so that Sheila can transfer the property to Brian "free and clear." She retains the remaining $60,000 as profit.

   Sheila's tax consequences: Sheila's realized gain on the transaction is $30,000, the difference between her amount realized ($100,000) and the adjusted basis of Blackacre ($70,000). Her recognized gain also will be $30,000, unless a Code provision limits recognition of that gain. The repayment of the principal amount of the loan is not a taxable event to Sheila.

   Brian's tax consequences: Brian takes Blackacre with a basis equal to his cost, or $100,000.

Friendly Bank: The repayment of the $40,000 principal amount of the loan is not income to the lender.

C. Buyer assumes the mortgage (or purchases the property subject to the mortgage)

1. **The transaction:** In this transaction, the buyer and seller agree that the buyer will become responsible for the mortgage on the property as part of the purchase transaction. When the seller transfers the property to the buyer, the latter either expressly assumes the debt or takes the property subject to the debt. The buyer pays the seller cash in the amount of the equity in the property, i.e., the difference between the property's fair market value and the amount of the debt. The property continues to secure the debt. For tax purposes, the buyer is treated as if the loan is now his or her own and that he or she has granted a security interest in the property to the lender. Ideally, the lender agrees to this transaction, because most mortgages contain a prohibition on transfer unless the mortgage is satisfied first.

2. **Tax effects:** When the buyer assumes a mortgage or takes property subject to debt, then for tax purposes the assumption is treated as a transfer of value to the seller. This is why the seller is treated as having an amount realized that includes the assumption of the mortgage. It is easy to see how this is the case for recourse debt because the seller directly benefits if someone else takes on the responsibility for the mortgage. But at one time it was unclear whether this same principle applied to nonrecourse debt, because the seller does not directly benefit when it is the lender, not the seller, that bears the risk of loss in a nonrecourse debt. The *Crane* and *Tufts* cases, discussed below, confirm that nonrecourse debt is included in the seller's amount realized.

3. **Nonrecourse mortgage amount is less than fair market value of property—*Crane v. Commissioner*, 331 U.S. 1 (1947):** Mrs. Crane owned an apartment building that was subject to a nonrecourse mortgage. Over the years, she claimed depreciation deductions. She sold it to a buyer subject to the debt. Mrs. Crane claimed that her only gain was her equity in the building. She argued that her amount realized could not include the mortgage assumed because she did not benefit from the buyer's taking the property subject to the debt. In *Crane,* the fair market value of the property exceeded the amount of the nonrecourse debt, and the IRS's argument was that to enjoy the benefit of the equity, she would have to either pay off the debt or have someone assume it. The Supreme Court held that when the fair market value of the property exceeds the amount of the mortgage, the seller's amount realized includes the debt assumed, regardless of the nature of the mortgage as recourse or nonrecourse. The Court explicitly did not rule on the proper result if the fair market value were less than the amount of the debt.

   a. **Seller's tax consequences:** The seller's amount realized will be the amount of money received, the fair market value of any property received, and the debt assumed by the buyer. The seller's realized and recognized gain or loss will be calculated under the usual rules.

   b. **Buyer's tax consequences:** The buyer will include in basis the amount of debt assumed plus the amount of money and the fair market value of property paid to seller.

   c. **Lender's tax consequences:** The lender will be unaffected by the transfer of property subject to the debt. From the lender's perspective, the loan remains outstanding.

   Example—Recourse mortgage: Sonny owns Parcel A of commercial real property, which is subject to a recourse mortgage to Friendly Bank of $40,000. Sonny has a basis of $60,000 in the property, and it is worth $110,000. Sonny sells Parcel A to Becca for $70,000 cash, and Becca agrees to assume the mortgage on Parcel A. Sonny's realized gain on this transaction is $50,000. His amount realized is equal to the cash received of $70,000 plus Becca's assumption of the mortgage of $40,000, or $110,000. The amount realized minus his adjusted basis in Parcel A ($60,000) produces his realized gain of $50,000. Becca's basis in Parcel A is her purchase price: $110,000 ($70,000 cash plus $40,000 debt assumption). The transaction is not a taxable event for Friendly Bank.

Example—Nonrecourse mortgage: Assume the same facts as in the previous example, except that the mortgage is nonrecourse in nature. The same tax consequences would result from this transaction because the nature of the mortgage as recourse or nonrecourse is irrelevant when the property's fair market value exceeds the amount of the debt.

4. **Nonrecourse mortgage amount exceeds fair market value of property:** Because the lender bears the risk of a fall in value of property for a nonrecourse mortgage, a buyer might well purchase a property subject to a nonrecourse mortgage with a face amount greater than the fair market value of the property.

   To aid understanding of this concept, consider *Commissioner v. Tufts*, 461 U.S. 300 (1983).

   a. **Facts:** *Tufts* involves complicated partnership taxation, so it is helpful to simplify the facts by ignoring the partnership and assuming that Mr. Tufts owned the property individually. Mr. Tufts purchased an apartment building in 1970 by making a small cash outlay and obtaining a nonrecourse loan of $1,851,500. During his ownership of the property, Mr. Tufts claimed depreciation deductions in a total of $439,972. By 1972, the fair market value of the property had fallen to $1,400,000, and Mr. Tufts's adjusted basis in the property was $1,455,740. Because no principal payments had been made on the debt, its outstanding balance remained at $1,851,500. In 1972, Mr. Tufts transferred the property to Mr. Bayles, who assumed the nonrecourse mortgage. Mr. Tufts reported a $55,740 loss equal to the difference between his adjusted basis in the property and its fair market value.

   b. **Issue:** How should the gain or loss on Mr. Tufts's sale be calculated? Specifically, must Mr. Tufts include in his amount realized the assumption of the nonrecourse debt by the purchaser of the property, even though he was not liable for it, and it would result in no benefit to him under the theory of *Crane*?

   c. **Result and rationale:** Mr. Tufts must include in his amount realized the debt assumed, so that he realized a gain on the sale of the property equal to the difference between the face amount of the debt ($1,851,500) and the adjusted basis of the property ($1,455,740), or $395,760. The majority opinion gives deference to the Commissioner's decision to treat a nonrecourse mortgage as a "true loan." This treatment allows the mortgagor to include the amount in basis, and requires the mortgagor to include the debt in amount realized if assumed. Although the economic benefit analysis relied on in *Crane* might suggest a different result when the mortgaged property falls in value below the balance of the debt, the Court does not rely on the theory of economic benefit. Instead, the taxpayer's tax-free receipt of the loan proceeds and the inclusion of those proceeds in the basis of the mortgaged property require consistent treatment upon sale of the property. Justice O'Connor concurred, but observed that the logical way to treat this transaction would be to bifurcate it into two different transactions: a sale of property and a discharge of debt. (See Figure 9C—Bifurcated Transaction—Justice O'Connor's Concurrence in *Commissioner v.*

Tufts.) This results in a net gain of the same amount as in the majority's opinion ($395,760), but the character of the loss and gain are different. The sale transaction produces capital gain or loss, while the discharge of debt is ordinary income. In addition, the discharge of debt may be subject to exclusion under §108 (see discussion in Chapter 4(VII)). However, in deference to the IRS's interpretation, Justice O'Connor concurred in the result.

Figure 9C
Bifurcated Transaction—Justice O'Connor's
Concurrence in *Commissioner v. Tufts*

Property Transaction		Discharge of Debt Transaction	
Amount realized =	$1,400,000 (FMV)	Face amount of debt =	$1,851,500
Less adjusted basis =	1,455,740	Debt satisfied =	1,400,000
Loss on sale =	− $ 55,740	Discharge of debt =	$ 451,500

D. Distressed real estate transactions involving recourse loans

As a practical matter, most mortgages are recourse. When property values fall, the owners of these properties can find themselves owing more on the property than the property is worth. They then face the difficult choice of deciding whether to continue to pay the mortgage. If they don't, there are a few different transactions that can occur. Often, the tax results will be different for principal residences than for investment properties because of §108(a)(1)(E), discussed in Chapter 4(VII).

1. **Renegotiating debt—discharge of debt income:** The debtor may negotiate a reduction in the mortgage amount with the lender and continue to pay the mortgage at its new amount.

    a. **Tax consequences to debtor:** The debtor has discharge of indebtedness income equal to the amount of the loan discharged, which is ordinary income and *may* be excluded under §108 if that section's requirements are met. In particular, if the property is the taxpayer's principal residence, §108(a)(1)(E) may apply to protect the debtor from recognition of discharge of indebtedness income.

    b. **Tax consequences to lender:** The lender has realized a loss in the amount of the debt forgiven. Unless some Code provisions prohibit it, the lender may deduct this loss.

2. **Transfer to creditor in satisfaction of debt:** In this transaction, the debtor negotiates with the lender to transfer the property to the lender in full satisfaction of the debt. The lender then sells the property for its fair market value.

    a. **Tax consequences to seller/debtor:** According to Treas. Reg. §1.1001-2(a)(2), and (c), Example (8), and Rev. Rul. 90-16, 1990-1 C.B. 12, this transaction is bifurcated (as Justice O'Connor's concurrence in *Tufts* suggested). The sale transaction produces gain or loss equal to the fair market value of the property minus the debtor's adjusted basis in the property. The excess of the debt over the fair market value of the property is discharge of indebtedness income, which may be excluded if the requirements of §108 are met.

b. **Tax consequences to buyer:** The buyer will take the property with a basis equal to the buyer's cost in purchasing the property from the lender.

c. **Tax consequences to lender:** The lender takes a basis in the property equal to its fair market value. The lender may claim a loss on the amount of the debt discharged. On sale of the property, the creditor calculates gain or loss in the usual fashion. If the sale occurs immediately (no change in fair market value), the creditor will realize neither gain nor loss on the sale.

Example: Sally owns Greenacre, which she holds for investment. Sally has an adjusted basis in Greenacre of $200,000, and its fair market value is $500,000. It is subject to a recourse debt of $900,000 held by Friendly Bank. Sally transfers Greenacre to Friendly Bank in full satisfaction of the debt. Friendly Bank then sells Greenacre to Ben for $500,000.

Sally's tax consequences: Sally must bifurcate this transaction into its sale and debt components. She realizes $300,000 of gain on the sale of the property, and also has $400,000 of discharge of indebtedness income that may be excluded if she can fit within any of the exclusions of §108.

Sale of Property Transaction		Discharge of Debt Transaction	
Amount realized	$500,000 (FMV)	Face amount of debt	$900,000
– Adjusted basis	– 200,000	– Debt satisfied	– 500,000 (FMV)
= Gain on sale	$300,000	Discharge of debt	$400,000

Friendly Bank's tax consequences: Friendly Bank may claim a loss equal to the amount of debt forgiven ($400,000). The bank takes Greenacre with a basis of $500,000 and, upon sale to Ben, realizes no gain or loss.

Ben's tax consequences: Ben takes Greenacre with a basis equal to his purchase price, or $500,000.

d. **Principal residence:** If the property is the taxpayer's principal residence, §108(a)(1)(E) may apply to exclude the discharge of indebtedness income and §121 may apply to exclude the gain on sale. However, in a state in which there is an antideficiency statute, the transaction may be transformed into a nonrecourse debt, in which case the analysis of *Tufts,* above, would apply, eliminating any discharge of indebtedness income.

3. **Foreclosure sale:** In this transaction, the debtor defaults on the debt, and the lender forecloses on the property, causing the property to be sold and using the proceeds to satisfy part of the debt. Because the fair market value of the property is less than the outstanding debt, a portion of the debt will not be repaid. This transaction is treated as two transactions: the foreclosure sale and the disposition of the remaining debt. These two transactions often occur in different taxable years. See, e.g., *Aizawa v. Commissioner,* 99 T.C. 197 (1992), *aff'd unpublished opinion* 74 A.F.T.R. 2d ¶ 94,5493 (9th Cir. 1994). The amount realized is the fair market value of the property, which usually will be the foreclosure price (although not always—see *Frazier v. Commissioner,* 111 T.C. 243 (1998)). The lender facing a post-foreclosure deficiency has two options: to forgive the remaining debt or to proceed against the debtor's other assets for full payment (if allowed under state law).

a. **Tax consequences to seller:** The debtor realizes gain or loss on the sale of the property equal to the fair market value of the property sold minus the seller's adjusted basis in the property sold. The application of the proceeds to satisfaction of the loan is not a taxable event. If the lender forgives the debt, the debtor has discharge of indebtedness income equal to the amount of the forgiveness, which *may* be excluded from gross income by §108. If the lender proceeds against the debtor's other assets, the transfer of assets to the lender in satisfaction of the loan may generate gain or loss, if those assets' adjusted bases are different from their fair market values. Payment of the debt, however, is not a taxable event to the debtor.

b. **Tax consequences to lender:** The full repayment of the loan is not a taxable event, but if the lender forgives any portion of the debt, the lender will be entitled to claim a loss on the transaction.

c. **Tax consequences to buyer:** The buyer of the property will take it with a basis equal to its purchase price.

Example: Selena owns Pinkacre, a commercial building, with an adjusted basis of $20,000 and a fair market value of $100,000. Pinkacre is subject to a recourse mortgage of $150,000 for which Friendly Bank is the mortgagee. Unable to make payments on the debt, Selena defaults, and Friendly Bank forecloses. At the foreclosure sale, Bruce purchases Pinkacre from Selena for $100,000, and this amount is paid to Friendly Bank and is applied to reduce Selena's debt. Friendly Bank discharges the remaining $50,000 debt at a time when Selena's total debt exceeds her total assets by $100,000.

Selena's tax consequences: Upon sale of the property, Selena realizes and recognizes $80,000 of gain, equal to the difference between the sales price ($100,000) and her adjusted basis in the property ($20,000). The repayment of $100,000 of the loan is not a taxable event to Selena. When Friendly Bank discharges the remaining debt, Selena has discharge of indebtedness income in the amount of $50,000. Because she is insolvent by at least that amount, Selena may exclude this amount from her gross income but must reduce certain of her tax attributes.

Friendly Bank's tax consequences: The repayment of $100,000 of the loan is not a taxable event to the bank. It may claim a loss equal to the amount of debt forgiven, $50,000.

Bruce's tax consequences: Bruce takes Pinkacre with a basis equal to its purchase price, $100,000.

Example: Assume the same facts as above, except that Friendly Bank does not discharge the remaining $50,000 of the loan. Instead, pursuant to a judgment obtained by the bank in the next taxable year, Selena transfers another commercial property, Whiteacre, to the bank in satisfaction of the remaining debt. Whiteacre has an adjusted basis of $70,000 and a fair market value of $50,000 in Selena's hand immediately prior to the transfer.

Selena's tax consequences: The tax consequences to Selena are the same as in the previous example, except that because Friendly Bank has not forgiven any part of the debt, she has no discharge of indebtedness income. In addition, however, in transferring Whiteacre to Friendly Bank, Selena realizes and recognizes (unless some loss recognition limitation applies) a loss of $20,000, equal to the difference between the debt satisfied ($50,000) and the adjusted basis of the property ($70,000).

Friendly Bank's tax consequences: As in the previous example, the repayment of the loan is not a taxable event to the bank. The bank takes Whiteacre with a basis equal to its purchase price (the amount of debt satisfied), or $50,000.

Bruce's tax consequences: As in the previous example, Bruce takes Pinkacre with a basis equal to his cost, or $100,000.

d. **Principal residence:** If the transaction occurs in a state with an antideficiency statute, the transaction could be treated as if the debt were a nonrecourse debt, if the requirements of the state statute are met.

4. **The so-called "short sale":** A short sale occurs when a taxpayer sells a home for less than the outstanding mortgage. This happens when the value of the property has fallen. Usually, the bank, owner, and buyer agree on a price which is less than the mortgage. The bank may or may not release the mortgagor from further liability on the mortgage. For tax purposes, this transaction is treated like a foreclosure sale.

VII. BASIS IN PROPERTY RECEIVED IN A TRANSACTION

A. Fully taxable transactions

If a taxpayer sells property for cash, it is not necessary to determine the basis of that cash. But if a taxpayer sells property by exchanging it for other property, it is important to assign a basis in the property received, because ultimately it will be sold and the gain or loss will have to be reckoned. In a transaction where all of the gain or loss is recognized, each taxpayer will take the property received with a basis equal to its fair market value.

Example: Tim owns Blackacre, with a basis of $100 and a fair market value of $1,000. Nan owns Whiteacre, with a basis of $1,200 and a fair market value of $1,000. Tim and Nan exchange properties. Tim will hold Whiteacre with a basis of $1,000 (his cost) and Nan will hold Whiteacare with a basis of $1,000 (her cost).

B. Tax-free or partially taxable transactions

In some cases, a taxpayer's realized gain or loss will not be recognized. Some of the statutes (discussed in Chapter 10) provide their own basis rules for determining the basis of property received in a tax-deferred exchange. If not, the general rules for determining basis will apply.

Example: Sam owns a home that he has used as a principal residence for many years. Sam has a basis of $100,000 in his home and it is worth $350,000. He trades his property for another home. What is Sam's basis in the new home? We assume that the new home is worth $350,000, as Sam has taken it in a trade without any cash or other property changing hands. His basis is his purchase price, the value of the home. The fact that the transaction is not taxable to him under §121 does not change that result.

VIII. CHARACTER OF GAIN OR LOSS

If gain or loss is recognized on a transaction, its character as ordinary or capital must be determined. Taxpayers generally prefer capital gain and ordinary loss, so this distinction is important. A full discussion of this issue is the subject of Chapter 12.

IX. NEED TO KNOW MORE?

This book's website *www.aspenlawschool.com/books/tax_outline* contains additional information, including:

- Practice problems in computing realized and recognized gains and losses.

- Examples of foreclosure and similar transactions in distressed real estate.

- Antideficiency statutes and their probable tax effects.

- And other materials that will help you become comfortable with property transactions.

X. WHERE ARE WE GOING?

This chapter has examined the principles for computing realized gain or loss on the sale or other disposition of property. In general, realized or recognized gain or loss is recognized, so that a taxpayer must include in his or her gross income realized gain and is entitled to deduct (subject to certain limitations) realized loss. However, certain statutory provisions defer the recognition of realized gain or loss until a future date, and the next chapter discusses those statutes in detail.

Quiz Yourself on *TRANSACTIONS IN PROPERTY*

91. As a favor to an old friend, Carolyn invested $1,000 in shares of WikiLearn, a web-based company that matches tutors with students needing help. She put the shares in a desk drawer and promptly forgot about them, until yesterday when she learned from her old friend that her shares were now worth $1,000,000. Panicked that she will owe taxes on $999,000 of income, she consults you. What is your advice? _____

92. What is the difference between "realized" gain and "recognized gain"? _____

93. Al and Sal are avid sports memorabilia collectors. Al owns a baseball signed by Mickey Mantle. Sal owns a football signed by Joe Montana. Both purchased these items years ago and they have appreciated in value. They trade. What are the tax consequences to them of this trade? Disregard any nonrecognition provisions of the Code. _____

94. Taylor owns a collectible sports car, which she purchased many years ago for $10,000. It has appreciated significantly in value. Taylor gives it to Melique in satisfaction of a debt she owes him. What are the tax consequences to Taylor of this payment? _____

95. What is the function of "basis"? Of "adjusted basis"? _____

96. Jessica buys Blackacre, an office building on two acres of land, for $395,000. She claims $10,000 of depreciation on Blackacre in Year 2. Is she correct? _____

97. Dick owns Bleak House, a bed-and-breakfast inn for literary types. He had an initial basis of $140,000 in this property, and has claimed $40,000 of depreciation deductions over the years. He agrees to sell the property to Tom for $300,000 cash. What are the tax consequences of this sale to Dick? _____

98. Assume the same facts as in the preceding question, except that Dick has a mortgage on Bleak House in the amount of $100,000. He agrees to sell Bleak House to Jerry. Jerry will pay Dick cash of $200,000 and Jerry's assumption of the debt on Bleak House. What are the tax consequences of this transaction to Dick? What is Jerry's basis in Bleak House? _____

99. Courtney purchased the Emerald Apartment Building for $1 million. She financed 100% of the purchase price through Very Friendly Bank, which loaned her the money on a nonrecourse basis. Over the years, she properly claimed $250,000 of MACRS deductions with respect to the property. Unfortunately, the value of the property declined and became a stone around her neck. One day she simply marched into the bank, gave them the deed to the property and walked away. She had paid off only $50,000 of the debt so her mortgage balance was $950,000 at that time. The bank ultimately sold the property for $600,000. Courtney reported a $150,000 loss on this transaction on her tax return. Was she correct? _____

100. Linda purchased The Bates Motel for $500,000, the entire amount of which she financed with a recourse mortgage from a bank. Over the years she claimed $100,000 in depreciation deductions. Some spooky things happened at the motel, and it declined in value because few visitors wanted to stay there. Linda was unable to repay the debt. Last year, when Linda had a mortgage balance of $450,000, the bank foreclosed on the property. The property was sold for $200,000, all of which was applied to Linda's loan. The bank tried to collect the remaining $250,000, but ultimately decided it was uncollectible because Linda's debts were well in excess of her assets. The bank wrote off the debt. What are the tax consequences of this transaction to Linda? _____

101. Would the result in the previous question be any different if the bank and Linda had simply agreed that she would transfer the motel to the bank in full satisfaction of the debt? _____

102. Would the result in Question 100 be any different if the property had been Linda's principal residence, not The Bates Motel? _____

103. Craig purchased a home, which he used as his principal residence, for $475,000. To purchase the home, Craig paid $75,000 in cash, and borrowed $400,000 from the Bank on a recourse basis. Later, the property increased in value, and the Bank loaned him an additional $120,000 as a home equity line of credit (HELOC) (also recourse). The value of Craig's home has fallen to $400,000, and he still owes $500,000 to the Bank ($380,000 on his original mortgage and $120,000 on the HELOC). What are the tax consequences if Craig:

(a) Negotiates a reduction in the HELOC to $20,000 and leaves the primary mortgage intact at $380,000? _____

(b) Negotiates a reduction in the primary mortgage to $280,000 and leaves the HELOC in place at $120,000? _____

104. Fred purchased an airplane, which he used for business 60% of the time and used for personal purposes 40% of the time. His original cost was $1,000,000. At the time that he sold the airplane for $500,000, he had taken $350,000 of depreciation deductions associated with it. Fred plans to report a $200,000 loss on this sale. Is he correct? _____

105. What is "tax cost" basis? Can you offer an example? _____

106. Darcy inherited a painting from her grandmother, who had purchased it for $100 from a starving artist in Paris. At her grandmother's death, the painting was worth $1,000,000. The grandmother's estate paid $350,000 of estate tax attributable to the painting. What is Darcy's basis in this painting?

(a) $100

(b) $1,000,000

(c) $1,350,000

(d) $350,100

(e) $0 because Darcy detests all Impressionist art.

Answers

91. You can tell Carolyn to relax. Although her shares have gone up in value, she has not "realized" any gain because there has been no transaction that qualifies as a realization event. If she sells or trades them, she will realize income at that time.

92. In a transaction involving a sale or other disposition of property, realized gain is the difference between the amount realized and the taxpayer's adjusted basis in the property transferred. Recognized gain is the amount of gain that the taxpayer must include in gross income as a result of that transaction. The two numbers might not be the same.

93. This trade is a realization event to both Al and Sal. What they received was different, qualitatively, than what they had before; they have different legal rights after the trade. Each has realized gain in the amount of the difference between the fair market value of what was received and the basis of what was transferred. That gain will be recognized unless they can find a nonrecognition statute that applies. (See Chapter 10.)

94. Taylor has used appreciated property to satisfy a debt, and will be treated as if she had sold the sports car and paid the debt with cash. Therefore, she will realize and must recognize gain on that transaction equal to the difference between the fair market value of the sports car and its adjusted basis. The amount of the debt may be easier to determine than the value of the sports car, so that amount will be the amount realized.

95. Basis represents the initial economic investment a taxpayer has in an item of property (or his or her deemed investment, as in the case of property received from a decedent or by gift). Adjusted basis reflects the initial basis, plus and minus, respectively, improvements made to the property after acquisition and the capital recovery claimed with respect to the property. In both cases, basis or adjusted basis is the starting point for measuring the capital recovery deductions a taxpayer may claim, and is the way of measuring gain or loss on ultimate disposition of the property.

96. It appears that Jessica has simply divided the purchase price by the recovery period for this kind of property (39.5 years) to produce the first year's MACRS deduction. There are two problems with this approach. First, Jessica must allocate a portion of the purchase price to the land. The land is not depreciable, and her basis in the depreciable office building will be the total purchase price minus the amount allocated to the land. Second, the mid-month convention will result in Jessica not receiving a full year's MACRS deduction in the first year, even if she purchased the property on Jan. 1 of that year.

97. Dick has a realized and recognized gain of $200,000, which is equal to his amount realized ($300,000) minus his adjusted basis in the property of $100,000 ($140,000 – $40,000).

98. Dick has a realized and recognized gain of $200,000, which is equal to his amount realized of $300,000 ($200,000 in cash plus assumption of the $100,000 mortgage) minus his adjusted basis in the property of $100,000 ($140,000 – $40,000). Jerry's basis is $300,000, which is equal to his purchase price: $200,000 in cash plus the assumption of the mortgage.

99. First, note that this is a *nonrecourse* loan. Courtney is incorrect. Courtney is thinking that her loss is equal to the difference between the fair market value of the property ($600,000) and her adjusted basis ($750,000). But this is incorrect. She should have reported a *gain* of $200,000. Under *Tufts*, Courtney is deemed to have sold the property and the amount realized is equal to the amount of the outstanding loan ($950,000). Her adjusted basis in the property is $750,000 ($1,000,000 – 250,000 of MACRS deductions). This produces a realized and recognized gain of $200,000. So, Courtney will have gain even though she will have no cash from the transaction with which to pay the tax.

100. First, note that this is a *recourse* debt. Linda has experienced two transactions. First, in the foreclosure sale, she realized a $200,000 loss. The Motel was sold for $200,000, and Linda had an adjusted basis of $400,000 in the property (her cost minus her depreciation deductions). This results in a $200,000 loss to her, which should be deductible under §165(c). Second, Linda also experienced $250,000 of discharge of indebtedness income as a result of the bank writing off the loan. This may be excludable from Linda's gross income, however, if she meets any of the exceptions of §108(a), such as the insolvency exception.

101. The result would be the same, assuming that the value of the motel was $200,000 on the date of transfer.

102. If the property were Linda's principal residence, the exclusion of §108(a)(1)(E) would likely apply to exclude from gross income the $250,000 of discharge of indebtedness income. She would not have depreciated a residence, so her basis would be her original cost of $500,000 (assuming no improvements). The sale for $200,000 results in a $300,000 loss, but this loss is not deductible under §165(c).

103. Craig's property is worth $400,000, and he and the lender are negotiating to reduce the total loan balance to this amount, which results in discharge of indebtedness income of $100,000. This question focuses on the exclusion from gross income for discharge of debt attributable to qualified principal residence indebtedness under §108(a)(1)(E). Only acquisition indebtedness qualifies for this exclusion (not the HELOC), so a reduction in the original mortgage (Scenario B) is more favorable for Craig. He will have to reduce his basis in the residence, but that won't matter because if he ultimately sells it he will presumably enjoy the exclusion of §121.

104. Fred is not correct: he actually has a $50,000 loss. Because Fred used the plane for both business and personal purposes, he had to bifurcate the purchase price of $1,000,000 based on use, so that the purchase price for the business portion of the plane was $600,000. The MACRS deductions are attributable to this portion, reducing the basis to $250,000. Then, on sale, the purchase price must again be bifurcated, into business (60%, or $300,000) and personal (40%, or $200,000). He has a gain of $50,000 on the business portion of the plane ($300,000 amount realized minus $250,000

adjusted basis) and a $200,000 personal (nondeductible) loss attributable to the personal portion of the plane ($200,000 amount realized minus $400,000 adjusted basis). See *Sharp v. United States,* 199 F. Supp. 743 (D. Del. 1961), *aff'd* 303 F.2d 783 (3d Cir. 1962).

105. When a taxpayer receives property and must include its fair market value in gross income, the basis of the property is its "tax cost," or the amount included in gross income. An example of tax cost basis is when a taxpayer is paid for services with property. The taxpayer includes the fair market value of the property in gross income, and takes the property with a basis equal to the amount included in gross income.

106. The proper answer is (b), the fair market value of the painting at the grandmother's death. IRC §1014(a).

Exam Tips on *TRANSACTIONS IN PROPERTY*

☛ Questions involving transactions in property involve sales, exchanges, trades, and other dispositions of property.

   ☞ *Look for:* A taxpayer giving up a property in exchange for something else—cash, other property, promises, services, assumption of liabilities.

   ☞ *Analyze:* Which taxpayer's tax consequences are you asked to analyze? Both, or just one of them? If both taxpayers are at issue, analyze them separately.

☛ **Careful:** Don't jump right to the question of gain included in income, or loss deductible from income. Make sure there is a realization event, and that there is realized gain or loss, before asking what gain or loss is recognized.

   ☞ If in doubt, consider a transaction a realization event. Most transactions are realization events.

   ☞ Compute realized gain by subtracting the adjusted basis of the property given up from the value of what the taxpayer receives. If the property received is difficult to value, refer to the value of the property given up.

☛ **Remember:** Rational, unrelated taxpayers will trade value-for-value and will adjust differences in value by paying or receiving additional property. If taxpayers are related, there may be a gift involved.

☛ Most realized gain is recognized (see Chapter 10). If in doubt, include it in income.

☛ Realized loss is recognizable only if there is a statute that allows it. See Chapters 6 and 7. Deductions are a matter of legislative grace and are interpreted narrowly. If in doubt, deny the deduction of the loss.

☛ Given recent economic events, tax professors may be interested in testing on foreclosures and related transactions involving distressed properties, particularly residences. Be ready to analyze these transactions.

 ## STATUTE SUMMARY CHARTS

Statute Summary—§1001
Realized Gain or Loss on Dispositions of Property

Parsing Step	IRC §1001
General Rule	Realized gain or loss on the sale or exchange of property is recognized.
Definitions	**Realization event:** exchange where taxpayer ends up with something different than he or she had before. **Realized gain or loss:** equal to the amount realized minus the taxpayer's adjusted basis in the property transferred. **Amount realized:** what the taxpayer receives in exchange. **Adjusted basis:** depends on how the taxpayer acquired the property, and depreciation/improvements.
Special Rules and Exceptions	When a purchaser of property pays the proportion of real estate taxes (or the seller is credited with that amount at closing), that amount is not included in the seller's amount realized.
Related Statutes	**§121:** Exclusion of gain on sale of principal residence **§453:** Installment sale of property **§§1031, 1033, 1041:** Gain/loss deferral statutes **§1221:** Character of gain or loss
Typically implicated when	A taxpayer owns property and sells or exchanges it for cash, other property, the assumption of liabilities, or other considerations.

CHAPTER 10

NONRECOGNITION TRANSACTIONS

ChapterScope ━━━━━━━━━━━━━━━━━━━━━━━━━━━━━━━━━━━━

The previous chapter addressed the computation of realized and recognized gain and loss from the sale or other disposition of property. As a general rule, gross income includes these gains, and a loss will generate a deduction if the other statutory requirements for a deduction are met. Congress has, however, determined that for some transactions, the time is not ripe for recognition of realized gain or loss. For these transactions, even though a realization event has occurred, recognition is deferred until a more appropriate time. Code sections that provide deferral of recognition of gain or loss for such transactions are called nonrecognition provisions and are the subject of this chapter.

- ■ **An approach to nonrecognition transactions:** The approach to sales or exchanges of property discussed in Chapter 9(III) is equally applicable here, with special emphasis on steps 2 (gain and loss recognition) and 3 (calculation of basis).

- ■ **Section 1031—Like-kind exchanges:** Section 1031 mandates nonrecognition treatment for exchanges of like-kind properties, such as real property for real property, if certain requirements are met.

- ■ **Section 1033—Involuntary conversions:** Section 1033 allows nonrecognition of gain for conversions of property as a result of thefts, disasters, and condemnation actions, if certain requirements are met.

- ■ **Section 1041—Spousal and divorce transfers:** Section 1041 provides for nonrecognition of gain or loss on transfers between spouses and on transfers between former spouses if "incident to a divorce" and if certain other requirements are met.

I. WHERE ARE WE?

We are continuing our computation of gross income from the dealings in property, or losses from such transactions allowable as a deduction. A special group of statutes defer the recognition of all or part of the gain or loss for some kinds of transactions. If any of these statutes apply, all or part of the gain or loss will not be recognized by the taxpayer in the year of sale or exchange, but will potentially be preserved in the basis of the property received. So, this chapter is about gross income and deductions, as well as timing of the recognition of gains and losses.

II. AN APPROACH TO THE NONRECOGNITION PROVISIONS

The approach to sales and exchanges of property discussed in Chapter 9 (see Figure 9A) is equally applicable to nonrecognition provisions. However, particular emphasis is placed on the calculation of gain recognition and the computation of basis of the property received.

III. LIKE-KIND EXCHANGES—§1031

A. Recognizing this transaction

1. **Basic transaction:** A *like-kind exchange* is exactly what it sounds like—a taxpayer exchanging one property for a property of like kind. Common examples include the exchange of real property for real property or the trade-in of equipment for other equipment. The taxpayer may also receive or transfer other types of property in the transaction and may assume or be relieved of liabilities in the exchange.

2. **A few terms of art:** Know the nomenclature surrounding these transactions. Your professor may use different terms than these (e.g., instead of "relinquished property" she or he may say "property transferred").

    a. **The relinquished property:** this is the property the taxpayer transfers in the exchange.

    b. **The replacement property:** this is the like-kind property the taxpayer receives in the transaction.

    c. **Boot:** Any money or nonlike-kind property the taxpayer receives in the transaction.

B. Policy

A variety of rationales are commonly offered for nonrecognition in like-kind exchanges.

1. **No change in investment:** The most commonly offered rationale is that because the taxpayer continues to hold the same kind of property, the time has not yet arrived to compute the economic gain or loss on the original investment.

2. **Liquidity:** Another rationale is that in a like-kind exchange, the taxpayer receives no cash, and thus paying the tax would be difficult. Notice that if boot is received, the taxpayer may have the cash (or other property that can be converted to cash) to pay tax. This rationale is criticized because taxpayers engaging in other types of trades do not have cash, but nevertheless must pay tax. See, e.g., barter transactions discussed in Chapter 2(III)(B).

3. **Fighting "lock-in":** The like-kind exchange rules may be a limited method of fighting the effect of *lock-in,* i.e., taxpayers holding on to property that would otherwise be sold simply to avoid paying tax. See discussion of lock-in in Chapter 12(II)(D).

C. Section 1031 statutory analysis—General rule

The general rule of §1031 is easy to state: A taxpayer engaging in a transaction that qualifies as a like-kind exchange recognizes neither gain nor loss on the transfer of property in the exchange, and takes the property received in the exchange with an exchanged basis. This general statement of the rule, however, captures neither the precise requirements for a like-kind exchange nor the full implications to the taxpayer of §1031 treatment.

1. **Five requirements:** A like-kind exchange occurs if—and only if—the following five requirements are met.

    a. **Exchange:** A taxpayer must exchange property for property. IRC §1031(a)(1).

    b. **Not prohibited property:** The relinquished property and the replacement property must not be inventory, stocks, bonds, notes, securities or other evidences of indebtedness, partnership interests, interests in a trust, or chooses in action. IRC §1031(a)(2).

   c. Use of property transferred: The taxpayer must have held the relinquished property for use in a trade or business or for investment. IRC §1031(a)(1).

   d. Like-kind properties: The replacement property must be like-kind to the property exchanged. IRC §1031(a)(1).

   e. Use of property received: The taxpayer must intend to hold the replacement property for use in a trade or business or for investment. IRC §1031(a)(1).

2. Tax consequences:

   a. Nonrecognition: In a qualifying like-kind exchange, the taxpayer does not recognize any of the realized gain or loss on the transfer of the relinquished property unless he or she receives ***boot,*** which is any nonlike-kind property. Section 1031's nonrecognition rule is mandatory; if a transaction qualifies as a like-kind exchange, the taxpayer recognizes neither gain nor loss.

      i. Boot received—Gain recognition: If the taxpayer receives boot, realized gain on the relinquished property is recognized to the extent of the fair market value of the boot received. IRC §1031(b). In other words, realized gain is recognized in an amount equal to the lesser of the realized gain or the fair market value of the boot received. The receipt of boot triggers gain recognition because it represents a partial sale of the property. While the taxpayer has continued his or her original investment in a portion of the property (represented by the like-kind property received), the taxpayer also has discontinued this investment to the extent of cash or nonlike-kind property received. Thus, the taxpayer is treated as having sold a portion of the original property for purposes of gain recognition.

      ii. Loss not recognized: Loss is never recognized in a qualifying §1031 exchange, even when boot is received. IRC §1031(c).

   b. Basis: A taxpayer transferring property in a like-kind exchange may receive two types of property in the transaction: like-kind property and boot. See Figure 10A—Basis Calculation for Like-Kind Exchanges.

Figure 10A
Basis Calculation for Like-Kind Exchanges

To calculate the basis of the replacement property received in a qualifying §1031 exchange:

Start with:	The basis of the relinquished property
Add:	Any gain recognized by the taxpayer on the transaction
Subtract:	The fair market value of any boot received by the taxpayer
Subtract:	Any loss recognized by the taxpayer on the transaction
Add:	Any additional investment made by the taxpayer (boot paid)

i. **Like-kind property:** The taxpayer's basis in the like-kind replacement property is equal to the basis of the relinquished property, plus the gain recognized, minus the fair market value of the boot received, minus any loss recognized on the transaction, plus any additional amount invested in the property acquired. IRC §§1031(d), 1012. This is a form of **exchanged basis**, in which the basis of the property acquired is determined by reference to the basis of the property transferred. See IRC §7701(a)(44). The resulting basis will preserve, as of the date of the exchange, the realized but unrecognized gain or loss inherent in the relinquished property. Thus, if the property's fair market value remains unchanged until sale, the taxpayer will ultimately recognize upon sale of the property the gain or loss that went unrecognized in the previous like-kind exchange.

ii. **Boot:** The taxpayer's basis in any boot received is its fair market value. IRC §1031(d).

iii. **Loss taken into account in basis calculation:** Since losses are never recognized in like-kind exchanges, how can the basis calculation require a subtraction for losses recognized? This can occur if the taxpayer transfers property to the other party to the exchange that has an adjusted basis greater than its fair market value, and the taxpayer recognizes a loss on the transfer.

Example: Kay owns Property #1, which has a fair market value of $90,000 and an adjusted basis of $50,000. Kay wishes to trade Property #1 for Property #2, and the exchange would qualify as a like-kind exchange. However, Property #2 is worth $100,000, and therefore Kay must transfer $10,000 in boot to the other party. She does so by transferring a painting that she held for investment, which has a fair market value of $10,000 and an adjusted basis of $15,000. Assuming no other loss restrictions apply, she recognizes $5,000 of loss on this transfer. In computing her basis in Property #2, Kay will begin with her basis in Property #1 ($50,000) and the boot she paid ($15,000), add the gain recognized (0), subtract the fair market value of boot received (0), subtract the loss recognized ($5,000), and add the boot paid (0) since she has already taken into account the painting in step 1). Thus, her basis in Property #2 will be $60,000. Another way to think about this problem is to imagine that Kay sold the painting to someone else for cash, recognized the loss independently of this transaction, and then exchanged properties, adding the cash from the painting sale to the mix. In that case, the basis of Property #2 would be the same ($60,000), calculated in a slightly different way: Start with the basis of Property #1 ($50,000), add the gain recognized (0), subtract the fair market value of boot received (0), subtract the loss recognized on this exchange (0), and add the boot paid ($10,000).

c. **Independent results for each taxpayer:** In order to qualify under §1031, a taxpayer must meet only the requirements discussed above. It is not necessary that any other party to the exchange meet these requirements. Thus, each taxpayer's tax consequences must be analyzed separately to determine whether he or she has made a qualifying §1031 exchange.

The following examples illustrate operation of §1031.

Example: Alex owns Blackacre, a parcel of raw land she holds for investment. She has a basis of $30,000 in the property, and it is worth $100,000. Brenda owns Whiteacre, also a parcel of raw land, worth $100,000. Alex and Brenda exchange properties. Alex intends to hold Whiteacre for investment. What are the tax consequences of this transaction to Alex? Applying the four-step approach of Figure 9A to this problem, consider the following questions:

Has there been a sale of exchange of property? Yes. Real estate certainly qualifies as property.

What is Alex's realized and recognized gain or loss? Alex's realized gain or loss is equal to the amount realized on the transfer ($100,000, the fair market value of Whiteacre) minus her adjusted basis in the property transferred ($30,000) for a realized gain of $70,000.

This transaction falls within §1031 because (1) it is an exchange of properties; (2) Alex held Blackacre for investment; (3) the properties received are like-kind (they are both raw land); (4) Alex intends to hold Whiteacre for investment; and (5) the properties exchanged are not prohibited property (they are real property). As a result, none of Alex's realized gain of $70,000 is recognized; she need not include any of this realized gain in gross income. Notice that Brenda's tax consequences are irrelevant to Alex's entitlement to like-kind exchange treatment.

What is the basis of Whiteacre in Alex's hands? Alex's basis in Whiteacre is equal to her basis in Blackacre ($30,000) plus the gain recognized if any (0), minus the fair market value of the boot received, if any (0), minus the loss recognized, if any (0). Thus, Alex's basis in Whiteacre is $30,000. Notice that this preserves the realized but unrecognized gain inherent in Blackacre at the time of the exchange. If, later, Alex sells Whiteacre for $100,000 in cash, she will recognize $70,000 of gain—precisely the amount that went unrecognized in the like-kind exchange. (If Whiteacre's value changes, of course, she will recognize a different amount of gain, but that amount will reflect her economic profit or loss on the investment of Blackacre *and* Whiteacre.)

What is the character of Alex's gain? This is not relevant because Alex has no recognized gain. See discussion in Chapter 12(III)(B).

Example: Assume the same facts as in the previous example, except that Whiteacre was worth only $90,000, so that in order to make the trade, Brenda would transfer Whiteacre plus $10,000 cash to Alex. What are Alex's tax consequences? In this situation, Alex's realized gain from the exchange is again $70,000. Her amount realized is the fair market value of Whiteacre ($90,000) plus the $10,000 cash, for a total amount realized of $100,000. Subtracting her adjusted basis in Blackacre ($30,000) produces the same $70,000 realized gain as in the previous example. For the reasons discussed in the previous example, this transfer of Blackacre for Whiteacre qualifies as a like-kind exchange. The receipt of boot does not disqualify the like-kind exchange; it does, however, require the recognition of realized gain to the extent of the boot received ($10,000). As discussed in Chapter 12, that gain will be capital. Alex's basis in Whiteacre is equal to her basis in Blackacre ($30,000) plus the gain recognized ($10,000) minus the fair market value of the boot received ($10,000). Thus, her basis in Whiteacre is $30,000. Notice that this basis preserves the realized but unrecognized gain inherent in Blackacre ($60,000) at the time of the exchange. Thus, if Alex later sells Whiteacre for its current fair market value of $90,000, she will recognize the $60,000 of gain that was deferred in the like-kind exchange.

Example: Assume the same facts as in the previous example, except that instead of giving Alex $10,000 cash to equalize the values of the two properties, Brenda transfers a sports car to her along with Whiteacre. The tax consequences to Alex will be the same as in the previous situation, except that she will be required to assign a basis to the sports car. That basis will be the sports car's fair market value, or $10,000.

Example: Christian owns DogAcre, a parcel of raw land. His basis in DogAcre is $40,000, but its fair market value is only $15,000. He trades DogAcre for David's parcel of raw land, CatAcre. CatAcre is worth $10,000, so David also transfers $5,000 cash to Christian. Christian held DogAcre for investment and intends to hold CatAcre for investment as well. What are the tax consequences of this transaction to Christian? This realization event causes Christian to realize a loss of $25,000, equal to the difference between his amount realized of $15,000 ($10,000 in the form of CatAcre plus $5,000 in cash) and his adjusted basis in DogAcre ($40,000). However, because this qualifies as a like-kind exchange, Christian will not recognize any of the realized loss. (Notice that this is the result even though Christian received boot.) Christian's basis in CatAcre will be equal to his basis in DogAcre ($40,000) plus the gain recognized, if any (0), minus the fair market value of the boot received ($5,000). Therefore, his basis in CatAcre will be $35,000. Thus, if Christian later sells CatAcre for $10,000, he will recognize the $25,000 loss that was deferred in the like-kind exchange. (Christian should have sold DogAcre, recognized the loss, and then purchased CatAcre for cash.)

D. Definitional issues

1. **Exchange:** The taxpayer must *exchange* his or her property for the other property; the transaction must not be—in form or in substance—a sale for cash followed by a purchase of like-kind property. The taxpayer cannot later change his or her mind and transform a sale of property for cash into an exchange. Nor can the IRS cast a bona fide sale for cash and purchase of new property at cost as an exchange. See *Bell Lines, Inc. v. United States*, 480 F.2d 710 (4th Cir. 1973).

2. **Sale/Leaseback:** Because §1031 is mandatory, if a transaction is a qualifying exchange, no gain or loss will be recognized. This sometimes arises in *"sale/leaseback"* transactions in which the taxpayer wants to recognize a loss on the sale. In a sale/leaseback transaction, a taxpayer owning property sells it to another person, who then leases it back to the original taxpayer on a long-term lease. When the dust settles, it can appear that nothing much has changed. The question is whether a real sale occurred, or was the transaction an exchange of like-kind properties? See Figure 10B—Sale/Leaseback Transaction.

   a. **The typical sale/leaseback transaction to recognize loss:** In *Jordan Marsh Co. v. Commissioner,* 269 F.2d 453 (2d Cir. 1959), the taxpayer owned property with a basis of $4.8 million and a fair market value of $2.3 million. The taxpayer sold the property for cash, and then immediately leased the property from the buyer for a 30-year term, with an option to renew for 30 years. The taxpayer claimed a deduction of $2.5 million for the loss on the sale portion of the transaction.

      i. **Issue:** Was this an "exchange" of like-kind properties (a fee interest for a leasehold that effectively constituted a fee because of its length), so that Jordan Marsh incorrectly reported a loss on the transaction? Or was it a "sale," giving rise to a properly deductible loss?

Figure 10B
Sale/Leaseback Transaction

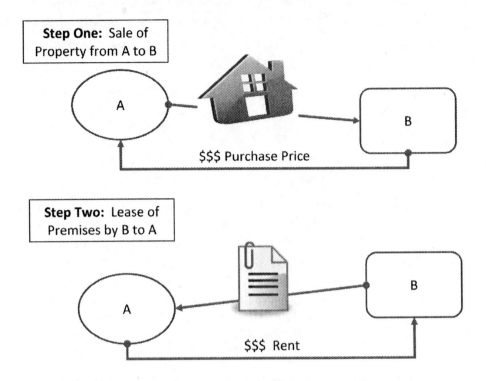

ii. **Result and rationale:** Jordan Marsh sold the property and properly reported the loss. The transaction constituted a true sale for fair market value, and the subsequent lease was a true lease for fair rental value. These bona fide transactions must be respected for tax purposes. Thus, the sale/leaseback transaction could not be recharacterized as an exchange.

b. **Factors important in sale/leaseback vs. exchange:** In *Leslie Co. v. Commissioner,* 539 F.2d 943 (3d Cir. 1976), another sale/leaseback transaction was analyzed. The taxpayer constructed property with a cost of $3.187 million and sold it to Prudential for $2.4 million, deducting the difference of $787,000 as a loss. Prudential then leased the property back to the taxpayer for a 40-year term with two 10-year options to renew and options to purchase the property during the term of the lease.

   i. **Issue:** Was the sale/leaseback, in substance, an exchange of like-kind properties so that Leslie incorrectly reported a loss on the transaction, or was it a sale giving rise to a properly deductible loss?

   ii. **Result and rationale:** Leslie sold the property and properly reported the loss. The court examined the different approaches of the Second Circuit in *Jordan Marsh* and the Eighth Circuit in *Century Electric Co. v. Commissioner,* 192 F.2d 155 (8th Cir. 1952). In *Century Electric,* the court held that no valuation of the fee interest and leasehold interest was necessary, and that an exchange was to be found if the transaction constituted a reciprocal exchange of properties. In *Jordan Marsh,* the court valued the two property interests; if the payments made were based on fair market value, the transaction would be considered a sale rather than an exchange of properties. In *Leslie,* the court adopted the *Jordan Marsh* approach, and because the sales price and the rental price reflected fair market value, the transaction was a true sale and lease rather than an exchange.

3. **Like-kind:** The analysis of qualifying like-kind property generates most of the controversy in §1031.

   a. **Statutory definitions:** Section 1031 itself provides that certain properties are not like-kind. Livestock of different sexes, and real property within and without the United States, are not like-kind. IRC §1031(e), (h).

   b. **Regulations' definition:** The regulations define like-kind as having reference to the "nature or character" of the property rather than its "grade or quality." Reg. §1.1031(a)–1(b).

      i. **Tangible personal property:** The regulations offer a safe harbor for determining whether depreciable personal property held for use in a trade or business is of like kind. The regulations and other administrative guidance divide the world of depreciable personal property into classes. An exchange of properties that are of the same class is considered a like-kind exchange. Reg. §1.1031(a)-1(b). Most trade-in transactions fall within this category. Exchanges of properties in different classes may still qualify as a like-kind exchange if the properties meet the general definition of like-kind. *Id.* But all properties may not be lumped together as a single asset. See Rev. Rul 72-151, 1872-1 C.B. 225.

      ii. **Other personal property:** Intangible and nondepreciable personal property, and personal property held for investment, must satisfy the more general like-kind test. The IRs's approach to personal property is apparently stricter than its approach to real property. See, e.g., Rev. Rul. 82-166, 1982-2 C.B. 190, in which an exchange of gold bullion held for investment for silver bullion held for investment was not a like-kind exchange, on the theory that silver and gold are intrinsically different metals and are used in different ways. See also Rev. Rul 79-143, 1979-1 C.B. 264 (exchange of numismatic-type coins for billion-type coins not a like-kind exchange).

      Example: Professional baseball Team A entered into a contract with Alex to play baseball. The team's basis in the contract is equal to the amount paid to Alex as a signing bonus. In the next year, Team A trades Alex to Team B in exchange for a contract that engaged Bob to play baseball. The contracts are depreciable personal property held for use in a trade or business and are like-kind contracts (even though they relate to different players). Therefore, the exchange qualifies as a like-kind exchange and no gain or loss is recognized. See Rev. Rul. 67-380, 1967-2 C.B. 291.

   c. **Real property:** State law is important, but not determinative, as to what constitutes realty or personalty. See *Commissioner v. Crichton,* 122 F.2d 181 (5th Cir. 1941). The regulations provide that an exchange of real property for real property qualifies as like-kind, regardless of the property's status as improved or unimproved, as like-kind relates only to the quality of the real property, not its nature or character. Reg. §1.1031(a)-1(b). Thus, a taxpayer may exchange city real estate for a ranch or farm. Reg. §1.1031(a)-1(c). The regulations treat a lease of 30 years or more as equivalent to a fee interest, so exchanges of a fee interest for a long-term lease will be considered like-kind exchanges. Occasionally, the transfer of an interest in real property of a shorter duration for a fee interest raises questions, and a court faced with such a problem will compare the exchanged properties to determine whether they are substantially alike, examining the physical characteristics of the properties, "the nature of the title conveyed, the rights of the parties, the duration of the interest, and any other factor bearing on the nature or character of the properties. . . ." *Koch v. Commissioner,* 71 T.C. 54, 65 (1978). In a related context, the IRS has asserted that a building and land are not like-kind. See Rev. Rul. 76-390, 1976-2 C.B. 243 (applying §1033(g), discussed in this chapter, Section (IV)).

Example: Marsha owns an office building and the underlying lot. She trades this property for a marina located on a 99-year lease of lakeshore property. This qualifies as a like-kind exchange, regardless of the different improvements and different uses of the two properties.

4. **Property held for investment or for use in a trade or business:** It is usually easy to identify property that is held for use in a trade or business, but sometimes whether property is "held for investment" is not so clear. It is also difficult to determine the taxpayer's intent with respect to the replacement property, and the best evidence of this is what the taxpayer actually does with the property. The taxpayer's intent at the time of the transaction is critical. In *Bolker v. Commissioner,* 760 F.2d 1039 (9th Cir. 1985), the taxpayer liquidated his corporation and received real property. He then exchanged that property for other like-kind property in what he hoped would be a valid §1031 exchange. The IRS challenged this as failing the requirement that the relinquished property be "held" for investment. The Court held that a taxpayer meets the requirements of the statute if he or she does not have the intention to liquidate the property or convert it to personal use. Similarly, in *Magneson v. Commissioner,* 81 T.C. 767 (1983), *aff'd* 753 F.2d 1490 (9th Cir. 1985), the taxpayers contributed the replacement property to a partnership. The Ninth Circuit considered this a mere exchange in form of ownership that did not invalidate the like-kind exchange.

E. **Special rules and exceptions**

1. **Deferred and three-party (*Starker*) exchanges:** *Deferred exchanges* and *three-party exchanges* are based on *Starker v. United States,* 602 F.2d 1341 (9th Cir. 1979), in which the court allowed like-kind exchange treatment for a transaction in which the taxpayer's transfer and receipt of property were separated by a significant period of time. The essential problem that these transactions address is that the taxpayer holds property he or she wishes to exchange in a like-kind exchange, but the buyer who wishes to acquire that property has only cash, not like-kind property.

    a. **Solution 1—Buyer acquires like-kind property:** In this transaction, the buyer purchases like-kind property that is acceptable to the seller and then exchanges it with the taxpayer. This transaction is treated as a pure like-kind exchange, as there is no delay between the transfer and receipt of properties. See Rev. Rul. 90-34, 1990-1 C.B. 154.

Example: Alvin holds Blackacre for investment and wishes to exchange it for like-kind property to be held for investment. Becky wants Blackacre, but has only cash. Cecilia owns Whiteacre, which is like-kind property to Blackacre, and would be happy to sell Whiteacre for cash. Alvin would be happy to exchange Blackacre for Whiteacre. In the first step of the transaction, Becky buys Whiteacre from Cecilia for cash. Then, in the second step, Alvin transfers Blackacre to Becky in exchange for Whiteacre. From Alvin's perspective, this is simply a like-kind exchange. Notice that Becky could not claim like-kind exchange treatment for this transaction because she acquired Whiteacre for the purpose of transferring it to Alvin, which would not qualify as holding it for use in a trade or business or for investment. However, this will not matter to Becky, because her basis in Whiteacre is its cost. Moreover, Becky's tax treatment is irrelevant to Alvin's ability to claim like-kind exchange treatment for his transfer of Blackacre. See Figure 10C—Alvin's Exchange of Blackacre for Whiteacre.

b. **Solution 2—Deferred exchange:** In a deferred exchange, the taxpayer could first transfer his or her property to the buyer, in exchange for the buyer's promise to acquire like-kind property and transfer it to the taxpayer within a specified period of time. This obviously doesn't work too well, because the taxpayer has to trust the other person to fulfill the second part of the exchange. The solution is the use of a qualified intermediary that acts as a kind of escrow for the parties. The intermediary will hold the property until the buyer acquires and transfers the like-kind property to the taxpayer or to the intermediary (who then transfers it to the taxpayer). Alternatively, the buyer may deposit funds with the

Figure 10C
Alvin's Exchange of Blackacre for Whiteacre

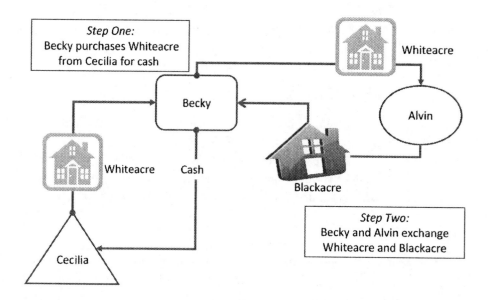

intermediary, who will acquire suitable property. If the intermediary is related to the taxpayer, this could be viewed as a transfer for cash, so care must be taken that the transaction fits the requirements of statute and regulations for a qualified intermediary.

Example: Alvin owns and wishes to exchange Blackacre for like-kind property. Becky wants Blackacre, but has cash, not like-kind property. Becky would like Alvin to convey Blackacre to her in exchange for her promise to acquire like-kind property within a stated period of time. Alvin, however, is reluctant to convey Blackacre to Becky for her mere promise. In the first step of the transaction, Alvin conveys Blackacre to an intermediary, and Becky places funds equal to the fair market value of Blackacre with the intermediary. The instructions to the intermediary are to acquire acceptable like-kind property (designated by Alvin) within a stated period of time. In the second step of the transaction, the intermediary acquires suitable like-kind property (Whiteacre) from Cecilia, paying Cecilia the cash previously deposited by Becky. In the third step of the transaction, the intermediary conveys Whiteacre to Alvin and Blackacre to Becky. In practice, Cecilia might directly transfer the property to Alvin, but in this illustration, the intermediary takes title and then transfers it to Alvin. See Figure 10D—Deferred Exchange with Intermediary.

c. **Statutory and regulatory requirements:** In order for a deferred exchange to receive nonrecognition treatment, the property to be received by the taxpayer must be *identified* within 45 days after the taxpayer relinquishes his or her property, *and* must be *received* before the earlier of (1) the 180th day after the date the taxpayer relinquishes his or her property, or (2) the due date of the taxpayer's tax return for the year of the transfer of the relinquished property. IRC §1031(a)(3). The 45-day period gives the taxpayer time to find the right property, and the 180-day period gives the taxpayer the necessary time to inspect it, make an offer, and close the transaction. Because the taxpayer doesn't know if he or she will be able to purchase a particular property (the taxpayer and the seller might not reach agreement on terms), the taxpayer may identify more properties than he or she will actually acquire. The taxpayer may identify (1) any three properties or (2) any number of properties, if the aggregate fair market value of the properties doesn't exceed twice the fair market value of the relinquished property. Reg. §1.1031(k)-1(c)(4). The regulations provide detailed rules regarding what constitutes adequate identification and receipt. Treas. Reg. §1.1031(k)-1.

Example: Ben transferred PeanutAcre to a qualified intermediary on August 1, Year 1. By September 14 (45 days from August 1), Ben identified Properties X, Y, and Z as potential exchange properties. By January 31, Year 2, Ben acquired Property Z through the intermediary. This is a deferred exchange that qualifies for nonrecognition treatment, assuming all other conditions are met.

d. **Another permutation—Reverse exchange:** At times the taxpayer may have identified the replacement property before deciding which property will be the relinquished property. In this situation, the taxpayer may receive like-kind property before he or she transfers like-kind property; this is known as a ***reverse exchange.*** The IRS has issued guidance creating a safe harbor for reverse exchanges in which a taxpayer may transfer property to a qualified intermediary while replacement property is being located, when the taxpayer has

Figure 10D
Deferred Exchange with Intermediary

Step One:
Alvin transfers Blackacre and
Becky transfers Cash to QI

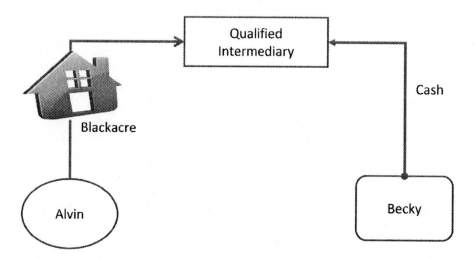

Step Two:
QI purchases Whiteacre from
Cecilia with Becky's cash

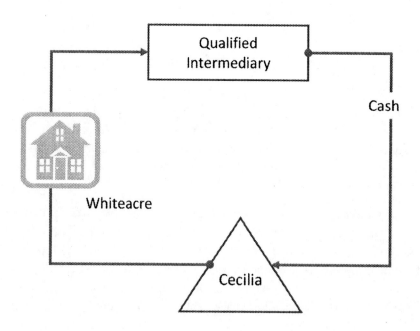

Figure 10D *[continued]*

Step Three:
QI transfers Blackacre to
Becky and Whiteacre to Alvin

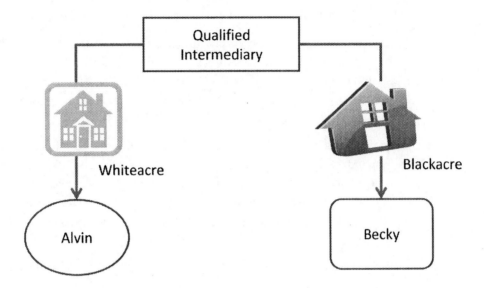

a genuine intent to engage in a like-kind exchange. *Rutherford v. Commissioner,* TC Memo 1978-505; Rev. Proc. 2000-37, 2000-2 C.B. 308, modified by Rev. Proc. 2004-51, 2004-2 C.B. 294.

2. **Effect of mortgages:** Property intended to be used in a like-kind exchange may be subject to a mortgage, and the first question in any exchange in which the encumbered properties are transferred is whether any party to the exchange is assuming those liabilities or whether property is being transferred subject to the liabilities. If so, special attention must be paid to the regulations setting forth the proper treatment of these liabilities.

   a. **The rules:** The IRS provides guidance on the treatment of mortgages in regulations that are generally taxpayer friendly, if somewhat complex.

      i. **Consequences to transferor of encumbered property:** A transferor of encumbered property must include the liabilities assumed by the other party to the exchange as part of his or her amount realized in calculating the realized gain or loss on the exchange. See §1001 and discussion in Chapter 9(V). In addition, the liability assumed by the other party is considered boot to the party to the exchange transferring the encumbered property. This results in gain recognition (but see ***mortgage netting,*** below) and must be treated as boot in the calculation of the basis of the like-kind property received.

ii.   **Consequences to acquirer of encumbered property:** The party assuming a liability of the other party to the exchange is treated as transferring property in the amount of the liability. Thus, the amount of the liability is added to the basis of the property transferred in the exchange in determining the realized gain or loss on the exchange. This amount is considered an additional investment in the property for purposes of calculating the basis of the property received in the transaction.

iii. **Mortgage netting:** When both properties are subject to liabilities, only the taxpayer with net relief from liabilities is treated as having received boot, for purposes of gain recognition only. Reg. §1.1031(d)-2, Example (2). The full amount of the mortgages are considered (i.e., are not netted) in computing realized gain or loss and basis calculation, although the result will be similar to netting. *Id.*

iv.   **Mortgage netting and boot:** The mortgage netting rule allows the party with net assumption of liability to avoid recognition of gain, but this applies only to the mortgage portion of the transaction. If that person receives other nonlike-kind property (boot), the usual gain recognition rules will apply. Reg. §1.1031(d)-1, Example (2). In addition, the party with net relief from liability may reduce the amount of gain recognized by any boot paid in the transaction. *Id.*

b. **Examples:** Consider the rules described above, as applied in the following examples.

Example: Heather owns Blueacre, which has an adjusted basis of $60,000 and a fair market value of $100,000. It is subject to a liability of $20,000. Heather exchanges Blueacre for Mickey's Pinkacre (worth $80,000) in a qualifying §1031 exchange in which Mickey assumes Heather's liability. Heather's amount realized is the fair market value of Pinkacre ($80,000) plus Mickey's assumption of her liability ($20,000). Subtracting Heather's adjusted basis in Blueacre of $60,000 produces a realized gain of $40,000. Heather's recognized gain is $20,000, equal to the liabilities Mickey assumed in the transaction. Heather's adjusted basis in Pinkacre is equal to $60,000, calculated as follows:

Heather's basis in Blueacre	$60,000
+ Gain recognized	+20,000
– FMV boot (A/L*)	–20,000
Basis of Pinkacre	$60,000

*A/L = assumption of liability.

Notice that Heather's $60,000 basis in Pinkacre preserves the unrecognized $20,000 gain on the original exchange. If Heather were to later sell Pinkacre for $80,000, she would realize and recognize the $20,000 gain.

Summary of Heather's Tax Consequences

Realized Gain	Recognized Gain	Basis of Pinkacre
$40,000	$20,000	$60,000 (basis of Blueacre) +20,000 (gain) −20,000 (boot) $ 60,000 Basis of Pinkacre

Example: Mildred owns Greenacre, with an adjusted basis of $40,000 and a fair market value of $80,000. Mildred exchanges Greenacre for Paul's Whiteacre in a qualifying §1031 exchange. Whiteacre has a fair market value of $110,000 and is subject to a mortgage of $30,000.

Mildred's realized gain is equal to $40,000, the difference between her amount realized ($110,000) and the sum of her adjusted basis in Greenacre ($40,000) and the amount of mortgage she assumes in the transaction ($30,000). Her recognized gain is zero because she received no boot in the transaction. Her basis in Whiteacre is $70,000, calculated as follows:

Mildred's basis in Greenacre	$40,000
+ Gain recognized	0
− FMV boot received	0
+ Additional investment	+30,000
Basis in Whiteacre	$70,000

Notice that Mildred's basis in Whiteacre preserves the realized but unrecognized gain ($40,000) on her transfer of Greenacre. If she later sells Whiteacre for $110,000, she will recognize $40,000 of gain on that sale.

Summary of Mildred's Tax Consequences

Realized Gain	Recognized Gain	Basis of Whiteacre
$40,000	0	$40,000 (basis in Greenacre) + 0 (gain) − 0 (boot) +30,000 (liability assumed) $70,000 Basis of Whiteacre

Example: Richard owns Blackacre, which has a basis of $100,000, a fair market value of $170,000, and is subject to a mortgage of $50,000. Richard exchanges Blackacre for Claudia's Yellowacre, which has a basis in Claudia's hands of $90,000, is worth $200,000, and is subject to a mortgage of $80,000. The exchange qualifies as a like-kind exchange under §1031 for both parties.

Richard Blackacre		Claudia Yellowacre	
FMV	= $170,000	FMV	= $200,000
AB	= 100,000	AB	= 90,000
Mortgage	= 50,000	Mortgage	= 80,000

Richard's tax consequences

▪ *Step 1:* **Calculate realized gain.** Amount realized minus adjusted basis of property transferred.

> $200,000 (FMV Yellowacre)
> +50,000 (Liability Claudia assumes)
> $250,000 Amount realized
> *minus*:
> 100,000 (Basis of Blackacre)
> + 80,000 (Liability Richard assumes)
> $180,000 Basis of property transferred
>
> Realized gain = $70,000

▪ *Step 2:* **Calculate recognized gain.** Richard takes on an $80,000 mortgage and is relieved of a $50,000 mortgage. Therefore, because Richard has net assumption of liability, he recognizes no gain.

▪ *Step 3:* **Calculate Richard's basis in Yellowacre.**

Basis in Blackacre	$100,000
+ Gain recognized	+0
− Boot received (liability assumed by Claudia)	−50,000
+ Boot paid (liability assumed by Richard)	+80,000
Richard's basis in Yellowacre	$130,000

▪ *Step 4:* Notice that this basis ($130,000) preserves the realized but unrecognized gain ($70,000) on the exchange of Blackacre.

Claudia's tax consequences

▪ *Step 1:* **Calculate realized gain.** Amount realized minus adjusted basis of property transferred.

$170,000 (FMV Blackacre)
+80,000 (Liability Richard assumes)
$250,000 Amount realized
minus:
  90,000 (Basis of Yellowacre)
+50,000 (Liability Claudia assumes)
$140,000 Basis of property transferred

Realized gain = $110,000

- *Step 2:* **Calculate recognized gain.** Because Claudia experiences net relief from liability (she gives up $80,000 of liability and assumes only $50,000), she recognizes gain equal to the net relief, or $30,000.

- *Step 3:* **Calculate Claudia's basis in Blackacre.**

Basis of Yellowacre	$90,000
+ Gain recognized	+30,000
– Boot received (Liability Richard assumes)	–80,000
+ Boot paid (Liability Claudia assumes)	+50,000
Claudia's basis in Blackacre	$90,000

- *Step 4:* Notice that this basis ($90,000) preserves the realized but unrecognized gain ($110,000 – 30,000 = $80,000) on the transfer of Yellowacre.

Summary of Richard and Claudia's Tax Consequences

	Realized Gain	Recognized Gain	Basis of New Property
Richard	$70,000	0	$130,000
Claudia	$110,000	$30,000	$90,000

Example: Assume the same facts as in the previous example, except that Claudia's property, Yellowacre, is worth only $190,000. Claudia transfers Yellowacre (subject to its mortgage) plus $10,000 cash to Richard in exchange for Blackacre (subject to its mortgage). Assume that the transaction qualifies as a §1031 exchange.

Richard			Claudia		
Blackacre			Yellowacre		
FMV	=	$170,000	FMV	=	$190,000
AB	=	100,000	AB	=	90,000
Mortgage	=	50,000	Mortgage	=	80,000
			Cash	=	10,000

Richard's tax consequences

- *Step 1:* **Calculate realized gain.** Amount realized minus adjusted basis of property transferred.

    $190,000 (Yellowacre)
    + 10,000 (Cash received)
    + 50,000 (Liability Claudia assumes)
    $250,000 Amount realized
    minus:
    $100,000 (Basis of Blackacre)
    + 80,000 (Liability Richard assumes)
    $180,000 Adjusted basis of property transferred

    Realized gain = $70,000

- *Step 2:* **Calculate recognized gain.** Richard recognizes $10,000 of the gain because he received that much boot in the form of cash, but the mortgage netting rule shields him from recognition of any gain on the mortgage.

- *Step 3:* **Calculate Richard's basis in Yellowacre.**

$100,000	(Basis of Blackacre)
+ 10,000	(Gain recognized)
− 10,000	(Boot received as cash)
− 50,000	(Boot received as A/L)
+ 80,000	(Boot paid as A/L)
$130,000	Basis in Yellowacre

- *Step 4:* Notice that this basis ($130,000) preserves the realized but unrecognized gain ($60,000) on the transfer of Blackacre.

Claudia's tax consequences

- *Step 1:* **Calculate realized gain.** Amount realized minus adjusted basis of property transferred.

    $170,000 (Blackacre)
    + 80,000 (Liability Richard assumes)
    $250,000 Amount realized
    minus:
    $90,000 (Basis in Yellowacre)
    +50,000 (Liability Claudia assumes)
    +10,000 (Boot paid)
    $150,000 Adjusted basis of property transferred

    Realized gain = $100,000

- *Step 2:* **Calculate recognized gain.** Claudia's net relief from liabilities of $30,000 would result in recognition of that amount of gain under the mortgage netting rule. However, Claudia may offset the $30,000 net relief from liabilities by the amount of boot she pays in the form of cash. Thus, she recognizes only $20,000 of gain.

※ *Step 3:* Calculate Claudia's basis in Blackacre.

$90,000 (Basis of Yellowacre)
+ 20,000 (Gain recognized)
− 80,000 (Liability assumed by Richard)
+ 50,000 (Liability assumed by Claudia)
+ 10,000 (Boot paid—cash)
$90,000 Basis in Blackacre

※ *Step 4:* Notice that this basis ($90,000) preserves the realized but unrecognized gain ($80,000) on the transfer of Yellowacre.

Summary of Richard and Claudia's Tax Consequences

	Realized Gain	Recognized Gain	Basis of New Property
Richard	$70,000	$10,000	$130,000
Claudia	$100,000	$20,000	$90,000

F. Related material

1. **Sale of principal residence:** If a taxpayer acquires property in a qualifying §1031 exchange, and subsequently converts its use to a principal residence, he or she must hold and use the property as the principal residence for at least five years in order to claim the exclusion under §121. IRC §1031(d)(10). See Chapter 4(VIII).

2. **Character of gain:** The character of any gain recognized in a like-kind exchange is determined under the rules discussed in Chapter 12.

G. Be alert for like-kind exchanges

Section 1031 is one of the most heavily tested areas in the basic tax class. Consider it whenever a taxpayer is exchanging property, even if the taxpayer also receives cash.

IV. INVOLUNTARY CONVERSIONS—§1033

Section 1033 potentially allows a taxpayer to defer, in whole or in part, recognition of gain on the involuntary conversion of property if certain statutory requirements are met. (Notice that §1033 applies only to gain; losses from the involuntary conversion of property (casualty losses) are the subject of §165(c)(3), discussed in Chapter 6(VII).)

A. Recognizing this transaction

Look for a taxpayer's property being destroyed by a natural disaster such as flood, storm, earthquake, etc. If the taxpayer receives similar property, or receives insurance proceeds or other compensation and reinvests in similar property soon after the event, gain may be deferred. Proceeds received in a condemnation action, or under threat of condemnation, also qualify. Look for a taxpayer's property being taken under eminent domain or a taxpayer selling property in light of a realistic threat of eminent domain.

B. Policy

The following two rationales are often proffered for §1033.

1. Same investment: The taxpayer has not liquidated his or her original investment and the type of investment remains the same, even though the particular property is different. A similar rationale is offered for deferral in like-kind exchanges, but this rationale is perhaps more compelling in §1033 because of the involuntary nature of the transaction. Because the investment remains essentially unchanged, the calculation of gain or loss on the investment will be deferred until the taxpayer fundamentally changes the investment, e.g., sells the property.

2. "Piling on": Another rationale is that a taxpayer experiencing an involuntary conversion has suffered enough, and thus gain recognition should be deferred.

C. Section 1033 statutory analysis—General rule

1. Three requirements: There are three requirements for the application of §1033.

   a. Property: The taxpayer's property converted in the transaction may be real or personal, fee or leasehold, and need not be held in a trade or business or held for investment. Cf. §1031, discussed above.

   b. Involuntary conversion: Only certain types of events trigger gain deferral. These are discussed below as definitional issues.

   c. Conversion and reinvestment: The taxpayer's property can either be converted into similar property or (more commonly) into money, usually insurance proceeds or damages for eminent domain. In the latter case, the taxpayer reinvests in similar property within the statutory two-year period to avoid recognition of gain. Conversion is the realization event for purposes of calculating realized gain or loss.

   Example: Garland owns a vase with an adjusted basis of $20,000 and a fair market value of $100,000. It is insured for its fair market value. The vase is stolen, and Garland's insurance company pays him $100,000. This is the conversion of property into money, which is also the realization event for purposes of calculating his realized gain of $80,000.

2. Tax consequences: If a transaction meets the requirements of §1033, there are two principal consequences: nonrecognition of gain and an exchanged basis for the property acquired.

   a. Conversion into similar property—Nonrecognition of gain: If the taxpayer's property is converted into property that is similar or related in service or use to the converted property, the taxpayer's realized gain on the involuntary conversion will not be recognized. IRC §1033(a).

   b. Conversion into money—Election: A taxpayer whose property is converted into money may elect to recognize only that portion of the realized gain attributable to money not reinvested in property that is similar or related in service or use to the converted property within a specific time period. IRC §1033(a).

c. **Basis:** A taxpayer may receive property that is similar or related in service or use ("qualifying replacement property") in an involuntary conversion and may also acquire nonqualifying property.

    i. **Similar property:** The basis of the qualifying replacement property in an involuntary conversion is an exchanged basis, calculated as follows:

> Basis of the converted property
> + Gain recognized
> – Amount of money not reinvested in
>   qualifying replacement property
> – Loss recognized
> _____
> Basis of qualifying replacement property

IRC §1033(b).

    ii. **Nonqualifying property:** Nonqualifying property has a basis equal to its cost, or fair market value. IRC §1012.

d. **Examples:** The following examples illustrate how §1033 works.

Example: Pete's vacation home is destroyed by earthquake. His basis in the home is $60,000 and it was insured for its fair market value of $100,000. He receives insurance proceeds of $100,000 and immediately invests $100,000 in a similar vacation home. What are the tax consequences of this transaction to Pete? Pete realized a $40,000 gain, equal to the difference between his amount realized ($100,000) and the adjusted basis of the property ($60,000). However, because this transaction falls within §1033, he need not recognize any of that gain. His basis in the new vacation home is equal to the basis of the old vacation home ($60,000), plus the gain recognized (0), minus the un-reinvested insurance proceeds (0), minus the loss recognized on the transaction (0), plus any additional amount invested in the property (0). Thus, Pete's basis in his new vacation home is $60,000.

Example: Melinda owns a marina in southern Oregon. One dark and stormy night, while Melinda is visiting friends in town, a freak wave washes the entire marina away. Melinda's basis in the marina is $100,000, and it was insured for its fair market value of $500,000. In due course, Melinda receives the insurance proceeds and immediately purchases a marina in Florida) for $300,000.

Realized Gain	Recognized Gain	Basis of Florida Marina
$500,000 Proceeds – 100,000 Adj. basis $400,000 Gain	$200,000 Proceeds not reinvested	$100,000 Old basis + 200,000 Recognized gain –200,000 Proceeds not reinvested $100,000

Notice that the basis of the Florida marina preserves the realized but unrecognized gain ($200,000) on the conversion of the Oregon marina.

D. Definitional issues

1. **Involuntary conversion:** An *involuntary conversion* includes all of the usual natural disasters—fire, storm, flood, and earthquake. Theft and condemnation, or imminent threat of

condemnation, also qualify as involuntary conversions, as does sale or destruction of livestock because of disease or drought. IRC §1033(d). Property that is rendered unsafe for its intended use as a result of chemical contamination is considered destroyed under §1033. Rev. Rul. 89-2, 1989-1 C.B. 259.

2. **Similar or related in service or use:** The replacement property must be *similar or related in service or use.* IRC §1033(a)(1), (2). However, for real property used in a trade or business or held for investment that is condemned or sold under threat of imminent condemnation, the replacement property may qualify as under the broader standard of §1031's "like-kind property" instead of the more restrictive standard of "related in service or use." IRC §1033(g).

   a. **Similar or related in service or use:** In order to qualify as similar or related in service or use, the property must generally have the same physical characteristics, must be used in the same way as the previous property, and the taxpayer must have the same relationship to the property as he or she had to the previous property. This determination is made based on all of the facts and circumstances of the situation, including an inquiry into whether the taxpayer essentially has continued his or her investment. See, e.g., *Liant Record, Inc. v. Commissioner,* 303 F.2d 326 (2d Cir. 1962).

      i. **Not similar—Rev. Rul. 76-319, 1976-2 C.B. 242:** The taxpayer owned a bowling alley that was destroyed, and the taxpayer replaced the bowling alley with a billiard parlor. The IRS determined that a billiard parlor and a bowling alley were not similar or related in service or use because of their physical dissimilarities and dissimilar functions.

      ii. **Similar—Rev. Rul. 71-41, 1971-1 C.B. 223:** The taxpayer owned land and a warehouse leased to others. After it was destroyed, the taxpayer erected a gas station and leased it. The IRS determined that the gas station was similar or related in service or use because the lessor was in substantially the same passive relationship to both properties. See also *Clifton Inv. Co. v. Commissioner,* 312 F.2d 719, cert. denied 373 U.S. 921 (6th Cir. 1963) (although a lessor, taxpayer engaged in different functions in the replacement property than it had with respect to the original property).

      iii. **Owner/investor vs. owner/user:** An owner/user must acquire similar property and use it for the same purposes. An owner/investor (who leases the property to others) appears to be under a different standard, whereby the properties must be similar, must present similar business risks, and must place similar demands on the owner—but the use need not be identical.

   b. **Like-kind standard for certain properties:** For real property used in a trade or business or held for investment that is condemned or sold under threat of imminent condemnation, the replacement property may qualify as like-kind instead of "related in service or use." IRC §1033(g). The definition of like-kind is the same under §1033(g) as it is in §1031. Reg. §1.1033(g)-1.

3. **Statutory replacement period:** The taxpayer must replace the converted property during the period beginning on the date of disposition of the property (or the beginning of the threat of condemnation) and ending two years after the close of the taxable year in which the taxpayer realizes any portion of the gain or conversion. IRC §1033(a)(2)(B). Gain is realized when insurance proceeds are received, for example. Longer replacement periods apply for certain kinds of properties and disasters. A taxpayer may apply to the IRS for an extension of the statutory period. IRC §1033(a)(2)(B)(ii).

Example—Statutory replacement period: Richard owned a warehouse in Dallas, Texas. On July 1, 2010, a fire destroyed the warehouse, and in August, Richard collected the insurance proceeds. The conversion resulted in a realized gain to Richard. To avoid recognition of gain, he is required to reinvest in qualified replacement property before January 1, 2012, which is two years after the close of the 2010 year in which he realized the gain on the conversion. If the insurance proceeds had not been paid until January 2011, his replacement period would continue until December 31, 2013 because he would not have realized any gain until 2011.

E. Special rules and exceptions

1. **Function of money received:** In Rev. Rul 89-2, *supra*, the government took a taxpayer's property by condemnation, and paid the taxpayer cash. However, the condemnation proceeding was a result of contamination (not the taxpayer's fault) and the proceeds did not take into account the reduced value of the property as a result of the condemnation. The IRS ruled that the money paid to the taxpayer must be allocated between payment for the condemnation (which is within §1033) and compensation for the destruction of the property.

2. **Ever wonder why the president declaring a disaster matters? Here's one answer:** A presidentially declared disaster is any disaster in an area where a taxpayer's property is located that resulted in a determination by the president that the area warrants assistance under the Disaster Relief and Emergency Assistance Act. IRC §1033(h)(2). If involuntary conversions occur as a result of such a disaster, taxpayers enjoy less stringent rules to qualify reinvestment for nonrecognition under §1033.

F. Related material

1. **Loss:** Section 1033 applies only to gains, not to losses. For individuals, losses from involuntary conversions *may* generate a deduction for a net casualty loss under §165(c)(3) or a trade or business deduction under §165(c)(1). The calculation of net casualty losses implicates §1033 because only *recognized* casualty gains are included in the definition of net casualty gains. See discussion in Chapter 6(VII).

2. **Section 121 exclusion:** An involuntary conversion of a principal residence of a taxpayer may generate gain that can be excluded (rather than deferred) under §121. See discussion in Chapter 4(VIII).

3. **Character:** For the character of recognized gain on the involuntary conversion of property, see generally Chapter 12.

G. Be alert for involuntary conversions

Section 1033 is potentially implicated whenever a taxpayer's property has been destroyed by some disaster, or has been taken in a process of involuntary conversion. The essential question is whether the taxpayer has realized gain (in which §1033 may apply) or loss (in which case §165(c) is implicated).

V. SPOUSAL AND DIVORCE TRANSFERS—§1041

A. Recognizing this transaction

Look for a transfer of property between spouses, or transfers made in connection with a divorce. Be careful to analyze cash payments separately if they qualify as alimony or child support.

B. Policy

Congress enacted §1041 in 1984 in response to three problems that arose when divorce transfers were treated as realization events. First, in a divorce, it is rarely clear exactly what a spouse "gives" in exchange for various items of property or other rights, thus the calculation of amount realized is unclear. Moreover, when what is exchanged is a nonmaterial right, basis calculation is impossible. Finally, taxpayers in community property and marital property states could be treated differently if such transfers are taxable events, which is a violation of the principal of horizontal equity. See Chapter 1(V)(C).

1. **Prior law—Divorces as taxable events:** In *United States v. Davis,* 370 U.S. 65 (1962), Mr. and Mrs. Davis were divorcing. Mr. Davis transferred 1,000 shares of DuPont stock to Mrs. Davis in satisfaction of all her marital rights under state law.

   a. **Issues:** Was this a taxable exchange, i.e., a sale? If so, what is the amount of gain recognized by Mr. Davis? What is Mrs. Davis's basis in the shares?

   b. **Result and rationale:** The transfer was a sale, resulting in a gain to Mr. Davis of the difference between the fair market value of the shares and his basis in them. Mrs. Davis took a cost (fair market value) basis in the shares. Mrs. Davis's rights in the stock under Delaware law were inchoate during marriage, not the rights of a co-owner. (This result might have been different in a community property state, where a spouse has a present interest in property.) Thus, she received the property by transfer from her husband. Since clearly this was not a gift, we must assume the parties acted at arms-length. She relinquished rights equal in value to the fair market value of the shares. As a result, both parties must treat the transaction as a sale. (The Court did not need to reach the question of the wife's gain, if any; it would be difficult to assign a basis to the marital rights she relinquished.)

2. **1984 change:** The 1984 change made spousal and divorce-related transfers nontaxable events.

   a. **Simplification:** This removes the difficulties of assigning an amount realized to property transfers and determining the basis of nonmaterial assets.

   b. **Uniformity:** Taxpayers in community and marital property states are treated equally under this approach.

   c. **Private ordering:** In their division of property, taxpayers may determine who will pay the tax on the gain inherent in various properties they divide between themselves.

C. Section 1041 statutory analysis—General rule

1. **Simple requirements:** For §1041 to apply, a taxpayer must transfer property to a spouse, or to a former spouse in a transfer that is ***incident to a divorce.*** IRC §1041(a).

2. **Tax consequences:** There are three consequences of a §1041 transfer.

   a. **Nonrecognition:** In a transfer meeting the requirements of §1041, the transferor recognizes no gain or loss. IRC §1041(a).

   b. **Basis:** The recipient of property takes it with the adjusted basis it had immediately before the transfer. IRC §1041(b)(2).

c. **Gift:** The recipient of property is treated as if he or she received a gift, and so the recipient need not include the value of the property in his or her gross income. IRC §1041(b)(1). However, the basis rules for a gift are not used (§1041 has its own basis rules), and the transfer is not treated as a gift for gift tax purposes. IRC §2516.

Example—Spousal transfer: Maria and Bob are married. Bob sells an office building with a basis of $50,000 to Maria. Maria pays him $100,000, the building's fair market value. Because this is a transfer between spouses, Bob does not recognize the $50,000 gain on the transfer, and has no income as a result of his receipt of $100,000. Moreover, Maria takes a basis of only $50,000 in the office building, even though she "paid" $100,000 for it.

Example—Divorce transfer: Consider the facts of the *Davis* case, discussed above, under current law. Mr. Davis transfers stock with a basis of $100 and a fair market value of $1,000 to Mrs. Davis in full settlement of their divorce. Under current law, Mr. Davis would not recognize the $900 gain inherent in the stock. Mrs. Davis would not include the $1,000 value of the stock in her gross income, and would take the stock with a basis of $100, the basis it had prior to the transfer.

D. Definitional issues

1. **Spouses:** State law determines the legal status of individuals as married or unmarried, except when specifically that law is preempted by federal law. Individuals of the same gender cannot be married for tax purposes under the federal Defense of Marriage Act, Pub. L. 104-199, §3 (1996), although this concept is currently being challenged in court.

2. **Incident to a divorce:** A transfer of property is incident to a divorce if it satisfies either of two tests.

   a. **One-year rule:** A transfer of property is incident to a divorce if it occurs within one year after the date the marriage is terminated. IRC §1041(c)(1).

   b. **Cessation of marriage:** A transfer of property is incident to a divorce if it is "related to the cessation of marriage." IRC §1041(c)(2). Transfers that are contemplated by the divorce decree and occur within six years of dissolution or thereafter if there is a good reason for delay are rebuttably presumed to be related to the cessation of marriage. Reg. §1.1041-1T(b),Q-7. A property transfer made after one year after the marriage is terminated that is not mentioned in the divorce decree is rebuttably presumed not to be related to the cessation of marriage. The divorce decree will include subsequent judicial modifications of the decree or actions to carry out the transfers contemplated in the decree. See *Young v. Commissioner,* 113 T.C. 152 (1999), *aff'd* 240 F.3d 369 (4th Cir. 2001).

   Example: Tim and Melissa are getting a divorce. Their divorce decree, issued July 1, Year 1, provides that Melissa will be awarded Blackacre, and title should be recorded in her name as soon as possible. However, Blackacre is the subject of litigation as to title, and in fact the transfer to Melissa does not occur until September Year 8. Regardless of the delay, this transfer would be related to the cessation of marriage and thus incident to the divorce because it was contemplated by the divorce decree, and there was good reason (litigation) for exceeding the six-year limit.

3. **Indirect transfers:** Indirect transfers of property may qualify for nonrecognition. A transfer to a third party on behalf of a spouse will qualify if it is specifically provided for in the divorce

decree, or if it is requested or ratified by the recipient spouse. Reg. §1.1041-1T(c), Q-9. This transaction will be treated as the transfer by a spouse to the other spouse, and a transfer by the latter to the third party. *Id.*

E. Special rules and exceptions—Nonresident alien transferors

Section 1041 does not apply to transfers by spouses or former spouses who are nonresident aliens. IRC §1041(d).

F. Related material

1. **Alimony:** Property transfers are analyzed under §1041, while alimony payments are analyzed under §§71 and 215. These Code provisions often intersect. In divorces where one spouse receives cash, either at the date of the divorce or thereafter, and the other spouse receives property, the cash settlements are likely candidates for designation as "nondeductible and nonincludable" in the divorce decree. If so designated, they will not qualify as alimony; instead, their tax treatment is governed by §1041. While the transfer of cash does not, of course, generate gain or loss, §1041(b)(1) applies to exclude the cash from the gross income of the recipient. If, however, the payments are not designated as nondeductible and nonincludable, they are likely candidates for being "front-end loaded," and thus will generate spellbinding tax consequences in the third year after separation or divorce. See discussion of alimony in Chapter 3(VI)(B).

2. **Child support:** The tax treatment of child support payments is largely independent of the tax treatment of property transfers. However, if a child support obligation is satisfied by a transfer of property from one former spouse to another, §1041 may apply. If the transfer *is* incident to a divorce, nonrecognition rules apply. If the transfer is *not* incident to a divorce, the usual recognition rules apply. See discussion of child support in Chapter 3(VI) and Chapter 4(XI)(A).

3. **Antenuptial settlements—*Farid-es-Sultaneh v. Commissioner,* 160 F.2d 812 (2d Cir. 1947):** The taxpayer received stock from her husband-to-be to induce her to give up any rights that she might have in a future divorce settlement. She later sold the stock, and the issue became the amount of her basis. The Court found that the transfer was not a gift and thus §1015(a) did not apply to assign her a basis equal to the donor's basis but instead the fair market value at the time of the gift. Note that §1041 does not apply to antenuptial transfers, so most of these transfers are now made, if at all, immediately after the wedding.

G. Be alert for property transfers between spouses/former spouses

Section 1041 is typically implicated as a critical part of transactions between divorcing spouses, which also implicates alimony and child support. But it also applies to married couples, preventing gain or loss recognition on the transfer of property between them.

VI. NEED TO KNOW MORE?

This book's website *www.aspenlawschool.com/books/tax_outline* contains additional information, including:

■ Practice problems with like-kind exchanges, including exchanges of encumbered properties and potential like-kind exchanges with vacation homes.

■ Practice problems with involuntary conversions.

- Coordinating the §1041 provisions with other spousal or divorce transfers.

- A summary of other nonrecognition provisions that crop up in the basic income tax class.

- And other materials that will help you understand nonrecognition transactions.

VII. WHERE ARE WE GOING?

This chapter concludes the discussion of sales and other dispositions of property and the computation of realized and recognized gain or loss from such sales. The character of recognized gain or loss is discussed in Chapter 12, but first Chapter 11 addresses questions of the proper taxable year for a taxpayer to include items of income, or deduct expenses.

Quiz Yourself on *NONRECOGNITION TRANSACTIONS*

107. Al and Sal are avid sports memorabilia collectors. Al owns a baseball signed by Mickey Mantle. Sal owns a football signed by Joe Montana. Both purchased these items years ago and they have appreciated in value. They trade. What are the tax consequences to them of this trade?

108. What are the rationales for the nonrecognition sections of the Code? _____

109. Katherine owns Blackacre, in which she has a basis of $40,000. It has a fair market value of $100,000. Spencer owns Blueacre, in which he has an adjusted basis of $30,000. It has a fair market value of $90,000. Both Blueacre and Blackacre are parcels of land held for investment by their owners. Both parties intend to hold the property received for investment. Katherine and Spencer trade their properties, and as part of the trade Spencer transfers a sports car to Katherine. What are the tax consequences of this trade to Spencer and Katherine? _____

110. Assume the same facts as in the previous question, except that Spencer did not hold Blueacre for investment, although he intends to hold Blackacre for investment. _____

111. Assume the same facts again as in Question 109, except that Katherine and Spencer are married at the time of the transaction. What are the tax consequences to Katherine in this situation?

_____

112. Jim owns Wineacre, a parcel of land on which he has unsuccessfully tried to grow grapes for years. The land has fallen in value, so that now his basis is $200,000 and the fair market value of Wineacre is $150,000. Jim is giving up the wine business. A friend of his is in the squash-growing business and offers to trade Squashacre for Wineacre. Jim agrees. How should he go about this transaction from a tax point of view? _____

113. Tony owns Rome Tower and Cleo owns Egypt Tower. Both are commercial office buildings. The properties have the following characteristics:

	Tony—Rome Tower	Cleo—Egypt Tower
Fair market value	$300,000	$180,000
Adjusted basis	$160,000	$200,000
Mortgage	$150,000	$ 0

Cleo transfers Egypt Tower to Tony. Tony transfers Rome Tower to Cleo, subject to its mortgage. Tony also transfers $30,000 to Cleo as part of this transaction. Both Tony and Cleo intend to hold their new properties for investment. What are the tax consequences of this exchange to Tony and Cleo? _____

114. Let's take another look at Tony and Cleo from the previous question. Assume the following alternative facts:

	Tony—Rome Tower	Cleo—EgyptTower
Fair market value	$300,000	$180,000
Adjusted basis	$160,000	$100,000
Mortgage	$180,000	$60,000

They exchange properties, each assuming the other's mortgage, with the lenders' approval. What are their tax consequences?

115. Harry and Sally are getting a divorce. Under the terms of their divorce decree, Sally will be deeded the marital home, which has a fair market value of $200,000 and an adjusted basis of $150,000. She will also receive stock in ABC Corporation with a fair market value of $100,000 and an adjusted basis of $175,000. Harry will receive the rest of the assets. What are the tax consequences to Harry and Sally of these transactions? _____

116. Ivanna and Steve are getting a divorce. In the divorce decree, the marital home is given to Ivanna in her sole name, with the proviso that it must be sold within eight years and the proceeds split 50/50. In the meantime, Steve must continue to pay the mortgage, taxes, insurance, and repairs. The home is sold eight years after the divorce and the proceeds are split between Steve and Ivanna. Steve insists that he has no gross income to report on the sale transaction. Is he correct?

_____

117. Don owned a commercial fishing boat in Miami in which he had an adjusted basis of $200,000. It had a fair market value of $600,000. The fishing boat was destroyed by a hurricane in December of Year 1. In January of Year 2, Don received insurance proceeds of $600,000 from the insurance company. He spent the rest of Year 2 looking for a suitable replacement. In December of Year 2, he purchased a new fishing boat for $500,000. What are the tax consequences of these events to Don? What if he decided that the commercial fishing business was an industry of the past and the new boat was designed to take tourists on deep sea fishing trips? _____

Answers

107. This familiar question (it's the same as Question 93 in Chapter 9) has a different answer now that we know about §1031. Al and Sal have realized gain attributable to the trade. However, assuming that these properties are held by Al and Sal "for investment," §1031 will probably apply to defer recognition of the gain. The football and baseball are properties of a like kind, and not the kind of property ineligible for like-kind exchange treatment (unless Al or Sal are in the business of collecting and trading memorabilia, in which case these items would be inventory to that person, and thus ineligible). If §1031 applies, Al and Sal will not recognize the gain associated with the trade, and will take a basis in the new item (the "replacement property") equal to the basis in the old item (the "relinquished property").

108. All of the nonrecognition provisions of the Code are about deferring the time at which gain or loss will be toted up and will appear on an income tax return. For like-kind exchanges, involuntary conversions and divorce transfers, there is a sense that the time is not ripe for taxing gains and allowing losses: The taxpayers have stayed in the same investments or kind of investments and no cash has changed hands (and if it does, recognition of gain does occur). For like-kind exchanges, there is the added rationale that nonrecognition combats the "lock-in effect," the tendency to hold on to property to avoid the adverse income tax consequences. (Perhaps this rationale could be extended to divorce transfers as well—a different kind of "lock-in.") For involuntary conversions and divorce transfers, there is the added rationale of not kicking someone when they are down—waiting until a better time, when property is actually sold, to assess the taxpayer's true gain or loss.

109. Spencer and Katherine's tax consequences are analyzed separately.

- *Katherine's tax consequences assuming qualification as like-kind exchange:*

Realized gain:	$60,000 ($90,000 + $10,000 − $40,000)
Recognized gain:	$10,000 (the value of the sports car)
Basis in Blueacre:	$40,000

- *Spencer's tax consequences assuming qualification as a like-kind exchange:*

Realized gain:	$60,000 ($90,000 − $30,000)
Recognized gain:	-0-
Basis in Blueacre:	$40,000 ($30,000 + $10,000)

The fair market value of the sports car must be $10,000 if the transaction is to involve a trade of value-for-value. If Spencer's basis in the sports car were different from its fair market value, he would realize gain or loss on the transfer of the car. Realized gain would be recognized, but it is doubtful that loss would be recognized. Katherine's basis in the sports car would be $10,000 (its fair market value).

110. If Spencer did not hold Blueacre for investment, all of his realized gain would be recognized because the transaction would not qualify as a like-kind exchange. This does not affect Katherine's ability to qualify for like-kind exchange treatment.

111. If Katherine and Spencer are married, §1041 prevents the recognition of *any* gain on the transaction for either party. Katherine will take any property she receives with the same basis as it had in the hands of Spencer.

112. If Jim trades Wineacre for Squashacre, his loss will not be recognized. Therefore he should not trade properties; he should *sell* Wineacre, recognize the loss, and *purchase* Squashacre.

113. This is a qualifying like-kind exchange. Therefore, the parties' tax consequences are as follows:

- *Tony's tax consequences:*

Realized gain/loss:	$140,000 ($330,000 – $190,000)
Recognized gain:	$120,000 ($150,000 – $30,000)
Adjusted basis in Egypt Tower:	$160,000

- *Cleo's tax consequences:*

Realized gain/loss:	($20,000) ($330,000 – $350,000)
Recognized gain/loss:	$ 0
Adjusted basis in Egypt Tower:	$320,000

114. Notice in this case that because the "equity" in each property is the same ($120,000) there will be no transfer of the additional $30,000 from Tony to Cleo. The tax consequences to Tony and Cleo are summarized in the chart below.

Tax Consequences to Tony and Cleo

	Tony	Cleo
Realized Gain/Loss	$140,000 Gain	$80,000 Gain
Recognized Gain/Loss	$120,000 (net relief from liability)	-0- (no net relief from liabilities)
Basis of New Property	$160,000 Old basis +120,000 Gain recognized −180,000 Cleo's A/L +60,000 Tony's A/L $160,000	$100,000 Old basis + 0 Gain recognized −60,000 Tony's A/L +180,000 Cleo's A/L $220,000
Is this correct?	If sold for FMV (180,000), using this basis, Tony would recognize the realized gain that was not recognized: $20,000.	If sold for FMV ($300,000), using this basis, Cleo would recognize all of the gain that went unrecognized: $80,000.

115. The transfers of property are almost certainly incident to a divorce, and therefore §1041 applies to defer recognition of any gain or loss. Neither Harry nor Sally will have income or deductions as a result of these transactions, and each will take the property he or she receives with the basis it had immediately prior to the transfer. Therefore, Sally will receive the marital home with a basis of $150,000 and the ABC stock with a basis of $175,000.

116. Steve is probably right. Remember that §1041 applies as between the parties to a divorce, not to sales to third parties. Who owns the property is a legal and factual question, and in this case, Steve has a strong case that Ivanna was the owner of the property so that its sale to a third party generated income to her, not to Steve. The division of the proceeds of the sale would probably be governed by §1041, however, resulting in no income or a deduction to either party. Ivanna would probably be able to claim an exclusion under §121, which Steve would not be able to do because he did not live in the home or own it for the time periods required. See *Suhr v. Commissioner*, T.C. Memo 2001-28.

117. The destruction of the fishing boat is a constructive sale of the fishing boat, in which Don realizes a gain of $400,000, which is the difference between the amount received from the insurance company ($600,000) and his adjusted basis in the boat ($200,000). However, he may defer recognition of this gain if he meets the requirements of §1033. In order to qualify, he must reinvest the proceeds in similar property within two years. In this case, he probably qualifies, as he has purchased a commercial fishing boat within the requisite period. However, he did not fully invest the proceeds. Therefore, he will recognize $100,000 of gain, and his basis in the boat will be his old basis ($200,000) plus the gain recognized ($100,000), or $300,000. If he reinvests in a tourist fishing boat, he runs the risk that this will not be considered property similar in use, and therefore he may have to recognize all of the gain. This is a close case, and the IRS would be likely to assert that commercial fishing and tourist deep sea fishing tours are not "similar" uses.

Exam Tips on
NONRECOGNITION TRANSACTIONS

☛ Be able to articulate Congress's reasons for nonrecognition treatment for some—but not all—transactions.

☛ The nonrecognition statutes are relevant only if there is realized gain or loss on the disposition of property.

    ☞ *Look for:* An exchange of one property for another, in which the taxpayer realizes gain or loss; usually in a situation in which the taxpayer hasn't fundamentally changed the nature of the investment.

    ☞ *Analyze:* Which taxpayer's tax consequences are relevant? One or both? Compute the realized gain or loss, and then ask if the requirements of a nonrecognition statute are met.

☛ Section 1031 is probably the most popular statute for testing, not only because it is important in tax law in general, but because it offers fertile ground for testing the student's knowledge of the requirements and consequences of the statute.

    ☞ *Look for:* Situations that raise questions about the taxpayer's use of the properties, or the like-kind nature of the properties.

    ☞ *Analyze:* Each requirement; make sure you analyze realized gain or loss, recognized gain or loss, adjusted basis in the property received in the exchange.

☛ **Remember:** Section 1031 is not optional. A taxpayer may not recognize loss on a transaction that qualifies as a §1031 exchange. A better way to recognize loss: Sell the old property and buy the new property with cash.

☛ Involuntary conversions can generate realized gain or loss.

    ☞ *Look for:* A disaster, or some event outside the control of the taxpayer that leads to the loss of property.

☞ *Analyze:* If realized gain (receipt of insurance proceeds or exchange of properties), do the requirements of §1033 apply?

☛ If loss is realized, §1033 doesn't apply to that loss. Does §165 allow a deduction for a casualty loss? Are there both casualty losses and recognized casualty gains? Offset them.

☛ Divorces also offer fertile ground for testing.

> ☞ *Look for:* Divorce or separation and the transfer of money or property pursuant to the divorce.

> ☞ *Analyze:* Is this a transfer of property, or is it alimony or child support? If a transfer of property, the nonrecognition rules of §1041 will usually apply, but watch for special circumstances that would disqualify the transaction. Be sure to determine the basis of property received in the divorce. Is there alimony or child support? If so, who gets the deduction, and who must include payments in gross income?

 # STATUTE SUMMARY CHARTS

Statute Summary—§1031
Like-Kind Exchanges

Parsing Step	IRC §1031
General Rule	No gain or loss is recognized upon qualifying exchange of certain property held for use in trade or business or for investment for like-kind property also to be held for these purposes.
Definitions	**Like-kind property:** real estate for real estate qualifies; personal property requires analysis of class of properties. **Boot:** any nonqualifying property received in an exchange.
Special Rules and Exceptions	If boot received, realized gain recognized to extent of FMV of boot Exchanged basis rule: old basis + gain recognized – FMV boot – loss + additional investment Deferred exchanges with qualified intermediary
Related Statutes	**§1001:** Calculation of realized gain or loss **§1221:** Character of gain
Typically implicated when	Taxpayer wants to defer gain on disposition of property by trading into like-kind property, or IRS wants to prevent recognition of loss.

Statute Summary Chart—§1033
Involuntary Conversions

Parsing Step	IRC §1033
General Rule	No gain is recognized if taxpayer's property is involuntarily converted, if taxpayer receives qualifying property or reinvests in qualifying property within two years.
Definitions	**Involuntary conversion:** fire, storm, earthquake, condemnation, or threat. **Qualifying property:** similar or related in service or use. **Two–year replacement period**
Special Rules and Exceptions	Certain kinds of disasters or properties receive more generous treatment in terms of length of period for reinvestment or type of property that qualifies for reinvestment.
Related Statutes	**§1001:** Calculation of realized gain or loss **§1221:** Character of gain **§165(c)(2), (c)(3), (h):** Recognition of loss
Typically implicated when	Taxpayer's property is destroyed by natural or human disaster, or condemnation and taxpayer wants to replace property to continue business or investment.

Statute Summary—§1041
Spousal and Divorce Transfers

Parsing Step	IRC §1041
General Rule	No gain or loss is recognized upon transfer of property between spouses or if incident to a divorce.
Definitions	**Incident to a divorce:** 1-year rule; related to cessation of marriage.
Special Rules and Exceptions	Property takes the same basis it had before the transfer (treated as gift).
Related Statutes	**§§71 & 215** Alimony and child support
Typically implicated when	Married taxpayers get a divorce, or rearrange their property holdings for other purposes (such as estate planning).

CHAPTER 11

TIMING OF INCOME AND EXPENSES

ChapterScope ▬▬▬▬▬▬▬▬▬▬▬▬▬▬▬▬▬▬▬▬▬▬▬▬▬▬▬▬▬▬

The previous chapters have addressed the issues of identifying and computing gross income and calculating available deductions. This chapter turns to the equally important question of *when* a taxpayer properly includes amounts in gross income or properly claims a deduction.

- **Importance:** Timing is important because of the understandable desire of taxpayers to defer for as long as possible the inclusion of items in gross income and to accelerate available deductions to the earliest possible year.

- **The annual accounting concept:** The federal income tax adopts an annual accounting system in which a taxpayer selects a taxable year and reports all income and deductions that occur in that year. The annual accounting concept can create results that seem unfair, particularly for transactions that do not fall neatly within a single taxable year. A number of doctrines and related Code sections have evolved to provide relief from the constraints of the annual accounting concept, including the claim-of-right doctrine, net operating loss carryovers, and the tax benefit rule.

- **Methods of accounting:** Every taxpayer has a method of accounting.

  - **Cash method:** Most individual taxpayers use the cash method of accounting, which provides simple rules based on receipt and payment for determining when to include items in gross income and when to deduct expenses.

  - **Accrual method:** A more accurate, but also more complex, method is the accrual method of accounting in which taxpayers include items in income or deduct expenses when the "all events test" is met. Special rules restrict the use of the cash method and impose limits on the deduction of expenses under both methods.

- **Accounting for inventories:** A taxpayer engaged in the business of selling goods will incur costs of acquiring or manufacturing the goods for sale. These costs, along with certain other costs of doing business, must be added to the cost of inventory in order to properly compute the taxpayer's income or loss from the sale of goods.

- **Installment method:** For certain sales of property in which payment is deferred, the taxpayer may elect to use the installment method of accounting, under which the gain is reported as payments are received under the contract for sale.

- **Section 83—Restricted property:** In certain situations, a taxpayer will receive property as compensation for services rendered, but the property will be restricted in some fashion to ensure the taxpayer's performance of the services. Section 83 provides specific rules for determining when the value of this property will be included in the taxpayer's gross income.

- **Restrictions on current deduction of losses:** Sections 465, 469, and 267 impose significant restrictions on the deduction of certain losses. Section 465 limits losses to the amounts a taxpayer has at risk in an activity. Section 469 limits the deduction of passive losses to the amount of the taxpayer's passive income, allowing a taxpayer to deduct deferred losses only at the termination of the investment. Section 267 prohibits the recognition of loss on sales or exchanges between related parties.

I. WHERE ARE WE?

Previous chapters have addressed issues surrounding identification of income and deduction and the computation of gain and loss. Embedded in all of these issues is a fundamental question that previous chapters have noted but have deferred for later consideration: *In which taxable year does the taxpayer include an item in gross income or claim a deduction?* For many transactions, the proper timing of income and deduction will seem obvious. But for some transactions, particularly those that span more than one taxable year, the choice of the proper year for reporting income and deductions is problematic. As discussed in detail in Chapter 15, taxpayers seek to defer the inclusion of income items in gross income and to accelerate deductions; this produces tax savings that can be invested during the period of deferral. Even if, later, the taxpayer must include an item in gross income, or income is not sheltered by a deduction, the taxpayer will usually be better off economically by deferring income and accelerating deductions. Congress and the IRS, however, have the daunting task of ferreting out and preventing inappropriate income deferral and deduction acceleration strategies, i.e., those that result in an inaccurate reflection of a taxpayer's ability to pay. This chapter addresses the principles that have evolved to govern the timing of income and deductions, beginning with that most basic of concepts—the taxable year.

II. THE ANNUAL ACCOUNTING CONCEPT

The annual accounting concept is the principle that a taxpayer reports all of his or her income and deductions on an annual basis, reporting these items based on the facts as they exist as of the close of the taxable year in question.

A. Taxable years

Every taxpayer has a **taxable year,** either a **calendar year** or *fiscal year.* IRC §441(b)(1). The taxpayer reports his or her income and deductions as they exist at the close of the taxable year.

1. **Calendar year:** Most individual taxpayers use the calendar year, which is a year that begins on January 1 and ends December 31. IRC §441(d).

2. **Fiscal year:** Some businesses use a fiscal year, which is a year other than a calendar year beginning on the first day of the month of any month but January (e.g., a year beginning July 1 and ending June 30). IRC §441(e). This is convenient for seasonal businesses (such as retailers) because this allows them to avoid year-end accounting during their busy season.

B. Why *annual* accounting?

The concept of **annual accounting** is merely an administrative convenience to allow the Commissioner to collect tax at regular, easily identifiable intervals. Reliance on annual accounting makes administrative sense, but this convenience often comes at the expense of a precise measurement of a taxpayer's ability to pay. Many of the issues raised by annual accounting illustrate the tension between the value of administrative convenience of an annual system of taxation and the value of fairness. See Chapter 1(V)(C). For example, an annual accounting system has difficulty accurately measuring the true increase or decrease in a taxpayer's ability to pay from transactions that span more than one taxable year. While other systems might be imagined, they do not eliminate this tension. For example, a "lifetime tax return" (one income tax return reporting lifetime income and loss, filed at death) would accurately measure a taxpayer's ability to pay over a lifetime. But its preparation (and audit) would be a nightmare, and such a system would be unlikely to generate the revenues at regular intervals needed by government. As described in the sections that follow, the unfairness of the annual accounting system is often mitigated by special Code provisions that require the reporting of income and deductions over various years to more accurately reflect a taxpayer's ability to pay.

C. Difficulties with annual accounting

1. **The problems:** The concept of annual accounting can create numerous difficulties because transactions rarely fall neatly into a single year. Instead, many transactions continue over several years. Events in one year may implicate a reporting position taken in the previous year, or a taxpayer may be aware of events that may occur in later years that will undermine the current reporting position. Nevertheless, annual accounting requires tax returns to be filed as if a year stands independently of all other years.

2. **Transactional accounting—*Burnet v. Sanford & Brooks Co.*, 282 U.S. 359 (1931):** The taxpayer was engaged in the business of dredging the Delaware River. During 1913–1916, it received payments and expended funds in this endeavor. In these years, it reported the payments from its customer as income and deducted its expenses. In most years it showed a net loss; in one year it reported a profit. In 1915, it abandoned the work and sued its customer, saying that the customer misrepresented the nature of the job to be done. In 1920, the taxpayer received damages of $176,271.88, which represented the taxpayer's total expenses over income from the project.

   a. **Issue:** Was the $176,271.88 includable in the taxpayer's gross income in 1920?

   b. **Result and rationale:** The $176,271.88 was includable in the taxpayer's gross income in 1920. Although the taxpayer argued that the amount could not be considered income because it experienced a loss on the entire contract from its inception in 1913, under the annual accounting system the events of other years are irrelevant in determining the tax consequences for the particular year. Thus, the Court rejected transactional accounting in favor of annual accounting.

   c. **Comment—Court of Appeals approach and §460:** The Court of Appeals was sympathetic to the taxpayer's argument and allowed the taxpayer to exclude the $176,271.88 from gross income on the condition that it amend its prior years' returns to eliminate the deduction of expenses in those years. The Supreme Court's rejection of this approach reflects a general preference for not reopening prior years' tax returns. Today, long-term contracts are governed by §460, which requires the income from such contracts to be reported during the years of the contracts based on the percentages of costs incurred in each year for the contract.

D. Net operating loss (NOL) deduction

Section 172 provides a method of mitigating the impact of annual accounting. Under §172, the excess of expenses over income in a particular year may be claimed as a deduction (known as the *net operating loss deduction,* or ***NOL***) in other years. In essence, the NOL rules allow a taxpayer "to set off its lean years against its lush years." *Lisbon Shops, Inc. v. Koehler*, 353 U.S. 382 (1957).

1. **Definition—Net operating loss:** A net operating loss (NOL) is the excess of allowable deductions over gross income, computed in accordance with special rules. IRC §172(c). In computing the allowable deductions, the following modifications must be made to the usual deduction rules.

   a. **No NOL deduction:** In computing the excess of deductions over income, no deduction is allowed for an NOL carryover from another year. IRC §172(d)(1).

   b. **No personal deductions:** In computing the excess of deductions over income of an individual, no personal deductions are allowed, including personal exemptions and nonbusiness deductions such as medical expenses, casualty losses, and charitable contributions. IRC §172(d)(3), (4). For a discussion of personal deductions, see generally Chapter 6.

   c. **Capital losses:** In computing the excess of deductions over expenses, the deduction for nonbusiness (i.e., investment) capital losses is allowed only to the extent of capital gains. IRC §172(d)(2). For a discussion of capital loss deductions, see Chapter 12(II)(B).

      Example: In Year 1, Zoe reported a profit (excess of income over deductions) of $15,000 from her business. In Year 2, Zoe has business income of $50,000 and business deductions of $40,000. She also has itemized deductions (mortgage interest, charitable contributions, and a personal casualty loss) of $15,000. Zoe does not have a $5,000 NOL in Year 2 to carry back to Year 1, because her nonbusiness deductions cannot generate a NOL.

2. **Carryover:** The NOL carries back to the two previous taxable years and forward to the succeeding twenty taxable years following the year of the loss. IRC §172(b)(1)(A). When carried to a particular year, it reduces taxable income in that year, potentially to zero. The loss must be applied to the earliest of the years first, and then in chronological order. IRC §172(b)(2). However, the taxpayer may elect to waive the entire carryback period and apply the loss only to later years. IRC §172(b)(3).

   Example: Zelco, a corporation formed in Year 1, has the following results in Years 1–6:

Year	Income or (Loss)
1	$10,000
2	$20,000
3	($50,000)
4	$10,000
5	($10,000)
6	$30,000

An NOL may be carried back two years and forward twenty years. Zelco may carry the Y3 loss first to Y1. It may then apply it to Y2, Y4, and Y6, in order. The Y5 loss may be applied only to Y6, because all other years' income has been eliminated. The following chart shows application of the NOL if Zelco chooses to apply any of it to previous years.

Year	Income/(Loss) before NOL	Application of NOL	Final Result Taxable Income
1	$10,000	($10,000)	0
2	$20,000	($20,000)	0
3	($50,000)	n/a	0
4	$10,000	($10,000)	0
5	($10,000)	n/a	0
6	$30,000	($10,000) Y3 ($10,000) Y5	$10,000

E. Claim of right doctrine

1. **Recognizing this transaction:** In *claim of right* situations, a taxpayer receives an amount that normally would be considered an item of gross income under the taxpayer's method of accounting, but there is some uncertainty about whether the taxpayer will later have to relinquish the income. In a later year, the taxpayer may have to repay the amount, in whole or in part.

2. **The problem:** The uncertainty about repayment raises the question whether the taxpayer should include the amount in gross income in the year of receipt or should wait and report the transaction when the uncertainty has been resolved. If the taxpayer must include the item in gross income, the question arises of how to treat the taxpayer if the funds must be relinquished later. While the taxpayer normally would be entitled to a deduction equal to the amount repaid, a deduction will not necessarily place the taxpayer in the same position as if he or she had never included the item in income, for two reasons. First, the taxpayer will have lost the use of the funds used to pay the tax from the first year. Second, if tax rates have fallen, the deduction will not generate a tax savings equal to the tax originally imposed on the same amount of income. (Of course, if tax rates have risen, the deduction will generate a greater tax savings, but this may or may not offset the loss attributable to *the time value of money.*)

3. **Claim of right doctrine—*North American Oil Consolidated v. Burnet,* 286 U.S. 417 (1932):** A taxpayer includes an item in gross income if he or she has a claim of right to it, regardless of uncertainties about subsequent relinquishment. A claim of right exists when the taxpayer has a colorable legal claim to the item of income and has it without restriction of disposition.

4. Examples

a. ***United States v. Lewis,* 340 U.S. 590 (1951):** In 1944, the taxpayer received a bonus of $22,000. In subsequent litigation, it was determined that he was not entitled to the full amount, and in 1946, he had to repay $11,000 to his employer. The taxpayer had use of the full $22,000 until repayment. The taxpayer was required to include the $22,000 in gross income in 1944. (As a corollary, when he had to repay the $11,000 in 1946, he was entitled to a deduction in that amount. The taxpayer received the income under a claim of right. The mistake as to his right does not relieve him of the obligation of reporting it in 1944, since he had a right to the income and received it without restriction. The subsequent event is addressed in the year it occurs.)

b. ***Inductotherm Industries, Inc. v. United States,* 351 F.3d 120 (3d Cir. 2003), reporting an unpublished District Court decision:** The taxpayer argued that the U.S. government's blocking order with respect to income earned in Iraq resulted in a restriction on the taxpayer's right to that income, so that it should not be included in income. In fact, the taxpayer didn't deposit the funds in a blocked account, and the government did not enforce the blocking order. According to the court, a dormant or potential restriction on the use of funds does not rise to the level of a restriction that would prevent inclusion in gross income.

5. Legislative response—§1341:
Section 1341 applies if a taxpayer has included an item in gross income in one year because it appeared that the taxpayer had an unrestricted right to that income, but in a later year the taxpayer had to repay some amount greater than $3,000. Section 1341 allows a taxpayer caught in a claim of right/repayment situation to pay the *lower* of two differently computed taxes: (1) the tax that would have been paid if the taxpayer had never included the amount in gross income, or (2) the tax that would have been paid if the taxpayer had included the amount in the first year and deducted the repayment in the later year. The statute does this by computing the tax in the year of repayment by reference to these two options. The details of §1341 are formidable, and its computations are beyond the scope of most basic tax courses. Recently, courts have disagreed on the basic requirement of whether there must be some dispute as to whether the taxpayer had a right to the income. See, e.g., *Cinergy Corp. v. United States,* 55 Fed. Cl. 489 (2002) (dispute must exist); *Dominion Resources, Inc. v. United States,* 219 F.3d 359 (4th Cir. 2000).

F. Tax benefit rule

1. Recognizing this transaction:
In a ***tax benefit rule*** situation, the taxpayer deducts an item or claims a credit, based on the facts as they existed in the year of deduction or credit, and in a later year an event occurs that suggests that the prior deduction was incorrect. The classic example of this is the deduction of a bad debt by the taxpayer. In a subsequent year, the debtor repays the debt, and the question arises: Does the taxpayer have income as a result of the repayment?

2. The problem:
The question raised by the tax benefit pattern is what impact the event in the later year should have on the taxpayer. One option would be to go back and amend the prior return. Not only would such an approach be administratively burdensome, it would also be theoretically incorrect if the taxpayer properly claimed the deduction or credit on the facts as they existed in that year. The proper result is to address the problem in the year of the

subsequent event, so that the taxpayer may have income in that year. Thus, in the bad debt example, the repayment should logically be income, to offset the prior deduction. See Reg. §1.166-1(f).

3. **Judicial development of tax benefit rule:** In *Alice Phelan Sullivan Corp. v. United States,* 381 F.2d 399 (Ct. Cl. 1967), the taxpayer made charitable contributions of property in 1939 and 1949. The property was subject to a reversion if the charitable donee did not make charitable use of the property. The taxpayer claimed deductions of $4,243.29 and $4,463.44 in those years, which created a total tax savings for the taxpayer of $1,877 in those years. In 1957, the property reverted to the taxpayer. The taxpayer originally did not include any amount in income as a result of the reversion, claiming that it was the nontaxable return of its own property, but ultimately asserted that the amount to be included in gross income in 1957 should be limited to the tax savings from the earlier years. This would essentially apply the earlier years' tax rate to the later recovery. The Commissioner argued that the sum of the prior deductions should be included in the taxpayer's gross income in 1957, thus requiring that the later year's tax rate be applied to the recovery.

   a. **Issue:** Should the amount included in gross income in 1957 be the tax savings from the prior year or the amount previously deducted?

   b. **Result and rationale:** The amount included in income in 1957 should be the sum of the deductions previously claimed. The court overruled *Perry v. United States,* 160 F. Supp. 270 (Ct. Cl. 1958), in which it determined that the recovery was income only to the extent of the prior tax savings. The annual accounting concept requires that income be determined without reference to events in other years and that the tax be computed without reference to earlier tax rates. While this may generate inequitable results, the court declined to legislate a different result.

4. **Statutory analysis—§111:** Section 111 is the codification of the tax benefit rule. As expressed, it is a rule of income exclusion and, conversely, a rule of income inclusion. It is discussed here in connection with timing rules because the annual accounting concept creates the need for such a rule.

   a. **General rule—requirements:** For the tax benefit rule to apply, there must be a *recovery* of an item in the current year that must relate to an item that was deducted or credited in a prior taxable year. IRC §111(a).

   b. **General rule—tax consequences:** The tax benefit rule of §111 may be expressed either as an exclusion from gross income or as an inclusion in gross income.

      i. **Exclusion:** Gross income does not include the recovery to the extent that the prior deduction or credit did not reduce tax in the prior year.

      ii. **Inclusion:** Gross income does include the recovery to the extent that the prior deduction reduced the tax in the year of deduction or credit.

      iii. **"To the extent":** The statute's use of "to the extent" is somewhat confusing, but the regulations clarify this. The amount of a recovery that is excluded from gross income is the "exclusionary amount." Reg. §1.111-1(a). The exclusionary amount is the amount of the prior deduction or credit that did not reduce tax in the prior year. *Id.* The rest of the amount of the recovery is included in gross income.

Example: Two years ago, Rashon incurred $25,000 in damage to his home from a windstorm. He submitted a claim to his insurance company for payment. The insurance company informed him that this damage was not covered under the policy for a variety of reasons. Rashon claimed the expenses as a deduction on his income tax return for the year of the loss, but because of the limitations on casualty loss deductions imposed by §165(h), he deducted only $15,000 of the expenses. His taxable income after this deduction was $62,000. Believing he was wrongfully denied coverage, Rashon sued the insurance company. This year Rashon won, and received $25,000 in payments from the insurance company. Rashon must include the payment in his gross income to the extent that the previous deduction reduced his taxes two years ago. His delight at winning the lawsuit, therefore, will be tempered by the understanding that he must include $15,000 of the payment in his gross income.

c. **Definitional issues—Recovery:** A recovery is an event that is inconsistent with the assumptions underlying the prior deduction or credit. *Hillsboro National Bank v. Commissioner,* 460 U.S. 370 (1983). To be a "recovery," the event must be functionally related to the original deduction or credit. The repayment of a debt previously deducted as worthless is obviously inconsistent with the assumption that the debt is uncollectible, and thus repayment is recovery. See Reg. §1.166-1(f). Other, less obvious, events also may be recoveries.

Example: Paula is an artist. She rents a loft warehouse as a studio in which she paints and displays her paintings for sale. In October of Year 1, Paula prepays nine months' rent, and properly deducts this amount as a business expense on her Year 1 tax return, which she files in Year 2. In March of Year 2 Paula decides to move into the loft and begins using half of it as her personal residence. The conversion of a portion of the loft from business to personal use is a recovery, because the use of the loft for personal purposes is fundamentally inconsistent with the assumptions underlying the deduction for rent, i.e., that the premises would be used exclusively for business purposes.

d. **Special rules and exceptions—Erroneous deduction rule:** A judicially created rule focuses on the impact of the propriety of the original deduction on the later recovery. The Tax Court has held that if the original deduction was erroneous, the later recovery is not included in gross income. See, e.g., *Streckfus Steamers, Inc. v. Commissioner,* 19 T.C. 1 (1952). However, the Second and Ninth Circuits have held that the propriety of the original deduction is not relevant in determining the inclusion of the later recovery for two reasons. First, there is no statutory authority for such an exception. Second, this places the IRS in the position of having to examine every return for errors in order to prevent recoveries from later being excluded from gross income. *Unvert v. Commissioner,* 656 F.2d 483 (9th Cir. 1981); *Askin & Marine Co. v. Commissioner,* 66 F.2d 776 (2d Cir. 1933).

e. **Related material**

   i.   **Section 61 and related statutes:** In addition to being a timing rule, the tax benefit rule is a rule of inclusion in and exclusion from gross income. Thus, it is similar to §61 and related statutes addressing the inclusion of various items in gross income and should be studied in conjunction with them. See generally Chapters 3 and 4.

ii. **Deductions and credits:** The application of the tax benefit rule requires that the taxpayer previously deducted or credited an item, and the propriety of that deduction or credit may also be implicated. Deductions and credits are discussed generally in Chapters 5 through 8 and 13, respectively.

iii. **Claim of right:** The tax benefit situation is the inverse of the claim of right pattern. In the tax benefit situation, there is a deduction in one year and income in a subsequent year. In the claim of right situation, the taxpayer has income in one year and a deduction in the later year. For a discussion of claim of right, see this chapter, Section (II)(E).

III. METHODS OF ACCOUNTING

A. Functions of a method of accounting

The taxpayer's *method of accounting* determines in which taxable year items of income, gain, loss, deduction, or credit will properly be reported. There are two principal methods of accounting, the *cash method* and the *accrual method.* While the specific rules of the two methods are very different, they both set forth the rules governing the inclusion of income and the deduction of expenses. A taxpayer is required to report net income based on his, her, or its usual method of accounting, unless that method does not, in the view of the Commissioner, clearly reflect income. IRC §446(a). The Commissioner may impose some other method to ensure a clear reflection of income, and in litigation of such matters, the courts will not usually inquire as to whether there is some better method of computing net income, but instead will focus on whether the Commissioner has abused his or her discretion in requiring a taxpayer to use a particular method to clearly reflect income.

B. The cash receipts and disbursements method

The cash method focuses on when the taxpayer receives income or pays expenses, regardless of when income or expenses are due or owing. A taxpayer using the cash method of accounting reports income in his or her gross income when the income is received, actually or constructively. Reg. §1.451-1(a). A taxpayer claims deductions when he or she actually pays them by cash, check, or credit card. Reg. §1.461-1(a)(1). All individual taxpayers use the cash method in their personal lives, and many businesses (particularly service businesses) use the cash method as well.

1. **Income—Actual receipt:** Actual receipt means that the taxpayer receives cash or other property and is usually easy to identify. Look for an inflow to the taxpayer, in cash or property.

   Example: Carla, an attorney, uses the cash method of accounting and is a calendar-year taxpayer. She sends out her bills, which are due in 30 days, monthly. In October of Year 1 Carla sends Client X a bill for $2,000, which is due in November. In fact, Carla receives payment from Client X in January of the next year. She properly reports the $2,000 in the year of receipt rather than the year the income was due or billed.

2. **Income—no actual receipt:** In some situations, a cash method taxpayer does not actually receive any money or property, but nevertheless an event has occurred that has made the taxpayer better off financially than he or she was before.

a. **Economic benefit doctrine:** A cash method taxpayer must include in gross income the economic benefit of a fund to which he or she has the absolute right, and which has been irrevocably set aside for the taxpayer in trust, if it is beyond the reach of the payor's creditors.

    i. *United States v. Drescher,* **179 F.2d 863 (2d Cir.),** *cert. denied,* **340 U.S. 821 (1950):** In that case, the taxpayer's employer purchased an annuity policy for the taxpayer's benefit. The issue in the case was whether the taxpayer had income in the year the policy was purchased. The court found that the taxpayer did have income in the year that the policy was purchased for the taxpayer under the economic benefit doctrine. See discussion of *Drescher* in Chapter 2(III)(B).

    ii. *Pulsifer v. Commissioner,* **64 T.C. 245 (1975):** A father purchased an Irish Sweepstakes ticket in his name and the names of his three minor children. Amazingly, they won. The administrators would not release the minors' shares of the winnings to the parent, but instead placed the funds in a bank account pending application by the minors' legal representative. The Court held that the minors were required to include the amounts in gross income in the year the funds were irrevocably placed in the bank for the minors' benefit, with the only requirement to obtain them being the application by the legal representative.

    iii. **Nonqualified deferred compensation plans—No economic benefit:** Employers will often promise to pay additional compensation to an employee in the future. A mere promise to pay, not represented by notes or secured in any way, does not constitute receipt of income for a cash method taxpayer. Rev. Rul. 60-31, 1960-1 C.B. 174. Because the employee is generally not satisfied with the employer's mere promise to pay, the employer will often set aside amounts that will be paid to the employee in a separate trust. If the assets earmarked for an employee remain subject to the claims of the employer's creditors, they do not constitute an economic benefit to the employee. The funds earn interest for the benefit of the employee. But because under the terms of the trust the assets of the trust remain subject to the claims of the employer's creditors, the employee need not include any amount in gross income until the amounts in the trust are paid to him or her. The employer is taxed on the interest earned by the trust, and the employer may not deduct any amount as compensation until payments are made to the employee. This arrangement is known as ***nonqualified deferred compensation*** because it is not subject to substantial rules applicable to ***qualified plans*** that allow the employer to deduct contributions as made, allow amounts to earn interest tax-free, and protect assets from the claims of creditors. *See Minor v. United States,* 772 F.2d 1472 (9th Cir. 1985). The trusts used in these arrangements are known as ***rabbi trusts*** because the first favorable ruling issued for such arrangements addressed a nonqualified deferred compensation plan for a rabbi. Section 409A now imposes additional requirements on nonqualified deferred compensation plans, which if not met will result in additional tax and penalties.

    Example: Debra accepts a job as CEO of Happy Trax, Inc. (Happy). She and Happy agree that she will be paid $100,000 per year and that Happy will contribute an additional $20,000 per year to a grantor trust under which she is the beneficiary, but the assets of which remain subject to the claims of Happy's creditors. Assume the arrangement meets the requirements of §409A. When she leaves Happy's employ,

Debra will be paid all contributions made on her behalf plus earnings attributable to those contributions. Under this arrangement, Debra will not be required to include any amount in gross income until she receives distributions from the trust. However, Happy will be taxed on the earnings of the trust and will not be able to deduct amounts attributable to the trust until distribution of the funds to Debra.

iv. **Compare—Qualified plans:** Qualified plans (as opposed to nonqualified plans) set aside retirement funds for the exclusive benefit of employees. Complex rules govern these plans. An employee is not taxed on amounts in the plan until they are distributed to the employee.

b. **Income—Constructive receipt:** The cash method rule that income is reported when actually received might tempt taxpayers to direct that income not be made available to them until a later taxable year, thus deferring income. The ***constructive receipt doctrine*** provides that a taxpayer will be considered to be in constructive receipt of amounts over which he or she has a legal claim, and which are available to the taxpayer without "substantial limitations or restrictions." See Reg. §1.451-2(a).

Example: Scott is a housepainter who uses the cash method and a calendar year. He agrees to paint Sue's house for a payment of $5,000, payable when the painting is complete. Scott completes the work in October, but when Sue starts to write the check, Scott says, "Sue, how about just holding off on that check until January, after the holiday rush, you know." Scott receives payment in January. Although the general rule of the cash method would require him to include the income in his gross income for the year of receipt he had a legal right to the income in the previous year, and in fact that income was made available to him in that year. As a result, he will probably be deemed in constructive receipt of the income for the earlier year.

i. **It's the legal arrangement entered into, not what could have been negotiated:** In *Amend v. Commissioner,* 13 T.C. 178 (1949), acq. 1950-1 C.B. 1, the cash method taxpayer entered into a contract for the sale of wheat in which he would be paid in the year following the year of sale. The Commissioner argued that he should be charged with income in the year of sale, not the year of receipt, because the taxpayer *could have* contracted for payment in the year of sale. Given that the sale arrangement was legitimate, the taxpayer was not in constructive receipt of the payment because the taxpayer had no legal right to the funds in the year of sale under the arrangement as negotiated. The constructive receipt doctrine does not inquire into what arrangements *could have* been negotiated; it looks to the legal rights of the taxpayer under the deal as struck, assuming that the deal is legitimate and not a sham.

ii. **Circumstances beyond the taxpayer's control:** In *Hornung v. Commissioner,* 47 T.C. 428 (1967), the taxpayer was a professional football player using the cash method of accounting. For 1961, he was selected as an outstanding player by *Sport Magazine.* The prize was a Corvette valued at the astonishing price of $3,331.04. The Corvette was typically made available to prize recipients in New York on December 31 after the football game in which they were selected as the outstanding player. However, in 1961, the December 31 football game was played in Green Bay, Wisconsin, and the taxpayer did not receive the car until the following Wednesday. The taxpayer did not include the value of the Corvette in his gross income for 1962, presumably on the grounds that it was a gift, and the Commissioner sought to include this value in the taxpayer's gross income. However, the taxpayer abandoned the gift approach in this controversy, relying instead (in an interesting procedural twist) on the doctrine of constructive receipt. By arguing that the Corvette was includable in his 1961 (not 1962) gross income, the taxpayer was seeking to defeat the Commissioner's notice of deficiency for 1962. (Although not explicit in the case, 1961 was probably closed by the statute of limitations.) The court found that the doctrine of constructive receipt did not apply, because the taxpayer did not have "unfettered control . . . over the date of actual receipt." The circumstances that led to the taxpayer not having the car in 1961 were not in the taxpayer's sole control—December 31 was a Sunday; the dealership had not arranged for title to be transferred to *Sport Magazine;* the taxpayer had no indicia of ownership as of December 31. Thus, the taxpayer received the car in 1962, as the Commissioner argued.

   iii. No constructive receipt (and facts too good to miss): In *Ames v. Commissioner*, 112 T.C. 304 (1999), the taxpayer was a spy for whom the Soviet Union agreed to set up a $2 million bank account in 1985. The taxpayer received funds in subsequent years and the IRS asserted deficiencies associated with these unreported amounts. The taxpayer argued that he was in constructive receipt of the funds in 1985, when the account was set up for him, not in later years when he was paid, presumably with funds from the account. The Court rejected this argument because the taxpayer had no control over the account and could not legally compel payment from the Russians.

3. Deductions: A taxpayer using the cash method of accounting claims otherwise deductible expenses when they are paid, whether by cash, check, or credit card. Reg. §1.461-1(a)(1); Rev. Rul. 78-39, 1978-1 C.B. 73. Look for the year in which there is an actual outflow of resources from the taxpayer to another person to determine the proper year of deduction.

Example: This year, William is in an automobile accident and incurs $15,000 of medical expenses for which he is not insured. In December of this year he writes credit line checks to the doctors and hospital for these expenses. He repays the amount on his credit line in the next year. He will be able to deduct these expenses this year, if the other requirements for deductibility are met, because he has paid them during this year. In using his credit line, he is viewed as borrowing the funds and using the borrowed funds to make payment of the medical expenses.

4. Restrictions on the cash method:

  a. Prepayments: The rule that a cash method taxpayer may claim a deduction for expenses when paid is limited by the capitalization requirement. If an expenditure creates an asset with a useful life extending beyond the close of the taxable year, a deduction is denied, and the taxpayer must capitalize the expenditure and amortize it over time. Treas. Reg. §1.461-1(a)(1). However, the courts have been more kind. In *Zaninovich v. Commissioner*, 616 F.2d 429 (9th Cir. 1980), the taxpayer was allowed to deduct twelve months of prepaid rent. This has led to the "one-year rule" in which, as a practical matter, if the prepayment doesn't extend for more than one year and serves a valid business purpose, a deduction may be claimed.

  b. Certain taxpayers: The cash method is unavailable to certain types of taxpayers and certain types of activities. These restrictions arose out of concern that certain taxpayers were using the cash method to defer income and accelerate deductions inappropriately.

Thus, farming corporations and farming partnerships with corporate partners must ordinarily use the ***accrual method*** of accounting. IRC §447(a). Section 448 has a much broader scope, disallowing the use of the cash method for tax shelters, certain corporations, partnerships with corporate partners, and unrelated business activities of nonprofit entities. IRC §448(a). Section 464 prohibits farming syndicates from deducting certain prepaid expenses, requiring deductions for items such as feed, seed, and fertilizer to be claimed as these items are actually used. IRC §464(a). These sections are rife with technical definitions, exceptions, and special rules, making the selection of a method of accounting for a business entity a tricky process.

C. The accrual method

The accrual method focuses on the ***all events test*** for both income and deductions, although the test is a bit different for the two items. Under the accrual method, a taxpayer includes an amount in gross income when "all the events have occurred which fix the right to receive such income and the amount thereof can be determined with reasonable accuracy." Reg. §1.451-1(a). A taxpayer using the accrual method deducts a liability (i.e., an expense) when all the events have occurred that establish the fact of the liability, the amount of the liability can be determined with reasonable accuracy, and economic performance has occurred with respect to the liability. Reg. §1.461-1(a)(2). The accrual method is sometimes said to "match" deductions with the income they produce in a taxable year to clearly reflect the taxpayer's net income in a particular year. Although this matching principle is not always the rule for income and deductions under the accrual method, a significant acceleration of deductions or deferral of income from related transactions is likely to draw IRS attention.

1. **The deposit doctrine—*Commissioner v. Indianapolis Power & Light Co.*, 493 U.S. 203 (1990):** Indianapolis Power & Light Co. (IPL) required certain of its customers to make deposits as a condition of providing electricity. When a customer terminated its electric service, it could either pay the entire bill and receive a refund of its deposit, or apply the deposit to the final bill. The power company did not include the deposits in gross income when received, and the IRS argued that they were income in that year.

   a. **Issue:** Were the amounts called "deposits" includable in the taxpayer's gross income as advance payments for electricity, or excludable as deposits?

   b. **Result and rationale:** The amount deposited by the electric customers were deposits and therefore were excluded from gross income of IPL. These amounts were most like a loan from the customer to IPL that could be applied to the purchase of electricity at termination of service. IPL's ability to retain the deposit depended on two events outside its control, i.e., the decision of the utility customer to purchase electricity and to ultimately apply the deposit against the final bill. See also *Westpac Pacific Food v. Commissioner*, 451 F.3d 970 (9th Cir. 2006), in which the taxpayer received cash advances from vendors as part of the taxpayer's promise to purchase certain quantities of goods. If the taxpayer did not live up to its promise to purchase those quantities, it would have to repay the advance. The Court viewed this as similar to the IPL case, but instead of deposits, the cash advances were loans that had to be repaid upon certain conditions, and thus were not income.

   c. **Comment:** These cases illustrate nicely the relationship between whether a taxpayer has income and when a taxpayer has income. If amounts called deposits or cash advances are income, they are included in gross income in the year determined by the taxpayer's method of accounting. If they are true deposits or loans, the income is properly taken into account when and if the taxpayer applies the deposit against the customer's bill (IPL) or when the debt is discharged (Westpac).

2. **Income—Accrual method:** Under the accrual method, a taxpayer includes an amount in gross income when "all the events have occurred which fix the right to receive such income and the amount thereof can be determined with reasonable accuracy." Reg. §1.451-1(a). The actual date of payment may be relevant to this test but is not determinative. There are two requirements of the all events test, one focusing on the taxpayer's right to receive income and the second on the determination of the amount to be received.

   a. **Right to receive income:** For income to accrue, the taxpayer must have the right to the income under its contractual or other arrangements, regardless of actual receipt. *Spring City Foundry Co. v. Commissioner,* 292 U.S. 182 (1934). Therefore, if the right to the income depends on one or more future events (including the passage of time), the taxpayer does not include the amount in income until the contingency has been resolved. However, purely ministerial or formal contingencies (e.g., clerk approval or issuance of a check) do not prevent accrual.

   Example: Luis, a calendar-year, accrual-method taxpayer, sells a shipment of artificial carnations to Emily under a contract providing that she will pay for the shipment within 30 days of her receipt of payment from her principal retail florist customer, Frank. In Year 1, Luis ships the flowers to Emily and sends her a bill for $30,000. In Year 2, Frank pays Emily. In Year 3, Emily pays Luis. Luis must include Emily's payment in his income for Year 2. He need not include it in Y1, for he has no right to the income because the contingency (Frank's payment to Emily) has not occurred. He has the right to the income (which of course can be determined exactly) in Y2, and payment in Y3 is irrelevant.

   b. **Determinable with reasonable accuracy:** The exact amount due the taxpayer need not be ascertainable, but the amount must be determinable with reasonable accuracy. Doubts about collectibility can affect this determination. In *Georgia School-Book*, 1 T.C. 463 (1943), the accrual-method taxpayer was a broker who sold books to the state of Georgia's school system. The broker was entitled to an 8 percent commission payable when the state paid the publishers. The only source of payment was the state's Free Textbook Fund, funded from an excise tax on beer, which was insufficient to pay the schoolbook obligations. The taxpayer did not include any commissions in income until it received them, on the theory that the commissions were not earned until payment and there was no "reasonable expectancy" that they would be paid (until receipt) because of the insufficiency of the excise tax fund. The IRS argued that the taxpayer should have included the amounts in income in the year the books were sold.

      i. **Issue:** In the year of sale, could the amount to be received be determined with reasonable accuracy, given the difficulty the state of Georgia was having paying for the books?

      ii. **Result and rationale:** The court concluded that the taxpayer was required to include amounts in income in the year the books were sold. The court agreed with the IRS that in the year the books were sold, all events had occurred that fixed the right to the income (the taxpayer had performed all its duties under the contract), and the amount thereof could be ascertained with reasonable accuracy. Collectibility would not affect this determination, according to the court, unless the right were in litigation or the debtor were insolvent. Even though the state of Georgia was having administrative problems with its fund, there was no reasonable expectation that the amounts due would not be paid.

c. IRS's discretion to change methods—Advance payments: If the IRS believes that a taxpayer's method of accounting does not clearly reflect income, the IRS may assert that the taxpayer needs to change his or her method of accounting or the treatment of a particular item. The courts are likely to respect the IRS's determination in making such a change, and a good example of this is found in the treatment of advance payments.

    i. *American Automobile Association v. United States,* **367 U.S. 687 (1961):** The AAA received prepayment of annual dues from members throughout each year. The payment of annual dues entitled the member to various services from AAA during the year, including towing, travel assistance, and other services. In accordance with its financial accounting methods, the AAA reported a portion of the prepayment as income in the year of receipt for tax purposes; amounts relating to the next year were reported in the following year. For example, if the annual dues were $60, and the AAA received the dues on October 1, 1952, the AAA would report $15 in 1952 and $45 in 1953. The IRS argued that the entire amount should be included in income in the year of receipt on the basis that the accrual of only a portion of the dues in the year of receipt did not clearly reflect income. The taxpayer's position was that only the portion of the dues allocable to services for a particular year should be included in gross income for that year, and that allocation of the dues between years matched income and deductions to clearly reflect income. The Court agreed with the IRS, on the basis that the uncertainty associated with the provision of services upon member demand and not at fixed intervals resulted in an artificial deferral of income. It also focused on Congress's apparent failure to enact a provision to change this result as indicative of Congress's approval of it.

    ii. Extension—*Schlude v. Commissioner,* **372 U.S. 128 (1963):** The taxpayers offered dancing lessons in exchange for cash payments, negotiable notes given by students, and contracts that provided for payment over time. The lessons did not occur at scheduled intervals, but were arranged between students and teachers at mutually convenient times. The taxpayer did not include the payments in income until lessons were given. The Supreme Court held that the principles of the AAA case, *supra,* applied, recognizing the IRS's authority to require the taxpayer to clearly reflect income by including the payments for lessons when those payments in the form of cash or negotiable promissory note were received.

    iii. Compare—when provision of services is scheduled: In *Artnell Co. v. Commissioner,* 400 F.2d 981 (7th Cir. 1968), the accrual-method taxpayer sold season tickets for Chicago White Sox games. The taxpayer reported as income on season ticket sales in a particular taxable year only the portion of the sales price that was attributable to games during that year; amounts attributable to games in the next year were deferred to that later year. The IRS predictably objected, relying on the theory that was successful in *American Automobile Association.* The court agreed that the deferral of prepaid income *may* not clearly reflect income (the principle of *American Automobile Association*), but rejected the IRS argument that deferral of prepaid income to a future year would not clearly reflect income in this situation. The court distinguished the *AAA* case in two ways. First, the time and extent of services to be performed in the *AAA* case were uncertain; in baseball, by contrast, the dates for games were certain, except for rain dates. Second, the *AAA* Court suggested that Congress was aware of the problem for automobile associations but chose not to act to change the law as it existed. There was no similar recognition of the problem for baseball ticket sales, and the court could not infer a congressional purpose to prevent deferral of prepaid income in that context.

3. **Deductions—Accrual method:** A taxpayer using the accrual method deducts a liability (i.e., an expense) when "all the events have occurred that establish the fact of the liability, the amount of the liability can be determined with reasonable accuracy, and economic performance has occurred with respect to the liability." Reg. §1.461-1(a)(2). The first two prongs of the test, fact of the liability and determination with reasonable accuracy, are often difficult to distinguish.

   a. **Fact of the liability—*United States v. General Dynamics Corp.,* 481 U.S. 239 (1987):** Under this test, all events must have occurred that fix the fact of the liability. The taxpayer must be under a legal obligation to make the payment, and that liability must not depend on future events, including the passage of time. As in the income situation, purely ministerial tasks will not prevent satisfaction of the all events test. For example, in *General Dynamics,* the accrual-method taxpayer maintained a self-insured medical reimbursement plan for its employees under which they submitted health-related expenses for reimbursement. The taxpayer was entitled to deduct as business expenses amounts actually paid under the plan as compensation. For 1972, the taxpayer claimed that it was entitled to deduct an additional amount that it actuarially estimated would be paid for medical expenses incurred by employees during the year, but for which claims had not yet been submitted, reviewed, or paid as of the close of the year. The IRS argued that such a deduction was not allowable because all events had not occurred (submission of the claim, review, and payment) that would establish the fact of the company's liability to the employee. The Court agreed with the IRS, on the grounds that the mere prediction that events were likely to occur was not sufficient to satisfy the all events test.

   b. **Determination with reasonable accuracy:** The exact amount of the liability need not be determinable, but there must be some reasonable method for estimating the amount. For example, in *Schuessler v. Commissioner,* 230 F.2d 722 (5th Cir. 1956), the taxpayer sold furnaces with a guarantee that he would turn them on and off each season for five years. Purchasers paid a premium for this guarantee, and the taxpayer offered proof as to the cost of performing this guarantee each year. The taxpayer sought to deduct in the year of sale of each furnace the estimated costs of performing the guarantee, and the IRS objected on the grounds that this did not clearly reflect income. The court agreed with the taxpayer, allowing the deduction even though the amount was not determinable with "mathematical certainty." *Id.* at 724.

   c. **Economic performance:** Section 461(h) provides that the all events test is not satisfied prior to the time *economic performance* occurs. What constitutes economic performance varies for the type of liability.

      i. **Services and property provided to the taxpayer:** When an accrual-method taxpayer incurs a liability to pay for services or property to be provided by another person, economic performance occurs when the other person provides the services or property. IRC §461(h)(2)(A)(i), (ii). If the liability is for the taxpayer's use of property, economic performance occurs as the taxpayer uses the property. IRC §461(h)(2)(A)(iii).

Example: Adrian, an accrual-method taxpayer, leases a loft for use as an art gallery. Under the terms of her lease, Adrian must prepay two years' worth of maintenance fees in the amount of $5,000. While the all events test may be satisfied because the liability is fixed, and the amount can be determined with reasonable accuracy, economic performance occurs as the maintenance services are provided to Adrian over the two-year period. Therefore, she will not be able to deduct the $5,000 in the first year.

ii. **Services or property provided by the taxpayer:** If the liability represents the obligation of the taxpayer to provide services or property, economic performance occurs as the taxpayer provides the services or property. IRC §416(h)(2)(B).

Example: Consider the *Schuessler* case discussed above. Today that case would be decided differently because of the economic performance requirement. The taxpayer would be considered as satisfying the all events test as he performed the guarantees over the five-year period, rather than in the year of sale of the furnaces.

iii. **Tort and workers' compensation claims:** For tort and workers' compensation claims, economic performance occurs as payments are made to the plaintiff or claimant. IRC §461(h)(2)(C).

Example: Paul sues Gresham for a personal injury sustained in Gresham's business. They settle the claim on the terms that Gresham will pay Paul $15,000 per year for five years. While under prior law Gresham might have been able to deduct $75,000 (or at least the *present value* of the five $15,000 payments) at the time of settlement, the economic performance requirement results in Gresham satisfying the all events test as he makes the $15,000 payments over the five-year period.

iv. **Certain nonrecurring items:** The economic performance requirement will not bar deduction of certain nonmaterial items if economic performance occurs within a relatively short period of time after the close of the taxable year. IRC §461(h)(3).

IV. ACCOUNTING FOR INVENTORIES

A taxpayer engaged in the business of selling goods incurs costs in manufacturing or purchasing these goods. Taxpayers would prefer to deduct these costs as they are incurred, but this practice can result in costs being deducted before income is earned (thus mismatching income and deductions and inaccurately reflecting the taxpayer's income). A more accurate reflection would occur if the costs of producing each item were taken as a deduction when that item is sold; the costs of production would be subtracted from the income from the sale to produce the taxpayer's net income or loss from that particular sale. While such an approach is feasible for sales of big-ticket items such as automobiles or large-carat gemstones, it is unmanageable for the sale of less expensive or fungible goods. Thus, a taxpayer must have a system for accounting for inventory.

A. Requirement for inventory accounting

Section 471(a) authorizes the IRS to require a taxpayer to account for *inventories* in accordance with the best accounting practice in the trade or business and to most clearly reflect income. The IRS generally requires inventories to be kept for manufacturing, mining, and merchandising businesses, and service businesses also may be required to keep inventories in certain situations.

B. General approach—Cost of goods sold

A taxpayer who must keep inventories will subtract the ***cost of goods sold*** from gross sales for the year. The cost of goods sold is equal to the taxpayer's opening inventory, plus purchases during the taxable year, minus the closing inventory.

Example: Collin is a sole proprietor engaged in the sale of cellular telephones. In his first year of operations, he began with no inventory, purchased $10,000 of inventory, and closed his first year with $8,000 of inventory on hand. Assume no other expenses of doing business. Collin's gross sales were $9,000. Collin must keep inventory because he is in the merchandising business. His cost of goods sold is computed by beginning with his opening inventory (0), adding the purchases for the year ($10,000), and subtracting the closing inventory ($8,000). Thus, his cost of goods sold was $2,000. His income from the business is $7,000, computed by subtracting the cost of goods sold ($2,000) from the gross sales ($9,000).

There are various methods for identifying the goods sold, such as "FIFO" ("first in, first out," meaning the inventory first purchased is considered sold first) and "LIFO" ("last in, first out," meaning the inventory purchased most recently is considered sold first).

C. Relationship to capital recovery

The notion of accounting for inventory is not only a timing rule, but also an example of capital recovery. (See discussion in Chapter 7(IV)(A).) A taxpayer is entitled to be taxed on his or her profit from business and to recover his or her economic investment in property. The cost of goods sold is the taxpayer's economic investment in inventory, and the process of accounting for inventory allows the taxpayer to recover that investment. It is presented here as a timing rule because accounting for inventories also determines the taxable year in which a taxpayer will report income from sales of inventory.

V. INSTALLMENT METHOD OF REPORTING INCOME

A. Recognizing this transaction

The ***installment method*** of reporting income is applicable to deferred payment sales, i.e., certain sales in which at least one payment occurs in a year after the year of the actual sale. IRC §453(b)(1). A deferred payment sale is really *two* interrelated transactions—a loan and a sale. When a seller agrees to deferred payments, the seller is actually making a loan to the buyer for the deferred portion of the purchase price. Therefore, the seller will expect to receive a market rate of interest on this loan, and will also expect full payment of the principal (the purchase price) under the terms of the contract. See Figure 11A—Deferred Payment Sale Transaction.

B. The installment method approach

In recognition of the two parts of any ***deferred payment sale,*** analyzing a deferred payment contract requires two steps.

1. **Interest:** If the deferred payment sale provides for adequate stated interest, that interest is includable in the gross income of the seller and *may* be deductible to the purchaser; the timing of inclusion of income, or the deduction of interest will be determined under the seller and

Figure 11A
Deferred Payment Sale Transaction

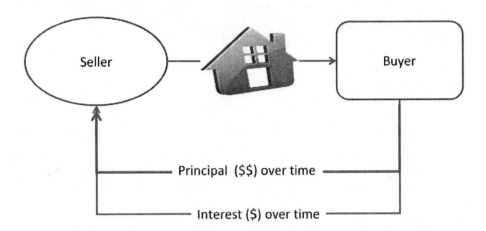

buyer's methods of accounting. If the sales contract does not provide for adequate stated interest, the Code may impute interest to the transaction (see discussion in Chapter 15 (III)–(V)).

2. **Principal:** The installment method is designed to allow the seller in a deferred payment sale to spread the recognition of gain from that sale ratably over the taxable years in which the seller receives payments under the sales contract. Thus, a portion of each payment received will represent a nontaxable return of the seller's basis, and the remaining amount will be income from the sale of the property. The details of this approach are discussed below.

C. Statutory analysis—§453

1. **General rule:** Section 453(a) requires that income from an installment sale be reported using the installment method. Section 453 does *not* apply to losses on such sales; these losses may be recognized in the year of sale if the other requirements for loss recognition are met. See IRC §165, and discussion in Chapters 6(VII), 7(III)(C), and generally in Chapters 9 and 10. Crucial to understanding this general rule is an understanding of the definitions of installment sale and installment method.

2. **Definitional issues**

   a. **Installment sale:** An installment sale is a sale of property in which at least one payment is due after the close of the taxable year in which the sale occurs. However, it does not include sales of inventory, sales by dealers of the property they hold for sale to customers, and sales of publicly traded stocks or securities. IRC §453(b)(2), (k)(2).

   Example: Maria owns Blackacre, a parcel of raw land that she holds for investment. She sells Blackacre to Chris for a sales price of $150,000. Under the terms of the contract of sale, Chris must pay Maria $50,000 upon sale, and the remaining $100,000 one year from the date of the sale with adequate interest. This is an installment sale because at least one payment is due after the close of the taxable year in which the sale occurs. If, however, Maria were a dealer in raw land, this transaction would not be an installment sale because dealer dispositions are not included within the definition of installment sales.

Figure 11B
Installment Method Calculation

Amount Included in Gross Income	=	Payment × Gross Profit Ratio

$$\text{Gross Profit Ratio} = \frac{\text{Gross Profit}}{\text{Total Contract Price}}$$

Gross Profit	=	Total Contract Price – Adjusted Basis of Property Sold

$$\text{Gross Profit Ratio} = \frac{\text{Total Contract Price} - \text{Adjusted Basis of Property Sold}}{\text{Total Contract Price}}$$

b. **Installment method:** The income from an installment sale for any particular year is equal to the payments received during that taxable year, multiplied by a fraction known as the ***gross profit ratio.*** IRC §453(c). The numerator of the gross profit ratio is the ***gross profit*** the denominator is the ***total contract price.*** See Figure 11B—Installment Method Calculation.

   i.   **Gross profit:** The gross profit is the selling price minus the adjusted basis of the property. Reg. §15a.453-1(b)(2)(v). The selling price is the gross sales price, without reduction for any selling expenses. Reg. §15a.453-1(b)(2)(ii). Interest is not a part of the selling price, as the interest portion of the transaction is addressed separately. The adjusted basis is the adjusted basis computed under the usual rules. See discussion in Chapter 9(V)(C).

   Example: Trisha owns Whiteacre, which has a fair market value of $150,000 and a basis of $30,000. Trisha sells Whiteacre to Patrick for $150,000 cash, payable over ten years in equal monthly installments (with adequate stated interest). The gross profit on this sale is $120,000, which is the difference between the sales price ($150,000) and Trisha's adjusted basis in Whiteacre ($30,000).

   ii.   **Total contract price:** The total contract price is the price to be paid under the contract. Reg. §15a.453-1(b)(2)(iii). For purposes of this computation only, the seller's expenses of sale, such as commissions and fees, are added to the basis of the property.

   Example: In the previous example, Trisha sold Whiteacre for $150,000 in cash, which is the total contract price.

   iii.   **Property encumbered by debt:** If the property sold is encumbered by debt, the application of the installment method changes. This is beyond the scope of most basic tax courses.

c. **Payment:** Payment includes the receipt of cash and property, but not promissory notes or other "evidences of indebtedness" unless they are payable on demand, readily tradable on an established securities market, or secured by cash or a cash equivalent. IRC §453(f)(3), (4), (5).

   Example: To compute the income of a taxpayer for an installment sale, first isolate and analyze the interest portion of the transaction. Then compute the realized gain, and determine the proper year for recognition by determining the gross profit ratio, which is the gross profit divided by the total contract price. Multiply the payments received during the year by the gross profit ratio. The resulting number will be the amount of the payment that is includable as gain from the sale for that year. The remaining amount of the payment will be a tax-free return of basis. By the last payment, the selling taxpayer will have recognized all of the realized gain on the sale and will have received a tax-free return of his or her basis as well.

Example: Jennifer sells Pinkacre to Sam for $150,000. Jennifer's basis in Pinkacre is $30,000. Under the terms of the contract of sale, Sam will pay Jennifer $50,000 in the year of sale and $50,000 on the first and second anniversaries of the sale with interest at 7% (which represents a market rate of interest).

Jennifer, a cash method taxpayer, will report her realized gain of $120,000 on this transaction using the installment method. She will first deal with the interest side of the transaction. Since the contract calls for adequate stated interest, she will report the interest earned using her method of accounting, the cash method. Thus, she will include the interest in her gross income when she receives it, actually or constructively.

Jennifer will then compute her gross profit ratio, as follows:

$$\frac{\text{Gross Profit}}{\text{Total Contract Price}} = \frac{\$150,000 - \$30,000}{\$150,000} = 80\%$$

Jennifer multiplies the gross profit ratio by the payments she receives each year to determine the portion of the payment that is income and the portion that is a tax-free return of basis. Her total income should equal her realized gain on the transaction, and she should receive a tax-free return of her $30,000 basis. The chart below summarizes these results.

Year & Payment	× Gross Profit Ratio	= Income	Tax-free Return of Basis
Year of Sale ($50,000)	× 80%	= $40,000	$10,000
1st anniversary year ($50,000)	× 80%	= $40,000	$10,000
2nd anniversary year ($50,000)	× 80%	= $40,000	$10,000
Total $150,000		**$120,000**	**$30,000**

3. **Special rules and exceptions**

   a. **Election out:** A taxpayer may elect not to apply the installment method by so indicating on his or her tax return for the year in which the sale occurs. IRC §453(d)(1), (2). If a taxpayer elects out of the method, the recognized gain must be included in gross income in the year of sale. IRC §1001(c). This would be an appropriate strategy if the taxpayer had losses in the year of sale sufficient to offset the gain from the installment sale or if the taxpayer believed tax rates to be climbing in future years (and had the funds with which to pay the tax).

   b. **Contingent price sales:** In some situations, the sales price under a deferred payment sale is expressed as a measure other than a specific sum. At one time, the courts applied the ***open*** *transaction* approach to such situations, allowing the taxpayer first to fully recover his or her basis in the property sold and, once basis was fully recovered, to report any additional amounts received as income. This ensured that the taxpayer would recover his or her basis tax-free, but allowed significant income deferral—a much too generous approach, in Treasury's view. It also created difficult questions about when the open transaction approach should be allowed. The courts typically applied it when the amount to be received under the contract did not have an ascertainable fair market value, a standard that created more controversy than it solved. See, e.g., *Burnet v. Logan,* 283 U.S. 404 (1931). The regulations now provide specific rules for three types of contingent payment transactions, essentially making the open transaction doctrine obsolete. In all three situations, the regulations supply an assumption necessary to compute the gross profit ratio even though the sales price is uncertain. See Prop. Reg. §15a.453-1(c). As a result, courts are usually unwilling to apply the open transaction doctrine, even when the ultimate economic result of transaction is quite uncertain. See *Bernice Patton Testamentary Trust v. United States,* 2001-1 USTC ¶50,332 (Fed. Cl.), *aff'd per curiam unpublished decision,* 2002-1 USTC ¶50,277 (Fed. Cir.).

4. Related material

   a. Realized and recognized gain: Inherent in the installment sale rules is the assumption that a realization event has occurred that has generated realized and recognized gain. See generally Chapter 9. A nonrecognition transaction (such as a like-kind exchange) in which a taxpayer receives boot after the close of the taxable year in which the exchange occurs can implicate both the nonrecognition rules and the installment sale rules, the correct combination of which takes tax complexity to new heights. See, e.g., IRC §1031(f). Fortunately this is beyond the scope of most basic tax classes.

   b. Disposition of installment obligations—§453B: If a taxpayer sells or otherwise disposes of an installment obligation, he or she realizes gain equal to the difference between the basis of the installment obligation and the amount realized on sale. IRC §453B(a). The basis of an installment obligation is its face value minus the income not yet recognized by the holder of the obligation. IRC §453B(b). The amount realized is (a) the satisfaction amount, if satisfied other than by payment in full; (b) the sales price, if sold; or (c) the fair market value if transferred other than by sale or exchange. IRC §453A(a).

   c. Character of gain: The character of the gain recognized under the installment method is determined under the usual rules as ordinary or capital. It will usually be capital, as sales of inventory or dealer property are excluded from the installment sale rules. For a discussion of the character of gain, see generally Chapter 12.

   d. Imputed interest: If an installment sale does not provide for adequate interest, a market rate of interest may be imputed, giving rise to income for the creditor (seller) and a potential deduction to the debtor (buyer). See discussion in Chapter 15(III)–(V).

VI. RESTRICTED PROPERTY—§83

A. Recognizing this transaction

As discussed in Chapter 2, gross income includes compensation received for services rendered whether the compensation is in the form of cash or property. The question of *when* the compensation is includable in the taxpayer's income is generally answered by the taxpayer's method of accounting. Special rules apply, however, when a taxpayer receives as compensation *restricted property,* i.e., property subject to significant restrictions on the taxpayer's ability to use or transfer it. Look for a compensation transaction in which the service provider receives not cash, but other property, and the property is subject to some restriction that makes it less valuable to the taxpayer. Transfers of stock or equity interests in other entities are frequently encountered in this context.

B. Whether, when, and how much

Transfers of restricted property raise significant questions not only of *when* the taxpayer must include the item as income but also *whether* the taxpayer has received income at all. The restrictions on the property may be so severe that in fact the taxpayer has not received any property interest at all. Moreover, *how much* income is also in question; the restrictions on use or alienability of the property will probably adversely affect its value. Section 83 resolves all of these difficulties by deferring taxation until it is clear that the taxpayer has received property that can be valued. It then specifies the proper year for inclusion as well as how much income must be included.

C. Statutory analysis—§83

1. **General rule:** A taxpayer who receives property in connection with the performance of services must include an amount in his or her gross income. IRC §83(a). The amount included is the excess of the value of the property received over the amount the taxpayer paid for the property. *Id.* The taxpayer includes this amount in gross income in the first year in which he or she may transfer the property, or the rights are not subject to a *substantial risk of forfeiture. Id.*

   Example: Sonny is the CEO of Regency Park, Inc. As part of its incentive compensation plan, Regency Park transfers 1,000 shares of its stock to Sonny on the condition that he remain as CEO for four years. The stock is nontransferable for ten years. The stock received by Sonny is restricted property within the meaning of §83, and Sonny need not include its value in his gross income until the first year in which he is entitled to the stock without the performance of future services or may freely transfer the stock. This will occur at the end of four years, at which time Sonny will include the fair market value of the stock in his gross income (unless he makes a §83(b) election, discussed below).

2. **Definitional issues**

   a. **Transfers of property:** Property includes items other than money and unfunded and unsecured promises to pay money in the future. Reg. §1.83-3(e). A transfer of property occurs when a person acquires a beneficial interest in the property. Reg. §1.83-3(a)(1). Property includes stock options, which is the right to acquire stock at a specified price. Companies often adopt stock option plans as a mechanism to attract and retain employees. There are two kinds of stock option plans: incentive stock option plans (which are subject to a medley of structuring rules) and nonstatutory stock option plans (which avoid these restrictions). Nonstatutory stock option plans are more frequently encountered. Stock options are beyond the scope of most basic income tax courses.

   b. **Substantial risk of forfeiture:** A substantial risk of forfeiture exists when the person receiving the property must perform substantial future services in order to have full rights in the property. IRC §83(c)(1).

Example: Mark agrees to manage the apartment buildings of ABC Partnership in exchange for a 20 percent partnership interest. However, his rights in the partnership interest are conditioned upon his performing management services for five full years. The partnership interest is subject to a substantial risk of forfeiture. (Indeed, he may not even be a partner because of this requirement, but that discussion is for another course.)

c. **Transferability:** A person may freely transfer property only if the transferee's rights in the property would not be subject to a substantial risk of forfeiture. IRC §83(c)(2).

d. **"In connection with" the performance of services:** Property is transferred in connection with the performance of services if it is transferred to an employee or an independent contractor who is obligated to perform services or refrain from performing services. Reg. §1.83-3(f).

3. **Special rules and exceptions**

a. **Restrictions that never lapse:** Certain restrictions on property will never lapse, and therefore it will be impossible to value the property under the usual fair market value standards. In these circumstances, the agreement of transfer will usually provide a formula for valuing the property. If so, the formula price will be the fair market value for purposes of determining the amount to be included in income. Reg. §1.83-5(a).

b. **Employer's deduction:** The employer takes a deduction with respect to the transfer of property when the taxpayer includes the amount in gross income. IRC §83(h).

c. **Section 83(b) election:** A taxpayer receiving restricted property may elect to include the value of the property in gross income at the time received, rather than waiting for restrictions to lapse. If the taxpayer makes this election, he or she includes in gross income the excess of the fair market value of the property (computed without regard to restrictions) over the amount the taxpayer paid for the property. *Id.* This would be a rational choice for property whose value is relatively low in the year of transfer but which is expected to increase substantially prior to lapse of the restrictions on transfer. However, if the property declines in value, the taxpayer may not revoke the election. In any event, the taxpayer has only thirty days after transfer to make the election. IRC §83(b)(2).

Example: Joe is the accountant for a fledgling company, Zippy, Inc. Joe agrees to take restricted stock in Zippy in exchange for (1) a capital contribution of $10, and (2) providing accounting and financial services to Zippy over ten years. Because the value of Zippy stock is low in its early years, Joe might well be advised to make the §83(b) election. He would then include in his gross income the difference between the fair market value of the Zippy stock in the year he receives it (valued without regard to the restrictions on transfer to which the stock is subject) minus the amount he paid for it ($10). Joe's basis in the stock will be equal to the amount he paid for it plus the amount he included in gross income. Ten years later, when Zippy is fabulously successful and the restrictions lapse, the stock will be much more valuable, but Joe will not include any amount in gross income because of the lapse of the restrictions and because he had already included the value in income in the year of transfer.

4. Related material

  a. **Basis:** The basis of property received as compensation for services is its cost. This includes the amount paid for the property plus the amount included in gross income as a result of §83. For a discussion of basis of property received as compensation for services, see Chapter 9(III)(C).

  b. **Constructive receipt:** An alternative theory for challenging certain deferred compensation arrangements is the doctrine of constructive receipt.

5. Be alert for restricted property issues:
Section 83 is implicated whenever a service provider receives property as compensation, and there are restrictions on the transfer or retention of that property. These issues are often tested in the form of a package of employment benefits for an executive, including restricted stock and fringe benefits.

VII. SPECIAL RESTRICTIONS ON LOSS DEDUCTIONS

Three statutory schemes potentially limit or disallow deductions for certain types of losses. These provisions are properly viewed as timing rules because they address a taxpayer's ability to claim a deduction for a loss in the year that it is incurred, and typically defer loss deductions to a later year. Although these provisions are technical in the extreme, a passing familiarity with them is important for the basic tax student.

A. Passive loss restrictions—§469

Section 469 prohibits individuals and certain other taxpayers from deducting a *passive activity loss* for any taxable year. IRC §469(a). A passive activity loss is the net loss (i.e., the excess of losses over income) from the taxpayer's passive activities. IRC §469(d)(1).

1. Identifying passive activities:
A passive activity is any activity of the taxpayer that is a *trade or business* but in which the taxpayer does not *materially participate.* IRC §469(c). For example, a passive activity does not include income from investments, because the holding of investments does not rise to the level of a trade or business, but a taxpayer's participation as a silent partner in a horse-breeding business would be a passive activity. In general, *any* rental activity is a passive activity generating passive income and loss, but there is an exception for rental real estate activities in which the taxpayer "actively participates," for up to $25,000 of otherwise passive loss. IRC §469(c)(7). Active participation is a slightly easier standard to meet, requiring that the taxpayer make management decisions, carry out services with respect to the property, or arrange for others to perform such services in a significant and bona fide manner.

2. Material participation:
The statute defines material participation as regular, continuous, and substantial participation, and provides a special rule that limited partners are not considered to materially participate except as provided in the regulations. IRC §469(h)(1), (2). The regulations' definition of material participation is extremely complex, offering a variety of different tests. The most familiar of these is the 500-hour test, under which the taxpayer is considered to materially participate in an activity only if he or she devotes 500 hours or more to the activity each year. Treas. Reg. §1.469-5T(a)(1).

3. Deduction of passive losses:
A passive loss may be deducted only against *passive income,* i.e., income from a passive activity. IRC §469(d)(1).

Example: Carol is a limited partner in a boxcar investment partnership and also is a member of a limited liability company that owns a coin laundry business. She does not materially participate in either venture. She has a $6,000 loss from the limited partnership investment, and she has $4,000 of income from the LLC owning the coin laundry business. Her passive loss of $6,000 may be deducted against the passive income from the LLC, but her $2,000 loss in excess of passive income is not deductible.

4. **Suspended passive losses:** Losses that cannot be deducted because of the passive loss rules carry forward indefinitely until a year in which the taxpayer has passive income. When the taxpayer disposes completely of his or her investment in the activity, suspended passive losses will not be treated as losses from a passive activity, and therefore will be deductible, subject to any other loss restrictions. IRC §469(g)(1). The amount of deductible loss is the excess of suspended passive losses over any net income or gain from all passive activities for the year. IRC §469(g)(1)(A).

    Example: Penny invests $100,000 in a cattle-breeding enterprise from which she anticipates tax benefits but in which she does not have to actually ever see, touch, or communicate with any cows. She has no other investments in passive activities. In the first five years of the project, her share of the enterprise's income and deductions produce a net loss to her of $30,000 per year. These are passive losses, because although the underlying activity is a trade or business, she does not materially participate in the activity. Therefore, Penny may not deduct the losses, as she has no passive income. If in year six she sells her interest in the cattle-breeding enterprise, she may deduct the excess of the suspended $150,000 loss over the income from disposition, and income from other passive activities will be treated as a loss from other than a passive activity.

B. At-risk limitations—§465

Section 465 limits the amount of loss an individual and certain other taxpayers may deduct from certain activities to the amount the taxpayer has *at risk* in the venture. IRC §465(a)(1). Section 465 applies to businesses involving films or video, farming, leasing of personal property, certain oil and gas endeavors, and the holding of real property. IRC §465(b)(6), (c). The amount the taxpayer has at risk is equal to the amount of money and fair market value of property that the taxpayer has contributed to the business, and the amount for which the taxpayer could be held personally liable for contribution to the enterprise (or its creditors), reduced by any losses deducted in prior years for which the taxpayer was at risk. IRC §465(b). For real estate activities, the taxpayer may also be considered at risk for certain qualifying nonrecourse indebtedness, which greatly increases the amount at risk for certain taxpayers. See IRC §465(b)(6). Any losses disallowed by §465 carry forward and may be deducted if and when the taxpayer has additional amounts at risk. IRC §465(a)(2).

Example: Kerry invests in a filming enterprise by contributing $50,000 and promising to contribute another $40,000 if needed. He is not liable under contract or state law for any additional amounts in the venture. Kerry's share of losses from the venture is $60,000 in the first year. He may deduct these losses, as he is at risk by the amount of money he has contributed ($50,000) and the amount he has agreed to contribute ($40,000). If in the next year, Kerry's share of losses were again $60,000, he would be allowed to deduct only $30,000 of these losses, as his total amount at risk for that year would be reduced by the prior year's losses. The remaining $30,000 nondeductible loss would carry forward and would be deductible if Kerry were to contribute more money to the venture.

C. Losses between related taxpayers

Section 267(a) provides that no loss may be recognized on the sale or exchange of property between related persons. The statute then defines related persons as including certain family members and entities and their owners. These rules defining related parties also include complex "constructive ownership" rules that cause persons to own interests in entities owned by others to whom they are related; these are beyond the scope of most basic tax courses. Even if §267 applies, all is not lost. If the purchaser in a transaction in which loss is disallowed later sells the property at a gain, the gain is reduced by the amount of the loss previously denied. IRC §267(d). The Supreme Court has held that the predecessor to §267 applies not only to actual sales between related parties, but also to indirect sales that are in substance sales between related parties. See *McWilliams v. Commissioner*, 331 U.S. 694 (1947).

Example: Dorothy purchased 100 shares of ABC stock for $100,000. When its value had fallen to $60,000, she sold it to her daughter Anne for cash. Dorothy may not recognize the realized loss ($40,000) because of §267(a). Anne's basis in the ABC stock is $60,000, her cost. If Anne sells it for $110,000 to an unrelated party, her realized gain of $50,000 will be recognized only to the extent that it exceeds the previously denied loss ($40,000). Therefore, Anne will recognize only $10,000 of gain on the sale.

VIII. NEED TO KNOW MORE?

This book's website *www.aspenlawschool.com/books/tax_outline* contains additional information, including:

- Stock options and restricted property.

- Contingent sales prices and the installment method.

- Encumbered properties and the installment method.

- And other materials that will help you recognize timing problems and solve them appropriately.

IX. WHERE ARE WE GOING?

Previous chapters have addressed the computation of gain or loss from the sale or other disposition of property, and this chapter has discussed timing of that income or loss (as well as timing of other items of income and deduction). But a full analysis of gain or loss from the sale of property requires a determination of the *character* of income or loss as capital or ordinary. Chapter 12 turns to this very important question.

Quiz Yourself on
TIMING OF INCOME AND EXPENSES

118. Why does the U.S. income tax system use an annual accounting system? _____

119. Jerry is a talk show host on a local radio station. He produces the show himself, and had income from advertising of $25,000 in each of Years 1, 2, and 3 from this activity. In Year 4, he experienced a loss of $30,000. In Year 5, the business had taxable income of $20,000. Can Jerry average these years' income to reflect his overall taxable income of $65,000? If so, how can this be done? _____

120. Sandy entered into a consulting contract for services with Rocky Corp. The contract said that Sandy was to be paid $100,000, but if its consulting services did not increase Rocky's sales of gravel and sand by 35 percent by the end of the next year, the consulting contract price would be reduced based on a formula. Sandy received $100,000 in Year 1, but had to repay $15,000 in Year 2. How should Sandy treat the receipt of income in Year 1? _____

121. Tom is a lawyer using the calendar year and the cash method of accounting. Tom performed work in December and gave the client his bill, but the customer didn't pay until January. When will Tom properly include this payment in his gross income? _____

122. Consider Tom from the previous problem. What if Tom's client had showed up at his office on December 31 with a check but Tom refused to let him in? _____

123. Pam, a calendar-year, cash method taxpayer, wants to claim a Year 1 deduction for the following payments. Which of the following, if any, will be deductible in Year 1?

    (a) Her check written and mailed on December 29, Year 1, for payment of state personal income taxes.

    (b) Her check written and mailed December 29, Year 1, but postdated January 1, Year 2, for a charitable contribution.

    (c) Her check written and mailed December 29, Year 1, for otherwise deductible trade or business expenses on an account for which she is aware there are insufficient funds to honor the check.

    (d) Same as (c), except that because of a levy against her account of which she had no knowledge there are insufficient funds in the account to honor the check.

    (e) Her check written December 29, Year 1, for alimony that will be due January 31, Year 2.

124. Opie is a motivational speaker, using the calendar year and cash method of accounting. He paid otherwise deductible expenses of $5,000 this year, by paying $2,000 by check and $3,000 by credit card. He also owed the local office supply store $4,500 as of year-end. When will Opie properly deduct these amounts? _____

125. Oils R Us, an aromatherapy store, opened the year with $10,000 of inventory on hand. It purchased another $25,000 of products from suppliers, and its year-end count shows $12,000 of inventory on hand. It had gross sales of $50,000. What is its net income considering only inventory expenses? _____

126. Adam works for BigCo. On each anniversary of his commencement of employment with BigCo, Adam receives 500 shares of BigCo stock from BigCo. However, Adam cannot sell the stock and if he leaves BigCo prior to the fifth anniversary of receiving the stock, he must forfeit all his rights to such stock. What are the tax consequences of Adam's receipt of the stock?

_____

127. GoTown Recording Studios uses the calendar year and the accrual method of accounting. It engages Soundbites Corp. to provide mixing services in Year 2 for a stated amount. GoTown will pay Soundbites in two payments, one at the end of Year 1 and the second six months later in Year 2. When will GoTown properly deduct the payments to Soundbites? _____

128. Samantha owned Hideaway Hills, a ranch in California. Samantha is not a dealer in such property and the ranch is not her personal residence. She has a basis of $300,000 in the ranch. She sold Hideaway Hills to Darin for $1,000,000. Darin will pay her $200,000 per year, plus interest at market rates, for the next five years. When will Samantha report the gain on the sale of the ranch? Is there any other income to report? _____

129. Sara paid $5,000 of state income taxes and deducted this amount on her federal tax return for Year 1. This entire amount reduced her tax. In Year 2, she received a refund of $2,000 of those state income taxes. What are the tax consequences to Sara of receipt of the refund in Year 2?

_____

130. Bev, a college basketball coach, inherited an apartment building from her mother. This year, it produced a net loss for tax purposes of $40,000. Bev wants to deduct this amount on her income tax return. May she do so? _____

131. Harry purchased 100 shares of XYZ Co. from his father for $10,000. His father's basis in the shares was $60,000. What is Harry's recognized gain or loss if he later sells the shares for:

(a) $150,000

(b) $60,000

(c) $40,000

(d) $10,000

(e) $5,000

_____

Answers

118. The government needs some way to measure a taxpayer's income and collect the tax in predictable, objective, and fairly frequent intervals. The taxable year concept provides that technique.

119. Income averaging *per se* is not possible, but Jerry may carry back his net operating loss of $30,000 in Year 4 to Year 2 (applying $25,000, reducing taxable income to zero) and Year 3 (applying $5,000, reducing taxable income to $20,000). He does this by filing amended returns, and this carryback has the result similar to "averaging" his income.

120. In this case, Sandy had a colorable legal claim to $100,000 and must include that amount in income in the year of receipt. In the next year, she can invoke §1341 to pay the lower of the tax resulting

from (a) computing the tax in Year 1 as if the $15,000 had never been included; or (b) including the income in Year 1 and deducting the repayment in Year 2.

121. Because Tom is a cash method taxpayer, he will include the payment in gross income in the year he receives it, Year 2. When he performed the services and sent his bill is irrelevant.

122. Tom would probably be in constructive receipt of payment, because he had access to the money and refused to take it.

123. These questions address the proper timing of deductions for a calendar-year, cash method taxpayer. A cash method taxpayer deducts amounts when paid.

   (a) For tax purposes, a timely mailing is a timely payment, so unless other factors exist that would prevent a deduction, Pamela may deduct payments made by check and mailed in Year 1 for otherwise deductible personal income taxes.

   (b) By postdating the check January 1, Year 2, Pamela prevents the check from being presented for payment until Year 2, and so the payment is not deductible until Year 2.

   (c) If the taxpayer is aware (or should be aware) that there are insufficient funds in the account on which the check is drawn, the mailing of the check does not constitute payment.

   (d) If the taxpayer had no knowledge (or reason to know) of the levy, mailing constitutes payment even if the check is dishonored.

   (e) Because the alimony isn't due until Year 2, Pamela cannot accelerate the deduction by prepaying it in Year 1.

124. Opie will deduct $5,000 for payments made, and it doesn't matter if they are made by check or credit card. He cannot deduct amounts owed at the end of the year because he has not yet paid them.

125. Oils R Us is required to account for inventories because it sells merchandise. It has $50,000 of gross income. Its cost of goods sold is computed by taking beginning inventory ($10,000), adding purchases ($25,000), and subtracting ending inventory ($12,000). Its cost of goods sold is $23,000. Therefore, its net income, considering only inventory costs, is $27,000 ($50,000 − $23,000).

126. Adam has received property for services, a transaction that generates compensation income to him (see Chapter 1). However, this property is "restricted": Adam cannot sell it and may forfeit his rights to the stock. Under §83, Adam will include the fair market value of the stock in his gross income (and the employer, BigCo, will take a deduction) on the first date at which the stock is transferable or the forfeiture provisions lapse. For example, if Adam receives 500 shares on January 2, Year 1, the transferability and forfeiture provisions will lapse on January 2, Year 6, and Adam would be required to include in his gross income the fair market value of the shares in his gross income in Year 6 (at their value in that year). Adam can make a §83(b) election to include the value of the shares in his gross income when he receives them, which would be a good choice if he expects the value of the BigCo shares to greatly increase in value.

127. As an accrual-method taxpayer, GoTown generally deducts expenses when all events have occurred that determine the fact of the liability and the amount of the liability can be determined with reasonable accuracy. This test would normally lead to GoTown deducting the expense in Year 1. However, the economic performance rules are an overlay on the all events test. They provide that deduction cannot occur prior to economic performance. For the purchase of services, economic

performance occurs when the services are provided. Therefore, GoTown may not deduct the payment until Year 2, when Soundbites provides the services.

128. Unless Samantha elects out of the installment method, she will report the gain realized on the transaction over the five-year period of payments. The portion of each payment that is income is determined by multiplying the payment ($200,000) by a fraction, the numerator of which is the gross profit ($1,000,000 – $300,000) and the denominator of which is the total contract price ($1,000,000). Thus, 70 percent of each payment, or $140,000, will be income. Moreover, Samantha must include the interest paid by Darin in gross income in the year it is received, assuming she is a cash method taxpayer.

129. Under §111, the refund of the state income taxes is a recovery that may lead to inclusion of amounts in Sara's gross income. The exclusionary amount—the amount of the total $2,000 recovery that can be excluded from gross income—is the amount of the original deduction that did not reduce tax in the prior year. Since the entire amount was used to reduce tax, the entire amount of the recovery is included in gross income.

130. This is probably a passive activity loss, as it is produced from the activity of rental real estate. Therefore, Bev may deduct it against passive income, and depending on her AGI, Bev may be able to claim $25,000 of it as a deduction (§469(i)). If she cannot deduct the loss, it will be suspended and will carry over to the future until she can use it against passive income or she sells the apartment building.

131. Harry's basis in the XYZ shares is his cost: $10,000. The gain or loss that he would recognize in each of the offered scenarios is:

(a) **$90,000.** Harry's realized gain is $140,000 ($150,000 – $10,000). But because Harry's father's loss of $50,000 was disallowed on the sale to his son, Harry's gain is reduced by the amount of the previously disallowed loss. His $140,000 gain is reduced to $90,000.

(b) **$-0-.** Harry's realized gain of $50,000 is reduced by the previously disallowed loss to eliminate the gain entirely.

(c) **$-0-.** Although Harry might be tempted to report a loss, he cannot do so under the rule of §267(d). A portion of Harry's father's disallowed loss is gone forever.

(d) **$-0-.** Harry has no realized gain or loss on the transaction. Again, Harry's father's disallowed loss is gone forever.

(e) **($5,000).** Harry has a realized loss of $5,000 and absent some other provision of the Code that would prevent recognition, such as the capital loss restrictions, he may recognize this loss.

Exam Tips on
TIMING OF INCOME AND EXPENSES

☛ Questions of timing arise only *after* you have determined that there is an item of income or an expense that may be deducted. Don't get ahead of yourself by jumping straight to timing issues.

    ☞ *Look for:* Is there an item of income, and if so, how much? Is there an expense or loss that is deductible, and if so, how much?

    ☞ *Analyze:* Then, and only then, ask *when* is the income includable in the taxpayer's gross income, and when is the expense or loss deductible?

☛ Know what taxpayers are trying to do: Defer income and accelerate deductions. (See Chapter 15.) So, what's the Commissioner trying to do? (Accelerate income and defer deductions, when taxpayers try to play games!)

    ☞ *Look for:* Taxpayers playing games by accelerating deductions and postponing income. Look for situations in which taxpayers have access to income, but don't report it, or haven't yet made an economic outlay of some sort but still claim deductions.

    ☞ *Analyze:* Statutory and regulatory response to those games.

☛ When the facts describe a transaction occurring over two or more years, timing issues are likely to be important. If a result seems "unfair" to a taxpayer because of multiple-year transactions, timing issues are likely to be a big issue.

    ☞ *Look for:* Income in one year, and deductions in another; profit in one year, and losses in another; recovery of previous deductions; repayment of amounts received in previous years.

    ☞ *Analyze:* Chronologically—address the first year first, then later years, in order. Explain how the years affect each other, if they do. Think about claim of right, tax benefit, and NOL issues.

☛ Some kinds of property transactions raise important timing issues.

    ☞ *Look for:* Sales of property with deferred payment, stock, or other property given to employees or others for services.

    ☞ *Analyze:* Over what period of time will income be recognized, or in what year will there be a sudden influx of income from property received in exchange for services?

☛ If a question describes the taxpayer's method of accounting, it may have important timing issues. Scan for the words "cash method" or "accrual method."

    ☞ *Look for:* When is an amount paid, or received? When is the obligation due? Is there uncertainty about the amount?

    ☞ *If in doubt:* Include an amount in income and defer the expense, particularly for accrual-method taxpayers.

☛ If a question describes the taxpayer's accounting year, it may have important timing issues. Scan for the words "calendar year" or "fiscal year."

☞ *Look for:* Transactions occurring at the end of one year and the beginning of the next.

☞ *Analyze:* Chronologically—analyze the first year first, then move to the next year. Explain how the two years affect each other, if they do.

 STATUTE SUMMARY CHARTS

Statute Summary—§453
Installment Method of Reporting Gain

Parsing Step	IRC §453
General Rule	Gain on installment sale is reported on the installment method (over period payments are received).
Definitions	**Installment sale:** at least one payment received after close of taxable year of sale. **Installment method:** payment × gross profit ratio = amount included in gross income
Special Rules and Exceptions	Election out optional. Not available to dealers in property.
Related Statutes	**§1001:** Calculation of realized gain or loss **§453B:** Disposition of installment obligation **§§483, 1272:** Imputed interest if none provided in contract
Typically implicated when	A taxpayer sells property for payments to be received over time.

Statute Summary—§83
Restricted Property

Parsing Step	IRC §83
General Rule	A taxpayer who receives property as compensation must include the excess of the value of the property over the amount paid for it in gross income in the first year in which the property is transferable or is not subject to a substantial risk of forfeiture.
Definitions	**Property:** typically stock, partnership interests, or options. **Substantial risk of forfeiture:** typically, lost if the employee leaves employment. **Transferable:** can be transferred to even one person that is not the transferor of the property.
Special Rules and Exceptions	Restrictions that never lapse. Employer's deduction §83(b) election.
Related Statutes	**§61:** Inclusion in gross income
Typically implicated when	Employer uses restricted property to create an incentive for an employee to remain in employment.

CHAPTER 12

CHARACTER OF INCOME AND LOSS

ChapterScope ▬▬▬▬▬▬▬▬▬▬▬▬▬▬▬▬▬▬▬▬▬▬▬▬▬▬▬

Previous chapters have addressed issues surrounding the calculation of taxable income, including the identification of items of gross income and the availability of deductions. Several chapters have focused specifically on the computation of gain and loss on the sale or other disposition of property. This chapter turns to the important question of the character of income and loss as capital or ordinary for these transactions.

- **Importance of capital/non-capital distinction:** Net capital gain is taxed at a preferential tax rate, while ordinary income is subject to higher rates. Capital losses are subject to special limitations, which make them less attractive to taxpayers. Capital losses incurred in any taxable year may be deducted only against capital gains for that year plus $3,000 of ordinary income, for individuals.

- **An approach to characterization problems:** If gain or loss is recognized from the sale or exchange of property, the character of the gain or loss must be considered. Figure 12A offers an approach to characterization questions.

- **Capital gain and loss:** Gain or loss from the sale or exchange of a capital asset produces capital gain or loss. A capital asset is defined in §1221 as any asset, regardless of its business use, except for specifically enumerated items. Capital gain and loss is divided into categories, depending on the type of asset generating the gain or loss.

- **Section 1231 assets:** Real property and depreciable property used in a trade or business are §1231 assets and are subject to special rules for characterization. While these assets are generally not considered capital assets under the definition in §1221, §1231 supplies a taxpayer-friendly netting rule that, with some exceptions, can characterize net gains as capital and net losses as ordinary. Figure 12D offers an approach to determining §1231 gain or loss.

- **Holding period:** The taxpayer's holding period for a capital asset determines whether gain or loss on sale will be long- or short-term capital gain or loss. Holding periods usually begin with the acquisition of an item, but in some transactions (such as gifts) the owner of the property will "tack" another holding period onto his or her own period of actual ownership of the property.

- **Calculation of net capital gain and net capital loss:** The calculation of net capital gain and net capital loss—and the tax rates applicable to net capital gain—requires a complex process from which the includable income or deductible loss is derived.

▬▬▬▬▬▬▬▬▬▬▬▬▬▬▬▬▬▬▬▬▬▬▬▬▬▬▬▬▬▬▬▬▬▬▬▬▬▬▬

I. WHERE ARE WE?

As we move to the computation of a taxpayer's actual tax, it is critical to identify the character of the individual's income or loss. This is because different kinds of income are subject to different tax rates, and some kinds of losses may be deducted only against certain kinds of income. The default category is ordinary income, but some income and loss may be capital in nature, raising these questions of tax rate and deductibility. This income and loss arises from the disposition of property, making the material in Chapter 9 critical as background to this discussion.

II. WHO CARES? THE CAPITAL/ORDINARY DISTINCTION

The distinction between capital and ordinary income and loss has implications for both gain and loss.

A. Income—Preferential tax rates for capital gain

The tax rates imposed by §1 of the Code on individuals on **ordinary income** range from 10% to 35%. However, the rates imposed on **net capital gain** range from 0% to 28%, creating the **tax preference** for **capital gains.** IRC §1(h). Taxpayers usually seek to characterize income as capital gain in order to take advantage of this preferential rate.

Example: Last year, Margie's taxable income was $200,000, and she was subject to the marginal tax rate of 33%. This year her tax situation is the same except that she sold some stock she held as an investment at a gain of $90,000. Because the stock is a capital asset in Margie's hands, its sale produces capital gain of $90,000. This will be taxed at a lower preferential rate rather than the 33% marginal rate applicable to Margie's other income.

B. Deductions—Limitations on deduction of capital loss

Section 1211 imposes significant restrictions on the deduction of **capital losses** for individuals. Individuals may deduct capital losses recognized in a taxable year only to the extent of their capital gains for that year, plus the lower of $3,000 or the excess of capital losses over capital gains. IRC §1211(b). Losses that cannot be claimed because of this limitation are called **net capital losses** and carry forward (but not back) indefinitely to the next succeeding taxable years. IRC §1212(b)(1). In each succeeding year, capital losses may be deducted to the extent of capital gain recognized in that year. In addition, in each succeeding year, the taxpayer is *deemed* to have a capital gain equal to the lesser of (1) $3,000 or the excess of losses over gains, whichever is lower; or (2) the taxpayer's adjusted taxable income. IRC §1212(b)(2)(A). "Adjusted taxable income" means taxable income increased by the lower of $3,000 or the excess of capital loss over capital gain plus the personal exemption. IRC §1212(b)(2)(B). This deemed capital gain allows the taxpayer to deduct capital losses carried forward to future years, to the extent of capital gains in those years plus $3,000 of ordinary income in each year.

Example: This year, Bill sold two blocks of stock. Sale of ABC stock produced a capital loss of $15,000. Sale of DEF stock produced capital gain of $5,000. He also had $50,000 of salary income. Bill will be able to claim $8,000 of his capital loss as a deduction in the year of sale, which is equal to the amount of capital gain in that year, plus $3,000 (the lower of $3,000 or the excess of capital loss over capital gain, $10,000). The remaining $7,000 of capital loss will carry forward to the next year, subject to these same limitations. If, for example, Bill's adjusted gross income (AGI) in that year were only $2,000, Bill would be allowed to take $2,000 of the loss in that year, and $5,000 of the loss would carry forward.

C. Taxpayer preference—Capital gain/ordinary loss

Given the favorable tax rates for capital gain and the restriction on the deductibility of capital losses, taxpayers typically prefer to characterize income as capital and loss as ordinary. The IRS typically responds that income is ordinary and losses are capital, and this conflict produces much of the judicial and administrative guidance in this area.

D. Policy

A number of rationales are offered for treating capital gain and loss differently than ordinary income and loss.

1. **Rationales for capital gains preference:** The following rationales are often offered for a capital gains preference. Each can be countered by questioning its empirical support, the related economic effects of the preference, and whether a more desirable route exists for addressing the particular problem.

   a. **General incentive:** This rationale suggests that reduction in the tax rate on investments will increase savings, investment, and economic prosperity.

   b. **Specific incentive:** This rationale suggests that a reduction in the tax rate for specific industries will increase investment in those industries.

   c. **Preventing "lock-in":** *Lock-in* occurs when a taxpayer holds rather than sells assets because of the tax that will be due on sale. Section 1014 increases the likelihood of lock-in, because holding an asset until death results in the heirs having a basis equal to the fair market value of the property on the date of death, thus avoiding income tax on the gain inherent in the asset. See Chapter 9(V)(C). A capital gains preference is said to reduce lock-in by reducing the tax associated with sale.

   d. **Bunching:** Capital gains often accrue over many years, yet the gain is recognized in a single year. This *bunching* effect can result in the taxation of gain at the highest marginal rate in the year of recognition, even though the incremental gains might have been taxed at lower rates had they been recognized in the years they accrued. The capital gains preference is said to mitigate the impact of the bunching effect by allowing a reduced rate in the year of sale.

   e. **Inflation:** The recognized gain upon sale of a capital asset may not represent real gain, but instead may represent inflationary gains. The capital gains preference is said to mitigate the impact of inflation by lowering the tax in the year of sale. (Indexing the basis of assets for inflation is a common proposal to reduce the effect of inflation.)

2. **Rationale for limitation on capital loss:** Allowing a taxpayer to deduct an unlimited amount of capital losses would arguably give the taxpayer too much discretion to adjust his or her taxable income by selling only those capital assets that have declined in value.

E. Definitions

Characterizing income or loss as capital or ordinary requires reference to a number of definitions. Ordinary income or loss is the default category, i.e., unless an item of income or loss qualifies as capital gain or capital loss, it will be ordinary in nature. Characterization issues involve the interaction of a number of definitional issues, which are summarized here and discussed in more detail later in this chapter.

1. **Ordinary income:** Ordinary income is any gain from the sale or exchange of property that is neither a capital asset nor §1231 property. IRC §64.

2. **Ordinary loss:** Ordinary loss is loss from the sale or exchange of property that is not a capital asset. IRC §65.

3. **Capital asset:** A capital asset is any property held by the taxpayer (whether or not connected with the taxpayer's trade or business) except for eight categories of property, of which five are generally important in the basic tax course. See IRC §1221.

4. **Capital gain net income:** Capital gain net income is the excess of gains from sales or exchanges of capital assets over losses from such assets. IRC §1222(9).

5. **Net capital gain:** Net capital gain is the excess of net long-term capital gain for the taxable year over net short-term capital loss for that year. IRC §1222(11).

6. **Net capital loss:** Net capital loss is the excess of losses from the sale or exchange of capital assets over the amount allowable as a deduction under §1211. IRC §1222(10).

7. **Section 1231 gain or loss:** Section 1231 gain or loss is net gain or loss from certain kinds of property used in the taxpayer's trade or business (§1231 assets). IRC §1231(a)(3).

III. AN APPROACH TO CHARACTERIZING GAIN OR LOSS AS CAPITAL OR ORDINARY

A. An approach to characterization problems

To determine the character of gain or loss, simply ask (and answer!) five straightforward questions. These are illustrated in Figure 12A—An Approach to Characterization Problems, and the references below to box numbers refer to that chart.

Figure 12A
An Approach to Characterization Problems

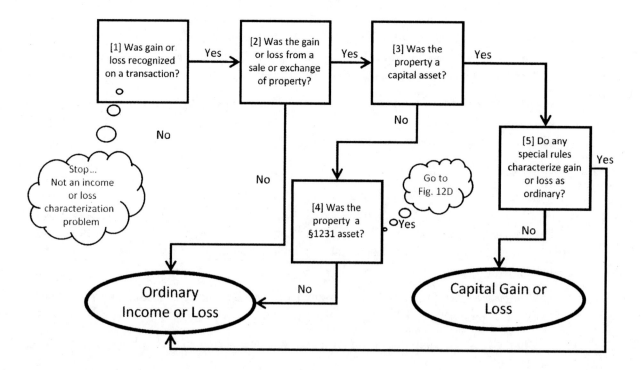

1. **Question 1 (Box [1])— Did the taxpayer experience a realization event from which income/gain or loss was recognized?** If the answer to that question is no, the problem is not one of characterizing gain or loss as capital or ordinary and one stops there. But if the answer is yes, there is recognized income or loss, we go on to the next question.

2. **Question 2 (Box [2])— Did the realization event constitute an actual or deemed sale or exchange of property?** If there is no sale or exchange of property, recognized gain or loss will be ordinary in nature. But if such a sale or exchange has occurred, we move on to the next question.

3. **Question 3 (Box [3])— Was the property sold or exchanged a capital asset?** The sale or exchange of noncapital assets usually generates ordinary gain or loss. However, it is important to distinguish between gains and losses at this step, because some gains that would otherwise be ordinary may be recast as capital.

4. **Question 4 (Box [4])— Was the property disposed of a §1231 asset?** Section 1231 assets are a specific kind of asset—generally, real estate and equipment used in a trade or business. If no, the gain or loss will be ordinary. But if the asset was a §1231 asset, gains can be characterized as capital and losses as ordinary—a taxpayer-friendly result. (Later in this chapter, you will see Figure 12D, which takes you through the §1231 analysis.)

5. **Question 5 (Box [5])— Do any special recharacterization rules recast capital gain or loss as ordinary?** If they do, the result will be ordinary income or loss. But if no recharacterization rules apply, the gain or loss is capital in nature.

B. Recognized gain and loss

For a taxpayer to have capital gain or loss, there must be a realization event (a sale or other disposition of property), and gains or losses from that sale must be recognized. This implicates §1001(a), which measures the realized gain or loss from the "sale or other disposition of property," and §1001(c), which requires recognition of gains or losses—unless otherwise provided in the Code. See Chapter 9(II). Moreover, the various provisions of the Code regulating the recognition of gain or loss, including the various nonrecognition provisions and §165(c), must be considered in determining whether realized gain is recognized. (See generally Chapter 10.)

Example—Gain: Janet owns Blackacre, a parcel of raw land, which she has held for investment for many years. She exchanges Blackacre for Whiteacre in a qualifying §1031 exchange in which she realizes $50,000 of gain but recognizes none of the gain. This realized gain is not capital in nature, because it does not result from a transaction in which gains are recognized. (Another way to express this is that the character of the gain is not relevant, because the gain is not recognized.)

Example—Loss: Chen owns a principal residence with a basis of $100,000 and a fair market value of $90,000. He sells it for $90,000, realizing a $10,000 loss. However, §165(c) prohibits the deduction of this loss, and therefore this loss is not a capital loss. (Another way to express this is that the character of Chen's realized loss is not relevant because the gain is not recognized.)

C. Sale or exchange requirement

Section 1222 requires that there be a "sale or exchange of a capital asset" in order to generate capital gain or loss. The sale or exchange requirement is different from, and independent of, the realization requirement implicit in §1001 (discussed above). The sale or exchange requirement is arguably a more stringent standard than the "sale or other disposition" language in §1001, and therefore a transaction might qualify as a sale or other disposition but fail to qualify as a sale or exchange.

1. **Judicial definition of sale or exchange:** The courts typically construe the term "sale or exchange" to have its ordinary meaning, requiring "a giving, a receipt, and a causal connection between the two." *Yarbro v. Commissioner*, 737 F.2d 479 (5th Cir. 1984).

   a. **Involuntary sales or exchanges—*Helvering v. Hammel*, 311 U.S. 504 (1941):** Even an involuntary or forced sale, as in the case of foreclosure, can qualify as a sale or exchange for purposes of measuring capital gain or loss.

   b. **Transfer to legatee—satisfaction of obligation:** In *Kenan v. Commissioner*, 114 F.2d 217 (2d Cir. 1940), a legatee was entitled to a payment of $5,000,000 in value from a trust established by a will. The trustees paid the legatee partly in cash and partly in appreciated stock. The court determined that the trustee's satisfaction of the legatee's pecuniary claim with the securities constituted a sale or exchange of those securities resulting in capital gain to the trust. This transaction is best viewed for tax purposes as a deemed sale of the securities by the trustees for cash, followed by a deemed distribution of cash to the legatee.

   c. **Contract rights and judgments:** In *Galvin Hudson*, 20 T.C. 734 (1953), *aff'd sub nom. Ogilvie v. Commissioner*, 216 F.2d 748 (6th Cir. 1954), the taxpayer purchased a judgment against a debtor. When the debtor settled the judgment by paying the taxpayer, the taxpayer claimed that he had capital gain to the extent that the amount received exceeded his basis (cost) in the claim. The court concluded that there was no sale or exchange when the taxpayer received payment, stating, "the judgment was extinguished without the transfer of any property or property right to the judgment debtor." Thus, the taxpayer had ordinary income in the amount of the receipt in excess of his investment in the judgment. The ***extinguishment doctrine*** continues to generate controversy. If a payment extinguishes a right altogether, there will be no sale or exchange. If a property right continues to exist, however, there may be a sale or exchange. *Gladden v. Commissioner*, 112 T.C. 209, 226 n.3 (1999) (water rights did not vanish where they reverted to the government; they survived, and "were reallocated to other users"), *rev'd on other grounds and remanded*, 262 F.3d 851 (9th Cir. 2001).

   d. **Connection to other transactions—*Arrowsmith v. Commissioner*, 344 U.S. 6 (1952):** The taxpayers liquidated their corporation and reported capital gain on the liquidating distributions. In a later year, the corporation was sued, and the taxpayers were held liable as transferees, i.e., recipients of the corporate property. Although there was clearly no sale or exchange in the later year when the taxpayers paid to settle the claim, the Supreme Court held that the transaction was so closely connected to the prior liquidation that it should have the same character—a capital loss instead of an ordinary loss. The scope of *Arrowsmith* is, and always has been, uncertain.

2. **Deemed sales by statute:** Some transactions would not qualify as sales or exchanges under judicial interpretations of the term, but Congress has deemed them to be sales or exchanges by statute. See Figure 12B—Statutory Sales or Exchanges.

Figure 12B
Statutory Sales or Exchanges

Code Section	Topic	What Event Is the Deemed Sale?	Here's an Example
165(g)	Worthless securities	When a security becomes worthless, it is deemed sold for $0.	Steve's 50 shares of ABC stock become worthless. He has a basis of $400 in them. He is deemed to have sold the stock for $0, realizing a loss of $400.
165(h)(2)(B)	Personal casualty losses and gains	If personal casualty gains exceed similar losses, the gains and losses are deemed to be from the sale of capital assets.	Pat has a casualty gain from a theft of insured property of $1,000 and a casualty loss from a flood of $600. The net $400 casualty gain would be capital.
166(a)	Bad debts	Partial or entire worthlessness of a bad debt is treated as a sale of the debt for its value.	Jody lends Bob $10,000. The debt becomes worthless. Jody is deemed to have sold the debt for its value, $0, realizing a loss of $10,000.
1234A	Certain terminations	Cancellation, lapse, expiration, or termination of certain property that is a capital asset to the taxpayer is treated as sale or exchange.	Brenda has the right to acquire 1,000 Euros for a stated price. This option expires, and she is treated as selling the option for $0.
1235	Patents	Patents transfer is treated as sale or exchange, even if payments depend on the productivity of an underlying asset.	Tara transfers her patent for a better mousetrap to Steve in exchange for $1,000 plus 2% of sales in perpetuity. This is a sale of the patent.
1241	Lease cancellation	A lessee who receives money for cancellation of lease or by a distributor for cancellation of agreement is treated as selling the lease or agreement.	Lane is leasing office space from Gar. Gar pays Lane $10,000 to cancel his lease. Lane has sold the lease for $10,000.
1253	Franchises, trademarks, trade names	A transfer of these items without retention of a significant interest is a sale.	Elyse transfers her trade name, Uncorked Wine Shop, to Emily for $1,000 with no continuing interest. Elyse has sold the trade name for $1,000.
1271	Debt instruments	Retirement of the debt instrument is a sale.	Prudence holds a note issued by ABC Co. ABC pays off the note. This will be treated as Prudence's sale of the note for the amount received.

D. Capital asset requirement

In order for capital gain or loss to be generated, the sale or exchange must be of a capital asset. Section 1221 defines a capital asset as "property held by the taxpayer (whether or not in connection with his trade or business)" except for eight enumerated categories of property, of which only five are usually important in the basic tax course. Thus, an item of property is a capital asset *unless* it falls within any of the five categories listed in (III)(D)(2), below.

1. **Property versus income:** To generate capital gain or loss, a transaction must involve a sale or exchange of property. While property is not usually difficult to identify, some transactions, while crafted as sales or exchanges of property, are actually only prepayments of income from that property. These kinds of payments do not constitute sales or exchanges of property. To distinguish property from prepayments of income, courts look to factors such as whether there has been substantial appreciation in the value of the so-called asset over time and whether there is an investment risk in holding such an asset.

   a. **Lease cancellation—*Hort v. Commissioner,* 313 U.S. 28 (1941):** The taxpayer was the lessor of property. He and the lessee agreed to cancel the lease in exchange for a payment of $140,000 from the lessee to the lessor. The taxpayer claimed a loss on the transaction, asserting that the cancellation payment was less than the value of the lease canceled. The IRS disagreed and included the entire $140,000 payment in the taxpayer's gross income as ordinary income. The Court agreed with the Commissioner, on the theory that the payment was merely a prepayment of rent, which is includable in gross income under §61(a)(5), regardless of the fact that the lease itself constituted a property interest. (Cf. §1241, in Figure 12B; lessees who receive a payment in cancellation of the lease are considered to have sold the lease and thus potentially receive capital gain treatment.)

   b. **Sale of life estate:** In *McAllister v. Commissioner,* 157 F.2d 235 (2d Cir. 1946), *cert. denied,* 330 U.S. 826 (1947), the taxpayer relinquished her life estate in a trust to the remainderman and agreed to the termination of the trust in exchange for a lump-sum cash payment. She reported a capital loss equal to the difference between the cash she received and the basis of her life estate, and the Commissioner disagreed, asserting that the entire payment was ordinary income to her under the principle of *Hort.* The court concluded that she had sold a property interest—her entire interest in the trust—citing *Blair v. Commissioner* for the principle that the gift of an income interest in the trust constitutes a valid transfer if it is not a "carved-out interest." See discussion of *Blair* in Chapter 14(III)(E). Thus, she realized a capital loss on the transfer.

   c. **Substitution of right to receive ordinary income periodically:**

      i. *Commissioner v. P.G. Lake, Inc.,* **356 U.S. 260 (1958):** A corporation owning a working interest in commercial oil and gas leases assigned to its president certain oil rights in exchange for the president's cancellation of a debt owed to him by the corporation. The debt was $600,000, and the right assigned was an oil payment right payable out of 25% of the oil from the corporation's working interest in two oil leases. The corporation reported the transaction as producing capital gain, and the Commissioner disagreed, asserting that the entire $600,000 should be included in the corporation's gross income as ordinary income. As in *Hort* (discussed above), the court viewed the transaction as the prepayment of income from the working interest, which should be taxable as ordinary income to the recipient.

      ii. **Lottery proceeds:** Lottery winners—unhappy with the long-term payout of their winnings—often assign their rights to a third party in exchange for a lump sum. While taxpayers have repeatedly tried to characterize their gain as capital, the IRS and the courts have resisted these efforts, on the theory that the proceeds are simply a substitution for their right to receive what would otherwise be ordinary income—the lottery winnings. See, e.g., *United States v. Maginnis,* 356 F.3d 1179 (9th Cir. 2004).

2. **Excluded categories of property:** Section 1221(a) excludes from the definition of capital asset properties in eight enumerated categories, of which five will be discussed here. A taxpayer generally will try to characterize property as *outside* these categories if its sale has generated a loss (in order to claim an ordinary loss), and property as *within* these categories if its sale has generated a gain (in order to claim capital gain). The challenge offered by the specific categories of §1221(a) is to determine whether a property fits within any one of them.

a. **Inventory/stock in trade:** Section 1221(a)(1) excludes from the definition of a capital asset stock in trade, inventory, and property held by the taxpayer for sale to customers in the ordinary course of business. These three types of property are referred to collectively as *inventory,* although there may be some arcane differences among the three. The rationale for excluding these types of property from the definition of a capital asset is that sales of such assets should generate operating business income or loss.

i. **Definition—*Malat v. Riddell,* 383 U.S. 569 (1966):** The taxpayer was a joint venturer in the purchase of a parcel of land, which was later subdivided and sold. The issue was whether the parcels sold were "property held . . . primarily for sale to customers 'in the ordinary course of his trade or business.'" Using the plain meaning rule of statutory construction, the Court defined "primarily" as "of first importance" or "principal," rather than using the IRS's proffered definition of "substantial." The Court remanded for reconsideration using this definition.

ii. **Investors, traders, and dealers:** In *Van Suetendael v. Commissioner,* 3 T.C.M. 987 (1944), *aff'd,* 152 F.2d 654 (2d Cir. 1945), the taxpayer's primary activity was the purchase and sale of stocks and other securities. The taxpayer reported the gains and losses as ordinary, on the theory that the assets were noncapital assets under §1221(a)(1). When the Commissioner asserted that the assets were capital, the taxpayer argued that he was a dealer in securities, and thus the securities were noncapital assets.

(a) **Issue:** Were the securities capital assets?

(b) **Result and rationale:** The securities were capital assets. The court viewed the issue as the nature of the assets themselves, as capital or noncapital, rather than the status of the taxpayer as a dealer. The nature of the securities depended on whether the taxpayer held them primarily for sale to customers in the ordinary course of business. Several facts suggested that the taxpayer did not hold the securities in this manner:

- He did not purchase them at wholesale;

- He purchased small quantities;

- His portfolio was diversified; and

- He resold most of the securities to or through the same broker from whom he acquired them.

iii. **Real estate factual inquiry—case-by-case:** In *Biedenharn Realty Co., Inc. v. United States,* 526 F.2d 409 (5th Cir.), *cert. denied,* 429 U.S. 819 (1976), the taxpayer purchased property in 1923 and over the years subdivided and sold parcels.

(a) Issue: Were the parcels capital or noncapital assets, i.e., were the lots property held by the taxpayer primarily for sale to customers in the ordinary course of its trade or business?

(b) Result and rationale: The lots were inventory (noncapital assets). The determination of this issue depended on the court's analysis of the seven factors enunciated in *United States v. Winthrop*, 417 F.2d 905 (5th Cir. 1969), as follows:

- *Number, extent, and continuity of sales:* The court considered this the most important factor, concluding that the number and ongoing activity relating to sales was sufficiently high to suggest that the property was inventory.

- *Extent of subdividing, developing, and advertising:* The taxpayer "vigorously improved" its subdivisions, as opposed to merely holding the property for appreciation; this factor supported inventory treatment.

- *Taxpayer's efforts to sell:* While the taxpayer did not engage in traditional advertising, the court found this was not necessary to noncapital treatment when business was brisk, and the development activity itself attracted customers.

- *Character and degree of supervision and control over agents:* While use of independent agents may at times shield a taxpayer from the activities of those agents, the court suggested that this applies only when the agents have complete discretion over sales, which these agents did not have. In addition, the taxpayer itself made some sales without agents. Together, these factors supported an inventory classification.

- *Time and effort habitually devoted to sales:* The taxpayer argued that its business manager devoted only 10% of his time to real estate dealings, and most of that time was for management of rental properties. The court discounted this factor, on the theory that the time devoted to sales will not be determinative when business is brisk.

- *Use of business office:* The taxpayer shared a business office and employed the usual accoutrements of business, suggesting that it held the property as inventory.

- *Nature and purpose of acquisition:* The Commissioner argued that the taxpayer's intent upon acquisition should be irrelevant, and the sole focus should be the activity at the time of sale. The court rejected this approach, preserving the possibility that prior investment intent will continue when external factors beyond the control of the taxpayer force sale of the property in circumstances that would otherwise suggest noncapital treatment. This did not save Biedenharn Realty Company, however, and the court concluded that the lots sold were noncapital assets (inventory) generating ordinary income.

iv. **Section 1237—Safe harbor:** Section 1237 provides a safe harbor for taxpayers other than C corporations that improve and sell parcels of land. If the taxpayer meets certain requirements relating to these assets, the taxpayer will be able to be certain of its claim to capital gain treatment on sale.

b. **Real and depreciable property:** Section 1221(a)(2) excludes from the definition of a capital asset real property used in a trade or business, or property used in a trade or business that is subject to depreciation under §167. This is called *Section 1231 property.*

c. **Creative works:** Section 1221(a)(3) excludes from the definition of a capital asset items such as copyrights, compositions, letters, or memoranda by a taxpayer who created them, hired others to create them, or received them in a transaction in which gain or loss was not recognized in whole or in part.

Example: Dave writes a book about federal court litigation. He holds the copyright. Big Publisher, Inc., wishes to acquire all rights to the book, and pays him $10,000 for the copyright. Because Dave created the work, the asset is not a capital asset in his hands and its sale generates ordinary income.

  i. **Exception—musical works:** A taxpayer who creates a musical work may elect to treat a musical composition or copyright in musical works as a capital asset. IRC §1221(b)(3).

  ii. **Making the election:** The taxpayer must make a separate election for each work, and must make the election before the due date of the return for the year of the sale of the property. Temp. Reg. §1.1221-3T(b).

d. **Accounts/notes receivable:** Section 1221(a)(4) excludes from the definition of a capital asset any accounts or notes receivable from the sale of inventory or stock in trade. In a sense, accounts or notes receivable of this kind are simply a transformation of inventory or stock in trade. Because sales of inventory or stock in trade generate ordinary income or loss, so too should dispositions of accounts or notes receivable from the sale of inventory.

Example: Connie's Crafts has accounts receivable of $40,000 for sales of silk flowers. As a cash method taxpayer, Connie's has a zero basis in the receivables. Connie's sells the accounts receivable to Friendly Bank for $35,000. This sale generates ordinary income rather than capital gain because the accounts receivable are not a capital asset.

e. **Supplies used in a business:** Section 1221(a)(8) excludes from the definition of a capital asset supplies customarily consumed by a taxpayer in his or her trade or business.

3. **"Related to" the trade or business—*Corn Products* and *Arkansas Best*:** Because sales of inventory and accounts receivable generate ordinary income and loss, the question arises whether other types of income or loss that are closely connected with the taxpayer's trade or business should also generate ordinary income or loss. In *Corn Products* (1955), the U.S. Supreme Court arguably allowed property closely connected with a trade or business to be considered a noncapital asset. In *Arkansas Best* (1988), the Court held that the relationship between the taxpayer's business and the asset is irrelevant and interpreted *Corn Products* very narrowly to mean that inventory may include "inventory substitutes."

a. *Corn Products Refining Co. v. Commissioner,* **350 U.S. 46 (1955),** *rehearing denied,* **350 U.S. 943 (1956):** The taxpayer was in the business of manufacturing products from grain corn. To ensure a long-term supply of corn at a favorable price, Corn Products purchased futures contracts in corn. A futures contract is an agreement to buy or sell a specific amount of a commodity at a stated price on a specific date in the future. Thus, when it entered into a futures contract, it agreed to purchase corn at a specific price. If the corn prices in the general market were favorable, Corn Products sold these futures contracts and purchased grain as needed. In some years it realized a profit on the sale of the futures contracts; in others, it realized a loss. Because Corn Products Co. had net gains during the years from these contracts, it claimed that the gains and losses on the sales of the futures contracts were capital rather than ordinary, arguing that because the contracts were separate from its business of manufacturing corn products.

    i.   **Issue:** Were the futures contracts capital assets, so that their sale generated capital gain or loss?

    ii.   **Result and rationale:** The futures contracts were noncapital assets, which generated ordinary income or loss upon disposition. According to the Court, they were an integral part of the profits and losses generated by the business, which Congress intended to be taxed as ordinary income or loss. The Court construed the exceptions to capital asset status broadly to effectuate its view of congressional purpose: to apply the preferential capital gains rate only to transactions that are not usual in the course of business.

  b. *Arkansas Best Corp. v. Commissioner*, **485 U.S. 212 (1988):** Relying on *Corn Products*, many taxpayers successfully classified items as "connected with" their trade or business (to produce ordinary loss) or "not connected with" their trade or business (to produce capital gain). Arkansas Best wanted to be one of these taxpayers. It purchased stock in a Dallas bank, which it ultimately sold at a loss. Some of the stock was purchased as an investment, but the taxpayer also purchased stock when the bank was having financial difficulties. The taxpayer asserted that the reason for these purchases was to protect its business reputation. The taxpayer argued that the latter block of stock was a noncapital asset, and thus the loss was ordinary because it was connected with its trade or business. The Commissioner asserted that all of the stock was a capital asset, generating a capital loss on sale.

    i.   **Issue:** Was the stock purchased while the bank was in financial difficulty a capital asset?

    ii.   **Result and rationale:** The stock was a capital asset. The Court rejected the interpretation of *Corn Products* as treating as noncapital any asset connected with a taxpayer's business, on the grounds that the specific language of §1221 ("whether or not connected with his trade or business") precludes any such inquiry. It thus rejected any inquiry into the taxpayer's motive in acquiring the stock. The Court viewed *Corn Products* as merely interpreting §1221(a)(1)'s inventory exception to capital asset treatment: the futures contracts were substitutes for the raw material from which inventory was created and therefore were a type of inventory. Since in *Arkansas Best* the stock was not in any sense an inventory substitute, it was a capital asset generating capital loss on sale.

E. Special recharacterization provisions—Related parties, recapture, and small business stock

Recognized gain or loss on the sale or exchange of a capital asset will usually be capital. However, specific Code provisions may in certain cases recharacterize all or a portion of this gain or loss as ordinary. This section discusses three of these provisions: sales or exchanges between related parties; recapture; and losses on the sale of small business stock.

1. Sales or exchanges between related parties: Section 1239 provides that a sale or exchange of property between related parties will generate ordinary income if the property, in the hands of the transferee, is subject to depreciation.

Example: Arthur owned Blackacre, an office building that he depreciated using the straight-line method. He sold it to his daughter, Beatrice, for $350,000, which was allocable $300,000 to the building and $50,000 to the land. Arthur had an adjusted basis of $100,000 in the building and $20,000 in the land underlying the building. Because Arthur and Beatrice are related parties, Arthur's $200,000 gain on the sale of the building will be characterized as ordinary income because the building is depreciable in Beatrice's hands. The sale of the land will generate capital gain because land is not depreciable.

2. **Recapture—General approach:** The recapture provisions potentially recharacterize gain on the sale of property as ordinary rather than capital as a means of "recapturing" (i.e., paying back) the benefit the taxpayer enjoyed when he or she claimed depreciation deductions with respect to the property, which reduces his or her ordinary income.

   a. **Section 1245—Personal property**

      i. **General rule:** Section 1245(a) provides that a taxpayer's gain on the disposition of "§1245 property" will be treated as ordinary income to the extent of the amount by which the lower of (1) the taxpayer's *recomputed basis* or (2) the amount realized (for sales) or fair market value (for transactions other than sales), exceeds the taxpayer's adjusted basis in the property. To put it more simply, the lesser of the realized gain or the depreciation claimed will be treated as ordinary income, and additional gain (if any) will be capital in nature.

      ii. **Definitional issues:** The key to understanding §1245 is grasping its definitions and applying them to the general rule.

        (a) **Section 1245 property:** Section 1245 property is personal property that is used in a taxpayer's trade or business and certain other property (but not buildings or structural components of buildings). IRC §1245(a)(3).

        (b) **Recomputed basis:** The *recomputed basis* of property is its adjusted basis plus all the depreciation attributable to the property taken by the taxpayer. IRC §1245(a)(2). For this purpose, depreciation includes all cost recovery deductions, including §179 deductions and any bonus depreciation. IRC §1245(a)(2)(C).

        (c) **Technique for calculating recapture:** For a three-step method for calculating the recapture, using the technical terms of the statute, see Figure 12C—Calculation of §1245 Ordinary Income (Recapture).

Figure 12C
Calculation of §1245 Ordinary Income (Recapture)

Step One: Is the transaction a sale? If so, compute the amount realized.
If not, determine the fair market value of the property at issue.

Step Two: Determine the "recomputed basis," which is equal to the adjusted basis of the property transferred plus the cumulative depreciation claimed on the property.

Step Three: Take the lower of the amount in Step One or Step Two, and subtract from it the taxpayer's adjusted basis in the property.

The result: The amount of recapture (ordinary income) on the transaction.

Example: Keith purchased a truck for $35,000 for business use. He added on $5,000 of after-market accessories that were needed for use in his business. He claimed $25,000 of the cost of the truck as a §179 expense in the year he purchased it, and later claimed $2,400 of MACRS deductions with respect to the truck. Keith then sold the truck for $15,000. His adjusted basis was $12,600 in the truck at the time of sale.

Step One: Is this a sale? Yes. The amount realized is $15,000.

Step Two: Determine the recomputed basis, which is equal to the adjusted basis of the property transferred plus the accumulated depreciation claimed. This is $40,000 (his adjusted basis of $12,600 plus accumulated depreciation (§179 deduction of $25,000 plus $2,400 of MACRS deductions)).

Step Three: Take the lower of the amount computed in Step One ($15,000) or Step Two ($40,000) and subtract Keith's adjusted basis in the truck ($12,600) from the lower of the two ($15,000). All of Keith's $2,400 gain on the sale will be treated as ordinary income.

Example: Assume the same facts as in the previous example, except that Keith sold the truck for $50,000. In that case, Keith's realized gain would be $37,400, of which the recapture amount (the ordinary income) would be $27,400 and the capital gain would be $10,000.

    iii. **Special rules and exceptions:** Recapture does not apply in certain transactions that are otherwise tax-free, including transfers by gift and at death. IRC §1245(b)(1), (2). For certain transactions that are generally tax-free to the transferors, the recapture amount is limited to the amount of gain recognized on the transfer. IRC §1245(b)(3). A special rule that applies to like-kind exchanges and involuntary conversions requires recapture in the amount of the gain recognized plus the fair market value of any non-§1245 property received that is not boot. See IRC §1245(b)(4).

    iv. **Related material:** Section 1245 is intimately connected with the notion of capital recovery through depreciation deductions. Depreciation is discussed in Chapter 7(IV).

  b. **Section 1250—Real property:** Section 1250 requires that "additional depreciation" taken with respect to *§1250 property* be cast as ordinary income upon the sale of that property. IRC §1250(a)(1). Additional depreciation is the depreciation claimed with respect to an item of property in excess of the amount that would have been allowable had the taxpayer used the straight-line method of depreciation. IRC §1250(a)(2). Thus, §1250 recaptures only the accelerated portion of depreciation. Section 1250 was at one time of more importance than it is today. Because all buildings and their structural components placed in service after 1986 are required to be depreciated using the straight-line method, there is generally no additional depreciation to be recaptured on buildings placed in service after 1986. Disposition of a building placed in service prior to 1987 will generate §1250 recapture, but for the most part, §1250 is not of major importance today.

3. **Small business stock—§1244:** As a special incentive to investors in small businesses, §1244 allows a taxpayer to treat losses on the sale or worthlessness of stock in certain small business corporations as ordinary rather than capital losses.

a. **Only individuals and partnerships:** Only individuals and partnerships may take advantage of this provision, and only if they are the original holders of the stock. IRC §1244(a).

b. **Dollar limitations:** The maximum amount of the loss that can be treated as ordinary is $50,000 for a single taxpayer or $100,000 for a married couple filing a joint return. IRC §1244(b).

c. **Qualifying business stock:** The corporation issuing the stock must be a *small business corporation*. It must issue the stock in exchange for money or other property (not services) and must have derived more than 50% of its income from active business sources within the five-year period ending on the date of the loss. IRC §1244(c)(1). A small business corporation is one whose capital does not exceed $1,000,000. IRC §1244(c)(3). Qualifying stock is often referred to as **§1244 stock**.

IV. SECTION 1231—REAL AND DEPRECIABLE PROPERTY USED IN A TRADE OR BUSINESS

As mentioned in the last section, §1221(a)(2) excludes from the definition of a capital asset real and depreciable property used in a taxpayer's trade or business. Alone, this would suggest that the disposition of such assets generates ordinary income or loss. However, §1231 offers the taxpayer-friendly rule that, for this kind of property, net gains are generally capital, and net losses are generally ordinary. Getting there, however, is a complicated process.

A. Policy

The taxpayer-friendly approach of §1231 was enacted to encourage taxpayers to sell or exchange their business properties during World War II to make these properties available for the war effort.

B. A systematic approach—§1231 gains and losses

Figure 12D—Section 1231 Gains and Losses—illustrates an approach to analyzing §1231. Again, five questions can assess the impact of §1231 on the character of gain or loss. The details of these rules are discussed later in this section.

1. **Question 1—Box [1]:** Did the taxpayer recognize any gain or loss on the disposition of §1231 property? Remember—for character to be relevant at all, there must be recognized (not just realized) gain or loss. Section 1231 only applies to this special kind of property (discussed in Section (IV)(C) of this chapter). If the property is not §1231 property, return to Figure 12A.

2. **Questions 2–3—Boxes [2] and [3]:** Did the taxpayer have any casualties relating to §1231 property? If the taxpayer had no casualty gains or losses from §1231 property, go to Question 4 –Box [4]. If the taxpayer did have casualties on §1231 property, net the gains and losses [Box 3]. If there is a net loss from these casualties, the net loss will be ordinary. If there is a net gain, then all of the casualty gains and losses on §1231 property are added together to be netted in the next step.

3. **Question 4—Box [4]:** Net all §1231 gains and losses to produce either net §1231 gain or net §1231 loss. If there is a net §1231 loss, that loss is ordinary. If there is a net §1231 gain, go to the next step.

Figure 12D
Section 1231 Gains and Losses

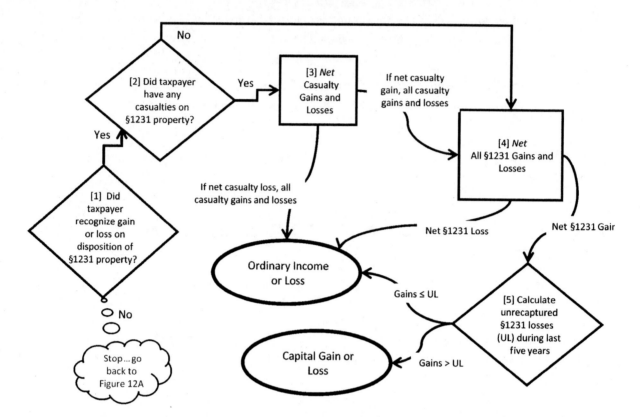

4. **Question 5—Box [5]:** Does the taxpayer have any unrecaptured net §1231 losses during the past five years? If so, any net §1231 gain will be recast as ordinary to the extent of those losses. If not, or to the extent that the net gain exceeds the unrecaptured loss, the §1231 gain will be capital gain.

C. **Statutory analysis—§1231**

1. **General rule:** The general rule of §1231 is deceptively simple to state: If §1231 gains exceed §1231 losses for the year, all §1231 gains and losses are treated as capital. If §1231 losses exceed §1231 gains for the year, all §1231 gains and losses are treated as ordinary.

2. **Definitional issues:** The key to applying §1231 is understanding the definition of §1231 gains and losses and applying this understanding to the process described in Figure 12D.

   a. **The disposition of §1231 property generates §1231 gains and losses:** There are two types of §1231 gains and losses.

      i. **Sales of business property:** The most common is recognized gain and loss that arises from the sale or exchange of real or depreciable property used in the taxpayer's trade or business. IRC §1231(a)(3).

      ii. **Conversions:** Section 1231 gain or loss also includes gain or loss recognized on the involuntary conversion (including condemnation) of property that was used in the taxpayer's trade or business or of any capital asset held for more than one year and held in connection with the taxpayer's trade or business. IRC §1231(a)(3).

b. Property used in the trade or business: Property used in the trade or business of the taxpayer means property that the taxpayer actually uses in the business, which is held for more than one year and which is either real property or property subject to depreciation, such as equipment. IRC §1231(b)(1). It does not include inventory. A home rented out in the trade or business of rentals would be a §1231 asset.

Example: Tajuan owns a restaurant. His §1231 assets include the building in which the restaurant is located, all of the kitchen equipment, the dining room furnishings and the vans his staff uses for catering events. Section 1231 assets do not include his beloved NBA basketball signed by his favorite team that he keeps in his office or the stocks and bonds he keeps for a rainy day.

c. Two-step netting process: *Netting* means subtracting losses from gains, and ending up with the net result, which is either a gain or a loss.

    i. First netting—casualty and theft gains and losses: If a taxpayer's recognized loss from the casualties or theft of §1231 property recognized gains from such events, the gain and the loss are excluded from the general process of netting §1231 gains and losses. IRC §1231(a)(4)(C); see Box [3] in Figure 12D. Instead, the character of these losses is determined under §1222 and related statutes, which will result in the taxpayer having an ordinary loss. Reg. §1.1231-1(e)(3). If such gains exceed losses, both gains and losses are included in the general netting process. IRC §1231(a)(4)(C). You will hear people refer to this as the "preliminary hotchpot." (In case you are wondering, "hotchpot" is a kind of pudding or broth made from many ingredients, and in law the term refers to a group of different properties.)

    ii. Netting of §1231 gains and losses: All §1231 gains and losses are added up, and losses are subtracted from gains. The net result is either a net §1231 gain or a net §1231 loss. Your will hear people refer to this as the "main hotchpot."

    Example: Warren experiences the following events with respect to properties A, B, C, and D, all of which are depreciable properties used in his trade or business. Property A is destroyed by fire, and Warren recognizes a $100,000 loss on this property. Property B is stolen, and Warren recognizes a $30,000 gain when he collects the insurance proceeds. He sells properties C and D, recognizing a $150,000 gain and $60,000 loss, respectively. In determining the character of these gains and losses, Warren will first net the gains and losses on the involuntary conversions of properties A and B. His recognized losses from such dispositions exceed gains. The character of the loss and gain on properties A and B will be determined under §1222. Since §1222 excludes from the definition of a capital asset depreciable property used in a trade or business, these assets are noncapital and produce ordinary gain of $30,000 and ordinary loss of $100,000. Warren will be able to deduct the loss attributable to property A under §165(g) and this will offset the ordinary income from property B. Properties A and B are excluded from the "main" netting process that will apply to properties C and D. Netting gains and losses from these two properties will produce a net §1231 gain of $90,000, which will be treated as capital, assuming Warren has no unrecaptured losses (see below).

3. Special rules and exceptions

a. **Unrecaptured losses:** If in any year, §1231 gains exceed §1231 losses, the general rule will characterize all §1231 gains and losses for that year as capital. However, the special loss recapture rule may limit this favorable characterization. If the taxpayer has had, within the previous five years, a §1231 loss that was characterized as ordinary, the current year's gain must be characterized as ordinary to the extent of that previous loss. IRC §1231(c)(1). This is known as an *unrecaptured loss,* which only needs to be recaptured once. *Id.*

Example: In Year 1, Sandy opened her sandwich shop business. In that year, Sandy had a net §1231 loss of $5,000, and she reported a $5,000 ordinary loss. In Year 2, she had §1231 gains in excess of §1231 losses in the amount of $7,000. This gain would be capital under the general rule of §1231, except that Sandy is required to recapture the previous loss, so that she must treat $5,000 of her Year 2 §1231 gain as ordinary, and the remaining $2,000 is capital under the general rule of §1231. If in Year 3 Sandy has a net §1231 gain of $3,000, all of this will be capital because she has already recaptured the previous year's loss.

b. **Effect of §1211:** As discussed in Section (II)(B) of this chapter, §1211 limits the deductibility of capital losses to the amount of capital gain for the year and, for individuals, $3,000 of ordinary income. However, in determining whether §1231 gains exceed §1231 losses, the §1211 limitation is ignored.

4. Related material:
Section 1231 is intimately related to §1221. The category of property removed from the definition of capital asset by §1221(a)(2) is the category specifically addressed by §1231. Thus, if one concludes that an item is not a capital asset because of §1221(a)(2), one must consider how §1231 characterizes the gain or loss upon the sale of the asset. Also, the treatment of §1231 gains and losses of individuals must be considered in connection with the different categories of capital gain income.

5. Summary

a. *Are we lost yet?* When the process described above and in Figure 12D is complete, the taxpayer should have a net §1231 gain or a net §1231 loss. (Along the way, recapture amounts, casualty losses, and gains may have been separately segregated and gains may have been recaptured; those are separate from the basic net §1231 gain or loss.) If there is a net §1231 gain, it is included in the computation of net capital gain or net capital loss described in Section V of this chapter. If the result is a net §1231 loss, it is an ordinary loss, which will be deductible as an ordinary loss on the taxpayer's tax return, unless some special rule denies or defers deductibility.

b. **Be alert for §1231 issues:** Section 1231 applies virtually every time that a taxpayer engaged in business sells property such as equipment or real estate used in the business. These issues are often bundled with other trade or business questions, such as ongoing expenditures.

V. CALCULATING NET CAPITAL GAIN AND NET CAPITAL LOSS

There are two final steps in dealing with the character of gain or loss. First, the taxpayer's net capital gain or loss must be determined. Then, the tax rate on net capital gain must be computed, along with the deductible net capital loss, if any.

A. A systematic approach

The ultimate tax on capital gains and the availability of a deduction for capital losses depends on a number of factors: how long the taxpayer has owned the property before selling it (the holding period), the type of asset, the taxpayer's tax bracket for ordinary income, and when the property was purchased and sold. If this sounds complicated—*it is*. The best way to approach the problem is to divide it into a number of smaller steps. The following sections discuss these steps.

▪ *Step 1:* First, identify and categorize each item of the taxpayer's capital gain and capital loss into four different categories: short-term capital gain and loss, 28% capital gain and loss, 25% capital gain, and 15%/0% capital gain or loss. (What's in these categories is described below.)

▪ *Step 2:* Next, net each category of gain and loss. *Netting* means subtracting losses from gains, and ending up with the net result. For example, short-term capital gain is netted against short-term capital loss, and the result is either net short-term capital gain or short-term capital loss. Because there are no losses in the 25% category, there is no netting in this category; it will always result in either zero or a gain. In addition, the 25% gain cannot exceed a taxpayer's total net §1231 gain.

▪ *Step 3:* Next, losses in each category are used to reduce any net gains in other categories. There is a precise order in which losses must be applied against income, and this approach is discussed below. The result is a net capital gain or a net capital loss in each category.

▪ *Step 4:* Finally: "*So what?*" Net gains in each category are included in gross income, but they are taxed at special rates depending on the category. Determining the correct rate to apply to net capital gain is important—and different rates may apply to different kinds of gain. If the result is a net capital loss, individuals may offset $3,000 of ordinary income per year with these net losses, and the losses carry forward to future years to offset other gains, retaining their character in those years.

B. Step 1: Categorize capital gains and losses

1. **Overview:** In this step, the taxpayer's capital gains and losses must be classified into two different kinds of gains or losses: short-term or long-term, and all long-term gains and losses must be classified as 28% capital gain or loss, 25% capital gain, or 15%/0% capital gain or loss.

2. **Holding period:** The calculation of net capital gain and net capital loss depends partly on the proper determination of the ***holding period*** (short- or long-term) for assets sold or exchanged during the taxable year. The period of time during which a taxpayer owns an asset (or is deemed to hold an asset) is the taxpayer's holding period. Holding an asset for one year or less qualifies as short-term, while holding it for longer than a year qualifies as long-term. IRC §1222. A holding period usually begins with the taxpayer's acquisition of an asset by purchase. For transactions other than purchases, however, a taxpayer may in certain cases be allowed to ***tack*** onto his or her actual ownership of an asset other periods of time during which he or she held other property, or another taxpayer held the property. For purposes of computing the holding period, the one-year period commences on the day after the day the asset is acquired and includes the day of disposition. Rev. Rul. 66-7, 1966-1 C.B. 188.

   a. **Exchanged basis property:** If a taxpayer receives property in an exchange that is totally or partially tax-deferred (such as §1031, §1033 and §1041), the holding period of the property received in the exchange will include not only the taxpayer's actual ownership period of the property received but also the period during which the taxpayer owned the property given in the exchange. IRC §1223(1). This only applies if the property exchanged was a capital asset or §1231 property. *Id.*

Example: In a qualifying §1031 exchange, Edward exchanged Greenacre for Paul's Whiteacre. Edward's basis in Whiteacre was determined by reference to his basis in Greenacre. Thus, Edward's holding period in Whiteacre included his period of actual ownership of Whiteacre plus the period of time during which he owned Greenacre.

b. **Transferred basis property:** If a taxpayer receives property in a transaction in which the taxpayer's basis is determined by reference to another person's basis in that same property, the taxpayer's holding period includes not only the period during which the taxpayer actually owns the property, but also the period of time during which the other person held the property. IRC §1223(2). This rule applies, for example, to gifts and property received in a divorce.

Example: Betty and Jim are getting a divorce. The divorce decree provides that Betty will take the house and Jim will take the stock in their family corporation in full satisfaction of all claims. In later determining the holding period of these assets, both Betty and Jim will include in their holding periods the period of time that they held the stock and house as a married couple. This is because §1041 calculates the basis of the property in each former spouse's hands by reference to the basis of the property in the hands of the marital unit.

c. **Property received from a decedent:** A special rule allows a taxpayer to treat property as having been held for more than one year (regardless of a lesser period of actual ownership) if the basis of the property is determined under §1014 (property received from a decedent), and the taxpayer sells the property within one year of the decedent's death. IRC §1223(11). This allows heirs promptly to dispose of property they receive by inheritance without short-term capital gain treatment.

Example: Vicki inherited 1,000 shares of ZAZEL, Inc., from her grandfather. She sold them six months after receiving them, when they had risen in value. Vicki's actual holding period is six months, but she will be considered to have held the stock for more than one year under the special rule relating to property received from a decedent.

d. **Identification:** A taxpayer selling some but not all of a group of assets may designate which items he or she sells.

Example: Peter purchased 100 shares of ABC stock in each month of Year 1. In February of Year 2 he sells 50 shares at a gain. He may designate these 50 shares as from the lot purchased in January of Year 1 in order to ensure that the gain is long-term capital gain.

3. **Types of long-term gain and loss**

a. **Overview:** All long-term (not short-term) capital gain and loss must be placed into one of three categories. Both gains and losses for a particular kind of asset go into that category, for later netting.

b. **28% capital gain and loss:** This category of gain and loss is made up mostly of gain and loss on the sale of "collectibles," such as coins, stamps, art, antiques, guns, gems, etc. This group also includes an amount equal to the gain excluded under §1202(a), which applies to certain sales of small business stock.

Example: Kate inherited a wine collection from her father. Her basis in the collection is $50,000 (the fair market value of this collection at the time of her father's death). She holds it for longer than one year and sells it for $80,000. The gain is 28% capital gain. If she had sold the wine collection for $40,000, she would have a $10,000 loss in this category.

c. **25% capital gain:** This category of gain is attributable to what is called ***unrecaptured §1250 gain.*** This is long-term capital gain, which is not otherwise recaptured as ordinary income, attributable to the taxpayer's previous depreciation of real property. Note that this category does not include any losses. However, the unrecaptured §1250 gain cannot exceed a taxpayer's overall net §1231 gain, which is the excess of §1231 gains over §1231 losses.

Example: Peyton has owned an apartment building for many years, which he purchased for $800,000 ($100,000 for the land; $700,000 for the building) His adjusted basis in the building is now $400,000 and $100,000 in the underlying land. This year, he sells the property for $900,000, allocating $275,000 to the land and $625,000 to the building. Peyton's total gain on sale is $400,000, of which $225,000 is attributable to the gain on the sale of the building is ($625,000 − $400,000) and $175,000 is attributable to gain on the land ($275,000 − $100,000). Assume no other transactions. This gain is capital, but to classify the gain into the proper categories, the amount of previous depreciation deductions that Peyton claimed with respect to the building must be determined. His initial cost was $700,000 and his adjusted basis at sale was $400,000, so he must have claimed $300,000 as depreciation. This amount is potentially 25% capital gain, but the overall amount of such gain is limited to his net §1231 gain (the gain on the sale of the building, or $225,000). Thus, of his total capital gain of $400,000, $225,000 is in the 25% category as unrecaptured §1250 gain and the remaining amount ($175,000) is in the 15% category.

d. **15%/0% capital gain and loss:** This category includes all capital gain and loss not included in the other two categories. In other words, it is the residual category; if gain or loss doesn't belong in either of the other two categories, it is placed in the 15%/0% category. Most taxpayers' capital gains and losses will be in this category. The 0% rate applies to taxpayers (only in the years 2008–2012) whose regular tax rate is 10% or 15%, thereby giving them a tax benefit for capital gains. Without such a break, if taxpayers whose normal tax rate is 10% were subject to a 15% capital gains rate, the capital gain rate would impose an additional tax burden on them, instead of giving them a benefit. Similarly, a taxpayer in a 15% bracket enjoys no benefit from a 15% capital gains tax. The 0% and 15% rates are scheduled to sunset on December 31, 2012.

e. **Section 1231 gains and recapture:** Special rules apply to §1231 property and recapture, which are beyond the scope of most tax courses.

C. Step 2: Netting within each category

In each category, including short-term capital gains and losses, the capital gains and losses must be ***netted.*** This means that gains are compared to losses, and the net result (positive, negative, or zero) is the "net" amount for that group. If losses exceed gains, the result will be a net loss. If gains exceed losses, the result will be a net gain. If the losses exactly equal the gains (not likely, but possible), the result will be zero. There are no losses in the 25% category, so that category will always have a positive or zero balance.

Example 1: Cindy has short-term capital gain of $10,000 and a short-term capital loss of $3,000. She has a net short-term capital gain of $7,000.

Example 2: Darla has a 28% capital gain of $50,000 and a 28% capital loss of $60,000. She has a net 28% capital loss of $10,000.

Example 3: Edward has a 25% capital gain of $30,000, a 15%/0% capital loss of $20,000, and a 15%/0% capital gain of $5,000. He has a 25% capital gain of $30,000 (there are no losses in this category), and a net 15%/0% capital loss of $15,000. (Since there can only be gain in the 25% category, there is no netting in that category.)

D. Step 3: Apply net losses against net gains in other categories

1. **Overview:** After Step 2, a taxpayer will have either a net gain or a net loss in each category. Net losses in each category are then applied to reduce gains in the other categories to zero (but not below zero) in a particular order. Losses must be applied to reduce 28% gain first, then 25% gain, and finally to 15%/0% gain, in that order.

2. **Step 3a—Apply (long-term) net 28% capital loss to gain in other categories:** If a taxpayer has a net 28% capital loss, that amount will be applied to reduce 25% capital gain, and then to reduce net 15%/0% capital gain. It does not offset short-term capital gain (STCG).

   Example: Gerry has the following:

Net short-term capital gain:	$40,000
Net 28% capital loss:	($30,000)
Net 25% capital gain:	$20,000
Net 15%/0% capital gain:	$4,000

   Gerry will apply the 28% net capital loss to reduce the 25% gain to zero, and will apply $4,000 of it to eliminate the 15%/0% gain entirely. He ends up with a net 28% capital loss of $6,000. The 28% loss does not offset the STCG category.

3. **Step 3b—Apply (long-term) net 15%/0% capital loss to gain in other categories:** If a taxpayer has a net 15%/0% capital loss, that amount will be applied to reduce net 28% capital gain, and then to reduce net 25% capital gain. It does not offset short-term capital gain.

   Example: Hilda has the following:

Net short-term capital gain:	$40,000
Net 28% capital gain:	$30,000
Net 25% capital gain:	$20,000
Net 15%/0% capital loss:	($40,000)

   Hilda will apply the net 15%/0 loss of $40,000 first to reduce the net 28% gain to zero, and will apply the balance to reduce the 25% capital gain to $10,000. It will not affect the net short-term capital gain.

4. **Step 3c—Apply short-term capital loss to gain in other categories:** If the taxpayer has a net short-term capital loss, and gains in any other category, the net short-term capital loss will be applied to reduce those gains. The short-term capital loss is first applied to reduce net 28% gains, if any. Then, if any loss is left over, it is applied to 25% gain, if any. Finally, if there is still short-term capital loss left over, it is applied to reduce net 15%/0% gain.

Example: Fritz has net short-term capital loss of $30,000. He has a $15,000 net 28% gain from the sale of collectibles, no 25% gain, and $50,000 of net 15%/0% gain. Fritz will apply the short-term capital loss to reduce the 28% gain of $15,000 to zero, and will then apply the rest of the short-term capital loss to reduce the 15%/0% gain by $15,000. As a result, he will have $35,000 of net 15%/0% gain, no short-term capital loss, and no net 28% loss.

5. **Wait! What about losses from the 25% category?** Because this category does not include losses, it will never generate a net loss that will be applied to the other categories. Gains in this category can, of course, be reduced by net losses from other categories, as illustrated in the above examples.

E. Step 4: Apply the correct tax rate (or claim the right deduction)

1. **Overview:** After all the steps described above are completed, the result will be a net capital gain or a net capital loss in each category. The final question is the maximum tax rate on each of these kinds of gain or whether the taxpayer will be entitled to a deduction for a net loss.

2. **Tax rates for net gain—in general:** The categories of capital gain and loss (28%, 25%, and 15%/0%) also define their generally applicable maximum tax rate. Thus, net 28% capital gain (after application of losses from other categories) is taxed at a 28% rate, net 25% capital gain is taxed at the 25% rate. Net 15%/0% capital gain is generally taxed at a 15% rate, unless the taxpayer's marginal rate is 15% or 10%, in which case he or she can take advantage of the 0% rate. However, that preferential rate is first applied to a taxpayer's ordinary income; only the excess of capital gain over ordinary income receives the special rate. Moreover, in each category, this rate is the maximum rate at which the gain will be taxed; if a taxpayer's rate applicable to his or her other income is lower, the gain will be taxed at that lower rate (after all, the tax preference for capital gains is intended to be a benefit to the taxpayer—not a punishment.) Net short-term capital gain is taxed at the rates applicable to ordinary income. See Chapter 13(II)(B).

3. **Deduction for capital losses:** If the end result of the netting and loss application process is a net capital loss, the restrictions of §1211 apply. This process has already applied losses against capital gains, and so the taxpayer will be entitled to offset up to $3,000 of ordinary income with the loss, and the rest will carry to other years. The loss retains its categorization in future years. For example, an unused net 28% capital loss will retain its character as such, and will be applied in the same manner in a future year as if it has arisen in that year.

F. Comprehensive Example

Eleanor is a veterinarian. She is in the 35% bracket for ordinary income, and experiences the following transactions in Year 1. Assume all assets are held for investment, unless otherwise indicated.

1. Sale of land held for more than one year: $60,000 loss.
2. Sale of XYZ Stock held for less than one year: $15,000 loss.
3. Sale of DEF Stock held for less than one year: $10,000 gain.
4. Sale of sports memorabilia collection held for more than one year: $10,000 loss.
5. Sale of wine collection held for more than one year: $15,000 gain.
6. Sale of Property #1, real estate that she had purchased for $100,000, allocating $10,000 to the land and $90,000 to the building. She used the property in her business, and had claimed $30,000 of MACRS deductions with respect to the building. She sold it for $140,000, allocating $25,000 to the land and $115,000 to the building.

7. Net §1231 gain on the sale of equipment used in her business and held for more than one year: $10,000.

8. Payment received from vendor in renegotiation of contract to provide canine blood plasma: $10,000.

Step One: Classification of gains and losses. All of Eleanor's gains and losses must be categorized into each kind of capital gain or loss. Eleanor has multiple kinds of capital gain and loss. Most are straightforward, but items #6, #7, and #8 deserve special mention. Item #6 is gain from the sale of real property, and requires a bifurcation into 25% gain and 15%/0% gain. Eleanor's total gain is $70,000, which is allocated $15,000 to the land (15%/0% gain) and $55,000 to the building. Because a portion ($30,000) of the total gain of $55,000 attributable to the building was previously claimed as MACRS deductions, this portion is 25% gain and the remaining gain ($25,000) is allocated to the 15%/0% category. Item #7 is net §1231 gain, which must be allocated within the categories. It is not gain from collectibles or from real estate, so it must be classified into the 15%/0% category. Item #8 is not capital gain at all; it is a release of a contract right, which neither the courts nor the IRS have considered to be a "sale or exchange" that can generate capital gain or loss.

Step Two: Netting within each category. In Step Two, the gains and losses in each category must be netted. Eleanor has:

Net short-term capital loss:	($5,000)
Net long-term 28% capital gain:	$5,000
Net 25% long-term capital gain:	$30,000
Net 15%/0% long-term capital loss:	($10,000)

Step Three: Apply losses against gains. Eleanor's losses in the 15%0% category and the short-term category are applied to reduce the gains in the other two categories, in the designated order. Eleanor will apply the $10,000 15%/0% loss: first to eliminate the gain in the 28% category and then to reduce the gain in the 25% category by $5,000. Once that is done, there is no 15%/0% loss left to apply. Then, she will apply the short-term capital loss to reduce the remaining gain in the 25% category by $5,000. At the end of this step, all the losses have been netted against gains, leaving $20,000 of capital gain in the 25% category.

Step Four: Result. When all these steps are completed, Eleanor is left with only $20,000 of 25% long term capital gain. This gain will be taxed at 25%.

VI. NEED TO KNOW MORE?

See *www.aspenlawschool.com/books/tax_outline* for additional information, including:

- Latest on the status of provisions scheduled to sunset in 2012.

- Practice problems in applying §1231.

- Practice in computing net capital gain or net capital loss.

- And other materials that will help you correctly characterize income, gain, and loss.

VII. WHERE ARE WE GOING?

This chapter concludes the discussion of the computation of a taxpayer's taxable income. By now, you probably are becoming a big fan of tax simplification. The discussion of tax rates on capital gains in this section will be revisited in the next chapter, as part of the larger discussion of tax rates on ordinary income and alternative minimum tax rates.

Quiz Yourself on CHARACTER OF INCOME AND LOSS

132. Your best friend is applying to be an IRS auditor. She's been studying for weeks and is very nervous about the upcoming test. She calls you and asks: "Why is it, exactly, that taxpayers seek to characterize income as ordinary and loss as capital?" Please answer her. _____

133. Wally is a sole proprietor engaged in the business of selling hand-carved duck decoys. Which of the following is *not* a capital asset in his hands: (1) his residence, (2) his supply of wood, (3) his stamp collection, (4) his antique tractor? _____

134. Laura won the lottery, and is entitled to receive $100,000 a year for 25 years. She did not want to wait for her money. So, just one year after the date she won, she sold her rights to receive the cash to Mr. X for $1,400,000. She claimed that the gain on sale (her lottery ticket cost $5, so her gain is $1,399,995) is capital and she is entitled to be taxed at 15% on the gain. Is she correct? _____

135. Lee sold stock in ABC Company for $10,000. He had a basis of $2,000 in the stock. He had a *capital* gain, right? If he had held the stock, he would have received dividends from ABC Company, which would be ordinary income. In fact, some people value stock by simply taking the present value of the future right to income from the stock. Under the rationale of *Maginnis,* why isn't Lee's gain ordinary income? _____

136. Wally (from question 133) also owns a van in which he travels to country fairs to display his ducks. He has an adjusted basis of $35,000 in the van. He sells it for $25,000. What is the character of his loss on the sale, and how will he be taxed on it? Alternatively, what if in the same year he sold his display cabinets at a gain of $35,000? _____

137. John is a singer and songwriter. He has a collection of guitars and other musical instruments that he acquired from a famous singer many years ago. He purchased them for $50,000, and has taken $30,000 of depreciation on them. The instruments have appreciated in value, and when his wife insists he get a "real job," John sells all of them for $100,000. What are the tax consequences to him of this sale? _____

138. Why are there two rates for the 15%/0% category of net capital gain? _____

139. Michael purchased a parcel of land in Hawaii for $2,000,000. He held it for several years, while he proceeded to get the proper zoning for homes of five acres or less, and put in streets and essential services, such as water and sewer lines. He then sold the entire parcel to Gwyneth for $5,000,000. Is he entitled to capital gains treatment? Why or why not? What if, instead of selling the entire parcel, he sold ten lots to people who proceeded to build vacation homes on the property? _____

140. Tillie has decided to become an investor in real estate. She plans to purchase a couple of rental homes, fix them up and rent them. When she retires, she plans to sell them. Tillie tells you that one reason this is a great plan is that she will be taxed at the very lowest rates on the appreciation in the homes on sale. Is she correct? _____

141. Andrea had the following transactions during the year:

(a) Sale of land held for investment and held more than one year: $5,000 loss

(b) Sale of ABC Stock held for more than one year: $15,000 gain

(c) Sale of NOP Stock held for less than one year: $25,000 loss

(d) Sale of stamp collection held for more than one year: $20,000 gain

Andrea is not a dealer in any of these assets. What are the tax consequences of these transactions to Andrea?

142. Bev is in the business of manufacturing basketballs. This year, the following events occurred with respect to equipment used in the trade or business:

■ Property A was destroyed by fire. Loss = $30,000.

■ Property B was sold. She recognized a gain of $45,000 of which $10,000 was §1245 recapture income.

■ Property C was sold. She recognized a $15,000 loss on that sale.

What are the tax consequences of these transactions to Bev?

143. In the previous question, what if Bev had experienced a net $5,000 §1231 loss in the previous year? _____

144. What are the principal arguments *for* having a tax preference for capital gain income? Against? Why are there substantial restrictions on the deduction of capital losses? _____

145. Brian, strapped for cash, sells his blood plasma. He makes two claims to reduce his taxes. First, he argues that he has no income at all from the sale because he is worse off—he feels terrible for days afterward. Second, even if he has income, it is capital gain, not ordinary income. Is Brian correct? _____

146. Why do the ordering rules for applying capital losses to reduce capital gains exist? Do they make a difference in actual tax due for taxpayers?

Answers

132. Tell her (gently) that she's got it backwards: Taxpayers seek to characterize income as capital and loss as ordinary. Capital gain income is eligible for preferential tax rates, which save the taxpayer significant amounts of money, as compared to the rates on ordinary income. On the deduction side,

there are restrictions on the ability of taxpayers to take deductions for capital losses, while ordinary losses offset ordinary income. Therefore, taxpayers try to characterize income as capital and losses as ordinary.

133. The wood is part of his inventory or supplies and is therefore not a capital asset.

134. Several courts (see *Maginnis, supra*) have held that a taxpayer who sells his or her right to lottery payouts does not qualify for capital gain treatment. If Laura had not sold the rights, she would have received ordinary income over 25 years; selling the rights is merely an acceleration of that income, and does not transform it from ordinary to capital.

135. *Of course* Lee has a capital gain. Distinguishing this from the sale of lottery winnings isn't difficult. Owning the stock grants Lee more rights than just the right to dividends—the owner of stock has a collection of rights, including the right to dividends, possibly the right to vote, and the right to share in liquidation proceeds on dissolution. So, the value of the stock incorporates all of these rights. By contrast, the sale of the right to lottery winnings is *only* the sale of the right to what otherwise would be ordinary income.

136. The loss on the sale of the van is a §1231 loss because it is attributable to the sale of a depreciable asset used in Wally's trade or business. If §1231 losses exceed gains, the net loss is deductible as an ordinary loss. If §1231 gains exceed losses, they are taxable as capital gain. In this case, if there is only a loss on the sale of the van, it will be an ordinary loss for him. If gains on the sale of the displays exceed the loss on the sale of the van, the gain will be considered capital gain (probably 15%/0% gain).

137. The easy answer is that John has an $80,000 gain on the sale of the instruments. This would be considered §1231 gain, which would normally be taxed as a capital gain, since there is no reported §1231 loss. However, §1245 will require recapture of the depreciation of $30,000 as ordinary income. The rest would be capital gain, and probably would be considered 15%/0% gain. However, if these are collectibles, the gain would be taxed at 28%. This becomes more difficult to analyze, however, because if they were collectible, John may have been incorrect in claiming MACRS deductions; they may not be subject to "wear and tear" and therefore non-depreciable.

138. The capital gains tax rate is supposed to be less than the rate for ordinary income. For taxpayers in the 15% or 10% bracket, a 15% capital gains rate would not be lower. Therefore, the 0% rate is available for taxpayers in brackets up to 15%.

139. The question for Michael is whether he has capital gain or ordinary income on the sale of the property, i.e., whether the property is a capital asset. If the property is inventory in his hands, it is not a capital asset, and he would have ordinary income on its sale. If he sells the parcel as a whole, he probably would not have ordinary income; he probably has a good argument that the parcel is an investment, not inventory. However, the more activity he engages in—installing services, plotting the lots, etc.—the closer he gets to the edge. When he subdivides and sells the lots individually, he likely has crossed the line into the world of inventory, especially if he takes all the usual steps to sell the lots, such as advertising, meeting with customers, etc. However, there is no bright line in this area. Section 1237 would have provided him with a bright line, but it appears that it is too late for Michael to take advantage of it.

140. Tillie's analysis is not exactly correct. The Code provides for a 25% rate on unrecaptured §1250 gain, which is the lesser of the taxpayer's §1231 gain or the depreciation deductions previously claimed with respect to the property. So, upon sale, it is likely that a portion of the gain will be taxed at the 25% rate, while the rest (as Tillie had hoped) will be taxed at the lowest rate.

141. Andrea's gains and losses must first be categorized. The sale of land generates a $5,000 long-term capital loss in the 15%/0% category. The sale of ABC stock generates a long-term 15%/0% capital gain in the amount of $15,000. The sale of NOP stock was held for less than one year, so it generates a short-term capital loss of $25,000. The sale of the stamp collection generates long-term capital gain of $20,000 in the 28% (collectibles) category.

Next, the gains and losses in each category must be netted. The only category that has both gains and losses in the long term is the 15%/0% category, so the $15,000 gain is netted against the $5,000 loss to produce a net long-term 15%/0% capital gain of $10,000.

In the next step, net capital losses in each category are applied against net capital gains in each category. The short-term capital loss is applied first to reduce the gain in the 28% category to zero, and then the remaining amount ($5,000) is applied to reduce the capital gain in the 15%/0% category.

Andrea's net result is a $5,000 long-term capital gain in the 15%/0% category.

142. All of these assets appear to be §1231 assets: They are depreciable property (equipment) used in a taxpayer's trade or business. Bev's casualty losses exceed casualty gains, so the loss is excluded from the computation of §1231 gains and losses (this loss is considered an ordinary loss). The gain on Property A is netted against the loss on Property B, but only $35,000 of the gain on Property A is included in the computation, because the recapture income is ordinary income and cannot be §1231 gain. The netting process produces a net gain of $20,000, which is considered capital in nature.

143. If Bev had experienced a $5,000 loss in the previous year that was characterized as an ordinary loss under §1231, a portion of her gain in the current year—up to that amount of loss—would be considered ordinary. Thus, $5,000 of her gain would be ordinary and the remaining $15,000 would be capital.

144. The principal arguments for having a capital gains preference (a lower tax rate on capital gain income) are: (1) a reduction in the tax rate on investments will increase savings, investment, and economic prosperity; (2) a capital gains preference is said to reduce lock-in (the tendency to hold on to assets rather than putting them to their best economic use) by reducing the tax associated with sale; (3) because capital gains often accrue over many years, requiring the gain to be recognized in a single year (the "bunching" effect) can result in the taxation of gain at the highest marginal rate in the year of recognition, even though the incremental gains might have been taxed at lower rates had they been recognized in the years they accrued, so a capital gains preference reduces the bunching effect; and (4) because the recognized gain upon sale of a capital asset may not represent real gain, but instead may represent inflationary gains, the capital gains preference mitigates the impact of inflation by lowering the tax in the year of sale.

The principal arguments against a capital gains preference is that it introduces new heights of complexity into the tax code, and of course, that it may not have the effects described above.

The rationale for a limitation on capital losses is that allowing a taxpayer to deduct capital losses without limitation would arguably give the taxpayer too much discretion to lower his or her tax rate by selling capital assets that have declined in value in years in which the taxpayer has significant ordinary income.

145. Brian is thinking like a tax lawyer—he would prefer an exclusion from gross income, but if he must have income, he'd like it to be taxed at a lower capital gains rate, rather than as ordinary income. Unfortunately for Brian, several courts have held that the sale of plasma and other body parts generates income, and no one has (yet) been successful in claiming that the sale is of a capital asset, as it is more likely to be considered inventory. See *Green v. Commissioner*, 74 T.C. 1229 (1980) (taxpayer claimed "depletion allowance"—a kind of capital recovery—to offset ordinary income on the sale of her rare blood, but the court rejected her claim).

146. With the proliferation of categories, some ordering rule is necessary to prevent chaos. The long-term loss/gain ordering rules are relatively taxpayer friendly, allowing losses to be applied to reduce gains, first, on the kinds of capital gain subject to the highest rates (28% and 25%). Thus, the overall rate of tax on capital gains should be lower than if the reverse applied—if losses were first applied to the 15%/0% category. The ordering rule that puts short-term capital losses at the end of the line—they cannot be applied against long-term capital gain until all long-term losses have been applied—makes it more difficult for taxpayers to use (or generate) short-term losses to offset long-term gains. The ordering rules work against taxpayers who have long-term losses and short-term gains, as the former cannot offset the latter.

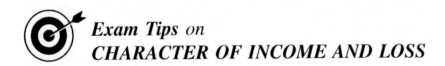

Exam Tips on
CHARACTER OF INCOME AND LOSS

☛ Warning: Different professors have varying degrees of interest in the technical aspects of calculating net capital gain or loss. Some are happy if you know the different categories of capital gain and are content to leave the rest to a computer program. Others insist that you know the exact process—and can explain it as well as apply it. *Ask your professor about his or her approach.*

☛ The same is true for §1231 gains and losses. Many professors simply want you to know that "net losses are ordinary; net gains are capital". Others require more detail. *Ask.*

☛ Questions of character arise only after there is a determination that gain or loss has been recognized. If there is no recognized income or loss, there is no question of character.

☛ Be able to recognize when a taxpayer is trying to characterize income as capital or a loss as ordinary—and know why. Make sure the requirements for capital gain or loss are met (see Figure 12A).

☛ If there is a sale or exchange of an asset, determine what kind of asset it is: capital, noncapital, or §1231 asset.

   ☞ *Look for:* Is the taxpayer engaged in a trade or business?

   ☞ *Analyze:* Business assets are likely to be inventory (noncapital) and §1231 assets. Nonbusiness assets are likely to be capital assets. But the connection with the business isn't the determinative factor. (See *Arkansas Best*.) Study §1221 carefully for the definition of capital assets.

☛ Is there a "deemed" sale or exchange? Even if there is no direct sale, there still may be a sale or exchange leading to capital gain/loss. See Figure 12B.

☛ Get to know the different kinds of capital gain: 28%, 25%, and 15%/0%.

☛ To get ready for any capital gain/loss calculation problem, have your friends pose various scenarios to you (and you to them). Don't stop until the process described in Figure 12A is easy for you.

 STATUTE SUMMARY CHARTS

Statute Summary—§1231
Section 1231 Gains and Losses

Parsing Step	IRC §1231
General Rule	If §1231 gains > §1231 losses, then all are capital. If §1231 losses > §1231 gains, then all are ordinary.
Definitions	**§1231 assets:** depreciable property used in trade or business.
Special Rules and Exceptions	Special two-part netting process—casualty gains/losses and all §1231 assets. Unrecaptured §1231 losses.
Related statutes	**§1221(a)(2):** Exclusion from capital asset definition **§165:** Losses in trade or business
Typically implicated when	A taxpayer in business sells equipment or buildings used in the trade or business.

CHAPTER 13

TAX RATES AND CREDITS

ChapterScope ▬▬▬▬▬▬▬▬▬▬▬▬▬▬▬▬▬▬▬▬▬▬▬▬▬▬▬▬▬▬▬▬▬▬▬

Previous chapters have discussed the computation of taxable income, including the identification of items of gross income and the allowances for deductions. This chapter turns to the crucial last steps in the calculation of the actual tax due—tax rates and tax credits.

Key concepts in this chapter include:

■ **Tax rates applicable to individuals and entities:** Taxable income is multiplied by the appropriate tax rate to determine the tentative tax due (before credits). Tax rates depend on the amount of taxable income and, for individuals, the taxpayer's status as single, married, or head of household. Net capital gain and certain dividend income are subject to special tax rates.

■ **Alternative minimum tax:** Certain taxpayers are subject to an alternate method of computation of taxable income known as the alternative minimum tax or "AMT."

■ **Tax credits:** A taxpayer subtracts available tax credits on a dollar-for-dollar basis to determine the actual tax due or refund owed the taxpayer. This chapter discusses the dependent care credit, the earned income credit, the first-time homeowner credit, and certain education credits in detail, and notes other available credits.

I. WHERE ARE WE?

In this chapter, we come to the end of the long process of calculating a taxpayer's tax liability: multiplying a taxpayer's taxable income by the appropriate tax rates (depending on type of income, amount of income, and the status of the taxpayer) and subtracting available tax credits. In many tax classes, the actual computation of tax is not emphasized, but embedded in that computation are important questions of the appropriate tax rates, the different taxing methods (regular versus AMT), and policy issues surrounding the appropriate tax rates.

II. TAX RATES

A. Policy

A variety of rate structures are theoretically possible, and selection of the appropriate rate structure generates a great deal of theoretical and political controversy.

1. **Progressive tax rates:** In a *progressive tax rate* system, the tax rate increases as taxable income increases, so that higher-income taxpayers pay proportionately more of their income as tax than lower-income taxpayers. The U.S. federal income tax system has historically been a progressive rate system. The major rationales for a progressive tax system include:

   a. **Ability to pay:** Taxpayers with more taxable income have a proportionately higher ability to pay.

    b. Decreasing marginal utility: Drawing from the insights of economics, a taxpayer is thought to derive less enjoyment from every additional dollar of income. Thus, the theory goes, it hurts a high-income taxpayer less to pay a higher proportion of his or her income as tax.

2. **Flat tax rates:** In a *flat tax rate* system, the same rate is applied to taxable income, regardless of level. Thus, all taxpayers pay the same proportion of their incomes as tax.

3. **Regressive tax rates:** In a *regressive tax rate* system, tax rates decrease as income rises. Thus, lower-income taxpayers pay proportionately more of their income as tax than higher-income taxpayers. Sales taxes are generally thought of as regressive.

B. Current tax rates on ordinary income—regular tax (not AMT)

The 2011 tax rate structure is progressive within a limited range from 10% to 35%. The actual rate of tax depends on the taxpayer's taxable income and filing status.

1. **Marginal rates:** The tax rates are expressed as marginal rates, i.e., the rate of tax on the last dollar of taxable income. A taxpayer is taxed on the first portion of taxable income at the lowest (10%) marginal rate, the next portion at the second lowest rate, and so on. As a result, the effective rate will be a blended rate of all applicable rates. (Fortunately, the IRS publishes tax rate tables each year to assist with this calculation.) When a taxpayer complains that additional income will "push me into a higher tax bracket" he or she is saying that the additional income is taxed at a marginal rate higher than the rate he or she previously experienced.

2. **Inflation adjustments:** The taxable income amounts designated in §1 are adjusted each year for inflation, and the IRS publishes the new amounts to reflect these inflation adjustments. IRC §1(f). See, e.g., Rev. Proc. 2011-12, 2011-2 I.R.B. 297.

3. **2011 tax rates:** The tax rates, and income levels to which they apply, are listed in Figure 13A.

Figure 13A
2011 Federal Income Tax Rates

2011 Regular Tax Rates on Taxable Income	Single	Married Filing Jointly
10%	$0 – $8,500	$0 – $17,000
15%	$8,501 – $34,500	$17,001 – $69,000
25%	$34,501 – $83,600	$69,001 – $139,500
28%	$83,601 – $174,400	$139,501 – $212,300
33%	$174,401 – $379,150	$212,301 – $379,150
35%	Over $379,150	Over $379,150

Example: Ian is single and has taxable income of $60,000 in 2011. His tax is computed as follows:

$$
\begin{array}{rcl}
\$8,500 & \times & 10\% = \quad \$850 \\
\$26,000 & \times & 15\% = \quad \$3,900 \\
\underline{\$25,500} & \times & \underline{28\% = \quad \$7,140} \\
\$60,000 & & \$11,890
\end{array}
$$

Ian's effective tax rate is 19.82%, a blended rate (11,890/60,000).

4. **Married filing separately:** A separate tax schedule is provided for married couples who file *separate returns.* These tax rates are usually unappealing, and you may have noticed that married couples filing separate returns also do not fully enjoy other tax benefits. Therefore, most couples file jointly. The primary reason couples file separately is to protect one spouse's assets from the other's tax liability (joint returns generate joint and several liability for the tax due, while separate returns do not).

5. **Surviving spouses:** *Surviving spouses* may use the more favorable tax rates for married taxpayers filing jointly. A surviving spouse is an unmarried taxpayer whose spouse died within the previous two years and who maintains a household for a dependent child. IRC §2(a).

6. **Heads of households:** Favorable rates are provided for *heads of households,* i.e., unmarried persons maintaining a household in which a dependent lives during the taxable year. IRC §2(b).

7. **Children:** Children file their own tax returns reporting their incomes. In some circumstances their parents may report the child's investment income on their returns, or children's investment income may be taxed at the parents' tax rate. See discussion of the *kiddie tax* in Chapter 14(IV)(A).

8. **Entities:** Corporations and other entities are sometimes subject to tax, but the taxation of these entities is usually beyond the scope of the basic tax course.

C. Tax rates on capital gains

1. **Maximum tax rates:** Preferential tax rates are available for net capital gain income. See Chapter 12. Net capital gain can be of any of three types: (1) collectibles gain, taxed at a maximum rate of 28% ; (2) unrecaptured §1250 gain, taxed at a maximum rate of 25%; and (3) all other net capital gain, taxed at a 15% rate, except for taxpayers whose regular tax rates are 15% or less, and in that case, the capital gain escapes tax altogether. These are *maximum* rates; if the taxpayer's regular tax rate is lower, that rate applies.

2. **Coordination with ordinary income rates:** The taxpayer's tax will be the *lower* of (a) the tax computed using the taxpayer's regular tax rate on all taxable income (including net capital gain) or (b) the tax computed using a bifurcated system: the regular rate on ordinary income and the various preferential rates on net capital gain.

D. Qualified dividend income

Although dividends qualify as ordinary income, certain dividend income is taxed at a special, preferential rate. *Qualified dividends* are taxed at 15% (or 0% for taxpayers whose effective rate is 15% or less). IRC §1(h)(11). A qualified dividend is a dividend (other than certain extraordinary dividends, or dividends from stock held for short periods of time) received from a domestic corporation or certain foreign corporations. This provision eliminates the disparity between the gain on sale of stock and the dividends from such stock.

E. Sunset 2012:

The 2010 Tax Relief Act provides for a sunset for these tax rates as of December 31, 2012. For tax years after that date, unless Congress otherwise acts, the applicable tax rates to ordinary income, capital gain, and qualified dividend income will be different. For updates see *www.aspenlawschool.com/books/tax_outline.*

III. THE ALTERNATIVE MINIMUM TAX

A. Overview

The *alternative minimum tax (AMT)* was enacted to increase the fairness of the tax system by ensuring that all taxpayers, even those with the kind of income or deductions that receive favorable treatment under the Code, pay some minimum amount of income tax. Calculating the AMT requires a separate determination of *alternative minimum taxable income,* which is the taxpayer's regular taxable income with some adjustments. The special AMT tax rates are applied to AMT income less an exclusion amount, and certain credits are subtracted. Then, a taxpayer's AMT is equal to the excess of the tentative minimum tax over the taxpayer's regular tax. A taxpayer subject to the AMT will pay two separate taxes: the regular tax and the AMT. The AMT is best thought of as a parallel tax system to the regular tax, which may impose a surtax on taxpayers.

B. Alternative minimum taxable income (AMTI)

To calculate AMTI, begin with taxable income computed in the regular manner, and make a series of adjustments that put back into taxable income some items that were excluded (see Chapter 4) or deducted (see Chapters 6–8). The following are the most important adjustments, although there are others that are not usually so important in the basic tax class.

1. **Add some items that were excluded from gross income:** To calculate AMTI, add back into taxable income certain amounts that were excluded from gross income in computing the regular tax:

    a. **Section 1202 stock:** Seven percent of the gain on the sale of §1202 stock that was excluded from gross income for regular tax purposes is added back into taxable income. IRC §57(a)(7).

    b. **Certain tax-exempt interest:** The tax-exempt interest on private activity bonds is added back into taxable income. IRC §57(a)(5). These include bonds used to finance mass transit, sewage facilities, and similar specialized activities.

    c. **Incentive stock options:** An incentive stock option gives an employee the right to acquire stock by exercising an option and paying less than the fair market value of the stock. The difference between the stock's market value and the exercise price is not included in regular gross income at the time of exercise, but it is included for AMT purposes, so it must be added back into taxable income. IRC §57(b)(3).

2. Add some items that were deducted in computing taxable income: For regular tax purposes, taxable income is the result of deducting certain items from gross income. These deductions are reversed in computing AMTI by adding back into taxable income deductions taken for the following:

    a. Personal deductions: Miscellaneous itemized deductions; standard deduction; personal exemption; state and local income, sales, and other taxes are not deductible for AMTI purposes. Medical expenses are deductible for AMT purposes only to the extent they exceed 10% (not 7.5%) of AGI, as computed for regular tax purposes. Interest on a home mortgage is deductible for AMT purposes, but special rules apply so that only "real homes" (houses, condos, etc.) will qualify as personal residences, not boats, RVs, and the like. For discussion of these personal deductions, see Chapter 6.

    Example: In 2011, Judy had AGI of $100,000 and had medical expenses of $16,000. For regular tax purposes, Judy may claim $8,500 of the medical expenses as an itemized deduction (16,000 − (7.5% × $100,000). However, for AMT purposes, she can claim only $6,000 as a deduction for medical expenses because the calculation of AMTI allows a deduction for medical expenses only to the extent that such expenses exceed 10% of AGI. Ten percent of Judy's AGI is $10,000, so only the amount of her expenses that exceed that threshold (i.e., $6,000) are deductible for AMT purposes.

    b. Depreciation: For AMT purposes, a taxpayer is generally required to use a longer, slower capital recovery method than for regular tax purposes. For three-, five-, seven-, and ten-year property, for example, a taxpayer would be required to use the 150% declining-balance method rather than the 200% declining-balance method. A taxpayer would then add the difference between the two in early years of ownership to taxable income in calculating AMTI.

        i.   Because real property is subject to straight-line MACRS deductions, no AMT adjustment is required for real property.

        ii.   Property subject to the §179 expense (see Chapter 7(IV)(F)) does not generate an AMTI adjustment.

    c. Losses: Certain restrictions apply to losses, including net operating losses (see Chapter 11(II)(D)) and passive activity losses. See Chapter 11(VII).

C. AMT tax rates

The first $175,000 of AMTI in excess of the applicable exemption amount is taxed at 26% IRC §55(b)(1)(A)(i)(I). Any AMTI in excess of this amount is taxed at 28% IRC §55(b)(1)(A)(i)(II). Special AMT capital gains rates also apply. IRC §55(b)(3).

D. Exemption amount

1. Relatively low amounts: The exemption amount was originally designed to exempt mid- and low-income taxpayers from the AMT. However, because the exemption amounts are not tied to inflation, over the years the usefulness of the exemption amount has fallen, and many middle-income taxpayers find themselves caught within the AMT web. For 2011, the exemption amounts are as follows:

Status	Exemption Amount
Single	$48,450
Married	$74,450

Example: Frodo, a single taxpayer, has AMTI of $75,000 in 2011. What is his tentative AMT? Frodo reduces his AMTI by the appropriate exemption amount ($48,450) and multiplies the result ($26,550) by 26%. His tentative AMT is $ $6,903. To the extent that this amount exceeds Frodo's regular tax, he will pay the difference as AMT.

2. **Phaseouts:** The exemption amounts begin to be phased out once AMTI reaches a certain amount. Once AMTI reaches $112,500 (for single taxpayers) or $150,000 (married taxpayers filing jointly) the exemption is reduced by 25% of the amount by which AMTI exceeds this amount.

   Example: Joanne, a single taxpayer, has AMTI of $250,000. While her exemption amount would normally be $48,450, her AMTI is above the threshold phaseout amount ($112,500), so that her exemption amount is reduced by 25% of the amount by which her AMTI ($250,000) exceeds the phaseout amount ($112,500). Therefore, her exemption amount is reduced (but not below zero) by $34,375 (25% × ($250,000 − $112,500)) so that her exemption amount is $14,075.

E. Minimum tax credit

Some of the adjustments to regular taxable income in computing AMTI are timing adjustments: Some disallow deductions in early years, pushing them to later years; others accelerate income into an earlier year than is required for regular tax purposes. In later years, the taxpayer's tax liability as a whole will be overstated as these timing adjustments reverse themselves. For example, consider a taxpayer who incurred AMT because he or she was required to take a longer, slower MACRS deduction period for AMT purposes. In later years, the regular tax liability would be higher (less depreciation would be allowed) and for AMT purposes, the AMT tax would be lower (more depreciation would be allowed). To alleviate this problem, §53 allows a taxpayer a minimum tax credit against regular tax liability. The computation of the minimum tax credit—fortunately—is usually beyond the scope of the basic tax course.

F. Comprehensive example

In 2011, Sabrina and Noah had a combined salary income of $150,000. Noah exercised a qualified stock option by paying $80,000 for stock worth $200,000. Their itemized deductions were $25,000 of which $6,000 was a miscellaneous itemized deduction (after taking into account the 2% floor) and $4,000 was a deduction of state income taxes. They each claimed an exemption of $3,500. Thus, Sabrina and Noah's taxable income for regular tax purposes was $125,000. Assume that their regular tax liability was $30,000. Calculating AMTI requires increasing taxable income as computed for regular tax purposes by adding: (1) the differential between what was paid for the stock option ($80,000) and the value of the stock itself ($200,000), or $120,000; (2) the miscellaneous itemized deduction of $6,000; (3) the deduction for state income taxes of $4,000; and (4) the personal exemptions of $3,500 each or $7,000.

This produces AMTI of $262,000.

Because AMTI exceeds $150,000 (the initial threshold amount for phaseout of the exemption), the exemption amount (otherwise $74,450) will be reduced by 25% of the amount by which AMTI exceeds this threshold amount, or $28,000. This leaves an exemption amount of $46,450. Their AMTI is $215,550.

The couple's tentative AMT is 26% of the first $175,000 of their AMTI (less exemption amount) and 28% of the excess AMTI. This produces AMT of $45,500 + ((215,550 − 175,000) × 28%) = $56,854. This exceeds their regular tax liability by $26,854, so the couple's total tax liability (before any credits) is $30,000 of regular tax and $26,854 of AMT for a total tax liability of $56,854.

When Noah sells the stock that he purchased through the stock option, the differential between option price and fair market value will be taken into account for regular tax purposes. At that time, he will probably be able to claim a minimum tax credit against regular tax to account for the timing differential in inclusion of income in the two taxes.

IV. TAX CREDITS—IN GENERAL

A tax credit is a dollar-for-dollar reduction in the amount of tax owed by a taxpayer.

A. Compare—Deductions

A deduction is a subtraction from gross income or adjusted gross income (AGI) in computing taxable income.

B. Why a credit? The upside-down subsidy problem

As a benefit to a taxpayer, a deduction is worth the amount of the deduction multiplied by the taxpayer's marginal tax rate. Therefore, in a progressive rate system, deductions are worth more to high-income taxpayers than to low-income taxpayers. Thus, deductions are occasionally referred to as "upside-down subsidies." By contrast, a tax credit is worth the same dollar amount to every taxpayer because it reduces tax on a dollar-for-dollar basis. Because a tax credit does not extend a larger tax benefit to higher-income taxpayers than to lower-income taxpayers, Congress may choose the credit vehicle in certain situations (e.g., the dependent care tax credit discussed below).

C. Refundable/Nonrefundable

A refundable credit can reduce the tax due below zero, generating a tax refund for the taxpayer. A *nonrefundable credit* can only reduce the tax to zero and thus will not generate a refund.

Example: Bo's income tax is $100, but he is entitled to a tax credit of $120. If the tax credit is refundable, he will receive a $20 refund. If the tax credit is nonrefundable, it will simply reduce his tax to zero.

D. Credit for tax withheld

Perhaps the most familiar credit is the credit for taxes withheld on wages. After computing the tax based on taxable income, the taxpayer subtracts from the tax due the amount of federal income tax withheld from wages, salaries, and bonuses. IRC §31(a)(1). This credit is a refundable credit, i.e., it can generate a tax refund.

V. DEPENDENT CARE CREDIT

The dependent care credit is designed to grant some tax relief to a taxpayer who incurs expenses to care for a dependent while the taxpayer works. (Remember that these expenses are not deductible because they are personal expenses. IRC §262.)

A. General rule

A taxpayer who maintains a household with at least one qualifying individual is allowed a tax credit in an amount equal to the "applicable percentage" multiplied by "employment-related expenses." IRC §21(a)(1). This is a nonrefundable credit with a maximum credit of $2,100.

B. Definitional issues

1. **Qualifying individual:** A qualifying individual is a dependent under the age of 13 for whom the taxpayer is entitled to a deduction as a dependent, or any other dependent or a spouse of the taxpayer who is physically or mentally unable to care for him- or herself. IRC §21(b)(1). The individual must live with the taxpayer more than half the year.

2. **Applicable percentage:** The applicable percentage depends on the taxpayer's AGI. For taxpayers with AGI of $15,000 or less, the applicable percentage is 35%. The applicable percentage drops by one percentage point for every increase of $2,000 (or fraction thereof) over $15,000 in AGI, but never falls below 20%.

3. **Employment-related expenses:** Employment-related expenses are expenses incurred for the care of a qualifying individual to allow the taxpayer to be gainfully employed. IRC §21(b)(2)(A).

   a. **Dollar limit:** Employment-related expenses are limited to $3,000 per year for one qualifying individual and $6,000 per year for two or more qualifying individuals. IRC §21(c). The maximum credit available is:

Adjusted Gross Income	Applicable Percentage	One Qualifying Individual	Two or More Qualifying Individuals
Up to $15,000	35%	$1,050	$2,100
$15,001–$17,000	34%	$1,020	$2,040
$17,001–$19,000	33%	$990	$1,980
$19,001–$21,000	32%	$960	$1,920
$21,001–$23,000	31%	$930	$1,860
$23,001–$25,000	30%	$900	$1,800
$25,001–$27,000	29%	$870	$1,740
$27,001–$29,000	28%	$840	$1,680
$29,001–$31,000	27%	$810	$1,620
$31,001–$33,000	26%	$780	$1,560
$33,001–$35,000	25%	$750	$1,500
$35,001–$37,000	24%	$720	$1,440
$37,001–$39,000	23%	$690	$1,380
$39,001–$41,000	22%	$660	$1,320
$41,001–$43,000	21%	$630	$1,260
$43,001 and over	20%	$600	$1,200

    b. Earned income limitation: Employment-related expenses are limited to the lesser of the earned income of the taxpayer or the earned income of the taxpayer's spouse. IRC §21(d)(1). Students and disabled taxpayers are deemed to have $250 per month in earned income for one qualifying individual or $50 per month for more than one qualifying individual. IRC §21(d)(2).

    Example: Timmy Sue has two children. She and her husband both work. Their adjusted gross income is $50,000. They incur $5,000 of expenses for the care of their children while they work. They may claim a tax credit of $1,000, equal to the applicable percentage (20%) multiplied by the employment-related expenses ($5,000).

C. Special rules and exceptions

A married couple must file a joint return in order to claim the credit. IRC §21(e)(2).

D. Related material—Dependent care assistance

Section 129 allows a taxpayer to exclude from gross income up to $5,000 of dependent care assistance provided by an employer under a qualifying dependent care assistance plan. (See discussion in Chapter 4(IX)(E).) Sections 129 and 21 share a common goal of providing a tax benefit for taxpayers who incur expenses for the care of dependents so that the taxpayer can work. They also share some common definitions (dependent care assistance) and limitations (earned income limitation). But §129 offers an exclusion from gross income, while §21 provides a tax credit. Moreover, a taxpayer cannot claim the benefits of both provisions for the same dollar of expense. No credit is allowed for any amount that is excluded under §129. IRC §129(e)(7).

Example: Paul is a single parent maintaining a household for his two children, ages six and eight. His adjusted gross income is $40,000, and he incurs $6,000 of expenses for the care of his children while he works. Paul's employer maintains a qualifying §129 dependent care assistance plan that reimburses Paul for up to $2,000 of his child care expenses. Paul may claim an exclusion of $2,000 under his employer's plan. He cannot claim a credit for the amount he excluded from gross income under §129. Thus, his employment-related expenses are $4,000. Multiplying these expenses by his applicable percentage (22%) gives him a credit of $880. Alternatively, Paul may choose to claim the $6,000 of expenses as wholly applicable to the tax credit, forgoing the dependent care plan benefit entirely.

E. Be alert for dependent care credit issues

Section 21 potentially applies whenever a taxpayer incurs expenses for the care of a family member to allow the taxpayer to work. It is commonly tested as part of a larger set of questions relating to compensation, because the dependent care credit must be coordinated with the dependent care exclusion of §127.

VI. EARNED INCOME TAX CREDIT

The *earned income tax credit* is designed to grant a tax benefit to low-income working taxpayers.

A. General rule

A taxpayer must be an "eligible individual" to claim the credit. Calculating the earned income credit can be complicated, and it often leads to mistakes on returns. To compute the amount of the credit, first multiply the "credit percentage" by the taxpayer's earned income, up to a certain amount known as the "earned income amount." Then, subtract from that figure the taxpayer's "phaseout percentage" multiplied by the greater of the taxpayer's earned income or modified AGI (MAGI), reduced (but not below zero) by the phaseout amount. These percentages and amounts vary depending on the year, income, and family status of the taxpayer. Confused? Just use the formula in Figure 13B using the numbers in Figure 13C.

Figure 13B

Begin with:	Credit Percentage × Earned Income Amount
Subtract:	Phaseout Percentage × (Earned Income − Phaseout Amount)
Equals:	Taxpayer's Earned Income Credit

Figure 13C
Earned Income Definitions and Amounts—2011

Item	No Qualifying Children	One Qualifying Child	Two Qualifying Children	Three or More Qualifying Children
Earned Income Amount	$6,070	$9,100	$12,780	$12,780
Maximum Credit	$464	$3,094	$5,112	$5,751
Threshold Phaseout Amount (Single or Head of Household)	$7,590	$16,690	$16,690	$16,690
Threshold Phaseout Amount (Married Filing Jointly)	$12,670	$21,770	$21,770	$21,770
Credit Percentage	7.65%	34%	40%	45%
Phaseout percentage	7.65%	15.98%	21.06%	21.06%

Example: Melinda, an eligible individual with no children, has earned income of $8,500. She may claim an earned income tax credit of $394.74, computed as follows:

Credit Percentage: 7.65% × $6,070   = $464.36

Less Limitation: 7.65% × (8,500 − 7,590) = − 69.62

Melinda's Earned Income Credit   **$394.74**

Example: Trudy and Stan, a married and eligible couple with one qualifying child, has earned income of $25,000. They may claim an earned income credit of $2,578 computed as follows:

Credit Percentage: 34%   × $9,100   = $ 3,094

Less Limitation: 15.98% × (25,000 − 21,770) =   − 516

Trudy and Stan's Earned Income Credit   **$2,578**

B. Definitional issues

1. **Complexity:** The earned income credit has been criticized as overly complex and impossible to comprehend by ordinary taxpayers. The complexity arises not just in the formula but also in the fact that the applicable numbers change each year and the definitions are exceedingly specialized. Taxpayers can use the earned income calculator on the IRS website [*www.irs.gov*] to determine their eligibility.

2. **Eligible individual:** An eligible individual is an individual with a qualifying child, or any other individual who meets the following three requirements.

   a. **U.S. residence:** The individual's principal place of abode must be within the United States for more than half the year. IRC §32(c)(1)(A)(ii)(I).

   b. **Age 25–65:** The individual must be at least 25, but not yet 65 during the taxable year. IRC §32(c)(1)(A)(ii)(II).

   c. **Not a dependent:** The individual cannot be claimed as a dependent on someone else's tax return. IRC §32(c)(1)(A)(ii)(III).

3. **Qualifying child:** The definition of a qualifying child is the same as the definition of a qualifying child for purposes of the personal exemption. See Chapter 6(XI).

4. **Earned income amount:** Earned income includes income from wages, salary, and self-employment, but does not include investment income, alimony, or pension benefits. IRC §32(c)(2).

C. Special rules and exceptions

1. **Disqualified income limitation:** A taxpayer may not claim the earned income credit if he or she has disqualified income in excess of $2,700. IRC §32(i)(1). Disqualified income includes tax-exempt interest income, dividends, net rental and royalty income, capital gain net income, and net passive income. IRC §32(i)(2).

2. **Mandatory joint return:** For either spouse to claim the earned income tax credit, they must file a joint return. IRC §32(d).

D. Related material

The earned income tax credit is part of an overall system designed to reallocate resources among taxpayers with different incomes. Thus, §32 is related to the system of progressive taxation and to welfare benefit systems outside the taxing arena.

E. Be alert for earned income tax credit issues

Section 32 potentially applies whenever a low-income taxpayer has earned income. Its startling complexity usually means that its details aren't tested on basic income tax exams, but the policy behind it and potential simplification proposals are fair game.

VII. EDUCATION CREDITS

A. In general

A number of Code sections provide special benefits for educational expenses. Two of these are in the form of nonrefundable tax credits: the HOPE/American Opportunity credit and the Lifetime Learning credit, both in §25A.

B. HOPE/American Opportunity tax credit

1. **Overview:** This is a credit of up to $2,500 (2011) per student for qualified expenses paid during the taxable year. IRC §25A(b)(1). The credit is available only for expenses for the first four years of postsecondary education at a qualified institution. IRC §25A(b)(2)(A). The expenses may be for the taxpayer, his or her spouse, or a dependent and is calculated on a per-student basis, so that a taxpayer can claim multiple credits if multiple qualifying students are involved.

2. **Calculation of credit:** The credit is calculated as 100% of the first $2,000 of qualifying expenditures, and 25% of the next $2,000, for a maximum credit of $2,500. IRC §25A(i).

3. **Qualifying expenses:** The credit is for expenses for tuition and fees, but not books, room and board, or nonacademic fees. IRC §25A(f)(1).

4. **Eligibility:** The student must be enrolled as a student in a qualified institution, and must be at least half-time. A student convicted of a drug-related felony will not be entitled to the credit. IRC §25A(b)(2).

5. **Phaseout:** Taxpayers with AGI in excess of $80,000 (single) or $160,000 (married filing jointly) (2011) will experience a reduction in the HOPE/American Opportunity tax credit.

6. **Sunset:** The HOPE/American Opportunity tax credit is scheduled to be significantly reduced on December 31, 2012.

C. Lifetime Learning tax credit

1. **In general:** The Lifetime Learning credit is equal to 20% of the qualified tuition and related expenses of up to $10,000. IRC §25A(c)(1). This is a maximum amount per return, not per student, so that only one credit may be claimed on a return.

2. **Duration:** The taxpayer may claim the credit for any number of years, not just the two years available under the HOPE/American Opportunity tax credit.

3. **Qualifying expenses:** The credit is for expenses for tuition and fees, but not books, room and board, or nonacademic fees. IRC §25A(f)(1). It is also available for expenses relating to any course of instruction at an eligible institution to acquire or improve job skills (but not as recreation). IRC §25A(c)(2)(B). The student need not be enrolled as a half-time student, but can take as little as one course.

4. **Phaseout:** The lifetime learning credit is phased out as modified AGI increases. This means that credit is only partially available to taxpayers with a certain modified AGI, and unavailable when modified AGI rises to a certain level. For 2011, the phaseout starts at modified AGI of $51,000 (single) and $102,000 (married filing jointly).

D. Coordination of the credits and deductions for higher education expenses

1. **No double credits for the same student:** While the taxpayer may claim both credits on the return for different students, the taxpayer cannot claim both credits for the same student. Prop. Reg. §1.25A-5(b)(1).

2. **Allocation to HOPE/American Opportunity credit:** Amounts of qualified educational expenses that qualify under both credits are first allocated to the HOPE credit, then to the Lifetime Learning credit. IRC §25A(c)(2)(A).

   Example: Ben and Ruth file a joint return reporting modified AGI of $25,000. Their son Adam is starting at a local community college this fall. They pay tuition of $5,000. Assuming Adam is a dependent of Ben and Ruth, these expenses qualify as both HOPE/American Opportunity credit expenses and Lifetime Learning credit expenses, so the first $4,000 is allocated to the HOPE credit. Ben and Ruth may potentially claim a credit of $2,500 of HOPE/American Opportunity credit. The remaining $1,000 is allocated to the Lifetime Learning credit, so that an additional $200 credit may be available.

3. **Deduction or credit for same expense:** A taxpayer cannot claim a credit and a deduction (under §222) for the same expense.

VIII. OTHER CREDITS

The Code provides for various other credits for certain types of taxpayers or activities. While these are beyond the scope of many basic tax classes, the tax student may be required to have at least a passing familiarity with them.

A. Child tax credit

Section 24 allows a $1,000 credit for each qualifying child, with phaseouts tied to modified AGI in excess of $110,000 (married filing jointly) and $75,000 (single taxpayers). This is a partially refundable credit for taxpayers with low amounts of earned income. It is scheduled to expire on December 31, 2012.

B. Blind/elderly/disabled tax credit

Section 22 allows a taxpayer to claim a tax credit if he or she is at least 65 years old, blind, or is permanently and totally disabled. IRC §22(a). The credit is computed by multiplying 15% by the "§22 amount," which is set forth in the statute as ranging from $3,750 to $7,500 depending on filing status. IRC §22(a), (c)(2). The §22 amount is reduced by amounts (such as certain social security benefits) that are excluded from gross income and is reduced as income rises. IRC §22(c)(3), (d). This credit is nonrefundable.

C. Adoption expense credit

A taxpayer is entitled to a credit for qualified adoption expenses up to $13,360 per child (2011). IRC §23(a)(1).

1. **Qualified adoption expenses:** Qualified adoption expenses include necessary adoption fees, court costs, attorney fees, and other expenses incurred for the principal purpose of the legal adoption of a child. IRC §23(d)(1)(H).

2. **When claimed:** The taxpayer claims the credit for adoption expenses incurred before the year of adoption in the year following the year they are paid, and for expenses incurred during or after the adoption year, in that year. For the credit for the adoption of special-needs children, the credit is available in the year of adoption. IRC §23(a)(2).

3. **Phaseout:** The credit is phased out for taxpayers with AGI greater than $225,210 (married filing jointly) (2011). IRC §23(b)(2)(A).

D. Energy credits

From time to time Congress enacts special incentives to encourage taxpayers to reduce energy consumption by purchasing energy-saving and green-energy devices, which can range from replacing windows in a home to purchasing an electric car. These are beyond the scope of most basic tax classes.

IX. NEED TO KNOW MORE?

This book's website *www.aspenlawschool.com/books/tax_outline* contains additional information, including:

- List of tax credits subject to phaseout.

- Chart of refundable and nonrefundable credits.

- How the phaseout of the lifetime learning credit works.

- Calculation of the earned income credit.

- And other materials that will help you understand and apply tax credits.

X. WHERE ARE WE GOING?

This chapter concludes the analysis of the computation of a taxpayer's tax. This process began with the identification of gross income, continued through the subtraction of deductions, and concluded with the application of tax rates and subtraction of available credits. This discussion has made a very important assumption: that the proper taxpayer has been identified. The next chapter turns to that issue, examining the types of taxpayers subject to tax and various strategies taxpayers employ to direct income to related persons.

Quiz Yourself on
TAX RATES AND CREDITS

147. How does a tax credit differ from a tax deduction? How does it differ from an exclusion from gross income? _____

148. What is the rationale for the AMT? Give two examples of AMT adjustments that support this rationale. _____

149. Of the following deductions, which are treated differently for AMT and regular tax purposes in computing the tax base for these taxes?

(a) State real property taxes and alimony

(b) Charitable contributions and MACRS

(c) State income taxes and miscellaneous expenses

(d) Personal exemption and charitable contributions

(e) None of the above

150. Catherine, a single taxpayer, had the following items of income and deduction in 2011

Salary income:	$97,200
Taxable interest income:	$3,000
Alimony payments:	$12,000
Interest on private activity tax-exempt bonds:	$2,000
Home mortgage interest on condo:	$5,000
State income tax:	$9,000
Medical expenses in excess of 7.5% of adjusted gross income	$1,000
Charitable deductions:	$2,000
Miscellaneous itemized deductions in excess of 2% floor:	$3,000

Will Catherine pay AMT? Why or why not? _____

151. Catherine, from the previous example, tells you that her obligation to make alimony payments will terminate at the end of 2011. Assuming that all of Catherine's other items remain the same, and the exemption amounts also remain unchanged, will Catherine's glee in having the alimony payments terminate be dampened by having to pay AMT? _____

152. A reckless newspaper reporter wrote a story about Becky that she was negligent in her duties as an employee of a child care facility. Becky sued the reporter and the newspaper for libel, and was awarded $300,000 in damages. Under Becky's agreement with her attorney, the attorney was entitled to one-third of this amount, or $100,000. What are the tax consequences of this transaction to Becky? _____

153. Candace is a single mother of two children, ages six and eight. Her AGI is $38,000. She spends $3,000 per year on child care while she works, and another $500 for their care while she travels as a volunteer for the American Cancer Society. What are the tax consequences to Candace of these expenditures? _____

154. Jordan has earned income $10,000 and is a single father of one child, age ten. To what earned income credit, if any, is he entitled? _____

155. Kara and Jim are married, filing jointly. They have three children. Their earned income is $43,000. Are they entitled to an earned income credit and if so, what is the amount of the credit? _____

156. In what significant way does the earned income credit, the paid-taxes credit, and to some extent the child credit differ from the dependent care credit? _____

157. David and Li have a child who is a sophomore in college, and have spent $10,000 this year on tuition and other qualifying expenses. "Well," says David, "at least we're going to get a tax credit of $4,500 as well as an above-the-line deduction for $10,000." Is David correct?

Answers

147. A tax credit is a dollar-for-dollar reduction in the amount of tax due, while a deduction is a reduction in the amount of gross income or adjusted gross income, upon which the tax is calculated. An exclusion ensures that some amount of what would otherwise be income never becomes part of the tax calculation at all. A deduction or exclusion potentially saves the taxpayer the amount equal to his or her rate multiplied by the dollar amount of the deduction or exclusion, while a tax credit potentially saves the taxpayer one dollar for every dollar of tax credit. Moreover, some tax credits are refundable, i.e., they generate a refund if the credits exceed the tax, which is not a characteristic of deductions or exclusions.

148. The rationale for the AMT is that every taxpayer—even those with activities that generate significant tax benefits in the form of deferred or excluded income or significant deductions—should pay some tax. For example, certain kinds of tax-exempt interest (from private activity bonds) are included in gross income for AMT purposes, while exempt for regular tax purposes. Also, depreciation on equipment is required to be claimed on a longer, slower schedule for AMT purposes than for regular tax purposes. Thus, taxpayers whose activities generate significant amounts of MACRS deductions, which reduce their taxable income and tax for regular tax purposes, will have larger AMTI in the early years of capital recovery.

149. The answer is (c). State income taxes and miscellaneous expenses (miscellaneous itemized deductions) are deductible for regular income tax purposes, but not when computing AMTI. The other answers include items that are both treated differently and not treated differently under the two tax systems.

150. To answer a question like this, it is helpful to have at hand certain figures that vary from year to year. To address Catherine's situation, it is helpful to know the personal exemption amount for 2011 ($3,700), the AMT exemption amount for single taxpayers ($48,450), and the regular tax rates for the year—See Figure 13A.

To determine whether Catherine is subject to the AMT, first compute taxable income and tax for regular tax purposes, as follows:

Salary income:	$97,200
Taxable interest income:	$3,000
Gross income:	$100,200
Minus: Alimony Payments:	–$12,000
Adjusted Gross Income:	$88,200
Minus: Itemized deductions	
Home mortgage interest:	$5,000
State income tax:	$9,000

Medical expenses in excess of		
7.5% of adjusted gross income:	$1,000	
Charitable deductions:	$2,000	
Miscellaneous itemized		
deductions in excess of 2% floor:	$3,000	
Total itemized deductions:	$20,000	($20,000)
Minus: Personal exemption		−$3,700
Taxable income for *regular* tax purposes:		**$64,500**
Tax on regular taxable income:		**$12,250**

Catherine's regular tax liability is equal to $4,750 plus 25% of the amount by which her taxable income ($64,500) exceeds $34,500

To determine whether Catherine will have to pay AMT, her taxable income is adjusted as follows to produce alternative minimum taxable income:

Taxable income for *regular* tax purposes:		**$64,500**
Plus:		
Tax-exempt interest on private activity bonds:	$2,000	
State income taxes:	$9,000	
Miscellaneous itemized deductions:	$3,000	
Medical expenses:	$1,000	
Personal exemption:	$3,700	
Total adjustments:	$18,700	+$18,700
AMTI		**$83,200**
Minus: Exemption amount		−$48,450
Tax base for AMT		$34,750
Multiply by: Tax rate for AMT (26%)		×.26
AMT		**$9,035**

Because Catherine's regular tax liability ($12,250) is more than her alternative minimum tax liability ($9,035), she will not pay AMT. (However, this does not excuse her from calculating the AMT liability to determine if she is subject to this surtax.)

151. No, elimination of the deduction for alimony won't increase Catherine's chances of being caught in the AMT net. It is not one of the tax preference items that trigger AMT concerns.

152. All of the award must be included in Becky's gross income, and her $100,000 of attorneys' fees is deductible on Schedule A as a miscellaneous itemized deduction for regular tax purposes, to the extent that these fees, plus any other miscellaneous itemized deductions, exceed 2% of her AGI. She cannot claim these as an above-the-line deduction because the award was not pursuant to the relatively limited category of claims that generate attorneys' fees eligible for such a deduction. See Chapter 6(X). For purposes of calculating her AMTI, however, none of the attorneys' fees are deductible because they are a miscellaneous itemized expense. This can generate significant AMT liability.

153. Candace can't deduct these personal expenses. IRC §262. However, she may be entitled to a nonrefundable tax credit for dependent care expenses. She appears to qualify: She maintains a household with children; they are under the age of 13; she incurs expenses to care for them while she works. The amount expended for child care while she works as a volunteer ($500) would not be eligible for the credit. The amount of the credit will be a percentage of the lesser of her earned income, child care expenses, or the specified dollar amount of the statute based on the number of children ($6,000 for two children). The percentage is based on AGI. In Candace's case, she will be entitled to claim 23% of her actual expenses of $3,000, or $690, as the child care credit.

154. Assuming that the myriad requirements of the earned income tax credit are met (and other facts are needed to make this determination), Jordan is entitled to claim the earned income credit because his income is within the earned income limitation. He has one qualifying child, and thus will be entitled to a credit of $3,094, computed as follows:

Credit Percentage:	34% × $9,100	= $ 3,094
Less Limitation:	15.98% × (10,000 – 21,770) = –	0
Jordan's Earned Income Credit		**$ 3,094**

155. Assuming that the myriad requirements of the earned income tax credit are met (and other facts are needed to make this determination), Kara and Jim may claim an earned income credit of $1,280. This is computed as follows:

Credit Percentage:	45% × $12,780	= $5,751
Less Limitation:	21.06% × (43,000 – 21,770) = – 4,471	
Kara and Jim's Earned Income Credit		**$ 1,280**

156. The difference between these two categories of credits is whether they are refundable or not. Some tax credits are refundable, i.e., they generate a refund if the credits exceed the tax, which is not a characteristic of deductions or exclusions. The taxes-paid credit, the earned income credit, and, potentially, part of the child credit are refundable. If these credits exceed taxes due, the taxpayer may receive a refund. The child care credit is not refundable; if the taxpayer has more credit available than taxes, the excess credit goes to waste.

157. No, David is not correct. First, David and Li must decide if they want to take the deduction or the credit, because they can't take both. If they decide that a credit is more favorable to them, they must allocate expenses first to the HOPE/American Opportunity tax credit ($4,000) for the tax credit of $2,500. The remaining $6,000 can be allocated to the Lifetime Learning credit, for a tax credit of $1,200 ($6,000 × 20%). If David and Li decide to opt for the deduction under §222, the maximum deduction will be $4,000. We have no facts on which to determine if these amounts (credit or deduction) will be limited or eliminated based on David and Li's income, but this should also be investigated.

Exam Tips *on*
TAX RATES AND CREDITS

☛ The computation of tax is the *last* step in analyzing a taxpayer's tax consequences. It is not usually the case that law students are asked to actually compute the tax, but instead are asked to understand the concepts involved in tax computation.

☛ Know the differential in tax rates on ordinary income and capital gain (see Chapter 12) and qualified dividend income.

　☞ *Look for:* A taxpayer with gain from dealings in property (not inventory) and other kinds of income, such as salary income.

　☞ *Analyze:* Differentiate between the types of income and note the different tax rates that apply.

　☞ *Note:* Most taxpayers one meets on exams have relatively high ordinary income levels, so that the preferential rates for capital gains will make a difference. However, when a taxpayer has low levels of ordinary income, and significant amounts of net capital gain in the 28% or 25% categories, the regular rates of tax will usually produce a lower rate than the capital gains rates. The capital gains rates are maximum rates; if the tax produced by the regular tax rates is lower, those rates will apply.

☛ Be able to explain the rationale for the AMT and to comment on its effectiveness

　☞ Different professors have different levels of interest in the actual computation of AMT. If your professor is interested in this, be ready to compute AMTI using taxable income as the starting place. Know the adjustments to taxable income. Look for taxpayers who have relatively high itemized deductions or tax-exempt income, or can take advantage of significant income deferrals.

☛ Understand the difference between a credit, a deduction, and an exclusion, and the impact of each on a taxpayer.

☛ Be familiar with the numerous credits available to taxpayers.

　☞ *Look for:* Adoptions, day care, low-income taxpayers.

　☞ *Analyze:* Have the taxpayers met the specific requirements for claiming the credit? If so, is it limited by the taxpayers' income level?

　☞ *Look for:* A taxpayer paying for higher education expenses, for the taxpayer or a spouse or child.

　☞ *Analyze:* What incentives are available: exclusions, deductions, credits, deferral devices (see Chapter 14)? Are the specific requirements of the statutes met? What limitations apply, particularly with respect to income levels? Don't let the taxpayer "double dip," i.e., claim two benefits for the same dollars.

STATUTE SUMMARY CHARTS

Statute Summary—§21
Dependent Care Credit

Parsing Step	IRC §21
General Rule	Taxpayers with at least one qualifying individual (child or other dependent) may claim a nonrefundable credit equal to the applicable percentage multiplied by the employment-related expenses, subject to a limit.
Definitions	**Qualifying individual:** child or qualifying dependent. **Applicable percentage:** from 20% to 35%, depending on income. **Employment-related expenses:** to allow a taxpayer to earn income.
Special Rules and Exceptions	Employment-related expenses limited to earned income. Cannot claim exclusion and credit for same expenses.
Related Statutes	**§129:** Dependent care assistance from employer
Typically implicated when	A taxpayer must work and pay another person to care for a child (or other dependent).

CHAPTER 14

IDENTIFYING THE TAXPAYER

ChapterScope

Previous chapters have focused on the computation of a taxpayer's taxable income and ultimate tax liability, from identification of income and deductions to the selection of the correct tax rate and subtraction of available credits. Thus far, the discussion has assumed that the taxpayer to report items of income and deductions has properly been identified. This is not usually a problem among unrelated taxpayers, whose individual self-interest will ensure that they do not overpay their taxes. However, related taxpayers may seek to transfer items of income and deduction among themselves in order to reduce the tax on the group as a whole. Both Congress and the courts have developed methods of combating this practice, which is the subject of this chapter.

- **Persons subject to tax:** Individuals and legal entities are potentially subject to tax and must properly compute their income, deductions, and credits.

- **Assignment of income principles:** Taxpayers in high tax brackets may attempt to shift (assign) income to a related person in a lower tax bracket. The assignment of income principle precludes many such attempts, taxing the assignor on the income.

- **Statutory approaches:** Congress has enacted several statutory schemes to ensure that the "proper" taxpayer reports items of income and deduction. This chapter discusses §1(g) (known as the kiddie tax) and §482.

I. WHERE ARE WE?

This chapter returns to a question that underlies all of the income/deduction/credit/tax rate issues discussed previously in this book: Who is the proper taxpayer to report income or claim a deduction or credit, or to pay tax at a certain rate? This issue is discussed near the end of this book because you need to understand what income is before we can identify transactions involving the games that taxpayers try to play to reduce their overall tax by "assigning" income to others. But, conceptually, it is one of the first questions in analyzing any tax question. This issue is embedded in all of the tax statutes studied so far, but doesn't normally become explicit except in a few Code sections such as the kiddie tax or §482. Therefore, it is up to the student of tax to ask the right question—Who is the proper taxpayer?—before tackling any tax problem.

II. PERSONS SUBJECT TO TAX

Both natural persons and legal entities are potentially subject to tax.

A. Adult individuals

Individuals are subject to tax at the rates described in §1 of the Code, generally ranging from 10% to 35% (See generally Chapter 13.)

1. **Single individuals:** Single persons file a tax return, reporting their own taxable income. IRC §1(b), (c).

2. **Married couples:** Married couples can file a joint return, reporting their income and deductions together. IRC §1(a). They have the option of filing separate returns, but this is generally a less desirable option. IRC §1(d). State law generally determines who is married for purposes of the federal income tax, unless federal law preempts this definition. See, e.g., 1 U.S.C.A. §7 (defining marriage as between a man and a woman). This is an area of law that is evolving daily. The parties must be married on the last day of the taxable year in order to be considered married, except for surviving spouses, who may file a joint return for the year of the death of their spouse. IRC §7703(a).

B. Children

If children have sufficient taxable income to generate a tax, they must file their own tax returns separately from their parents.

1. **Child's services income:** Section 73 provides that a child's income from the performance of services is to be taxed to the child, not to the parent. IRC §73(a). This is true regardless of the parent's rights to the child's income under state law. Similarly, expenditures made to earn this income are considered those of the child regardless of whether the parent or child makes the expenditure. IRC §73(b).

2. **Kiddie tax:** Special tax rates may apply to a child's investment income, and in limited situations a child may report his or her investment income on his or her parents' return. See discussion in this chapter, Section (IV)(A).

C. Entities

A legal entity—such as a corporation, partnership, estate, or trust—may be subject to tax and thus may be required to report items of income and may properly claim items of deduction or credit.

III. ASSIGNMENT OF INCOME

The IRS may challenge taxpayers' attempts to assign income to another. The question in these situations is "Who must include an amount in gross income?"

A. Definition

Assignment of income is the attempt by a taxpayer to shift income to another person. This usually occurs only when taxpayers are related, because the "assignor" of income is perfectly happy to have a relative enjoy the benefits of the income. That same assignor would be unlikely to arrange for an unrelated party to receive what is essentially a gift. Assignment of income issues do occasionally arise between unrelated parties.

B. Why assign income?

Progressive tax rates and the system of separate returns for related persons, taken together, create an incentive for a taxpayer in a high tax bracket to assign income to related taxpayers in lower brackets. The greater the progression in rates, the more incentive is created for assignment of income. Because related persons such as parents, grandparents, and children potentially file separate returns, it is possible to lower the overall tax of the group by reporting income on the separate tax return of a low-bracket member of the group.

Example: Alvin is a freelance artist. He is a taxpayer in the 33% marginal tax bracket, i.e., every additional dollar of income is taxed at 33%. His 21-year-old daughter, Beatrice, is in college and is in a 15% tax bracket. Alvin was planning to give Beatrice a $2,000 gift. Instead, he arranges for one of his clients to pay Beatrice (rather than Alvin) the purchase price of $2,000 for his latest project. By doing so, Alvin attempts to have the $2,000 taxed at Beatrice's lower rate than at his own higher rate. This will not work—Alvin must include the $2,000 in his gross income, and will be deemed to have made a gift of $2,000 to Beatrice. (However, if Alvin hired Beatrice to perform services, he could deduct reasonable amounts paid to her as compensation, and she would include those amounts in her gross income. This would achieve Alvin's desired result.)

C. Policy—Protection of integrity of progressive rates

The Code seeks to impose tax fairly on taxpayers, taxing similarly situated persons similarly *(horizontal equity)*. The tax rates are an integral part of identifying who is similarly situated to whom: Persons with similar taxable incomes are similarly situated and should be taxed similarly (at the same rates). If taxpayers could choose, without limitation, the person to whom income is taxed, the integrity of the progressive rate system would be undermined. As a result, the fairness of the system would be endangered.

D. Assignment of income from services

A taxpayer entitled to compensation income may attempt to shift that income to another person by private contract with the payor or assignee. Another route to the same result is the argument that state law gives another person significant rights to the income, and thus taxation should follow those state law rights by taxing that income to the other person.

1. **Diversion by agreement:** In this situation, a taxpayer enters into an agreement under which salaries or fees otherwise due the taxpayer will be paid to another person.

   a. **Rule:** Income is usually taxed to the person who earns it, regardless of arrangements made to channel it to another person. But not always . . .

   b. **Husbands and wives—*Lucas v. Earl*, 281 U.S. 111 (1930):** Mr. Lucas, an attorney, entered into a contract in 1901 with his wife that all property and salaries acquired by either of them would be "received, held, taken, and owned . . . as joint tenants, and not otherwise, with the right of survivorship." Mr. Lucas earned salary as an attorney in 1920 and 1921 and reported only half of it on his own return (at that time, husbands and wives filed separate returns).

      i. **Issue:** Should Mr. Lucas have reported the entire salary on his own return, or does the contract entered into with his wife vest half the income in her for federal income tax purposes?

      ii. **Result and rationale:** Mr. Lucas should have reported all of the income on his own return. Income is taxed to the person who earns it, regardless of "contracts however skillfully devised."

   c. **Parents, employers, and children:** In *Armantrout v. Commissioner*, 67 T.C. 996 (1977), *aff'd per curiam,* 570 F.2d 210 (7th Cir. 1978), an employer established and funded a trust that paid the college tuition of children of employees. The parents (employees) had no rights in the trust, and if their children did not use the funds by age 21, they were no longer entitled to them.

    i. **Issue:** Should the parents have included in their gross income the trust distributions used to pay for their children's college tuition?

    ii. **Result and rationale:** The parents were required to include in their gross incomes the amount paid by the trust for the children's tuition. The trust arrangement constituted a device by which the parents attempted to divert compensation income they earned to their children. The parents earned the income, and they must be taxed on it.

    iii. **Related issues:** This case raises interesting economic benefit and timing issues. The parents received an economic benefit (payment of their children's college education, for which they might otherwise be liable) and therefore had an increase in their incomes. But *when* should the parents have included the amount in income? Three choices are: (1) when the plan was established, (2) when the rights vested, and (3) when the benefits were paid. The court did not address this issue.

  d. **Gratuitous diversions?** Under certain circumstances, a person will voluntarily forgo payment. The IRS uses principles of constructive receipt to assert that the person constructively received the money or property, even though he or she renounced it.

    i. *Commissioner v. Giannini,* **129 F.2d 638 (9th Cir. 1942):** The board of a corporation voted to give a director/president 5% of the profits. After the first payment, the director/president refused further payment, encouraging the corporation to "do something useful with it." The IRS asserted that the taxpayer had constructively received the amounts that the corporation designated for him. The Court found that the taxpayer unqualifiedly refused the payment and this was sufficient to avoid inclusion in gross income.

    ii. **Rev. Rul. 74-581, 1974-2 C.B. 25:** Taxpayer faculty members assist in clinical law programs and receive attorneys' fees in some cases. However, under their contracts with the law school, they are bound to give these amounts to the school, because the clinical duties are part of their teaching responsibilities and they are compensated by their salaries. In this situation, the taxpayer faculty members are not required to include the fees in gross income.

2. **A contrast—Diversion by operation of law:** In some cases, governing law (state, federal, or foreign) sets forth rights of persons in items of property or income. The taxpayer may rely on these independently defined rights to assert that another person should report income.

  a. **Rule:** State, federal, or foreign law determines the legal rights and duties from which federal tax consequences flow. If state law limits the rights of an individual to income in favor of another, that limitation will also limit his or her individual taxation.

  b. **Could not have received income legally:** In *Teschner v. Commissioner,* 38 T.C. 1003 (1962) (nonacq.), a parent prepared an essay for a contest and entered it on behalf of his child. The essay was selected and the child received a prize. The IRS sought to include the value of the prize in the income of the parent, but the Tax Court disagreed, because under the terms of the contest the parent could not receive the prize—only the child. The court relied on the principle that the mere right to direct income does not lead to inclusion of the income in the gross income of the person with the right of direction.

c. **Community property—*Poe v. Seaborn,* 282 U.S. 101 (1930):** Husband and wife were residents of Washington, a community property state. Under Washington law, each spouse had an equal interest in community property, although the husband managed the property. They owned real and personal community property and had income from salary, interest, dividends, and the sale of real estate. Husband and wife each reported one-half of the income on their separate returns. (At that time, husbands and wives filed separate returns.)

   i. **Issue:** Was the husband and wife's reporting position correct, or should the husband have reported *all* the income?

   ii. **Result and rationale:** Each spouse was entitled to claim half of the income on his or her separate return. Under Washington law, each spouse had a right to half the income; the husband's rights to management were those of an agent. The right to the income under state law was dispositive of the incidence of taxation. *Poe v. Seaborn* arguably ignored the holding of *Lucas v. Earl* with respect to Mr. Seaborn's salary. However, the opinions might be reconciled by suggesting that state law determines who earns income; in the Seaborn situation, the community earned the income, not Mr. Seaborn.

   iii. **Related issues:** *Poe v. Seaborn* led many states to adopt community property systems, and ultimately to Congress enacting the joint filing system for married persons.

d. **Recent developments—domestic partners.** In Chief Counsel Advice 200608038, the IRS ruled that ***registered domestic partners*** may not split their combined incomes; instead, each domestic partner must report his or her earned income. In Private Letter Ruling 201021050, the IRS reversed this position, on the basis that in 2007 California extended the community property system to registered domestic partners. From 2007 on, each domestic partner must report one-half of the partners' income, and is entitled to one-half of the credit for taxes withheld.

E. Income from property

In these situations, an owner of income-producing property (e.g., stocks, bonds, real estate) gives the income or property to another person. The issue is which person—the donor or the donee—should include the income attributable to the transferred interest in gross income.

1. **Rule:** Attempts to transfer income of property independently of the property itself generally will be respected only if the income interest is transferred for its entire duration. Otherwise, the donor will be taxed on the income, and will be deemed to have made a (nontaxable) gift to the donee.

2. ***Blair v. Commissioner,* 300 U.S. 5 (1937):** William created a trust giving his son, Edward, a life estate in income of the trust. Edward assigned to his daughter, Lucy, an interest of about $9,000 per year in the trust. Edward later made similar assignments to his other children. The trustees distributed income directly to Lucy and the other children. The children reported the income they received from the trust in their gross incomes, but the IRS asserted that Edward should have included the income in his gross income.

   a. **Issue:** Should Edward have been required to include the income in his own gross income, or were the children correct in their reporting positions?

     b. Result and rationale: The children were correct in reporting the trust income in their gross incomes; Edward was not required to include it in his income. Edward transferred to his children the property interest he owned (an income interest in the trust), not the income from that property.

     c. Comment: This case illustrates the difficulty in distinguishing between property and income. Since the fair market value of property is simply the present value of its future income stream, the two are inextricably connected, thus creating this confusion.

3. *Helvering v. Horst,* 311 U.S. 112 (1940): Dad owned negotiable bonds with interest coupons attached. Just before some of the coupons matured, Dad detached them and gave them to son. The son negotiated them, received the interest payments, and reported the income. The IRS asserted that Dad, not son, was the proper taxpayer to include the interest income in gross income.

     a. Issue: Who—Dad or son—should include the interest income in gross income?

     b. Result and rationale: Dad should have reported the interest income. The court relied on the realization concept, that Dad's gift of the coupons constituted enjoyment of the income, and thus income should be taxed to the person who obtains enjoyment of it. This rationale is not favored today.

         i. Ripe fruit hanging on trees: Dad essentially earned the income, because the coupons were so close to maturity when they were transferred. This case is the origin of the fruit-and-tree metaphor, which is vivid but generally unhelpful in analyzing assignment of income issues.

         ii. Carved-out interest: A better rationale is that Dad gave away only the income from the property, not the property itself, for less than the entire duration of the income stream. Thus, this was an inappropriate assignment of income.

     c. Related issues

         i. Income/property distinction: The Court focused on the different interests in the bond: a capital interest (the right to be repaid the amount loaned) and the interest income (annual payments of interest to compensate the lender for the loan). While certainly both economics and tax law make a distinction between capital (principal) and income (interest), in fact the principal is merely the present value of the future income stream. Distinctions that rely on some essential difference between capital and income are probably destined to failure.

         ii. Timing: In *Horst,* the interest payments were made in the same year as the transfer. If the interest payments had been made in the next year, the question would arise whether the transfer would have accelerated the income to Dad, i.e., required him to report the income in the year of transfer, even though the interest had not yet been paid. Subsequent cases have reached varying results on this issue.

         iii. Gifts—§§102 and 1015: Recall that a donee excludes from gross income the value of property received by gift and generally takes the donor's basis in the gift property. IRC §§102 and 1015, discussed in Chapters 4(IV) and 9(V)(C), respectively. The combination of these rules allows a donor to transfer to the donee the unrealized appreciation in property, if the gift is of the full property. Special rules for the donee's basis in loss property, however, restrict the transfer of losses.

4. Qualified dividend income: With tax rates on qualified dividend income at a low 15%, the incentive to transfer stock from high-bracket to low-bracket taxpayers is diminished.

5. What's good for the goose . . . : In *Est. of Stranahan v. Commissioner,* 472 F.2d 867 (6th Cir. 1973), the taxpayer was entitled to a large interest deduction in 1964, but he didn't have enough income in that year to use the deduction. The taxpayer agreed with his son to transfer to the son the father's right to dividends on certain stock owned by him, in exchange for a payment equal to the present value of the future dividend income. The taxpayer, relying on assignment of income principles to work for his benefit, included the payment in income and deducted the interest payment. Naturally, the IRS objected. The Tax Court found the transaction lacking in business motive, and essentially a loan, not a sale. It found that the taxpayer did not realize income as a result of the transaction with his son.

  a. Issue: Did the taxpayer realize income on the sale, pursuant to assignment of income principles?

  b. Result and rationale: Yes. Even though the tax benefit was the sole motive for the transaction, it was a bona fide sale with all of a sale's attendant risk and reward. The nongratuitous nature of the transaction distinguishes it from *Helvering v. Horst* and related cases, and it must be respected for tax purposes. The taxpayer did assign the dividends, and receive payment in exchange, and the payment is includible in the taxpayer's gross income.

F. Transformation of services into property

In this situation, a taxpayer's services result in some item of income-producing property (often intellectual property) that he or she then gives to a related person. The issue is which person—the donor or the donee—should be taxed on the income from the property.

1. Rule: The assignment of the right to income alone arising from property created by services is an invalid assignment of income: The donor will be taxed on the income. By contrast, the transfer of the income-producing property itself is valid, resulting in the donee being taxed on the income. In order to qualify as property, the transfer must include some bundle of legally enforceable rights (other than the right to collect income) given to the donee by the donor.

2. Commissions—*Helvering v. Eubank,* 311 U.S. 122 (1940): A retired insurance agent assigned renewal commissions to others, who subsequently collected the commissions. The court relied on *Horst,* holding that the insurance agent was taxable on the commissions when paid to the assignees.

3. Patents: In *Heim v. Fitzpatrick,* 262 F.2d 887 (2d Cir. 1959), Mr. Heim invented a better mousetrap and applied for a patent. He then transferred the invention and patent application to a corporation owned by family members. Under an agreement with the corporation, Mr. Heim was entitled to certain royalties, retained some control over use of the invention, and retained a reversionary interest in the patent. He then transferred a portion of his interest in the agreement to his wife, son, and daughter (donees). The corporation paid royalties to Mr. Heim and the donees.

  a. Issue: Who should be taxed on the royalties due under the agreement—Mr. Heim or the donees?

  b. **Result and rationale:** The donees should be taxed on the income from the invention. Mr. Heim transferred income-producing property rather than merely assigning income from services rendered. The donees received not only the right to the royalties but certain legally enforceable rights relating to the invention and patents, including the power to bargain for royalties on new uses of the patent and the reversionary interest in the invention and patents.

G. What about transfers of property?

1. **Does the doctrine apply?** So far, the assignment of income doctrine has been applied to the transfer of services income, and the transfer of property that is essentially the culmination of a taxpayer's services. Will it apply to transactions purely in what is thought of as traditional "property"? Maybe. This also raises questions about what property really is.

2. *Salvatore v. Commissioner,* **29 T.C.M. 89 (1970)**

   a. **Facts:** Mrs. Salvatore inherited real property operated as a service station from her husband. She and her children ran it, dividing the income among themselves; she received what she needed for her support, and the children divided the rest. Texaco offered to buy the property, and Salvatore agreed. The sales price was to be divided, by family agreement, between Salvatore, up to the amount they estimated she needed for her lifetime support, and the rest to her children equally. To accomplish this, just before the sale, Salvatore made a gift of one-half of the property to the children, and she reported the gain only on her remaining one-half of the property.

   b. **Issue:** How much gain on the sale of the property is Mrs. Salvatore taxable on—all of it, or just one-half? In other words, who has income on the sale of the property: Mrs. Salvatore only, or Mrs. Salvatore and her children?

   c. **Result and rationale:** Mrs. Salvatore is taxable on all of the gain. She impermissibly assigned one-half of the income from the sale to her children. The children were treated as "mere conduits" for the income.

      i. **The gift:** The gift of the property was valid under state law; the deeds were recorded and all formalities respected. Mrs. Salvatore even paid gift tax on the gift. But the amount of the gift was conditional upon Mrs. Salvatore's need for income: If she had needed more, the gift would have been less.

      ii. **Fundamental principles:** If you continue in the study of tax, you'll see versions of this transaction again, in corporate tax (*Court Holding Company v. Commissioner,* 342 U.S. 331 (1945)) and throughout estate and gift tax. The fundamental principles: The substance of a transaction, not its form, governs its federal income tax consequences, and familial transfers are subject to special scrutiny.

3. **Choses in action:** A taxpayer may transfer to another the right to prosecute a claim and receive a recovery. If the transfer occurs when recovery is contingent and uncertain, the transferor will not be considered to have assigned the income. If the transfer occurs when payment is relatively certain, the transferring taxpayer must include the amount in gross income, and then is deemed to have transferred that amount to the transferee. *When* the right to payment becomes certain is a question of fact. See, e.g., *Doyle v. Commissioner,* 147 F.2d 769 (4th Cir. 1945).

H. Contingent fee awards—*Banks v. Commissioner,* 543 U.S. 426 (2005)

When a taxpayer hires an attorney on a contingent fee basis, such as in a personal injury lawsuit, the recovery is usually paid to the attorney, who deducts his or her fee and gives the balance to the client. In a personal physical injury case, of course, none of this amount is includible in gross income. But for nonphysical injury cases, all of the recovery must be included in gross income. Prior to *Banks,* many taxpayers argued that the amount paid to the attorney as fees was not included in gross income, and some courts agreed. In *Banks,* the Supreme Court held that all of the award—including the amount paid to the attorney—is included in the client/plaintiff's gross income for a nonphysical injury.

1. **What's the problem?** The taxpayer may claim a deduction for the attorneys' fees, but these are miscellaneous itemized deductions. This creates two problems. First, miscellaneous itemized deductions are subject to the 2% floor, rendering some of them nondeductible. See Chapter 6(X). Second, none of the miscellaneous itemized deductions are deductible in computing the AMT. See Chapter 13(III). As a result, many taxpayers receiving apparently large awards end up paying tax on all of the award, even though they didn't receive the portion attributable to attorneys' fees.

2. **Statutory response:** For certain kinds of nonphysical injuries, Congress has allowed an above-the-line deduction for attorneys' fees. See Chapter 6(II)(G) and Chapter 13(III)(B) (AMT issues).

I. Be alert for assignment of income issues: Related taxpayer have an incentive to act as one economic unit. Be alert to situation in which a taxpayer in a high income tax bracket tries to lower the rate on the overall group by assigning it to someone in a lower bracket. Consider also the issue of gifts in this context.

IV. STATUTORY RESPONSES TO ASSIGNMENT OF INCOME AND RELATED PROBLEMS

The previous sections have set forth the judicially developed assignment of income principles. Congress has also responded in a limited fashion to assignment of income problems.

A. Section 1(g)—The Kiddie Tax

Children are often in a lower tax bracket than their parents and grandparents, and this creates an incentive for parents and grandparents to transfer income-producing property to them so that the income from the property is taxed at the child's lower rate. This type of planning is not precluded under assignment of income principles because the property itself is transferred to the child.

1. **Tax at parents' rate:** The kiddie tax reduces this incentive by taxing the child's ***unearned income*** at the parents' tax rate. IRC §1(g)(1).

2. **Only certain income:** The kiddie tax applies only if the following conditions are met.

   a. **Age/status of child:** It is applicable to children 18 years of age and under, with at least one parent living. IRC §1(g)(2). It also applies to students age 19–23 if they do not provide over half of their support through earned income.

   b. **Unearned income:** The kiddie tax applies only to investment income, not earned income such as income from a paper route or film salaries. IRC §1(g)(4).

    c. Dollar amount: The kiddie tax applies to investment income in excess of $1,900 (2011), so that the first $1,900 (in 2011) of the child's investment income is taxed at his or her lower rate. IRC §1(g)(4).

    d. Include in parental return: The kiddie tax has a special option for parents to include their children's investment income on their own tax returns, in which case the child's income is taxed to the parents. IRC §1(g)(7).

B. Reallocation of income and deductions—§482

Section 482 is a broad statute, allowing the IRS to *reallocate* among members of commonly controlled businesses items of income, deduction, and credit if necessary to prevent evasion of tax or clearly to reflect income of the businesses. Although a detailed analysis is beyond the scope of most basic federal income tax courses, §482 should be noted as an effective tool for the IRS in ensuring that the appropriate taxpayer pays tax on various items of income.

V. NEED TO KNOW MORE?

This book's website *www.aspenlawschool.com/books/tax_outline* contains additional information, including:

- How identification of the taxpayer "fits" with the basic concepts of income, gain, loss, deduction, and credit.

- Overview of how entities are taxed.

- Calculation of the kiddie tax.

- And other materials that will help you identify the proper taxpayer.

VI. WHERE ARE WE GOING?

This chapter has concluded the discussion of the computation of a taxpayer's tax liability (by identifying the proper taxpayer) and has introduced a common technique of tax planning (assignment of income). The next chapter turns to a fundamental financial concept—the time value of money—that motivates much of tax planning and generates congressional response to that planning.

Quiz Yourself on IDENTIFYING THE TAXPAYER

158. What is the tax incentive for a taxpayer to assign income? If tax rates become more progressive, is there a greater or lesser incentive to engage in assignment of income strategies?

---

159. Danielle writes romantic novels. Her daughter Tiffany is 12 years old. Danielle requests that her publisher (the owner of the copyright to Danielle's works) pay all the royalties on the book to be published this year to Tiffany, so that Tiffany can begin saving money for college. Her publisher does so, and reports Tiffany as the taxpayer on the required Form 1099. Is this correct? _____

160. Will Danielle be successful in having the royalties taxed to Tiffany if she owned the copyright and transferred it to Tiffany? _____

161. Retired lawyer Peter assists his friend, Lawyer Dan, in a case. Ultimately, Dan arranges a settlement in which his fee will be $300,000. Dan wants to split this fee with Peter, but since Peter no longer has his license, this would be unethical under the rules of the state in which Peter and Dan live. Not needing the money, Peter says to Dan "Just make a $50,000 gift to my favorite charity, and we'll call it even." If they go forward with this plan, who will be taxed on the legal fee and why? Is there a charitable deduction to be had, and if so, who is entitled to it? _____

162. Sam is Peter's grandfather. Peter's parents are living. Sam owns a number of bonds and regularly receives interest payments on these bonds. Sam directs the company that issued the bonds to pay Peter, rather than Sam, the interest on the bonds for two years. The company does so. Who is taxed on this interest, and why? _____

163. Assume the same facts as in the previous question, except that the bonds are tax-exempt private activity bonds. Why would it matter who is taxed on these interest payments if they are tax-exempt? _____

164. Barbara is George's mother. Barbara owns a ranch in Texas. In Year One, she transferred an undivided 50% interest in the ranch to George, as a gift. In Year Ten, a buyer purchases the ranch for $2,000,000. Barbara and George each report one-half of the gain on the sale. Is this correct? _____

165. Brian files a lawsuit against Rob alleging defamation of character. Prior to trial, Brian's health starts to fail. He assigns his rights in the action to Steve for a payment of $500,000. The trial and subsequent appeals result in an award of $5 million. Who, if anyone, must include this amount in gross income? _____

166. Kayla sues her employer for race discrimination. She hires an attorney on a contingent fee basis to represent her. Ultimately, the court enters a judgment of $500,000 against the employer. The lawyer's share of that is $165,000 for fees and $35,000 for costs, and Kayla receives $300,000. How should she treat this transaction for tax purposes? _____

167. Assume the same facts as in the previous question, except that the action was for slander rather than discrimination. What changes, if anything? _____

168. Spencer is age 12. He has a paper route, from which he makes $3,600 per year. He also has investment income of $3,000 per year from stocks and bonds given to him by relatives over the years. Spencer's parents are living. How will Spencer be taxed on his income? _____

169. Spencer's brother, Corbin, is age 20. He is a student at the local community college and has a part-time job at a local coffee house. He has investment income of $5,000 per year. How will Corbin be taxed on this income? _____

Answers

158. Taxpayers "assign" income in order to direct it to a person in a lower tax rate than their own and to avoid paying gift taxes. If a father is in the 33% bracket for ordinary income and his son is in the 15% bracket, it makes sense for the father to try to direct income to the son, as the family as a unit will save 18% in taxes if the attempt is successful. As tax rates become more progressive (i.e., there is a larger spread between the lowest and highest rates), there is a greater incentive to engage in assignment of income strategies.

159. Danielle has probably engaged in an inappropriate assignment of income. She transferred income from services (transformed into "property"—the intellectual property that gives rise to the income) to her daughter, who did not perform the services. However, she would argue that there is no impermissible assignment because she transferred all of the income stream. However, without also transferring the intellectual property that gives rise to the income, she retains power over that income stream that would defeat her argument.

160. If Danielle can transfer the intellectual property (the copyright) to Tiffany, she will be able to direct the income to Tiffany as well. Of course, the transfer of the copyright to Tiffany will be a gift (not includible in Tiffany's income for income tax purposes (§102), but a gift for gift tax purposes).

161. In these circumstances only Dan could legally receive the legal fee under the rules of the state bar. Therefore, he would be required to include the entire $300,000 fee in gross income. His transfer of $50,000 to the charity would not likely generate a charitable deduction for him, as he would be making the contribution as a quid pro quo for Dan's services. The more likely characterization is that Peter would be deemed to have paid Dan a $50,000 fee for services, which Peter would be required to include in gross income. The charitable deduction would inure to Peter, who is deemed to make a donation of the amount received. (Whether this arrangement is ethical is a separate question.)

162. Sam is taxed on the interest. He cannot give away just the interest element. If he wants Peter to be taxed on the interest, then Sam must give Peter the bonds.

163. If the income is tax-exempt interest, it won't matter who is deemed to own it for regular tax purposes. But this kind of interest income may be included in alternative minimum taxable income, and therefore the assignment of income doctrine will apply.

164. It is probably correct. Although the *Salvatore* case might raise questions, in this case (1) the length of time between gift and ultimate sale; and (2) the absence of facts suggesting that Barbara's share was uncertain supports the taxpayers' position that the transfer was bona fide and that the substance of the transaction is a sale by both Barbara and George of the property.

165. Brian's assignment of his claim will probably not result in an assignment of income because the claim is contingent and doubtful at the time of transfer. Thus, the transferee will properly include the amount in gross income. Because Steve has a basis in this action of $500,000, he will include only $4,500,000 in gross income; the rest will be a return of capital. Steve will argue that this is capital gain, but is unlikely to prevail. See Chapter 12(III).

166. Under *Banks*, Kayla must include the entire amount of the award ($500,000) in her gross income when she receives it. (Section 104(a) doesn't apply to exclude this award because this is a nonphysical injury.) However, Kayla will be allowed an above-the-line deduction (a deduction from gross income in computing AGI) for her attorneys' fees and costs.

167. In this case, Kayla must still include the $500,000 in her gross income, but is not allowed an above-the-line deduction in computing AGI for her attorneys' fees and costs. Instead, she can claim these as a miscellaneous itemized deduction, subject to the 2% floor of §67.

168. Spencer will probably file his own tax return, but he does have the option of filing with his parents. His regular tax rate (10%) will apply to his earned income and up to $1,900 of his investment income. But the remaining amount of investment income will be taxed at his parents' marginal rate.

169. Corbin's situation is a little more difficult to analyze than Spencer's. At his age, for the kiddie tax to apply, Corbin must be a full-time student for at least five months of the year and must not provide more than one-half of his support during the year in question. If those two conditions apply, the kiddie tax will apply to Corbin and all of his investment income in excess of $1,900 will be taxed at his parents' rate. If not, Corbin's regular tax rate will apply to all of his income, earned and investment.

Exam Tips *on*
IDENTIFYING THE TAXPAYER

☛ Even though the discussion of the assignment of income doctrine comes close to the end of this book, it is conceptually one of the first questions you should ask yourself in analyzing tax questions.

    ☞ *Look for:* Intrafamily transfers, usually from a senior generation to a younger generation, with the opportunity to lower taxes on the overall economic unit.

    ☞ *Analyze:* Has there been an impermissible assignment of income from one person to another? What is the result of this assignment? Is there a judicial doctrine or statutory "fix" that prevents this assignment?

☛ Use the smell test: Does it seem that the taxpayer is "getting away with something" by transferring income or property to another person? If so, the question probably involves an assignment of income problem.

☛ The assignment of income doctrine applies most often to services income.

    ☞ *Look for:* One person who performs services, but another receives the compensation, in money or other property. That other person just happens to be in a lower tax bracket.

    ☞ *Analyze:* Compensation income is taxed to the person who performs services. Then, that person is considered to have made a gift to the person who ended up with the income. However, if state, federal, or foreign law divides the income between two people—that will usually be respected.

☛ The assignment of income doctrine also applies to income arising from property.

    ☞ *Look for:* Assignments of dividends, interest, rent, royalties, etc.

☞ *Analyze:* Did the assignor transfer the underlying property or just the income stream? If only the income stream, it is likely to be an impermissible assignment of income.

☛ The *Banks* case is good fodder for testing, not only because it is a recent Supreme Court tax case, but also because it combines issues of gross income, deductions, and the AMT. Make sure you understand *Banks* and the stakes of the controversy.

☛ Remember two fundamental principles:

☞ Familial transfers are subject to particular scrutiny.

☞ The substance of a transaction governs its federal income tax consequences—not its form. If it seems too good to be true, it probably is.

CHAPTER 15

TIME VALUE OF MONEY: PRINCIPLES AND APPLICATIONS

Chapter Scope

The previous chapters have focused on the issues surrounding the calculation of a taxpayer's tax liability; from identifying items of income, deduction, and credit, to identifying the appropriate taxpayer and tax rate. This chapter turns to a more general principle, the time value of money. The time value of money, simply expressed, is the notion that a sum of money will earn interest when invested. Thus, a dollar invested for one year at 8% interest will be worth $1.08 one year in the future (ignoring inflation). Time value of money principles are important in tax law for two reasons. First, some Code sections specifically incorporate time value of money principles in prescribing the proper tax treatment of certain transactions, principally those dealing with loans and similar undertakings. More generally, the time value of money often motivates taxpayers to engage in certain tax-planning strategies, and understanding how the time value of money operates helps one understand these common strategies. This chapter explores both the specific and general applications of the time value of money in tax law.

Key concepts in this chapter include:

- **Time value of money:** This chapter introduces the basic concept of the time value of money and the calculation of present and future values.

- **Specific applications:** The Code specifically invokes time value of money concepts in prescribing the tax treatment of loans, debt instruments, and similar arrangements.

- **Deferral of income and acceleration of deductions:** Recognizing time value of money concepts, taxpayers typically seek to defer income as far into the future as possible and accelerate deductions to the earliest possible year. These principles form the basis of many common tax-planning strategies.

I. WHERE ARE WE?

The focus of this chapter isn't the Code, or technical questions of income or deduction or credit. Instead, we now turn to a principle underlying much of tax planning and legislative responses to that planning: the time value of money. As with the assignment of income principles discussed in the previous chapter, time value of money concepts appear explicitly only in a few places in the Code, mainly dealing with loan transactions. However, understanding how time value of money principles inspire taxpayers to take certain tax-planning steps, and why the IRS and Congress are motivated to block these steps, is critical to understanding tax law in general.

II. TIME VALUE OF MONEY PRINCIPLES—THE BASICS

A. In general

The essence of the time value of money is expressed in the old adage, "A penny saved is a penny earned." But this works only if the saver doesn't stash the penny in a mattress. The alert saver will lend his or her penny to someone else, and that borrower will pay the lender for the privilege of using the penny during the period of the loan. Thus, the penny will earn more pennies for the saver, and given sufficient time, the saver will have dozens of pennies. The saver will have dozens, not just a few, because of the "miracle" of *compound interest.* Compounding means that the lender earns interest not only on his or her principal sum but also on the interest earned. As a result of compounding, the investor will end up with many more pennies than the average person expects. The longer the investment period, and the higher the interest rate, of course, the more pennies will be earned. Add a few zeros, and this process becomes very interesting indeed.

Example: Leslie, age 50, invested $2,000 in an IRA. It earned interest at 12% compounded annually, tax-free. By the time she retired at age 60, her single $2,000 investment had grown to $6,211. Had Leslie made her investment at age 40, allowing 20 years for her investment to grow, she would have had $19,321 in her nest egg. Had she invested $2,000 at age 20, allowing 40 years of growth, she would have had $186,916 at retirement.

B. Interest

Interest is the cost of using money. A lender charges a borrower interest for the privilege of using the lender's funds during the period of the loan, and thus the lender is said to earn interest on the loan. Interest is expressed as a percentage of the principal amount of the loan for a stated period, usually a year.

1. **Simple interest:** *Simple interest* is calculated as a percentage of the principal sum.

2. **Compound interest:** *Compound interest* is computed by applying the interest rate to both the principal sum and the accrued, but unpaid, interest. Compounding can occur at various intervals—typically daily, monthly, half-yearly, or annually.

   Example: Steve lends Andy $1,000 at 10% interest to be repaid in a lump sum in two years. If the loan provides for simple interest, the loan will generate $100 in interest each year that it is outstanding. If the loan provides for interest compounded annually, in the first year the loan will generate interest of $100. In the second year, the loan will generate interest of $110, which is calculated by adding the interest on the principal amount ($1,000 × 10% = $100) and the interest on the accrued but unpaid interest ($100 × 10% = $10).

3. **Market rate of interest:** A typical loan carries a *market rate of interest,* i.e., the interest rate at which loans of the same type are made in the general lending market. The interest rate depends on a variety of factors, including the repayment risk (a higher-risk loan comes with a higher interest rate) and the general availability of funds. It is not always easy to determine the market rate of interest for any specific loan, but the IRS makes things easy by publishing tables that can be used for tax purposes. See this chapter, Section II(F)(1).

C. Future value of a stated sum

We can calculate what amount will eventually be created for any amount today, if we know the rate of return (interest rate) and period of time of investment. This is the *future value* of the principal sum (or any investment), calculated using the following formula:

$$FV = PV(1+i)^n$$

FV = Future value
PV = Present value of invested (or loaned) amount
  i = interest rate
  n = number of years invested (or loaned)

Example—Loan: Larry lends Bob $10,000 at 10% interest compounded annually for five years. At the end of five years, Bob will pay Larry $16,129, calculated as follows:

$$FV = \$10,000 \times (1+ .10)^5$$

$$FV = \$10,000 \times (1.1)^5$$

$$FV = \$10,000 \times 1.6129$$

$$FV = \$16,129$$

D. Present value of a future sum

Present value is the mirror image of future value, based on the same principles and derived from the same formula. Present value is the current value, given an assumed interest rate, of a right to a stated amount in the future. Differently expressed, it is also the amount that must be invested today, at a given interest rate and for a given period, to produce a stated amount. Present value can be computed using the following formula, which is simply the future value formula algebraically rearranged to solve for present value.

$$PV = \frac{F}{(1 + i)^n}$$

PV = Present Value
FV = Future Value
  i = interest rate
  n = number of years

Example: Brenda is planning for her daughter's college education. She predicts she will need $100,000 in ten years and can earn 6% on her investment. She calculates how much she will need to invest ($55,800) as follows:

$$PV = \frac{\$100,000}{(1 + .06)^{10}}$$

$$PV = \frac{\$100,000}{1.7921}$$

$$PV = \$55,800$$

Example: Kate's employer offers her a bonus of either $75,000 today or $150,000 due in five years. Current interest rates are 8%. Disregarding taxes (and constructive receipt!), which offer is more valuable? To answer this question, the present value of the $150,000 five years hence must be calculated. Kate does so as follows:

$$PV = \frac{\$150,000}{(1 + .08)^5}$$

$$PV = \frac{\$150,000}{1.4684}$$

$$PV = \$102,150$$

The calculation shows that the five-year offer is the more valuable of the two, suggesting that Kate should accept the five-year offer.

Figure 15A
Present Value Table

Year	2%	3%	4%	5%	6%	7%	8%	9%	10%	12%	15%
1	.980	.971	.962	.952	.943	.935	.926	.917	.909	.893	.870
2	.961	.943	.925	.907	.890	.873	.857	.842	.826	.797	.756
3	.942	.915	.889	.864	.840	.816	.794	.772	.751	.712	.658
4	.924	.888	.855	.823	.792	.763	.735	.708	.683	.636	.572
5	.906	.863	.822	.784	.747	.713	.681	.650	.621	.567	.497
6	.888	.837	.790	.746	.705	.666	.630	.596	.564	.507	.432
7	.871	.813	.760	.712	.665	.623	.583	.547	.513	.452	.376
8	.853	.789	.731	.677	.627	.582	.540	.502	.467	.404	.327
9	.837	.766	.703	.645	.592	.544	.500	.460	.424	.361	.284
10	.820	.744	.676	.614	.558	.508	.463	.422	.386	.322	.247
15	.743	.642	.555	.481	.417	.362	.315	.275	.239	.182	.123
20	.673	.554	.456	.377	.311	.258	.215	.178	.149	.104	.061
25	.610	.478	.375	.295	.233	.184	.146	.116	.092	.059	.030
30	.552	.412	.308	.231	.174	.131	.099	.075	.057	.033	.015
35	.500	.355	.253	.181	.130	.094	.067	.049	.036	.019	.008
40	.453	.307	.208	.142	.097	.067	.046	.032	.022	.012	.004

To determine the present value of a future sum, multiply the sum by the figure at the intersection of the row indicating the year in the future and the column representing the interest (discount) rate.

To determine the future value of a present sum, divide the sum by the figure at the intersection of the row indicating the year in the future and the column representing the discount rate.

E. Using present value tables

Instead of using the formulas above, the present and future values may be derived from commonly available tables. See Figure 15A. Today, of course, many useful websites offer calculators for computing present value and future value.

1. **Future value:** The future value of a sum invested today is calculated using the tables by locating the entry found in the table at the intersection of the column representing the given interest rate and the row representing the given number of years to maturity. The sum to be invested is divided by that figure to determine the future value of the beginning sum.

   Example: Peter has $10,000 to invest at 10% for 20 years. To determine the future value of this sum, i.e., the amount he will have at the end of the 20-year period, divide $10,000 by 0.149. Thus, Peter will have $67,114 at the end of this period.

2. **Present value:** The present value of a sum available in the future also can be determined using the tables, given an interest rate and the number of years to maturity. To do so, multiply the sum available in the future by the entry found in the table at the intersection of the column representing the given interest rate and the row representing the given number of years to maturity.

   Example: Katherine is planning to retire in 20 years and estimates that she will need $1 million at that time. She can earn 8% on a one-time investment made today. How much must she invest today to have $1 million in 20 years, i.e., what is the present value of $1 million 20 years hence at 8%? To determine this, multiply $1 million by 0.215 to produce $215,000. Katherine must invest $215,000 today in order to have $1 million at retirement.

F. The Code's use of time value of money principles

Although the Code does not import time value of money principles on a global scale, it does recognize these principles in a number of specific transactions principally relating to loans and similar undertakings.

1. **Federal rates:** Every month, the IRS publishes interest rates (known as the *applicable federal rate* or *AFR*) that are used for computations under various Code provisions. There are many different rates, used for different purposes, but the major categories are the federal *short-term rate* (for obligations designed to be outstanding for fewer than five years), the *mid-term rate* (five through nine years), and the *long-term rate* (ten years or more).

2. **Tax over- and underpayments:** If a taxpayer overpays tax, the government will pay interest on the overpayment at a rate of the federal short-term rate plus 3%. IRC §6621(a)(1). If a taxpayer underpays tax, the taxpayer must pay interest at a rate of the federal short-term rate plus 3%. IRC §6621(a)(2).

3. **Loan transactions:** Much of the time value of money material in the Code addresses loan transactions. When one unrelated party lends money to another, the lender charges interest on the loan at market rates. However, related parties may want to make interest-free loans to transfer value to the borrower, and sellers and buyers of property may want to characterize income as capital gain rather than ordinary income. Various provisions of the Code prevent this by imputing interest (which is ordinary income, of course) to loan transactions.

III. ORIGINAL ISSUE DISCOUNT (OID)

Most basic tax courses do not involve any discussion of original issue discount. The materials that follow discuss only the policy and general approach of the OID rules.

A. Policy

Sometimes a debt instrument will not provide for market interest payable annually during the period of the debt, but instead will build the interest payment into the final payment (repayment) of the debt. This strategy would offer two tax benefits for investors (creditors), the second of which specifically invokes the time value of money principle. First, the repayment in excess of the original amount loaned might be considered capital gain on the repayment of the debt. Second, the creditor might defer the inclusion of any amount in gross income as interest until the end of the investment. The OID and related rules seek to preclude both of these misstatements of the economic realities of the loan.

Example: Steve, a cash method taxpayer, lends Andy $1,000,000 at 10% interest, compounded annually, to be repaid in a lump sum in two years. Thus, at the end of the two years, Andy will repay Steve his principal of $1,000,000 and interest of $210,000. Steve might argue that the $210,000 should be treated as capital gain, which, as you know from Chapter 12, would not be a winning argument. More importantly, Steve would argue that because he did not receive his payment until Year 2, he should not have to include any amount in gross income until that year. This would offer him the opportunity to defer the tax on the first year's interest, achieving significant tax savings.

B. What the OID rules do

The OID rules require the holder of a debt instrument who doesn't actually receive interest to include in his or her gross income the amount of interest that is accruing. Using the previous example, assuming the OID rules apply, Steve would be required to include in his gross income interest of $100,000 in Year 1 and $110,000 of interest in Year 2 and Andy may be able to deduct that interest if it qualifies for a deduction. The OID rules contain complex mechanisms for computing the amount of interest and the timing of its inclusion in gross income.

IV. IMPUTED INTEREST—§483

Section 483 imputes to the creditor interest on certain loans made in connection with sales or exchanges of property that are not subject to the OID provisions. Unlike the OID provisions, basic tax courses often involve a discussion of §483, particularly in connection with sales and exchanges of property (see Chapters 9 and 10).

A. Policy

A taxpayer who sells property to another for payments to be received in the future is essentially engaging in two different transactions—the sale of property and the lending of funds to the buyer. Because of the time value of money, a lender would be expected to charge interest on the loan. However, in the context of the sale of property, the tax preference for capital gains creates an incentive to "hide" interest in the purchase price of the property. This is because interest received by a creditor is included in gross income and taxed at the usual rates, but net capital gain from the sale of property will be taxed at a maximum 28%. As a result, sellers of capital assets might well attempt to characterize all or a large part of what is received as the sales price for property rather than interest. Section 483 prevents this by imputing to the transaction a market rate of interest.

Example: Jeff owns Blackacre with a basis of zero and a fair market value of $100,000. Blackacre is raw land that Jeff holds for investment. Wendy wishes to buy Blackacre, but cannot pay the entire $100,000 today. At a time when interest rates are 10%, Wendy agrees to pay Jeff $110,000 for Blackacre one year from date of sale, but the contract provides for no interest to be paid. Because Jeff is in the 35% bracket, he would like to characterize the entire $110,000 as net capital gain subject to the maximum 15% tax rate. However, economically this transaction is a sale of Blackacre for $100,000 and the payment of interest of $10,000. Thus, Jeff will have $100,000 of capital gain and $10,000 of ordinary income after §483 is applied to the transaction.

B. Statutory analysis—§483

1. **General rule:** Section 483 applies when there is a contract for the sale or exchange of property under which at least one payment is due more than one year after the date of the contract and there is ***total unstated interest.*** IRC §483(c). If §483 applies, the total unstated interest will be included in the creditor's gross income. IRC §483(a). The creditor will determine the timing of that inclusion based on his or her regular method of accounting. Reg. §1.483-1(a)(2)(ii).

2. **Definitional issue—Total unstated interest:** Total unstated interest is the excess of the total payments due under the contract over the sum of the present values of those payments and the present value of any interest payment provided for in the contract, using a discount rate equal to the applicable federal rate under §1274(d). IRC §483(b).

   Example: Betty, a cash method taxpayer, owns Whiteacre with an adjusted basis of $100,000. At a time when market interest rates are 7%, she agrees to sell Whiteacre to Carl for $250,000 on the following terms: No cash down, the entire $250,000 due in three years, and no interest on the loan.

   Section 483 applies to this transaction because:

   - The contract is for the sale or exchange of property,

   - There is at least one payment due more than one year after the date of the contract, and

   - The OID rules do not apply because the price is not more than $250,000.

   Section 483 requires that Betty include in her gross income the total unstated interest ratably over the period of time she holds the contract. The total unstated interest is equal to the excess of the payments to be received under the contract ($250,000) over the present value of those payments ($204,000, assuming a 7% interest rate). Thus, Betty must include in her gross income the $46,000 of interest on the contract when she receives it. The remaining amount ($204,000) will be payment for Whiteacre.

   Correlative effects of recharacterizing the transaction:

   - Carl may be able to deduct the interest deemed paid on the contract.

   - Carl's basis in the rental property is $204,000 (the imputed principal amount).

   - Betty's gain on the sale is Carl's purchase price of $204,000 minus her basis of $100,000, or $104,000.

3. **Special rules and exceptions**

    a. **Price limitation:** Section 483 does not apply to sales with purchase prices not exceeding $3,000. IRC §483(d)(2).

    b. **Maximum interest rate:** For a qualified sale (sale or exchange of land to a related party) with purchase price not exceeding $500,000, the maximum imputed interest is 6%, compounded semiannually. IRC §483(e)(1).

4. **Related material**

    a. **Coordination of §483 with OID rules:** Section 483 does not apply to any debt instrument for which an issue price is determined under the OID rules of §§1273(b) or 1274. IRC §438(d)(1).

    b. **Below-market loans:** Certain transactions not subject to §483 may be subject to the below-market rules of §7872. See this chapter, Section (V).

    c. **Deduction for imputed interest:** A debtor who is deemed to pay interest under §483 may be entitled to deduct that interest, if the other requirements for interest deductibility are met.

    d. **Calculation of basis to buyer and realized gain to seller:** Section 483's recharacterization of the transaction necessarily affects the calculation of the amount realized and basis of the property.

5. **Be alert to imputed interest issues for property sales:** Imputed interest rules can apply whenever a loan (whether explicit or implicit) is created and does not carry a market rate of interest. Section 483 potentially applies to any sale or exchange of property without total unstated interest.

V. BELOW-MARKET LOANS—§7872

Section 7872 provides that when a person makes a loan to another that provides for interest at a rate below the market rate of interest, the transaction may be recharacterized in order to ensure that the creditor includes the market rate of interest in gross income.

A. Policy

Low- or no-interest loans are often an important feature of a number of other relationships. For example, employers can compensate employees by providing them with interest-free or low-interest loans. Section 7872 seeks to make the tax consequences of these arrangements match their economic substance, by imputing a market rate of interest to the loan and requiring certain correlative tax consequences as well (such as payment of compensation or the making of a gift).

B. Statutory analysis—§7872

1. **General rule:** Below-market demand, term, and gift loans are recharacterized so that the creditor includes the appropriate amount of interest in gross income. IRC §7872(a)(1).

    a. **Recharacterization of gift loans and demand loans:** Section 7872 treats the forgone interest as transferred from the lender to the borrower, and retransferred from the borrower to the lender on the last day of the taxable year. IRC §7872(a)(1)(A), (B). Each leg of the transaction must be characterized in accordance with its substance, i.e., gift, interest payment, compensation, etc.

b. Recharacterization of other types of below-market loans: Section 7872 identifies the excess of the amount loaned over the present value of all payments to be received under the loan. It treats the lender as transferring this amount to the borrower on the date the loan is made. The below-market loan is then treated as having OID in the same amount. IRC §7872(b). The deemed transfer from the lender to the borrower must be characterized in accordance with its substance (as, for example, a gift or compensation). The characterization of the loan as having OID means that the creditor must include a ratable portion of the OID in gross income over the term of the loan.

2. Definitional issues

a. Demand loan: A demand loan is a loan payable on demand of the creditor. IRC §7872(f).

b. Term loan: A term loan is a loan payable on a certain date fixed or determinable by the loan instrument. IRC §7872(f).

c. Gift loan: A gift loan is a loan in the context of which the creditor's forbearance of interest is properly viewed as a gift. IRC §7872(f).

Example—Gift loan: Donna loans her son Edward $50,000 for two years, and the note provides for no interest at a time when the applicable federal rate is 10%. Since it is likely that Donna's forbearance of interest is intended as a gift, this is a gift loan. Section 7872 will characterize this transaction as a gift each year of $5,000 by Donna to Edward, and an identical payment of interest by Edward to Donna. As a result, Donna will include the $5,000 of interest income each year in her gross income.

d. Below-market loans: A demand loan is below market if its stated interest is less than the applicable federal rate at the time of the making of the loan. IRC §7872(e)(1)(A). A term loan is a below-market loan if the amount loaned is greater than the present value of the payments due under the loan, using the applicable federal rate as the discount rate. IRC §7872(e)(1)(B).

3. Special rules and exceptions

a. Small gift loans: Section 7872 doesn't apply to gift loans between individuals if the total outstanding principal amount for all loans between them does not exceed $10,000. IRC §7872(c)(2).

b. Income limitation: If the total amount of gift loans between two related parties does not exceed $100,000, the amount recast as interest income to the lender is limited to the investment income of the borrower. IRC §7872(d)(1). Investment income includes interest, dividends, royalties, and gains from the disposition of investment property.

c. Small employee loans: Section 7872 doesn't apply to compensation-related and corporation-shareholder loans if the total outstanding principal amount of all loans made to the employee/shareholder does not exceed $10,000. IRC §7872(c)(3).

4. Related material

a. Coordination of §7872 with §§483 and 1274: Section 7872 does not apply to any loan to which either §1274 or §483 applies. IRC §7872(f)(8).

b. Gifts, compensation, dividends, and related transactions: Section 7872 recharacterizes a below-market loan in accordance with its economic substance. The tax consequences of this recharacterization must be analyzed in terms of the transfers deemed made, as gifts, compensation, dividends, or other transactions. See generally Chapters 2 through 4.

5. **Be alert for imputed interest on loans:** Section 7872 potentially applies to any loan (usually between related parties) in which market interest is not charged. A loan can exist even without an explicit promissory note. It is critical to distinguish between situations in which §483 and §7872 apply, respectively.

VI. THE BASIC TAX STRATEGIES—DEFERRAL OF INCOME AND ACCELERATION OF DEDUCTIONS

A. In general

Time value of money principles inspire the most basic of tax-planning strategies—the deferral of income and acceleration of deductions. A taxpayer who includes an amount in gross income without offsetting deductions must pay tax at his or her applicable rate. The amount of the tax is therefore unavailable for investment. If, however, the taxpayer can avoid the tax by deferring the income or accelerating deductions to reduce taxable income to zero, the amount that otherwise would be paid in tax will be available for investment, earning interest over the period of time before tax is due (if ever). Even if the taxpayer must ultimately pay the deferred tax, he or she will usually come out ahead by the end of the investment period, unless tax rates rise dramatically over the period of investment.

Example: Compare the tax and economic situations of two taxpayers, Alvin and Betty. Alvin has $100,000 in income, with no offsetting deductions and is taxed (for illustrative purposes) at a flat 30%. He pays $30,000 in tax, leaving $60,000 for investment. Assuming he invests this amount for five years at 6% (after tax), he will have $80,292 at the end of the five-year period.

Betty has the same $100,000, but is able to invest the full amount for five years, paying the $30,000 tax only at the end of the five-year period. At the end of five years, having invested the $100,000 at 6% (after tax), Betty will have $133,820. When reduced by the $30,000 tax, this will give her $103,820. The tax deferral has given Betty a benefit of $23,528 over Alvin. Even if tax rates were to rise over the five-year period, Betty would still come out ahead, unless rates were to rise to over 54%.

B. Achieving tax savings

To take advantage of the time value of money, the taxpayer seeks to generate tax savings through deferral of income and acceleration of deductions. Income deferral requires that the taxpayer have a sufficient ownership interest in funds so that they will be invested for his or her benefit, but that taxation of these funds do not occur until a later year. Acceleration of deductions allows a taxpayer to offset current income, thus sheltering that income from tax and generating tax savings to be invested. Each of these is simply a timing strategy, moving to the future a tax that might be paid today. The time value of money suggests that this is a rational move, for the present value of a tax to be paid in the future is less than the same tax to be paid today. By contrast, the relentless taxpayer searching for exclusions from gross income and for tax credits seeks to forever exempt a sum from taxation and thus increase either investment or consumption without the necessity to plan for payment of a future tax.

C. Income deferral strategies

Taxpayers employ a wide variety of income deferral strategies. Congressional, administrative, and judicial responses to these strategies are embodied in various Code provisions and their interpretations. The following sections point out some common income deferral strategies.

1. **Method of accounting:** A taxpayer's method of accounting determines the proper taxable year for the inclusion of income in gross income. The cash method will allow deferral of income until amounts are actually or constructively received, and a taxpayer in a business where customers are slow to pay might well prefer the cash method as a deferral device.

   a. **Limitations on cash method:** Congress has placed a number of restrictions on the use of the cash method in situations where abuses of this method may arise. See Chapter 11(III)(B).

   b. **Constructive receipt:** A cash method taxpayer may seek to defer the inclusion of income by arranging a transaction so that he or she does not actually receive the income. This strategy is limited by the doctrine of constructive receipt. See Chapter 11(III)(B).

2. **Realization principle:** The realization principle, which requires a realization event to occur before gains in property are recognized, defers gains to future years. While the realization principle itself is not a taxpayer strategy, it perhaps encourages taxpayers to make investments in properties (such as growth stocks or real estate) that tend to appreciate in value over time. That appreciation will not be included in gross income until a realization event occurs. (Of course, the realization requirement also works to prevent recognition of losses on such investments prior to a realization event, but taxpayers can usually overcome this by simply selling loss property in the year they wish to take the loss.) For a discussion of realization, see Chapter 9(IV)(B).

3. **Nonrecognition provisions:** Various nonrecognition provisions specifically allow a taxpayer to defer the inclusion of income in gross income if certain specific requirements are met.

   a. **Like-kind exchanges:** Section 1031 of the Code allows a taxpayer to defer the recognition of gain on the exchange of certain property for like-kind property. See Chapter 10(III).

   b. **Involuntary conversions:** Section 1033 allows a taxpayer to defer income from the involuntary conversion of property into similar property. See Chapter 10(IV).

   c. **Divorce transactions:** Section 1041 allows a taxpayer to defer income from the division of property in divorce. See discussion in Chapter 10(V).

4. **Retirement planning:** Most of retirement planning is based on the notion of income deferral. For example, in a qualified plan, the employer's contribution to the plan is not included in the employee's gross income at the time of the contribution. The contribution earns interest, without tax, and the total amount is taxed to the employee as he or she withdraws it at retirement. Similarly, a taxpayer establishing an individual retirement account (IRA) will deduct (if qualified to do so) the contribution to the account. The contribution will earn interest without tax during the taxpayer's working years, and the entire amount will be included in the gross income of the taxpayer when he or she withdraws it at retirement.

5. **Education savings:** The Code offers a wide variety of incentives for education savings. Some of these involve deferral of income techniques, in which saving can occur in ways that the income from the investment of funds is not subject to tax currently—or perhaps ever.

a. **Education savings accounts:** Formerly known as "Education IRAs," these are accounts, usually held by banks or other custodians, to which taxpayers may contribute up to $2,000 per year per beneficiary. These accounts name a beneficiary, who is the person whose education is being funded. The account owner can direct investments, i.e., purchase individual stocks or mutual funds. No deduction is available for these contributions, but income earned in these accounts is not subject to tax. IRC §530(a).

   i.   **Cash/Age 18:** Contributions must be in cash and made before the beneficiary turns 18 (unless the beneficiary has special needs). IRC §530(b)(1).

   ii. **Treatment of distributions:** Any distribution is allocated between invested capital (tax-free) and income (potentially taxable) based on the rules of §72, discussed in Chapter 3(V)(F). IRC §530(d)(1). The income is tax-free (i.e., excluded from gross income) to the extent that it is used to fund qualified education expenses. IRC §530(d)(2). If qualified education expenses are less than the amount distributed, the expenses are deemed to come proportionately from invested capital and income. IRC §530(d)(2)(B).

   iii. **Qualified education expenses:** These are expenses for tuition, fees, books and supplies, not only for higher education but also for K-12 in a private, public, or religious school. IRC §530(b)(4).

   iv. **10% penalty tax:** Amounts of income not used for qualified education expenses are subject to an additional 10% penalty tax, with certain exceptions. IRC §530(d)(4).

   Example: Brittany receives a distribution from an Education Savings Account of $2,000. Assume that under the rules of §72, this is considered to consist of $500 of principal and $1,500 of income. Her qualified education expenses for the year are $1,000. Three-fourths of the qualified education expenses are considered to come from income (1,500/2,000 × 1,000 = $750) and one-fourth from principal (500/2000 × $1,000 = $500). Therefore, of the $1,500 of income, she used only $750 for qualified education expenses, and must include the rest in gross income and must pay the 10% penalty tax as well on this amount.

   v.   **Income limitations:** Contributions to education savings accounts are subject to income limitations, which may apply to reduce or eliminate the benefit of Education Savings Accounts.

b. **Section 529 Plans:** A second type of savings vehicle is the *§529 plan,* which is a plan established under state law allowing college savings. Under this type of plan, the account owner designates a beneficiary, and cannot direct the investment, although usually choices are given based on investment preferences. There is no deduction for contributions, but the investment earnings accrue tax-free, i.e., are not includible in the gross income of either the account owner or the beneficiary. IRC §529(c)(1). Many states offer tax deductions for investments in their §529 plan.

   i.   **Cash:** Contributions must be made in cash. IRC §529(b)(2).

   ii. **No contribution limits:** Each plan establishes its own limits on contributions, which are usually well over $25,000 per year. There is no federal limit on contributions.

iii. Treatment of distributions: Any distribution is allocated between invested capital (tax-free) and income (potentially taxable) based on the rules of §72, discussed in Chapter 3(V)(F). IRC §529(c)(3). The income is tax-free (i.e., excluded from gross income) to the extent that it is used to fund qualified education expenses. If qualified education expenses are less than the amount distributed, the expenses are deemed to come proportionately from invested capital and income (as in education savings accounts).

iv. Qualified education expenses: These are expenses for tuition, fees, books, and supplies, not only for higher education but also for K-12 in a private, public, or religious school. IRC §530(b)(4). It also includes the cost of room and board, within certain limits, for students who are enrolled at least half time. IRC §529(d)(3)(B).

v. 10% penalty tax: Amounts of income not used for qualified education expenses are subject to an additional 10% penalty tax, with certain exceptions. IRC §530(d)(4).

vi. No income limitations: Unlike most other education savings tax incentives, there are no income limits on the §529 plan, so taxpayers of any AGI amount can take advantage of this kind of plan.

D. Acceleration of deduction strategies

From a taxpayer's perspective, claiming deductions should follow the voting-in-Chicago rule: *early and often.* A taxpayer expending funds for a deductible item wants to claim the deduction for that item in the earliest year possible and to the greatest extent possible. And if deductions can be claimed before (or without) an actual cash outlay, the taxpayer will be even better off. The following sections describe some common deduction acceleration strategies.

1. **Method of accounting—the faster the better:** A taxpayer's method of accounting determines the proper taxable year for claiming a deduction.

   a. **Cash method strategies—Prepayments:** A cash method taxpayer cannot claim a deduction until an actual cash outlay is made, precluding a taxpayer from claiming a deduction prior to the year an actual cash outlay is made. But cash method taxpayers may try to accelerate deductions by making large prepayments (for rent or supplies, for example) applicable to several taxable years. The Code places certain restrictions on this strategy. See Chapter 11(III)(B).

   b. **Accrual method—Economic performance:** Accrual-method taxpayers may seek to deduct amounts they owe before they actually pay them. While this is an acceptable practice under accrual-method accounting, the Code prohibits certain deductions for accrual-method taxpayers until economic performance occurs. See Chapter 11(III)(C).

2. **Capital recovery:** The taxpayer's preference for accelerated deductions is clear in the area of capital recovery. Under the theory of depreciation, a wasting asset actually becomes less valuable over its useful life, and the wise owner will be contributing to a fund each year the amount necessary to replace the property at the end of its useful life. (In reality, however, few owners actually establish such a fund, in part because the asset may actually be increasing in value or because the owner's planning horizon is not sufficiently lengthy to make this fund worthwhile.) The capital recovery period allowed for tax purposes on the property, however, may be shorter than its actual useful life, thus accelerating deductions for the taxpayer.

a. **Section 179 expenditures:** Section 179 allows a taxpayer a deduction for the cost of certain otherwise capitalizable assets in the year of purchase. See Chapter 7(IV)(F).

b. **MACRS:** The recovery periods for assets covered by MACRS is set forth in the Code and administrative rulings. If the recovery period for an asset is shorter than the actual useful life of the asset, the taxpayer will enjoy an acceleration of deductions. See Chapter 7(IV)(G).

c. **Other capital recovery provisions:** Sections 195 (addressing pre-opening expenses) and 197 (addressing the amortization of intangibles) provide capital recovery for expenditures that may benefit taxpayers. See Chapter 7(II)(B), (IV)(H).

3. **Loss limitations:** Various loss limitations restrict the ability of taxpayers to accelerate deductions by recognizing losses.

a. **Capital loss restrictions:** An individual may deduct capital losses only to the extent of capital gains plus $3,000 of ordinary income. See Chapter 12(II).

b. **Passive loss restrictions:** Passive losses may be deducted only to the extent of passive income; any additional amounts carry forward and may be deducted against future passive income or against any income at the termination of the investment. See discussion in Chapter 11. See also the discussion of tax shelters, this chapter, in Section (VI)(B).

c. **Nonrecognition provisions:** If the requirements of the various nonrecognition provisions are met, taxpayers may not recognize loss on the transaction. See generally Chapter 10.

VII. NEED TO KNOW MORE?

This book's website *www.aspenlawschool.com/books/tax_outline* contains additional information, including:

- Directions to useful websites to calculate present and future value.

- Examples of calculations of present and future value.

- More on original issue discount.

- Examples of below-market loans.

- And other materials that will help you understand how the time value of money operates in the tax arena.

VIII. WHERE ARE WE GOING?

This chapter has begun the process of "pulling it all together" by showing how the time value of money principle inspires some of the most basic tax-planning strategies. The next chapter finishes that process by introducing a way to look at tax problems from a transactional viewpoint, to ensure that one asks the right questions in formulating tax advice.

Quiz Yourself on
TIME VALUE OF MONEY

170. Why should (and do) taxpayers care about the time value of money? _____

171. What is the present value of a promise to pay you $10,000 in five years, if the appropriate interest rate is 5%? What if the interest rate were 9%? _____

172. How much would you have to invest today to have $10,000 in eight years, if interest rates held steady at 6%? At 12%? _____

173. If you had $3,000 to invest today, and interest rates held steady at 4%, how much would you have at the end of 10 years? 15 years? 30 years? _____

174. Your rich aunt gives you a choice of receiving a gift of $50,000 today or a gift of $70,000 five years from now. Interest rates are holding steady at 8%. Which should you choose, assuming you are a rational taxpayer? _____

175. Grandmother is considering making a gift to her granddaughter, who is heading for college in a few years. She could either give the granddaughter $5,000 or contribute the same amount to a 529 plan for the granddaughter's benefit. From a tax perspective *only,* which plan would be better for Grandmother to implement? _____

176. Beverly is a doctor with a large income taxed at the highest federal and state tax rates. She tells you about an interesting offer that she has heard about from her broker. She has an opportunity to invest in a venture to locate and communicate with alien life forms. This has dazzling commercial potential. Start-up costs would be large, and she would have to invest $75,000, but this would result in over $300,000 of losses, that would serve as deductions to her over the next five years. She could use them to offset her salary income. Beverly consults you about this idea. What do you say?

_____

177 Of the following, which one is *not* an income deferral strategy?

(a) Investing in real estate

(b) Use of the cash method

(c) Categorizing payments to a former spouse as alimony rather than child support

(d) Engaging in a like-kind exchange

178. Identify two methods the Code and/or courts and IRS use to combat inappropriate income deferral strategies. _____

179. Ronald owned the Flying Z Ranch. Due to failing health, he sold the ranch to his good friend James for $900,000. The contract called for payment in a single lump sum in five years, with no provision for interest. Ronald's basis in the ranch was $400,000, so he simply reported $500,000 of capital gain in the fifth year when he received payment. At the time the contract was entered into, the applicable federal rate was 6%. Was Ronald's reporting position correct? What is James's basis in the ranch? _____

180. Joe's mother wants to lend Joe $10,000, interest-free. What will be the tax consequences of this loan? What if the loan were $100,000? $1 million? _____

181. Elmo purchases a bond from Monster Cookies, Inc., in the face amount of $15,000. In five years it will pay him a lump sum of $21,037. Elmo thinks he doesn't have to report any income until he receives it; after all, he is a cash method taxpayer. Is Elmo correct? _____

Answers

170. Taxpayers should (and do) care about time value of money principles because these principles affect the amount of tax they owe—specifically, by affecting the timing of taxes. Taxpayers seek to defer income as far into the future as possible (while still having access to it) in order to defer the tax on this income. Taxpayers want to contribute money to tax-deferred savings vehicles such as IRAs for this reason. A tax-deferred vehicle may be a tax never paid (consider the impact of §1014) and the present value of that future tax is less than its face amount. Taxpayers also want to accelerate deductions as much as possible, because these deductions reduce the taxes owed now.

171. The present value of a promise to pay you $10,000 in five years if the appropriate interest rate is 5% is $7,840. If the appropriate rate is 9%, the present value is $6,500. The appropriate interest rate should take into account the riskiness of the promise. A promise by the U.S. federal government (as in a savings bond) is essentially risk-free and would have a low interest rate. By contrast, a promise by a deadbeat (high risk) would carry a higher interest rate.

172. This is just another way to ask for the present value of a future sum. If you know you have a debt to pay in eight years of $10,000, you might set aside the present value of that debt (assuming an interest rate) and let that sum grow during the term so that you would have just the right amount to pay off the obligation. This is often how people save for college educations for children or for their own retirement, although they generally do that through periodic savings rather than putting aside a lump sum. At 6%, the amount you would have to put aside is $6,270. At 12%, you would only have to put aside $4,040.

173. If interest rates held steady at 4%, you would have:

10 years:	$4,437
15 years:	$5,405
30 years:	$9,740

174. To answer this question, you must compare the present values of the two gifts: the present value of $70,000 five years in the future or $50,000. Because gifts are not included in gross income, there are no taxes to figure into the equation on the gift itself. You should take the gift today because the present value of the future gift is $47,670, less than the current gift. The present value is calculated as follows:

$$PV = \frac{FV}{(1 + i)^n}$$

$$PV = \frac{\$70,000}{(1 + .08)^5}$$

$$PV = \$47,670$$

This can also be calculated by using the table: multiply the future gift by the number at the intersection of 8% and five years, or 0.681. This produces the same number. (It's a relatively close case. You should also consider whether the stated interest rate doesn't reflect the riskiness of this gift—your rich aunt might "forget" to make it! The riskier the promise, the higher the interest rate properly used in calculating present value, and the lower the present value of the future gift.)

175. Putting aside non-tax issues such as whether the granddaughter is mature enough to handle a $5,000 gift, Grandmother should seriously consider using the 529 plan. If the granddaughter invests the money, she will be taxed (perhaps at her parents' rate) on the income from the gift. If the money is placed in a 529 plan, it can grow tax-free and this income will not ever be taxed if the money is used for educational purposes. However, in making that decision, Grandmother should consider any fees associated with the plan and the likely rate of return in the plan.

176. Beverly should run—not walk—away from this so-called opportunity. Leaving aside the wisdom of such a venture, she will not be able to use the losses from the venture to offset her income from private practice. This would constitute a passive activity because it is certain that Beverly, a doctor, will not be actively involved in the business of contacting alien life forms (plus, the structure of the investment will probably ensure that it is a passive activity for her). The passive loss rules prevent a taxpayer from using "passive losses" to offset nonpassive income, so that the deductions from the venture would be useless to her until she disposes of the activity.

177. (C) is not an income deferral strategy. Investing in real estate takes advantage of the realization principle: increases in the value of the real property are not taxed until the property is disposed of in a realization event. Use of the cash method can defer income until it is received. A like-kind exchange defers the gain on the exchange of property until the replacement property is sold. But the characterization of a payment to a former spouse as alimony results in a deduction to the payor (thus, a deduction strategy) and the payee spouse must include it in gross income when received.

178. Each Code section that allows for potential deferral (e.g., like-kind exchanges under §1031) contain myriad rules to confine the technique to its intended scope. The doctrine of constructive receipt is an example of a non-Code method of preventing inappropriate use of the cash method to defer income. A cash method taxpayer cannot exclude income if he or she has the right to it, even if he or she does not claim it.

179. No. The Code will impute interest to this transaction. There are three potentially applicable Code provisions (§483, §7872, and §1272 and its related statutes). Of these, §483 applies because this involves a sale or exchange of property for which the purchase price is less than $1 million.

Section 483 provides that the unstated interest must be calculated by subtracting from the total deferred purchase price the present value of the future payments, using the applicable federal rate. In this situation, the AFR is 6%. Using present value formulas (or the chart on p. 338), the unstated interest is calculated to be $227,700, and therefore the purchase price for the ranch is $672,300. Ronald's gain on the transaction is $272,300 (the sales price minus his basis). James's basis in the ranch is $672,300, the same as Ronald's selling price.

180. Joe's mother may lend him a total of $10,000 without interest because of the de minimis exception for gift loans. IRC §7872(c)(2)(A). If the loan is $100,000 or less, the transaction will be cast as a gift of the forgone interest (calculated at the applicable federal rate for long-term obligations) but the amount treated as included in the mother's income will be limited to Joe's investment income (i.e., his total of dividends, interest, etc.). If the loan is $1 million, neither of these exceptions apply.

In that case, each year Joe's mother will be deemed to have made a gift of the forgone interest to Joe, who in turn transfers it to his mother as interest, which she must include in her gross income.

181.   Elmo is incorrect. He (it?) must include in his gross income a proportionate amount of the interest on the bond each year, and this will be ordinary income to him. The interest rate is 7% on this bond.

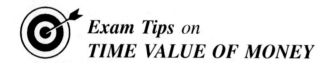

Exam Tips on
TIME VALUE OF MONEY

☛ Most law exams do not ask pure time value of money questions like Questions 171 through 174 in "Quiz Yourself" of this chapter. Time value of money principles are embedded in other kinds of questions.

  ☞ *Look for:* A taxpayer's choice between two alternative receipts, or an opportunity to defer income or accelerate deductions.

  ☞ *Analyze:* Discuss time value of money principles to explain why a taxpayer would choose one alternative or plan over another.

☛ The statutory rules (OID, 483, 7872) are all based on making a loan transaction reflect economic reality: Interest would be charged, and must be imputed if it is not stated.

  ☞ *Look for:* Loans, sales of property, etc. without an adequate stated interest rate.

  ☞ *Analyze:* Which section applies; what exactly does it impute; what are the results to the taxpayers? Analyze each side of the transaction separately.

☛ The Education Savings Accounts and §529 plans are just two of many education incentives, but the two are available to relatively higher income taxpayers. Consider these two benefits in connection with education deductions, the HOPE credit, and the Lifelong Learning Credit. See Chapters 13 and 16.

☛ *Math anxiety?* Forget running the numbers. Discuss the theory of the time value of money, and what it causes taxpayers (and Congress) to do in a particular situation.

STATUTE SUMMARY CHARTS

Statute Summary—§483
Imputed Interest on Sales of Property

Parsing Step	IRC §483
General Rule	The lender and borrower will be treated as having received and paid interest, respectively, on sales or exchanges of property with total unstated interest.
Definitions	**Total unstated interest** = total payments due – PV of payments plus stated interest
Special Rules and Exceptions	Doesn't apply to sales ≤ $3,000. For a qualified sale (price ≤ $500,000), maximum 6% rate required.
Related Statutes	**§§1272–1275:** OID rules **§7872:** Below-market interest rate loans **§§163 and 61:** Interest deduction and inclusion in gross income **§453:** Installment sale method of reporting income
Typically implicated when	A deferred payment sale in which the interest charged is nonexistent or is below the market rate of interest.

Statute Summary—§7872
Imputed Interest on Loans

Parsing Step	IRC §7872
General Rule	Below-market loans will be recharacterized to take into account payment of interest by borrower and receipt of interest by lender.
Definitions	**Below-market loan** **Demand loan** **Gift loan** **Term loan**
Special Rules and Exceptions	Small loans excepted. ≤ $100,000 loan between related parties interest limited to investment interest
Related Statutes	**§§1272–1274:** OID rules **§483:** Imputed interest on sales or exchanges of property **§§163 and 61:** Interest deduction and inclusion in gross income **§102:** Gifts
Typically implicated when	A related person (relative, corporation, employer) makes a loan to another person and doesn't charge a market interest rate.

CHAPTER 16

PUTTING IT ALL TOGETHER: RECOGNIZING AND ANALYZING COMMON TAX PROBLEMS

ChapterScope ════════════════════════════════════

Previous chapters have addressed the issues surrounding the calculation of a taxpayer's tax liability, from identification of income to the subtraction of tax credits. Chapter 15 broadened the perspective by focusing on the principle of the time value of money, showing how this concept informs common tax planning strategies as well as specific tax statutes. This chapter concludes the outline by offering a method to help the tax student approach unfamiliar tax problems systematically. It then applies this approach to five types of problems, showing how groups of Code sections and tax concepts work together in commonly encountered transactions. Once you have a grasp on the substantive issues of tax law, use this chapter to make sure you understand how they fit together.

Key concepts in this chapter include:

- ■ **A systematic approach to the tax consequences of a transaction:** A tax problem can be approached systematically to ensure that all the issues are adequately addressed.

- ■ **Commonly encountered transactions:** This chapter introduces five kinds of transactions that are commonly encountered in the real world and on tax examinations. These are compensation transactions, transactions in property, personal expenditure transactions, business transactions, and intrafamilial transfers. This chapter discusses the Code sections and tax concepts potentially applicable to each type of transaction.

════════════════════════════════════

I. WHERE ARE WE?

Unlike previous chapters, this chapter *isn't* about the determination of a taxpayer's tax liability. Instead, it is about tax problem solving. Use it to systematize your approach to tax problems, and review it before doing practice problems. After you have completed some problems, review it again to see how you could improve your answers.

II. A SYSTEMATIC APPROACH TO TAX PROBLEMS

Tax issues do not arise from a taxpayer's private contemplation of the universe, but from two or more taxpayers engaging in some sort of transaction. In the broadest terms, a transaction is an event between two or more people in which some value changes hands. The goal of tax students and tax professionals alike is to determine the proper tax consequences to these transactions, either from a planning point of view in which the transaction has yet to occur or from a reactive point of view in which a transaction has occurred, but its tax consequences are unclear.

A. A systematic approach

Determining the tax consequences of various transactions can be expressed as a process, parts of which are already familiar to tax students from other courses, and some of which are unique to tax. See Figure 16A—A Systematic Approach to Tax Problems. This approach is intended for use in both exams and the real world. But use of this method for exam taking must be tempered by a student's understanding of his or her professor's emphasis on material in class. For example, the development of a reasonable return position is of crucial importance for a practicing tax lawyer in a planning situation but receives differing degrees of emphasis in the tax classroom. Some tax professors focus on this issue in discussing the ambiguity of tax law; some professors note the standard only in passing; others never mention it at all. The observant student will incorporate his or her tax professor's emphasis into studying for and writing exams.

Figure 16A
A Systematic Approach to Tax Problems

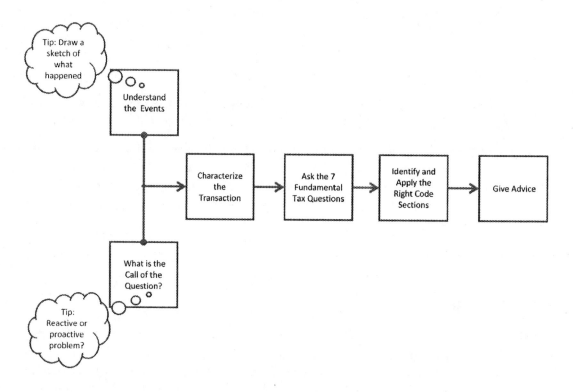

B. Understand the events

The very first step in any tax problem is to understand what events have occurred that are giving rise to the problem at hand. Just like most other law school exams, most tax exam problems pose a series of events that have occurred in the past. Make sure you understand who did what, when, why, how, and with whom. Property, money, or other items or services may change hands in unexpected ways, and therefore it is often helpful to sketch a picture of the transaction. In some tax problems, the events are of a more general character, such as taxpayers taking certain actions that a legislator or IRS sees as inappropriate.

C. Understand the call of the question

In some situations, a professor (or client) may pose a very specific tax question. The question may be "Are these expenditures deductible?" Much more common in essay exams and in the real world, however, are calls for a general discussion of tax issues. These are posed as questions such as "Discuss the tax consequences of these events" or "Advise the taxpayer." These types of questions call for a broader range of advice in two different potential settings—the reactive problem and the proactive (planning) problem.

1. **Reactive problems:** In a *reactive problem,* events have already occurred, and the problem is to determine the proper tax consequences of those events. This is the most common type of problem on tax exams. When representing the taxpayer, the specific problem presented is typically either to create a return position for a transaction that has already occurred (i.e., determine how to report the transaction on a tax return), or to react to a challenge on audit. When representing the government, the typical problem is to determine if and how to challenge a taxpayer's return position or how to respond to a proposed transaction in a private letter ruling request. This type of problem is also occasionally raised as a government-client question in which the government seeks to draft legislation or regulations to combat a particular taxpayer strategy. This type of problem does not offer the option of changing the facts, but different interpretations of the existing facts are possible and indeed are the focus of such problems.

2. **Proactive (planning) problems:** In a *proactive problem,* a taxpayer typically is contemplating a transaction and seeks advice on how best to structure it. In this type of problem, there is flexibility to change some, but usually not all, of the facts. The specific task will be to develop a plan that meets the taxpayer's goals and results in a reasonable return position. This type of problem is also sometimes presented as a government-client question in which the government seeks to draft new legislation or regulations to implement a new tax policy.

D. Recognize the transaction: what *is* it for tax purposes?

Most transactions can be characterized as a common type of transaction, which allows the problem solver to reduce the universe of potentially applicable Code sections and concepts to a manageable size for analysis. To illustrate, suppose that in a particular transaction, the student grasps that Sue transferred property to Alvin in exchange for Alvin's performance of services. In analyzing these facts, the student recognizes this as a typical compensation transaction and a sale property transaction, allowing the student to consider a discrete number of Code sections and tax concepts for analysis. But remember these three tips in giving a name or type to a transaction.

1. **Only a hypothesis!** Giving a name to the facts is simply a hypothesis that a transaction is of a certain type. As with any hypothesis, it can later be revised if further analysis suggests that the Code sections selected do not apply, or other facts are discovered to suggest that another type fits the transaction more precisely.

2. **Complex transactions—More than one type:** A complex transaction may have two or more parts, of different types. Or a transaction may potentially fit within two different types, and its tax consequences must be considered under both. In such a situation, the tax student must decide which label is most appropriate for the transaction.

Example: Mildred transfers a car to Sam to pay him for painting her house. He uses the car in business. He trades the car for a light truck, also to be used in the business. This is a compensation transaction, followed by a transaction in property (a possible like-kind exchange under §1031).

3. **Recharacterization:** Because the U.S. tax system is a self-assessment system, it is the taxpayer's responsibility initially to name or characterize his or her transactions. The taxpayer does so by taking a position on the tax return. Although the taxpayer is usually (but not always) estopped from later changing *(recharacterizing)* this characterization of the transaction, the IRS may recharacterize all or a portion of the transaction in accordance with its economic substance. It is the substance, not the form, of a transaction that governs its federal income tax consequences. As a result, one must consider the possibility of the IRS asserting a different label if the economic substance of a transaction is different than its form.

Example: As in the example above, Mildred transfers a car to Sam, and we now discover Sam is Mildred's son. While the transfer of the car may be compensation income, it might instead be a gift. The alert tax student would analyze the transaction under both labels and would search for additional facts that would allow a definitive characterization.

E. Ask the seven fundamental tax questions

In Chapter 1, we introduced the seven fundamental tax questions (and these should make a lot more sense at the end of the basic tax course than at the beginning!). In analyzing any tax problem, these seven questions can be applied, in order, to begin the analysis.

1. **Who is the relevant taxpayer?** In all transactions, there are at least two taxpayers, and in some transactions, there are many more. As a general rule, the tax consequences to each taxpayer should be analyzed independently. Which taxpayer is your client? Or, in an exam-taking situation, in which taxpayer is the professor interested? Are the taxpayers involved in the transaction related to one another? Are there children participating in property or service transfers? Has any taxpayer attempted to "assign" income to another? These questions focus attention on which taxpayer's tax consequences must be considered. See generally Chapters 1, 13, and 14.

2. **Does the taxpayer have income?** This issue raises questions of whether a taxpayer has income in a theoretical sense—has the taxpayer experienced an economic benefit? See generally Chapter 2. Once theoretical issues are resolved, §61 requires the inclusion of all income in gross income, but specific statutes may apply to exclude amounts from gross income. See generally Chapters 3 and 4.

3. **What deductions may the taxpayer claim?** This issue raises the question of whether the taxpayer has made an outlay or incurred a loss that is potentially deductible. If so, the question is whether there is a specific statute to support the taxpayer claiming a deduction for the outlay or loss, and whether any limitations apply to the deductions. In general, deductions may be business related or personal. Personal expenditures are not deductible without specific statutory authority. (See generally Chapter 6.) The usual expenses of doing business are generally deductible, but important constraints are also imposed on business deductions. See generally Chapters 7 and 8.

4. **When must the taxpayer include an item in gross income, and when may the taxpayer claim a deduction?** Timing questions raise issues about when a taxpayer must include an item in gross income, and when the taxpayer may claim a deduction. Time value of money principles and taxpayers' planning strategies feature prominently in timing questions, raising technical questions regarding the taxpayer's taxable year, method of accounting, and various nonrecognition provisions. See generally Chapters 10, 11, and 15.

5. **What is the character of the taxpayer's income or loss?** If the taxpayer has income or loss, the gain or loss must be characterized as capital or ordinary. Ordinary income is subject to tax at rates up to 35%, but net capital gain is subject to a preferential tax rate as low as 5%, and can, for certain taxpayers, escape tax altogether. Moreover, capital losses are subject to significant restrictions and may be deducted only to the extent of capital gains plus, for individuals, $3,000 of ordinary income. See generally Chapter 12.

6. **To what tax rate(s) is the taxpayer subject?** Remember that capital gain is taxed at varying rates, and differently from ordinary income. The taxpayer may also be subject to the AMT. See Chapters 12 and 13.

7. **Is the taxpayer entitled to any tax credits?** A taxpayer might have paid estimated taxes, or may be entitled to an earned income credit, or dependent care credit, or some other kind of tax credit. See generally Chapter 13.

F. Identify and apply the applicable Code sections

Code sections often work together in families of related statutes, and some of these are discussed later in this chapter. Identification, however, is necessary but not sufficient. The student must examine the specific requirements of potentially applicable concept and statute to determine whether a particular rule applies to the facts at hand.

G. Give advice

In other words, *answer the question.* In this final step, recall that the point of tax information in the real world is to advise a client—whether the taxpayer or the government—on tax issues. In this step, the student returns to the tax problem posed, offering advice to the client. In developing this advice, the student considers the interests of the client and the constraints the client is under within the particular facts, as well as whether the problem is reactive or proactive. This step challenges the student to exercise that lawyerly skill of providing advice while changing perspectives—giving advice to taxpayers, or the IRS, or to legislators.

1. Advice to a taxpayer

a. **Return position:** If a client is seeking advice on the proper reporting of a transaction on a tax return, the student offers advice on an appropriate return position. See Chapter 1(III).

b. **Transaction structure:** If a client is seeking advice on the proper structure of a transaction, the student offers that advice with a discussion of why a particular structure is the most appropriate. This can also implicate the taxpayer's return position, because only a transaction that results in a reasonable return position is acceptable.

c. **Tax controversy:** If a taxpayer is embroiled in a controversy, the student offers advice on possible responses to the controversy, including procedural issues (e.g., in which forum to litigate the matter; see Chapter 1(II)(D)) and substantive issues (e.g., the proper interpretation of the facts and law).

2. Advice to the government: Although most tax exams involve advice to taxpayers, it is not unheard of to be asked to take the IRS's perspective or a legislator's perspective on a factual situation.

a. IRS advice: The IRS's job is to properly administer the tax system. It does so in two ways: pursuing tax controversies with taxpayers and promulgating administrative guidance with respect to the Code. In tax controversies, the IRS's role is to ensure that the taxpayer has properly included items of income and claimed the appropriate deductions and credits. Thus, advice to the IRS will center on the propriety of the taxpayer's return positions, and in controversies the IRS is likely to take positions that are mirror images of those taken by the taxpayer. In promulgating administrative guidance, the IRS's role is to issue "reasonable interpretations" of the Code, and in doing so, it will be considering the policy implications of the proposed guidance. See Chapter 1(V).

b. Legislator's advice: A legislator will be examining the wisdom of a proposed change to the tax code. In doing so, he or she will consider the policy implications of a particular provision. See Chapter 1(V). In addition, a legislator may be reacting to a particular taxpayer strategy and IRS response, and must be cognizant of those strategies and interests. See generally Chapter 15.

III. APPLYING THE SYSTEMATIC APPROACH TO COMMON TYPES OF TRANSACTIONS

The following sections analyze five types of transactions that are common both in the real world and on tax exams. The discussion assumes that the student understands the events that have occurred and has identified the call of the question. The discussion focuses on recognizing the transaction as one of the familiar types, asking the right tax questions, and identifying/applying the appropriate Code sections. Charts illustrate the Code sections and tax concepts for the six fundamental tax questions raised by each type of transaction.

IV. COMPENSATION TRANSACTIONS

A very common transaction is the performance of services in exchange for something of value—cash, property, or some other benefit, including other services.

A. Recognizing this transaction

Look for a person performing services in exchange for value or a promise to transfer value. The most common transaction is payment in cash or check for services performed, but value also may be transferred in the form of property or other services. In some situations, payment may be deferred (which raises important timing issues). Be sure to distinguish compensation transactions from services performed as a gift in which the service provider receives no tangible value beyond the satisfaction of a good deed done (such as driving a friend's children to school).

B. The seven fundamental tax questions

Pay attention to the call of the question for the important preliminary question: who is the taxpayer? Does the question focus on the service provider or the service recipient? In some cases, the tax consequences of a compensation transaction must be considered from the perspectives of both the person who receives the benefit of the services (the payor) and the service provider. A compensation transaction essentially poses two tax questions. First, will the payor be entitled to a deduction for payment for services? Second, will the service provider include an amount in gross income, and if so, when?

1. **Tax issues for the service recipient/payor:** The essential tax question for the payor is whether a deduction is available for the amount paid for services. The answer to this question depends in large part on whether the payment is related to the payor's trade or business. A deduction is generally not allowed for payments for services incurred for personal use. (See discussion in Chapter 6.) Payments for services relating to business, however, are generally deductible. If a deduction is allowed, important timing questions also arise.

   a. **Income:** The payor generally does not have income questions arising from payment for services. In some situations, however, the nature of income that can be offset by the deduction is important. See discussion in Chapter 11(VII).

   b. **Deduction:** The essential question for the payor in compensation transactions is whether the payor will be entitled to claim a deduction. A deduction will be available for the payment if it qualifies as an "ordinary and necessary business expense." (See discussion in Chapter 7(II).) Important questions arise if the payment has some connection with the taxpayer's personal life; if so, its deductibility may be restricted. (See generally Chapter 8.) If the payment for services constitutes a capital expenditure, the amounts paid must be capitalized and included in the basis of the asset to which they relate (e.g., legal services to establish title to a parcel of real property). See discussion in Chapter 7(IV)(D).

   c. **Timing:** If a deduction is available for an expenditure, the subsidiary question is when the deduction is allowable. This will depend on the taxpayer's method of accounting and taxable year. A cash method taxpayer will generally deduct an amount in the taxable year when it is paid. An accrual-method taxpayer will generally deduct an amount in the taxable year when all events have occurred that fix the fact of the liability, and its amount can be determined with reasonable accuracy, subject to the economic performance rules. See discussion in Chapter 11(III). The payor's deduction for deferred compensation depends on the nature of the deferred compensation plan. See discussion in Chapter 11(III). If deductions exceed income, the net operating loss may carry forward or back. See discussion in Chapter 11(II)(D).

   d. **Character:** A deduction for amounts paid for business-related service is a deduction from gross income from business, unless it is a capital expenditure.

   e. **Rates and credits:** Rates and credits for payors are not generally at issue. Note, however, the possibility of the dependent care credit for payors for dependent care services. See discussion in Chapter 13(V).

2. **Tax issues for the service provider:** The essential tax questions for the service provider are: How much income, and when?

   a. **Income:** A service provider usually has income in the theoretical sense, as he or she receives something of value. If there is compensation income in the theoretical sense, it usually (but not always) is income in the sense of §61, which is the cornerstone of compensation transactions for service providers. (The major exception is imputed income from the provision of services for oneself or one's family, which may be income in a theoretical sense but which is not included in gross income. See Chapter 2(IV).) In addition, specific exclusionary statutes must be considered.

i.   **Section 61(a)(1):** Section 61(a)(1) provides that gross income includes "compensation for services including fees, commissions, fringe benefits, and similar items." Under this rule, the service provider must include in his or her gross income all types of compensation. See discussion in Chapter 3(II).

ii. **Amount included:** Cash is included in gross income, of course, at its face value. When the value paid to the service provider is property or services, the service provider includes the fair market value of the services or property in gross income. See discussion in Chapter 3(II). The amount included becomes the basis in the property (known as "tax cost basis"). See discussion in Chapter 9(V)(C).

iii. **Exclusions and deferrals:** Specific Code sections address particular types of compensation income. Some offer an exclusion (such as payment for health insurance premiums or certain fringe benefits). Others offer deferral (as in deferred compensation arrangements).

b. **Timing issues—income:** Individual service providers are typically cash method taxpayers using a calendar year. Therefore, they report income in the calendar year in which they receive it. Payment by cash, check, or credit card is considered payment in cash, but a mere promise to pay is not income to these taxpayers until it ripens into something of value. See generally Chapter 11.

i.   **Restricted property:** If the property transferred to the service provider is subject to restrictions relating to the service provider's continued services, the service provider may either include it in income in the year of receipt at its value or include it in gross income in the year the restrictions lapse at its fair market value at that time. See discussion in Chapter 11(VI).

ii. **Retirement benefits:** The employee in a properly structured retirement plan does not include any amount in gross income until he or she receives payments under the plan. When distributions are made from the retirement plan, the employee includes the amount in income that has not been previously taxed. See discussion in Chapter 11(III).

c. **Deductions:** A service provider in the marketplace is considered engaged in a trade or business and therefore may claim the usual expenses of doing business. Unreimbursed employee business expenses, however, are subject to the limitation that such expenses are deductible only to the extent that they (along with certain other miscellaneous expenses) exceed 2% of the taxpayer's AGI. See discussion in Chapter 6.

d. **Rates and credits:** Service income is ordinary income subject to progressive tax rates for individuals. Two specific credits are potentially applicable to service providers. First, the earned income tax credit is available for low-income taxpayers. See discussion in Chapter 13(VI). If the service provider in turn must hire dependent care services in order to work, the service provider may be eligible for the dependent care credit. See discussion in Chapter 13(V).

C. Applicable Code sections

Once theoretical questions of whether the service provider has income and whether the payor has made an outlay are resolved, a variety of Code sections potentially apply to these transactions. See Figure 16B—Compensation Transactions.

Figure 16B
Compensation Transactions

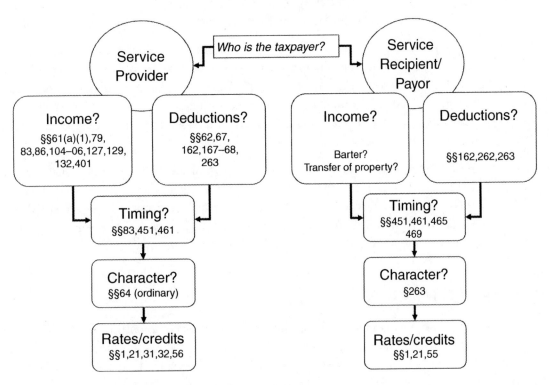

D. Advice

1. Advice focusing on the service recipient/payor:

a. **Advice for a taxpayer:** The payor is usually seeking to increase and accelerate deductions associated with the payment of compensation. A typical issue in this area involves the different treatment of payors in qualified and nonqualified deferred compensation plans. In qualified plans, the payor may claim a deduction in the year a contribution is made to the plan, but in a nonqualified plan the payor cannot claim a deduction until the compensation is actually paid to the service provider. Notice here the differing interests of the payor and the service provider. See discussion in Chapter 11(VI).

b. **Advice for the IRS:** The IRS will be determining whether the taxpayer is entitled to the deductions claimed in the year that they are claimed. In a controversy, the IRS will be likely to argue that the payor is not entitled to a deduction, or must defer the deduction to a future year.

c. **Advice for a legislator:** A legislator must consider the propriety of changes in the tax law that would change payors' ability to deduct or claim a credit for amounts paid for services.

For example, a common question for legislators is whether a deduction should be currently allowed for compensation to be paid in the future, under various sorts of retirement and related benefit plans.

2. Advice focusing on the service recipient:

a. Advice for a taxpayer: Service providers seek to exclude items from gross income as their first choice in tax planning. But because exclusions are relatively rare for compensation income (beyond fringe benefit rules), service providers will seek to take advantage of the time value of money by deferring inclusion of compensation until future years. Consider the use of retirement plans and restricted property as methods of accomplishing this goal.

b. Advice for the IRS: In examining a return, the IRS will be determining whether a taxpayer should have included an amount in gross income that he or she claimed was properly excluded or deferred. Thus, the IRS will be seeking to include items in gross income and to accelerate items of compensation income to the current year that the service provider claims are deferred to future years. The IRS may also challenge a taxpayer's deductions attributable to the business of providing services.

c. Advice for a legislator: A legislator would be faced with a change that either includes certain service providers' income in gross income that is currently excluded, or excludes items that are currently included. For example, a legislator might be faced with the possible expansion of fringe benefits or other exclusions from gross income, or the amendment of timing rules regarding the inclusion of compensation income.

V. TRANSACTIONS IN PROPERTY

Transactions in property constitute a second major category of common transactions. These include sales, taxable exchanges, and various types of wholly or partially tax-free exchanges. The tax consequences of these transactions must be determined for the person who disposes of property (called here the seller) and for the person who acquires it (called here the buyer).

A. Recognizing this transaction

Look for a transaction in which there is an exchange, and the seller ends up owning an interest in property that is different than he or she had prior to the transaction.

B. The seven fundamental tax questions

Pay attention to the important and preliminary tax question: who is the taxpayer? The tax consequences of the transaction to buyer and seller of property are usually independent. In some cases, the tax effects to both parties to the transaction—the seller and the buyer—must be considered in property transactions. In both cases, the fundamental tax issues most often implicated are: whether the taxpayer has income or loss, the timing of recognition of that income or loss, and the character of that income or loss. The seller's realized and recognized gain or loss must be determined, and the buyer's basis in the property acquired must be computed. If the seller has also acquired property in the transaction, the seller's basis in that property must be determined.

1. Tax issues for the seller: The essential tax question for the seller of property is determination of the amount and character of the gain (income) or loss on sale. (Notice that a purchaser of property can also be a seller if the purchaser transferred property rather than purchasing for cash.)

a. Income: The starting point for the seller's income is §61(a)(3), which requires that the taxpayer include in gross income all gains from dealings in property. The seller's realized gain is equal to his or her amount realized minus the adjusted basis of the property transferred. Realized gain is generally recognized unless there is a statutory provision to the contrary. See discussion in Chapter 9(IV).

    i. Amount realized: The seller's amount realized includes the money received, the fair market value of any property or services received, and the amount of any liabilities assumed by the taxpayer. Transfers of encumbered properties whose fair market value are less than their associated debt raise particularly challenging issues in determining amount realized. See Chapter 9(V).

    ii. Adjusted basis: The seller must compute his or her initial basis in the property transferred and adjust it upward for improvements and downward for depreciation. See generally Chapter 9.

    iii. Basis of property received: If the seller has accepted property other than cash in the sale, the seller must determine the basis of that property. The basis will usually be the cost of the property (fair market value of the property given in exchange) unless a nonrecognition rule requires a specially computed basis. See Chapter 9(V)(C), and generally Chapter 10.

b. Deductions: Losses on the sale or exchange of property constitute a deduction, if allowed by statute. Potential restrictions on the deductibility of such losses abound within the Code. See discussion in Chapters 6(II)(D) and(VII), 7(III)(C), 11(VII), and 12(III).

c. Character: The character of the gain or loss as capital or ordinary will be determined by the nature of the asset sold and its holding period. Capital assets will generate capital gain and loss, and noncapital assets will generate ordinary gain and loss. Special limitations apply to the deduction of capital losses. See generally Chapter 12.

d. Timing: The inclusion of income or deduction of loss will depend on the taxpayer's method of accounting and taxable year. See discussion in Chapter 11(II) and (III). In addition, certain nonrecognition rules may apply to defer, in whole or in part, the inclusion of income or deduction of loss. See generally Chapter 10.

e. Rates and credits: A preferential rate for net capital gain may apply to recognized gain on the sale of property. See discussion generally in Chapter 12. Credits are not usually at issue for the seller.

2. **Tax issues for the buyer:** The essential tax question for the buyer is generally his or her basis in the property acquired.

    a. Income: A purchaser who pays only cash or the assumption of liabilities never has any gain or loss on the purchase transaction. But a purchaser who transfers property will have realized gain or loss if the adjusted basis of the property transferred is different than its fair market value. In that situation, the purchaser is treated as having sold or exchanged the property, and the tax consequences are determined under the rules applicable to sellers. See generally Chapter 9.

    b. Deductions: Deductions are not usually at issue in the sale or exchange of property, as expenses of sale paid by the purchaser are considered part of his or her purchase price. If the property is depreciable in the hands of the purchaser, the purchaser may begin to take depreciation or amortization deductions after placing the property in service. See discussion in Chapter 7(IV)(F), (H).

c. Character: Character of income or loss is not usually at issue for the purchaser of property. If he or she has transferred property and recognized gain or loss, the gain or loss will generally be capital. See generally Chapter 12.

d. Timing: The basis of the property acquired is equal to its purchase price unless a nonrecognition provision requires a special computation of basis. See generally Chapters 9 and 10. The timing of the purchase is important for determining the beginning of the depreciation period for depreciable assets. Real property purchased for use in a trade or business or for investment is considered placed in service at the midpoint of the month in which it is actually purchased. Personal property purchased for use in a trade or business or for investment is considered placed in service at the midpoint of the taxpayer's year in which the property is actually purchased. See discussion in Chapter 7(IV)(G).

e. Rates and credits: Tax rates are not usually an issue for the purchaser of property. If, however, the purchaser has recognized gain on the transfer of property to acquire the other property, that gain may be subject to a preferential rate for net capital gain. Credits are not usually at issue for the purchaser of property except in certain circumstances that are typically beyond the scope of the basic tax course.

C. Applicable Code sections

Once theoretical questions for the seller and buyer of property have been resolved, a variety of Code sections potentially apply to these transactions. See Figure 16C—Property Transactions.

Figure 16C
Transactions in Property

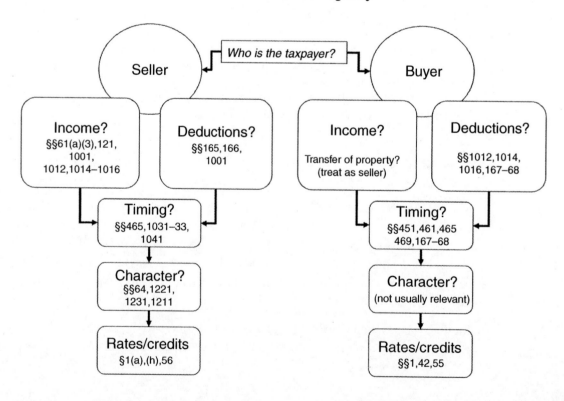

D. Advice

1. Advice focusing on the seller

a. **Advice to a taxpayer:** For a seller of property, tax advice generally focuses on the reduction and deferral of recognized gain and the acceleration of recognized loss. For example, a taxpayer contemplating sale of gain property held for investment might well be advised to engage in a like-kind exchange with respect to the property, in order to defer recognition of gain. Similarly, a taxpayer contemplating an exchange of loss property in similar circumstances would be better off selling the property and recognizing the loss rather than deferring it through a like-kind exchange. Alert tax advisors will also be on the lookout for strategies to exclude gain from gross income altogether, such as the exclusion of gain on the sale of a principal residence offered by §121. See discussion in Chapter 4(VIII).

b. **Advice for the IRS:** The IRS will be determining whether a taxpayer properly calculated the realized and recognized gain or loss on a transaction, properly claimed a loss on sale of property, properly deferred items of income, and properly characterized the gain or loss as capital or ordinary. The IRS is likely to take positions that are mirror images of those taken by the taxpayer, claiming, for example, that gain is ordinary rather than capital.

c. **Advice to a legislator:** A legislator would be faced with the wisdom of changing the calculation of realized gain or loss, or the recognition provisions. For example, a legislator might well be faced with amendments to §1031 or §1033, expanding or limiting the reach of such statutes.

2. Advice focusing on the buyer:

Because a purchase for cash is not a taxable event, taxpayers generally require tax advice not on the computation of gain or loss created by the event but on the timing of purchases to maximize MACRS and other capital recovery deductions. Buyers also may seek advice on the proper structuring of property exchanges if they are not to pay the entire purchase price in cash.

VI. PERSONAL EXPENDITURE TRANSACTIONS

A third major category of transactions involves situations in which the taxpayer makes expenditures or experiences losses not related to his or her trade or business or investments.

A. Recognizing this transaction:

Look for expenditures by the taxpayer for personal and living expenses, and in particular, items such as medical expenses, charitable contributions, savings for various future needs, interest and taxes, child care, education, and adoption expenses. Look also for any other event that causes the taxpayer's personal (as opposed to business or investment) finances to be adversely affected, for these events may generate losses. Particularly relevant are losses from natural disasters such as storms, earthquakes, and fire. Consider as well the situation in which the taxpayer has received some sort of reimbursement, through insurance or otherwise, for expenditures or losses. In all of these situations, the professor is usually interested in the tax consequences to the person making the expenditures and perhaps receiving reimbursement, not others with whom the taxpayer interacts in making these expenditures.

B. The seven fundamental tax questions

In this type of transaction, the call of a question usually focuses on one individual (or a married couple or family), not the various others that provide services (such as medical services, or education). The central question in the personal expenditure situation is whether the taxpayer may deduct any part of his or her expenditures or losses. If the taxpayer has received reimbursement for any loss or expenditure, a related question is whether he or she must include that reimbursement in gross income. Relevant to both questions are timing questions: *When* may the taxpayer claim a deduction, and when must the taxpayer include an amount in gross income? Timing issues raise important time value of money issues, as taxpayers seek to defer income and accelerate deductions.

1. **Income:** A taxpayer must include all income from whatever source derived in gross income. See generally Chapters 2 and 3. However, certain exclusions from gross income are particularly relevant in this context. These include compensation for personal physical injuries of §104 and for amounts received from accident or health plans. (See discussion in Chapter 4(VI).) In addition, the tax benefit rule may apply to include in gross income (or exclude from gross income) recoveries of amounts that were deducted in previous years. Finally, certain savings vehicles (such as HSAs, IRAs, and education savings plans) offer the opportunity to defer—or even exclude—amounts from gross income. See Chapter 6(II)(C), (F).

2. **Deductions:** A taxpayer may not deduct family and living expenses. See discussion in Chapter 5(III). However, the Code allows deduction of certain expenses, such as medical expenses, extraordinary casualty losses, qualified residence interest, certain taxes, and certain charitable contributions. In order to ensure a deduction, the taxpayer's facts must fit precisely within the requirements of these statutes. See generally Chapter 6.

3. **Character:** The character of income and deductions associated with this type of transaction is not usually an issue. Income, if included, will usually be ordinary.

4. **Timing:** The taxpayer's method of accounting will generally determine when the taxpayer may claim a deduction or must include an amount in gross income. Since this type of transaction deals with a taxpayer in his or her personal life, normally the cash method of accounting will apply. The taxpayer will include amounts in gross income when received and will deduct amounts when paid by cash, check, or credit card. See discussion in Chapter 11(III)(B).

5. **Rates and credits:** The preferential tax rate for capital gain is not usually applicable to this factual situation. However, the Code allows certain tax credits for amounts that are not deductible. These include the tax credit for dependent care expenses and the tax credit for adoption expenses. See discussion in Chapter 13(V), (VIII).

C. Applicable Code sections

Once theoretical questions of income and deduction have been resolved, a variety of Code sections potentially apply to these transactions. See Figure 16D—Personal Expenditure Transactions.

Figure 16D
Personal Expenditure Transactions

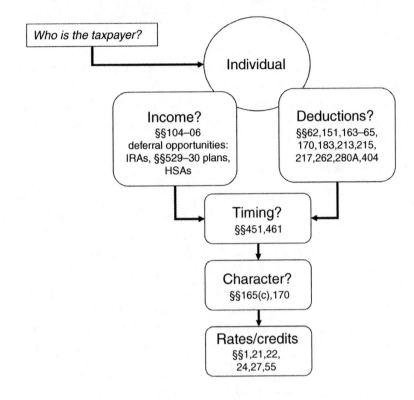

D. Advice

1. **Advice to a taxpayer:** Advice to taxpayers in these situations generally centers around determining whether they are entitled to a deduction and, if so, accelerating that deduction to the earliest possible year to allow a taxpayer to take advantage of the time value of money. For example, if a taxpayer incurs a liability to pay medical expenses in an amount that would generate a deduction for the taxpayer but does not have the cash to pay the bill currently, the taxpayer might be well advised to pay these expenses by credit card in December of one year rather than paying the bill in cash in the following year. This would accelerate the deduction to the current year.

2. **Advice to the IRS:** In examining a taxpayer's return, the IRS must determine whether the taxpayer is entitled to the personal deductions claimed and, if so, when those deductions should be allowed. Thus, the IRS may be making arguments that are the mirror image of those of the taxpayer, denying deductions and credits altogether or deferring them to future years.

3. **Advice to a legislator:** A legislator might well be faced with a proposal either to eliminate a current personal deduction (such as home mortgage interest) or credit or enact a new deduction or credit. In analyzing such a proposal, the legislator must consider the tax policy, revenue, and political implications of the amendment.

VII. BUSINESS TRANSACTIONS

A fourth type of commonly encountered transaction is the taxpayer engaging in sale of services or inventory for profit.

A. Recognizing this transaction:

Look for a taxpayer potentially engaged in business—the regular undertaking of business activity for profit. A taxpayer in this context may be an individual engaging in business as a sole proprietor, or may be an entity such as a partnership or corporation. A fundamental question is whether the activity truly qualifies as a business, or whether it is merely a hobby. Look for sales income and for outlays for items used in the business.

B. The seven fundamental tax questions:

Typically, the call of these kinds of questions focus on the taxpayer engaged in business (or arguably engaged in business) rather than the various other people (such as employees, vendors, or customers of that taxpayer). The essential tax questions for business transactions are how much a taxpayer must include in gross income as income from business, when he or she must include it, what expenditures are deductible, and when they are deductible. Business transactions also can involve sales of property other than inventory, and these should be analyzed separately as sales or exchanges of property. In a business transaction, there will potentially be many other taxpayers involved (customers, suppliers, employees, and competitors), but business transaction questions typically focus on the net result of business activity to the taxpayer engaged in business.

1. **Income:** Section 61(a)(2) is the starting place for business taxpayers, who must include gross income derived from business in their gross incomes. See Chapter 3(III).

2. **Deductions:** A business taxpayer is entitled to a number of business-related deductions. The taxpayer is not entitled to a deduction for capital outlays but will claim capital recovery with respect to these items during ownership of the asset. See generally Chapter 7. Often embedded in business transaction questions are issues of whether an expenditure is truly a business expenditure or is a personal expense and therefore nondeductible. Deductions may be limited if the activity is not engaged in for profit or if the deduction is attributable to listed property or other specially treated items (such as home offices or business entertainment). See generally Chapter 8.

3. **Character:** The character of business income is ordinary. It is important also to characterize the gains and losses on sales of property used in the business as §1231 property, which can lead to the taxpayer-friendly rule of gains as capital and losses as ordinary. See Chapter 12(IV).

4. **Timing:** In computing the net profit from sales of inventory, the taxpayer will deduct the cost of goods sold. See discussion in Chapter 11(IV). Amounts paid as capital expenditures will not generate a deduction but will generate capital recovery during ownership of the property. See discussion in Chapter 7(IV). Finally, the taxpayer's method of accounting and taxable year will determine when he or she includes amounts in gross income or claims deductions. The cash method taxpayer will include income when received and claim deductions when they are paid, subject to certain limitations. The accrual-method taxpayer will include amounts in income and claim deductions when the all events tests are met, again subject to certain limitations. See Chapter 11(III).

5. **Rates and credits:** Net business income, as ordinary income, is taxed at the usual rates, and the business owner may be entitled to claim certain business-related tax credits.

C. Applicable Code sections

Once theoretical questions of business income and deduction have been resolved, a variety of Code sections potentially apply to these transactions. See Figure 16E—Business Transactions.

Figure 16E
Business Transactions

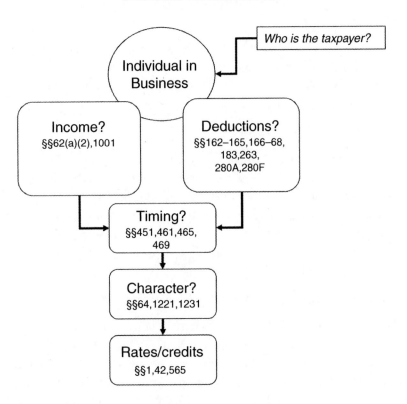

D. Advice

1. **Advice to a taxpayer:** Most advice to business centers around identifying available deductions and helping accelerate those deductions to the earliest possible year to allow the taxpayer to take advantage of the time value of money. In giving this advice, the lawyer must provide guidance on the important questions surrounding the identification of capital expenditures and deductible expenses, the computation of MACRS and other capital recovery deductions, and the selection of an inventory identification method.

2. **Advice to the IRS:** In examining a taxpayer's return, the IRS must determine whether the taxpayer has properly included all items of business income and claimed the proper deductions in the appropriate year. Thus, in a controversy, the IRS is likely to make arguments that are the mirror images of those made by the taxpayer: accelerating income, denying deductions and credits altogether, and deferring deductions and credits to future years.

3. **Advice to a legislator:** A legislator might well be faced with proposals that increase or decrease the number of business-related deductions. Deductions that have a personal flavor to

them (such as meals and entertainment) are perennial congressional favorites for tinkering. In analyzing a proposal to change the deductibility of an item, the legislator must consider the tax policy, revenue, and political impact of the measure. In addition, Congress has shown interest in changing the timeframe for capital recovery, shortening the period to stimulate the economy. Some professors may test your ability to discuss the wisdom of these efforts.

VIII. INTRAFAMILIAL TRANSFERS

A fifth commonly encountered type of transaction is intrafamilial transactions.

A. Recognizing this transaction:

This type of transaction is usually easy to recognize if you treat each individual as a separate taxpayer, even if they are related to one another (e.g., a parent and child). Look for a transfer of value among family members (broadly defined) and, in particular, transfers from the elder to younger generations.

B. The seven fundamental tax questions

1. **Who is the taxpayer?** This is the tax issue most often implicated in intrafamilial transactions. A taxpayer may attempt to assign income to a related individual in a lower tax bracket. Attempted assignments of services income will not be respected, and assignments of income from property will be respected only if they are not "carved-out interests" in property. See generally Chapter 14. The transfer of property to a child under the age of 14 may implicate the kiddie tax under which the child is taxed at his or her parents' tax rate on certain investment income. See discussion in Chapter 14(IV).

2. **Income:** When a taxpayer receives value from a family member, does he or she have income?

    a. **Gifts:** The transfer of property as a gift is not a realization event to the transferor, and therefore he or she does not recognize the gain or loss inherent in the property. The recipient of a gift need not include any amount in gross income, although the recipient must include any income from the gift in gross income. See discussion in Chapter 4(IV). The recipient of a gift generally takes the property with a basis equal to the basis the property had in the hands of the donor, increased by a portion of any gift tax paid by the donor. A special basis rule applies, however, to certain loss property. See discussion in Chapter 9(V)(C).

    b. **Bequests, devises, and inheritances:** The distribution of property pursuant to a specific or residual bequest, devise, or inheritance is generally not a taxable event to the estate, but if the estate transfers property to satisfy a monetary obligation, it may realize and recognize income. See discussion in Chapter 9(V)(B)–(C). The recipient of property pursuant to a bequest, devise, or inheritance will exclude the value of that property from gross income. See discussion in Chapter 4(III). The recipient will take the property with a basis equal to the fair market value on the date of the decedent's death or at the alternative valuation date six months later, if that date is elected. See discussion in Chapter 9(V)(C).

    c. **Life insurance and annuities:** The recipient of life insurance proceeds by reason of the death (or chronic or terminal illness) of the insured may exclude these amounts from gross income. See discussion in Chapter 4(III). Annuity payments are taxed in accordance with the rules of §72 that require a portion of each payment to be considered income and a portion as recovery of capital. See discussion in Chapter 3(V)(F).

    d. Divorce—Property settlements and alimony: Neither spouse will recognize gain or loss on the transfer of property in a divorce-related transfer, if the requirements of §1041 are met. Neither spouse has income as a result of the receipt of property, and neither spouse claims a deduction for such transfers of property. Alimony, but not child support, is included in the gross income of the recipient.

3. **Deductions:** It is unusual to see a deduction for an intrafamilial transfer. For example, the donor of a gift does not receive any deduction as a result of the gift. The exception is alimony, which is deductible by the payor if certain conditions are met. See discussion in Chapters 3(VI) and 6(III). The Code is full of exceptions that apply to transfers between related parties, such as the denial of deduction for losses on sales to related parties (see discussion in Chapter 11(VII)(C)).

4. **Character:** The character of income or deductions is not usually an issue in interfamilial transfers. However, upon certain transfers of property between related parties, gain can be recast as ordinary rather than capital in certain circumstances (see discussion in Chapter 12(III)(E)).

5. **Timing:** Timing issues are typically tested indirectly. For example, in a gift situation, the donee takes the donor's basis in the property received, and this will preserve the inherent gain or loss in the property for later recognition.

6. **Rates and credits:** The principal tax rate section that is important for intrafamilial transfers is §1(g), otherwise known as the kiddie tax. See discussion in Chapter 14(IV)(A).

C. Advice

1. **Advice to a taxpayer:** In advising families on intrafamilial transfers, attention should be focused on ensuring that the transfer itself is not a taxable event and that the recipient will not have unintended items of gross income. Care must be taken to properly compute the basis of the property transferred. In particular, advice in the divorce setting must take into consideration the inherent gain or loss in property transferred (which will ultimately be recognized upon sale of the property) and the impact of deductible alimony (and nondeductible child support) payments.

2. **Advice to the IRS:** In examining intrafamilial transfers, the IRS may assert assignment of income principles, along with determining whether the transfer fits within an exclusion or deferral statute.

3. **Advice to a legislator:** A legislator is likely to be faced with changes that make intrafamilial transfer more or less "taxing." The evolution of the kiddie tax is an example of the kind of question a legislator would be faced with, and in connection with which the legislator would be required to consider policy, revenue, and political implications.

Exam Tips on
PUTTING IT ALL TOGETHER

☛ The two process steps of understanding the events and considering the call of the question are interrelated. Many students prefer to scan for the call of the question first, but others prefer to understand what happened first—it can prevent tunnel vision that results from a preconceived idea of what the call of the question is. There is no one right approach.

☛ In solving a reactive problem, don't spend time on how the taxpayer should have structured the transaction, unless specifically asked to do so. Instead, fully consider the tax consequences of alternative interpretations of the facts and conclude as to which interpretation is most appropriate. Ethical issues (such as what would constitute an appropriate return position) can be embedded in this type of problem.

☛ When addressing a proactive problem for a taxpayer, consider first the taxpayer's tax and non-tax goals and then consider alternative ways of accomplishing those goals, within the facts that are flexible. Propose alternative paths to solve the taxpayer's problem and analyze the tax consequences of each path. Choose the path that produces the best overall consequences for the taxpayer and explain why the other paths are less suitable. Ethical issues, including conflicts of interest and development of reasonable return positions, may well be embedded in proactive problems.

☛ It is not always possible to properly characterize a transaction at the outset of the analysis. A working hypothesis is fine. Or, if unable to even reach some initial characterization, jump right into the seven fundamental tax questions, which will likely trigger the necessary characterization.

☛ Beginning tax students often lament: *"How do I know which Code sections apply?"* This is a valid question, because wasting time on inapplicable sections can mean the difference between a successful and unsuccessful exam. This chapter has offered an approach. Another approach is the one of this outline as a whole—remembering which Code sections apply to each of the seven fundamental tax questions.

☛ At the heart of many tax questions lies a statutory ambiguity in its terms that raises questions about whether the facts fit within its statute. In some cases, the facts themselves are ambiguous, which also raises questions about whether a statute applies. These types of situations usually deserve an in-depth analysis in an exam situation, engaging in the process of statutory interpretation of ambiguous terms, or discussing alternative interpretations of the facts that cause them to fall within or without the statute.

☛ In addressing the tax consequence of applying a particular concept or statute, discuss each step in your analysis carefully. If performing some arithmetic feat, show how you reached your conclusion. If you have identified some ambiguity in the statute that causes you to be uncertain as to whether it applies, be sure to discuss the effects in the alternative of falling within and without the statute's reach.

☛ Many tax professors are relatively uninterested in the calculation of the tax due and focus instead on an understanding of the progressive rate regime (in contrast to other potential tax regimes), the determination of taxable income, and various tax credits.

Essay Exam Questions

QUESTION 1: *Oh, it's good to be the President of the United States.* Sure, you have to deal with wars, looming deficits, natural disasters, and Congress, but there is a nice salary and some *very* nice perks. For example, the President has the use of Camp David as a private retreat and the use of Air Force One for travel. Five chefs at the White House (and three at Camp David) provide meals to the First Family, on demand, twenty-four hours a day. In addition, U.S Code, Title 3, Chapter 2, §§102, 103, and 104 (*as edited or invented*) provide as follows:

§ 102. Compensation of the President

The President shall receive in full for his or her services during the term for which he or she shall have been elected compensation as an employee of the United States in the aggregate amount of $400,000 a year, to be paid monthly, plus health insurance, life insurance in the amount of $500,000, and disability insurance and in addition an expense allowance of $50,000 to be used exclusively in defraying expenses relating to or resulting from the discharge of his or her official duties. He or she shall be entitled also to the use of the furniture and other effects belonging to the United States and kept in the Executive Residence at the White House as well as unrestricted access without charge to all National Parks, National Monuments and National Museums.

§ 103. Traveling expenses

There may be expended for or on account of the traveling expenses of the President of the United States such sum as Congress may from time to time appropriate, not exceeding $100,000 per annum, such sum when appropriated to be expended in the discretion of the President.

§ 104. After leaving office

After leaving office, the President shall be entitled to an annual stipend of $250,000 for his or her lifetime, as well as health insurance. Personal protective services shall be provided as requested or as recommended by the Secret Service.

Mrs. X has just been elected President of the United States, after serving two terms as a senator from a southwestern state. She is married to Mr. X, and they have two children, ages 8 and 10. Mr. X recently retired as a corporate executive in order to assist his wife on the campaign trail. The couple has just attended the obligatory human resources orientation, where they learned about the compensation package. You have been the longtime tax adviser to the X's and they have come to you for advice as to the federal income tax consequences of their "new job." Please advise them.

QUESTION 2: Several recent tax reform proposals have suggested the repeal or scaling back of IRC §163(h). Please comment, from a tax policy point of view, on how such proposals might be structured and whether they are a "good idea."

QUESTION 3: Brian owns Whiteacre, an apartment building, which he holds for investment. He has an adjusted basis of $400,000 in Whiteacre, and it is subject to a mortgage of $260,000. Anita owns Blueacre, a commercial office building, which she also holds for investment. It is worth $800,000 and is subject to a mortgage of $350,000. Anita has an adjusted basis of $400,000 in Blueacre.

   A. Brian and Anita exchange Whiteacre for Blueacre and Brian transfers a painting worth $10,000, in which he had a basis of $2,000, to Anita as well. Each assumes the other's liabilities. What are the tax consequences of this exchange to each taxpayer?

   B. Would your answer change if Anita had recently acquired Blueacre as an inheritance?

QUESTION 4: Spencer, a single taxpayer, is the owner of an Internet research business organized as a sole proprietorship. He uses the cash method of accounting. Last year, he recorded on his books $150,000 in sales of information to customers. As of December 31, he had received $125,000 in payments and $25,000 in oral promises to pay within thirty days from clients. He also incurred the following expenses:

Compensation to employees	$25,000
Advertising	5,000
Rent	12,000
Telephone & Internet	2,500
Taxes	2,000
Business entertainment	1,000
Insurance	3,500

He purchased a computer for $5,000 for exclusive use in the business and sold a used computer that had a basis of zero for $1,500. He had originally purchased the computer for $10,000. Spencer also had a theft this year of some office equipment, with a fair market value of $1,500 and basis of $2,500. He received no insurance proceeds for this, as it was below his deductible amount. A flood destroyed some of his office art, which had a basis of $5,000 and a fair market value of $8,000. His insurance company paid him $8,000 for this loss.

Please advise Spencer on the tax consequences of these transactions. Do you have any suggestions for him to reduce next year's taxes?

QUESTION 5: Big Law Firm has a dress code, which is strictly enforced. Much to the delight of attorneys and staff, the Big Law Firm managing board issued the following edict on January 2:

> Commencing this week and throughout the rest of the year, attorneys and staff may wear jeans to the office on Fridays (and only on Fridays) but only if such jeans-wearing person makes a donation to the Big Firm Charitable Fund by 10 am of the Friday on which jeans are worn. Donations may be made at the Human Resources Office.
>
> Attorneys are encouraged to donate to the Fund not less than $10, and staff are encouraged to donate not less than $5, for each Friday that the person wears jeans. At the end of the year, the Big Law Firm Charitable Fund will be donated, on behalf of the participating attorneys and staff, to a variety of public charities from nominations by the participating staff members.
>
> Ragged jeans, jeans with holes, jeans bedecked with rhinestones, denim miniskirts and the like will not be tolerated. The Board would like to take this opportunity to remind attorneys and staff of our established dress code, which remains in effect for all other days (excepting Sundays) or for persons who have not made an appropriate donation.

This year Attorney G wore jeans on fifty Fridays and contributed $800 to the Big Law Charitable Fund. On December 31, the entire fund was donated to a qualifying §501(c)(3) charity. Big Firm gave Attorney G a report showing his $800 deduction. G wishes to claim a charitable deduction on his tax return for the year. May he do so?

QUESTION 6: Peter and Gabrielle divorced in Year 1. Their divorce decree provided that Peter was to pay Gabrielle the following amounts:

$40,000	Year 1
$20,000	Year 2
$10,000	Year 3 and each year thereafter

In addition, Peter transferred to Gabrielle the following assets:

100 shares of XYZ stock, in which Peter had a basis of $50,000.

The family home, for which the couple paid $200,000. It was worth $175,000 at the time of the divorce subject to a mortgage of $150,000.

Peter was obligated to pay the mortgage on the home each month until it was repaid or Gabrielle sold the home or ceased to use it as her principal residence, whichever came first.

A. In each year, Peter deducted the amount he paid to Gabrielle, including the amount paid under the mortgage and the value of the XYZ stock. Gabrielle included these amounts in her gross income. Is this treatment correct?

B. In Year 6, Gabrielle moved out of the home and gave it to her daughter, Trendee. At that time, the property was worth $160,000 and was subject to a mortgage of $90,000. What is Trendee's basis in the home?

Essay Exam Answers

SAMPLE ANSWER TO QUESTION 1

This is obviously a compensation question, in which the focus is on the taxpayer's compensation package.

Who is the taxpayer?

As an initial matter, we are talking about a married couple who will likely file a joint return. No facts indicate income or deductions for Mr. X or the children, so the primary focus will be the tax consequences to Mrs. X of her compensation package.

Income Issues

Of course, Madam President and her family will experience the thrill of being President and the First Family. This thrill may be offset, perhaps, by the continual demands of the job, not to mention the hassles of the constant presence of the Secret Service. Fortunately, however, neither of these need to be measured because noneconomic benefits are not considered "income" in our federal income tax system and noneconomic detriments do not generate deductions.

Madam President will receive several items that constitute an "economic benefit" to her, which do constitute income in a theoretical sense. These include (1) salary; (2) meals and lodging at the White House and Camp David; (3) health, life, and disability insurance premiums; (4) an expense allowance; (5) use of the property of the United States at the White House; (6) an annual pass to the National Parks, etc.; and (7) use of Air Force One plus up to $100,000 in traveling expenses. In due course, when she leaves office, Mrs. X will enjoy (1) the annual retirement stipend, (2) health insurance, and (3) protective services. All of these items constitute gross income in the sense of Code §61. They must, at some point in time, be included in Madam President's gross income, unless a specific statutory provision excludes them.

There is no exclusion for salary and the retirement stipend, even for the President of the United States. However, various fringe benefit provisions may be available to exclude other items, as follows:

Meals and Lodging: Section 119 allows an employee to exclude the value of meals and lodging provided to the employee on the business premises of the employer, if those meals and lodging are provided for the convenience of the employer. The locations where the President and her family will reside are the White House and Camp David, both of which are owned by the employer (the United States) and are places where the United States conducts business. The "convenience of the employer" test should be met, for two reasons. Like the hotel manager in *Benaglia*, the President is on call twenty-four hours a day, seven days a week. Plus, it is more convenient for the United States to protect its President and First Family by having them live in a place that has already been secured. Although there is no specific statutory language supporting this, the lodging exclusion is considered as including the use of the employer's furnishings at the lodging. Therefore, the First Family's use of the White House property, such as the famous dinnerware, is likely included in the meals and lodging exclusion.

A related question is whether the meals and lodging exclusion extends to the meals and lodging provided to family of the employee. Section 119(a) fortunately answers this question in the affirmative, so that the value of such benefits provided to the employee's "spouse or any of his dependents" is excluded from the employee's gross income.

Therefore, the value of the meals and lodging provided at the White House and at Camp David should be excluded from the gross income of the President.

Health, life, and disability insurance: Sections 79 and 106 of the Code allow an exclusion from gross income for premiums for life, health, and disability insurance provided by an employer to an employee. However, there is a $50,000 limit on life insurance, and it must be group term life insurance. Therefore, the premiums for health and disability insurance should be excluded from the President's gross income, but all or a portion of the life insurance premium will be included in her gross income (more facts are needed about the type of insurance). In addition, post-employment health insurance coverage can be excluded from gross income, because it will be provided in connected with previous employment.

$50,000 expense allowance: If the $50,000 is provided as part of an accountable plan, the amount can be excluded from the President's gross income. An accountable plan requires that the employee account to the employer for the expenditures, and that any excess amount advanced be returned to the employer. If there is no accountable plan, then the employee must include the amount in gross income (see deduction issues, below).

Use of Air Force One, traveling expenses, and protective services: The use of Air Force One, the $100,000 in traveling expenses, and the protective services would likely be excluded as a working condition fringe benefit under Section 132 of the Code. If the President were self-employed, these are the kind of expenses that would be deductible, and therefore qualify as working condition fringe benefits.

Annual National Park/Museum Pass: There is no specific exclusion in the fringe benefit Code sections for a pass for the National Parks and Museums. However, this might be considered either (1) a de minimis fringe benefit, as its value is de minimis in connection with the overall compensation package; or (2) a working condition fringe benefit, if part of the President's job is to visit and support these national institutions. If so, the amount would be excluded from Mrs. X's gross income. If not, the value of the pass must be included as part of her compensation income.

Deduction Issues

Moving expense deduction: The President and the First Family will be moving into the White House. Mrs. X has served two terms as a senator from a southwestern state, and it is likely that her tax home was in that state. If so, she will be moving more than 50 miles to a new place of employment and may claim an above-the-line deduction for her moving expenses (19 cents per mile, and the cost of moving her belongings). If, however, her tax home had been in Washington, D.C. she would not qualify under the 50-mile rule and the moving expense deduction would not be allowed.

$50,000 expense allowance: If the expense allowance is included in gross income, amounts expended for legitimate employee business expense may be deducted, but only as miscellaneous itemized deductions subject to the 2% floor. For example, assuming that the President's AGI were $500,000, any amount of employee business expenses would have to exceed $10,000 to be deductible as an itemized deduction.

Other deductions: There are no other facts to suggest other deductions, such as mortgage interest on a principal residence in the President's home state or real estate taxes, but these should be explored. The President will likely claim the itemized deduction and will be entitled to an exemption amount for herself, her husband, and her two children.

Timing Issues

Like most individuals, Madam President is a cash method taxpayer who will include her items of gross income when she receives them. In particular, the retirement stipend will likely be included as she receives it. It is unclear whether the stipend qualifies as deferred compensation that would be subject to §409A, but this is an item that bears further scrutiny when more facts are available.

Character

The income that the President includes in her gross income will be ordinary income, because it is compensation income, not income from the disposition of property.

Rates

Because the income is ordinary income, it will be subject to marginal rates of 35% (in 2011).

Credits

The First Family includes two children under the age of 13, and so the question arises of whether the President and Mr. X will be entitled to claim a dependent care credit for expenses incurred in caring for their children while they work. The dependent care credit is available even at high income levels, and is a nonrefundable credit equal to the applicable percentage (here 20%) multiplied by the earned income of the lower-earning spouse. It appears that Mr. X will not be earning a salary, as he is retired and there is no mention of a salary for anyone but the President. If that is the case, no dependent care credit can be claimed, even if the couple must engage a child care provider to care for their children while they both work—after all, both of them will have significant public duties. If, however, Mr. X becomes part of the President's staff, and therefore employed, a dependent care credit will be allowed to the extent described above for child care expenses.

SAMPLE ANSWER TO QUESTION 2

Author's Note: There is no one "right" answer to this policy question. An answer to a policy question should show that the student (1) knows what the affected Code section does; (2) can speak to what reform might look like; and (3) can analyze the potential effects of tax reform in terms of raising revenue, the three major tax policy concerns, and practical politics. (If you are reading this after Congress has already acted with respect to §163(h), check the book's website at www.aspenlawschool.com/books/tax_outline *for an alternative question/answer.)*

IRC §163(h) allows taxpayers who claim the itemized deduction to deduct interest on debt that qualifies as acquisition indebtedness (up to $1,000,000 of debt) and home equity indebtedness (up to $100,000 of debt). Without going into detail, this allows a taxpayer who takes out a mortgage to purchase a home a deduction for the interest paid each year (plus, in certain cases, points paid and even mortgage insurance premiums). It also allows a taxpayer to access the equity in his or her home by taking out a home equity loan, and deducting the interest on this loan.

A repeal of this provision would eliminate this itemized deduction, making mortgage and HELOC (home equity line of credit) interest nondeductible like most other kinds of personal interest. Possibilities for scaling §163(h) back could include, for example, reducing the amount of debt that could qualify, eliminating home equity indebtedness but keeping some amount of acquisition indebtedness, or (the perennial congressional favorite) reducing the benefit of the deduction as AGI rises.

The deduction for home mortgage interest of §163(h) is a major tax expenditure, with estimated revenue loss of $62 billion annually. Recalling that the income tax code is how the U.S. government raises money, repealing or even scaling back §163(h) could result in a significant increase in tax revenues. However, given the issues discussed below (see economic effects), Congress can expect major pushback if it tries to repeal this Code section.

Apart from a tax provisions' ability to raise revenue, a tax provision can be evaluated in terms of its effect on fairness of the Code, its effect on administrative practicality, and its expected economic effects, as compared to current law.

Fairness: The tax code is intended to tax people based on their ability to pay, and a proposed change can be evaluated based on whether it makes the system more or less "fair." Fairness is typically described in terms of horizontal equity: taxpayers with similar abilities to pay should pay similar amounts of tax. So, a provision that would make the tax system fairer would (1) more accurately measure ability to pay; or (2) results in a greater degree of horizontal equity (a better fit between tax and ability to pay) than current provisions of the Code.

Repealing or scaling back the deduction for acquisition indebtedness could lead to greater fairness in the tax system. Consider "twin" taxpayers A and B who have identical salaries and live in identical houses along the same street. Taxpayer A purchased the home, taking out a $200,000 30-year mortgage at 5%, and makes a monthly mortgage payment of about $1,000. Taxpayer B rents her home for $1,000 per month. Allowing A to deduct the interest portion of the loan will reduce A's taxable income as compared to B, but they are in precisely the same situation in terms of salary and housing. Allowing the deduction, therefore, appears to violate principles of horizontal equity. Its repeal could lead to greater fairness between renters and owners. The problem with this analysis is that it is often difficult to determine if A and B are really "similarly situated." An argument can be made that they are not, as A has undertaken the commitment desired by society to home ownership, but this begins to bleed over into economic effects, as discussed below.

From a fairness point of view, the deduction for *home equity indebtedness* interest deduction is almost unsupportable. Consider twin taxpayers C and D, alike in every way, including a desire to buy a $50,000 boat, but without ready cash. C has access to a HELOC, secured by a home, and D has access to an unsecured line of credit at the bank. C can borrow to buy the boat, and that purchase will be subsidized by a tax deduction for the interest, making the boat cheaper for C to buy. D also borrows to purchase the boat, paying for it with a practically identical line of credit, except for security, but the purchase is not subsidized. Both C and D have equal abilities to pay, but the tax system draws a distinction between them, suggesting that C's ability to pay is less than D's. This obvious glitch in the tax system makes at least this aspect of §163(h) a ready target for the chopping block.

Administrative practicality: The desirability of a tax provision can be measured in terms of how practical it is to administer, and the costs of administration. An outright repeal of §165(h) would likely reduce the complexity of the Code, and thereby reduce overall compliance and administrative costs because fewer taxpayers would likely itemize, i.e., if they could not claim this deduction, they might opt for the standard deduction. Therefore, repeal would not create an administrative burden, and would probably create an administrative benefit. Scaling back §165 could increase complexity, however, because at least some of the solutions (eliminating the deduction as AGI rises, for example) would draw finer lines between taxpayers as to eligibility for the deduction.

Economic effects: Any proposed tax provisions should be evaluated based on the expected economic effects of the provision. In this analysis, we make the assumption that taxpayers respond to tax incentives by taking certain actions. Section 163(h) is an important component of a larger group of tax and other federal law provisions that benefit the U.S. housing market and encourage taxpayers to purchase and own homes. The theory is that a nation of homeowners is likely to be more stable than a nation of renters. The economic effects of acquisition indebtedness and home equity indebtedness are likely different, however, and must be analyzed separately.

Acquisition indebtedness*:* Presumably, the deduction for interest of §163(h) factors into taxpayers' decisions to purchase homes (although whether it is a deciding factor would be a good question for economists to answer) Specifically, §163(h) makes purchasing a home less expensive than if the deduction were not available. Therefore, as compared with a tax system without §163(h), a tax code with this provision is likely to result (1) in more taxpayers purchasing homes, and (2) taxpayers purchasing more expensive homes than they would otherwise desire because the after-tax cost of a home is less than its price without a tax subsidy. Given the recent housing meltdown and the continuing foreclosure crisis, one can question the policy of encouraging "home ownership by all" through the tax code or any other means. So, repealing the provision could implement a policy decision to remove taxes as a subsidy to home ownership. However, that is not the end of the story. A repeal of §163(h) could lead to fewer people willing to purchase homes and could accelerate the decline in value of homes (with fewer buyers engaged in the market and less willing or able to pay high prices for homes due to the absence of the tax subsidy). This could lead to a decline in home prices. Obviously, there would be some political pushback to repealing §163(h) from the construction industry, realtors, and even regular folks who see their home values dropping even further. That said, some scaling back of the deduction might not have adverse economic effects. The current limit of $1,000,000 on acquisition indebtedness seems high, given that the average home price in the United States is about a quarter of that amount. Presumably, people purchasing million-dollar homes are not motivated solely by tax considerations and there just aren't that many million-dollar homes. At the other end of the scale, the elimination of the deduction for mortgage insurance premiums (already scheduled for 2012) could have the desirable economic effect of causing home purchasers to increase their down payments.

Home equity indebtedness: The policy foundation for the deduction for interest on home equity indebtedness is not as strong as for its cousin, acquisition indebtedness. The deduction for interest on home equity loans is a leftover from a time when all personal interest was deductible, and perhaps it is designed to boost consumer spending at a time of rapidly rising home prices. This provision arguably contributed to the foreclosure crisis, by encouraging taxpayers to take out "second mortgages" on their homes. These factors suggest that it is ripe for repeal or scaling back.

SAMPLE ANSWER TO QUESTION 3

This is a question that involves a transaction in property, in which the major issues will be the realization and recognition of gain and loss to the taxpayer.

Who is the taxpayer?

This question focuses on the tax consequences to both taxpayers. In property transactions, each taxpayer's consequences are usually independent of each other, and must be analyzed separately.

Part A

Will Brian and/or Anita recognize income as a result of this transaction?

In exchanging Whiteacre and Blueacre, Brian and Anita have each experienced a realization event. Section 1001 measures their realized gain or loss as the difference between their amounts realized and their adjusted bases in the property transferred. (See calculation below.) Section 1001 requires recognition of this gain (which is includible in gross income under §61) unless another Code section excludes or defers it. There is no applicable exclusion statute for commercial property, but potentially §1031 will allow deferral of gain if its requirements are met.

A taxpayer will not recognize gain or loss on an exchange of property if the requirements of §1031 are met: an exchange of qualifying property of like-kind, when the taxpayer has held the surrendered property for investment or for use in a trade or business and intends to hold the property received for investment or in a trade or business.

The two properties are like-kind (real property for real property, regardless of use) and this kind of property qualifies for a like-kind exchange. Assuming that each of these taxpayers held the properties for investment or for use in a trade or business and intends to hold the acquired properties for either of these uses, these requirements are met. If so, neither taxpayer will recognize gain or loss, except to the extent of nonlike-kind property received (boot). Net relief from liabilities is treated as boot. The basis of the property received in the transaction is equal to the basis of the property transferred, plus the gain recognized on the transaction, minus the fair market value of the boot received, plus the fair market value of the boot given.

Anita's equity in Blueacre is $450,000 (its fair market value of $800,000, minus the debt of $350,000). Therefore, Whiteacre must be worth $700,000, because Brian will trade Whiteacre (with equity of $440,000) for Blueacre plus a painting worth $10,000. Therefore, the tax consequences to the two taxpayers are as follows:

	Brian	Anita
Amount Realized	$800,000 Blueacre +260,000 A/L **$1,060,000**	$700,000 Whiteacre +350,000 A/L + 10,000 Painting **$1,060,000**
Basis in Property Surrendered	$400,000 Whiteacre +350,000 A/L + 10,000 Painting **$760,000**	$400,000 Blueacre +260,000 A/L **$660,000**
Realized Gain or Loss	**$300,000**	**$400,000**
Recognized Gain or Loss	**$8,000** gain on painting	$10,000 Painting + 90,000 Net Liab. Relief **$100,000**
Basis of Property Received	$400,000 Basis of W/A + 10,000 Painting − 260,000 A/L +350,000 A/L **$500,000 Basis of Blueacre**	$400,000 Basis of B/A +100,000 Gain Recog −350,000 +260,000 −10,000 **$400,000 Basis of Whiteacre** **$10,000 Basis of Painting**

Will Anita and Brian have any deductions associated with this transaction?

As described above, both Anita and Brian realized gain on the transaction, not loss. They will undoubtedly have expenses associated with the sale, which will be included as part of their basis in the properties transferred. In addition, there are real estate taxes and mortgage interest to be allocated and deducted in the year of sale. Each will be entitled to his or her share of real property taxes as a deduction.

When will Anita and Brian recognize gain?

The essence of §1031 is that it requires recognition of gain in the year of the transaction to the extent that the taxpayer "cashes out" of the investment, but defers any other gain to future years. The recognized gain described in the chart above must be recognized in the year of sale. If in a future year, Anita or Brian sell Whiteacre or Blueacre, they will compute their amount realized based on the property's values as of that date, and their adjusted basis will be computed based on the exchanged basis rule described above, adjusted further for depreciation.

What is the character of the gain recognized by Anita and Brian?

Both Anita and Brian held their respective properties (including the painting, in Brian's case) for investment, rather than as part of a trade or business. Each property constitutes a capital asset with respect to its owner under §1221, because the property does not fall within any of the excluded categories of that section. The exchange by the taxpayers qualifies as a "sale or exchange" and thus the recognized gain will be capital in nature. The gain recognized by Brian on the transfer of the painting will be classified as 28% capital gain. The gain recognized by Anita will be either 25% or 15%/0% capital gain.

What are the tax rates to be paid by Anita and Brian?

As noted above, the capital gain that each recognizes will be taxable at different rates, because of the nature of the gains. Each taxpayer must take the gain into account in computing net capital gain.

Are Brian and Anita able to claim any tax credits?

This kind of transaction does not typically generate any tax credits.

Part B

If Anita had received the office building as an inheritance, the theoretical question arises of whether she held it for investment or for use in a trade or business. There is no definitive answer to this; it depends on her intentions as revealed by her use, the period of time she held the property, and similar factors. However, it may not matter (or matter much) to Anita, because if she had recently received Blueacre as inheritance, her basis would be the fair market value on the date of death, and therefore she would have little if any gain or loss in the property. Anita's situation does not affect Brian's ability potentially to qualify his side of the transaction as a §1031 exchange; each taxpayer's situation is analyzed independently.

SAMPLE ANSWER TO QUESTION 4

This question raises issues relating to business income and expenses.

Who is the taxpayer?

Spencer is a sole proprietor of a business. Sole proprietors report the income and deductions attributable to their businesses on Schedule C of their tax returns. Net income from business is includible in gross income (§61(a)(2)), and net loss generates a deduction (§165(c)(1)), subject to some limitations.

Does Spencer have income? If so, what is its character?

Spencer begins by including in his gross income his receipts from sales of information. In addition, Spencer has had several property transactions during the year (both voluntary and involuntary) and he may have net gain or loss from these. Because the character of this income or loss is so closely tied to its computation, these two major issues are considered together. Spencer's information sales are ordinary income, but the character of the property transactions depends on the proper application of §1231 and related Code sections.

Sale of computer: Spencer's sale of the computer used in his business is the sale of a §1231 asset. However, we must first apply the recapture rule of §1245 to recast as ordinary income any amount of accelerated depreciation claimed on the computer. It is not clear from the facts how much that would be, but let us assume for purposes of illustration that the recapture amount is $100. That amount is treated as ordinary income. The rest ($1,400) is §1231 gain.

As such, we must add up the §1231 gains and losses for the year, netting the two. Spencer had a theft loss of the equipment, with a basis of $2,500 and a fair market value of $1,500. If property used in a trade or business or for the production of income is totally destroyed, and if the fair market value of such property immediately before the casualty is less than its adjusted basis, the adjusted basis of such property is the amount of the loss. Reg. §1.165-7(b)(1)(ii). Therefore, Spencer's casualty loss is $2,500 on the theft. He also had a casualty gain of $3,000 due to the flood. Because Spencer's casualty losses are not greater than his casualty gains, all of the gains and losses are included in the computation of §1231 gains, as follows:

Sale of computer:	$1,400 gain
Theft loss:	$2,500 loss
Flood gain:	$3,000 gain
NET	**$1,900 gain**

This gain would be capital in nature. There is no indication that Spencer has unrecaptured losses in previous years that would treat any of this as ordinary income. This capital gain income would be taxed at 15%, or 0% depending on Spencer's income. Because Spencer's net income from business (ordinary income) exceeds the amount that would be subject to the 15% rate, this capital gain will be taxed at the 15% rate.

Which deductions may Spencer claim?

In order to qualify for any deduction, an expenditure must meet the specific requirements of a deduction statute. Potential deduction statutes are discussed below.

Ordinary and necessary business expenses: Section 162 allows a deduction for all "ordinary and necessary business expenses." This requires that the expenditure be usual in the trade ("ordinary"), have a reasonable likelihood of generating profit ("necessary"), be incurred for business and not personal reasons, and be incurred while the taxpayer is engaged in a trade or business ("trade or business"), and not be a capital expenditure ("expense"). Spencer's expenditures for compensation (if reasonable in amount), rent, advertising, and telephone/Internet would all seem to meet this requirement.

Business entertainment: While business entertainment may also seem to fall within the category of §162 expenses, special rules limit deductions for business entertainment. First, Spencer must establish that the entertainment item was "directly related to" the active conduct of his trade or business, or if the activity immediately preceded or followed a bona fide business discussion, was "associated with" the active conduct of his trade or business. IRC §274(a). Even if he meets this requirement, only 50% of the amount expended will be deductible. IRC §274(n). Spencer must substantiate his deductions for entertainment expenses, and additional information would be necessary to determine if he is eligible for any deduction.

Purchase of computer: The purchase of the computer is an outlay for a capital expenditure, because the computer is likely to generate benefits beyond the close of the taxable year. IRC §263. Thus, Spencer cannot take a deduction under §162 for this outlay. He may, however, deduct the cost of such items up to the lesser of $500,000 (in 2011) or the net income of the business disregarding this expense. IRC §179. If he elects to deduct the cost of the computer under §179, its basis will be reduced by the amount of the deduction (if he fully deducts the amount, the basis will be zero).

Taxes: Section 164 allows a deduction for income, real property, personal property taxes, and sales taxes, at least in some years. It is not clear what kind of tax Spencer paid, and further information is necessary to determine the deductibility of this expense.

Retirement Planning: To generate an additional deduction in future years, Spencer might consider establishing some sort of retirement plan for his business to defer income to future years, or prepaying some expenses (within the limits imposed on prepayments) to accelerate deductions to earlier years.

When must Spencer include items in gross income and when may he claim deductions?

Since Spencer uses the cash method of accounting for his business, he will include income in the year he receives it and claim deductions in the year they are paid. Therefore, he will include $125,000 in gross income, not including the $25,000 of promises. For deductions, "payment" includes payment by credit card, even if Spencer does not pay the balance to the credit card company. Thus, he should deduct those expenses that have been paid during the year and include income that he has received, but not the promises to pay from clients.

To what tax rates will Spencer be subject?

Spencer's net ordinary income will be taxed at rates ranging from 5% to 35% (in 2011). His capital gain will fall into the 15% category and will be taxed at 15% unless his other income is subject to tax at 5%, in which case the capital gain will escape tax altogether.

Will Spencer be entitled to claim any tax credits?

None of the facts suggest Spencer's entitlement to any kind of tax credit.

SAMPLE ANSWER TO QUESTION 5

This is a question tightly focused on personal deductions, specifically the charitable deduction. For that reason, only the "deduction" question of the seven major tax issues will be discussed.

A charitable deduction is allowable as part of the itemized deduction for donations by individuals of cash and property (within specified limits) to qualifying §501(c)(3) public charities.

In this case, a preliminary question is whether Attorney G made a donation to the qualifying charity, or whether the donation properly belongs to Big Law Firm. Although Attorney G did not directly donate to the charity, or select the charity himself, the edict says that the Fund will be contributed "on behalf of participants" to qualifying charities, and the Firm did give Attorney G a statement of his donation. Therefore, Attorney G should be viewed as the donor.

The second question is whether the donation is available when it directly results in a benefit to the donor, which in this case is the privilege of a day of exemption from the strict firm dress code. A charitable deduction is allowable for a donation only if the donor does not receive a "quid pro quo" for the donation. In *Ottawa Silica*, for example, a donation for the value of land to the local school district was denied because the donor received the benefit of significant improvements to surrounding land through public improvements. In that case, the benefit was economic and substantial.

In this case, Attorney G made an $800 contribution, when the "suggested" contribution was only $500 for 50 weeks of jeans-Fridays. There is no question that the $300 "additional" contribution is not for a quid pro quo.

Moreover, the managing board's edict included only a "recommended" donation. In theory, Attorney G could have donated just a penny every Friday for the privilege of wearing jean, because only a "donation" is required. Whether Attorney G succumbed to peer pressure, or sensibly decided to exceed expectations, or simply wanted to give more out of a sincere charitable impulse, the fact remains that he exceeded what was required as a condition of wearing jeans.

Finally, this should not be viewed as a "quid pro quo" in the same sense as in *Ottawa Silica* and similar cases, because it is not the kind of economic benefit usually taken into consideration in the tax code, and whether it is "substantial" depends on the subjective view of the donor. It could be likened to the naming of a building for a major donor to a college, for example, which is not viewed as a disqualifying quid pro quo for a charitable deduction.

In conclusion, Attorney G should be entitled to the charitable deduction of $800.

SAMPLE ANSWER TO QUESTION 6

This question focuses on a specific kind of intrafamilial transfer, i.e., transfers that occur as part of a divorce situation. In this situation, the primary questions are (1) the income to a former spouse; (2) the deductions available to the other former spouse; and (3) the basis of any property that changes hands in the divorce.

Part A

In general, the payor of alimony may deduct it from his or her gross income, and the recipient must include it in gross income. However, for this treatment to occur, the payments must qualify as alimony under the federal definition of alimony (state law labels don't matter). Alimony must be paid in cash, must be pursuant to a divorce decree or written instrument pursuant to divorce, must not be designated as nondeductible and nonincludible in the decree, must not be paid while the couple are living together, and must terminate upon the death of the payee spouse. In addition, the payments cannot be disguised child support.

The question in this situation is whether the payments deducted by Peter and included by Gabrielle are "alimony" as defined in §71.

XYZ stock: Because alimony must be paid in cash, the transfer of the XYZ stock does not qualify as alimony. So this amount cannot be deducted by Peter, nor must it be included in Gabrielle's gross income. Instead, it is a transfer of property incident to a divorce, and is governed by §1041.

Mortgage payments: It is possible for payments made to a third party to qualify as alimony (see Treas. Reg. §1.71-1T, Q-6). These payments required some scrutiny to see if they would terminate upon Gabrielle's death. The decree provides that they will continue until the earlier of the sale of the home, the payoff of the mortgage, or when Gabrielle ceases to use the home as her principal residence. Peter has a good argument that the payments qualify because upon Gabrielle's death, she will no longer be using this residence as her principal residence. The parties would have been better off to state explicitly in the decree that the payments do or do not end upon Gabrielle's death.

Cash—Front-end loaded alimony? The cash payments appear to meet the definition of alimony, but the question is whether there is front-end loaded alimony. If so, the excess alimony payment will be included in the payor's gross income in the third post-separation year and will be deductible by the payee spouse in that year.

Step 1	Calculate the excess alimony payment for the *second* post-separation year. $20,000 − ($10,000 + $15,000) = -0-
Step 2	Calculate the excess alimony payment for the *first* post-separation year. $$\$40,000 - \left[\left\{ \frac{\$(20,000-0)+\$10,000}{2} \right\} + \$15,000 \} \right] = \$10,000$$
Step 3	Calculate the excess alimony payment: The sum of steps 1 and 2: -0- + 10,000 = $10,000
Step 4	Determine the consequences to payor and recipient in the third post-separation year: $10,000 deduction from AGI to Gabrielle $10,000 inclusion in gross income for Peter

Part B

The transfer of the family home to Gabrielle in the divorce is governed by §1041. That section provides that she receives this as a gift (and therefore has no income) and takes the basis of the home equal to the couple's basis in it immediately before the divorce, i.e., $200,000. When Gabrielle gives it to her daughter, Trendee, she takes the home with a basis equal to the donor's basis ($200,000), except that for purposes of determining loss on any sale by Trendee, her basis will be the fair market value on the date of the gift, i.e., $160,000.

Table of Internal Revenue Code Sections

Table of Treasury Regulations Sections

Table of Cases

Table of Administrative Authorities

Index